ST. MARY
ST. MARY

W9-ACG-872

98605

THE HISTORY OF
EGYPT

SECOND EDITION

P. J. VATIKIOTIS

THE JOHNS HOPKINS UNIVERSITY PRESS
BALTIMORE

© 1969, 1980 by P. J. Vatikiotis
All rights reserved
Reprinted 1976
Second edition 1980

Second edition published in the United Kingdom, 1980, by
Weidenfeld and Nicolson
91 Clapham High Street London SW4

Second edition published in the United States of America, 1980, by
The Johns Hopkins University Press, Baltimore, Maryland 21218

Library of Congress Cataloging in Publication Data

Vatikiotis, Panayiotis J   1928–
    The history of Egypt.

    (Asia Africa series of modern histories)
    Bibliography: p. 500
    Includes index.
    1. Egypt–History–1798–   I. Title.
DT107.V38   1980   962   79–21412
ISBN 0–8018–2339–0
ISBN O–8018–2340–4 pbk.

Printed and bound in Great Britain

CONTENTS

ACKNOWLEDGEMENTS   viii
NOTE ON TRANSLITERATION   ix
PREFACE TO THE FIRST EDITION   x
PREFACE TO THE SECOND EDITION   xii

INTRODUCTION Background to the Development
of Modern Egypt

1 Land and people   3
2 The establishment of Islam in Egypt   12
3 The first European impact   30

PART I The Social and Political Foundations of
Modern Egypt, 1805–82

4 Muhammad Ali, the modernizing autocrat   49
5 Ismail, the impatient Europeanizer   70
6 Modern education and the first Egyptian intellectuals   90
7 Constitutionalism, rebellion, and occupation   124

PART II Conservative and Liberal Response to
Europe, 1882–1914

8 The British in Egypt   169
9 Journalism and the press   178
10 Religious reform and Islamic political sentiment   188
11 Stirrings of secular liberalism   215

PART III Society, Government and Politics,
1919–39

12 The struggle for independence, 1919–22   247
13 Experiment in constitutional government, 1923–39   271
14 The attack upon tradition   296

Contents

PART IV   From the Old Order to the New, 1930–79

15 The failure of liberalism and the reaction against
   Europe, 1930–50   317
16 Prelude to revolution, 1939–52   343
17 Revolution and republic, 1952–79   372

PART V The Search for a Modern Culture and Society

18 Education and culture   433

Notes   467
Bibliography   501
Maps   515
Index   518

MAPS

(*pages* 515–17)

Modern Egypt
Egypt, Sudan, Libya, Sinai
The Middle East and North Africa

ACKNOWLEDGEMENTS

I wish to thank Professor Bernard Lewis, editor of this series, for his generous advice and criticism throughout the preparation of the book. He read the complete draft manuscript and offered valuable suggestions. Dr Roger Owen of St Antony's College, Oxford, and my colleague Dr P. K. O'Brien made helpful suggestions regarding the relevant aspects of the economic history of modern Egypt.

The generosity of the Guggenheim Foundation permitted me to spend the academic year 1961–2 planning the book. My colleague Michel Mazzaoui, Near East Bibliographer at Indiana University in 1962–5, made available to me Arabic sources on nineteenth-century Egypt that would otherwise have been difficult to secure. His interest and help in my work were most generous and I am deeply grateful to him. James Pollock, Cataloguer for the Arabic collection at Indiana University at that time, provided answers to many bibliographical queries. Dr Derek Hopwood of St Antony's College, Oxford, and Mr Geoffrey Schofield of the School of Oriental and African Studies Library provided me with equally kind assistance on bibliographical matters.

I also wish to thank Indiana University for the secretarial assistance it gave me from time to time during the preparation of the book; Mrs Valerie Thorpe and Miss B. Fleming for typing portions of the manuscript.

Between the first and second edition I have had the benefit of reading the more recent works of Tariq al-Bishri, Abdel Azim Ramadan and Aliy al-Din Hilal Desuki, who represent a new generation of modern Egyptian historians. I also benefited greatly from work done by my own research students at the University of London who prepared doctoral theses under my supervision on the modern history and politics of Egypt, among them Walid Kazziha, Muna Abul Fadl and Mustafa el-Feki. Occasional, lengthy conversations with Dr Louis Awad, Dr Abdel Malek Awda and Maitre Tawfiq al-Hakim have been of invaluable assistance in convincing me of the work that still remains to be done on the history of Egypt in the nineteenth and twentieth centuries. Any shortcomings in this work are mine.

NOTE ON TRANSLITERATION

Generally in the text I have followed a simple transliteration of Arabic names, terms, and titles. Also, in the text I have rendered some well-known names in the form they have appeared in the English press and other publications. I have however followed a more formal transliteration system in the footnote citations.

PREFACE TO THE FIRST EDITION

Egypt has been a popular country with authors ever since Herodotus wrote his famous *History*. So many books about Egypt have been written recently that the reader may impatiently question the reasons for yet another one. I can perhaps justify this added volume by stating briefly its limited scope and aim.

This is neither a detailed history of modern Egypt nor a detailed account of the economic, political, and diplomatic record of that country from 1800 to the present. It is rather a book *about* the history of modern Egypt: an introduction to the development of the country and the evolution of Egyptian society over the last hundred and fifty years. As such, it is presented not strictly to the specialist but primarily to the lay reader in the hope of acquainting him with the general characteristics of the country and the people, of Egyptian society and its leadership. Within this general context, the book also tries to depict the response of Egyptians to the forces of the modern world, and to show how these affected them.

Egyptian leadership has had a wide impact upon the Arab peoples of the Middle East in the last twenty-five years. Behind this impact has been the Egyptian claim to leadership as the most advanced Arabic-speaking Muslim state today. Egyptians have based their claim to Arab leadership in part upon the varied resources of their society, in part on their social, economic, technological, cultural, and political achievements over the past hundred and fifty years.

The main problem in writing a general introduction to the development of modern Egypt is not what to include in the discussion, but what to leave out. Egypt has the longest national history of any independent state in the Arab Middle East today. Moreover, modern Egyptian writers have been more numerous and more prolific than those of any other Arabic-speaking country: the mere volume of published works pertinent and useful to any inquiry into the history of modern Egypt is staggering.

The narrative favours three major themes. The first is the continuity in Egyptian society from ancient times to this day, deriving ultimately from the interplay between physical and human environment, between man and earth, man and river. The second is the processes by which this continuity, influenced and modified by Islam and the Arabic language, has shaped the collective and individual beliefs of the Egyptian people, their view of the world, their relations with one another and with their rulers. The third theme is the encounter in the nineteenth and twentieth centuries between an awakened Egypt on the one hand, and European civilization on the other. Important aspects of this last theme are the dislocation and uncertainty wrought by changes in the socio-economic, cultural and political life of Egypt; the contrasted enthusiasm and antagonism of different groups of Egyptians for the new way of life from Europe; the ambivalence of leaders in their choice of new social-political philosophies and ideologies; and the emotional disturbance of the masses resulting from the onslaught of technology, of modern economic and social activity.

Throughout the book the emphasis is on internal developments. The very important question of the policies of European states towards Egypt, especially since 1875, is adequately discussed in numerous published works. It is not therefore dealt with here in any great detail. Similarly, I avoided repeating the detailed story of the Suez Canal. Financial and administrative matters, so crucial in the period 1883–1923, have been touched upon only when necessary. Their treatment by British authors especially has been detailed. Since the purpose of the book is to survey the social, cultural, and intellectual development of modern Egypt, more technical considerations of economic and fiscal matters have not been highlighted. The importance of these matters cannot of course be minimized, yet their inclusion in a volume such as this was deemed distracting. Moreover, treatment of an important aspect of modern Egyptian history, namely, the Sudan in the nineteenth century, has been omitted.*

* See the volume in this series, *The History of the Sudan* by P.M. Holt and M.W. Daly (London and New York, 1980).

PREFACE TO THE SECOND
EDITION

A volume of this size dealing with the modern history of such an old country as Egypt is best left unrevised. Any extensive or real improvement in the writing of the history of modern Egypt deserves a new book. However, in revising this book, first published ten years ago, I ask the reader to bear in mind that it remains only a general survey of the modern history of Egypt.

More material has been added to the parts of the book dealing with the nineteenth century. Thus, I have more or less rewritten Chapter 3, dealing with the first European impact on Egypt. I re-arranged some of the material in Chapter 5 dealing with Khedive Ismail, and added a new section which surveys Western or foreign views of the Khedive. Students, I felt, may find some of that literature on Ismail's Egypt interesting.

Subheadings have been introduced in several of the chapters for easier reference. These are particularly useful for Chapter 7, which has been expanded to include a reappraisal of the Orabi Revolt on the basis of the literature written about it fairly close to the event.

Part Two of the book is introduced by a new chapter, 'The British in Egypt'. It is not a narrative or record of the British occupation of the country from 1882 to 1956. Rather it is an attempt to highlight its circumstances, peculiarities and broad consequences, many of which are surveyed or discussed in the chapters that follow.

I regret that Professor Afaf Lutfi al-Sayyid Marsot's work on Muhammad Ali has not appeared as yet. Pending its publication, however, I believe that, on balance, my depiction of Egypt's histori-cal experience in the nineteenth century remains, on the whole, real-istic. There is, needless to say, much monographic work to be done on several aspects of nineteenth-century Egypt (as well as its eigh-teenth-century background). Khedive Ismail, for example, deserves a serious study – one hopes before the centenary of his death (1995). Equally important and, in terms of economic, social and administra-tive history, perhaps more significant, would be a study of Ali Pasha

Mubarak. His contribution to the transfer of modern technology in the development of modern Egypt is possibly unsurpassed.

The narrative in Chapter 16 has been slightly expanded in order to cover the period up to the death of President Nasser in 1970. This additional narrative is a very broad survey and general outline of events and trends. The whole of Part Four of the book, however, should be read in the light of my recent work, *Nasser and his Generation* (London and New York, 1978).

The chapter on Education and Culture has been left more or less, intact. To add to it would have meant going beyond 1970 to survey the effusion of post-Nasserite writing.

Certain books that have appeared since 1969 have been added to the bibliography. These, as the reader will readily notice, are, with very few exceptions, mainly about the period since 1952.

P. J. V.

May 1979

INTRODUCTION

Background to the Development of Modern Egypt

CHAPTER 1
LAND AND PEOPLE

Egypt is the home of one of the most ancient civilizations of mankind. The beginnings of this civilization are not our present concern; yet they have some relevance to the modern history of Egypt, and a brief glance at ancient origins may help in the understanding of recent developments.

Situated at the meeting point of two continents, Asia and Africa, Egypt is a geographical phenomenon. Although the total surface of the modern state of Egypt is over 363,000 square miles, habitable and historical Egypt – the Nile Valley and Delta – occupies but a narrow strip of land between vast deserts. Yet the Valley of the Nile is one of the oldest meeting places of man, and the fertile ground upon which one of the first civilizations developed and flourished for over 4,000 years. To speak of the living Egypt, therefore, is to speak of the 15,000 square miles upon which 98 per cent of Egyptians live, work, procreate and die – an area slightly less than 5 per cent of the total surface of geographical Egypt.

Until our Egyptian contemporaries or their successors in the future can conquer the desert and make it productive, Egypt proper will remain the Nile Valley. The Nile traverses over a thousand miles from Wadi Halfa in the south to the Mediterranean in the north, without a single tributary joining the river across the country. The Egyptian landscape sharply emphasizes the precarious border line between life and death, habitation and wilderness. Travelling overland eastwards or westwards from the brilliant river valley, one hardly notices when the green ends and the brown and yellow begin, for the two often blend with uncanny harmony; the contrast is driven home only by the teeming masses that press upon the river banks and the surrounding fields. No wonder then that this immortal Nile has beckoned man to its banks from time immemorial to enjoy the life-giving qualities of their muddy brown earth. Once there, man managed to establish one of the most crowded settlements in the world. Under the decaying rule of the Mamluks in the eighteenth century, the population of the Nile Valley dropped down to the low

3

figure of two and a half million inhabitants in 1800.[1] Since then, Egypt's population has been growing with uniform, though alarming, speed, so that in 1979 nearly forty million Egyptians are squeezed into this historical Valley of the Nile. It is estimated that at the end of this century over sixty million people will inhabit it.

No one accepts the ancient dictum 'Egypt is the gift of the Nile' more readily than the Egyptian himself. But no student of Egypt can fail to qualify this dictum by adding that productive Egypt has also been the fruit of incessant toil and back-breaking labour by the *fellah*, the peasant cultivator, literally the one who breaks up the soil, the largest identifiable social class in the country with unbroken historical continuity through the ages. Inhabiting an essentially rainless land, confined to the banks of the river, and trapped between waterless deserts – the Arabian to the east and the Libyan to the west – the Egyptian's struggle for life has been fixed with rare regularity: to use and harness the waters of the river in such a way as to extract the best livelihood for himself and his family, and to ensure a measure of security. But also fixed, for many thousands of years to come, were his personality, beliefs, fears, habits of thought and behaviour. 'The good earth' – the silt and mud deposited by the Nile – became his one overriding obsession: it was the source of all his happiness, but also the greatest single cause of his misery. Now, however, with the Aswan High Dam, the silt and mud have gone.

Exposed as he is to what Lawrence Durrell called a 'flat and unbosomed land', the Egyptian has lived for centuries attuned to the river. Until the explorations of the upper reaches of the Nile in the nineteenth century he was ignorant of its source, but fully realized that its presence meant incessant toil for him in order to survive against the vast desert emptiness around him, which he believed to be 'overpopulated' by demons and the Devil. He observed, year in and year out, that in the month of June the river began to rise, so that by September its banks and surrounding fields were inundated: this was the annual flood. He now had to work some fifteen hours a day digging canals and building dams to direct and preserve the waters of this flood for cultivation. Frantically he tried to utilize as much of the river waters as possible. In mid-October he observed the water level going down, until by April and May it was at its lowest mark. Such rhythmic periodicity of the river's behaviour affected the rhythm and regularity of the Egyptian's occupation as a farmer, and his life.

Rarely seeing rain, always basking in sunshine, constantly

4

threatened by unchanging desert, and yearly visited by an inundated river, the Egyptian was not only convinced of the fact that his security lay in his proper treatment and utilization of the Nile waters, but became confident that all of these phenomena were manifestations of an eternal being. Thus, the river that gave fertility to his land was a god; so was the sun which permitted him to work without need of shelter all year round. Both these gifts of Nature, which emphasized the inevitability of Time with its unbearable weight upon man, also outlined the Egyptian's hope of defeating Time through immortality. They constituted the essential variables in victory over death. What else could the unfailing annual flood imply but an annual resurrection for the tiller of the soil?

Witness the Nile systematically living and dying once each year: death and resurrection, resurrection and then death.[2]
... Resurrection is Egypt's eternal anthem,[3]

for 'Egypt's plight is Time ... that great struggle between Man and Time ... and the victory of the spirit over Time and Place.'[4]

The Nile, helped by the sun and directed by the incessant toil of the fellah, the Egyptian peasant, sustained some seven to ten million Egyptians in Pharaonic times; over ten millions in Graeco-Roman and Christian times; and today helps to support some forty millions. The river does this after having flowed some 3,300 miles before entering Egypt, to continue another 1,000 miles of its course to the Mediterranean Sea. It traces the unique silhouette that is Egypt as seen from the air, and which is emphatically characterized by a north–south axis: as if by coincidence the palm-tree shape of the river parallels the famous and popular date tree of Egypt. The bare trunk explodes with its branches just north of Cairo to form the Delta, until the river joins the Mediterranean through Rosetta (Rashid) in the west and Damietta (Dimyat) in the east. The 250-odd miles between these two extremities of the river's juncture with the sea represent one of the world's most densely populated areas – almost 1,000 people per square mile. A string of lakes, Mariut, Edkou, Borollos and Manzaleh, meet the river on its final spill into the sea.

This sharp delta formation of the Nile north of Cairo established since ancient times the socio-political separation between the two Egypts: Lower and Upper Egypt, *Bahri* and *Qibli*, the theme in Pharaonic history of the Memphis of the God Ra versus the Thebes of the God Ammon, until the two Egypts were united by Menes in

3400 BC into one kingdom. The separation between Lower and Upper Egypt is also of great historical significance. Upper Egypt, narrow and within immediate contact with the desert, was limited in its outlook towards Africa. People lived and worked on the five-to-twenty-mile-wide band of black earth, and when they died they were buried in the sands and hills of the surrounding desert. The tombs and temples at Luxor, Aswan and Edfou are some of the most prominent finds in our retracing of ancient Egyptian history. The sand and dry climate preserved these monuments for thousands of years, so that Egyptologists came to know more about ancient Egypt's religious worship and beliefs, mortuary and funerary practices and art than about its social and political organization, administration and commerce – a fact which led many to exaggerate the ancient Egyptian's preoccupation with death.[5]

Lower Egypt, on the other hand, occupied the wide Nile Delta, richly agricultural, marshy and intensively habitable. Facing outwards to Asia, Europe and the Mediterranean, the Lower Egyptian must have been in commercial and other contact with various peoples: Hebrews, Phoenicians and Greeks. Unfortunately, very little information has come down to us about the interaction of these peoples in the Delta and about its cultural effects. This is perhaps due to the continuous destructiveness of the muddy, flooded earth of the Delta through the centuries. It is thus possible that our view of ancient Egypt could have been different had not the historical evidence available been so disproportionately and overwhelmingly from Upper Egypt. Nevertheless, it is safe to speak of a dual Egyptian 'psychology' down to this century as a result of this geographical division of Egypt: an Asian–Mediterranean versus an African-orientated Egyptian.

Cutting across the dichotomy of the two regions of Nilotic Egypt, there is the further contrast between town and countryside. Although this kind of distinction is more apparent and significant today, it was nurtured by the historical evolution of Egyptian society. While the priests and clergy of ancient Egypt were the depositories of tradition since Pharaonic times, and the *ulama* the standard-bearers of traditional Islamic knowledge and the Sacred Law, the educated urban élite, influenced by European ideas and conceptions, tended to become the agents of change. The rural masses, on the other hand, remained for a long time isolated in their village existence, in constant communion with earth and nature. These country folk, especially, constituted a society in which the rituals

6

of family and village hierarchy and solidarity were buttressed by an elaborate structure of ethical and moral standards, based on myth and belief. This structure survived successively under Christian and Islamic hegemonies.

Isolationism and conservatism were the mainstays of fellah existence. Paradoxically though, the fellah has easily adapted to the most advanced methods of cultivation. The latter of course were brought to him by his city brothers, who learned the secrets of the machine and its benefits. Nonetheless, the fellah continued to construct his views and images of the universe, the mystery of life, and his relation to both of these through the earth and the mighty river. Thus his folklore reflected the sharp influence of these two environmental phenomena around him. Until very recently, the fellah's contact with the city was either through the intermediary of the tax-collector, the foreign merchant and the money-lender, or through his *nazir* (agricultural field foreman), who supervised his work in the fields while protected from the valley's merciless sun by the parasol (*shamsiyya*) – the traditional emblem of authority. Whether under Christianity or Islam, the fellah has been attracted to popular religion: in his veneration of saints and his adherence to religious brotherhoods. Such popular religious practices were not merely ceremonial; they were a source of solace, and a means of social intercourse in the village, or, as in many cases, among a number of villages. Whereas all of this tended to make the peasant's belief, his personal conduct and social relations highly formalistic and ritualistic, it provided him with a psychologically satisfactory formula for a relatively contented existence – and for sanity.

The First World War, with its agitation for political independence, brought the rural communities into close contact with their urban fellow-citizens. Nationalist leaders, in adopting some forms of European political organization, descended among the fellahin (who represented the vast majority of Egyptians) to seek political support. This did not imply that the peasants were now entering a dynamic era of modernity. It simply meant that they were being made the objects of new socio-political arrangements, exclusively directed and operated by an urban élite. In the cities of Egypt, until recently, an indigenous Muslim population lived side by side with enterprising foreign colonists settled in, but not attached to, the land or country. These consisted of foreign and indigenous minorities directing economic, commercial and service enterprises to the whole population for profit. Such were the Jewish, Greek, Armenian, Italian and

7

French communities in Egypt, especially during the nineteenth century and the first half of the twentieth century.

Until quite recently, these contrasts were accentuated by the excessive density of the rural population, when 75 per cent of the country's inhabitants lived in rural areas, huddled in nearly four thousand villages. The unequal distribution of landownership, which until recently permitted two million peasants each to own under one *feddan* (1·03 acres) of land, and over 500,000 peasants each to own between one and two *feddans*, was not mitigated by the crucial importance of cotton in Egyptian agriculture as a cash export crop.

After 1870, almost everyone who owned or rented land in the Delta grew cotton. Since it was the most certain means of obtaining cash, middlemen were willing to finance it. Yet most of the profit from this lucrative cash crop ended in but a few hands, due partly to the unequal nature of land holdings and partly to the land rental system. The foremost beneficiaries in this situation were the landowning capitalists living in the city, who directed production for maximum gain. Their speculation was further encouraged by favourable conditions obtaining in Egyptian agriculture, namely, fertile land, dependably good climate, excellent state-built irrigation systems, and cheap agricultural labour. The latter had been so cheap that, despite the 1959/60 minimum agricultural labour daily wage law of PT 18 (approximately 10 pence or $0.20), the labourer during the period 1960–2 rarely realized over PT 12 during good seasons and never over PT 10 in actual wages on average. Until 1952, 2 per cent of Egyptians owned 50 per cent of the land, encouraging the speculative nature of Egyptian agriculture to develop still further.

The inhabitants of rural Egypt have until recently been poor, sick, and on the whole unattuned to the requirements of modern life. Their relatively short life expectancy, moreover, prevented them from contributing appreciably to the economy of the country as they never survived to reach the peak of their productive years. In this sense they constituted for a very long time, as human resources, an economic loss to the country. Their poverty derived from the peculiar agricultural-economic structure mentioned briefly above; their sickness, especially in the form of bilharzia and ankylostoma, came with the perennial irrigation introduced by Muhammad Ali in the nineteenth century. Yet there was little concern with agrarian or land reform in Egypt despite the attainment of formal political independence in 1922. The agrarian reform activities of the 1920s in Eastern Europe did not influence Egyptian attitudes enough to deal with their own problem. It was only after the Second World War that discussion of agrarian reform gained some prominence among leaders of the Egyptian intelligentsia, and only after the Free Officers coup in 1952 that drastic agrarian reform was attempted.[6]

Although the urban population of Egypt has increased by 50 per cent since 1918, in contrast to a population increase of only 20 per cent in the countryside, the isolation of the peasantry from the urban centres that direct the national revival remains a serious obstacle to the evolution of a cohesive national community. The customs and traditions of group and local loyalties, whether to city, village, province, occupation, or religious community, are still strong. Conservatism and insularity are manifested in the social practices of villagers, in their attachment to old agricultural methods, in their patience in adversity that derives from religious belief ('if life is unpleasant on earth, it will be better in the hereafter!'). Social intercourse continues to be collective between families; so do conflict and vendetta. Egypt, in Father Ayrout's phrase, has been largely 'rural, dense and sedentary'. Even the migrants to the towns and cities perpetuate their rural ethos.[7] This may be significant when of the country's forty million population, 42 per cent are under fifteen years of age; when the working population constitutes barely 25 per cent of the total population of the country; and when nearly half of this working population is still engaged on the land. Hardly 20 per cent of it is occupied by industry. The remainder mans the service sector of the economy.

Conservatism, isolation and a long-established traditional social structure comprise what one might call Egypt's permanent 'Egyptianity'. The essential feature of this Egyptianity has been that of an overwhelmingly rural nation, whose existence was regulated by the flow of the Nile. Egyptians formed the first unified nation known to history. Their unity and characteristic response to foreign influences at all times have not been the result of any speculative thought on their part. Rather these have been a reflection of their historical conditioning and their style of life: their unity in suffering while clinging to the traditions and beliefs of their society, to their arts and crafts. This constitutes perhaps the essence of the continuity in their history.

A series of invasions by foreign conquerors – Hyksos, Persians, Greeks, Romans – has presumably affected this Egyptianity. Three epoch-making events in its history, however, underlie the emergence and development of modern Egypt: the Arabic–Islamic conquest in the seventh century; the non-Arab Islamic conquests from the twelfth to the sixteenth centuries, namely Kurdish, Turkish and Ottoman; and the European encroachments beginning with the Napoleonic expedition to Egypt in 1798. The legacies that these influences have left in Egypt in the areas of social and cultural change and adjustment constitute perhaps the essential and crucial elements of development.

The importance of the Arab conquest of Egypt, led by Amr Ibn al-As in AD 641, lay in the imposition upon a Christian Egypt of a new faith, Islam, and a new language, Arabic. The natives relinquished Coptic and Greek in favour of Arabic, and abandoned Christianity for the faith of Allah. Theories regarding this massive shift in religion and language have preoccupied scholars of this period for a long time. There is strong evidence to support the argument that the native population was alienated by the Byzantine attempt to establish one monothelitic creed in the Empire at all costs, including persecution and torture of heterodox sects such as the Coptic majority of monophysites in Egypt. Some scholars contended that Amr's benevolent and tolerant administration, which gave tax relief to the Egyptians, served as an added attraction of Islam. Regardless of the reasons for the mass acceptance of Islam by the Egyptians, after the seventh century Egypt gradually became part of the Islamic–Arab tradition and civilization, and eventually its very centre.

Students of Egyptian history have often asked 'Are the Egyptians Arabs?' Racially, this question is improper; moreover, it was barely ever raised fifty years ago. More appropriate for consideration is whether the Egyptians have for the last thirteen centuries partaken of a basically Islamic–Arab culture and civilization. Here, too, one must be careful to qualify this cultural involvement of Egyptians through the language in which the faith of Islam was propagated; for one cannot assume that Egyptians also adopted indiscriminately the social and cultural standards of conduct emerging or deriving from the Arabian Peninsula – the earliest base of the Islamic movement. Even if one accepts the argument of Taha Husayn[8] that Egyptians have been more influenced by their earlier participation in what he called a Mediterranean–Hellenic civilization, it is evident that the greatest stamp upon thirteen centuries of their history has been the Asian–Islamic ethos. On this premise alone, it is useful to examine briefly this heritage which evolved in Egypt until the first European encroachments heralded by Napoleon. In doing so, we may also be able to outline the peculiarly Egyptian influences upon this adopted civilization and heritage, for in this confrontation between a conquering religion and an old established society, as the one found in Egypt in the seventh century, the interaction and impact were bound to be mutual.

Similarly, although the country's evolution and development over the last thirteen centuries has been closely identified with the history and the fortunes of the Islamic world, Egypt was one of the first Arabic-speaking countries in the Middle East to come under direct European influence. Moreover, Islamic rulers based in Egypt sought to extend their dominion and power over the traditional Islamic world. Both Saladin (1169–92) and the Mamluk Sultan Baybars (1260–77) led their Kurdish and Turkish armies from Egypt in battle to repel Christian conquerors from the West and Mongol and Tartar invaders from the East. Again in 1820–39, Muhammad Ali used Egypt as a springboard in his quest for aggrandizement and the extension of his dominion at the expense of the Ottoman Empire, and to exclude European influence. The revolutionary leadership of the Egyptian Free Officers in the 1950s sought in the name of Arab Nationalism and Arab Socialism to lead at least the Arab Islamic world to development and power and, in doing so, to exclude Western Europeans and Americans – some would argue outsiders in general – from exerting influence or control in the Middle East.

In the so-called nationalist style of politics, the Egyptians have been the first among the Arabs in the use of resources, articulate mass communications media, and in the short-lived determination to forge a united Arab nation, preferably under their own leadership and hegemony. They have also exhibited a capacity to vary their Arab policy to suit their national state interest.

CHAPTER 2

THE ESTABLISHMENT OF ISLAM
IN EGYPT

The Muslims sought the conquest of Egypt as a rich source of revenue and food supplies for the Hijaz in Arabia, and a strategic base for future expansion. It is reported that the famous Arab general Amr Ibn al-As suggested the conquest of Egypt to Caliph Omar, for he considered it a country as wealthy as it was defenceless.[1]

The conquest itself was spectacular in so far as the Arabs had no navy or knowledge of naval warfare at that time. Thus the relatively small army of four thousand horsemen that conquered Egypt overland from the east in 639–41 attests to the military and political disarray of the Byzantine forces in Egypt. Perhaps the Byzantines underestimated the military ability and vitality of the Arabs under the banner of Islam, still believing that the Arabs were mere raiders, interested in pillage and plunder. Yet the speed with which Graeco-Roman culture decayed in Egypt after the Arab conquest was paralleled by the rapid growth of a new Islamic civilization in the country. By AD 710 Arabic had replaced Greek as the official language of the administration, while Coptic, after lingering on for several centuries, is used today only in monasteries in the desert and for church liturgies.[2]

The imprudent policy of religious conformity followed by the Byzantine authorities had weakened the bonds of loyalty to State and Church among all subject peoples. In 636 the province of Syria had fallen to the conquering Muslim Arab armies. The Egyptians especially felt that their monophysite Coptic creed had been crushed by the harsh repression of Cyrus (631–41), Byzantine Prefect of Egypt and Bishop of Alexandria. The cruelty of their repression further alienated the last vestiges of loyalty to Constantinople. The Egyptians craved religious freedom which, under the circumstances, also meant political freedom from Byzantine tyranny. This irreparable division between imperial rulers and subjects in Egypt partly accounts for the ease with which Amr's handful of warriors crossed the Sinai from Gaza into Egypt to occupy Pelusium in 639.

Almost a thousand years earlier the Egyptians had welcomed

another conqueror, Alexander the Great, as their deliverer from hated alien rule. The ready acceptance of Christianity under Roman rule, for example, as an integral part of Egyptian deliverance from Ptolemaic and early Roman persecutions, was now turned into an even readier acceptance of Islam as a protest against Christian misrule. Looked at differently, a new and powerful force had arisen in the East to challenge both the Persian conquerors and Byzantine oppressors of Egypt. To Islam, therefore, the Egyptians looked for relief.

The early years of Arab rule, especially under Amr, were marked by a liberal policy towards religious worship. The Muslims were concentrated at first in Alexandria and Fustat, the town Amr founded, whereas the countryside remained predominantly Christian for over a hundred years. The Arab conquerors set out to rule Egypt as a province of the Islamic Caliphate, and, as in the case of Syria, they made no drastic changes in Egypt's administration. Instead, they were content to accept the allegiance of, and collect the revenue from, the various districts and provinces of the country under the old organization of village headmen and district governors.

By 650, however, the caliphs and their governors were bent on extracting as much revenue from Egypt as possible. Consequently, the tolerant and prudent administration inaugurated by Amr was gradually replaced by one of harsh financial policies which produced a succession of peasant rebellions early in the eighth century. Soon the Arab ruling class was so weakened that by 860 Egypt came to be controlled by a series of Turkish governors, whose forceful establishment in power cost the Baghdad Caliphate the control of the province altogether. However, any oppression exercised by Muslim governors in 'milking' the Egyptian cow was not motivated by religious hatred or antipathy for the Christians. Simply because the majority of the peasants were Christian the oppression was mainly borne by them.

However, the Egyptians did not convert to Islam as readily and massively as is usually supposed. In 725, there were still five to six million Christians – almost 98 per cent of the country's total population. The temptation to escape the poll-tax payment required of non-Muslims by a simple conversion to Islam did not seem very strong at first. The slow spread of Islam among the natives was contrary to the expectations of the conquerors. It gained momentum with the importation of Arabs from the tribes of Arabia, such as Qais, Kanz,

Juheina, Himyar and Lakhm. Most of these were settled in the eastern part of the Delta, known in Arabic as the Hawf. Each of the
ninety-two governors who ruled Egypt from 641 to 750 brought with
them an Arab army estimated at five thousand. Together with the
tribes who had migrated into Egypt, these eventually settled in both
Lower and Upper Egypt, intermarried with Christian Egyptians, and
acquired land. Although at an earlier stage of Islamic rule Arab
Muslims were forbidden to acquire land – a measure calculated to
maintain their status as a warrior class – the restriction was eventually lifted, and they become landowners. Considering their privileged
position with the government, the new settlers must have brought
tremendous social and economic pressure to bear upon Christians
to convert to Islam, adopt Arabic names and Arabic speech.

The Abbasid revolt which overthrew the Umayyad Caliphate of
Damascus in 750 ushered in an empire whose seat in Baghdad was
the centre of Islamic civilization for another two centuries. Further
court practices, especially those borrowed or imported from Persia,
and the efflorescence of learning in the eighth and ninth centuries
quickened the pace of conversion to Islam in all the imperial
dominions. For a hundred years the Baghdad Caliphs appointed a
series of mostly Arab governors whose terms of office were usually
very brief. By 856, they began to send Turkish governors to Egypt,
or to give the government of the Egyptian province in fief to one
or another commander of their Turkish praetorian guard in Baghdad. This guard was soon after 850 replacing the Arabs as the warrior
caste in Islam. Heavy burdens of taxation and religious discrimination against the Christians of Egypt were prominent policies in
the reign of Caliph al-Mutawakkil in 850, and may have possibly
accelerated the rate of their conversion to Islam.

The mid-ninth century marks the beginning of a system of government in Egypt which, with the exception of a few interruptions,
lasted until 1800: namely, the control of the country by autonomous
and semi-independent Turkish, Kurdish and Circassian princes.
Rule was autocratic – at times benevolent, but often tyrannical. But
it also accelerated the growth of Islam in Egyptian society, until by
1300 Egypt had become the strongest centre of Islamic power and
civilization. The Mongol conquest in the East and the destruction
of Baghdad by Hülaku in 1250 gave Egypt a central position in
Islamic culture: she became the centre of Arabic letters and the depository of Islamic religious tradition, as well as the greatest bulwark
of the Islamic world against Christian attack.

Ibn Tulun, the first Turkish governor of Egypt to establish an autonomous dynasty which lasted for some thirty-seven years (868–904), brought prosperity and a stable rule to Egypt. He embarked upon a brilliant age of building, including the famous mosque in Cairo; and he extended the frontiers of Egypt to Syria in the north, and Libya in the west.

Chaos and insurrection prevailed in Egypt for about thirty years after the fall of the Ibn Tulun dynasty. The slave soldiery and officers imported by Turkish governors to Egypt became the chief determinants of political power, and dominated the government. The Caliphs in Baghdad were unable to impose any authority over the province. In 935, Muhammad b. Tughj, known as al-Ikhshid, another Turkish mercenary, secured control over Egypt, and like Ibn Tulun before him, founded a short-lived dynasty. Although we know relatively little about his rule, he was, like Ibn Tulun, a great builder and patron of the arts, and paid great attention to the improvement of irrigation canals. He too brought peace to a country seething with insurrections, and established a hereditary principality recognized by the Caliph. His two sons who succeeded him were too weak to govern, and the government of Egypt passed in 965 into the hands of a Negro eunuch, Kafur, a man whose strong rule became, it seems unjustly so, a by-word for all dictatorial rule in the Arab world since.[3] Upon his death in 968, Egypt reverted to weak rule and thus became easy prey to the conquering ambitions of the rival Fatimid caliphate in North Africa. A series of low Niles resulted in famine and general economic crisis which further weakened the country, and facilitated its conquest by the Fatimid general Jawhar in 969.

The Fatimid invasion of Egypt in 969 was the crowning event in the success of the Ismaili (shiite) movement against orthodox Islam which was then politically represented by the Abbasid state. With the acquisition of Egypt, the Fatimid dynasty which had first established its rule in North Africa was now able to extend its dominions eastwards and challenge its rivals in Baghdad for the control of the whole Islamic community. Their rule in Egypt from 969 to 1171 represents a brilliant period of Islamic civilization, which not only speeded and completed the influence of Islam in Egypt, but rendered the country the most prosperous and illustrious centre of Islamic culture.

Two accomplishments of the Fatimids in Egypt stand out as

epochal in the Islamization of the country: the founding of the city of Cairo by Jawhar and the erection of the Azhar mosque and university in it. The heretics of Islam challenged their rivals in Spain and Baghdad from magnificent Cairo on the Nile in their bid for supremacy in the Muslim world.

Like those rulers who governed Egypt before them, the Fatimids were foreigners to the country. While interested in power and wealth, they were heads of a significant Islamic sect aiming at the leadership of all Islam. The first two caliphs, Al-Muizz (969–75) and Al-Aziz (975–96), were energetic, benevolent and prudent. The Egyptians, on their part, accepted the new régime with their habitual forbearance and good humour. Authority was again claimed by a powerful Islamic conqueror.[4] Unlike their predecessors or their Mamluk successors, the Fatimids led by Muizz asserted their hegemony over Egypt for two centuries not only by force, but also by virtue of their belief in the legitimate cause of their dynasty and the righteousness of their sectarian faith. Although the Fatimid Ismaili creed tended at first to be more tolerant in matters of religion, the power of the caliphs was based primarily upon the loyalty of their armies, which consisted of Arabs, Berbers, Negroes and other foreign legions. The unhappy reign of the controversial al-Hakim (996–1021) with his persecutions and harsh measures against certain sections of the population, was soon overshadowed by the relatively brilliant and long career of al-Mustansir (1036–94), during whose reign Egypt enjoyed tranquillity and prosperity with the exception of a seven-year-long and terrible famine (1066–72). It is reported as an indication of this ruler's appreciation of learning and letters that al-Mustansir's library numbered over one hundred thousand books.

There is no doubt that the Fatimids gave Egypt, and especially its capital Cairo, its permanently Islamic character, which best survives in the architecture of their mosques, especially al-Azhar, and the famous gates of the city.[5] In the period 960–1170, Egyptian historians and interpreters of the religious law flourished, setting forth a tradition of local Arab–Islamic scholarship which reached its greatest development in the fifteenth century. Such were al-Kindi (d. 961) of Fustat, his student and collaborator, Ibn Zulaq (d. 997), a native Egyptian, and the historian al-Musabbihi (d. 1029).

Like their rivals, the Abbasid caliphs in Baghdad, the Fatimid rulers of Egypt succumbed to the rising power of their slave bodyguards until, by the end of the eleventh century, they had been reduced to mere pawns in the hands of their feuding army generals.

The Kurd, Saladin, who with his uncle, Shirkuh, had come to the aid of Egypt against the Franks, succeeded to the office of *wazir*, or Chief Minister, to the Fatimid caliph in 1169. Two years later he supplanted the Fatimid ruler to found the Ayyubid dynasty of Egypt and inaugurate ninety glorious years in the history of Muslim domination in Egypt.

Over five hundred years had passed since the Arabs first occupied the Nile Valley. The natives appeared at first to cling tenaciously to their religious faith, but soon and with amazing docility adopted both the Islamic faith and the language of their new masters. Yet most of the memorable and commanding figures in Egypt continued to be foreigners: Ibn Tulun, al-Ikhshid, Jawhar, al-Aziz. Materially, the condition of the populace remained unchanged. Cultivation and irrigation continued as before with few and rare instances of public initiative for their extension or improvement. On the whole, the new rulers were mainly interested in collecting the revenue necessary to support their opulent existence, their army and their expeditions. The Egyptian historian, al-Maqrizi, reports occasional drops in land-tax yield, an indication of the rulers' neglect of agriculture – the major source of income in the country. Although the courts of the Turkish governor Ibn Tulun, or the slave despot Kafur, and the Fatimid caliph al-Mustansir may have attracted some men of learning and stimulated architectural and artistic activity, most of these aspects of their rule were of benefit to the cities and towns but not to the countryside – a condition true of Egypt until our time. It was not until the political 'dark ages' of the Mamluks that Islamic Egypt reached the height of its achievement: a strange alliance between the political autocracy of exclusive slave dynasties on the one hand, and intellectual and cultural activity on the other.

Salah al-Din al-Ayyubi, or Saladin (1169–93) – often the hero of present-day Egyptian–Islamic–Arab nationalism – was essentially a Kurdish warrior, whose interest in war dictated his policy at home. Being a stranger to Egypt, he depended for support, in addition to his own Kurds, upon his imported, or purchased, Mamluk slave guards. Also, influenced by the fortified cities in Syria, he built the famous Citadel in Cairo. His interest in a Holy War against the Crusader Franks prompted him to extend his sway over Syria and Mesopotamia as a base from which to strike at the infidels of Europe. Although his dynasty, the Ayyubid (1170–1250), was short-lived it had a great impact on the social and political evolution of Egypt.

First, it marked the coming of the Mamluks to the country in ever-increasing numbers, and secondly, it promoted the gradual emergence of Egypt as a centre of Islamic learning and culture. The first development had serious consequences for that country's political evolution; the second speeded up the processes of Islamic influence in Egyptian society and fixed its ideological and spiritual orientation for a long time to come. Saladin's *madrassas*, or collegiate mosques, for instance, were an innovation (copied from Persia) of great importance. In this tradition one may view the later collegiate mosque of Sultan Hasan (1347–51, 1354–61) built in 1362. Saladin considered himself the champion of Islam against the Christians, and aspired to extend his rule over a vast Muslim kingdom. The Holy Places, Mesopotamia and Syria, all came under his sway, and it was not until the third Crusade in 1191 that the Christians could retaliate, though unsuccessfully. The dynasty Saladin founded in Egypt came to an end in 1250 but, at least according to most Arab historians, Ayyubid rule had been relatively good for Egypt. The country was opened to European trade, especially to Venetians and Pisans, and the sultans were friendly to Christians.

Successive conquerors ruled Egypt as a garrison state. Under the later Fatimid caliphs, soldiers came to monopolize the chief administrative posts. Saladin militarized his administration even further. Upon his accession to power he abolished, for instance, the Fatimid army consisting of Negro slaves, and officered by Armenians, Egyptians and Arabs, and replaced it with Kurds and Turks. The financial demands of his numerous campaigns were so great that the treasury could not always meet the pay of the army and its officers. Saladin, and the Mamluk sultans after him, resorted freely to a practice begun by the Abbasid caliphs long before them, namely the granting of land to military officers in return for services. Thus, whereas under the early Umayyads the lands of a province were the property of the State to be rented out to cultivators and tax-farmers, now a new class of landowners who were also fighting mercenaries arose. By the fifteenth century, most of the land in Egypt was the property of the sultan and his military commanders. Peasant cultivators were soon converted into mere agricultural workers, tied to the soil as vassals of the fief holders. The latter had no particular interest in the peasants other than their ability to produce the desired revenue. In turn, the sultan had no interest in the welfare of the peasants either, so long as his feudatory commanders paid their share of the tribute to the exchequer.[6]

By 1250, therefore, the rulers of Egypt were recruited from a class of warriors who were either imported or came to Egypt in the first instance as slaves. A chief Sultan – usually the strongest, cleverest and most ruthless among them – presided over a pyramidal structure of power whose base consisted of soldiers and retainers of the military commanders, while the latter, the princes, occupied the middle ranges of that pyramid. All of them knew one occupation only – war. With Saladin came many Kurds and Turks, who later became the dominant military caste and grabbed power. This was essentially an Asian Turkish-speaking caste which imported into Egypt the manners and customs of Asian life.

Ever since the end of the ninth century waves of peoples from Asia had infiltrated the Islamic empire, first slowly, then as armed tribes, and finally as paid mercenaries. What the caliphs of Baghdad began as a means of protecting themselves against Arabs aspiring to power eventually developed into a new élite corps of non-Arab Muslims that became the basis of dynastic power in the provinces, particularly in the case of the Mamluks in Egypt. Thus the only identity left to society was that of a religious community, the community of Islam.[7]

The state of Egypt became the private domain of the Mamluks and only those who bore arms seemed to have any political rights. The Mamluk system, moreover, depended for its support and perpetuation upon the importation of more of their kind. No Mamluk sultan was secure in his position or sure of the succession of his heirs without the loyalty of his satisfied retainers. With the recession of the Mongol threats at the beginning of the fifteenth century the influx of Turkish slaves and mercenaries into the Islamic provinces and Egypt diminished. The decreased flow was partly responsible for the weakening of Mamluk rule in Egypt and their ultimate defeat by the Ottomans in 1517.

The word 'mamluk' means 'owned', but the circumstance of Mamluk 'slavery' was an avenue to political power in view of the basically military function of these so-called slaves. Moreover, the relationship of the 'mamluk' to his master was one of kinship, not necessarily of servitude; so that the slave frequently succeeded his master in a position of authority and power.

The official Mamluk control of Egypt lasted from 1250 to 1517, although their virtual control was not decisively destroyed until 1811 (see Chapter Four), and is divided into two periods: the state of the Bahri or River Mamluks (1250–1382), who were mostly Turks, and that of the Burji or Citadel Mamluks (1382–1517) who were pre-dominantly Circassians. By murdering the Ayyubid Turanshah in 1250, the Bahri Mamluks acceded to power. The most famous among them was Baybars (1260–77), whose strict but relatively en-lightened rule left a deeper impression upon the Egyptians than that of Saladin. Not only did he secure Egypt against certain invasion by the Mongols and Franks, but he also managed to control his army princes by centralizing the military system, inaugurating a postal sys-tem, and elevating the function of the religious judges (*qadis*) of the four orthodox schools to a position of eminence and respect. In fact, his munificence and strong personality are still extolled in the folk-tales of the Egyptian public along with Abu Zeid al-Hilali and other legendary heroes.

Equally significant was his concern with learning and the endowment of mosque colleges and other religious institutions. He was thus not only the founder of the Egyptian Mamluk state but also its most brilliant sultan, the defender of Islam against the Mon-gols at Ain Jalut in 1260 before his accession to power. Determined to recapture and extend the power and prestige of the imperial base founded by Saladin in Egypt, Baybars proceeded to consolidate his position as the leader of an Islamic Empire based in that country by reinstating al-Mustansir, a descendant of the Abbasids who had survived the sacking of Baghdad by the Mongols in 1258, as Caliph in Cairo. This perfunctory restoration of the Caliphate did not merely lend legitimacy to the authority of Baybars, but also served to rally Muslim sentiment against the Mongol menace.

By the beginning of the fourteenth century the dominion of the Mamluk sultans of Egypt had extended to the Arabian Peninsula, so that the Sharifs of Mecca and Medina were appointed by them.[8] Even independent Yemen under the Rasulid kings was obliged to send tributary presents from time to time to Cairo. Frequent expedi-tions to Nubia brought slaves. The *khutba*, or Friday prayer, was said as far west as Tripoli and Tunis in the name of the Mamluk sultan. Egypt under the Mamluk sultans with their extraordinarily efficient army had become a power to be reckoned with throughout the Islamic world, even though the actual authority of the Mamluk sultan may not have extended directly over distant parts, i.e., beyond the Syrian desert and the Euphrates in the east and northeast, or Aswan in the south.

Generally, the Mamluk sultans were not unduly harsh on their Christian subjects in Egypt. Copts continued to be employed in the various offices of the State and administration – indeed, they were apparently preferred over Muslim subjects for their aptitude in business and accounting matters. Moreover, the era of the Mamluks is generally regarded as one of learning. The fertile soil of the country afforded wealth to the sultans and their courtiers which they were able to use in the patronage of architecture, the arts and letters. At the same time they did not altogether ignore public works, which under Nasir's reigns (1293; 1298–1308; 1309–14) received great attention in the building of irrigation canals, bridges, dams and aqueducts. Commerce and trade with Europe, on the other hand, also enhanced the fortunes of the sultans and indirectly brought a measure of prosperity to the population at large.

Under the sway of the Citadel Mamluks (1382–1517), Egypt's political fortunes declined, primarily as a result of the extreme and violent factiousness among them and their followers. No sultan was able to establish a hereditary dynasty as stable and illustrious as that founded, for example, by the Bahri Qalaun. The unruly factions could no longer be controlled by the sultan: they could therefore turn their unbridled excesses upon a helpless public. Despite such political disarray in the ranks of the Circassian Mamluks, they were able to show superb qualities as a fighting force, especially in their confrontation with Timur (Tamerlane) at the end of the fourteenth century, and to retain their control over Egypt and Syria. Their founding sultan, Barquq (d. 1399), for instance, was not only an able sultan and warrior, but left splendid monuments (a *madrasa* and his tomb mosque) as testimony to his taste in art and his piety in faith. His successors were able to conquer Cyprus and render that island a tributary of Egypt until the Ottoman conquest.

Among these Al-Ashraf Kait Bey stands out as the most successful (1468–96). Like other Mamluk sultans he was a bought slave who rose in the ranks of Mamluk soldiery to a 'prince of a thousand' and commander-in-chief. Obsessed by the idea of restoration of all public monuments, and over-zealous in his ambitious public works programme, he caused the people to suffer the heavy cost of his many works. During his reign it became clear that the Ottomans in the north were seeking an opportune moment to nibble away at the Syrian dominions of the Mamluks. This rivalry, interspersed with minor wars in the dominions, heavy taxation at home, and serious plagues (especially in 1492), forecast the economic disaster that gripped Egypt for the next twenty years. Fierce contests broke out between the Mamluks themselves, so that order was not restored in the realm until 1501 under the leadership of Ashraf Kansuh al-Ghuri (1501–16) who levied catastrophically burdensome taxes, heavy customs duties, and even appropriated *waqf* (religious endowment and charitable trust) properties. Badly needed revenue for the state coffers was offset by the general impoverishment of the people. As usual, Kansuh spent most of this revenue purchasing more Mamluks to strengthen his position, erecting his mosque and college as was the custom with many Mamluk sultans, and constructing fortifications.

In 1512 Selim I, known as the Conqueror, succeeded his father Bayazid II to the Ottoman throne in Constantinople. Ambitious and warlike, he defeated the Safavi Shah Ismail of Persia in the battle of Chaldiran in 1514 and was now ready to move westwards and southwards to Syria and Egypt. On a minor pretext that Kansuh was harbouring renegade princes of the Ottoman house, and that he was aiding the enemy of the Ottomans, i.e., Ismail of Persia, Selim I proceeded to invade Syria, a dominion of Egypt. Failing to recognize the importance of an alliance with Ismail of Persia against the Ottomans until too late, the ageing Kansuh marched against the Ottomans. The two armies met in Marj Dabiq, north of Aleppo, in 1516, where the Mamluk Egyptian army was routed by the Turks. Killed in battle, Kansuh was succeeded in Cairo by his slave and viceroy Tuman Bey who, at the insistence of the Mamluk princes, refused Selim's offer of a deal: to recognize Selim in the prayers and coinage in return for his appointment as Ottoman viceroy of Egypt. By January 1517, the Turks entered Cairo. Selim the Conqueror himself entered the city on 26 January 1517.

The Ottoman conquest of Egypt marked the end of the independent state of the Mamluks as well as of their empire. Egypt now became a province in the Ottoman Empire to be ruled by viceroy *pashas*, or *walis*, of the Ottoman Sultan. These governors appointed by the Sultan and supported by a corps of Janissaries were not, however, able to maintain their control over the country for very long. The revived strength of the Mamluk Beys, headed by their chief prince, usually the governor, or *shaykh al-balad*, of Cairo, rendered the Turkish pashas captives to their desires and demands and reduced their position to that of nominal representatives of Constantinople but with virtually no real power in the country.

The Mamluk legacy of Egypt is perhaps one of the strangest in the country's history. A group of foreign slaves, imported into the

country to buttress the authority of ruling princes and dynasties, ultimately supplanted their masters and ruled the country for over two
hundred and fifty years. Undergoing rigid training as a warrior caste,
the Mamluks kept themselves quite apart from the Egyptian people
whom they governed. In this they constituted a militarized oligarchy
par excellence. Even though they were internally divided in their
ranks, at no time were the Egyptians in a position to challenge their
authority. They were a force that supported a sultan, a ruler, but
not a nation. The allegiance of Mamluk troops was to their commanders who, in turn, remained loyal to the sultan, so long as he
satisfied their appetite for revenue-producing land fiefs and other
forms of wealth. Thus the Mamluks were a feudal military organization separated from the bulk of the native population, so that regardless of the practices or ideas developed in the courts of the Mamluk
sultans, these could scarcely influence the social and traditional
structure of the native masses.

The Arab invasion marked a turning point in Egypt's history, for
it introduced two original factors in her future development: a new
religion and a different language. The tremendous impact of Islam
and Arabic on Egyptian society cannot be underestimated, for Egyptians became, within a period of five hundred years, Arabic-speaking
Muslims in thought, belief and tradition. By the ninth century, Egypt
was essentially an Arab Muslim society. Egyptians even tried to
obscure their pre-Islamic past. This desire was reflected in their
numerous historical and religious studies during the Mamluk period.
The Egyptians now joined the peoples of Asia and gradually became
isolated from Western Europe until the first fierce confrontation with
the Crusades.

Just as the Roman wave culminated in the evolution of a Christian
society in Egypt, so did the Arab wave bring about an Islamic society
in its place. Despite Egypt's loyalty to the native church under the
Byzantines, the Arab conquest with its subsequent establishment of
Islam produced a society defined along even broader religious lines.
Loyalty to Islam became paramount over loyalty to Egypt, so that
the proliferation of Islamic states and dynasties within Egypt – Fatimid, Ayyubid, Mamluk, Ottoman – represented dynastic–religious
divisions and differences rather than national entities. Indeed, slaves
from the Caucasus and Transoxania could come to Egypt as rulers.
The State and its rulers depended for their existence and the pursuit
of their objectives upon warrior classes to the exclusion of the bulk
of the citizenry, who were strictly expected to provide the food and

other necessities of these privileged ruling groups. Thus the tribal Arabs sustained the early Islamic state in its expansion; Kurds, Turks and Circassians guarded the Islamic Empire and ruled its provinces; Persians, Jews, Armenians and other Christians administered for long periods the non-military offices of the State; native merchants, artisans and craftsmen held together the fabric of the economy; and learned men of religion provided the judicial and often financial services of the State. The direction of Egypt's political fortunes thus passed from Arabs to Maghribis (North Africans), to Kurdish, Turkish and Circassian Mamluks, to Ottomans, French and British, without any real sense of organic social or national consciousness on the part of the mass of its inhabitants until the late nineteenth century.

The rural–urban dichotomy mentioned in the first chapter was not only maintained but, in political-economic terms, sharpened after the Arab conquest of Egypt. The Pharoah Menes, who had unified Upper and Lower Egypt, centralized political control and administration. This enabled him to undertake public works on a large scale and to enforce his authority throughout the land with the aid of an official state religion. His was essentially a military rule, supported by a state religion whose systematic expansion of irrigation and cultivation utilized the fertile Nile Valley to support a densely populated country. Power and social status were associated with landownership, and the relationship of the peasant farmer to his ruler was determined by his relationship to the land. The ruler allotted land to his generals and army officers, priests and bureaucrats. The 'gift-land' practice of a series of conquerors – Persians, Romans, Byzantines, Arabs, Mamluks and Ottomans – initially strengthened a military group of landowners. The various governments of this period depended upon this type of patronage for their rule, thus completely transforming the Egyptian land tenure system. From a situation where all the land of the country belonged to the crown, which had the right to parcel it out in the form of gifts as well as to reappropriate it, a semi-feudal arrangement gradually emerged by which large tracts of land were granted to soldiers, religious leaders and others who were now masters of their cultivation and disposition.

The condition of the fellah under these circumstances was almost one of bondage, and his rights – if he had any – were denied. The Royal Lands of the Pharaohs cultivated by the Royal Tenants became the Sultan's or Caliph's lands; whereas under Islam, *waqf*, or Religious Institution, lands became the equivalent of the Lands of the Temple. Under the Mamluks, the slave warriors, the military chiefs, became the nucleus of a landowning class. Although the Otto-mans attempted to ease the tax burden of the fellahin as an induce-ment to stay on the land and increase production, improved irriga-tion systems and restored fallow land to cultivation, they soon failed to maintain a centralized administration of taxation that would have enabled this situation to prevail. Their cadastral survey, the first for many centuries in Egypt, provided the basis for a more efficient tax system, and tax collection was first entrusted to salaried agents of the central government. Less than a hundred years after their con-quest of the country, the tax agents were replaced by *multezims*, or tax-farmers, 'who were required to pay to the Imperial Treasury a fixed amount of land tax in return for their right, and who could keep the balance of the annual collection as profit for themselves'.[9]

The chief function of the fellahin remained that of cultivating the land and returning in taxes the bulk of their produce. The steady decline of Ottoman central authority and the re-emergence of the landed class, especially that of the Mamluks, simply multiplied the amount of local taxes the fellahin had to pay. Where once the land of Egypt was divided into *iltizams*, or tax farms, under the control of the *multezims* who in a way owed allegiance and paid a required tribute to the Ottoman viceroy (*wali*), the units now became *muqa-ta'at*, or possessions, of various landed gentry, who could bequeath these lands to their heirs. Both systems of land tenure, however, per-mitted the exploitation of the land and the peasants. Administrative matters were delegated to officials at the village level, and villagers were directly responsible to the *multezim* or the *muqata'ji*. This further isolated the villagers.

For three centuries (1250–1520), Egypt was the centre of cultural and intellectual activity in the Arabic-speaking part of the Islamic world. The other two centres of Islamic power, Baghdad and Anda-lusia, had succumbed to external attack. Especially during the fif-teenth century, Egypt witnessed a period of historical, topographical and other writing. This intellectual activity did not slacken until after the Ottoman conquest when Istanbul became the centre of Islamic spiritual and temporal authority. Nevertheless, Islamic teaching and culture continued in the religious institutions of the country, led by the Azhar.

The tradition of Arabic historical writing in Islamic Egypt begun by Abd al-Hakam in the ninth century continued down to the famous chronicler Abd al-Rahman al-Jabarti of the early nineteenth century. These historians provide a basic source for the study of the early history of Muslim Egypt. A serious school of historical writing inaugurated by the arrival of the North African historian Ibn Khaldun as a judge in Cairo at the beginning of the fourteenth century was further developed by the Egyptian al-Maqrizi (d. 1442), a Cairene, who is best known for his monumental topographical and historical work on Egypt, and his history of the Fatimid Caliphs and Ayyubid Mamluk dynasties.[10] Two major chroniclers of the same period should be mentioned: Jalal al-Din al-Suyuti (d. 1505) of Asiut, and his student Ibn Iyas (d. 1524).[11] It is in the tradition of these chroniclers that, much later, al-Jabarti wrote his famous history of the eighteenth and early nineteenth centuries, indispensable for a study of the Napoleonic expedition and the rise of Muhammad Ali to power. Following Jabarti, the nineteenth century was well chronicled and topographically described by Ali Pasha Mubarak (d. 1893), a French-trained military engineer.[12]

One of the most interesting consequences of the interaction between Islam and Egypt was the development of mystical teachings and organizations among the Egyptians. Whereas in Mesopotamia and the Arabian Peninsula the mystics, or *Sufis*, evoked continuous opposition from orthodox religious leaders, in Egypt the various mystical brotherhoods (*tariqas*) established themselves and flourished until our day. The Egyptian mystic Dhu'l-Nun al-Misri (d. 860), the Cairene poet Ibn al-Farid (d. 1234), and the later leaders of mystic orders often achieved positions of social and political leadership over the Egyptian people. The Egyptians moreover introduced much of the heroic and romance literature into Islamic society, the most celebrated examples of which are the *Thousand and One Nights*, the legends of Abu Zeid al-Hilali and the Mamluk Sultan al-Zahir Baybars. The art of story-telling became a source of popular entertainment among the people.

The salient phenomenon of Ottoman rule in Egypt was the distribution – in fact, sharing – of power between the Ottoman Viceroy and the Mamluk Beys. Both centres of power, however, were unconcerned with the condition of the population. The only group to which the public could look for aid and comfort under these circumstances was that of the religious teachers, the ulama, judges and heads of religious institutions. Traditionally the religious institutions, and especially the Sharia judges, were independent from and highly respected by the rulers. Consequently they were usually able to influence, if not limit, the power of the governors. By virtue of this privileged position and in their capacity as the focus of religious authority, they were viewed by the public as their ultimate resort against the excesses of the rulers. At the same time, certain prominent members of the religious institutions, such as Shaykh Ali al-Bakri (d. 1793), were taking a keen interest in the reform of these institutions. Their major targets of attack were the various religious sufi orders, through whose activities the Islamic faith had become one of excessively superstitious group ritual and ceremony.

One of the ready weapons in the hands of reforming shaykhs against the mystic orders was the *fatwa*, or juridical ruling regarding the Sacred Law. Jabarti reports the activities of the eighteenth-century poet Hasan al-Badri al-Hijazi in connection with his criticism of these social conditions. Jabarti also informs us that the preachers attacked the excessive adoration and worship of saints so common in Egypt at that time, especially as manifested in the visitation of tombs. Thus we can assume a vigorous, though as yet incipient, campaign for some religious and social reform on the part of certain religious leaders and scholars, contemporary to the puritan Wahhabi movement in Arabia. This took the form of an attack upon 'popular religion', especially its mystical orders, and a criticism of superstitious folk accretions to the faith.

Concern with the condition of society was shown by some of the Egyptian religious leaders, and a modest intellectual activity was acquiring some momentum towards the end of the eighteenth century. This first stirring was not influenced either by East or West. Thus in the field of mathematics and astronomy we read about the famous Shaykh Hasan al-Jabarti, father of the celebrated chronicler. In language and poetry, there emerged the Azharite Shaykh Hasan al-Attar, teacher of a new generation of reformers and intellectual leaders of whom more later. Prominent in linguistic and religious studies was Shaykh Muhammad Murtada al-Zabidi (d. 1791). One wonders how this Egyptian intellectual revival movement would have developed had it not been abruptly interrupted by the appearance of conquering Europeans in 1798. The latter event gave rise to an educational and intellectual movement on completely different and modern lines.

Militarized ruling oligarchies, provincial governors, and landowning feudatories constituted the ruling establishments in Egypt for thirteen centuries. While Islam and Arabic took root in Egyptian society, at no time did the foreign rulers of Egypt, largely Turks, superimpose their language or customs upon Egyptian society. Secure in their city courts, citadels and garrisons, their contact with the native population was at a minimum. The latter, on the other hand, maintained a highly ordered and independent existence in their villages, craft and merchant guilds, religious orders and institutions. Society was divided into two separate groups: the rulers and the subjects. The former were mainly soldiers and officials; the latter were merchants, craftsmen, artisans and farmers. Contacts between the two groups were formal and minimal so long as revenue was forthcoming to the Central State Treasury.

The architectural and building activities of the Fatimid Caliphs and the Mamluk Sultans after them produced the exquisite city of Cairo. The combination of a court in a brilliant city did not, however, reach out with its benefits to the countryside. The age-old dichotomy, the social division between rural and urban Egypt, was maintained: all the institutions of central government were directed towards the perpetuation of this condition. The subjects continued to supply the needs of the governors. Moreover, the eternal conflict between central authority, represented since 1517 by the Ottoman Pasha, or Viceroy, and the feuding ambitious Mamluk Beys rendered the population victims of these disorders. At no time was the Ottoman Sultan in fact capable of exercising strict control over his representatives in Egypt. So long as the tribute, or set sum of money, was dispatched to the Central Treasury annually, the Sultan took little interest in the actual governing of the province. When, moreover, the power of his viceroy in Egypt declined in contrast to that of the Mamluk Beys, the Sultan was hardly in a position to assist him. Only in 1775 was an expedition sent to Egypt under the leadership of the Capudan Pasha Hasan to deal with the separatist activities of Ali Bey the Great.

Essentially the primary interest of the Ottoman Sultan in Egypt, or for that matter, in other provinces, was the exploitation of the country for the benefit of the Imperial Treasury and the Imperial Army. While the Sultan was obliged to defend his empire with all its provinces from external attack and to enforce the observance of the Sharia, the task of governing the province of Egypt and maintaining its internal security belonged to the provincial administration, headed by the Viceroy. Simultaneously, the local Beys and military leaders exacted their revenues from their lands by imposing heavy taxes upon the peasants who worked on them. By the eighteenth century, these Beys returned only a small portion of this revenue to the provincial governor as tribute. The rest they retained for their own use. Military requirements, moreover, called for greater exactions of revenue from the agricultural workers.

In the relations between the Beys, tax-farmers and other exploiters on the one hand, and the fellahin on the other, the governors maintained a position of neutrality. They were merely interested in collecting that portion of the revenue necessary to maintain their nominal authority and to pay the tribute to the Imperial Treasury in Istanbul. A foreign military ruling caste coexisted with a native bureaucracy operating between it and the population. So long as this closed economic, social and intellectual order was not disturbed or challenged by disruptive forces the equilibrium of that society was maintained. By 1750, however, economic difficulties within the country, as well as economic pressures from the outside, together with military difficulties, rendered the existing system incapable of coping with new situations.

What indeed took deep root in Egypt was that consciousness of the Arabic language which accompanied the acceptance of the Islamic faith with its Holy Book, the Koran. Through it, the Egyptian joined millions of his co-religionists in the Muslim world to partake of Islamic tradition and culture. Like them, however, he was ruled for many centuries by a conquering caste of warriors, the Turks and their satraps. Although somewhere deep in the recesses of his memory he felt that he was Egyptian, and therefore different from his rulers, the Egyptian hardly influenced government and authority, or its institutions. Fortunately, the Islamic framework with its religious tradition, orders and institutions, operating on the whole within the limits of the Sacred Law, afforded him an ordered and relatively contented existence. Towards the end of the eighteenth century it was not only the political authority and military power of his rulers that were destroyed, but more significantly the coming of a European conqueror to Egypt undermined his traditional order and subverted his loyalty to it.

CHAPTER 3

THE FIRST EUROPEAN IMPACT

The Ottoman conquest in 1517 put an end to the Circassian Mamluk dynasty. Selim I proceeded to lay down the foundations of a new political order by which the country was to be governed for almost three centuries. According to the Egyptian chronicler Ibn Iyas, this order was based on the existence of competing power groups in the country. Thus, Selim first appointed a viceroy, or governor, to represent imperial authority; second, he left in Egypt a body of Janissaries, ostensibly to serve as the imperial military force in the country but actually to checkmate any ambitions of the viceroys. The battalions and companies of these troops were led by officers known as *ocaklis*, and the chief among these officers was the *Agha*. The *ocaklis* constituted the Viceroy's, or Pasha's, Council (*Diwan*). Finally, Selim permitted a third group to exist, namely those Mamluk Beys who had declared their allegiance to the Sultan, by appointing them governors of various provinces in Egypt. Al-Jabarti refers to these as the 'Egyptian Princes'. The rivalry that ensued between these three groups eventually led to the ascendancy in power of the local Mamluk Beys, or Egyptian princes, so that by 1700 the Turkish Viceroy in Egypt was a mere pawn in their hands.

Mamluk supremacy in Egypt was further advanced by the coincidental decline of Ottoman power in the late seventeenth and early eighteenth centuries as a result of continuous warfare and the weakening of internal political administration. Moreover, the quick succession of Ottoman Viceroys in Egypt prevented any one among them from attaining unrivalled political strength, or great influence in the country. The rival Mamluk Beys, on the other hand, managed to retain their exclusiveness and *esprit de corps*, for they were able to continue to import their slaves and thus to swell the ranks of their private armies. The Janissaries were slowly assimilated into the country and their loyalty to the Ottoman Sultan was soon eroded. They were thus unable to act as defenders of the Sultan's interests in Egypt. Soon all civil and financial administration came into Mamluk hands, enabling them to distribute lands and other gifts to officers and thus attract them to their side. All these developments undermined the authority of the Ottoman governors, while the influence of the Beys increased. Led by a Bey of their own choice, the Chief Mamluk of Cairo, better known as *shaykh al-balad*, or Governor of Cairo, the Mamluks became the actual rulers of Egypt.

Throughout the eighteenth century – at least until the French conquest – Egypt presented a spectacle of an Ottoman dominion over whose possession and control local chiefs fought with one another continuously. Rebellion was practically endemic. Peasant and tribal uprisings were so violent – and occasionally well organized – that civil war broke out between the Huwara tribesmen led by their Shaykh Humam in Upper Egypt and the troops of the Cairo Mamluk Beys, which lasted on and off for over thirty years (1736–69). It practically detached Upper Egypt from the rest of the country when Humam set up his own government.[1]

The financial system of the country was just as disruptive. Although initially the Sultan considered all lands in Egypt his property, ownership gradually passed to the various Beys and, as military and other financial necessities arose, much land also passed to the tax-farmers (*multezims*), who had total control over the fellahin and their lands. The peasant cultivator was thus at the mercy of the tax-farmer who, in turn, was at the mercy of the Beys. During this period *waqf* (charitable trust and religious endowment) properties increased, for it was one of the best means of ensuring that such property would escape appropriation by the Beys.

The judicial system also was changed under the Ottomans. Before the conquest there were four judges (*qadis*), representing the four rites of orthodox (Sunni) Islam. Sultan Suleyman (1520–66), however, abolished these and replaced them by one Chief *Qadi*, an Ottoman Turk, appointed from Istanbul.

Ottoman governors and Mamluk Beys alike neglected irrigation and related agricultural works, allowing the country's economy to deteriorate. Similarly, trade and industry, arts and crafts suffered as a result of the general political conditions in the country and because Selim had transported many of the leading craftsmen and artisans with him to Istanbul. In the eighteenth century the French traveller Claude Étienne Savary, however, reported that even though the Ottomans had neglected agriculture and irrigation, he found that commerce flourished. Thus Alexandria, a city of 6,000 people, was 'very commercial, an advantage it owes to its situation'.[2] 'Guilds of artisans marched under banners,'[3] suggesting a thriving community of craftsmen. After a nine-month stay in Cairo, he wrote, 'Grand Cairo is a modern town.'[4] He suggested, however, that the city had undergone a sharp decline after the Ottoman conquest:

Grand Cairo until the fifteenth century was one of the richest and most flourishing capitals in the world. It was the emporium of Europe and Asia. Its commerce extended from the straits of Gibraltar to the lower parts of India. The discovery of the Cape of Good Hope, and the consequences of the Ottomans, have robbed it of a great part of its splendour, and its opulence.[5]

Education was equally neglected.[6]

In mid-eighteenth century, the Beys were not unaware of the difficulties of the Ottoman Sultan arising from his wars against Russia and Austria. A desire for independence from Istanbul grew among them, best expressed in the separatist policy of Ali Bey the Great (*al-kabir*), who had been chosen *shaykh al-balad* in 1763.

Ali Bey was born in Anatolia in 1728, the son of a Greek priest. He was christened Joseph. At thirteen he was carried off and sold to Ibrahim Kaiaia, a lieutenant of the Janissaries in Cairo. After the usual training, he became *selikhdar aga*, a swordbearer, and *kafradar* or treasurer. At twenty-two, he was a *kāshif*, a lieutenant of the Mamluk Beys, commanding towns and districts, and befriended the Ottoman Viceroy Ragheb Pasha. By the time he was barely thirty he was a Bey in the Governing Council, or *Diwan*. When in 1758 his patron was murdered by a party of his rival Ibrahim, the Circassian, Ali sought revenge, and in 1763 was chosen *shaykh al-balad*. Exposed to the intrigues of other Mamluk Beys, he was forced to flee the country to Arabia and Acre more than once, but his old friend Ragheb Pasha, now in Istanbul, helped him recover his position in Egypt in 1766. He proceeded to pack the Governing Council with his own Beys, including Ismail, Murad and Ibrahim, and a certain Muhammad Abu Dhahab as *Agha* of the Janissaries. He purchased 6,000 Mamluks and 10,000 Maghribis (North Africans) to strengthen his army. Having improved security, he encouraged the development of agriculture. In the meantime, he married Maria, a Russian woman, gave customs houses exclusively to Syrian Christians (whom he preferred to the Jews) and favoured European merchants in the country. He also appointed the famous Copt, Muallem Rizq, Controller of Revenues and Finances.

When war broke out between Russia and Turkey in 1768, he proceeded to declare Egypt's independence, and proposed to enter the war on Russia's side. He thus wrote to Count Alexis Orlov at Leghorn asking for a treaty of alliance with Russia. He proposed a similar treaty of alliance with the Republic of Venice. At the same time he refused to pay the tribute to the Imperial Treasury in 1769, ousted the Ottoman viceroy, coined his own currency, invaded the Arabian Peninsula, and sent his follower Muhammad Abu Dhahab to invade Syria. The latter, though, as soon as he had conquered Damascus, turned against his master and agreed with the Sultan to restore Egypt to Ottoman control. This he achieved in 1773 (in which year also Ali Bey was killed) with the help of the Mamluk Ismail Bey who betrayed Ali. Moreover, on his circuitous way back to Cairo from the Red Sea and Upper Egypt, Abu Dhahab publicly accused Ali of being a Christian at heart. He was soon succeeded by the dual local control of the Mamluk Beys Ibrahim and Murad. Under their rule the Ottoman Viceroy continued to be powerless until the French invasion of 1798.

Ali Bey and his successor Abu Dhahab also attempted to extend their power and secure their autonomy by taking advantage of Anglo-French rivalry in the East. The rivalry over trade and imperial possessions had become sharper in the eighteenth century. In 1775 a trade treaty was concluded between Abu Dhahab and Warren Hastings, Governor of Bengal. When Murad Bey came to power in Cairo (1775–98), the French succeeded in turn in concluding a treaty with him to counteract British trading privileges in the Red Sea area. It was, however, abrogated by Murad a few years later, who proceeded to conclude a new trade agreement with the British Consul in Egypt. Thus the Mamluk rulers of Egypt were, towards the end of the eighteenth century, embroiled in the vicissitudes of Anglo-French imperial rivalry. England, on the one hand, was interested in Egypt primarily because of India. France, on the other, hoped to curtail English supremacy in the East. In this sense the Napoleonic expedition to Egypt was a French attempt to gain the upper hand in this imperialist contest by hitting directly at English economic and strategic interests short of invading the British Isles.

The demise of the rebellious Ali Bey the Great in 1773 and the death of his treacherous Mamluk and ally Abu Dhahab in 1775 brought a curious duumvirate of Mamluks to power in Egypt. This was the notorious reign of Murad and Ibrahim Beys, which lasted from 1775 until the French invasion in 1798: twenty years of allegedly irresponsible and tyrannical rule. The ill-effects of this dual control laid Egypt prey not only to the European conquerors, but also to the scheming ambitions of an imaginative and shrewd adventurer. It was a period characterized by internecine Mamluk squabbles at the expense of the subjects on one hand, and the weak attempts of a group of religious leaders to intercede and arbitrate between these warring rulers and the oppressed subjects on the other. Maladministration and exploitation were aggravated by environmental disasters ranging from flood and famine to plague and pestilence. Frequent wars between an expanding imperial Russia and a weakening Ottoman state rendered the latter's imperial political and administrative organization ineffective in checking the excesses of its provincial satraps. The steeper this decline became, the greater the benefit to the Mamluk chiefs in Egypt in terms of unbridled power.

Jabarti informs us that the misrule of Murad and Ibrahim was largely responsible for the easy invasion of Egypt by Napoleon. The Mamluk Beys were not too concerned about the impending French invasion, since they believed they could trample over the French with their horses. Murad he depicts as harsh, tyrannical and ignorant. Ibrahim, on the other hand, was weak and easy-going. As Qaimaqam (Deputy Governor) of Egypt, he administered the political affairs of the country, presumably with the assistance of a Council in which the Chief Judge and other ulama, or religious leaders, participated. Plagues, inflation and poverty, however, characterized their misrule.[7]

Savary described life in Cairo under the joint rule of Murad and Ibrahim as 'more a passive than an active existence ...'[8] and the country as one 'where death may prove the consequence of the slightest indiscretion'.[9] He reports that since 1775,

Mourat Bey and Ibrahim Bey are the most powerful princes of Egypt. Ambition which is their ruling passion has disunited them. They have been at war with each other. The equality of their forces again made them friends. At present, Mourat Bey, prevailing over his colleague, has obliged him to fly into Upper Egypt...[10]

The town, Savary exclaimed, 'groans under their yoke'.[11]

By 1775 then, the Mamluk Beys, actual rulers of the country, depended largely on the sword for the perpetuation of their control. Savary quaintly refers to Mamluk rule as 'Republican' in contrast to the monarchy of the Ayyubids, mainly because the Mamluk princes elected a chief.[12] Their power, however, initially rested on the specific privileges which Sultan Selim I, conqueror of Egypt, granted them in a treaty. In return for this privileged position, the

Mamluk Beys were required to raise a number of troops in case of war, and to contribute a certain number of purses and bushels of wheat and barley as annual tribute to the Sultan's treasury. But they were allowed to coin money in the name of Egypt and elect a chief Bey, the celebrated *shaykh al-balad*, among them. Although certain revenues in the Egyptian province were exclusively earmarked for the Ottoman Viceroy (e.g., customs revenues at Suez, especially on merchandise from the Arabian Sea), the ambitious Mamluk Beys engaged in a kind of 'payola' in order to corrupt the Viceroys and so erode their authority. Since only twelve to fourteen thousand Janissaries were allowed under arms during peacetime in Egypt, it became relatively easy for the Mamluks to prevail in the country.[13]

The Mamluks constituted a fixed class in so far as Egyptians could not enter its ranks. At the opposite end of the social spectrum was another fixed group, the peasant cultivators, the fellahin. Between these two extremes there was a more open and mobile constellation of Egyptian social groups, namely, the religious leaders, the ulama, the merchants and traders, artisans and craftsmen. The judges among the ulama, for instance, were granted fiefs of land by the Mamluks. Whereas these occupational and trade groups suffered the same burdens of taxation at the hands of the Mamluks as did the peasants, their more discrete level of organization and developed sense of occupational solidarity permitted them a measure of influence and restraint upon the all-too-ready excesses of the rulers. Because of their better economic condition, they often 'bought' from their Mamluk masters a better treatment for the mass of their less fortunate peasant brethren. The ulama in particular acted throughout the eighteenth century as political middlemen between the Mamluk Beys and the Egyptian masses.

Savary expresses surprise at the nature of the relation between the Egyptians and the Mamluks. In reporting his reaction to the sight of scores of thousands of peope who had come out to see Ibrahim and Murad Beys march with their Mamluks in 1778, he wrote

I could not help being surprised at seeing so numerous a body of men voluntarily submitting themselves to seven or eight thousand foreigners, who have no other employment than their destruction. But the natives of Egypt, gentle and peaceable, without force, and without energy, seemed destined to eternal bondage.

But for ages under the yoke of despotism they suffer every sort of misery, without lifting up their heads. . . . In spite of their wretched destiny, they passionately love their country, and nothing can tear them from it.[14]

The fact that four million Egyptians were governed by a handful of Mamluks Savary explains by invoking Strabo's assertion that the Egyptian is numerous but by no means warlike, and therefore easy to govern. In noting their lack of energy he attributed it to a 'long slavery'. His suggestion that the country needed a wise administration to revive it may constitute a hint as to his possible wish for a French conquest.[15]

At the time of the Napoleonic expedition, Egypt's population numbered between three and four million, and was divided into rulers and subjects.[16] The former consisted primarily of Mamluk Beys supported by an army of approximately fifteen thousand soldiers and officers. The subjects consisted of the majority of the population, divided into two main religious communities – Muslims and Copts – and organized into at least four social strata: religious leaders, judges and teachers who exercised spiritual and moral control over the other classes and were considered by them as their political leaders; the propertied classes and merchants, living mainly in cities and comprising ex-Ottoman *ocaklis* who had been assimilated, public officials of the bureaucracy, members of Egyptianized Turkish families, property owners, especially notables in the provinces, and merchants who were usually better off than the other classes; craftsmen and artisans organized in guilds headed by shaykhs, active in the food, clothing and building trades; and the peasant cultivators, the fellahin, who made up the poorest class.

The Copts were in addition employed by the State and the Beys as financial inspectors in the provinces and villages, recording produce and assessing taxes. In this capacity they wielded some power, and individuals among them, such as Muallem Rizq and Muallem Girgis al-Gawhari, achieved high financial office in the State.[17] In reporting the composition of the population, Savary distinguishes as Copts those who were mainly engaged as secretaries to the Beys, tax-collectors who kept commercial accounts in Coptic. Under the category Arab, he lumps the peasants, Beduin and shaykhs. He also mentions the Maghribis or North Africans, who were mainly in the army and in commerce, whereas the real Turks, Savary observes, were very few, most of them Janissaries. Among the Christians he includes Syrians and Greeks, engaged mainly in commerce and money exchange. In passing, Savary remarks that these had no integrity. As for the Jews, according to Savary, they were mainly goldsmiths and cloth merchants.[18]

There was also a small foreign community. Its members were

mainly engaged in war industries, sword and other weapon-making for the Mamluks. Some of them were in the cotton-spinning and weaving trade, centred already on Mehalla al-Kubra. A few Swedes, Italians and Frenchmen were in medicine and pharmacy. The foreign communities increased in size, however, with the French occupation of the country. Thus Ali Mubarak reports that the population of Cairo in 1798 was 260,000 and that some four hundred foreigners came into the country with the French. Moreover, the local Syrians, Maronites, Armenians and Greeks numbered over 25,000.[19]

Jabarti pens for us a vivid picture of conditions in Egypt around the time of the French invasion, when he writes of the high cost of living, low Niles, and the resultant misery of the fellahin. But he also describes the great festive celebrations of the *mulids* (birthday anniversaries of saints and religious martyrs), such as al-Hussayn, al-Sayyid Zeinab, al-Imam al Shafei, al-Sayyida Nafisa and Ibrahim al-Dasuqi. There was also widespread belief among the people in all kinds of legends, superstitions and miraculous personalities. Thus, throughout the eighteenth century, stories circulated in Egypt about the Day of Judgement, prophets and anti-Christs. The chronicler alleges that the Azhar shaykhs exploited this ignorance among the public, so that when, as he reported, *al-Waiz al-Rumi*, a religious preacher calling for reform, came to Egypt from Anatolia, the Azharites and the Ottoman Chief *Qadi* stood against him.[20]

Intellectual activity was confined to the Azhar. Some of the rich families, however, encouraged a measure of cultured social and genteel intellectual exchange. Literary salons were not uncommon in the homes of the richer merchants, who often acted as 'patrons of the arts'.[21] From the writings of Volney, Savary and Jabarti one gets the impression that opulence and extravagance were not limited to the Mamluk Beys, for they tell us that Murad Bey's palace was matched in appearance by the palatial home of the head merchant al-Mahruqi. Even the leading notables and ulama, among them Muhammad al-Sadat, Mustafa al-Sawi, Muhammad al-Jawhari and Shaykh al-Bakri, enjoyed similar comforts. Those close to the rulers, whether tax agents and collectors or accountants and secretaries, such as the Copt Muallem Ghali, were just as privileged. Savary and Jabarti describe vividly the 'guild floats' in the parades honouring the circumcision ceremony for the grandson of Omar Makram, *Naquib al-ashraf*, in Egypt.[22] They also detail the vast sums expended by the local nobility when they participated in the receptions honouring the arrival of a new Pasha (Ottoman Viceroy or

Governor) from Istanbul. Even among the poor there was a tendency to borrow money for indulgence in extravagant celebrations – weddings and other festive occasions – and the so-called 'public processions'.

Generally then, on the eve of the French invasion, Ottoman authority in Egypt was at a low ebb, despite the successful expedition in 1784–5 which thwarted premature Egyptian plans for secession and autonomy. Real power lay in the hands of the two chief Mamluk Beys, Murad and Ibrahim. Unrest and some disaffection with social and economic conditions were beginning to find expression among a few enlightened religious leaders. According to Jabarti, there was chaos in the countryside: people were massacred, villages were pillaged and plundered. The Beys imprisoned European merchants in the Citadel; Christians were searched and harassed. 'The masses wished to kill Christians and Jews, but governors prevented them from doing so.'[23] Savary, incidentally, was unhappy about the treatment of Europeans in Cairo, further promoting the justification for a French expedition against Egypt.[24]

The Ottoman–Islamic order was not resilient enough to withstand new shocks. Its system had become so rigid that it could not meet successfully the rising power of Europe, the commercial activities of Europeans, and the potential effect of the new maritime empires that began to appear at that time. Magallon, French consul in Egypt, secretly urged his country to conquer Egypt, in order to strike a direct blow at British commercial and imperial interests. Egypt was a ripe prey, for neither were its Mamluk Beys strong enough to protect it, nor was its nominal master, the Ottoman Sultan, free from other problems to defend it.

Napoleon's invasion of Egypt in 1798 is significant primarily for two things: first, it discredited the authority of the Mamluk Beys and severed for all practical purposes the province of Egypt from the Ottoman realm; second, it introduced educated Egyptians to the ideas of the French Revolution. The latter with its secular ideology was alien and abhorrent to Muslim Egyptians, but it generated a gnawing and uncomfortable feeling among them that the *umma* (the Islamic community) of Egypt at least was not as perfect and as strong as they had imagined. Such uncertainty was the basis for new ideas and conceptions. Until that time the Muslims in Egypt were disdainful of the little they knew of Europe, as is reflected in their notables' reaction to the news of an imminent French invasion. One of the Mamluk princes is reported to have exclaimed:

'Let the Franks come; we shall crush them beneath our horses' hooves!'[25]

In destroying the military power of the Mamluks, Bonaparte was anxious to stabilize his occupation of Egypt by attracting the co-operation and, hopefully, the loyalty of native Egyptian leadership – in this case, consisting mainly of the ulama and the notables. His proclamation in Arabic which began with the traditional Muslim invocation, 'In the Name of God, the Merciful, the Compassionate; there is no God but Allah, He has no offspring, and no partner,' combined a cordial invitation to friendship with a firm declaration of French power. The purpose of the French occupation was the destruction of the Mamluk oppressors who had denied Egyptians their rights, not the destruction of the Islamic faith. As the French believed that all men were free and equal before God, distinguished only by reason, virtue and knowledge, Napoleon came to liberate Egypt from tyranny so that the leaders of the *umma* – ulamas and notables – would assume the task of government and thus improve the conditions of their nation.

O Shaykhs, *qadis*, *imams*, and officers of the town, tell your nation that the French are friends of true Muslims, and proof of this is that they went to Rome and destroyed the Papal See which had always urged the Christians to fight Islam; then went to Malta and expelled from it the Knights of Malta who claimed that God required them to fight the Muslims. Thus, the French at all times were sincere friends of the Ottoman Sultan and enemies of his enemies. The Mamelukes refused to obey the Sultan, and obeyed him only as a means to satisfy their greed. Blessed are those Egyptians who agree with us...[26]

This appeal to local religious sentiment was followed by five conditions to be met by Egyptians in villages and towns, if they were to escape the application of strict measures and harsh treatment by the French forces.

Whatever the response of the Egyptians, we must note that the idea of a local native government proposed by Napoleon in his proclamation was novel to Egypt. Regardless of the propaganda objectives of Napoleon's policy, the invitation to the shaykhs, ulama and notables to participate in a French-controlled government of Egypt seemed to identify a native leadership and to invoke a local patriotism. Napoleon made it plain that he considered these shaykhs and notables as the leaders of the Egyptian people, and proceeded to negotiate with them the establishment of the *Diwan* or Administrative Council. Although he appointed its members by decree in July

1798, he ordered them to elect a president from among themselves.[27] The *Diwan* was to be responsible for civil government in Cairo, although its power was not final but subject to approval by the French military governor. While the French authorities retained the right to appoint certain high civil officials without consulting the Council, the latter did possess the broad power of appointing all other officials under the French directors. Another limitation upon the Council was the participation of French members. Nor could its authority extend beyond Cairo in fact, for Napoleon organized a system of Provincial Councils in the rest of the country, to which he appointed French representatives as well as natives. He also wished to bring together the representatives of the provinces with the leaders in Cairo and, for that purpose, in September 1798, he ordered the meeting of a General Council (*Diwan Am*).

One of Bonaparte's alleged purposes was to familiarize Egyptian notables with the processes of advisory councils and representative government; another of his intentions was to assess the reaction of these native leaders towards his system of Administrative Councils; to devise a civil and penal judiciary best suited for his purposes in Egypt; to promulgate the kind of legislation that would accommodate orderly laws of inheritance; and to plan the type of reform necessary for landownership, land surveys, and the devising of a proper taxation system. All these measures were moreover designed to win local support for the French against the Ottomans.

Jabarti reports that the purpose of this General Council was to examine and discuss three matters: religious (*sharia*) courts and the judicial system; landownership; inheritance laws. Moreover, Napoleon insisted that the Council devise its own internal rules and elect its own officers. In his opening address to the first meeting of the Council in October 1798, Bonaparte referred to Egypt's wealth and the desire of other states to control it; he also referred to the destructive consequences of oppressive Ottoman rule, thus expressing for the first time his disapproval of the Ottoman Sultan.[28] The latter indiscretion was prompted no doubt by the recent decision of Turkey to seek the aid of England in ousting him from Egypt. He was anxious to secure the friendship and loyalty of Egyptians against this impending attack.[29] Nevertheless, the plan for the establishment of these Adminstrative Councils exposed Egyptians for the first time to the idea of popular rule even if this were confined to the novelty of vote by secret ballot – an experience hitherto unknown to them.

While Bonaparte's expedition to Egypt can ultimately be adjudged a military failure, the scientific and educational consequences of his adventure for both Egypt and Europe were monumental. Besides his innovations in the government of Egypt, Bonaparte founded the Institute of Egypt to serve as the academic organization for the scientists, historians and men of letters who accompanied his expedition from France. Significantly, the Institute was meant to have a direct relationship with, and bearing upon, the administration of Egypt. In decreeing its establishment on 22 August 1798, Napoleon outlined the Institute's purposes as follows: (1) to work for the advancement of science and knowledge in and about Egypt; (2) to study the natural, industrial and historical sciences relevant to Egypt; and (3) to consult with, and advise, the government on specific matters pertaining to policy. He moreover divided the Institute into four sections: Mathematics, Physical and Natural Sciences, Political Economy, Literature and the Arts. The Institute furthermore was to publish the findings of its studies every three months.

The importance of the Institute can be appreciated from some of the work it did during the brief sojourn of the French in Egypt: studies of the problem of fuel, water power, and the raw materials available in the country for the manufacture of gunpowder; legislation and the question of civil and penal jurisdiction; the state of education and its possible reform; agricultural projects such as the cultivation of grapes and wheat, and drilling of water wells in the desert. The Institute, moreover, set up laboratories for chemical and physical experiments, initiated archaeological studies and excavations over a wide area, drew topographical and other maps of the country, including the Nile and its canals and banks, and studied animal and plant life, as well as the available minerals and the geological formation of the soil, oases and lakes.

Much of this work did not have a real impact on the Egyptians until later. What impressed many of them, especially members of the Council, however, was the systematic method of study utilized by French scholars. Jabarti, who visited the Institute, recorded his admiration of the laboratory equipment and the rich library. He also reported the disbelief of many Egyptian shaykhs when they witnessed chemical experiments performed by French scientists. They apparently accused the latter of magic and devilry. In the long run, however, the activities of the Institute played a significant role in undermining the Egyptian's traditional view of the world.[30]

The French introduced two things which were to have a wide impact upon the intellectual and political evolution of Egypt in the nineteenth century. One was an Arabic printing press; the other was the organization of an official press when the French started publishing the *Courrier de l'Egypte*, a political journal, and *La Décade Egyptienne*, a monthly scientific and economic journal which reported findings and discussions of Institute members. As for the printing press, it appears that Napoleon secured Arabic letters for it from the Vatican, and appointed the Orientalist Marcel to direct it. He designated it the National Press, and it was used for the printing of French proclamations to the population in Arabic, and the printing of the two journals just mentioned.

Meanwhile, French scientists and engineers worked diligently under the governorship of General Menou on the improvement of roads, and the construction of arsenals and factories, including the erection of a theatre. They expended great efforts in the service of science and the arts. Although the Institute closed with the departure of the French from Egypt in 1801, it was reinstated in Alexandria in 1859 under the honorary chairmanship of Jomard. Later a new Institute was founded in Cairo, presumably to carry on in the scholarly tradition begun by the French.

While many exaggerated reports of Bonaparte's devotion to Islam have come down, perhaps what he sought was to show a philosophical neutrality about all religions, deriving from his French Revolutionary creed: an equality among religions. With his Institute he was, on the other hand, portraying the power of the civilization he was bringing to Egypt and the strength of the ideas released by the French Revolution. Toleration of religion was an aspect of this new rational attitude. The inevitable contradiction, however, between his professed friendship to Muslims and their Sultan-Caliph in Istanbul on the one hand, and his occupation of the country which was a province of the Ottoman Empire, as well as his campaigns in Syria against another Muslim governor, Ahmad Pasha al-Jazzar of Acre, on the other, was apt to confuse the Islamic population of Egypt and provoke antagonism against him.

Napoleon's ultimate aim was the colonization of Egypt for the benefit of France. Given these circumstances and the fact that he represented a foreign and Christian power, opposition to his rule, irrespective of its highly enlightened goals – even methods – for the time, was inevitable. At the same time, certain harsh measures of taxation to raise funds for the support of the French occupation forces, once they had been cut off from France by virtue of the blockade effectively erected by the Anglo-Ottoman fleets in the Mediterranean, exercised Egyptian public opinion to the point that they were willing to risk open rebellion, as in fact they did in October 1798. Needless to say, the rebellious mood of the Egyptians was encouraged by the proclamations emanating from the Ottoman Porte against the 'infidel' French. Thus, in a proclamation in Arabic distributed in Egypt, Syria and Arabia, the Ottoman government condemned French revolutionary doctrine as anti-religious and evil.[31]

The Ottoman government countered Bonaparte's appeal to Egypt's Islamic faith by challenging his sincerity and pointing out his apparent disavowal as a French revolutionary of any religious creed, including his own Christian faith. Although the French defeat in Aboukir, the Ottoman declaration of war on France, the speed with which Britain came to Turkey's aid, and the impending Anglo-Ottoman expedition all had their undermining effect upon Napoleon's position in Egypt, the actual rebellion of the Cairenes and, soon thereafter, of the rural population, was a direct result of the heavy financial burdens imposed by the French occupiers on merchants, artisans, villagers and cultivators alike. Looting by French troops and harsh retaliatory measures against the population, including some atrocities, further excited the rebellious spirit of Egyptians against the foreign occupiers of the country. The hanging of Muhammad Kurayyim, Governor of Alexandria, left no doubt in Egyptian minds about the readiness of the French to take harsh and repressive measures when their interests so required.[32]

What is significant about the Cairo rebellion of 1798, and the general aspect of popular resistance to the French occupation, is the fact that the centre of the resistance was the Azhar, and its leaders the ulama, shaykhs and notables. The pre-eminence of the Azhar, as the leading institution of Muslim learning and culture throughout the political annals of Egypt, is a matter of record. In 1798 and throughout the nineteenth and twentieth centuries it has stood not only as the depository of tradition and the stalwart guardian of an essentially Islamic–Arabic educational system, but has also produced eminent Egyptian social and political leaders. Thus the first reformers and intellectual leaders of modern Egypt in the nineteenth century were Azharites who became exposed to the teachings of Europe. What is also significant is the fact that Egyptians recognized the shaykhs of the Azhar as the natural leaders and protectors of the community. This basically Islamic view of the 'nation' as the community of believers and respect for the religious institutions, in counterdistinction to the political establishment which was often of foreign composition, has been the source of both strength and weakness of many Islamic countries.

Jabarti tells us that Cairo rebelled primarily against the high taxation imposed by the French, the expropriation of property and other financial burdens. He also reports that native members of the Council protested against such measures to the French members and Bonaparte. Unsuccessful in their protests, the religious leaders formed an *ad hoc* revolutionary headquarters centred in the Azhar mosque to organize opposition to the French. Shaykhs al-Sadat, al-Sharqawi and other well-known religious personalities led this opposition. The rebellion nevertheless was suppressed by overwhelming force including the bombardment of the Azhar quarter by French artillery ensconced on high ground in the Muqattam hills. Even though Bonaparte's army had destroyed the hated Mamluks, his stern measures and ruthless suppression of the Cairo uprising seemed to convince Egyptians that there would be no respite, that one tyrant had been replaced by another.

Meanwhile, at the instigation of Britain, the Sultan was prompted to issue a *firman*, an Imperial Decree, denouncing the French Republic as the enemy of the Ottoman Empire and the atheist antagonist of the Islamic faith. General mobilization was ordered, and two armies were assembled, ready to attack the French forces in Egypt. One was to move from the Island of Rhodes, the other from Syria. To prevent the attack from Syria, Bonaparte took the initiative by launching his Syrian campaign that got bogged down in Acre in June 1799. Back in Egypt, influential notables in the provinces of Sharqiyya and Beheira were inciting the people to rebellion, and the calls to prayer from the mosque minarets were used as a form of secret verbal telegraph to foment antipathy against the French.

Even so, Bonaparte was able to defeat the badly commanded army from Rhodes which had landed in Aboukir Bay, and then secretly leave for France in August. Kléber, his successor as head of the French forces in Egypt, came to terms with the Anglo-Turkish force at El Arish in December, agreeing to evacuate Egypt. Britain, however, rejected the convention signed by Sir Sidney Smith, and Kléber had no choice but to defend Egypt; and this he did successfully. But his success was temporary at best, and, after his assassination, Menou assumed French leadership in Egypt.

Lacking the ability and fortitude of a Kléber, let alone a Bonaparte, already a convert to Islam, and badly supplied from France,

'Abdullah' Menou's position began to look hopeless. The Anglo-Turkish expedition under Abercrombie began its march upon Cairo in March 1801, and, with the help of the Mamluk Beys, overwhelmed the French garrison. Menou accepted surrender terms, and the last French soldier left Egypt at the end of September 1801. With this, the Sultan of Turkey reasserted his sovereignty over Egypt, and a chaotic Egypt it was. From this chaos arose the modern Egypt under Muhammad Ali; and from it followed the transformation of the country from a medieval Ottoman–Islamic province to a semi-Europeanized, albeit traditional, state searching and striving for a new order.

Much of the French influence on Egypt was not the direct consequence of the brief three-year occupation, 1798–1801. The impact of this occupation was gradual and indirect, and lasted long after the French had evacuated Egypt. Even in that brief period Menou's administrative reform measures, for instance, left the greatest impact upon the future Egyptian state. Reforms in public health and sanitation (the registration of births and deaths, for example), inheritance taxes which were previously set at the discretion of the *qadis*, the termination of involuntary servitude and the institution of a regularized system of wages for workers, all seemed to contribute to a solid beginning for the proper administration of Egypt.

The occupation also made a certain impact upon the country's social life. Thus, it is reported that the mixing of the sexes in public occurred for the first time after 1798 in the Ezbekiyya park, the theatre and cafés. Intermarriage between soldiers or other Frenchmen and Egyptian women was not uncommon. Consequently, a certain incidence of conversion to Christianity among such women was noticeable. Jabarti, at least, objected to these infidel developments, and deplored the general loosening of Egyptian morals. The presence of foreign troops, he claims, had a deleterious effect upon the population.[33] Cafés and taverns abounded everywhere for the amusement of a pleasure-seeking public. The government collected an amusement tax from these establishments, as well as from prostitution (*al-khawati*). *Bakhshish*, or hand-out, collection every Friday by the employees of the governor was not only a commonplace, but highly organized.[34] Such practices continued with greater incidence, especially when Ottoman rule returned to Egypt briefly in 1801.

The French occupation of Egypt was perhaps disappointing in its result for France. None of the Directory's objectives were fulfilled: English commercial supremacy continued unchecked, Ottoman sovereignty returned to Egypt. In addition, England was introduced to Egypt, marking an association which led ultimately to the British occupation of the country for some seventy-five years. On this basis, the French venture was a dismal failure. Yet this would be an unfair evaluation; for the brief occupation left a permanent mark upon the country. Not only were the Egyptians impressed by the military prowess and genius of Bonaparte, who so easily defeated the feared Mamluks, but the ideas inspired by the French Revolution which he brought with him – whether in the form of the Institute or the Cairo Council – were to influence Egyptians for the next hundred and fifty years and to form the basis of their cultural renaissance and national development. The science and technology of post-Enlightenment Europe shook Egyptians from their slumber and traditional rigidity, and infused in the minds of the alert among them just the right amount of gnawing uncertainty about their condition and state of indolent ignorance. It simply showed them that there was another world, outside their own, which had certain things to offer that would make material existence better, and political life perhaps more powerful.

Egypt's response to this first massive impact of modern Europe was therefore a cautious and ambivalent one: it was cautious in so far as Egyptians did not quite know what to make of this new force other than consider it the harbinger of new and, as always, foreign ruling institutions. It was ambivalent in so far as the French with their science, administration and political ideas were received with mixed feelings of admiration, awe, perplexity, dismay, but also of disbelief, religiously provoked antagonism, and overt enmity. To be sure, no self-respecting Muslim in eighteenth-century Egypt wished to be governed by infidel foreigners regardless of how harsh and unjust his Mamluk and Ottoman masters may have been – at least they were members of the community of believers, brothers in the faith. At the same time, he sensed that the powerful ability of the infidel was made possible by some kind of new knowledge and an efficacious pattern of attitudes and scale of values. About all this the Egyptian became curious. He spent most of the nineteenth century satisfying his curiosity.

PART ONE

The Social and Political Foundations of Modern Egypt
1805–82

CHAPTER 4
MUHAMMAD ALI, THE MODERNIZING AUTOCRAT

Muhammad Ali came to Egypt in 1801 as a young officer with the Albanian detachment in the Turkish expeditionary force against the French. He participated in the battles involving Ottoman, British and French troops. Allegedly illiterate, but with some experience in tobacco trading in his Macedonian home-town of Kavalla, Muhammad Ali was shrewd enough to recognize that the Turkish force represented a backward army raised and equipped by a declining power, the Ottoman State. On the other hand, he observed that both the British and French armies were technically superior to the Turkish forces, and represented two advanced, but rival, powers competing for the control of Egypt at the crossroads of East and West. This kind of perception, backed by several years' experience of the reform programme introduced into the Empire by Sultan Selim III (1789–1807) in 1792–3,[1] influenced Muhammad Ali's understanding of politics and guided his diplomacy throughout his long reign in Egypt, from 1805 to 1848.

While he ruled in the name of the Ottoman Sultan, he practically detached Egypt from Turkey, especially after he had destroyed the Mamluk Beys and their power between 1805 and 1812. Like the French who were only briefly in Egypt, he was, throughout his reign, faced with the same adversaries, namely, Turkey and England. Economic reasons apart, Muhammad Ali recognized, as much as those who had governed Egypt before him – Ibn Tulun, the Fatimids, Saladin, and Bonaparte – the strategic importance of Syria and invaded it to protect his eastern flank. More significant though were his continuous efforts to reform the administration and develop agriculture, irrigation, public works and industry – in general, his insistence upon the massive introduction of European technology in all the activities and functions of the State.

With the *nizam jadid* (new order) which Sultan Selim III introduced to the Ottoman State in the 1790s as a model, Muhammad Ali proceeded to impose a New Order in Egypt in the first three decades of the nineteenth century. The New Order became the basic framework for that country's drive towards modernity for the next hundred years. It aimed first at the organization of a modern army, and required reform and innovation in several areas of state activity: agriculture, administration, education and industry. Muhammad Ali inaugurated policies that changed the patterns of landownership and agriculture in order to increase productivity and yield greater wealth to the State. He introduced a system of state education in order to provide the trained and skilled manpower required by the services of his state, and especially his armed forces. He reformed the administration in order to secure efficient, strict and economical control over the functions of state and government. He embarked upon an ambitious programme of industrialization which produced the first state factories in Egypt in order to make his armed forces self-sufficient in materials and supplies.

The French evacuation of Egypt in October 1801 left a power vacuum in the country in which a struggle for control among competing groups developed immediately. It was from this struggle that Muhammad Ali emerged victorious as the ruler of Egypt. Ottoman troops, consisting of Turkish, Albanian and other elements, were dissatisfied because of arrears in pay. They soon rebelled against the Turkish Governor, Khusraw, who fled to Damietta. Tahir Pasha, head of the Albanian contingent, succeeded Khusraw as Governor, but was killed within a matter of weeks. Finally, Khurshid was appointed Governor, staying in that office for less than a year and a half. During this period Muhammad Ali actively campaigned to secure the governorship of Egypt, especially after having succeeded his chief Tahir as commander of the Albanian battalion.[2]

During Khurshid's tenure of the gubernatorial office in Egypt, Muhammad Ali was already well versed in the weaknesses of the political situation in the country. He observed that the Mamluks were anxious to restore their power in the country, which they could only do at the expense of the legitimate authority of the Sultan's appointed representative. But the local population, and particularly the notables and religious leaders among them, were not anxious to see a Mamluk restoration. His choice of a plan of action was therefore clear: to make such necessary alliances at various stages of his campaign as to eliminate one group of contenders for power after another. And this is exactly what he did.

First, Muhammad Ali studied the Mamluk camp for rivals and found that it was divided against itself. Elfi Bey and Bardisi Bey appeared the two major contenders for Mamluk leadership and both had to be dealt with. Both of them were Mamluks of the notorious Murad Bey. Elfi at least was seriously interested in a Mamluk-ruled independent Egypt. He contemplated, on the one hand, the possibility of British assistance which would serve as an external guarantor of an independent Egypt. In order to frustrate Muhammad Ali's ambitions, he sought, on the other hand, an alliance with the local population which was then represented, if not led, by Omar Makram. Muhammad Ali, in turn, tried to forestall such an eventuality by approaching Bardisi to enlist his support against his rival Elfi.

Second, the inability of the Mamluks to unite against Muhammad Ali was in large measure due to the latter's success in channelling public hatred against both the Ottomans and the Mamluks, especially against Bardisi. Meanwhile, he tried to convince the same public that disorder in the country was also due to the inefficiency of the Turkish governors, whereas the dissatisfaction of the troops he also ascribed to the governors. By securing the support of the ulama and, through them, that of the merchants and the public, Muhammad Ali emerged as the champion of the people against both groups of 'oppressors': Ottomans and Mamluks. In this way, his appointment to the governorship of Egypt seemed to carry the stamp of public acclamation. In May 1805 he was appointed *wali* by decree from Istanbul; in 1807 both Elfi and Bardisi died. Muhammad Ali was rid of, if not the two serious rivals to his power, at least two sources of potential trouble. Between March and September of the same year he weathered the British occupation of Alexandria. Moreover, by 1807 the reforming Selim III was in serious trouble in Istanbul and could not have influenced greatly the outcome of this struggle in Egypt. His attempted reforms of the administrative and fiscal structure of the Ottoman State were by then meeting violent opposition from the old *derebeys* – valley lords – and conservative religious groups. The main thrust of his New Order – to organize a new corps of regular infantry, trained and equipped on European lines – ran foul of the fanatic opposition of the powerful old corps of Janissaries. Thus, Selim III was deposed in May of that year. The political situation in Istanbul remained turbulent until Mahmud II succeeded in destroying the Janissaries in 1826.[3]

While Istanbul, then, was seething with unrest and political upheaval, Muhammad Ali was consolidating his power in Cairo. Very soon, by 1811, he was being asked by his suzerain in Istanbul to send an expedition to Arabia to punish rebels there. On the occasion of the departure of the expedition that year, he staged the wholesale massacre of the remaining Mamluk princes and leaders in the Cairo Citadel.

Although Lane, who lived in Egypt when it was governed by Muhammad Ali Pasha, considered the years 1834–5 the best period of his rule, he was not an enthusiastic admirer of the Pasha. He criticized the Pasha's monopolistic economic system and agricultural policy which impoverished the people.[4] An Egyptian historian, M Sabry, on the other hand, concluded that irrespective of his shortcomings, Muhammad Ali's rule was a tremendous impetus for the emergence of modern Egypt.[5] Professor Henry Dodwell concludes his study with a great deal of admiration for the Pasha as a ruler, if not for his rule as such.[6] Although he calls him 'universal master, universal landlord, universal merchant', Dodwell credits Muhammad Ali with having brought Egyptians into closer touch with Europe through his military, educational, economic and other measures, and thus having laid the foundations of a modern Egyptian state. Dodwell, in fact, points out that the failure of Muhammad Ali's schemes to survive his death was due primarily to the weaknesses of the generations of rulers that followed the great Pasha.[7]

That Muhammad Ali founded an independent dynasty in Egypt in fact if not in law; laid the foundations of a modern Egyptian state, and a society whose educated members desired to emulate at least the external trappings of European civilization; set up the framework of modern government and the transaction of public business in organized fashion; revolutionized education and opened the way to instruction in the modern arts and sciences, no one can deny. In short, Muhammad Ali gave Egypt the organizational basis and the human cadres for the emergence of a modern state. He effected a revolution in internal government and administration by becoming the sole landowner and only merchant in the country. To manage as large a farm as Egypt itself, as well as his commercial and industrial monopolies, he developed an effective bureaucracy. To control the countryside and maintain order he divided Egypt into provinces to which he appointed governors. These became members of a new aristocratic political class. 'Thus Egypt became nearly one great farm, held at a nominal rental of the Sultan. From this Muhammad Ali derived his usufruct; his bureaucracy were the overseers, and the population of Egypt the servants.'[8] If, as many claimed, the Ottoman Sultan, the French and the British were all interested in destroying the Mamluks in Egypt, only Muhammad Ali succeeded. And this he achieved by murdering them.[9]

Muhammad Ali was the first ruler in Islamic lands to undertake massive economic development: he embarked upon the transformation of the Egyptian economy. This he tried to do by expanding agriculture which constituted the major source of the country's economic strength, while at the same time introducing large-scale industry. By revolutionizing agricultural methods he expanded cultivation to increase production, and by establishing manufacturing industries he wished not only to increase trade and commercial capabilities but also to increase tax revenue and to ensure the potential economic independence of his state. At no time did Muhammad Ali, however, favour the free trade of liberal economic ideas of Europe: he designed his economic development plans under a state-controlled programme of monopolies.

Before his accession to power, most of the land belonged to the State. In the seventeenth and eighteenth centuries, however, state ownership was rendered a legal fiction by the wide spread of the *iltizam*, or tax-farming, system. Throughout the sixteenth century, the tax-farmers were mainly *ocaklis*, who held state land in return for the payment of a set land tax. They were, however, permitted to retain any amount over this tax they could extract from the peasant farmers who worked on the land. Beyond this financial arrangement, the tax-farmer virtually ruled the peasants on his *iltizam* land inasmuch as he could exact forced labour from them and in so far as he settled any disputes that arose between them.

By the end of the eighteenth century, the *iltizam* system in Egypt comprised Mamluks, many ulama, public officials, Beduin shaykhs, or tribal leaders, and other notables. These had come to replace in great measure the earlier Turkish military group of *ocakli* tax-farmers. The *derebeys*[10] of Anatolia – valley lords, hereditary landlords, and virtually autonomous provincial rulers – by the eighteenth century came to have their practical counterpart in Egypt in the tax-farming landholders.

Whereas initially *iltizams* were granted for a limited period of a few years, by 1800 many of them were held for life and, in certain cases, as alienable and heritable property. A favourite method to achieve the latter condition was the institution of agricultural *waqf* land.

The earliest measures of the Pasha's agricultural policy, therefore, had to be directed against tax-farming and the tax-farmers. This system of agricultural holdings had to be abolished for two principal reasons. First, tax-farming diverted a large proportion of agricultural income away from the State, and second, it afforded the tax-farmers considerable power over the cultivator peasants, thus enabling them to become a source of potential opposition to the Pasha's total control in Egypt. Similarly, Muhammad Ali viewed with misgivings the influence and power accruing to the ulama as a result of their control over the administration of, and income from, charitable or religious trust properties (*waqfs* and *rizaq ahbasiyya*); which, in turn, deprived the State of considerable revenue.[11]

Very early in his reign, Muhammad Ali imposed taxes on *iltizam* lands. Soon tax-farmers found it increasingly difficult to meet these tax payments, especially when income from their land holdings was low. Gradually, more and more of their lands were confiscated by the State, that is, the Pasha. A year after he had staged his famous massacre of the Mamluks in the Citadel, Muhammad Ali confiscated the remaining *iltizam* lands of the Mamluks in the country. Instead of transferring them (i.e., their tax leaseholds) to other tax-farmers, Muhammad Ali retained these lands as state property.

The net social and political consequences of this agrarian policy were to undermine – and soon eliminate – the influence of Mamluk and other tax-farmers over the peasant cultivators. The role and influence of religious leaders and institutions, especially the Azhar, in education over society at large were weakened by Muhammad Ali's policy of levying taxes on *waqf* land property (buildings, gardens and mosques were excluded from taxation) between 1809 and 1814. Following the cadastral survey in 1814–16, a new taxation system was introduced by which land was registered in the name of the village community. The latter now became responsible for the payment of taxes directly to the State. More significant was the fact that villagers, i.e., the fellahin, did not acquire ownership or inheritance rights over land. They merely had lifetime rights to use the land which was owned by the State. Yet the right to farm certain lands did pass from father to son; a practice already common in the eighteenth century.

Within ten years of his coming to power, therefore, Muhammad Ali succeeded in virtually nationalizing land in Egypt by destroying the agrarian position of the privileged classes he found in the country. The rapid development of agriculture within the next thirty years was, on the other hand, partly responsible for a less monopolistic agrarian policy on his part.

Having destroyed the *iltizam* system, Muhammad Ali distributed land to the peasants and village headmen.[12] While allotting small tracts of land to peasants (3–5 *feddans*) for cultivation and permitting them to dispose freely of the produce, the Pasha did not give them legal ownership. Economic and other conditions in the next twenty years, however, tended to erode Muhammad Ali's, or the State's, monopoly over landownership in favour of private ownership. The latter development was especially rapid in the case of an emergent class of big landowners.

In 1829–30, Muhammad Ali began to make free grants of large tracts of uncultivated land to high officials of the State and others. In doing so, he exempted them from taxes on condition that the recipients cultivated these lands and increased the country's agricultural production. At first, these land grants, known as *ibadiyya*, did not confer ownership of the land upon the recipient; they merely gave him the right to use the land. In 1836, however, such land grants became heritable by eldest sons of the grantees, and by 1842 the latter acquired complete rights of ownership. A decree in 1846 made the transfer, mortgage and sale of such land property legal.

Besides these land grants to high officials and notables, Muhammad Ali adopted the Ottoman *ciftlik* system of gifting large tracts of land, buildings and other property to his family and relatives. This practice led to the concentration in the hands of members of the ruling family of vast agricultural holdings which by the beginning of the twentieth century represented about one-sixth of the country's cultivated land.

Military campaigns, especially in the 1830s, caused the partial depopulation of several villages. Conscription was heavy and continuous to meet the demands of the army. The burden of taxation, on the other hand, led to the accumulation of tax arrears in many villages. With the failure of his foreign ventures at the hands of the Powers and Turkey, Muhammad Ali's treasury was in urgent need of replenishment. He instituted the system of *uhda* lands by which high officials, army officers, provincial governors, and notables would receive control over lands covering whole villages in return for their assumption of the tax liability on this land. *Uhda* differed from the old *iltizam* in that the *uhda* holder was expected to pay in the tax rate decreed by the Pasha and could not levy any further tax upon the cultivators. He did, however, acquire a parcel of land for each *uhda* that was tax free. On this parcel of land, moreover, he was entitled to unpaid labour by the farmers.

Thus, while all three systems of land distribution and grants, *ibadiyya*, *ciftlik* and *uhda*, were originally conceived by Muhammad Ali as limited types of landownership for individuals other than the State, i.e., himself, they all contributed to the emergence of private ownership of land and large landed estates in the country. A combination of economic conditions and financial difficulties of successive rulers – especially Khedive Ismail – made it relatively easy for holders of such lands to acquire hereditary ownership over them, and accumulate further holdings. If one also considers the practice of rulers of granting land gifts to their servants and advisers in return for – and in appreciation of – their services, or, as often occurred, in lieu of pensions, the accumulation of landed wealth in the hands of a new group of Egyptians developed rapidly in the nineteenth century. At the local or village level headmen who became part of the civil administration hierarchy also found their way to landed wealth.[13]

Under Said Pasha (1854–63), a decree was promulgated permitting the fellahin who had usufruct rights to land (and who by 1846 were allowed to mortgage it) to inherit it. Another decree in 1858 recognized inheritance rights for male and female heirs to such land. The same law also authorized foreigners to purchase land in Egypt.

However, Muhammad Ali's major concern during the early years of his rule was not over the improvement of Egyptian agriculture. Rather his first priority was the creation of a strong army to secure his power and buttress his rule. Everything else – whatever plans he already contemplated, or developed later – was contingent upon the attainment of this goal. Like Selim III in Istanbul before him, and Mahmud II after him, Muhammad Ali made the building-up of a strong army, equipped and trained on European lines, the foundation of his New Order. Soon this army became the basis for all reform in the country. Every other accoutrement of modernity and European innovation was to be a corollary and complementary activity to fill the needs of the new military institution. In short, the Pasha thought of civilization (at least, European civilization) as a set of devices to organize, arm and maintain his army, which in turn, was the best guarantee of his independence. The first Medical School opened under the supervision of the French doctor Clot Bey, for instance, was originally intended to train doctors and other medical aides for the armed forces. The extensive development of industry was also primarily designed to fill the needs of the armed forces.

Before 1820, the Pasha's army consisted of irregular troops, often unruly and mutinous. At first he tried to reorganize these troops with up-to-date training, but found this an impossible task, and nearly lost his life in the attempt. Albanian and other elements among the undisciplined troops mutinied and proceeded to pillage and plunder the local inhabitants and their commercial establishments. With his usual shrewdness, Muhammad Ali paid ample compensation to Egyptian merchants and other groups that suffered from the mutiny, based on the estimate calculated by Sayyed Muhammad al-Mahruqi, Chief of the Merchants Guild in Cairo. Compensation served to increase and extend his popularity among the local public. With such popular support against the irregular troops, the Pasha was able to expel them gradually from the capital and disperse them about the country, making it difficult for any sizeable force among them to concentrate in one place. They were posted to such harbours in the Mediterranean as Rosetta and Damietta. With them he sent two of his own sons, Toussoun Pasha and Ismail Pasha,[14] as well as some of his most trusted army officers.

The Pasha's first step in the creation of a modern army was the founding of a military school in Aswan to train officers. But to train officers in the art of modern warfare required the importation of European military and other instructors. While the Pasha's need for such personnel was great and urgent, the supply was no less abundant. The demise of the Napoleonic Empire in 1815 left many brilliant French officers unemployed. One of these was Colonel Sève, whom the Pasha engaged to build his modern army. Having been converted to Islam, Sève came to be known as Soliman Pasha al-Faransawi (the Frenchman) (d. 1860).

The first batch of cadets to be trained at Aswan were chosen from among the Pasha's own Mamluks. Aswan was perhaps carefully selected as the site of the college for its distance from the centre of things and therefore liable to keep ambitious Mamluks away from intrigue. But training officers alone was not enough for the organization of an army. The officers had to have troops to command, and recruitment of soldiers presented serious difficulties for the Pasha. How to recruit them and from what classes or groups in society were two rather difficult matters. He ruled out the recruitment of Turks and Albanians in the modern army for reasons mentioned above: discipline and direct obedience would be uncertain at best. To conscript natives, who had not seen military service for centuries, would have constituted too abrupt and disconcerting an experience for the

Egyptians, and might create civil disturbances. It is also possible that Muhammad Ali intended to spare the Egyptian population for the intensive agricultural work he planned in order to increase production. For a while he therefore turned to the Sudan as a possible source of recruitment, and one of the motives in the conquest of Kordofan and Sennar was perhaps the manpower needs of the new army, although Nubia was first conquered in pursuit of fleeing Mamluks. Twenty thousand Sudanese were conscripted, but many of them perished as a result of climatic and endemic disease conditions, and the experiment proved to be a total failure. By 1823, therefore, we find the Pasha resorting to the recruitment of Egyptians for the army, and the first six battalions of the organized modern army were mustered that year, officered by the first batch of Aswan graduates.[15]

In addition to military schools and colleges, the Pasha founded a War Department (*nizarat al-harbiyya*), also known as the War Council (*diwan al-jihadiyya*), which became responsible for the staff, command and administrative organization of the armed forces. Modelled on French military organization, it was also responsible for logistical support to the army: supplies, armaments, munitions and other services.

In order to provide the skills and services required for the maintenance and fighting effectiveness of a modern army which were not available in Egypt at this time, Muhammad Ali invested money and effort in the creation of a native educated élite. As in the organization and training of his army, in education too he created a European-style state school system in Egypt. At first, it was staffed partly by Europeans, but eventually entirely by Egyptians who had been trained in Europe. In 1816, Muhammad Ali began to send Egyptians on educational missions abroad, namely, to Italy, France and England for technical and academic training.[16] Bearing in mind the prevailing traditional Azhar-supervised school system (koranic schools and theological institutes attached to mosques), Muhammad Ali's state school system was a revolutionary innovation. His desire for modernity, which was a precondition of his power ambitions, led the Pasha to by-pass the traditional cadres of Egyptian leadership in education, who were also the arbiters of social norms, by prompting the rise of a state-trained, European-influenced native élite of public officials, teachers, technical, scientific and administrative officers. The Pasha was also unwittingly sowing the seeds of an intellectual, cultural, social and political renaissance led by his Egyptian protégés in the second half of the nineteenth century.

Education was not the only field in which Europe could teach the Pasha's subjects the secrets of modern life. There were already beginning to appear the desirable fruits of industrial invention, production and its concomitants of power and comfort. Industrialization seemed a precondition of a powerful independent state. It was natural, therefore, that Muhammad Ali should associate military power and its need for modern educated personnel with the establishment of an industrial complex to supply and equip his army; to increase his wealth and independence as well as to support the apparati of a strong state.

The industrialization of Egypt was not, however, an original idea of Muhammad Ali. One reads that Napoleon's *Commission des Arts* studied, and reported on, the industrial potential of the country in 1799–1800. They canvassed, for example, village shaykhs throughout the country and discovered that an industrial substructure already existed in the primary industries of villages, namely, linen manufacture, pottery, oil pressing, alcoholic beverages, perfumes and sugar. The famous *Description de l'Egypte*[17] documents the extensive field research and theoretical work conducted by the French savants to assess and evaluate natural resources in Egypt, industrial possibilities and agricultural projects. They recommended that a basic industrial task was the search for power to move machinery, and that, at the outset, concentration should be on agriculture-based industry, including irrigation works. In fact, during their brief stay in Egypt, the French did erect factories in Cairo for gunpowder, beer, hats, arsenals for field guns, tanneries and windmills to make flour – all intended for the supply of the occupation troops.

The French reportedly had hopes of making Cairo into a 'Manchester of the East'. Those among them who remained behind and found employment with the new ruler of Egypt, and those who flocked to Muhammad Ali's court from Europe for the first time, must have entertained similar notions, for it is quite possible that much of Muhammad Ali's industrialization plan was influenced by his European technical and other expert advisers. A group of these were followers of Saint-Simon, while others were consular representatives of various European states.[18] Whoever these Europeans may have been, there is no doubt that Muhammad Ali was greatly influenced by the recommendations of the French savants who had anticipated the ability of Egypt to become part of commercial and industrial Europe.

By 1820, the Pasha was about to transform the whole basis of the Egyptian economy: his monopoly over agricultural cash crop production and whatever native small industry existed was virtually complete. He was now ready to intensify the cultivation of a highly marketable cash crop, for which Egyptian conditions were most favourable: cotton. With the help of the famous French expert Jumel, the intensive cultivation of cotton not only increased its production for export, but enabled Muhammad Ali to expand his textile industry in an unprecedented manner. His monopolistic ownership of cotton-cultivated acreage, together with his monopoly over the textile industry, afforded the Pasha vast revenues which he spent on his armed forces and other projects. By 1830–1, all private textile manufacturing endeavour in the towns and villages was officially suppressed; an Office of Factories Control was established in 1832, which was superseded by a Department of Industry to stabilize, direct and control all activities in this sector of the economy. Large-scale monopolistic industrial methods obviously militated against the perpetuation of existing artisan and small craftsmen guilds. Members of these guilds soon became wage-earning labourers in the ruler's enterprises.

One could argue that the suppression of guild corporations was a step in the right direction towards modernity. Whereas capital and labour were linked in the guild, Muhammad Ali was now providing all the capital, and rendering the guild members wage-earning labour. The latter became completely dependent upon the Pasha as the new industrial 'tycoon' and submitted to his control. Moreover, whereas under the guild system not everyone could become an artisan or craftsman member, its suppression theoretically laid all types of labour skills open to every Egyptian. One set of figures indicates that by 1840 there was a 260,000 strong labour force in industrial concerns of the State, and that during the period 1816–50 no less than 450,000 Egyptians passed into industry. One could even make a case that while in England, say, wages of labourers during the period under discussion depended upon market fluctuations, Muhammad Ali, through his centralized monopoly, kept them at even level. This would presumably have been to the labourer's advantage, especially if such a monopoly could have also stabilized prices. Yet, because of centralization, inevitable and major administrative abuse (e.g. frequent arrears in salary and wage payments) resulted.

Yet another dimension of industry's impact upon Egypt consisted of the increased immigration of Europeans to Egypt. Soon sizeable foreign communities – French, Italian, Greek – settled in Egypt, which began to dwindle seriously only after the Second World War, and disappear rapidly after 1956. Frenchmen, Italians and Greeks were employed in the military arsenals, gun factories and shipyards. The famous French engineer from Toulon, Lefebure de Cerisy, erected the Alexandria Arsenal in 1829–33, and commanded the Navy War College there.[19] Italian textile factory artisans, dyers and mechanics, abounded from the beginning of the industrialization programme. A paper factory, for example, erected in 1834, was directed by the Italian Camiagi. An English engineer led the construction of a large foundry in Bulaq. In Cairo, between the Citadel, Bulaq, and the Island of Roda on the Nile, was concentrated a formidable military-industrial complex, producing armaments, military dress and equipment. Alexandria had become a self-sufficient naval arsenal. From its yards came frigates, corvettes, and other classes of men-of-war. From Assiut to Rosetta, sugar factories, tanneries and chemical factories worked to meet the growing needs of a ruler whose army had been on campaigns of conquest almost continuously for twenty-five years.

Communications and transport, especially canals, were developed to facilitate foreign trade, conducted under the Pasha's monopoly system. He bought crops from farmers at fixed low prices and resold them to foreign exporters at great profits. Similarly, he directly imported for his private account almost two-fifths of all goods into Egypt. In the industrial sector, the Pasha was investing by 1838 some twelve million pounds, keeping busy in his factories over 40,000 workers. He had also by this time created the nucleus of a growing governmental and state apparatus namely, an army, a navy and a bureaucracy.

Through his monopolies, Muhammad Ali was not only the sole industrialist and agricultural master of Egypt, but also its only entrepreneur. Although he permitted an incipient wage-earning labour force to emerge in the country, financial and commercial classes among the Egyptians did not arise until the twentieth century. Between 1850 and 1930, financial and commercial services and enterprises were largely owned and operated by foreigners, who were protected by the Capitulations.[20]

Despite the rise of an administrative and technical cadre among Egyptians as a result of Muhammad Ali's reform and educational policies, the imposition of a settlement by the European Powers upon the Pasha in 1839–41 undermined the industrial state mono-poly complex he had erected. Interested as they were in free trade at a time of imperial expansion, the European Powers encouraged economic specialization, whereby a country like Egypt became the supplier of agricultural raw materials, mainly cotton, for the indus-trial expansion of British textiles and related manufacturing enter-prises. Egypt's economy became export-oriented – in this instance with a cash crop – until the attempt by the Free Officer régime after 1952 to create a complex industrial formation. Indeed, this type of economy was to govern and affect Egypt's relation with Europe, and particularly Britain, as well as its domestic social-political evolution, for the next hundred years.[21]

Muhammad Ali's methods of government and administration were absolute and strictly centralized. All power delegated by authority of the Sultan in Egypt was vested in him. Contrary to previous Otto-man governors appointed by the Sultan to Egypt, Muhammad Ali appeared original in so far as he imposed his authority over all other power groups in the country. There were no longer such contenders for power with the Viceroy as the *shaykh al-balad*, the Mamluk chiefs, or the religious leaders from the Azhar. Instead of delegating the command of his troops to Albanian or other officers Muhammad Ali placed his sons – Toussun, Ibrahim and Ismail – at their head. His youngest son, Said Pasha, commanded the naval forces; his grandson, Abbas, was in charge of the Cairo governorate. Other members of his family – nephews and grand-nephews – filled military and civil administrative positions in the conquered dominions, especially Syria and the Hijaz. He centralized the control of the vari-ous provinces in Egypt by reorganizing their administration into governorates, provinces, districts and departments for which he appointed governors, sub-governors, inspectors and mayors in a chain of command relationship. In the central administration, in-stead of Defterdars, Kazandars and Silahdars Egypt now had execu-tive heads of departments responsible for specialized functions of the government. These ministers were close and immediate colla-borators of the Viceroy, directly responsible to him, and loyal only to his person, not to a system. Their staff consisted of officials re-cruited both from among Europeans and from the native population that was now receiving education and training under the Viceroy's modern scheme.

For the first time in modern Egyptian history, the country had in 1833 a Ministry of Foreign Affairs headed by the Armenian Boghos Bey. In 1837 six ministries were organized: Interior, entrusted to the Christian Habib Effendi, Public Instruction, headed by one of the early trainees in France, War, Finance, Foreign Affairs and Commerce and Navy. All of this reflected the desire of the Viceroy to handle affairs of state by systematic direction and supervision. Moreover, heads of these ministries were in effect his private secretaries. On the other hand, Muhammad Ali abolished the so-called legislative and consultative bodies established by the French occupation, such as the Cairo Council (*Diwan*), the provincial councils and the General Council of Egypt. Instead, he preferred to have a Council of State and a Private Council, consisting of the corps of high public officials and ministers, acting as executive aides rather than as representatives of the public. [22]

Religious leaders, notables and judges, or doctors of the religious law were confined to the exercise of their limited functions in society. These were consulted by the Viceroy only in times of crisis; otherwise they were entirely subjected to the control of a state bureaucracy and lacked serious influence upon his constituted power.

Muhammad Ali continued to conduct his government and administration in the Turkish language, and to appoint to high civilian administrative and military command positions only those among his Albanians and Turks who were most loyal to him, as well as white Mamluk slaves. The Arabized natives were not favoured for such positions, even though some of them were to be found in the middle and lower ranks of both the civilian administration and military hierarchy. After 1845, however, Arabic gradually replaced Turkish for the conduct of public affairs and Arabic-speaking Egyptians replaced Turks and others in most, if not all, high positions. Of course many of these ex-Turks had become assimilated into the native population, and the Viceroy's educational policy led to the accelerated revival of the Arabic language, and its literature.

The work of Muhammad Ali would have suffered amidst a disorderly country and population. He therefore viewed as primary tasks the establishment of order and the proper administration of justice. A feature of the Pasha's insistence upon public order and security was his policy of religious toleration. Christians – Armenians, Copts, Greeks and other Europeans – held key posts in his administration. Although throughout his reign the Sharia Courts (Islamic religious courts) remained the sole judicial system in the country, he initiated the study of French-modelled civil, criminal and commercial codes, which were to be adopted later under his successors.

While doing all this in Egypt, Muhammad Ali came to the aid of his suzerain master in Istanbul. During the period 1811–23, he quelled at the request of the Sultan the rebellions of the Wahhabis in Arabia, thus exposing his troops for the first time to sustained military campaigns and extended war. His control over the Holy Cities, Mecca and Medina, afforded the Viceroy a potentially immense influence over his co-religionists everywhere, while at the same time it tended to undermine the supreme religious authority of the Sultan who was also the Caliph.

Motivated partly by the need to recruit slaves for his new army, and partly by his search for mineral resources, Muhammad Ali decided to conquer the Sudan. Immediately upon the final defeat of the Wahhabis, he ordered, in 1820, two small armies into the Sudan, one commanded by his son Ismail, and the other by his Defterdar, to conquer Dongola and Sennar respectively. In 1822 he founded Khartoum at the confluence of the two (the White and Blue) Niles, and by 1830 the first Egyptian governor of the Sudan was installed there. Later, the Egyptian domination of the Sudan was extended to include Suakin and Massawah, linking Egypt's possessions in Arabia to those in Africa via the Red Sea. This achievement aroused English suspicions of Egypt under Muhammad Ali, and the British government under Palmerston opposed the Pasha successfully in the 1830s.

It was only natural that, having secured his dominion and control to the southwest of the Ottoman Empire, Muhammad Ali should turn his attention to the immediately contiguous flank of the centre of Turkish authority, namely Syria. But in the meantime he was to assuage his suzerain's fears by coming to his aid in the Morea, where the Greeks were seeking independence from the Empire by force of arms. Under his son, Ibrahim, the Egyptian armies conquered Crete and the Morea, only to be defeated by the combined fleets of France and England in Navarino Bay in 1827.

Recovering quickly from the defeat in Greece, Muhammad Ali was ready in 1830 with a larger army and navy, to turn against his Sultan in Syria. He realized the intrinsic decay of Ottoman power and foresaw the quick decline of its dominion. If he could now achieve a delicate diplomatic balance between England and France, by playing one against the other, Muhammad Ali was ready to risk an all-out attack against the Empire for the extension of his dominion.

Within three years, 1830–3, the Viceroy's armies commanded by his son Ibrahim had reached as far as Konya in Turkey. It was apparent that the Ottoman Sultan would not be able to resist his vassal's military push successfully and he sought the aid of the Powers to stop him. Shrewd as he was, Muhammad Ali in turn realized the time was not opportune to defy the European Powers. He therefore satisfied himself with the gains made by the Treaty of Hunkar Iskelesi in July 1833. These included the Pashalik of Acre, which included Jerusalem and Nablus, Damascus, Aleppo and Adana. He was now master of Palestine and Syria and the passes of the Taurus Mountains at the gates of Turkey. This gave him the flexibility necessary to mount a final attack on Constantinople whenever the opportunity presented itself. The suzerain was now at the mercy of the vassal, and Muhammad Ali was for all practical purposes politically, economically and financially independent of the Ottoman Empire, even though he continued to pay tribute to the Imperial Ottoman Treasury.

The years 1833–9 represent perhaps the apogee of Muhammad Ali's reign. He had developed the strongest state in the Ottoman Empire by introducing to that part of the world European agents and methods of change to transform a strictly Muslim society into, at least, a mixed Islamic-European one. Similarly, the Sultans in Istanbul too had begun to introduce European methods for the reform of their army and administration as early as 1792. But the conservative opposition to reform in Turkey was stronger, creating serious difficulties for a succession of rulers that could not be overcome until later.

Despite the formal jurisdiction of Ottoman sovereignty over the entire area, the successes of Muhammad Ali had a tremendous impact throughout the Levant. The unity of the Ottoman empire was now merely a theoretical one, for in fact it was so fragmented that Muhammad Ali's empire extended from the Sudan in the south to Arabia in the east and Syria in the northeast. Despite the continued tributary relationship with the Porte, this empire was now a distinct state in which power rested exclusively with the Pasha in Cairo. Moreover, its population was predominantly Arabic-speaking. They were in effect separated from Turkey and attached to Egypt. The political axis for these areas now shifted from Istanbul to Cairo. Meanwhile, heightened nationalist sentiment led to political separatist movements in the Balkans, the European dominions of the Ottoman Empire, which partly provided the model to be followed later by the Arabic-speaking ones. Indeed, Ottoman sovereignty was undermined to the extent that until 1839 no imperial decrees (*firmans*) issued by the Sultan to agents of foreign states or their representatives could apply in Egypt or in the dominions of Muhammad Ali without his approval. Much of this defiance on the part of the Pasha was possible by virtue of his material and military superiority over the Ottoman Sultan. Indeed, he now had his own foreign ministry, and received diplomatic representatives accredited to his court.

Despite all these achievements Muhammad Ali's overriding ambition during these six years was to secure the hereditary title of the Pashalik of Egypt for his successors. To achieve this he suggested to the Powers (England and France) – who by now were intensely interested in guarding their interests against his growing power in the Levant – a plan by which he would help regenerate and strengthen the Ottoman Empire against the imperial designs of Russia. He proposed to form a league between Persia and himself against Russia which might help retrieve lost Turkish territory along the Black Sea. Meantime, he justified his occupation of Syria as a measure to safeguard the integrity of the Ottoman Empire. But he also demanded the recognition of his independence.

England and France were primarily concerned with the maintenance of the *status quo* in the East. The Pasha's demands for independence and a hereditary title to Egypt could conceivably undermine this situation. Initially, therefore, both Powers were opposed to the idea. In 1837, the Porte approached Muhammad Ali with the proposal that his family could have hereditary title to Egypt and retain Arabia on condition that he relinquished the remainder of the territories he had conquered thus far. Muhammad Ali rejected this offer. Then in 1839 two important events occurred: the British occupied Aden at the south-western tip of the Arabian peninsula, driving a wedge between the Pasha's Arabian dominion and his African possessions. Simultaneously, Palmerston, who was then Prime Minister, favoured a *status quo* policy in the East, i.e. the maintenance of the integrity and independence of the Ottoman Empire under the Sultan. With this knowledge, Sultan Mahmud II renewed hostilities against the armies of Muhammad Ali. The last stages of armed conflict (April–August 1839) ended in a decisive victory for Egyptian arms against the Turks in the Battle of Nizib, and the Ottoman fleet defected to Egypt. This almost total collapse of Turkish military power in the face of the Pasha's superior forces prompted England and France to take joint action against the Governor of Egypt. Their collective Note to Muhammad Ali in July 1839 was designed to forestall direct negotiations between the Pasha and the Porte that might increase the power of the Viceroy. Such direct negotiations between the Porte and the Pasha – when the latter had the upper hand – could conceivably have further undermined the Sultan's authority and the integrity of his empire and, in England's view at least, endangered British imperial communications to India.

An Egyptian historian has argued that Muhammad Ali foresaw the incipient movement among his subjects for national independence, and that he designed much of his policy on the basis of this perception.[23] This is a tendentious contention. Similarly, certain writers who were contemporaries of Muhammad Ali and some later historians too have concluded from his Syrian campaigns that he was leading an 'Arab national movement' against the Turks.[24] But nationality was an unknown concept to the Pasha. It was equally unknown to the Arabs of the Fertile Crescent at that time. The available evidence rather suggests that all Muhammad Ali perceived was an enfeebled Ottoman State and the possibility of extracting ever greater concessions from the Sultan; or simply the extension of his power and authority as the governor of an Ottoman province at the expense of his master in Istanbul. That he was aware of earlier separatist movements in Egypt, especially the one led by Ali Bey the Great in the preceding century, is possible. But separatist movements then had no bearing upon, or relation to, national independence notions. These did not begin to appear and crystallize until later in the century. That Muhammad Ali liked to hear what Machiavelli had to say about the prince and his power, what Alexander accomplished in the East, and what Bonaparte designed for Egypt does not imply that he had similar visions of a message for the Eastern world. Rather, throughout the history of the Islamic Middle East, the tendency was for local and provincial governors to aspire to greater power at opportune moments when central authority appeared weak.

The Syrian dominions, for instance, offered Muhammad Ali – in addition to their strategic value – a certain economic-military advantage. They were a potential source of conscription for the Pasha's army; an additional and lucrative area of agricultural wealth; a source of raw materials, such as minerals and timber from their forests for a demanding naval arsenal in Alexandria; a rich commercial entrepôt; and an additional export centre. The articulation – especially by Muhammad Ali's son, Ibrahim Pasha – of the desire for an independent Egyptian state, or empire, extending to Syria under the Muhammad Ali house, did not imply the adoption of a *nationalist* cause. Any such imputations to the Muhammad Ali episode, especially in Syria, have been the result of subsequent 'over-reading' by historians, and particularly nationalist historians.[25] It is furthermore doubtful if the Pasha's military campaigns in Syria were, as some have suggested, motivated by his desire to reform the Ottoman State and deliver the faithful from the tyranny of the Turkish Sultan. Rather reports of travellers and others at the time indicated the extent of opposition to Muhammad Ali both in Egypt and in Syria, especially in response to his policy of heavy military conscription.[26] In short, there was no politically sophisticated public that identified Muhammad Ali as their 'national leader'. It is also possible that later Arab historians and publicists of the Arab national cause attributed to Muhammad Ali the leadership of an early 'Arab national independence movement' after reading of Palmerston's unbending opposition to the ambitions of the Pasha against the Ottoman Sultan.

What can be safely said about Muhammad Ali's foreign policy is that he tried to balance his position against that of the Sultan *vis-à-vis* the European powers, particularly Britain and France. He played one against the other, until the pro-Muhammad Ali policy of King Louis Philippe was abandoned by the French government in favour of a coalition with England to save the independence and integrity of the Ottoman State. The British bombardment of the Pasha's positions in Beirut and Acre was a prelude to the London Treaty of 1840 (and 1841). While he lost his Syrian possessions, Muhammad Ali secured, as a result of the Sultan's *firman* in 1841, the title of Viceroy of Egypt and the hereditary succession to this title by his lawful heirs. Whereas until that point France regarded herself and was, in turn, regarded by the Egyptian government as the champion of the Muhammad Ali dynasty on the one hand, and Britain as the prime protector of Turkish suzerainty over Egypt on the other, conditions changed in such a way as to lead England to establish closer relations with Egypt and in fact, before the end of the century, to dominate the country.

It would be wrong, therefore, to attribute such modern sentiments to Muhammad Ali as nationalism, whether Egyptian, Arab or Ottoman. He was simply a Muslim ruler whose conceptions about society and the relations among men were basically religious, with a strong instinct for domination and command. He was not conversant with, sympathetic to, or concerned with such modern European concepts as the emancipation of the people, popular sovereignty and representation. People to him were subjects who obeyed a forceful ruler who, in turn, ruled alone and absolutely without their participation.

Nor was Muhammad Ali concerned with the inherent goodness or badness of modernization. He simply understood, and came to accept, the formula that modernity presented indispensable advantages for his attainment of power and the establishment of a strong dynasty. If these required certain reform measures and other conditions, he never hesitated to take the former and create the latter. Nevertheless, the consequences of the Pasha's pursuit of power and dominion constituted the essential foundations of the development of modern Egypt – both as a state and a society.

CHAPTER 5

ISMAIL, THE IMPATIENT
EUROPEANIZER

In working to achieve complete independence from the Ottoman Sultan, Muhammad Ali and his son Ibrahim Pasha depended mainly on military power. Said Pasha, son of Muhammad Ali, who succeeded his rather colourless nephew Abbas Pasha in 1856, is credited with the further separation of Egypt from Turkey by encouraging the emergence of Arabic as the official language of the country. Ismail, on the other hand, is considered to have encouraged the emergence of an educated Egyptian élite that first rebelled against him, later was in intermittent controversy with his son King Fuad, and ultimately deposed his grandson, King Faruq.

Europeans became directly involved in the struggle between the Muhammad Ali House and the Ottoman Porte; they served as leading experts in the development of the economic and other aspects of modern Egyptian life; they were instrumental in fostering the tendency among educated Egyptians to emulate Europe, and their countries exerted political pressure and control upon the rulers of Egypt until very recently. The European powers also caused the deposition of Ismail as Khedive of Egypt by the Sultan before the newly formed educated class in Egypt could coalesce into a national interest group, or groups, with functioning institutions. In short, the state system founded by Muhammad Ali – based on his New Order – was not permitted to develop to its fullest possibilities, as a result of the events that led to Ismail's fall and the subsequent British occupation of Egypt. The latter influenced the next generation of the élite created by Ismail in such a way as to channel their thinking and action along ideas of limited rule, responsibility and accountability of public power, a desire for representative and constitutional forms of government. These attitudes – if not values – which the new Egyptian aristocracy learned from Europe caused a conflict within their own society. Politically at that time this conflict may be described as one arising from the desire of the new aristocracy to participate and share in power on the one hand, and the traditional autocratic rejection of such notions by the ruling house on the other.

Whether the Egyptians considered Muhammad Ali as simply another governor, or whether his military and other successes had the effect of stirring a national instinct and popular spirit among them, is an indeterminate and really an unimportant question.[1] The fact is that at the end of his reign, Egypt's population had almost doubled – from two and a half to over four and a half million – commerce had increased almost six-fold, and the nucleus of an educated class began to form, gradually undermining and eventually displacing in the 1900s the privileged aristocracy of Turks, Mamluks and Albanians, to lead and direct the further development of modern Egypt.

During the interval between Muhammad Ali and Ismail reigned three successive Pashas: Ibrahim for a mere six months, Abbas I (1848–54), and Said (1854–63). We are told that Abbas I, the oldest male heir in the Muhammad Ali family and a grandson of the Pasha, was generally reactionary and despotic. He had no interest, or desire, to continue the reform and other works of his illustrious predecessor, as he was suspicious of not only the many Europeans already in the service of his grandfather, but also the few Egyptians in government service who had been trained in the modern schools opened by Muhammad Ali and in the educational missions to Europe. His policy amounted to a deliberate arrest of the process of modern change – a process just as deliberately initiated by his predecessor. Moreover, he suspected and disliked his half-brothers and brothers so intensely as to cause them to leave the country for Istanbul and European capitals for the duration of his reign.[2] In fact, he tried to change the law regarding the succession to the Egyptian viceregal throne so that his own son Ilhami Pasha would succeed him. He was generally given to secrecy and preferred to live in isolation and seclusion away from the capital. For this purpose he built palaces in Abbassia, Benha and elsewhere.[3]

Despite his enmity towards Europeans, and especially the Suez Canal project which at the time was being proposed by Frenchmen, Abbas permitted the improvement of road communications between Cairo and Suez, and the extension of railroads between Cairo and Alexandria. The railroad projects were in turn supported by the British in view of their interest in the lines of communication to India, and the first railroad between Alexandria and Cairo was built by Robert Stephenson in 1852. Schools, factories and other enterprises were, however, neglected by Abbas. The armed forces, moreover, deteriorated in quality and organization, even though their activities were revived briefly when the Sultan Abd al-Majid in 1853 requested military aid from Abbas in the Crimean War. A twenty thousand strong expeditionary force was transported by the Egyptian Navy to that battlefront. Yet, when Abbas died in 1854 – allegedly murdered by his own servants – he had left no appreciable mark on Egypt, except for a reputation as the dismantler of his grandfather's edifice.[4]

His successor, Said Pasha, who ascended the throne in 1854, was the son of Muhammad Ali. For his military training, Said was assigned to serve in the navy and later was appointed Navy Commander-in-Chief. Many of his tutors were Europeans and particularly Frenchmen, and he is said to have acquired a great fondness for Europeans in general. In sharp contrast to Abbas, he appeared kind, lenient and merciful. But he was also weak, lacking in willpower, and ready to be swayed by the advice of the man closest to him at the moment. Possibly under outside influence, Said proceeded to revive the works in agriculture, irrigation and education begun by his father. More than this, he found himself succumbing to the pressure exerted by the dexterous and charming Ferdinand de Lesseps by granting him in November 1854 the famous concession to dig the Suez Canal.

In the field of agriculture Said promulgated the first comprehensive law governing private landed and immovable property in Egypt, in 1858, and abolished the system of monopoly over agricultural products that prevailed during his father's reign. By this act, Said granted farmers the right to dispose freely of their produce, as well as the freedom to choose what crops to cultivate on their land.[5]

Similarly, irrigation occupied much of Said's attention. He widened, deepened and kept serviceable major irrigation canals, such as the Mahmudiyya. He was just as interested in extending communications, especially railroads and telegraphs, as well as in drawing detailed maps of Egypt for which he used Egyptian engineers and topographers. One of his most important accomplishments was the introduction of uniform military service. Under Muhammad Ali peasants were conscripted into the army forcibly and for indefinite periods. Consequently, the bulk of these conscripts came from the poorer and lower classes of society. On the other hand, Said limited military service to one year and recruits were recommended by village headmen and notables. In the field of civil administration, Said introduced the first organized pension scheme for public servants, which became the basis for all subsequent pension schemes in the

Egyptian government. A consequence of European influence upon Said was the founding of the first River Navigation and Transport Company in Egypt in 1854, and a commercial Navigation Company in 1857 to buttress Egyptian foreign trade.[6]

When Ismail came to power

the country was practically devoid of any social institutions capable of supporting the reform; the old ones had broken down and no new ones had yet come into existence as a result of the introduction of western ideas. So far, there was only imitation of western civilization. There were no public men, there was no public spirit; the bureaucracy was servile and corrupt; the people, the agricultural classes, were subjected to every kind of injustice and oppression and were not only without the means of redress but were completely ignorant of political rights; even the more enlightened elements in the population were politically ignorant.[7]

Abbas Pasha was, it seems, against any modern advance in the country which was to be accomplished with the assistance of Europeans. He even prescribed conditions to restrict the residence of foreigners in Egypt. Said, on the other hand, was pro-European, somewhat anti-Ottoman, yet like his immediate predecessor, Abbas, he was not highly motivated by political ambition. Ismail, however, marks a turning point in mid-nineteenth-century Egypt in so far as he was not only excessively pro-European, but had vast and definite political ambitions both within the country and abroad. Ismail was obsessed with the ambition to transform Egypt into a European country, and to transform its capital city Cairo into a dazzling European city. He believed that only Europeans could help him attain these goals. His main foreign policy aim was to achieve greater independence from Turkey and to continue the plan begun by his grandfather of conquering all of the Sudan and its outlying areas, so that Egypt could command an African empire.

Whereas Muhammad Ali believed that the firm establishment of his rule and that of his heirs in Egypt depended upon a policy of European-style reform, his grandson, Ismail, wanted to make Egypt a part of Europe. 'My country is no longer in Africa, it is in Europe,' Ismail is reported to have said to one of the members of the European control commission. While he managed eventually to make Egypt part of Europe in the sense that it came under European financial control first, and direct British occupation later, Ismail's reign also provided the basis for the genesis of a Europeanized Egyptian élite in government, education and letters. The membership of this élite soon expanded and its knowledge increased appreciably until it became the leader of the reform and later nationalist movements of the early twentieth century. Paradoxically the reign of Ismail (1863–79) was an age of great advancement in the building up of an, at least outwardly, European-looking Egypt through the extension of public works, the opening of the Suez Canal, the encouragement of education and the arts. All these accomplishments awakened Egyptians to the advantages of the modern world. But they also brought financial ruin to the country leading to foreign control and domination – literally the loss of the virtual independence Egypt enjoyed from the Ottoman Porte for seventy-five years.

Many writers have already considered Ismail as the root of all evil in Egypt, past and present; other have lauded his accomplishments and the blessings he brought to the country.[8] Speculating on Ismail's ambitions, one of them said:

> He [Ismail] saw himself in his mind's eye the greatest sovereign on the African continent. He looked forward to the day when, in the event of the impending collapse of the Ottoman Empire, he might become the virtual, if not the nominal, successor of the Sultan; and he was carried away by the delusion that if he could only secure the continuance of European financial support, he might extend his sovereignty from the Nile to the Bosphorus.[9]

Whatever his ambitions, the effects of Ismail's rule on the development of modern Egypt have been great indeed.

In order to achieve greater independence from the Sultan, Ismail had to alter the conditions imposed upon Egypt by the Imperial Decrees of 1840 and 1841, sanctioned by the Powers who had decided to prevent Muhammad Ali from endangering the independence and integrity of the Ottoman Empire. He had to deal simultaneously with both the Porte and the European Powers. Whereas his grandfather dealt with the Sultan from a position of strength and depended on his military might to extract certain concessions from Istanbul, Ismail on the other hand chose to achieve similar results by money – gifts, bribery and other informal arrangements. He was therefore interested in establishing close relations with the Sultan Abdel Aziz as a prelude to other things. Among the latter was Ismail's desire to change the rule of succession in the viceregal family from the oldest surviving male heir in the Muhammad Ali family as was the Ottoman rule, to direct male primogeniture in his family. He thus spent much money in inviting Abdel Aziz to Egypt on a state visit. No Ottoman Sultan had visited Egypt since Selim I, the conqueror

of the country, who was there briefly in 1517. Now in 1863 the Ottoman sovereign of Egypt was received with great pomp, ceremony
and expense.

Ismail, who, unlike Abbas or Said, had been to Europe as a
student, and travelled widely between Istanbul and Paris, had known
the Sultan Abdel Aziz in the 1850s when the latter had appointed
him to various offices in the judicial councils of the State. His diplomatic experience was enhanced when Said Pasha entrusted him with
a special diplomatic mission to the court of Napoleon III in Paris.
During the state visit of his sovereign master, the Sultan, to Egypt,
Ismail approached him and his entourage with a view to changing
the rule of succession to the Egyptian viceregal throne. After lavish
expenditure and outright bribes to Ottoman courtiers allegedly
amounting to some three million pounds sterling, a *firman* was issued
by the Sultan in May 1866 decreeing the rule of succession in Ismail's
favour, but extracting in return the increase of the Egyptian annual
tribute to the Ottoman Treasury from 400,000 to £750,000. The decree, however, also permitted Ismail to increase the size of the Egyptian Army, as well as to coin his own currency and bestow state
decorations and titles to individuals – Egyptian and foreign – up
to a certain rank.

In this connection it is interesting to refer to Mustafa Fazil Pasha,
brother of the Khedive and until 1866 his heir to the Egyptian vice-
regal throne. The new *firman* excluded Mustafa Fazil from succession. It was suspected that at the instigation of Ismail the Sultan
removed Mustafa Fazil from the office of President of the Treasury
Council in Istanbul in February 1866. Soon Mustafa came to be
associated with a conspiracy of opposition against the Sultan, probably a group of Young Ottoman 'liberals'. Asked to leave Istanbul
in April, Mustafa joined other Turkish exiles in Paris where, in
March 1867, he published an open letter to the Sultan in the paper
Liberté. This took the form of a manifesto demanding constitutional
reforms. It has also been suggested that the Sultan Abdel Aziz was
anxious for a similar law of succession favouring his own family in
Istanbul. Thus, in addition to the possible adherence of Mustafa
Fazil to the liberal notions of the Young Ottomans from conviction,
he had perhaps a vital personal interest in attacking what he referred
to in his letter as despotism and tyranny in the Ottoman State. Yet,
after the renewed difficulties between the Khedive and the Sultan
in 1869, Mustafa Fazil was rehabilitated by his master in Istanbul
as President of the High Court and later Minister of Finance, before

he died in 1871.[10] Another interesting aspect of this episode that may have some bearing on developments in Egypt is that of the formation of the first legislative assembly in Egypt in 1866.[11]

Closely related to the efforts of Ismail to render his rule more secure within his family was his ambition to acquire the more formal accoutrements of sovereignty *vis-à-vis* his master and the European Powers. From a mere *wali*, a representative of the sovereign Sultan in Egypt, he managed, after further lavish expenditure in Istanbul, to secure a special Imperial Decree bestowing upon him the formal title Khedive, which, as ranks go, elevated his standing to a position closer to royalty. A more important concession that Ismail received along with this title was the virtual internal independence of Egypt and her right to enter into special treaties and agreements governing posts, customs and trade transit. These provisions were to give Ismail freedom in the financial, administrative and judicial arrangements of the country.

It was inevitable that Ismail's newly won, though relative, independence should get him into difficulties with the Sultan, for he used it to deal directly with the European Powers for the strengthening of his finances, his armed forces, and related matters. His pursuit of his conquests in the Sudan, his massive and continuous borrowing abroad to finance both his public projects and private affairs, the expenditures entailed in the digging and opening of the Suez Canal in 1869, all led to near bankruptcy and the imminent interference of certain European powers in the affairs of Egypt. Thus in November 1869, as soon as the celebrations inaugurating the Suez Canal had ended, the Sultan issued another *firman* limiting the concessions granted by the previous one in 1866. It dealt largely with the borrowing power of the Khedive: it ordered that Ismail could not contract any new loans without the Sultan's permission. It has been alleged in this connection that the Sultan was indignant at the Khedive's rumoured plan to announce the independence of Egypt during the Suez Canal opening ceremonies, and that the reason Ismail had not done so was the advice of the European representatives in Cairo against such a course of action. Ismail placed great stock in his special cordial relationship with the court of Napoleon III which, he believed, could help him achieve many of his plans both in Egypt and against the Sultan. Unfortunately for Ismail, the Empire fell when Napoleon's régime was overthrown after the French defeat in the Franco-Prussian War of 1870–1. Consequently, Ismail had to mend his fences in Istanbul once again, especially when at that time he found himself in serious financial straits and somehow had to find new sources of money.

Curtailed as he was in borrowing by the 1869 *firman*, he considered a lavish investment in a visit to Istanbul a wise one. Thus in the summer of 1872, accompanied by his financial adviser and confidant, Ismail Pasha Saddiq, known as al-Mufattish, and his foreign minister, Nubar Pasha, the Khedive arrived in Istanbul affecting great opulence by bearing very expensive gifts to the Ottoman court. By September of that year he had secured a new *firman* rescinding the provisions of the 1869 decree and restoring to him the freedom to raise money, i.e., borrow as he wished without Ottoman approval. Still Ismail was not satisfied. Suspicious by nature, like most other princes and rulers of his time and milieu, he was anxious to extract one more decree from the Ottoman suzerain that would incorporate all the rights and privileges he had already secured for his family in Egypt by the previous *firman* – rule of succession in his immediate family, financial and administrative autonomy, military independence and so on. After distributing enormous bribes to Istanbul courtiers and other influential personages, Ismail secured a *firman* in June 1873, incorporating all the previous gains. Yet despite such guarantees the Sultan did not hesitate to side with the European Powers only six years later in 1879 to depose the Khedive from the Egyptian throne.

Ismail's European policy, however, presented serious problems. England, for instance, was not as impressed by, or friendly to, the Khedive; first, because of her opposition to the Suez Canal project, which was sponsored and directed by the Frenchman Ferdinand de Lesseps, and supported by the French imperial court, and second, because of her traditional adherence to a policy that would secure and perpetuate the integrity and independence of the Ottoman Empire as the best guarantor of British imperial communications to India. France was in a rather privileged position in Egypt, not only as a result of the long presence of Frenchmen as advisers in the court of Muhammad Ali, but also because of Ismail's own preference for their advice. Moreover, such a privileged relationship afforded France a means of opposing British imperial interests. But when France's fortunes ebbed with the defeat in 1871, Ismail began to look towards England for support.

This outward change in the Khedive's policy coincided with a new concern of the British government, namely, apprehension over their imperial interests in the East after the opening of the Suez Canal. While Ismail tried deliberately to interest England in his country by granting engineering contracts to British firms for the expansion and improvement of Alexandria harbour and other works, the British, in turn, welcomed the infiltration of their influence after 1871. Moreover, the dramatic purchase in 1875 of the Khedive's Suez Canal Company shares for a cash payment of four million pounds sterling by Disraeli on behalf of the British government eased temporarily and very slightly the Khedive's desperate need of cash but also made the British government overnight the largest single shareholder in the Company. This single and most abrupt though shrewd act by the then British Prime Minister more than any other act of policy cast the die of British vital interests in Egypt. Two years later, in an apparent effort to appear enlightened but also in order to secure British sympathy, Ismail signed a convention with Britain outlawing slavery and the slave trade in his dominions. In the meantime, a series of expeditions to the Sudan, Equatoria, Uganda and other parts of Africa, led by British and American officers, seemed to satisfy Ismail's plan for an African empire. In fact, one Egyptian historian argued that Ismail conquered the great lakes in Africa, the Congo Valley and Ethiopia in the hope that he could proclaim himself Emperor of Africa.[12]

Even though Ismail's pursuit of his ambitions brought financial ruin to Egypt, it also produced real advances in its economic and social development, as well as in its physical appearance.[13] Expensive change (the Khedive had no compunction at living beyond his or his country's means) generated tangible advances. The Consul General of the United States reported in 1876 that the improvements introduced into Egypt by Ismail during the period 1864–76 were remarkable and without precedent. Even Mr Cave, of the famous Cave Mission, sent to investigate the condition of Egyptian finances in 1875, admitted that the productive forces of the country under the government of the Khedive had made great progress. Thus in 1864 the annual revenues of Egypt were estimated at just under five million pounds sterling; in 1875 they had risen to 145·9 million pounds sterling. Exports for the same period rose from 29·6 million pounds sterling to almost 62 million. Undeniably, the material value of Ismail's work was great, for it augmented the economic capabilities of the country.

In the field of agriculture Ismail expanded and further developed the cultivation of cotton as a cash export crop. A leading farmer himself, and owner of a large part of the arable lands of Egypt, he managed by personal action, initiative and an imaginative programme to render Egypt one of the leading producers in the world and the essential one for the provision of the European cotton industry. Moreover the first years of his rule coincided with the second half of the Civil War in the United States (1861–5). From 596,000 kantars of cotton representing a value equal to 143,088,000 piastres exported from Egypt to foreign markets in 1861, the export figure for 1865 was two and a half million kantars worth 1,544,312,000 piastres. All of this, in turn, represented unprecedented prosperity for Egypt. But cotton being a commodity the income from which depends mainly on fluctuating world markets, such profit and prosperity could not always be guaranteed. What perhaps was of more permanent benefit to the country was the fact that during his reign Ismail brought an additional one and a quarter million acres under cultivation, representing a sizeable rise in production and an increase in terms of income (over eleven million pounds sterling). Population increased by one million during Ismail's reign.

Closely related to the advance in agriculture and its economy was Ismail's attention to public works. 112 canals, 8,400 miles long, were dug to expand irrigated areas in the country. Of these the largest was the Ibrahimiyya Canal, leaving the Nile at Assiut in Upper Egypt and thus bringing wider areas of that part of the country under cultivation. Another important canal with salutary consequences for transport, water supply to cities, and other benefits was the Ismailia Canal joining the Nile with Suez, and Cairo with Ismailia. Some four hundred bridges were constructed across the Nile at various points, the most famous today being the Kasr el-Nil bridge joining Kasr el-Nil in Cairo to Gezira. Telegraph lines were put up amounting to five thousand miles. By 1870 Ismail had increased the railway mileage from five hundred to eight hundred and by the end of his reign there were eleven hundred miles of railway connecting towns and cities that were central to the economy of Egypt, its trade and commerce. One of his important achievements was the establishment of a national postal service. Until his accession to the throne, postal services were conducted privately by Europeans, and especially Italians. Moreover a variety of foreign concerns had their own postal services. By setting up a governmental postal service, Ismail succeeded in gaining admission to the Postal Union in Switzerland and this enabled him to abolish all foreign postal services in his country.

Attentive as he was to the development of profitable agricultural projects, especially the cultivation of cotton, one would suspect that Ismail was not too concerned with the revival, or further expansion, of industry begun by his grandfather. One industrial sector he did, however, develop profitably was related to the expansion of irrigated areas in Upper Egypt, permitting the introduction of wide-scale sugarcane planting, which strengthened the sugar industry in Egypt. Ismail opened at least fourteen new sugar factories in various parts of the country.

Ismail gave serious and devoted attention to modernizing the major cities and towns of Egypt by expanding the municipal services to the public. Water distribution, transport, street lighting, gas supply and other amenities of modern living were established and organized in his time. The design and construction of residential quarters in the cities, of city and town squares and parks was one of his major concerns in the building up of modern cities.

Yet all these works would have been incomplete without the provision of financial arrangements for increased commerce, trade and other enterprises that make up life in a modern civilized society. Financial societies appeared at his encouragement which conducted banking operations and commercial transactions to exploit further industrial and agricultural development. River and maritime transport also flourished under Ismail. The earlier and smaller Nile Navigation Company founded by Said Pasha under the name Madjidieh Company, was absorbed by a new one, the Azizieh el-Masria Company, which was bought by Ismail and renamed the Khedivial Company. A Bank of Egypt was founded in 1856, which became the Anglo-Egyptian Bank in 1864. The Ottoman Bank appeared in Egypt in 1867 and the Crédit Lyonnais set up offices in 1875. Foreign capital investment was encouraged for the creation of various enterprises. With the establishment particularly of the Mixed Tribunals in 1877 – largely by the efforts of the intelligent Nubar Pasha who wanted both to curtail the unbridled power of the sovereign through a regularized legal apparatus on the one hand, and to render foreign interests more secure but less abusive to Egypt on the other – long-term investment by foreign capital, the granting of long-term credit and mortgage facilities became a common inducement to economic development.

The development projects of Ismail Pasha were of such a new and technical nature as to require skills not available among the Egyptians themselves. Rather he carried them out by the wide use of European technical talent. In fact, Egypt had rarely before seen such an impressive immigration of European talent into the country. Ismail issued a blanket invitation to Europeans, especially Frenchmen, Englishmen and Italians, to participate in the development of Egypt. He similarly called upon foreign, particularly British and American, military talent to lead the extension of Egyptian domination in Africa. The English Samuel Baker Pasha led Ismail's expeditions into the Sudan and was later succeeded by the celebrated Gordon Pasha. General Stone, an American army officer, was Chief of Staff of the Egyptian Army and, along with other American Army officers, performed great cartographic services in mapping unexplored areas in Egypt and the Sudan, besides training Egyptian staff officers.

Under Muhammad Ali and Said Pasha French talent and influence were preponderant in the administration of the technical services of the State, public works enterprises, and thus in the general evolution of modern life in Egypt. But Ismail, more than either of his predecessors, increased such French influence in both his administration and the general education of Egyptians. During his reign Catholic missions were permitted to establish orders in the country. His patronage extended to such household names in Egypt (until very recently) as the Sisters of the Bon Pasteur, the Jesuits, the Dames de Sion, the Sisters of Saint-Vincent-de-Paul, the Filles de Charité, the Frères de la Doctrine Chrétienne. All of these were to have an educational and cultural influence upon Egyptians in both their speech and thought which not even direct British occupation was able to completely eradicate in the next seventy-five years.[14] Although Muhammad Ali introduced a modern state school system fashioned along the French model of public instruction he did not, however, permit the establishment of private European-directed schools parallel to his own. Ismail did so with great patronage and seemingly a total lack of religious prejudice. Some have argued that all of this Europeanization and tolerance in favour of Christian advisers and confidants was motivated in Ismail by his desire to appear progressive and thus solicit the aid of European Powers in his struggle for complete independence from his Ottoman suzerain.[15] Much of his affected approval and patronage of constitutional reform for a more limited and representative government were also given in the hope of marshalling local support against the intervention of the Powers in his financial affairs.

Be that as it may, Ismail's domestic policy and his extensive development projects made it possible for the number of Europeans settled in Egypt to increase from a few thousand in 1860 to over a hundred thousand in 1876. Egyptians had seen and come in contact with Europeans seventy-five years earlier when French armies invaded and occupied the country briefly. But the members of the European communities in Egypt in 1876 were not army troops; they were civilians engaged in various state enterprises, in private educational and economic activities. Moreover, only a very small number of Egyptian religious leaders and notables had really come in contact with the French conquerors in 1798–1801. Now an ever-increasing number of Egyptian state officials, engineers, lawyers, teachers and others, trained in European-modelled schools in Egypt as well as through educational missions in European capitals, were themselves in daily contact with members of local European communities.

Himself more fond and appreciative of occidental ways of life than any of his predecessors, Ismail was personally most active in leading the way for his subjects in the acquisition of Western manners and habits of life. European dress was adopted by the educated Egyptians in the professions and government services. His efforts in the introduction of European methods in education, public works and urban construction were reflected in the multifold increase of the State's budget for these projects. Indeed, his programme of public instruction constitutes an epochal departure in mid-nineteenth century Egypt. He founded specialized schools for lawyers, administrators, even religious shaykhs, engineers, technicians and linguists, teachers and craftsmen. Ismail gave his special attention to education when he entrusted its improvement and expansion to the Swiss Dor Bey. By 1875 there were a hundred thousand pupils in these schools, especially after the autocrat Ismail permitted in 1874 the entry of children from the peasant classes into his public schools. Moreover, until this time, female education was confined to private foreign schools and to the personal efforts of princesses and noblewomen. It was an aspect of their charitable work. Ismail, again, was the first ruler in Egypt to bring the education of girls under government supervision and eventually integrate it with the general state school system.

Affecting further his adoption of the European style, Ismail inaugurated by his personal patronage the development of state-supported activities and organizations for arts and letters: archaeology, music, poetry, public libraries and museums, learned societies and scholarly research. For instance the interest in Egyptology and related historical studies about Egypt which began under the French – especially Bonaparte's Institute – was not revived until Ismail took a personal interest and the initiative in patronizing and encouraging such activities. In 1875 he founded the Geographical Society which made great contributions in the fields of geography, history and ethnography. He founded a national library[16] and an observatory in Cairo as well as a museum in Bulaq. The direction of the latter he entrusted to the famous archaeologist Mariette Pasha whose interest in Egyptology was in the tradition of the great Champollion who had deciphered the Rosetta Stone in 1822, thereby establishing once and for all the study of hieroglyphics. To make Egypt's commitment to an identification with Europe more positive and acute, Egypt under Ismail participated in the Paris World Exhibition of 1867.

It is difficult for the student of this period in Egyptian history to reject the proposition that the work of Ismail constituted the real socio-political basis of modern Egypt. Despite everything, his administration shaped the framework of the future conduct of public affairs in Egypt. His agricultural and economic policy influenced subsequent Egyptian policy in these two fields for almost one hundred years. He, more than any other member of the Muhammad Ali dynasty, impressed upon the Egyptians that Islamic–Ottoman methods of administration and public organization for the State should from then on be abandoned in favour of European methods. There was to be, so to speak, no turning back. Much of this impression was created by the fact that Ismail himself adhered to these methods by example. What is interesting, however, is that he maintained highly Oriental methods of political manipulation and power control – an area that constituted the major lag in this so-called Europeanization of Egypt, and which lag persists in large measure until today.

Though only eight years younger than his immediate predecessor Said Pasha, Khedive Ismail belonged to a new and different generation which rose along with him to assist him in his political power ambitions – a generation in which East and West seemed to be fused in a better and happier balance than before. Yet, one must conclude that the immense value of his works was largely material. Although Ismail must take much of the credit for the decisive development of new social and intellectual conditions in Egypt, the changes he was able to induce in these areas of Egyptian life, thereby appreciably

affecting the characteristics of the Egyptian nation, were not so profound as to drastically change the nature of political power, authority, or the political community in the country. He was impatient
to achieve eminence as a ruler and reformer by European standards,
and the changes he introduced into the country were perhaps both
too sudden and rapid to be managed and absorbed by the elements
of his administration.

WESTERN VIEWS OF KHEDIVE ISMAIL

No ruler of Egypt, however, until that time had stirred greater controversy and generated more argument than Ismail. He provoked
passionate divisions among Egyptians and Europeans alike over his
behaviour and policies. Europeans were divided in their views as to
whether Ismail was a great ruler, reformer, developer and administrator on one hand, or a 'reckless spendthrift, voluptuary and thief',
whose actions and policies benefited himself and his family, not
Egypt. Only the Arab-Israel conflict of the last thirty years has produced the same passionate division of views. Yet more books were
written on Ismail and Ismail's Egypt – the Suez Canal, his finances, the
pros and cons of European control – by non-Egyptians than perhaps
any other single man, episode or event in the history of modern Egypt.

As for the image of Ismail amidst the controversy surrounding
him, there were basically two main views. There was a thoroughly
anti-Ismail one, held really after his deposition and exile – even
after his death – and mainly by English administrators in Egypt, such
as Cromer, Milner, Colvin and a few others. It was a simple and
highly biased view. It held that Ismail, with the assistance of his
notorious finance minister, Ismail Saddiq, known as al-Mufattish,
squeezed the population for money by oppressive taxation and the
use of the *kurbaj* (whip).

The other view, held mainly by journalists in the 1890s, by American consuls in Egypt, such as Edwin de Leon and Elbert Farman,
argued that Ismail inherited a difficult situation from his uncle Said
Pasha (1854–63). The latter, with his simple-minded attraction to
Europeans, his friendship with Ferdinand de Lesseps and their common love of *pasta*, was hoodwinked into signing the Suez Canal concessions in 1856, with its unfavourable provisions: for example, the
supply of forced labour (*corvée*), the making over to the new Company of 60,000 *feddans* of land along the way, and the construction of the Sweet Water Canal. In addition, Said left a £3 million

state debt, and a £7 million personal one. This view further argued that Ismail's efforts to modify the Suez Canal concessions, whose provisions he clearly anticipated would undermine Egyptian sovereignty, cost money and involved him in European entanglements, Ottoman intrigue and, above all, borrowing. Eventually, this view concluded, the demands of European creditors forced Ismail to squeeze his people for more revenue.[17]

The question, however, which writers in those days invariably tried to resolve was one of responsibility and guilt: Who was responsible for the 'ruin of Egypt', as the fashionable phrase of the epoch put it – Ismail with his ambition to make Egypt independent, part of Europe and highly productive; or European creditors, bondholders and the Powers behind them, in particular Britain and France with their rivalry in the Mediterranean, Africa and the East? What was the role of the Sultan in all of this? How did he view his vassal, ruling a province which, since Muhammad Ali's time, had been virtually independent and which, even as far back as 1517, very soon after Sultan Selim's conquest, remained independent under the Mamluk Beys?[18]

Baron de Malortie, one of the more moderate critics of Ismail, writing in 1883, described the reign of Ismail as one of 'great projects, great results, and great expenditure'.[19] A vast development of public works – canals, railways, harbours, public utilities – accompanied the fantastic expansion of commerce and the extension of the area of cultivated land (4–5 million *feddans*). The further conquest of the Sudan and parts of Central Africa was followed by the exploration and survey of the new dominions. Public education was reorganized; so was the planning and construction of cities and their services. In short, Ismail laid the intricate foundation of the modern state which Muhammad Ali had carved out of chaos with his sword. The achievement dazzled the Europeans, and attracted many of them in search of quick profit. By 1876 all these great works had been hypothecated, mortgaged to European creditors. Thus, while Ismail spent over £10 million in bribes in Istanbul in order to extract a greater measure of autonomy from the Sultan, more millions to reorganize and modernize his army and administration and improve the judiciary by founding the Mixed Tribunals (1875), he undermined this autonomy by inviting European control. Great engineering works, such as the Canal, were soon transformed into burdensome financial problems. Egypt herself became a European financial question.

Muhammad Ali mistakenly assumed that power lay in economic autarky. Ismail, on the contrary, plunged willingly into economic dependence, into the mainstream of European economic and trade patterns, into deficit spending to promote development. Rapid development inflated the bureaucracy.

Everything we know about Ismail before he ascended the Khedivial throne points to a man dextrous in administration and financial management, a keen and methodical agriculturalist. He was perhaps the most brilliant member of the Muhammad Ali dynasty until his son Fuad became king of Egypt in 1923. His three passions, for real estate, ambitious public works projects and the more visible accoutrements of sovereignty, should not detract from these attributes.

It should be remembered that if Ismail was a typical Oriental despot, desperate to play the role of reformer and wishing to regenerate the country he ruled, he was doing so under immense disabilities and in the face of great obstacles. Without them, he might not have gone bankrupt. There were, for instance, the Capitulations, rather different in their actual working in Egypt from Turkey. These precluded Ismail from taxing about 100,000 foreigners living in Egypt, or bringing them under the jurisdiction of the native administration of justice. They constituted an *imperium in imperio*. At the same time, his policy of development projects attracted European creditors, behind whom stood their respective consuls and governments. Thus of a £90–£100 million debt Ismail incurred in sixteen years, his treasury realized a mere 50 per cent of that amount, such were the exorbitant charges and interest rates levied by foreign creditors. And yet Cave's Report in 1876 adjudged Egypt solvent on the basis of her resources. All she needed to get back on her feet was time and the proper servicing of the debts. Bluntly, European creditors – and above all, France for her own purposes – would not allow this. Five and a half million Egyptians paid in 1875 some £7 million in taxes which were imposed and forcibly collected with the sanction of European power.[20]

Whatever the arguments over Ismail's finances, the fact remains that he separated Egypt from Turkey. He became the real father of Egyptian independence, substituting a measure of legality for arbitrariness by instituting a semblance of cabinet government, a chamber of notables and the Mixed Tribunals. He created a new cadre or élite of Egyptian leaders, and flirted with new ideas and institutions,

ranging from education, financial accountability and control, more
equitable taxation and the abolition of the slave trade and forced
labour.

The English lion, French tiger, Egyptian ox, Greek jackal, all seemed designed
for the life of the country under Ismail – a Bachanalia of follies – making
Egypt a hot-bed for parasites of civilization. A Cairene bureaucracy battened
on the fellah and a foreign Alexandrian plutocracy battened in turn on the
Khedive.[21]

How accurate or distorted is such a description of Egypt in 1876
or 1879? Foreign bankers and creditors were the croupiers in Ismail's
baccarat game of public expenditure. They held the bank, so that
in Ismail's time the country was caught up in a European whirlpool,
a helpless victim of its force.[22]

Pierre Crabitès, a leading apologist for Ismail, asserts that the
image of Ismail held by Europeans is an 'historical heresy'. Others
who share his view have charged the Europeans with the rape of
Egypt. One of Ismail's famous ministers, Nubar Pasha, asserted that
it was in the time of Said Pasha that the débâcle began. Lord Cromer
echoed Nubar when he reminded us that it was Said who first invited
European adventurers to prey on Egypt. Viscount Milner may have
been nearer the mark when he depicted Ismail's Egypt as a 'carnival
of extravagance and oppression'.[23] How accurate is Crabitès's
definition of Ismail's predicament in general when he wrote that his
'ambition and independence, wielded and satisfied unlike his grandfather by his sword of gold, rather than steel, was opposed by the
European powers for their own designs'? The French, after all, loved
Egypt under Ismail's immediate predecessor, Said Pasha, because
they thought they were paramount there and the country a virtual French dependency. By 1870, though, Ismail had replaced
Frenchmen in his army with veteran Confederate officers from the
United States, and hired British engineers for his public works projects.

It is, anyway, irrelevant to argue as some have that Ismail was
a despot, for he was, after all, a product of his environment. *Bakhshish*, the *kurbaj* and the *corvée* were all integral features of that environment.

Instead, in inquiring into Ismail's reign one might do better to
consider whether he was, as some have suggested, a pathfinder of
the mid-nineteenth century, or whether Egypt in his sixteen-year rule
advanced (however advance is defined) more than in the two

hundred years before. He appeared to have a definite programme which, despite its dire financial consequences, wittingly or unwittingly introduced ideas associated with modernity. Ismail himself may well have been their instigator in a last desperate attempt to ward off European interference. The coming of European Dual (Financial) Control may have been the stimulant to the bubbling native reaction, culminating in the Orabi Revolt. At the end, Ismail may have been the victim of the European money élite.

One difficulty in assessing Ismail's reign derives from the contradictory judgements about it. It has been argued that he made the European the man of possession in his country, and that his submission to European control amounted to a confession of failure, bankruptcy and wrongdoing. He has been harshly compared to his grandfather who, it has been contended, was a statesman with perceptive qualities, whereas Ismail was a foolish adventurer. His extreme detractors have asserted that his was a dismal, degrading story of a country's ruin by its absolute ruler, affecting only a veneer of civilization; that he was a parvenu and parvenus are hard masters as a rule. According to them, Ismail the Khedive levied blackmail on pashas, the pashas on the headmen of villages, the headmen on the fellah and so on through an endless system of extortion.[24] One of them wrote,

Ismail was the French Tartuffe, the English John Diddler and Arab Son of Sin, and merely the occupant of a splendid house of bondage. Under him the powers became bailiffs for the European money-lending confraternity.[25]

All that can be said with any degree of certainty about Ismail's reign and as a general reaction to these contradictory judgements is that there was a rich Egypt in mid-nineteenth century which remained poor on account of its ruler's debts. There was a quasi-independent country which was none the less the tool of Europe. Its population was nominally free, yet practically in bondage. It had a constitution and a chamber of delegates that were paralysed by European financial control and undermined by native autocracy. Its government was, for a while, administered by presumably responsible ministers advised by non-responsible Europeans and shackled by several communities of privileged resident foreigners over whom it had no jurisdiction. Its native subjects were over-taxed whereas foreign residents escaped taxation.

In the final analysis, what makes Ismail interesting is the fact that the magnitude of his accomplishments as well as his mistakes have kept the outside world busy with and interested in Egypt for a long time. After him new men and subsequent events in Egypt – the British occupation, the Anglo-Egyptian question, Anglo-French rivalry – commanded the world's attention. These were all integral aspects of Egypt's relations with the outside world. It was the financial question, after all, in which Ismail featured so prominently, that furnished Europe with the excuse and opportunity to interfere in the affairs of Egypt for so long. He had perhaps succeeded in making Egypt a part of Europe.

All the same, whereas Muhammad Ali created the modern state of Egypt and inaugurated the renaissance of the society in it, Ismail forcefully stimulated, by his ambition and even his financial recklessness, the emergence of modern Egypt and outlined its future development. To an assessment of Ismail's stimulation of, and impact upon, the emergence of the modern Egyptians who became the leaders of the cultural, social, intellectual and political regeneration of his country, we now turn.

CHAPTER 6

MODERN EDUCATION AND THE FIRST EGYPTIAN INTELLECTUALS

The reign of Khedive Ismail constituted a decisive epoch in modern Egyptian history in so far as Egyptians learned to adopt modern European methods in many fields of private and public endeavour. In fact, the period 1863–82 was most crucial in the evolution of modern Egypt, for the vast educational and intellectual strides made by Egyptians after 1882 had interesting and, in many ways, enduring cultural, social and political consequences.

Generally, the period of the Mamluk dynasties from the thirteenth to the sixteenth centuries, as well as of the Ottoman–Mamluk control of Egypt which succeeded them, had reduced the country to a monopolistic source of income for the various rulers and their clients. Until the French occupation, the native population had been subjected to a series of continuous economic and political hardships which frequently led them to revolt. Their rebellions, whether in the cities, towns or the countryside, were no more than desperate reactions against oppression ranging from heavy taxation to forced labour.[1]

In these circumstances, the intellectual and cultural life of the country was bound to suffer. In fact, it stagnated. Apart from the occasional encouragement of cultural and artistic activity by the odd ruler in Mamluk Egypt in the thirteenth and fourteenth centuries, literary activity came to be limited to traditional forms of poetry and a body of folklore about saints and other local religious ceremonies. Jabarti described Egyptian society before the French expedition as intellectually barren and culturally stagnant. Although Arabic was the spoken language of the people, Turkish was that of the rulers and their courts. The quality of the Arabic language and its letters was, by neo-classical standards, low indeed. Some of the more prominent chroniclers and historians like Ibn Iyas and later, Jabarti, wrote mainly in the colloquial, and apparently made no attempt to use the classical idiom. The use of the latter remained confined to Azharite teachers and students who were generally concerned with the preservation of traditional Islamic learning.

Amidst foreign rulers, the Azhar stood for centuries at the apex of an educational system in Egypt consisting of village and town Koranic schools (*kuttab*), many of which were attached to mosques. The teachers in these schools were shaykhs who had studied at the Azhar or at one of its many religious institutes scattered around the country and supervised by the Azhar hierarchy. The *kuttab* taught students the rudiments of reading, writing and some arithmetic. Often the learning of these disciplines was only of secondary importance, the primary task and purpose of the *kuttab* being to get students to memorize the Koran, the Holy Book.

Despite the increasing contacts between Europe and the Ottoman Empire after 1600, the Azhar remained insulated from any outside non-Islamic influences. Cairo became relegated to the status of a provincial city in the Empire, whereas Istanbul emerged as the new cultural and intellectual centre to which the most ambitious and successful scholars were drawn. Thus the educational and intellectual position of the Azhar declined under Ottoman rule. More detrimental still was Azharite ignorance of the scientific and philosophical consequences of the Renaissance and Reformation in Europe, so that when Egypt was directly confronted in 1798 by the armies and administration of France – one of the most enlightened European states of the time – the educational and intellectual standards of the Azhar were really backward in comparison, even though the first stirrings of a revival had begun.

Yet, in seeking to assuage the impact of his conquest of the country upon Egyptians, and to effect their liberation from the yoke of Mamluk tyranny, Napoleon Bonaparte had to appeal directly to the Azhar and its chiefs in their capacity as the intellectual and social leaders of Egypt, as opposed to the Mamluk intruders. The Cairo Council which Bonaparte created to govern Cairo consisted of nine to ten shaykhs, or religious leaders. Azharites were the first Egyptians invited by Bonaparte to witness the chemical and physical experiments conducted by the French scientists at the famous *Institut*.

The Azhar was thus the educational and intellectual mainstay of Egypt until 1800. What is more important is the fact that it soon contributed from its ranks the first Egyptians to make their mark in the modern educational and intellectual renaissance begun during the long reign of Muhammad Ali. Its more sensitive and intelligent members, for instance, reacted to the French presence, and particularly to the scientific and intellectual attainments of the French savants, with astute introspection. Despite their opposition to, and dislike of, an infidel conqueror, Shaykh Abd al Rahman al-Jabarti, the famous chronicler of modern Egypt, Shaykh Hasan al-Attar, the famous grammarian and noted teacher of Rifaa Rafii al-Tahtawi, another luminary of the intellectual regeneration in the nineteenth century, and Shaykh al-Sharqawi, a melancholy lamentor of 'passing tradition', were all Azharites who deplored the condition of their society and the backwardness of their people. As a reaction to the first direct contact with Europeans, the response of these men alone constituted an admission, though not necessarily an understanding, of the deficiencies of their system and a reluctant admiration for the efficacy of European learning. It was enough as a beginning to encourage later Azharites to seek the advantages of a modern European education.

Al-Jabarti, in describing the intellectual life of Egypt before the French invasion as well as during the first ten years of the reign of Muhammad Ali, has paid special attention to his friend Shaykh Hasan al-Attar (d. 1833). The importance of Shaykh al-Attar in the intellectual renaissance of Egypt is not so much due to his own writings as it is due to his spirited teaching of young Azharites, one of whom was Shaykh Rifaa al-Tahtawi. Attar had travelled widely in Arab lands before his first contacts with the French in Cairo. He soon became interested in the work which French scholars were doing in Egypt and had a chance to observe them very closely. Many of the French savants engaged al-Attar as their Arabic tutor, and he is said to have taken lessons in French from them. His general response to the French impact upon his country reveals his sensitivity to the weaknesses of Egyptian society as well as his instinct for political survival. 'Conditions in our country must change,' he is reported to have said. 'We must introduce new knowlege that is yet unknown in Egypt.'[2]

Al-Attar reportedly sought to improve teaching methods in the Azhar and to interest his students in new knowledge. He deplored the rote mothod of learning, and sought to replace it by a more analytical approach to study. He was apparently unhappy with the emulative nature of Islamic pedagogy and writing, and sought to free himself and his students from its shackles. He left a collection of essays, *Al-Rasa'il*, first published in Cairo in 1866, on a wide range of subjects, such as law, logic and grammar, medicine and other sciences. His proclivity towards innovation and his sympathy with modern change brought him close to the court of Muhammad Ali. The latter appointed him Shaykh of the Azhar and first editor of the official government newspaper *Al-Waqa'i al-Misriyya*.

Another religious leader of that time was Shaykh al-Sharqawi who was three times President of the Local Council of Notables established by Napoleon. He also left a major work, *Tuhfat al-nazirin fiman waliya misr min al-wulat wa al-salatin* (A Survey of the History of Governors and Sultans of Egypt), first published in Cairo in 1865. In it Sharqawi both refers to the low cultural level of his countrymen and expresses his views on the French. He deplored the fact that Egyptians were not serious by nature; that they were cunning, deceitful and possessed of weak character; that they were impatient under adversity and fearful of authority.[3]

Some advance had also been made by 1800 in the study of Arabic. Not a native Egyptian, Muhammad Murtada al-Zabidi, the famous lexicographer and grammarian, came to the country in his early twenties and devoted most of his time to the preparation of the massive lexicon-dictionary of the Arabic language, *Taj al-arus min sharh jawahir al-qamus*, published in 1870. This, together with Jabarti's *Chronicle*, and the final Egyptian version of the *Thousand and One Nights*, are perhaps the most important literary works of that epoch.[4]

A few poets, among them Hasan al-Badri al-Hijazi (d. 1718), and Ismail al-Zuhuri (d. 1793), composed verses that satirized and occasionally criticized directly the religious and social life of the times. Neither language nor art was of the best quality. All the same, their poetry reflected a certain preoccupation with the low cultural level of their society and the freedom to express such views.[5]

These then were some of the intellectual luminaries at the end of the eighteenth century in Egypt. Their work manifests a glimmer of dissatisfaction with their spiritual and cultural environment and a touch of annoyance – if not impatience – with the weighty tradition. The latter stood in the way of their desire for innovation and possibly reform. Yet it was not until a totally alien agent of intellectual and cultural advancement was introduced into Egypt that these Azharites – the standard-bearers of Islamic traditional culture in society – sought to reform their own establishment.

THE EDUCATIONAL POLICY OF MUHAMMAD ALI

To achieve a powerful state in Egypt Muhammad Ali directed his attention to Europe and what instruments of power he could learn, borrow and adapt from there. Thus he employed European experts and technicians, organized modern state schools, and dispatched

Egyptians on educational missions to Europe, to be trained in the modern sciences so as to provide the skills required by the various departments of the state. Since all this modern knowledge was available in European languages – English, French and Italian – a crucial means for Egyptians to acquire it was its translation into Arabic and/or Turkish. Throughout the nineteenth century, Egyptians who had studied in Europe as members of the State's educational missions, or who had been trained in the famous School of Languages in Cairo, undertook the translation of basic works in the various sciences from leading European languages.

The initial educational policy of Muhammad Ali thus had limited goals. It aimed primarily at the formation of a group of technicians capable of performing specific tasks for the State, especially its armed forces. For this reason, Muhammad Ali insisted upon total government supervision over education, and over the selection of students for the schools who were then treated as soldiers under military supervision. Education, in his view, was simply a means to an end. Nonetheless, there is a direct link between the results of the Pasha's educational programme and the emergence of the first Egyptian intellectuals. His state educational programme produced eventually the conditions under which the beginnings of an intellectual group were made possible in the reign of Khedive Ismail.

Foreigners trained the armed forces and instructed Egyptians in technical skills necessary for the operation of state factories and public works. Professional schools of engineering, agriculture and medicine were staffed until 1845 mainly by Europeans and Levantines, and the preparatory schools founded by the Pasha to prepare recruits for the higher professional colleges were for a long time supervised by Europeans too. Yet even if the opening of schools in Egypt, beginning with the Medical School in 1827, required the engagement of foreign instructors, it also raised the question of the language of teaching – the matter of plain communication between teachers and students. Since not all Egyptian students could be sent abroad to study the appropriate languages, nor could the State wait for some years until they acquired a knowledge of them, an elaborate scheme of groups of translators was devised for each professional school. To train these translators both for the classrooms and for the preparation of manuals and texts for student use, the Pasha founded a School of Languages (*madrasat al-alsun*) in 1835 which, for the next twenty years, had the most direct influence of any institution over educational and cultural matters in Egypt. The first trainees of the School were Azhar students and teachers who knew Arabic well. Moreover, newly trained Egyptian medical doctors, engineers, agriculturists and scientists were assigned specific translation tasks once they had learnt not only the particular science of their specialty but also the appropriate foreign language in which many of its sources were written.

Italians, for example, had had strong commercial relations with Egypt since the Middle Ages, and were to be found living in the port cities of Egypt and throughout the Levant. According to Yaqub Artin Pasha, Italian was the most commonly used foreign language in Egypt until 1820.[6] Italian was also the first foreign language taught to officer cadets in the early Citadel school erected by Muhammad Ali. The very first Egyptian students to be sent abroad under Muhammad Ali's educational missions programme in 1809 and 1813 went to Leghorn, Milan, Florence and Rome to learn such trades as printing, letter-making and shipbuilding. The first educational missions in the period 1809–16 were conceived with a view to training Egyptians in the art of printing. The state printing press at Bulaq was in operation by 1822, and the first book was published that year: an Italian–Arabic dictionary prepared by Father Rafael Zakhur.

One observes a gradual advance in the quality of translations by Egyptians between 1820 and 1860. Until Egyptians became proficient in European languages, the first group of translators for the State were mainly Christians from Syria. Although conversant with European languages, these Syrians were allegedly weak in Arabic. Consequently, their translations were of poor literary quality to Muslim taste. A second group of translators recruited from among those Egyptians who had studied various scientific and technical subjects, or the military arts, understood their specialized subjects better but still produced awkward Arabic translations. With the training of professional translators by the School of Languages it appears that quality translations of European works in a variety of fields of knowledge came of age.

The need for translated texts and their availability to the many state schools did not merely prompt the training of a generation of Egyptian translators and the founding of a Government Press. It also generated an interest, in Muhammad Ali and in those students who had studied abroad, in the collection of European books. And this interest, in turn, led to the creation of the first small state libraries in the country. Uthman Nur al-Din, one of the first Egyptian students in France, selected and brought back with him a sizeable collection of French texts. These he was ordered to house in a library at the Bulaq palace of Ibrahim Pasha, which may well have been the first state library in the reign of Muhammad Ali. The Armenian minister and confidant of Muhammad Ali, Boghos Bey, bought books during his travels in Europe for the libraries of the armed forces. So did the French Consul Drovetti, a close adviser of the Viceroy. Tossizza, a prominent Greek in Egypt and a friend of the Viceroy, brought books to Egypt from Smyrna in Turkey.

The year 1822 was not only significant as marking the beginning of Egyptian book publishing activities, but also for the organization of a committee responsible for the setting of curricula for all the military schools. This committee was the nucleus of a wider and more elaborate commission for the control and supervision of the state education system in the country. Similarly a committee presided over by the French scholar Jomard looked after the educational and personal well-being of Egyptian students in France.

If it appears that the earliest foreign language influence in Egypt under Muhammad Ali was Italian, and that the first educational missions from Egypt were to Italy, one may ask, why was Italian abandoned in favour of French by 1830? One can only speculate on the causes for this shift from the available evidence. By 1825 there were in Egypt two important Frenchmen in the court of Muhammad Ali. One was Colonel Sève, who was entrusted with the training of a modern Egyptian army; the other was Dr Clot Bey, who was given the responsibility of all public health and medical projects in the State, including the founding in 1827 of the Medical School in Cairo. It was natural that these two leading figures engaged in the formation of such crucial institutions should exert some influence over the Viceroy. More important was the ready availability of French military experts, teachers and professional men after the fall of Napoleon in 1815, and until the Restoration in 1830, which facilitated their commission by Muhammad Ali for various state services. The peculiar rivalry between England and France in the Near East via the Ottoman Porte which was developing during the first forty years of the nineteenth century caused successive French governments to pay special attention to the Pasha.[7]

In the professional and technical fields of education the French influence introduced by Muhammad Ali in the 1820s continued unimpeded until 1920, despite the predominance of Italians in the court of Ismail after 1860, the massive influx of Italians in the textile trade and industry, and such services as Posts and Telegraphs beginning in the same year, and the British occupation of 1882. The French impact was generally cultural, permeating all classes of educated Egyptians. This was, in turn, fostered further by the activities of French mission schools during the second half of the nineteenth century. Thus, the famous Engineering School at Bulaq (1844) was modelled after the Paris *Polytechnique*. So were the technical and industrial schools for Chemistry (1831) and Minerals (1834).

By 1835, Egyptians trained in Europe were already teaching in the professional colleges of Egypt. Such early graduates as the medical doctors Ibrahim al-Nabrawi and Muhammad al-Shafi achieved eminence on the teaching staff of the Medical School and after 1845 replaced Europeans as heads of the School itself. The engineer and mathematician Muhammad al-Bayyumi was, by 1836, a leading member of the Bulaq Engineering School teaching staff. In 1849 another prominent Egyptian engineer, and later educator, Ali Pasha Mubarak, became principal of the same Engineering School.

It was noted earlier that many of the students of the preparatory, secondary, technical and professional schools, including those sent on educational missions to Europe, were recruited from the Azhar. Ex-Azharites became doctors, engineers, translators and pharmacists. In a way, this is a tribute to the Azharite's openness to new learning and his basic literacy.[8] In another way, such recruitment was instrumental later in the sharp division between those Azharites who, having been trained in the modern arts and sciences, argued for the reform of Azharite institutions and their curriculum on the one hand, and those who clung to the traditional methods on the other. This essentially educational, but in fact widely socio-political controversy, was to preoccupy Egyptian leaders, government and public for two and three generations, erupting occasionally in serious political conflicts.

One would assume that such massive attention, sustained over a twenty-five-year period, by the Egyptian ruler to the learning, the arts and the technology of Europe should have produced a permanently European-type élite of Egyptian leaders, strictly secular in outlook and totally uninterested in the Arab–Islamic heritage to which they so far belonged. Significantly, though, it revived interest in the literature, history and tradition of the Arab–Islamic civilization and culture. Just as the work of Champollion and Mariette Pasha in Egyptology and ancient Egyptian history gradually elicited the interest of Egyptians in their own local past, the new era in education prompted a renewed interest in the systematic study of Islamic history and literature. Meantime, Oriental and Islamic studies were coming of age in Europe, especially in France, with the interest of European powers in the Islamic Near East; and the work of Orientalists gradually began to have an effect upon Egyptians similar to that which came from the Egyptologists. Alongside the translation of European works a new interest in the critical editing and printing of Islamic and Arabic classics developed among Egyptians. Serious work in this direction did not, however, fully blossom until after 1875, by which time a revival of the Arabic language and letters was being led by Syrians and Lebanese throughout the Levant and Egypt.

The net effect of these early efforts in education and translation was not so much a process of Europeanization in Egypt. Rather the effect consisted of a growing interest among Egyptians in systematic learning, education generally, and more important still scholarship. The latter came eventually to be applied equally to both the knowledge of Europe as well as to Arabic and Islamic studies – history and literature. It was in this way that Egypt ultimately emerged as the centre of both modern technological learning borrowed from Europe and Arab–Islamic culture in the modern Arab world.

In terms of education and the beginning of a scholarly and intellectual milieu in Egypt, the founding of a printing press and the School of Languages and Translation were perhaps the two greatest achievements of the Muhammad Ali period within Egypt. And this should not detract from the importance of the educational missions overseas. Apparently the interest of Muhammad Ali in a government press rose with his concern for the issuance and wide distribution of laws, regulations, order and ordinances throughout the country: a press, so to speak, for government documents. He was also concerned with the provision of textbooks and manuals for his armed forces and newly founded schools. The machines, paper and other essential materials for the press were first imported from Italy, including Arabic, Italian and Greek letters. Soon, ink and paper were being manufactured in Egypt, dispensing with their importation from Italy. The first technicians for both the press and the related factories of paper and ink were Syrians, Armenians and Italians. The Pasha considered the printing press one of the best means of transferring European knowledge to Egypt and, later, attached smaller printing establishments to some of the military schools. Government administrative departments were also given their own printing facilities.[9]

In addition, the publication of government decrees, orders and regulations facilitated more regular communication between central authority and the provinces, and perhaps helped integrate a more effective administration. After four years of study in Milan in the techniques of printing, Nicola Masabki returned to set up the first Arabic press *Sahib al-saada* in the Alexandria Arsenal. This was later moved to Bulaq. Soon there were printing presses in the Tura Artillery School, in the Medical School at Abu Zabal, in the Cavalry School at Giza and in the Citadel. Generally, at this stage, Muhammad Ali considered the printing press another important facility for strengthening his rule in the country.

In 1827, there appeared the *Khedivial Journal* printed in both Turkish and Arabic at the Citadel Press. A limited daily edition (perhaps not more than a hundred copies) was printed for distribution to high government officials and provincial governors. In its content the *Journal* was confined to news covering the ruler's decrees and decisions; a sort of daily report issued by the Office of the Pasha. The following year saw the publication of the Official Gazette (*al-waqa'i al-misriyya*). This was a more detailed report of events, decisions and regulations throughout the country, and had a wider distribution. It solicited subscriptions from high public officials, army officers and the educated 'class'. But it was also distributed widely and gratis among students in the state schools. The *Gazette* was also published in both Turkish and Arabic. Unlike the *Journal*, the *Gazette* was not a daily publication at the beginning, and rarely appeared more than three times a week.

A third paper, *Le Moniteur Egyptien*, appeared in French in 1832–3, printed at the Ras al-Tin press in Alexandria. Apparently this was founded by members of the foreign community in Alexandria with some support from Muhammad Ali who hoped that it would serve as an organ for the defence of his policies to foreign readers, and so counteract perhaps *Le Moniteur Ottoman* which was inimical to him in those days. But the paper did not appear after March 1834 until it was revived by Khedive Ismail in 1874 in an effort perhaps to serve the same end in his case. After the British occupation, *Le Moniteur* was reinstated as *Le Journal Officiel* and merged with the Arabic *al-waqa'i* to become the *Official Newspaper* (Journal) (*al-jarida al-rasmiyya*) of the government.

Yet all three papers at this early stage did attempt, in addition to their coverage of official news, the treatment of some literary and educational subjects in a very limited way.[10]

With printing and a small official press, translation became a source of direct enlightenment for Egyptians in many areas of knowledge.[11] Whereas the French occupiers had at the turn of the century introduced such administrative practices as the registration of births and deaths, and sanitation measures in the cities, Muhammad Ali now embarked upon massive state programmes of translation from European languages – mainly from French – of manuals on public health, sanitation and children's diseases for dissemination among the public. For a long time, however, the bulk of the translation effort was confined to specialized works in medicine, engineering and other applied sciences.

What is interesting, however, is that printing and translation led to the revival of the Arabic language and Arabic studies generally, which ultimately resulted in a neo-classical tradition. This, despite the fact that the court of Muhammad Ali was Turkish-speaking and most government business was conducted in Turkish. Translation, however, led to the preparation of Arabic–French, Arabic–Italian and Arabic–English dictionaries and the formulation of technical terms in Arabic, in order to facilitate the teaching of scientific and technical subjects to Egyptian students. A further interest in other Oriental languages, such as Persian, must be noted, so that Arabic language and culture benefited greatly from the originally limited policy of the Viceroy over a period of twenty-five years. On the one hand, translation made available to Arabic readers major works and classics in the sciences and arts of Europe. On the other, the publishing of books in Arabic became the basis of further educational, cultural and social advances and change in Egypt.

Obviously, in this early period of Egyptian efforts in translation and publishing, the direction was strictly scientific and educational, rarely extending beyond the confines of schools and colleges. The education of the masses was still very much a concern of the traditional Ahzarite institutions, which perpetuated the social and cultural values of Islam in Egypt. In fact, many Azharites were ill-disposed towards the new state educational programmes, though many of them as we saw were recruited into the state schools and professional colleges. Others among them, moreover, were directly involved in the translation of European works. All the same, their presumed objection to and disapproval of state educational policy were ineffective to stop the growth and eventual leadership of the state school system in the evolution of modern Egypt. Given their habit of acquiescence and their loss of power early in Muhammad Ali's rule, they were unable to convince the Pasha, or his more energetic successors, to abandon their new programme in favour of support for the traditional Azharite institutions.

The support Muhammad Ali gave to the early efforts of Egyptians in the fields of translation and publishing made it possible for a new generation of Egyptian intellectuals to supplant the Azharite shaykhs as the educational and cultural leaders of modern Egypt. It was left to this new group of Egyptians, trained in European languages and sciences at the direct expense of the ruler, to disseminate this new knowledge and its usefulness to a wider sector of the population. It is through them that the effect of the Muhammad Ali policy on Egyptian society can be assessed, for its first fruits began to appear in the second half of the nineteenth century beginning with the reign of the Khedive Ismail, i.e., the period roughly between 1860 and 1880. These first intellectuals arose from the ranks of officials in the loyal service of the ruler and his state, entrusted as they were by him with specific tasks and duties in the fields of teaching, translation and technical services.[12]

EDUCATIONAL DEVELOPMENT UNDER ISMAIL

Although such institutions as the Schools of Medicine, Pharmacy, Midwifery and the War College remained open, there was a hiatus of fifteen years in Egyptian educational activity between the death of Muhammad Ali and the accession of Ismail to the viceregal throne of Egypt. Neither Abbas I (1848–54) nor Said Pasha (1854–63) showed any marked interest in this field of endeavour during their relatively short reigns. The administrative machinery of the state school system was neglected and many of its capable employees were transferred to other posts, retired or sacked. Ismail not only revived and strengthened this administrative establishment particularly with the reconstitution of the Council of Schools (*Diwan al-madaris*) which was to become later the Ministry of Education, but also entrusted its direction to a series of most energetic and dedicated men such as Ibrahim Adham Pasha and Ali Pasha Mubarak. Under the guidance of these two men, new schools and professional colleges were founded, primary and secondary education was expanded and strengthened to the point where it became the accepted standard system of education in modern Egypt. Their activities and interests extended further to deal with other crucial educational and cultural needs of Egypt: learned societies, libraries, academies, teachers' colleges and the reform of religious education as found in the Azhar.[13]

One of the most important educational developments under Ismail was the reopening of the famous School of Languages and Administration founded in 1835 but closed down by Abbas I in 1850. In 1886 this school became the first secular Law School under the direction, until 1891, of Vidal Pasha, a French jurist. From it graduated the first Egyptian lawyers and jurists who led Egypt in the field of civil and criminal legal studies, as well as in politics. Another epochal development was the opening of *Dar al-Ulum* teachers' college in 1872 to train Arabic teachers for the state primary and secondary schools. Like many of the earlier schools and colleges founded by Muhammad Ali, *Dar al-Ulum* also recruited its first students from the Azhar. For the next fifty years it played a leading role in the revival of Arabic literature and studies in Egypt.

A number of trade and vocational schools for training Egyptians in technical subjects were opened in the 1860s. Schools for specialized training in land surveying, accountancy, archaeology and hieroglyphics were also founded in the 1870s. New and better secondary schools were built by the State in Cairo and Alexandria and over twenty primary schools throughout the country. Educational missions to Europe begun by Muhammad Ali were resumed under Ismail. During his reign some hundred and seventy-five Egyptian students were sent to study abroad. The Khedive approved a tenfold increase in budget expenditure for education during his reign, from £6,000 to £75,000 annually, while education in most schools remained free.

A strengthening factor in this educational activity under Ismail came from private local and foreign educational institutions, foundations, missions and establishments. Community parochial schools were founded by the leading Christian minority of Copts. Generally directed by the Patriarch of the Copts – at that time, the famous Anba Kyrillus IV – these schools were further strengthened by direct grants from the Khedivial government in the form of land, farms and cash. The Greek, Armenian and Jewish communities also formed their own schools. Thus, the Greek community in Alexandria maintained for a hundred years some of the best *lycea* in the history of Greek education abroad or in Greece. Although these were heavily endowed by rich Greek entrepreneurs and professional men, the system of dues levied on all gainfully employed members of the Greek community rendered these schools financially solvent.

The vast influx of Europeans into Egypt in the period 1860–70 was accompanied by the increased activity of European religious missions in Egypt. These concentrated their efforts in the field of teaching and founded, in this period, some sixty to seventy primary, secondary and vocational schools. Generations of Egyptians trained by Italian, French, British and American mission schools came to constitute the membership of the modern Europeanized group of government officials, professionals and politicians. Their political and cultural preferences to a large extent were determined by their early training in these schools. They came to speak and think in terms of European-inspired models of life and society, and often stood in direct opposition to the traditional cultural norm represented by the Azhar and its institutions, which were relatively untouched by this foreign influence.

While schools – state, parochial, communal and foreign missionary – raised the student population of Egypt in the primary and secondary levels, the intellectual and cultural advancement of Egyptian men of affairs and social leaders was accomplished in part by the appearance of numerous cultural societies, academies and research organizations. Remembering the Institute founded by Napoleon in Cairo in 1798, Egyptians under Ismail tried to encourage scientific research under the auspices of an Egyptian Academy. In fact, the old French *Institut* had been reopened in Alexandria in 1859 during the reign of Said Pasha. It continued to flourish in Ismail's reign with its publication of several findings of scientific and other research. More widespread in its effect was the *Jamiyyat al-maaref* (Society of Knowledge) formed in 1868 to spread culture and education via writing, translation and publishing. Founded by Muhammad Aref Pasha, the Society aimed at the dissemination of scientific knowledge mainly through the publication of important works. Patronized by the Khedive and his successor, Tawfiq Pasha, the Society was financed by a public subscription of shares. Its early success permitted it to build its own press, as distinguished from the Government Press at Bulaq.[14]

What was significant about the Society was its attention to the editing and publication of Arabic Islamic classical texts. A look at the first list of its subscribers, moreover, is a Who's Who of the first modern Egyptian intellectuals, men of letters, and of public affairs: Ibrahim Adham, Ibrahim al-Muwailihi, Shaykh al-Marsafi of the Azhar, Ahmad Faris al-Shidyaq, publisher of the famous newspaper *al-Jawaib*, Amin Bey Fikri, and many members of the Consultative

Assembly of Delegates during Ismail's early representative legislative experiments. Yet the Society did not survive the frequent political vicissitudes of the reign of Ismail.

One of the academic institutions that has survived to our day is the Khedivial Geographical Society, later under King Fuad I (1923–36) and King Faruq (1936–52) the Royal Geographical Society, and since 1952 the Egyptian Geographical Society. It was founded by the Khedive Ismail in 1875 to conduct, sponsor, finance and supervise geographical research on Egypt, the Sudan and the African continent generally. It has perhaps been one of the most successful scientific-academic ventures in modern Egypt. Comprising a mixed membership of Egyptian and European scholars – Mahmud Pasha al-Falaki, General Stone Pasha, Prof. Schweinfurth – it has published important research findings in cartography, irrigation and water problems of the Nile, desert studies, cotton cultivation, and so on.

Not all cultural and educational endeavour was sponsored by the Khedive or his government. It is significant that organized response to this new age also came from certain leaders of Egyptian society outside the government. The response was, in part, prompted by a characteristically Muslim reaction to the overwhelming influence of Europe over this new government-directed intellectual and cultural renaissance. Thus in 1878, a group of Muslim Egyptians, led by the orator-journalist Abdullah al-Nadim,[15] formed *Al-Jamiyya al-khairiyya al-islamiyya* (The Islamic Philanthropic Society)[16] with the primary aim of organizing private community schools for boys and girls. These schools were to educate Muslim children gratis, but at the same time aim at giving them an Islamic moral training. Although the Society received some government grants, their amount and regularity must have been meagre and infrequent, because the Society disappeared after a few years, during the Orabi Revolt.

In mid-nineteenth-century Egypt, female education in primary and secondary schools was unknown. A traditional Islamic society at that time was literally a male society. Even the School of Midwifery founded by Muhammad Ali recruited its first students from among Sudanese and Ethiopian Negro girls, since work so close to the processes of nature was considered too crude for squeamish Egyptian girls. The richer families of notables, court officials and aristocrats confined any literate training for their daughters to the privacy of tutors at home. And that took the superficial form of 'finishing' a girl in preparation for marriage. Ismail, however, encouraged and financed the opening of the first girls' school by his third wife Jashem Afet Hanum in 1873. Known as the Suyufiyya Girls School, it admitted the following year (1874) four hundred pupils. Its curriculum combined fundamental subjects such as arithmetic, geography, history and religious knowledge with training in practical household crafts such as sewing and weaving.

Bold innovation in this period did not merely consist of introducing Egyptians to the desirability and, eventually, necessity of educating their girls, but significantly of reforming the traditional religious training of their spiritual mentors provided for so long by the Azhar and its institutions. For the first time in generations an Egyptian ruler took a keen interest in the reform of the Azhar curriculum, and of the educational and moral standards of its trainees. A spirit of reform began to infiltrate that venerable institution, beginning in 1870 under the leadership of its Shaykh Muhammad Al-Abbasi al-Mahdi.[17] Although, as was mentioned earlier in this chapter, certain individual Azhar scholars were dissatisfied with Azharite education in general and sought to imbue a different educational and intellectual outlook and spirit in their students, systematic efforts at reform which were to preoccupy governments, rulers and reform leaders for the next seventy-five years began in 1870. In 1872, for instance, a more rational scheme of examinations for certificates for the ulama was instituted.

THE NEW GENERATION OF INTELLECTUALS IN LITERATURE AND THE ARTS

The forcefulness of Muhammad Ali in reform and the determination of Ismail to Europeanize Egypt awakened Egyptians to a consciousness of Europe and the modern age. The parallel confrontation of the Ottoman State with Europe and reform stirrings there, together with the interest of European Powers in the Near East, accelerated this process. In many ways, the cumulative effect of these forces and influences over a period of a hundred years (1820–1920) constitutes a striking experience in Islamic history: the construction of a modern state in Egypt. Yet, despite the massive importation of technical and scientific knowledge and skills from Europe, the renaissance under Ismail and his successors drew its inspiration heavily from Arab–Islamic sources. The reforms of Muhammad Ali and the ambitious Europeanization programme of Ismail tended, however, to overlook the Azharite institutional bulwark of tradition. To this extent, the

Azhar was left outside the evolution of modern Egypt until the pro-mulgation by the Nasser régime in June 1961 of the Law for the Reorganization of the Azhar. Yet this is true only in so far as the newly educated leaders in Egyptian society replaced Azharites in the fields of Arabic letters, the interpretation of Islamic culture, and the upbringing of a new generation of Egyptian students and leaders. Thus, attention was now paid to the training of Arabic teachers in *Dar al-Ulum*, an institution forming prart of the state school system, instead of the Azhar. There was now a state or national library, *Al-maktaba al-khidawiyya*, later *Dar al-kutub*, founded in 1872.

Whereas the Arabic language and its literature remained weak under both Muhammad Ali and Ismail, this renaissance had the direct consequence of strengthening this very aspect of Egyptian cul-tural and intellectual advance. For even under the Khedive Ismail, apart from translation and the improved organization of education, Arabic literary activity was slight. In the 1870s one witnesses an eruption of this activity beginning with the emergence of the Press and journalism, which flourished even further under the British occupation. Yet, for the first time under Ismail, Egyptians were exposed to the artistic aspects of European culture via the modern theatre, opera and related arts. Attracted by the relatively European-inspired reign of Ismail, Syrians for example, came to Egypt and introduced dramatic performances on the stage. Salim al-Naqqash and Yusuf Khayyat led Syrian theatrical troupes into Egypt. The Egyptian Othman Galal (1828–98) – a student of Shaykh Rifaa al-Tahtawi – translated Saint-Pierre's *Paul et Virginie*, and the fables of La Fontaine. He also rendered some of Molière's comedies into colloquial Egyptian Arabic.[18]

James Sanua, an Alexandrian Jew, better known by his pen-name *Shaykh Abu Naddara* (d. 1912), was active during this period in both journalism and the theatre. In addition to his numerous and short-lived satirical newspapers, he organized the first local popular theatre group in Egypt, in 1869–71. He wrote most of the plays per-formed by this group in either colloquial Egyptian Arabic or in Ita-lian (viz., *Hukm Garaqush*, a satire on government). He was, it seems, the first Egyptian in the 1870s to perfect political satire both in his publications and his plays, using vernacular expressions and names for political figures, including the Khedive (e.g., *shaykh al-hara* for the Khedive, *Abu'l-ghulb* for the fellah). In this way he claimed to satirize political tyranny in Egypt. When he fell out with Ismail and his theatre group was disbanded, Sanua organized two 'progressive associations', *Mahfal al-taqaddum* and *Mahfal muhibbi al-ilm*. In his publications he also attacked foreign financial control in Egypt. In 1878 he went in exile to Paris, where he continued to publish a series of anti-Khedive publications. Considering his connections then and later with Afghani, Abduh and Orabi, these societies and publications could have served as front organizations for the old National Party.[19]

On the occasion of the inauguration of the Suez Canal, Ismail built the Opera House in Cairo. Moreover, he encouraged band music in the armed forces and the entertainment of the public by them in the many parks and recreational areas of the city. Egyptians were now exposed to the tunes of European music. On the other hand, Ismail also patronized native Egyptian singing artists and performing groups, thus contributing to the development of a popular – and to some extent, original – *genre* of Egyptian music. The emergence of such Egyptian singing stars as Sayyed Darwish, Abd al-Wahhab, Um Kulthum, Asmahan, Hafez Abd al-Halim and others popular today throughout the Arab world has its beginning in the early success of Abduh al-Hamuli, Muhammad al-Aqqad, Mahmud Othman and the girl Almas, all of whom were handsomely patronized by the Khedive Ismail. Abduh al-Hamuli particularly (1845–1901) was instrumental in producing a popular Egyptian musical *genre* which synthesized Turkish music with local Egyptian folk music forms. Born in Tanta, the son of a small coffee merchant, he left home early to become a singing apprentice with a variety of troupes. In addition to setting the framework of Egyptian popular music, al-Hamuli was largely responsible for making his music acceptable to the Turkish ruling house and aristocracy.[20]

The fine arts of drawing, painting and sculpture received their first impetus during this period. Mechanical and other drawing in the engineering and trade schools resulted in the introduction of drawing into the curriculum of most state primary and secondary schools, taught by graduates of the technical colleges. Architecture and building decoration advanced as is evidenced in the palaces and public buildings constructed in that period.

The 1860s were a relatively prosperous decade in Egypt as a result of the lucrative world cotton market, rendered more lucrative because of the American Civil War (1860–65), and the mass entry of Europeans into Egypt with their interest in the financial and economic development of the country heralded by the building of the Suez Canal. One can assume, therefore, that the 1860s was also a decade of increased social entertainment and that the environment was generally conducive to the development of the arts.

A year before the opening of the Opera in Cairo in 1869, Ismail supported the erection of a Comedy Theatre in Ezbekiyya Gardens. Together these two theatres attracted over the next ten years a number of European theatrical and musical companies who performed in Egypt. *Rigoletto* was the inaugural performance at the Opera in November 1869. The première of Verdi's *Aïda* took place in December 1896. In the 1870s Alexandria boasted two theatres, *Zizinia* and *Alfieri*. Syrians, who were in closer touch with the European – namely, French – theatre, were encouraged by Ismail's patronage of the arts to come to Egypt. Thus Yusuf Khayyat's troupe appeared in Alexandria and Cairo in 1878. Their performance of socially and politically significant plays, some alluding to authority and tyranny, elicited the ire of the Khedive, and their sojourn in the country was consequently short. None the less, these early excursions into the dramatic arts form the basis of later Egyptian interest in the theatre, playwriting and the cinema. Moreover, without the extensive translation efforts of Egyptians in this period, the fine arts of Europe would have not become as well known to the literate Egyptians at this early age.

During this period there grew up a new generation of Egyptian public officials, army officers and intellectuals who, though supported by and working for the Muhammad Ali dynasty, constituted the nucleus of a class in society seeking to share in power. It is doubtful if any of these – even the European-trained ones – deviated from their view of authority as resting in the basically Muslim-conceived benevolent ruler. Despite their exposure to and admiration of European concepts of authority and legitimate power, they never questioned the legitimacy of their own rulers.

The concern of the first Egyptian intellectuals of this period was the need to acquire European methods of education, for they considered these essential to the emergence of a modern state in Egypt. They were especially concerned with modern methods of organization in areas of public policy: education, administration, public health, irrigation and so on, for the successful adoption and adaptation of such methods and techniques was the prerequisite to state power and strength. They did not, however, at this stage entertain the implementation in their own country of socio-political values which underpinned European culture and society or political systems.

The task of transmitting European knowledge to Egypt over a period of forty years (1830–70) – if one excludes the work of Europeans actively in the service of the Egyptian State – was dominated by two men: Shaykh Rifaa Rafi al-Tahtawi (1801–71) and Ali Pasha Mubarak (1824–93). Both men studied in France with one of the educational missions. Both were native Egyptians, belonging roughly to the same social class. Although both held military ranks[21] and occupied senior administrative positions in the government, Rifaa received his formative education in the traditional Azharite milieu. Until he was chosen by the Viceroy to go to Paris as spiritual preceptor, *imam*, of the 1826 mission, the ambition of Rifaa was perhaps confined to becoming a competent interpreter of the religious law, a respectable member of the class of ulama, and a teacher in the Azhar. Mubarak, on the other hand, received his early schooling in the new state schools (*amiriyya*), studied at the new Engineering School, went to the Army Engineers' School at Metz, participated in the Crimean War (1854–6) as a member of the Egyptian contingent fighting on the side of Turkey against Russia, and returned to occupy positions of high responsibility in the development of engineering and public works in Egypt, as well as in the educational establishment. He desired from the start to join the new class of educated government officials. It is reported that while a young boy, he heard that members of the new ruling class were recruited from the new state schools, and determined there and then to enter these schools. He received all his formal education in the militarized school system founded by Muhammad Ali.

In Tahtawi and Mubarak we have on the one hand the man of languages and letters and on the other the technically trained administrator-educator. Tahtawi was the sieve for European ideas, whether through his translations or his own writings. Mubarak was the practical implementor of science and engineering for the material well-being of his country. Yet both men were educators and writers of some significance for the history of modern Egypt. Mubarak wrote many manuals and textbooks in engineering and military fortifications for the use of students. But he also wrote the most extensive topographical study of Egypt to date, *Al-khitat al-tawfiqiyya*, a sort of encyclopedia on Egypt: its history, geography and topography. Modelled perhaps after the famous *Khitat* of al-Maqrizi in the fifteenth century, the twenty parts in four volumes by Mubarak constitute the most detailed reference work on nineteenth-century Egypt. It contains topographic information about cities, places, town quarters, mosques; biographical data on celebrities, officials and rulers; technical data on dams, barrages, irrigation matters relating to the Nile, agriculture and industry. In short, this work of Mubarak is a primary source for the study of the social, technical, and, therefore, political history of modern Egypt.

Another important work by Mubarak dealt with the agricultural problems and policy of Egypt. Entitled, *Nakhbat al-fikr fi tadbir Nil misr*, it deals mainly with the irrigation and agricultural problems that arise from the nature of the Nile. Yet, in this treatment, Mubarak tried to relate these problems to the desired tasks and policies of any Egyptian ruler and of the society itself. He tried, so to speak, to apply his specialized technical knowledge of irrigation and agricultural problems to a socio-economic assessment of the relation between the natural resources and terrain of Egypt to government and state policy. In a less known book, *Alam al-din*, Mubarak introduced the reader, in what may be considered one of the earliest critiques of European Orientalism, to a series of imagined confrontations and conversations between an Azharite scholar and an English Arabist visiting Egypt.

Yet the greatest contribution of Ali Mubarak was not in the area of intellectual and literary innovation, but in administration, and particularly that of education, public works and *waqfs*. He was a reformer within the government by virtue of continuous and sustained service over a period of forty years. He may be considered the leader of the transfer of modern European technology and its application in Egypt by Egyptians for the common good and in the public interest.

Mubarak was not an intellectual critic outside the government. Rather he accomplished reforms in education and the administration of various state functions within the limits of the ruler's permission and desires. Thus, if Ismail desired to improve, by Europeanizing, the material appearance of Egyptian towns and cities, Mubarak implemented the desire of the ruler by initiating, extending, improving and administering the public works necessary for its fulfilment. One might almost say that Ali Mubarak was brought up by the State, and grew up in its service from the day he entered the Kasr el-Aini School as a twelve-year-old boy in 1836, through Engineering School, 1840–5, his advanced training in France, and his service in the Army Corps of Engineers. He moved from one government position to another, from Instructor in the Tura Artillery School to chief of the Alexandria fortifications projects, from an engineer with the

Aswan cataract works and the Delta Barrage near Cairo, all the way up to the posts of Minister of Education, Director-General of the State Railways, Minister of *Waqfs* and Minister of Public Works. In all these posts, Ali Mubarak worked energetically for the modernization of his country. His rulers, in turn, compensated him handsomely by gifting him land and other estate properties – the best form of wealth in Egypt in those days. Mubarak was a reformer, not a political revolutionary in the sense of a man alienated from the established authority of the times. Yet his reform programme and achievements were in a sense revolutionary for Egypt. Beyond his acceptance of the necessity for modern schools, engineering works and a proper administrative order, it is doubtful if Ali Mubarak had any fully developed, intellectually conceived political ideas, or revolutionary sentiments.

Mubarak was a practical, not a book, reformer. He was essentially realistic about his society, its capabilities, and its environment. While he worked for modern education he also appreciated the role of the *kuttab*, or Koranic schools, in the moral formative training and upbringing of the masses. Consequently he sought to reform them. Having studied himself in state schools, Mubarak saw the necessity of separating civilian from military schools, the former under a civilian administration and the latter under a military one. Civilian education he considered as the means for elevating the cultural level of the society that should therefore take priority in the attention of the State. In order to accommodate traditional schools within the general state educational policy he subjected their curricula, despite their independent financial sources from religious and pious endowments, to the Ministry of Education. Simultaneously he reformed the financial organization of *waqfs* so that educational expenditure in the religious schools was more rational and orderly.

Two educational matters preoccupied Mubarak. One was the question of training competent teachers for the government schools. The other was his concern with the availability of reference and other textbooks for use of students, i.e., a library. To meet the first problem he was instrumental in founding *Dar al-Ulum*. Its main purpose really was to give a more modern training and preparation to selected Azhar students who would qualify for the teaching of Arabic in government schools. As an aid to learning and teaching he worked for the establishment of the first major state library, *Dar al-Kutub*.

Perhaps some of his greatest achievements were in the field of public works and irrigation. Mubarak considered public works the most crucial field of economic endeavour in Egypt, as it affected directly the wealth of the country. For, besides the erection of buildings, construction of roads, bridges, city and town services and irrigation schemes, public works had a direct bearing upon the agricultural wealth of Egypt – the extension of cultivable lands, the mechanization of agricultural methods, and so on. In all these areas, Mubarak seemed to combine the technical knowledge of the engineer and the competence of the brilliant administrator on the one hand, with the vision of the reformer on the other.

Ali Pasha Mubarak was a reformer in the social and economic sense. Some of his Egyptian biographers have ascribed to him a nationalist preoccupation too. In the sense that Mubarak sought the advancement and well-being of his country, he was no doubt what Westerners would have called a patriot. Nowhere, however, in the history of his life and work does one find a concern with undermining existing rule and authority, or sympathy for and subscription to the notion of popular rule, and a participant citizenry. On the contrary, Mubarak was a loyal servant of the ruling dynasty. He seemed convinced that the reformation and regeneration of Egypt could be attained by the salutary efforts of a benevolent ruler and his stable, though reform-oriented, administration. In fact, he was opposed to the Orabi Revolt as disruptive of this constructive work. A son of a Muslim shaykh and village religious leader in the Delta, Mubarak, through energetic and effective work, came to dominate the most constructively creative period in modern Egyptian history as an administrator, educator and reformer. This, in itself, reflects the same great social mobility in mid-nineteenth-century Egypt as that which prevailed in the Ottoman–Islamic world generally. He died before the new forces unleashed by the new techniques of mass media and liberal mass ideologies began to bombard and dismantle the stable edifice of autocratic but benevolent rule in Egypt. Yet, the dismantlers continued to benefit from his work.[22]

Rifaa Tahtawi played a different role in this cultural renaissance. In fact, the period 1830–70 in the evolution of education and culture in Egypt was dominated by Rifaa and Mubarak not simply by virtue of their respective efforts, but also because of the rivalry between them. Thus Abbas I patronized and encouraged Mubarak so that Rifaa was in eclipse during his reign. It was a time of exile for Rifaa in the Sudan. Said Pasha on the other hand favoured Rifaa and reinstated him in Cairo, while Mubarak was sent off with the Egyptian expeditionary force to the Crimea. Both men, however, were fully occupied with their respective state functions under Ismail: Mubarak in various administrative posts and Rifaa in the field of translation, journalism and writing. Both men were handsomely remunerated with royal endowments and gifts.

Unlike Mubarak, when Rifaa went to Paris he was already a trained Azharite. He was not just a religious man, but a man of religion too. His response and reaction to France and Europe was more contemplative, reflective and intellectual than that of Ali Mubarak. His mind pondered over what he had seen, heard, and learnt. His training was not as confining as that of the engineer or technician, for a glance at the curriculum of studies and reading list he covered in Paris between 1826 and 1831 indicates a wide variety of subjects in the humanities and sciences. Thus he informs the readers in his *Rihla* (Journey to Paris) that in philosophy he read Condillac, and Burlamanqui's work on natural rights; in literature he read Voltaire, Racine and Rousseau, and especially Montesquieu's *Lettres Persanes*. In social and political philosophy he mentions Montesquieu's *Esprit des lois* and Rousseau's *Contrat Social*. In mathematics and geometry he lists the authors Bezout and Legendre. Rifaa, perhaps, received the widest possible liberal education of any of the mission students in France at that time. Though a professional translator, his interest in European works extended beyond the mere task of translation into a reflection on the value of European knowledge in itself as well as for Egypt.

Like Mubarak, Rifaa returned to Egypt in 1831 to serve the ruler and his state in their efforts to modernize Egyptian government and administration through education and related activities. Having impressed both his French tutors and, through their reports, the Viceroy, Rifaa was soon in a position to influence his master in the establishment of institutions like the School of Languages (1835) for the training of a generation of professional translators. His accomplishments in this area over a period of fifteen years brought him military promotion (all civilian government officials at that time were given military rank) to Brigadier (Amiralai) and landed wealth.

In his work as a translator, Tahtawi was exposed to most fields of study: medicine, geography (he translated Malte-Brun's *Geography*), the military arts and sciences, history, literature (he translated Fenelon's *Aventures de Télémaque*), politics (in his Paris Journal, Tahtawi includes translated excerpts of the 1830 French Constitution: *La Charte* which he renders *al-sharta*), secular legal studies and jurisprudence (he translated the French Civil Code). The last field became especially important under Ismail who was anxious to copy European legal codes. Rifaa's intellectual interests were therefore wide and, as he proved in his own writings, rather sustained and imaginative. He is best known for his direction of the School of Languages in its various forms during the three distinct phases of its career, 1835–49, 1864–8 and 1868–71, and the translators, jurists and administrators whom it trained. Graduates of this School have reportedly translated a total of some two thousand European works. Yet the writings of Rifaa command a distinct interest in themselves. He wrote and translated more than twenty-five works in a variety of fields ranging from history to mathematics and poetry. Three of his own writings are relevant to the narrative, namely, *Takhlis al-ibriz fi talkhis bariz* (more commonly known as the *Rihla*, or *Paris Journey of Rifaa*: 1st ed. Bulaq 1834, Turkish trans., 1840; 2nd ed. 1849; 3rd ed. 1903–5; new ed. Cairo 1958); *Al-murshid al-amin fi tarbiyat al-banat wa al-banin* (Bulaq 1873); and *Manahij al-albab al-misriyya fi manahij al-adab al-'asriyya* (1st ed. Bulaq 1869; 2nd ed. Cairo 1912).[23]

The first volume is based on the record of his five-year sojourn in Paris, 1826–31. It seems that Rifaa, on the advice of his teacher and mentor Shaykh al-Attar, kept a diary from the day he sailed from Alexandria until his return to Egypt. Whether it was meant to be a guide for Egyptian students travelling to and in France, or as a reference volume on France for the use of Egyptian readers, one cannot say. It is, however, the first book by an Egyptian on France, written as an autobiographical expression of the response and reaction of an Azharite to that country. As such, it consists mainly of sketches on various aspects of French life, topography, customs, legal, educational and political institutions, including among the latter the French Constitution and events of the 1830 Restoration movement which Rifaa witnessed. These sketches are not necessarily connected as a discussion of one theme throughout the book. They are based on his own observations and discussions with prominent French academics, including the Orientalist Sylvestre de Sacy, supplemented by published French sources on the subjects under discussion. Undoubtedly Rifaa meant his book to introduce Egyptian readers to the civilization and culture represented and led by France, its high level of achievement and the contrasting backwardness of Islamic society.

In describing the French constitution and the political institutions of France generally, Rifaa was, in a way, introducing Egyptian readers to the notion of secular authority, the concept of law as deriving from other than divine sources. Similarly, he was apprising them of such ideas as political rights and liberty. He was the first Egyptian to report fairly systematically and intelligently to his compatriots on the general outlines of European political institutions, the ideas of the Enlightenment and the French Revolution which underlined them. To this extent, Rifaa inaugurated the interest of the modern Egyptian in the liberal social and political ideas of Europe which found their widest dissemination in the country during the first two decades of the twentieth century. In this sense also, an Azharite reported admirably on the rationalism of enlightened Europe and opened the way further for his successors' massive attack upon tradition.

As a result of his translation and educational work, Rifaa saw for himself a role as a didactic moralist. He was not apparently satisfied with the transference and transmission of European scientific knowledge and technical know-how to Egypt. He was impressed by the moral content of European education, and realized that the material aspects of modern civilization could take root in and benefit a society only if the latter deliberately sought education and culture for their own sake. His second volume, *Al-murshid al-amin*, represents an attempt by Rifaa to convince Egyptian students of the enjoyment and benefit that can be derived from refined reading, and the delightful results of intellectual curiosity. He was trying to inculcate an intellectual bent into Egyptian students. Rifaa was seemingly convinced that a civilized society could emerge only on two bases: first, by the sound moral training of its members' characters to inspire them with human virtue, and second by the social organization and administration of the public good to be derived from the natural wealth of the country, i.e., the improvement of social conditions. Thus, civilization must be both material and spiritual, or cultural. There can be no civilization without culture. Hence his interest in public instruction and the state school system.

Encouraged by the interest of the Khedive in education, culture and the arts, including the education of girls, Rifaa tried in this volume of essays on morals, virtue and related subjects to present in readable form to Egyptian boys and girls what he thought the bases of civilized modern society to be. Thus the pursuit of knowledge was crucial to a civilized existence; the invention of machines and other artifacts a facility for the advancement and comfort of this civilized life; the improvement of agriculture, industry, trade and commerce the material and social means for public welfare. Above all he advanced the idea of the rule of law and a stable order as the most important manifestations of a civilized society. To this extent, Rifaa was interested in describing to his compatriots the 'good life' and the 'good society or polity'. What is a civilized and, therefore, a good Egyptian was also his concern. He tried to describe this kind of Egyptian in this volume of essays by discussing ideas on education, the political order, reform principles, social problems and religious morality.

In the third volume, Rifaa was specifically trying to identify for the Egyptians what constituted the public interest and public good, in so far as these concepts were essential to the advancement of civilization. What public interests should be pursued so as to best serve the advancement and happiness of Egypt and its society? Material wealth he considered important, but inadequate without a virtuous society. Work, earnestness, diligence, perseverance and service he considered virtuous attributes in a cultured man, as proper and equitable social arrangements for the common good were essential to a civilised society.

Because in his books Rifaa touched upon political questions – equality among citizens irrespective of religious creed or belief, natural rights, legislative assemblies, pride in and loyalty to the fatherland, and the good citizen – he has interested many later writers both Egyptian and Western.[24] More recently, in Egypt, there has been a noticeable concentrated interest in the work and writings of Rifaa. In 1945, the Egyptian historian Jamal al-din al-Shayyal published what may be considered the first biography (as distinguished from biographical sketches of Rifaa which appeared in many reference works and articles earlier) of Rifaa. In 1950, Ahmad Badawi came out with a longer biography. In 1957–8, the UAR Ministry of Culture and National Guidance commissioned a new edition of Tahtawi's *Rihla* by Allam, Badawi and Luqa, which was published in 1958.

Why this wide interest in Rifaa, and not in Mubarak or others of their contemporaries? The very nature of educational-literary work by Tahtawi interests the student of the history of modern Egypt. The work done by Mubarak was of a practical administrative nature, unspeculative and hardly appealing to the student who looks for historical links between, and the origins of, socio-political movements and ideas. The contemporary Egyptian is perhaps struck by the boldness with which Tahtawi discussed European culture, its achievements and possibilities for advancement in certain areas of civilization. This is a legitimate impression and a useful one. But the contemporary Egyptian also assumes that Tahtawi was a nationalist, one of the precursors of modern Egyptian and Arab nationalism, because he used such terms as *watan*, meaning the fatherland or *patrie*, rights and duties of individuals, and equitable rulers and administration. It is one thing to speak of these things in the 1850s and 1860s in a didactic tone, and another to outline and suggest schemes of nationalist thought and movements. The fact that he translated the French Constitution and in doing so introduced Egyptian readers to a new political vocabulary did not make Rifaa a disaffected protestor against existing rule and political authority. That he admired the rule of law and freedom of the Frenchman does not necessarily imply that he wished the same political arrangement for the Egyptian.

In fact Tahtawi is explicit in his insistence upon the necessity of a ruling power for civilized orderly existence. Despite his adumbration of Montesquieu's idea of the separation of powers, Tahtawi conceived of a class society in which the ruler was to be plainly obeyed. The ruler, in turn, was bound by the Sacred Law and the general principles of equity and justice. In this sense, the political views of Rifaa remained largely within the traditional limits of Islamic society and culture, despite his admiration and respect for representative European institutions and constitutional systems of government. What he proposed in modern terms for the first time were ideas of civic rights and duties as well as the conception that the members of a political community should be instructed and trained in civic virtue from an early age. His understanding of politics, moreover, specifically related to the principles and rules of administration, or statecraft. 'The management of the kingdom' and *bolitiqa* 'is everything which deals with the state, its government, rules and regulations, its relations and connections with other states'.[25]

Tahtawi was not writing about 'the people' in the contemporary conception of the nation and nationalism. Nor was he protesting against unjust or tyrannical rule and calling for its overthrow. On the contrary, Tahtawi viewed his masters, Muhammad Ali and Khedive Ismail, as benevolent rulers without whose leadership 'Egyptians would not have arrived at their level of advancement'.[26] He credits them with destroying the isolation of Egypt and her insularity from the world by linking her to Europe and helping her develop towards modernity. They cured her of her ignorance. And as

Tahtawi put it, 'Muhammad Ali rendered the Egyptian community (*milla*) knowledgeable; awakened it through the educational missions to France and other European countries.'[27]

So all one can say about Tahtawi is that he was a patriot in the sense that he wished the advancement and cultural edification of his compatriots. At no point did he suggest that they should rule in place of the Muhammad Ali dynasty. Nor did he doubt the legitimacy of these rulers or their authority because they were of foreign extraction. In fact, the educational and social views of Rifaa were consciously limited by his awareness of the Islamic ethos of his country and community. Egyptian nationalist revolutionaries of the twentieth century were not inspired by the work of Tahtawi, for it emphasized individual virtue, order, respect for authority and stability. The work of Tahtawi suggested too evolutionary a model for social change. Instead the twentieth-century nationalists adopted more alien ideas of national liberation that were mass-oriented. By that time, moreover, Egyptians were in large measure under alien British rule. Liberation was therefore more urgent, and collective or group purposes more appealing than the preoccupation with the status of the individual, or the tedious processes of law and order.[28]

As a man of action, involved in the delicate resolution of matters of policy and administration, Mubarak, on the other hand, could scarcely appeal to the articulators of Egyptian nationalism, even though his contribution to the national welfare of Egyptians has been immense. Perhaps his apparent ability to govern and administer and, because of it, his fastidious respect for law and order, excites even less the modern nationalist. It is known, for instance, that he objected to the Orabi Revolt, 1881–2, for its disruption of the orderly development of the country. Even though Tahtawi was also associated with the ruling class, his writing had greater appeal to the romantic nationalist, and was more readily identified with the opinion-makers in the Press. His writing appeared more speculative and abstract. Moreover, he never experienced the responsibility of power in the sense and to the extent that Mubarak did as a government minister, entrusted with the task of making policy in such important fields as education, public works, irrigation and *waqfs*.

Yet both these men exerted great influence over the early development of science, law and literature in the country. Mubarak, for example, with his administrative guidance of the engineering, technical and other schools in Egypt, made possible the work of the earliest group of Egyptian mathematicians, doctors, astronomers and chemists in mid-nineteenth-century Egypt. Thus Mahmud Pasha al-Falaki (1815–85), who was perhaps the leading scholar in mathematics and engineering science in that period, was a product of the state school system founded by Muhammad Ali and improved by Mubarak. Falaki did important work in archaeology, topography and engineering, and served in both the Ministry of Public Works and Education. Similarly Ismail Pasha al-Falaki (d. 1901) studied astronomy in Paris and returned to Egypt where the Khedive appointed him director of the Abbasiyya Observatory. He rendered important engineering services to the Egyptian railways, and represented Egypt in the International Congress of Statisticians in Moscow in 1873. He published a number of works on astronomy and mathematics.

In medicine, Muhammad Duri Pasha (1841–1900), a product of the state schools and a graduate in surgery from Paris, was, during the reigns of Khedives Ismail and Tawfiq, the leading surgeon and professor of surgery at Qasr el-Aini hospital. He wrote a standard work in four volumes on general surgery and a smaller volume on preventive medicine. Before him, there were other famous medical men: Muhammad Ali al-Bulqi Pasha, and Muhammad Shafii Bey.

Tahtawi and his School of Languages had a great impact on the emergence of the first lawyers and jurists in Egypt. One of the tasks assigned to the School by Khedive Ismail was the translation of European legal codes, e.g., The Napoleonic Code. Muhammad Qadri Pasha (1821–86) was a graduate of the School who interested himself in the study of comparative law, Islamic jurisprudence and legislation in general. He wrote standard works on Personal Status Law in Islam and *waqf* Equity. He later became Minister of Justice in the 1881 cabinet of Sharif Pasha during the Khedivate of Tawfiq Pasha. While in this cabinet post Qadri Pasha drafted the judicial system for the *Ahli*, or National, courts which began their work in 1883, including the civil and commercial codes for them as well as the procedure for civil and penal cases. He also served on the Commercial Court in Alexandria, translated into Arabic the legal codes of the Mixed Tribunals founded by Nubar Pasha in 1875, and co-translated with Tahtawi the Napoleonic Code. One of Qadri's greatest academic achievements consisted of his codification of Sharia law in the style of European legal codes in three volumes.[29]

Many of the scholars in law and the sciences might not have been able to train and accomplish these difficult tasks for the times had it not been for the tireless administrative efforts of Mubarak to strengthen educational programmes, or the almost religious devotion of Tahtawi to professional translation. From a mere £6,000 annual budget under Said Pasha, Egypt was by 1875 spending over £75,000 annually for education. Mubarak made much of this possible by the intelligent collection, distribution and allocation of revenue from various sources. Mubarak and Tahtawi encouraged further the work of these scholars by the launching and financing of scholarly and academic journals as publication outlets for their researches, as exchange forums for their ideas, and as media for information generally. Taking advantage of Khedivial patronage of academic societies, they encouraged through them the development of an academic *esprit de corps* among these early scholars and first intellectuals.

The field of language and literature benefited even more from the constructive educational efforts of these two men and from the support of the Khedive. Many of those trained as translators in the School headed by Tahtawi – products of both the Azhar and the state schools, and usually public officials – emerged as the new leaders in the fields of arts and letters. Abdullah Abu al-Suud Effendi (1820–78) was a typical trainee of the School who became a famous history master at *Dar al-Ulum*, the teachers training college founded by Khedive Ismail and Mubarak. Besides writing school textbooks in history and translating Mariette Pasha's *History of Ancient Egypt* from the French, Abu al-Suud also participated in the translation of the Napoleonic Code. He became the first editor of the newspaper *Wadi al-Nil* in 1868.

A more famous student of Tahtawi and graduate of the School of Languages was Muhammad Bey Othman Galal (1828–98), a product of the state schools, who specialized in the translation of European – mainly French – fiction: short stories, romances, plays, essays and novels. He thus helped introduce a new *genre* of European literature to Egypt; one which Egyptians came to master so well later in the twentieth century. Like most of his contemporaries, Othman Galal was a public servant, a government official who occupied a variety of posts, including towards the end of his career a judgeship in the Mixed Tribunals. He published with Ibrahim al-Muwailihi the short-lived (only two issues of it appeared) weekly paper *Nuzhat al-afkar* in 1869. Galal is best known for his translation in verse of La Fontaine's *Parables* (*Al-uyun al-yawaqiz*) and plays by Molière such as *Tartuffe*, to which he gave a local colour and twist (*Al-shaykh maltuf*).[30]

Another illustrious student of the School of Languages was Saleh Magdi Bey (1827–81). Besides his work in the translation of several works in mathematics, engineering and military sciences, and teaching in government schools and colleges, Magdi Bey was an able poet. Like Othman Galal he participated in the translation of the Napoleonic Code, and was actually in charge of the section dealing with the translation of the code for criminal investigations. Along with his contemporaries, Saleh Magdi contributed to the early scholarly journals like *Rawdat al-Madaris*, founded by Ali Pasha Mubarak. In 1876 he was appointed a judge in the Mixed Tribunals in Cairo, a post he held until his death.

Famous Arabic and Islamic scholars from the Azhar were also prominent at that time. Shaykh Ali al-Laythi (d. 1896) was the court poet of Khedive Ismail. A leading member of the Azhar ulama, Shaykh Hassan al-Tawil (d. 1899) became a famous teacher of logic and mathematics at *Dar al-Ulum* Teachers College. Shaykh Hasan al-Marsafi (d. 1889) was another leading teacher of language and literature at the same college. He left a book entitled *Al-kilam al-thaman* (*The Eight Words: nation, fatherland, government, justice, tyranny, politics, liberty, education*). These representatives of tradition were equally encouraged, patronized, and supported in their work by the Khedive Ismail.[31]

The first educators and intellectuals in nineteenth-century Egypt were essentially state officials performing specialized tasks of teaching, translation and writing. Their aim was to transmit knowledge from Europe in the service of the State, and they were selected by the ruler to perform these tasks. Their primary duty for a period of fifty years (1830–80) was to instruct an ever-increasing number of Egyptians to become qualified, competent public servants. It was not their role or function as intellectuals to question or to criticize, in order to undermine, the prevailing political order. For all practical purposes, Egypt was at that time an independent state, despite the diluted suzerain sovereignty of the Ottoman Sultan over it. European influence, financial control, and later occupation were external forces whose impact was not felt directly until 1882.

But it is clear that their work was in great measure the result of the ruler's wish and will. It was Muhammad Ali who responded to the impact of the French invasion, and later the Khedive Ismail who became convinced about the desirability of European ways. These first intellectuals were the direct products of the efforts by these rulers to model their state and government along European lines. To this extent, there was hardly an independent, or independently organized, response to modernity on the part of individual Egyptian scholars and intellectuals as distinguished from the desired programme of the ruler. This is not to say that as individual students, whether in the state schools of Egypt or as members of the Egyptian educational missions in Europe, Egyptians did not react and respond to these new and alien ideas and conditions in various and different ways. But their conceptions of the relationship between ruler and subject, the individual and the State, still remained within the framework of Islamic and local tradition. Yet their own work and public activity laid the foundations of a questioning and reforming spirit in the generation that followed them, aided by the revival of Arabic letters, the expansion of educational facilities and their availability to greater numbers of Egyptians, the development of such mass media as the newspaper and magazine press, and through them the dissemination of ideas detrimental to the existing socio-political order.

Loyal servants of the State and its ruling dynasty introduced Egyptians to ideas of material progress and brought them to the threshold of social ferment. Perhaps unknowingly these first intellectuals revived an Egyptian identity that later clashed against a foreign dominating power and ruling dynasty both of which had done so much to improve the public and private levels of Egyptian society. The new élite of Egyptians trained and educated at the expense of the ruler soon recognized its capacity to rule and eventually demanded this role as a right. It realized, with pride, its advance over the traditional leadership groups found among the Azharites and other notables. Having been recompensed with vast landed wealth by the ruler for their services to the State, they now came to command not only cultural, educational and technical skills but also economic power.

These fifty years (1830–80) in the history of modern Egypt represent a supreme rapprochement between governing authority on the one hand, and the intellectuals, the experts, the men of ideas on the other. The response to the technological, cultural and political supremacy of Europe was at this stage a positive constructive one. Such response was possible because Egypt was relatively a strong autonomous state, the Ottoman Empire still afforded a Commander for the community of the faithful, and massive European military might was not to appear physically on the Egyptian scene until 1882.

Ambivalent and rancorous attitudes to the apparently superior cultural achievements of Europe did not set in until the danger of its direct domination became imminent.

Yet the very rise of this new intellectual class in Egypt made the clash between certain groups in it and lesser members of the ruling dynasty – by then seriously limited by European control – an early certainty. Given the financial difficulties of the country in 1880, European rivalry over the control of imperial communications in that area, and the general decline of Ottoman imperial power, Egypt became an arena of local power struggles. These, in turn, were for the first time expressed and reflected in a proliferation of nationalist reform ideas aided by a changing social structure. Given the secure and stable administration provided by the British occupation between 1882 and 1914, the same ideas received a far more intensive treatment than would have otherwise been the case. To these and related matters – the rise of the Press and stirrings of public opinion, early attempts at constitutional government, rebellion and reform movements – we must now turn our attention.

This near Golden Age in Egyptian cultural and intellectual advance was not strictly self-generated, but mainly power-directed. An acquaintance with the outside world – in this instance with Europe – its power and prestige, motivated a ruler, in a similar pursuit of power and prestige, to emulate this outside world. He had to do this by utilizing local material. He therefore ordered the fashioning of this material in the service of his state and dominion. In doing so, he and his more energetic and imaginative successors laid the social, political and intellectual foundations of modern Egypt.

CHAPTER 7

CONSTITUTIONALISM, REBELLION, AND OCCUPATION

It is clear that the strongest desire of the generation of Egyptian leaders who were affected by, and benefited from, the modernizing experiments of Muhammad Ali and Khedive Ismail was to emulate Europe in their search for a better life and a stronger state. Educated in Europe and in Egyptian state schools in the modern sciences and arts, they acquired, besides technical and professional skills, a taste for Western political ideas and institutions. They considered the acquisition and application of European knowledge for the reform of their society not only essential to end their backwardness and subordination, but also necessary to attain power and prosperity. Among these European ideas, which by the 1860s were spreading eastwards across the continent of Europe and into Turkey, constitutionalism and its principle of representative government appealed to the new educated classes of Egypt. It inspired them to seek its adoption and application in their own country in the belief that it would easily lift them to the level of a European power.

Consultation of community leaders by the ruler, however, was not unknown in Islam. To this extent the idea of deliberation and consultation in the exercise of executive power was not totally alien to Muslims. Yet, given the rule of forceful, though modernizing, autocrats like Muhammad Ali and Ismail, the political climate of nineteenth-century Egypt was not conducive to the development of representative institutions or constitutional ideas. Tahtawi may have acquainted some Egyptians with the ideas of the French Revolution and with the constitutional development of France. Translators of French literature among the first Egyptian intellectuals and the early journalists may also have iterated the ideas of civil liberty and the rights of man, and called attention to the injustices of authority. But the idea of freedom is not peculiarly of European origin. Some will argue that it has universal appeal – that, in fact, it is a universal desire. Yet freedom in the abstract is not the crucial element in constitutionalism and representative government. What was peculiarly Western European and new to the Egyptians – indeed to all Muslims

– was the genius of the institutions devised by European man for the realization of this freedom as a right, not merely as a mercy vouchsafed by a benevolent ruler; the limitation and control of public power; and the availability to the individual of mechanisms and processes with which to secure his civil liberties.

Muhammad Ali managed within a period of thirty-five years to strengthen further the independence of Egypt from Turkish rule. From then until 1914, Turkish sovereign control over Egypt was nominal. The penetration of European influence under Muhammad Ali and Khedive Ismail, and later under the British, tended to supplant within less than a century even the remnants of lingering Turkish social and cultural influence. By the 1860s Arabic had replaced Turkish as the official language of the State; native Egyptians became the new class of officials, educators, technicians and professionals. Soon the impact of Europe proceeded from the educational, cultural and administrative fields to the emerging political awareness and interests of the educated Egyptians. The more sustained the adoption of European methods of administration, finance and legislation the more preponderant and lasting became the impact of Europe upon political life. An aspect of this impact was the introduction of Egyptians to experiments in constitutional and representative government: legislative councils, parliaments and parties. With the exception of Tunisia in North Africa, Egypt was one of the first Arabic-speaking countries to adopt these European political forms and has had the longest history in working them. It was also in Egypt that the most dramatic collapse of these essentially borrowed foreign institutions occurred in 1952.

Political developments in the period 1866–82 cannot, however, be fully appreciated outside the context of the educational and cultural advances of the same period, or outside the context of the financial difficulties which brought about European control of the Khedivial government. To attribute early constitutional developments in nineteenth-century Egypt to the maturation of liberal political ideas among Egyptians is to misrepresent the real political conditions of the time. To confine the explanation of these developments on the other hand to the inspiration and machinations of the ruler alone is to underestimate the force of circumstances and necessity which compelled him to experiment with constitutional measures. The peculiar relationship between the legal status of Egypt and the Ottoman Porte on the one hand, and the financial interest of Europeans and their governments in Egypt on the other, were additional crucial factors in the strange political events which for the first time produced a local opposition to the Khedive: a series of interventions by Egyptian Army officers in the affairs of the State, the deposition of Khedive Ismail by the Sultan at the insistence of the European Powers in 1879, an armed rebellion, and the British occupation in 1882.

There was not, therefore, a strictly self-generated Egyptian constitutional movement in the sense that Egyptians spoke of, wrote about, and put forward in a systematic or sustained fashion ideas of representative, limited government before the formation (for very practical reasons of state) by Khedivial decree of the first Assembly of Delegates in 1866. Despite the reporting of such institutions in France in his *Rihla*, Tahtawi did not write a reasoned appreciation of representative institutions for Egypt until 1869;[1] and then only in order to praise the Khedive for creating an Assembly. Once again then Egyptians were introduced to, and given their first experience in, borrowed European institutions by an act of their ruler. Nonetheless, a series of Assembly sessions between 1866 and 1881, several political difficulties generated by the financial recklessness of the Khedive, and mounting European pressure all contributed to the beginnings of a limited Egyptian public involvement in politics distinct from the régime. Those Egyptians who became involved soon dared to criticize the policy of the ruler and to demand a greater share in power, if not total power itself.

Only a very small group of Egyptians were actively involved in these developments, namely, the new class of educated and semi-Europeanized among them who, since 1820, were trained largely at the expense of the ruling dynasty. Furthermore, much of their political agitation was possible because of the growing weakness of the ruling house, undermined as it was by foreign financial demands and political intervention, and perhaps also by its incredibly lavish expenditure in Istanbul when it sought to extract a greater measure of autonomy from the Sultan. It was thus the European powers who secured the deposition of Khedive Ismail in June 1879, not the so-called nationalist forces. It was similarly European armed intervention that quashed the first serious bid for power by the so-called nationalists.

KHEDIVE ISMAIL'S CONSTITUTIONAL POLICY

Ismail's idea of creating an Assembly with limited powers was not totally new in Egypt. Both the Council of Napoleon and the Ad-

visory Council of Muhammad Ali (*Majlis al-mashwara*) were pre-
cedents. Organized in 1829, the latter served as a consultative council
that assisted Muhammad Ali in the administration of the country.
The Assembly of Delegates created by Ismail in 1866 was significant
not so much as a legislature (for it had no real legislative functions)
but in its effect on the later development of constitutionalism in
Egypt. It came at a time when the Khedive sought to associate the
notables of the country, mainly village shaykhs and headmen
(umdas), with his financial policies and, through these, with his diplomatic moves to thwart foreign intervention. He did not necessarily
desire the political enfranchisement of any sector of the public since
he viewed his authority as absolute. To this extent he was motivated
by the need to obtain more funds both from taxation and by the
contraction of fresh European loans. Associating representatives of
the Egyptian propertied classes with his policy was a protective
measure against outside objection and interference, whether the latter came from Istanbul, Paris or London.

Briefly, two decrees were issued by the Khedive on 22 October
1866. The first provided for a representative assembly of seventy-
five members elected indirectly for a three-year term and to be called
Majlis shura al-nuwwab (Consultative Assembly, or Council, of
Deputies). It also provided a fundamental law (*la'iha asasiyya*) consisting of eighteen articles setting out the functions of the Assembly
and the electoral procedure for deputies. The second decree contained an 'organization law' (*la'iha nizamiyya*) for the internal organization and regulation of the Assembly, rules of debate and related
matters. This Assembly first met on 25 November 1866. It was
suspended in 1879.

The financial entanglements of the Khedive, however, moved with
relentless complexity to a political crisis in the years 1876–9. Instead
of saving him, his constitutional measures opened a Pandora's
Box from which emerged the first Egyptian rebels. Generally, the
membership, mode of election of the Delegates and functions of the
Assembly permitted very limited representation of a particular
group of the Egyptian public. Its members were primarily concerned
with a discussion of taxes, education, public works and agriculture.[2]
While their concern with these matters was strictly deliberative, it
marked the beginning of communication and debate between the
Assembly and the Executive. Created as it was by the ruler, the
Assembly could not possess real powers to check him or his policy.
There was no comparable demand on the part of enlightened

Egyptians for constitutional government at the time. Outside the land-owning élite, representation of the merchant and artisan classes was negligible. Nor had the Press progressed beyond the first stages of development, and most of the papers were government-sponsored, or subsidized by the Court. Moreover, the climate for the expression of free views on such political matters was not conducive to the emergence of a public demand for constitutionalism. There were no legal or institutional safeguards to support free discussion of political ideas. The meetings of the Assembly for the first ten years of its existence (1866–75) were, therefore, perfunctory, controlled by the Khedive and essentially serving his purposes. One Egyptian writer has described Ismail's real purpose in creating the Assembly as 'to appear a constitutional monarch, permitting some public participation in power, to avoid the charge of absolutism'.[3] The same writer related the story that when the Secretary of the Assembly called on the Delegates to divide themselves into three groups – pro-government on the Right, opposition on the Left, and moderates in the Middle – all the Delegates crowded on the Right murmuring, 'How can we be opposed to the Government?'[4]

The year 1875 marks a turning point in Egyptian political history as reflected in the constitutional movement and its effect upon the emergence of new patterns in political activity. Desperately in need of money, the Khedive took certain measures to raise it (1871–5), which were to prove disastrous to himself. In 1871, he promulgated the Muqabala Law by which the government invited landowners to pay six times the annual land tax in advance in return for a perpetual reduction of one half of the tax. When, by 1874, not enough landlords opted for this scheme, the Khedive made the Law's provisions compulsory. The whole scheme apparently was the work of the notorious Ismail Saddiq Pasha al-Mafattish, the Khedive's Finance Minister, foster-brother and confidant. It was, moreover, a catastrophic financial measure as it sacrificed half the main land revenue to secure temporary relief which reportedly did not exceed two and a half million pounds. The expenditure the Khedive incurred in securing the 1873 Imperial Decree from the Porte granting him greater autonomy in Egypt was also prohibitive. By 1875 he had practically exhausted all of his borrowing capacity; his credit rating in Europe simply vanished. He was now on the verge of bankruptcy. Selling his 176,602 shares in the Suez Canal to the British government for an immediate cash payment of four million pounds was another very temporary financial palliative which merely staved off the crisis for another year. Yet the Disraeli coup in purchasing the shares for England had far-reaching political consequences. First, it implied the increasingly more direct interest of England in Egypt. Second, it marked the beginning of the decline of French influence there, for England was now the largest single shareholder in the Canal Company. It was a great political victory for England at the relatively cheap price of four million pounds.

Given this short breather, Ismail was now seriously concerned with the alleviation of the financial situation. Unsuccessful campaigns in Abyssinia and a costly military involvement in Crete contributed to the deterioration of the general situation. He therefore requested British help in fiscal reform and Britain responded by sending Steven Cave, MP, to investigate. The latter reported that a Control Commission over Egyptian finances must be established and that it should be headed by an Englishman seconded from the British government. The Commission would approve all future loans.

Fearing the effect of the report if publicized, Ismail prevented its publication and suspended payment of interest on his loans.[5] His creditors in England and France suspected insolvency and appointed Mr Goschen and M Joubert respectively to represent their interests in Egypt and to negotiate new arrangements with the Khedive. Three things were accomplished. The Goschen–Joubert mission brought about the unification of the funded debt. To guarantee payment, the Khedive agreed to the appointment of two European Controllers, an Englishman and a Frenchman. The *Caisse de la Dette*, a special department with representatives from the various European creditor states to ensure the service of the debt, was formed in 1876. It was on this body that Major Evelyn Baring, later Lord Cromer, represented British creditors. Revenue from the most productive provinces went straight into the *Caisse* and by 1877 over 60 per cent of all Egyptian revenue went to the servicing of the national debt.

Under the pressure of these enormous debts, the burden of taxation fell heavily on the fellahin. A low Nile in 1877–8 did not help matters. Although Egypt serviced the debt fully and faithfully in 1877, European creditors were apprehensive and suspicious of the Khedive's ultimate willingness to satisfy them. Litigations in the Mixed Tribunals frequently rendered judgements in their favour and against the Khedivial government. But judgements were rarely enforced. Foreign commercial and financial interests increased their representations to the Consuls against the Khedive. The latter, in turn, became apprehensive at this strong European opposition in Egypt, and tried to meet and quash it by decreeing the appointment of a Commission of Inquiry in January 1878. The outstanding members of this Commission were two Englishmen, Sir Rivers Wilson and Major Baring. Riad Pasha represented the Khedive on the Commission, which was empowered to examine all sources of revenue and all expenditures. This meant the right of the Commission to ask any Egyptian official or government department to testify before it, as well as to subpoena all records. Such powers also implied the dilution of Egyptian sovereignty by Europeans.

The first report of the Commission was a plain indictment of the Khedivial government, and implied the limitation of Ismail's power as a first step to the solution of the financial problems of the country. This was sought first in the sacrifice by the Khedive of his and his family's private properties. The Khedive accepted these conditions, as well as the first indirect political intervention by Europeans, and agreed to recall Nubar Pasha from Europe to head a cabinet in which European ministers were to serve for the first time. The mixed cabinet was committed to the implementation of the recommendations of the Commission of Inquiry, implying a European mandate for power. In addition to Sir Rivers Wilson as Minister of Finance and M de Blignières as Minister of Public Works, Nubar appointed many European officials at high salaries. It is reported, for instance, that thirty British officers were appointed to the Land Survey department alone.

What is more important is that Ismail was forced to accept the principle of ministerial responsibility for the first time. The ministry that Nubar was invited to form was to be the first executive cabinet (*majlis al-nuzzar*) in modern Egyptian history. The Khedivial decree of August 1878 formally delegated the responsibility of government to it. In his letter to Nubar, dated 30 August, asking him to form a government, Ismail informed him that 'he intended that the administration be reformed and organized on principles similar to those observed in the administration of the states of Europe'.[6] The decree limited to some extent the power of the Khedive in that the cabinet, or 'Council of Overseers', was to be independent of the ruler and responsible for the administration of the country. The ruler, in turn, undertook to accept the collective advice of his cabinet. Moreover, the members of the Council were to be collectively responsible for their policies; their decisions were to be taken by majority vote; and meetings of the Council were to be presided over by the Chief Minister (i.e., the chairman of the Council), not by the Khedive.

These developments marked the beginnings of the political crisis that soon engulfed the Khedive, members of the Assembly and the Egyptian Army officers, and were an indication of the chaos which ensued. It soon became clear that neither the Khedive nor the politically ambitious Egyptians approved of the Nubar ministry which clearly reflected European control. The Khedive thus worked for its overthrow in the hope of freeing himself from foreign control, while political factions, including elements in the Egyptian Army officer corps, agitated against it. To attain his purposes, the Khedive seemed to encourage such agitation, while Egyptian journalists fomented general opposition and antagonism to European influence and control among the public. Financial difficulties, European attempts to protect creditors, rivalry between Britain and France in Egypt, Ottoman hopes of retrieving paramount sovereignty over Egypt – all of these factors and other events were to work in such a way as to throw Egypt into political turmoil.

The financial crisis of 1875–7 unavoidably undermined the authority of the Khedive. This condition was soon reflected in the bolder criticisms of his policy by some of the delegates in the Assembly and a restless army officer corps. Foreign financial control was not simply viewed by the Egyptians interested in political power as a curtailment of Khedivial power but also recognized as a propitious situation in which to increase their own share in government at the expense of the ruling house. Economy measures introduced by the Nubar mixed cabinet in the army and the expenditures of military schools resulted in the retirement of Egyptian officers to the inactive list. Officers' pay and benefits were, as a result of the financial situation, in arrears. At the same time the reform programme required the appointment of ever-increasing numbers of British officers, especially from India. Resentment and bitterness among the Egyptian officers against both the European Powers and the Khedive grew. It was gradually echoed in the sessions of the Assembly, the embryonic Press, secret national societies and military conspiracies.

The discontented aimed at the expulsion of foreign control and the overthrow of the Khedivial government. In a way, both these aims were interrelated. For a time, however, they took the form of demands for greater governmental accountability to a more liberal constitution, including ministerial responsibility to the Assembly.

The latter was of such composition and character as not to be effective in achieving this end. Ultimately the use of force, that is, the intervention of the military in politics, threatened to overthrow the dynasty. And the military coup and its leaders were, in turn, subdued by force of British arms.

The Khedive caused the Assembly to meet in August 1876 primarily for the purpose of strengthening his hand in effectively implementing the collection of the Muqabala tax. In order to approve such policy delegates demanded an explanation of the government's financial operations in general, implying criticism of them, as well as the desire of the Assembly to supervise and control government expenditures. It is possible that some of them were influenced by developments outside Egypt, especially in Turkey. The promulgation that year of the first Constitution – the so-called Midhet Constitution – in Turkey was an event of great political significance throughout the Empire even though the constitution itself was very short-lived.

The Nubar ministry with the two Europeans in it had been in office since August 1878, creating difficulties for the Khedive, but also affording the Assembly Delegates cause for bolder intervention. When the Assembly met in session, January–July 1879, certain of its members put forward even bolder proposals regarding their rights in the control of financial matters: e.g., the reduction of taxes, the accountability of European ministers to the Assembly, and so on. Meanwhile, Nubar's drive for economy, which greatly affected the army, had serious consequences. A group of army officers led by Latif Bey Salim organized a protest march on the Ministry of Finance to demand the redress of wrongs. The immediate pretext for the military demonstration on 18 February 1879 was the placement of two and a half thousand officers on half-pay as part of the government's economy drive. The armed officers, accompanied by troops and followed by a crowd, went up to Nubar and Sir Rivers Wilson who were riding in a cab, insulted and rough-handled them. They also occupied the Ministry building. Only the intervention of the Khedive, supported by the European consuls, saved the situation.

Ismail not only successfully appeared on the scene to order the rebels to disperse, but also found himself at an enviable political advantage. Faced with demands from the Assembly for greater ministerial responsibility and a restless officer corps rebelling against Nubar's mixed cabinet, the Khedive perceived an ideal chance to rid himself of both a European-controlled ministry and a demanding Assembly. His success in placating the rebellious officers was crucial, for it elevated his prestige and strengthened his hand. He could now point to the inability of Nubar to maintain order and the disrupting effect of a querulous and clamouring Assembly. Nubar resigned on 19 February and the Assembly was prorogued a month later on 19 March. Judging from the neat way in which matters fell into his own hands, it is possible that Ismail was as much the instigator of the crisis, or at least the demonstration, as he was its beneficiary.

For a while, the Khedive hoped to head his own government by becoming Prime Minister. To this the European consuls objected strenuously, until the Crown Prince, Tawfiq Pasha, was accepted as a compromise premier. He formed a cabinet on 10 March in which both Sir Rivers Wilson and M de Blignières were included. European financial control, therefore, continued, and Ismail had failed to be rid of it.

During the month that elapsed between the resignation of Nubar and the formation of the Tawfiq cabinet, the Assembly continued its deliberations of government policy and the financial crisis. Both European ministers now pressed for the abolition of the Muqabala Law and the declaration of the government's insolvency. To achieve this they favoured the dissolution of the Assembly. When Riad Pasha, Minister of the Interior, was delegated to appear before the Assembly with a Khedivial decree dated 27 March ordering its dissolution, he was met with strong protests from the members, who refused to disperse. A sharp exchange took place between Riad and Abd al-Salam Bey al-Muwailihi, leader of the Assembly, in which the latter insisted that the delegates were representatives of the nation and would not relinquish their mandate at the orders of the Khedive, influenced and pressed as he was by foreign powers.

Whether this was a reflection of a wider and more mature national opposition movement, or merely a protest by landed notables, *ulama*, and other members of the propertied classes against impending measures detrimental to their interests (after all, the Muqabala Law was to their advantage) or the result of Khedivial encouragement one can only speculate. Their action was perhaps motivated by a combination of interests. Consequently, the delegates prepared a petition in the form of a manifesto dated 29 March which they presented to the Khedive protesting against the action of the Council of Ministers to usurp their powers and delegated authority. They specifically objected to the proposed financial bill abolishing the

Muqabala Law and declaring insolvency, stated their determination to reject the measure, and petitioned the ruler to reconsider matters in view of their declared position.

It is rather difficult to reconstruct the exact composition of the so-called national groups, organized or not, which represented at the time demands for greater participation in power and opposition to European financial control. The landowners, state officials, army officers and journalists were aware of the nature of the financial crisis and its political implications. There is no conclusive evidence, however, that any of them were at that time openly interested in overthrowing the Khedive. On the contrary, many of them were active on his behalf. Agitation for increased legislative power by the expansion of the functions of the Assembly and the demand for ministerial responsibility to it were ostensibly directed against European interference and control. To this extent this so-called first national political movement was anti-foreign, but still very much directed and led by a small group of Egyptian landowners and high-ranking army officers. To the extent that the elimination of foreign control required the curtailment of Khedivial power, this agitation was also directed against the authority of the Viceroy. How much of the sentiment of the delegates against foreign ministers was national and how much it was their immediate reaction to safeguard their private interests is difficult to say. This is a difficult question in politics anywhere.

Meanwhile, with the knowledge and active support of the Khedive, Egyptian journalists between 1876 and 1879 increased their attacks upon foreign control over the financial affairs of the country. By March 1879, the Press campaign had accelerated and secret societies among army officers and national societies comprising Assembly delegates were formed. How co-ordinated the efforts of these groups were is not too clear. If the direct clash later (1881–2) between the National (Party) Society led by Muhammad Sharif Pasha (also known as the Helwan Society) in the Assembly and the political group in the army led by Orabi is any indication, these two sections of early Egyptian political leadership often worked at cross-purposes and ultimately against one another.

STIRRINGS OF OPPOSITION TO ISMAIL'S RULE AND HIS DEPOSITION

Much has been written about the influence of the popular Islamic reformer and political agitator Jamal al-Din al-Afghani on young

Egyptian intellectuals, political leaders, Azharites and journalists of
this time. His influence has been more realistically assessed in recent
research based on fresh evidence.[7] It is generally assumed that Afghani, who came to Egypt in 1871 and was expelled from the country
by Tawfiq Pasha in August 1879, instructed his Egyptian disciples
in the necessity of reform as the basis of national solidarity and as
the only way to strengthen their position *vis-à-vis* European
encroachment and control. Younger journalists like Adib Ishaq,
Ibrahim al-Laqqani and Abdullah al-Nadim, as well as younger
Azharites like Muhammad Abduh and Saad Zaghlul, were
impressed by his argument about the need for reform as a prelude
to power. Instruction mixed with agitation against an inferior political condition struck a responsive note among the young intellectuals
and the disaffected army officers. Anti-European preaching appealed
to the beleaguered Ismail; for it explains in part the sojourn of Afghani in Egypt during these crucial nine years. Generally, the first
attempts at organized – if not concerted – political action took the
form of secret societies both among civilians and army officers.

Secret and conspiratorial political groups were not alien to Islam.
Nor were they unknown in its political history if one recalls the early
Shiite movement against the Umayyads (665–748) soon after the
murder of Ali, son-in-law of the Prophet and fourth Caliph of Islam.
In the 1850s, 1860s and 1870s societies were springing up in Turkey,
Egypt and Lebanon, aimed initially at the promotion of learning
and the organization of native schools. Soon they came to embrace
social and political aims: reforms ranging from demands for equality
before the law, to ministerial responsibility and certain aspects of
civil liberty. Later, societies seeking to reform, strengthen and unite
the Islamic world appeared in certain countries of the Middle East.[8]
These may be considered the forerunners of political parties in
Egypt, for instance, in the period 1906–13.

By 1876, secret groups consisting of notables, ministers and journalists had been organized in the country. At first, these reflected
perhaps no more than the coming together of certain individuals all
of whom considered it in their interests to oppose the newly instituted European control over Egyptian finances and administration. For this reason too, their formation was not without the knowledge of Ismail – or possibly with his encouragement – even though,
featured among their demands, was also the call for a curtailment
of the ruler's powers.

The Mixed Ministry of Nubar marked a turning point in Egyptian political history. Until that time the country had been governed directly by the Khedive, aided by some notables heading his administrative departments, and courtiers directly responsible to him. Faced with growing European control, Ismail encouraged the objectives of any anti-European group, whether in the Assembly, among the journalists, the Azharites, or – as it turned out, disastrously – the army. Interest among Egyptians in the Russo-Turkish War of 1877, in which some thirty thousand Egyptian troops were involved, led to the belief among some of them that continued Turkish suzerainty over an autonomous Egypt, ruled by a Khedive responsive to certain of their demands, was the best guarantee against foreign domination.

Afghani, for instance, had joined a secret Masonic lodge whose members presumably deliberated modernist and reformist ideas. Its membership allegedly included Abd al-Salam al-Muwailihi, leader of the Assembly, Shaykh Muhammad Abduh, the Jewish publicist James Sanua, the journalists Adib Ishaq, Ibrahim al-Laqqani and Salim al-Naqqash, the ostensible leader of the constitutionalist movement and influential courtier of the Khedive Ismail Muhammad Sharif Pasha, the then Prince and heir apparent Tawfiq, and the leader of the February 1879 army rebels Latif Bey Salim.

About the same time, the existence of a secret informal group in the army was suspected. It was led by a group of disaffected officers with a variety of complaints ranging from pay and promotion, to social and class discrimination. Latif Bey Salim, a Freemason, Muhammad Sami Pasha al-Barudi, another officer and Freemason, may have been members of this group. It has been alleged that Halim Pasha, last surviving son of Muhammad Ali the Great, living in exile in Istanbul since 1868, was the real leader of this conspiracy as he hoped to succeed to the Khedivial throne.

Thus by 1879 three groups were actively agitating in the political affairs of Egypt: the army, the intelligentsia consisting of landowners, newspaper editors, ulama and others (in part inspired by Afghani), and members of the Assembly. Only the last group was in a position to act openly regarding the crisis of March–April 1879.

Having refused to comply with the order of dissolution, the Assembly delegates continued to meet privately in the homes of Sayyid Ali al-Bakri, *Naqib al-Ashraf*,[9] and Ismail Raghib Pasha, President of the First Assembly of 1866, an ex-Minister of Finance, and the spokesman of the Assembly in financial matters. It was here that some of the prominent members of the Assembly formed a secret National Society (not to be confused with the Army National

Committee, or the later National Party founded by Mustafa Kamil in 1907) to oppose the acts of ministers and the abolition of the Muqabala Law. Later in the year when the same group, under the leadership of Sharif Pasha, opposed the policies of Riad and the new Khedive Tawfiq it came to be known as the Helwan Society for it met secretly in Helwan. With rising disaffection in the army which culminated in the mutiny led by Orabi against Riad and the Khedive in 1881 a link, if not a merger, was effected between Orabi militarists and the National Society. It appears that this expanded group assumed the name of *Al-hizb al-watani al-ahli* (The National Popular Party). The Turco-Egyptian and Circassian elements in the army and the court of the Khedive referred to this group as *Hizb al-fellahin* (The Party of the Peasants), whereas the group itself in presenting its demands and issuing its pamphlets referred to these as 'the demands and aims of the National Party and the Army (*al-jiha-diyya*)'.[10]

If, on the whole, all these groups and societies – whether in the Assembly, the army or among journalists and Afghanists – sought to rid the country of European control, then their aims were similar to those of Ismail. This explains in part the involvement and close association of many of these personages (especially Sharif Pasha) with the Khedive. Thus, after Ismail's deposition they begin to appear as the 'party' of the deposed Khedive.[11]

Be that as it may, this National Society demanded in March 1879 the formation of a national government excluding European ministers (they claimed this exclusion was not motivated by religious fanaticism). They also drew up a programme for the resolution of the financial crisis counter to that proposed by Sir Rivers Wilson. Sharif Pasha soon emerged as the obvious leader to represent and implement these demands. He was a natural choice as he was known to have defied, when previously in the Cabinet (and probably with Ismail's encouragement), the demands of European Debt Commissioners and those of the controllers. He was, furthermore, acceptable as the Khedive's 'man'.

A National Project of Reform (*La'iha wataniyya*) was drawn up which contained the scheme for meeting the financial crisis contrary to that proposed by Sir Rivers Wilson. Central to this scheme was the recommendation that Egyptians should take the initiative to relieve the financial crisis, independently of foreign advice and control. Any of the latter should be introduced at the discretion of the ruler. Furthermore, Dual Control was to be restricted to the actual administration of finances in the country. More significant was the demand incorporated in the Project for the revision of the Organization Law governing the Assembly so as to give the latter greater control over government affairs. In this connection, the Project suggested the extension of ministerial responsibility introduced in August 1878 from the cabinet to the Assembly. To this extent one might consider the Project a step in constitutional reform.

Ismail's disarming – and calculated – acceptance of these demands came as a surprise to both the Assembly and the European Controllers and Consuls. It was a clever political move – almost a coup.[12] The Khedive now took the initiative from the Assembly 'nationalists' to turn their action to his advantage against the British and French Controllers. On 6–7 April he summoned the Consuls to confront them with the seething discontent of his legislators, the disaffection in the army, and the general uneasiness among the public. He cavalierly informed them that he would now act in accordance with the resolutions of the Assembly, namely, that he would reject the proposal by Sir Rivers Wilson to declare Egypt bankrupt and would undertake to meet all obligations to the creditors. He ordered the cabinet headed by his son Tawfiq Pasha to resign and invited his favourite – and Nubar's and Riad's rival – Sharif Pasha (a leader in the Helwan, or National, Society and a so-called constitutionalist) to form a government.

Ismail's sudden national-constitutional enthusiasm was reflected in the opening sentence of his letter to Sharif, 'In my capacity as head of the government and an Egyptian, I consider it my duty to comply with the opinion of the nation ...'[13] He declared his intention to retain the principle of ministerial responsibility instituted the previous year under pressure from the Control Commission. His ex-critics among the Assembly delegates and army rebels had been peacefully disarmed. Nubar, a restraining influence upon the more reckless moments of the Khedive, fled to Europe; and the austere administrator Riad Pasha was at a safe distance in Paris. The Egyptian detractors of the Khedive were meanwhile appeased by the formation of an all-Egyptian cabinet. A draft constitution of forty-nine articles – the most liberal thus far – was submitted to the Assembly and there was Egyptian jubilation all round. But the exhilarating atmosphere did not last very long. Other forces were already at work against the Khedive and therefore against the overall 'national' strategy of which he was in great measure the author.[14]

The report by Sir Rivers Wilson proposing to declare Egypt bankrupt also recommended concrete, realistic measures to deal with the financial crisis: a liquidation law, lower interest rates on loans, and the disqualification of the decisions of the Mixed Tribunals against the Khedive, that is, those in favour of creditors. Obviously, such measures were to Ismail's advantage. He was, however, determined to rid himself of European financial control as a prelude to maintaining his freedom of political action. His campaign tactics to achieve this are interesting.

Using the Press, including his own French language paper *Moniteur Egyptien*, Ismail sought the sympathy of every group involved in the affair. He aired his objection to lower interest rates on loans hoping to secure the support of creditors. He appealed to the disaffected groups in the Assembly and the army by whipping up their anti-foreign feelings on the basis of a vague Islamic sentiment. Thus, he manœuvred the welding of an alliance with landowners, ulama, and army officers and demanded a 'national budget' which would meet all debt obligations.[15] So far, the Khedive showed brilliant tactical political sense, although as it turned out later, poor strategy. Cornered by the demands of European creditors, he embarked upon a triple political game to extricate himself. He proceeded to 'democratize' his rule by subjecting it on paper at least to popular account. This he thought would earn him popular support for his international position in return. He then baited the creditors with his objection to lower interest rates. Finally, he affected a situation in which European infidels were seeking to undermine an Islamic ruler. In the process, he had not only neutralized the truculent members of the Assembly, but inexorably involved them in his own fight for survival against the European Controllers.

European reaction, however, was against the Khedive. It was alleged, at the time, that both Nubar and Riad Pasha who had fled to Europe – the former because of his support of a mixed cabinet, the latter for his straightforward investigation into the Khedivial finances – pressed the French at least to act against Ismail. They argued that only the deposition of the Khedive could save the financial situation in Egypt and thus safeguard the interests of the creditors. Whether the European powers accepted these alleged representations of Nubar and Riad is difficult to say. Other considerations entered into the decision of the Porte to order the deposition of the Khedive.

Despite the temporary alliance Ismail succeeded in effecting between himself, the Assembly and others in the guise of a 'nationalist' government headed by his front-man Sharif Pasha, the army remained restless. Secret factions among the discontented existed. Certain journalists and intellectuals – among them Adib Ishaq and Abdullah al-Nadim – banded together in 1879 to form a secret society in Alexandria. Borrowing its name from the famous Italian patriotic society Young Italy, they called it Young Egypt (*Misr al-fatat*). They published their own periodical by the same name, in which they attacked foreign influence in Egypt. James Sanua in his paper *Abu Naddara* supported this group by his attacks on the Khedive.[16] Afghani moreover urged those around him, especially the journalists, to criticize the government of the Khedive. In the same year, some Egyptian officers formed their own secret 'National Society' (perhaps more of a cabal of disaffected officers than a serious political group) to combat foreign influence in the country and to promote their interests in the army. This group was later to be linked to the civilian National (Helwan) Society.

England and France were not impressed by the apparent solidarity of all those factions now led by the Khedive in their determination to withstand foreign financial control. Although they did not minimize the dangers inherent in the possible success of the so-called constitutionalists or the army rebels, both powers were more interested now in the deposition of the Khedive. The only question was whether to depose him directly or via the Ottoman Porte. Neither the last-ditch entreaty to the Sultan that his deposition by the Powers would establish a precedent for their interference with Ottoman authority, nor his momentary consideration to declare Egypt independent, seemed to save the Khedive from exile. The Porte after a fresh war with Russia (1877–8) was in no position to defend such action. Nor was the Khedive sure of his own position within Egypt. Moreover, he had no military or financial resources to back up his independence once he had declared it. After dismissing the European ministers, Sharif Pasha and his all-Egyptian cabinet tried desperately to reassure and reconcile the European creditors. His suggestion that dual Anglo-French control over Egyptian finances be resumed was rejected by the Powers. When on 22 April 1879 the Khedive decreed the financial arrangement recommended by the Assembly, which was contrary to the one recommended by the European Commission, reaction in Europe was swift and forceful.

Strangely enough the reaction of European creditors to the 22 April decree did not come first from France or England, but from Germany. Bismarck invited the interested Powers to act on behalf of creditors against the illegal action of the Egyptian Viceroy. By May the Germans were warning Ismail that his decree constituted a direct violation of international agreements and should be rescinded. All the other powers seemed to support the German move. In June, England and France took the initiative by advising the Khedive to abdicate in favour of his son. Meantime, they made sure that the Sultan in Istanbul would not be swayed by the Khedive's representations. The Sultan was perhaps anxious to rid himself of a Viceroy who was ambitious enough to throw off even the last vestiges of Ottoman suzerainty and, on 26 June, ordered the deposition of Ismail and the accession of his son Tawfiq Pasha to the vice-regal throne. Ismail left Egypt to live in exile in Naples and subsequently in Istanbul, where he died in 1895.

How far Ismail anticipated the acquiescence of England and France in his scheme to restore his independence in financial matters cannot be known. What is certain is that he misjudged the possible reaction of other European states, e.g., Germany. What is also certain is that despite the temporary alliance between him and his opponents in Egypt, the European states were convinced of his bankruptcy. To this extent their ultimate intervention was prompted by the consideration of protecting their financial interests. In doing so, however, England and France seriously undermined the authority of the Khedivial house and so contributed to the political upheavals of the next three years which culminated in the occupation of Egypt by British forces.

PRELUDE TO THE ORABI REVOLT AND THE BRITISH OCCUPATION

The situation in July 1879 was a critical one. The report of the European Commission had declared Egypt insolvent. On the one hand, the Assembly was demanding greater control over government policy, and on the other a mutinous army was pressing on with its own demands. The military group was, moreover, encouraged in its agitation by its successful intervention in February 1879. While the new Khedive, with the help of European representatives, tried desperately to re-establish a sound administration that would restore his authority, the movement led by the militarists to impose their will on future governments went on unabated. Nevertheless, the centre of events shifted at this time away from the activities of nationalist agitators to the matter of finding a government that could, first, successfully restore relations with the Porte, and second, re-fashion its relationships with the European financial controllers.

Realizing the precarious position of the new Khedive, the Ottoman Sultan saw an opportunty to tighten his control over Egypt. In deposing Ismail, Sultan Abdul Hamid had simultaneously repealed the 1873 Imperial *firman* by which the deposed Khedive had, at great expense, secured a further measure of autonomy for his country, including the right to conclude commercial treaties, contract loans, and increase the strength of the army as required by security needs. Moreover, the Ottoman practice relating to succession had been modified in favour of male primogeniture within the immediate family of the Khedive. Now the Sultan wished to abolish all this and limit the strength of the Egyptian Army to eighteen thousand officers and men. Only the intervention of Britain and France forced the Sultan in August 1879 to issue a new decree restoring the conditions of the 1873 *firman* with the exception of the army strength limitation which was retained. Nonetheless, the Sultan was to continue his interference in the Egyptian crisis until the First World War.

When the new Khedive Tawfiq invited Sharif Pasha to form a government, the latter laid the adoption of his project for a new and more liberal constitution as his minimum condition for accepting the responsibility. Suspicious of a strengthened Assembly, Tawfiq did not accept Sharif's conditions and instead proceeded to act as his own Prime Minister. But realizing the need for a strong Chief Minister, he soon recalled Riad Pasha from Europe, who returned to form a government in September. Its strong measures, especially in permitting the European Controllers to push through the fiscal reforms which led to the July 1880 Law of Liquidation, seemed momentarily to ease the crisis. Although the functions of the European Controllers were limited to inspection and verification, the formation of an International Commission to settle the Debt meant vast European control over the disposition of Egyptian finances.[17]

Riad pressed for other reforms by suppressing odious taxes, abolishing the *corvée*, or forced labour, prohibiting flogging and whipping, the *kurbaj*, and initiating a scheme to reorganize the National Courts. Considering the repeal of the Muqabala Law in January 1882 and these other reforms, landed and other notables looked with disfavour upon Riad's policy, for it affected their immediate interests. They felt that under a more 'constitutional' government, headed by Sharif Pasha, their interests could be better safeguarded. But Riad was not well disposed towards constitutional government, or towards satisfying their demands. To this extent the tough policy of absolute rule followed by Khedive Tawfiq and his first minister Riad Pasha contributed to the more serious crisis of January–February 1882, in so far as it permitted the Orabists to marshal wider support among the landowners and other members of the Assembly. Whether this policy was also responsible for the organization of a National Party aiming to overthrow the government and combat European control cannot be ascertained. That Riad suspended such critical newspapers as *Misr* and *Tijara* is a matter of record. The National Society, led by the Sharifists, then subsidized Adib Ishaq to publish an anti-Riad paper, *Misr al-Qahira*, in Paris.

It seems though that the leaders of the Assembly headed by Sultan Pasha, Sulayman Abaza and Mahmud Fahmi held secret meetings to co-ordinate their campaign with the anti-Khedive army officers, Orabi, Abd al-Al Hilmi, and Ali Fahmi. Their Manifesto of 4 November was not only a reaction to the deposition of Khedive Ismail, but also an attempt to seize the opportunity to assert control over the new one. Its proposals directly contradicted European financial recommendations, and demanded further autonomy and freedom from European control. At this time, the militarists and civilian 'nationalists' appeared united in their efforts to achieve greater control over the new Khedive and to exclude European influence from Egypt. They were further encouraged by the knowledge that the Sultan was anxious to undermine Khedivial authority in Egypt through the possible use of the armed support of the military dissidents and that the diplomatic action of the Powers would be slow. The civilian elements did not, however, fully appreciate the extent of their submission to Orabist control.

Meanwhile Tawfiq, through both his Chief Minister and the Circassian Minister of War, was seeking means to curtail and destroy the power of the mutinous army officers. In addition to the economy cuts in army personnel which affected primarily Egyptian officers and men, a July 1880 Khedivial Decree limited military service to four years. The Orabists interpreted this to mean that, given such short-term service, no Egyptians would be able to rise from the ranks to commissioned grades. Moreover, Osman Rifqi Pasha, the Minister of War, embarked upon a vast scheme of promotions, transfers and replacements among officers, all intended to weaken, by dispersing, the Orabist officers.

Encouraged by the support forthcoming from the Assembly, Orabi now organized a movement to petition Riad Pasha for the dismissal of the Circassian Osman Rifqi and the appointment of an Egyptian as Minister of War. The candidate of the Orabists for the post was Mahmud Sami Pasha al-Barudi (1839–1904), a soldier, poet, Freemason and statesman. As Officer Commanding the Vice-regal Guard of Khedive Ismail, Barudi had undertaken military missions to London and Paris, participated in the quelling of the 1864 uprising in Crete, the Russo-Turkish War in 1877, and joined the Helwan Secret National Society. In 1879, he had initiated the re-organization of the Army General Staff. Although at first willing to remain in the cabinet after Sharif had resigned in August 1879, Barudi now saw in an alliance with army rebels the opportunity eventually to head the government.

By the end of January 1881, the government decided to arrest the petitioners and put an end to their movement. News of this decision, however, was leaked to the conspirators who took appropriate steps for their regimental troops to mutiny in case of their arrest and court-martial. And in fact this is what happened on 1 February 1881. While the three colonels were being court-martialled, their regimental troops stormed the Ministry of War, arrested the military judges and freed their commanders. The Khedive was forced to dismiss Rifqi Pasha and appoint the army candidate, Barudi, in his place. He then proceeded to consider the remainder of army grievances and demands. Chief among the latter was the revision of pay scales and new law regulating promotions more favourable to Egyptians. By April, most of these demands had been met. But by July mutinous acts committed by troops in Alexandria engendered a fresh crisis between the Khedive and the army. The offenders were punished and the rebel leaders ordered Barudi to convey their displeasure to the Khedive. For this, Barudi was dismissed, and the Khedive replaced him with his brother-in-law, Daud Pasha Yeken.

Barudi's removal augured ill for the Orabists. They now felt that their position as well as their personal safety were in danger. The new Minister of War, moreover, proceeded to clamp down on their activities with orders for their dispersal and surveillance. The Khedive was thus encouraged to suppress conclusively the army rebels and their movement, and readily approved the measures taken by Daud Pasha against the officers. It was clear that Orabi and his companions were cornered. Their alternatives for action were not, however, exhausted. The policy of Riad Pasha had earned him the enmity of many delegates in the Assembly. An alliance with the latter could serve Orabist purposes in affecting a united popular front against a tough government which was aided and abetted by Europeans. They also counted upon assistance from the Sultan who did not particularly wish to see Khedivial authority in Egypt strengthened. The Orabists may also have been encouraged by the French Consul-General.[18] Moreover, their recent successful coup in February 1881 had impressed upon them the idea that, short of foreign armed intervention, the Khedive could not withstand their new demands especially if these were backed by force. The prospect of overthrowing the government appeared to them now more feasible than ever. A fresh demonstration against the Khedive was planned accordingly.

The extent of the impact of the February 1881 military intervention upon civilian dissidents can only be conjectured. That it pushed Orabi and his accomplices into the forefront of national news is certain. After all, their action had cowed the Khedive into temporary submission, removed a harsh Circassian Minister of War, produced better conditions of pay and promotion for the army and gave the military group a forceful say in government policy. This was an impressive array of accomplishments; at least impressive enough to awe the spectator public. It also encouraged army officers towards renewed disobedience of government orders.

When Daud Pasha ordered the transfer of the Third Regiment from the Cairo Citadel to Alexandria, Orabists urged that the order be ignored. Meantime, they spread the rumour abroad that the real intention of the government was to do away with all the Egyptian military leaders. A demonstration of all regiments in force at Abdin Palace was organized for 9 September, to present the Khedive with a new set of demands, among them the dismissal of the Riad Pasha ministry, the convocation of the Assembly and the increase of army strength. This time, however, Orabi was acting as a 'representative of the Egyptian army officers', and proceeded to inform the representatives of the European Powers of his intention as leader of the national movement to safeguard European lives and property and to honour their interests. This was in effect a usurpation of power by Orabi. But the uneasy armed confrontation between Orabi forces and the Khedive in the courtyard of Abdin Palace ended once more in the latter's total submission to army demands. Moreover, the tone of Orabi's address to, and conversation with, the Khedive and Cookson, the acting British Consul-General, indicated clearly that he considered the army as 'the implement by which the nation will attain its ends, and we shall stay here till we are satisfied'.[19]

Once again Sharif Pasha, the ostensible leader of the constitutional movement at that time, the rival of Riad, and the deposed Khedive Ismail's favourite courtier, was asked to form a government as he was then acceptable to the military rebels – although the latter might have preferred Barudi. Sharif, however, refused to form a government under pressure from the rebels, for he realized he would be no more than a pawn to their designs. It looked then as if what the Orabists failed to achieve by force they would gain by default, namely, the overthrow of the Khedive. Not a very astute politician, however, Orabi erred at this point by ordering the Assembly delegates to meet in Cairo, and threatening them to get in line with his policy and plans. This approach immediately put the delegates on their guard and alienated enough of them to withhold all-out support for the army in its plans against the Khedive. Simultaneously Orabist threats and demands cut no ice with Sharif Pasha, who demanded as a condition of his acceptance to lead the government, a guarantee that there would be no interference by the military in the affairs of the State. Afraid of losing everything, Orabi and his group were now intent to see Barudi appointed Minister of War in any new cabinet headed by Sharif. They dropped their other demands.

The brief honeymoon between Orabists and anti-Khedive, i.e., anti-Riad, anti-European and, in many instances, pro-Ismail, elements in the Assembly, now seemed ended. Nonetheless both continued in their diluted, though still inimical, attitude towards the government. Sharif, however, was confident that he could proceed from strength to restore normal governmental activity. But his enthusiasm for constitutional reform was dampened by the situation. Instead, he reinstated effective Dual Control over finances and set out to regain legitimate authority to govern with a minimum of interference from the military and civilian factions. Though frantic, his efforts between September 1881 and January 1882 were fruitless for three main reasons. First, there was the renewed attempt by the Sultan to interfere in Egyptian affairs in the hope of attaining great control over the country. Second, the European Powers vacillated over supporting a policy that could have maintained law and order and guaranteed their financial interests, in part because of their suspicion that Sharif still harboured a desire for the ex-Khedive's restoration. Third, the Orabi faction in the army never ceased to agitate against the Sharif government, despite the fact that he had for some time been identified with their interests. The Orabists had tasted some power throughout 1881 in their ability to remove and appoint governments, and were now anxious to accede to total power.

Orabist agitation that Egypt was about to fall into European hands as a result of the subservient policy of the Khedive aroused the interest of the Sultan in regaining control over the country. Even if he contemplated the dispatch of an expeditionary force, it would have failed because of French opposition and of the knowlege that Britain would not countenance the deposition of Khedive Tawfiq. The Sultan, therefore, settled for a double-faced diplomatic game by sending two emissaries simultaneously to investigate the situation. One of these, Ali Fuad Bey, was instructed to support the Khedivial forces, and the other, Ali Nizami Pasha, was ordered to attract the Orabist faction. Britain, meanwhile, encouraged Sharif and the Khedive to work for the complete alienation of the Assembly from the Orabists. Unfortunately, Sharif did not possess the sanctions or necessary force to deal with the situation, and the Orabist agitation was able to continue unchecked. In October, Orabi addressed a crowd in Zaqaziq during which he defiantly asserted the need for reform, harangued the audience against the employment of Europeans in the Egyptian government, and threatened to use force to secure these ends. He moreover reminded representatives of the European powers that the army was capable of achieving these aims as effectively and swiftly as they had dictated the acceptance of their demands on two previous occasions, namely, February and September 1881. In short, the Orabists were assuming the role of spokesmen for a national revolution against the Khedive and his European supporters. The Arabic Press meantime sharpened its attacks upon the government. *Misr* and *al-Tijara* set the tone for an Islamic revulsion against infidel influence in Egypt. The decisive action of Sharif – and that of Riad before him – to muzzle the Press only increased his unpopularity.

This was then the situation at the end of 1881: a Khedive humiliated by the army, and the latter now more than ever wishing to assert its authority. Sharif Pasha, a politician motivated to some extent by the necessity for constitutional reform in order to forestall a victory of the Orabists, was anxious to restore the legitimate authority to govern of a discredited executive. Civilian leaders flirted with a more cohesive military conspiratorial group in order to gain leverage against the Khedive, and the Press appealed to the religious sentiment of its readers against the European supporters of the

Viceroy. Whether Sharif could have attracted the ulama, landowners and other elements in the Assembly led by Shahin Pasha, Muhammad Sultan Pasha and *Naqib al-Ashraf* Al-Sayyid Ali al-Bakri to his camp and away from the Orabists is not certain. Nevertheless, in December 1881 he appeared to be holding his own against them and on the way to restoring full control over the situation. But in January 1882, an unsolicited Joint Note from Britain and France assuring the Khedive of their support changed the situation.

Tawfiq Pasha had, on 26 December 1881, formally opened the Assembly, and the response of the delegates to his opening speech indicated a real possibility of close collaboration between them and the Sharif government. Had this possibility materialized it would have isolated the Orabists in the army. The receipt of the Joint Note on 8 January did not only come as a surprise to Sharif, but dealt a serious blow to his efforts to paralyse and isolate the army rebels. The Orabists immediately pointed out the mischievous intent of the Powers in interfering in Egyptian domestic affairs by aiding the establishment of a Khedivial dictatorship. The delegates, on the other hand, lost their capacity to co-operate with Sharif and veered towards a renewed alliance with the Orabists. Indeed, the net effect of the Note was to weaken Sharif, isolate him politically, and render his resignation inevitable. But the Note also made ultimate European military intervention a certainty.[20]

Agitation by Orabists, nationalists – in fact, anti-Khedivists generally – was now possible not only within the limited terms of specific demands for a legislature and a more liberal constitution, but also in terms of opposition to foreign influence in general. Another level of this agitation took the form of Egyptian versus Turco-Circassian preponderance in the army, the administration and particularly the officials of the Court. Even though the Turco-Circassians were as Muslim as the Egyptians, their influence in the government and the army was resented by ambitious Egyptians, and agitation against them was associated with the campaign against all foreign influence upon the Khedive. While his Turkish entourage encouraged Tawfiq to oppose the demands of the Assembly and the Orabists, the latter successfully acquired the support of delegates in pressing their demands. By force, they were able in September–November 1881 to impose Orabi as Deputy Minister of War. In the absence of either European or Ottoman military intervention, the only organized force in Egypt at the beginning of 1882 was the Egyptian Army, and this was controlled by Orabi and his Egyptian colleagues. Having apparently undermined the authority of Sharif Pasha with their Note of January 1882, the European Powers opened the way for a total Orabist victory.

Orabists were disturbed by the cordiality – brief though it was – which marked the early relations between the Assembly and the Sharif government (December 1881). The Note, however, made their task of overthrowing Sharif easier. In February, Tawfiq Pasha had no choice but to ask the Orabist candidate, Burudi, to form a cabinet in which Orabi himself was to serve as Minister of War. The Orabists were victorious at last. Orabi immediately proceeded to strengthen his position in the army further by pushing through mass promotions of Egyptian officers and up-grading their scales of pay. Simultaneously, he sought to bring the Assembly under his control. He forced Barudi to dismiss European officials from the government as a prelude to removing all European influence from Egypt, and in fact, upbraided him for not doing this with celerity and firmness. Undoubtedly Barudi was now to be used as the broom for the Orabist clean-up campaign, and Orabi looked forward to the day when he would succeed Barudi as Prime Minister.

With the mass promotion of Egyptian officers and the general Orabist ride on the wave-crest of success came rumours of Turco-Circassian reaction in the army. An alleged plot to assassinate Orabi and his comrades was uncovered in March and a military council tribunal appointed to try the ringleaders. Some fifty officers were found guilty, among them Osman Rifqi Pasha, ex-Minister of War, and arch-enemy of Orabi. Stiff sentences exiling many of them were passed. This action by Orabi, however, encouraged a general defiance of authority by army ranks throughout the country. These behaved in a disorderly manner in the provinces, terrorizing many inhabitants. It also produced a crisis in the government more serious than any before, for it led to a penultimate show-down between Orabi–Barudi militarists on the one hand, and the Khedive on the other. When Tawfiq Pasha insisted that the sentences passed upon the guilty officers be submitted to the cabinet for review and approval, Orabi refused. Encouraged by the Powers to reject the sentences, the Viceroy compromised by commuting some and lightening others. There was now an open rift between Khedive Tawfiq and the Barudi ministry. It is likely that Barudi would have accepted the compromise were he free of Orabist control. Orabi, instead, urged Barudi to convene the Assembly as a source of added support against, and in further defiance of, the Khedive. Tawfiq objected to the convening of the Assembly without his consent and Barudi resigned on 15 May. The Khedive was now in great danger, short of foreign intervention on his behalf.

Orabi could still use Barudi, and the militarists threatened that they would not be responsible for the maintenance of law and order if the government resigned. Thus, despite the resignation of his favourite Prime Minister, Orabi and the remaining ministers refused to resign. The Assembly delegates, meanwhile, were apprehensive at the turn of events. Rumours circulated that the militarists had met in the home of Orabi to plan the deposition of Khedive Tawfiq, and to exile the ruling family. Counter-rumours of a tribal uprising in support of Tawfiq Pasha confused matters further, leading to a state among the public approaching panic. While the delegates regretted their facile abandonment of Sharif Pasha the previous year and their unwitting exposure to the mercy of Orabists now gone wild, the Viceroy feared for his own personal safety.

The power confrontation between Khedive and Orabist rebels invited an outside arbiter. Fearing a successful bid for power by Orabi assisted by elements in the Assembly, Britain and France saw their financial interests in jeopardy. They accordingly informed the Viceroy of their intention to guarantee his safety and his authority by dispatching an Allied fleet to Egyptian waters. This they were prepared to do on condition that he dismissed the remaining members of the Barudi ministry and recalled Sharif to form a new government. But opposition to the Anglo-French proposals came not only from Orabi but also from the Porte. The Sultan objected to Anglo-French action in Egypt, even if this were intended to protect the Khedive from total defeat and deposition. Evidence that the Sultan encouraged Orabi in his intransigence emerged a few days later.

Realizing that the government would not resign unless the naval units were withdrawn, Britain and France demanded, on 25 May, not only the resignation of the government, but more significantly the temporary retirement of Orabi from Egypt and the withdrawal of his two closest associates, Ali Fahmi and Abd al-Al Hilmi, to the interior of Egypt. Orabi became apprehensive that without support in the country or from the Sultan, his own safety was uncertain. He therefore circulated a document among army officers and the public claiming that the European Powers planned to occupy Egypt. He blamed the Khedive for this, and referred to him as a public enemy and a traitor. The government resigned the following day in protest against the Khedive's betrayal of the country to foreign powers.

Meanwhile, England and France urged the Sultan to join them in support of the Khedive and suggested he send a commission of inquiry to Egypt. To make matters worse, Sharif declined to form a new government in the face of continued Orabist agitation. Deputy ministers were appointed to carry on as acting ministers and the Khedive was precariously poised against an imminent rebellion, led and organized by Orabi. Between May and June 1882, it became quite clear that Orabi could not be suppressed short of foreign power intervention in force.

The army insisted upon its demands for the reappointment of Orabi as Minister of War. When delegates in the Assembly met privately in the home of Sultan Pasha to consider the crisis, Orabi with his troops surrounded the premises, and threatened to storm Abdin Palace and depose Tawfiq Pasha if the delegates refused to support his movement. The delegates were non-committal. Yet they decided to urge the Khedive to restore Orabi to the War Ministry in the hope of curtailing his other activities. This was done on 27 May, and the Powers immediately sought the necessary assurances from Orabi. But the Khedive was not assured of his own safety and, on 31 May, moved to Alexandria to be near the Anglo-French fleet. The return of Orabi to the cabinet did not, however, placate the Orabists who now pushed harder for a total take-over of power. Moreover, Orabi in Cairo was the virtual governor of Egypt. Anticipating aid from Istanbul, he proceeded to strengthen the defences of the country by a series of military measures. These terrified the Assembly delegates who feared that Orabi might expropriate their wealth and property. Christian minorities were seized by a similar fear and started to flee towards Alexandria.

With Orabi in control it appeared as if European efforts to strengthen the Khedive would be ineffective and superfluous. The effect of the apparent triumph of Orabi was to elicit the support of civilian elements, among whom the journalists provided the necessary publicity for his cause. To the public, Orabi was presented as a hero who could rid Egyptian Muslims of foreign control and free them from a heavy debt.[21] Such publicity excited further the frustrations of the poor, ignorant masses and egged them on to commit irresponsible acts of hooliganism.

In this tense atmosphere, communal troubles broke out in Alexandria which culminated in an armed clash between Europeans and

Muslims on 11 June, with considerable loss of life in both communities.[22] It appeared that Orabi's security forces were either unable or unwilling, or both, to contain the mobs. Meanwhile, the Ottoman emissaries, Darwish Pasha and Ahmad Es'ad Effendi, were not able to accomplish very much since their arrival in Egypt on 7 June. As usual, the Sultan continued to play his double game of supporting both parties to the dispute simultaneously. To the Khedive, Darwish Pasha declared he had come to Egypt to strengthen his authority and help him negotiate with the European Powers in the country. He further intimated to the Khedive that he would support him if he proceeded to arrest Orabi and his fellow-rebels, to dissolve the Assembly, and to request a military expedition from Istanbul if necessary. To the Orabists on the other hand – and especially in the case of Es'ad Effendi – the Turkish representatives indicated the Sultan's sympathy and willingness to help them in thwarting the plans of the representatives of foreign powers in Egypt, and in rallying the support of ulama and landowners (including Assembly delegates) for their Sultan and Caliph in Istanbul. The mission of these emissaries was thus, under the circumstances, destined to fail.[23] Orabi was in military control of the country and Darwish Pasha was powerless to do anything. Simultaneously, Orabi continued his preparations for a military confrontation with the European fleet in Alexandria. In this he hoped to attract direct military assistance from Turkey, for he speculated that the Sultan would be loath to see England or France, or both, occupy Egypt. Unfortunately, the military preparations of Orabi also elicted repeated demands from Seymour, Commander of the British naval units in Alexandria, that construction of shore defences be abandoned.

Briefly in early July the consideration of the fate and future of Egypt shifted to Istanbul. In view of the magnitude of the crisis, England at least was anxious to internationalize the Egyptian question by involving more of the interested European states. A Conference of the Powers met in Istanbul on 7 July with the purpose of strengthening the authority of the Porte and the Khedive to restore law and order in Egypt. Knowing that the Khedive preferred Turkish support, the Conference invited the Sultan to send an expeditionary force to Egypt. Sultan Abdul Hamid, however, refused either to participate in the Conference or to send troops to Egypt. His emissaries in Cairo had managed to set up an interim but weak government headed by Ismail Raghib Pasha, and he desperately hoped they would succeed in resolving the crisis. But this government was dominated by Orabi, the Minister of War. While the European conferees in general were anxious to avoid actual intervention in Egypt, Britain persisted in her demands that Orabi be dismissed and Dual Control be restored. She also reserved the right to act to protect British lives and property in Egypt.

The situation in early July was alarming. The Viceroy, Khedive Tawfiq, had taken refuge in Alexandria, stripped of all power and duly terrorized. Orabist troops went about their task of leading a 'national struggle for liberation', conscripting troops, building up defences, and generally lording it over the population. The land-owners and other civilian elements contributed to the financing of the Orabi rebellion apparently more out of fear and less out of confidence in the Orabist cause. A strong British fleet was now poised in Alexandria harbour whose commander was growing daily more impatient in the face of Orabist defiance. A series of ultimata – between 3 and 10 July – to the Orabists to desist from fortifying shore defences and to dismantle gun emplacements had gone unheeded. When England notified the Powers and Turkey that she intended to bombard Alexandria early on 11 July, the French withdrew their naval squadron. At 7 am Sir Beauchamp Seymour (later Lord Alcaster) ordered his ships to open fire. And so began an unintended British military operation that sealed the fate of the Orabists and which left such resentment in Egypt until 1956.

Events now moved quickly. The Khedive urged Orabi not to oppose England. Characteristically, the Colonel ordered general conscription and declared war on Britain. He moreover sought to depose the Khedive. Following the burning of Alexandria and its occupation by British marines, the Khedive was safely installed in Ras el-Tin Palace, in close touch with the British naval command. He immediately decreed the dismissal of Orabi on the grounds of mutiny. Orabi, in turn, secured a religious dispensation, a *fatwa*, signed by three Azhar *shaykhs*, deposing Tawfiq for being a traitor who brought about the foreign occupation of the country and who betrayed his religion. The general directive by Orabi to all provincial governors and district officers demanding financial support, conscripts for the army, and supplies is eloquently traditional: 'to safeguard honour, faith and fatherland is a religious duty. All those who fail in their duty shall be punished according to military law and will be anathematized in this world and in the hereafter.'[24] The Khedive countered this proclamation by declaring the Colonel a rebel, and depriving him of all political rights. 'All who persist in his aid and company would be treated as criminals against God and us.'[25]

As Sir Garnet Wolseley and his army of twenty thousand strong were about to land in August, Egypt had two governments: a Khedivial one whose power and authority were confined to the already British-controlled Alexandria, and the Orabist rebel government in full control of Cairo and the provinces. The latter was not, however, always able to keep the mob, or its own troops, in check, so that massacres and plunder in provincial towns and villages were common occurrences. Sir Garnet was authorized to crush the Orabists by every means and the campaign of clearing the country of rebels began in earnest. Moving quickly along the Canal, British troops were soon in Ismailia and on their way to the fateful encounter in Tel el-Kebir, where on 13 September the Orabists were routed and their movement collapsed.[26]

The military operation was supplemented by a political drive to wean the civilian population away from the Orabist cause. The British Army was declared a Khedivial force which had come to rid Egypt of rebels and to uphold the authority of the legitimate ruler, Tawfiq Pasha. Money was freely distributed among the tribes and provincial landowners to desist from assisting the Orabi forces. By the end of August a government was formed by Sharif Pasha who, upon taking office, insisted that after the authority of the government over the people had been restored a constitution should be drafted. In the meantime, he acted firmly in support of the anti-Orabi operation. Cairo fell to the British Army on 14 September and Orabi and his chief aides, Tulba Ismet and Barudi Pasha, were arrested on the 15th. By 19 September, the Orabist army had been dispersed and the cause, as well as the fate of Orabi, moved to the courts.[27]

THE ORABI REVOLT: A REAPPRAISAL

If the reign of Khedive Ismail engendered so much controversy and attracted so many authors to write about it, the Orabi episode constitutes a watershed in modern Egyptian history. Ismail pawned himself and his country with European creditors to the tune of £98 million and invited European control over Egypt's finances – a constraint in itself not merely on the country's fiscal freedom, but also a serious fetter on its administrative and political freedom of action, too. To this extent he also endangered the dearly bought independence of Egypt from the Ottoman Sultan, and threatened the continued development of social, educational and other projects in the country. Many resources were diverted to, and vast sums strictly earmarked for, the servicing and redemption of loans contracted over a period of twenty to twenty-five years. Since the major powers with the highest financial stake in the bankrupt Egyptian Treasury were England and France, it was inevitable that they should dominate the European supervision of Egypt's finances and administration. Such was the task with which were associated Mr Rivers Wilson, M de Blignieres, Sir Evelyn Baring (later Lord Cromer), Sir Auckland Colvin and Baron de Ring.

Orabi, on the other hand, a simple soldier with ambitions beyond his capabilities, found himself at the head of a military conspiracy against a weak Khedive, misjudged the forces at play, indulged in brinkmanship when confronting superior powers and lost. His, however, was a more disastrous failure, for it ended the autonomy of Egypt and subjected it to occupation by a foreign power for the next seventy-five years.

The period from 1879 to 1882 constitutes one of the best illustrations, or historical case-studies, of complex forces at play; of the impact of imperial rivalries on a society in the process of revival; of the grim consequences of the creation of a 'modern' military establishment in an otherwise weak state, and its involvement in politics. In pure Egyptian terms, the Orabi affair facilitated the ascendancy of the military in the country's political affairs in the absence of an otherwise strong ruler and/or foreign power control. It also nurtured the proclivity to conspiracy – a Mamluk style of politics – and encouraged the dangerous use of soldiers by politicians for their own purposes.

It is therefore instructive to recall the historical experience that was the Orabi episode. Usually one can approximate that, if the evidence is straightforward. However, in the case of the Orabi affair it is not. Like Nasser, seventy years later, Orabi attracted a band of sympathizers, myth-makers and supporters among the rising new generation of liberals of the time, especially in England. The English had not forgotten Byron and Philhellenism or the terrible Turk, 'Abdul the Terrible', with his Balkan and other atrocities. Even in those days, Western liberals had visions of saving the downtrodden of the world. Above all, they were beginning to feel guilty about the vast empire they were acquiring (even though most of the great Black African possessions were yet to come). They were tortured perhaps by their Victorian hypocrisy. Such were the mysterious, engaging W. S. Blunt (whose wife, Anne, was a granddaughter of Byron), Napier, Sir William Gregory and the Swiss Ninet. Yet they took their cue from Gladstone who, throughout most of the century, unlike Palmerston or that presumed arch-imperialist Disraeli, flagellated himself and his Liberal followers over the Empire, injustice in the world and related causes. Ironically, it was under a Liberal government, headed by Gladstone and his astute Foreign Secretary, Lord Granville, that Britain occupied Egypt with the express purpose of restoring the authority of the Khedive and thus sustaining the relationship of Egypt to the Sultan, suppressing the military mutiny of Orabi, and protecting the lives of the European community in Egypt.

When Ismail left Egypt permanently in June 1879, he was remembered for the distressing financial mess he left behind. What is more relevant to our story is the fact that he left behind on the throne a weak son, Tawfiq, at a time when Europeans were bustling anxiously everywhere to lay their lands on the coffers of the State, and when whatever army the Khedive disposed of was in a state of disarray and disaffection – ill-fed, ill-clad and ill-paid. More serious was the fact that Ismail had already injudiciously used that army conspiratorially, earlier that year, in a desperate attempt to get rid of his Prime Minister Nubar Pasha and his mixed Egyptian–European government. While he succeeded in getting rid of Nubar, he failed to escape European control. Meanwhile, he unwittingly permitted his soldiery to discover the advantages of forceful intervention in the affairs of state.

Similarly, for his own purposes, Ismail had devised an incipient legislature as far back as 1866 – the Chamber of Deputies, not to speak of his encouragement of the Press, thus unwittingly providing the conditions for new areas and sources of conflict between the governing, administrative and military classes of the State on one hand and his successors on the other. Shackled by the requirements of Dual Control, abandoned by his suzerain in Istanbul, preyed upon by European power rivalries, plagued by the class-racial antagonism between Turks and Circassians on one hand and lower-class native Egyptian officers in his army on the other, his son Tawfiq was simply unable to cope. In addition, the new landed, commercial and administrative élites created,. promoted and enriched by his great-grandfather's *New Order* were demanding a greater share of power, as well as a bigger slice of the already mortgaged Egyptian cake. Pulled and buffeted by these conflicting forces, Tawfiq tended to be at the mercy of his more forceful subjects and their conspiracies. He dared not solicit the aid of his Turkish suzerain for fear of losing his independence. To submit to the demands of his so-called constitutionalists among his subjects, such as Sharif Pasha and his cohorts in the Chamber, would have meant the erosion of his Orientally conceived power. To give in to the military power of Orabi and his fellow Egyptian officers would have been tantamount to becoming a pawn in the hands of the soldiers. To seek the assistance of the European Powers, as he finally did, entailed, as it turned out, the occupation of his country by foreign forces.

Twice in 1881, in February and September, Orabi and his fellow-colonels extracted from the sovereign concessions involving changes of government, by the threat and use of force. Conceivably, had it not been for the involvement of the European Powers, Tawfiq could have become the head of an Egyptian national movement – or its victim. What is certain is that without the complex and subtle involvement of the Powers, Orabi's movement would not have acquired the dimensions that it did, requiring its suppression by force. The inflexibility of the Khedive, caught as he was on one side between the demands of the rebels, the requirements of European financial control and the intrigues of the Porte on the other, allowed the movement of the colonels and their secret military society to acquire a wider appeal and following among wealthy Egyptians, as well as the lower classes and peasants. Their grievances came to be expressed in a resentment against European financial control as the source of all their ills. Since the source was infidel, the resentment also acquired a religious form, that of Islam versus exploiting Christendom. The precipitate interference of England and France in January 1882 in support of a weak, discredited Khedive constituted in the minds of the rebels further evidence of ill-intentions. And this was equally exploited by the Orabists and the Sultan in Istanbul. Ismail's Pandora's Box of 'modernity' was now wide open, letting out all its *jinn* in their full fury, ranging from religious and racial fanaticism to intimidation, murder and plunder. In the heyday of imperial power, however, there was only one response, that of military intervention.

Nor were the European Powers united over their policy towards Egypt. England stuck to its support of the *status quo* in Egypt, and preferred that Turkey should handle Egyptian disturbances. France was opposed to any Turkish interference in the affairs of Egypt, hoping to come to terms with the military party of Orabi and to avoid complications over her Tunisian venture. Turkey was reluctant to do anything beyond intriguing with all Egyptian groups involved in the hope of retrieving its control over the Egyptian province. In the event, like many episodes in history, a combination of accident and design conspired towards an unexpected outcome, namely, the British occupation of Egypt.

Who was this Colonel Ahmad Orabi who styled himself *al-Misri*, 'the Egyptian'? Was he briefly the leader of a seditious military conspiracy, or mutiny; or was he the heroic standard-bearer of an Egyptian national movement against 'indigenous foreigners' – Turks and Circassians, European interference and an autocratic Khedive? And whether he was one or the other, what were his motives? Needless to say, the popular Egyptian view of him was that of a national hero, even a *mahdi*, who had come to rid Egypt of tyrannical rule and save her from infidel subjugation. To the Europeans in general he represented native fanaticism and heralded the future destruction of their communities in Egypt. To the Khedive he was the crude though popular Egyptian peasant-soldier anxious to relieve him of his job. The Ottoman Sultan considered him a useful rebel who could perhaps, if dextrously manipulated, help him regain control of Egypt. Subsequent Egyptian national movements, that is, those against Britain, did not necessarily consider Orabi a respectable precursor; it was not until 1952 that the successful soldiers under Nasser's leadership implicitly adopted him as a worthy hero and progenitor. The particular élite which came to govern Egypt from 1923 to 1952, especially those of its members who had entered it during the British occupation, did not consider him worthy of a place in their national pantheon.

In its barest outline, the Orabi movement was the outcome of the erosion of Khedivial power, and the imposition of European financial control over the country. It also reflected a weakened Ottoman State and an empire in decline. Yet it was perhaps more fundamentally the by-product of a ruler's modernization policies which required the training of a new generation of natives who later led the opposition to his power and authority. Orabi and his fellow-conspirators, such as Ali Fahmi and Abdel Al, were native Egyptian officers from humble social backgrounds, sons of conservative, traditional, provincial families. They owed their careers and status to the ruler's pleasure who, in his desire to be free of outside control, had to turn to them for assistance. At a certain point, their interest in either curbing the power of their master or wresting it from him converged with similar aspirations on the part of Egyptian landowners, government ministers and religious leaders. That is, it coincided with the emergence of a new constellation of native forces in Egypt.

The first attempts by these officers to challenge constituted authority were not in any way, in 1879, related to national matters. On the contrary, these were conceived with crassly mundane considerations relating to pay, employment and maltreatment. Even in 1881, their bold show of force against the Khedive was primarily intended literally to save their lives from the executioner. It was the fortuitous convergence of greater events having to do with European power rivalries and financial interests which lent Orabi's movement the kind of wider native support it came to have in the spring of 1882.

Undoubtedly, the army and civil bureaucracy resented the Circassians and Turks who occupied the highest posts in the army and the administration, while the natives were relegated to lesser positions. They equally resented the proliferation of European advisers. More generally and vaguely, they resented the known and unknown array of foreign money-lenders who had something more than their Egyptian 'pound of flesh', and were only too obviously resolved to have yet another. In these circumstances, it was relatively easy for Orabi and his friends to point out to the fellah the iniquities and injustices of *Effendina* (the Khedive), especially the taxes he exacted in order to pay those greedy foreigners, and to convince him that there was a good chance of changing all this. In addition – and for good measure – Orabi assumed the role of the champion of Islam, and presented himself ambiguously and alternately as the agent of the Khedive and the defender of the Sultan's prerogative in Egypt against infidel aggression.

Thus in 1879–81 there was an army threatened with a reduction of its ranks, a native official class that detested European interference, a peasantry reeling under taxation, and a privileged class whose privileges were being curbed by European financial controllers. There were privileged foreigners in the country and a Khedive whose power and dignity had been seriously impaired. There was, that is, smouldering discontent among all strata of society and branches of the administration.

A temporary coming together of native soldiers and other Egyptian leaders in the spring of 1882 gave the Orabi affair the appearance of a national movement. It also elicited the sympathy of outsiders, and a campaign in Britain on behalf of Orabi (especially after he lost) reminiscent of contemporary lobbies. Such were the activities of Blunt and his colleagues in arguing the destruction of a genuine national movement in Egypt by the British, a view expressed today not only by Egyptian historians such as Rafii but also by European writers such as Berque and Rowlatt.[28] We have yet, though, to determine accurately whether the Orabi movement was any more than a military mutiny motivated primarily by the bureacratic and personal considerations of the soldiers.[29] At least Sir Edward Malet, HM Agent and Consul-General in Egypt from 1879 to 1883, thought so.[30] So too did Sir Auckland Colvin, Controller-General of Egyptian Finances, and most other officials on the spot.[31] The French were more ambivalent, guided by their aggressive North African policy, their anti-British posture in the East, and their resistance to any re-involvement of Turkey in Egyptian affairs. With regard to the Orabists, one feels they kept their options open, invariably intriguing with several interested parties in the hope of coming out on top in Egypt.

It is certain that by 1882 the Orabists had managed to mobilize the natives against the foreigners, the indeterminate foes of the faith and allies of their oppressor, the Khedive. There are those, on the other hand, who have argued that this was accomplished to a great extent by intimidation and force.[32] As for the temporary alliance between the soldiers and notables, including such ministers as Mahmud Sami Pasha al-Barudi, there is evidence that this was a marriage of convenience. In it lurked the usual mistrust, intrigue and treachery. What is not in doubt is that the Orabists were determined to depose the Khedive, whether with Turkish support or without it. But they had to contend with superior, though hopelessly divided, European power which, in the end, in the shape of British Ironclads and Redcoats, suppressed the Orabi Revolt at Alexandria and Tel el-Kebir.

Orabi was too shallow and incompetent a soldier to succeed in his brinkmanship, not to speak of his and his country's other weaknesses and shortcomings at the time. A perusal of his putative autobiography, edited by his son, as well as his statements, letters and depositions to his lawyers during his trial in December 1882, reveal an unsophisticated though cunning man.[33] His temporary success in 1881–2 tended to inflate his ego and drive him to excessive acts beyond his capacity to manage or control. The writings of Blunt, Broadley, Adams, Baron de Malortie and Dicey all point to a twilight position for Orabi: one between personal resentment and foolish brinkmanship, and a visceral rapport with widespread native discontent.[34]

Francis Adams, for example, argued in 1893 that the peaceful 'just dear little chap' Egyptian would not fight

... until Arabi, who was a fellah himself, and the first one who had risen from the ranks to even such a command as that of colonel of a regiment, came to concentrate the vague hatred and resentment of endless suffering that seethed in the race, and the fellah, still a little dubious, but incontestably appreciative, trickled in to fill up the ranks of the army that was to shed its sweat and blood to give Egypt to the Egyptians.[35]

But did the simple fellah, as Adams claimed, '... The Nilot ... indeed grasp the main features of the situation'?[36] Adams believed that Egyptians under Orabi

shook off temporarily their hereditary instincts of submission, and stood up for a regular, organized struggle. But when it comes to the 'peine forte et dure' their courage fails them. At the anguish of the first blow, the slave in them reasserts himself, and they cry and cower.[37]

He went on to assert that only a miracle could have saved Egypt from the disastrous legacy of Khedive Ismail. Alas, '... whatever else they may call him, no one can call Arabi Pasha a miracle'.[38]

Other English writers of that period were less complimentary to Orabi and his cause. Baron de Malortie, for instance, was only mildly less unkind than that unabashed and polemical imperial publicist, Edward Dicey. In his *Egypt; native rulers and foreign interference* (London 1883), de Malortie lashed out:

Recently some political amateurs tried to produce Arabi in the garb of an enlightened reformer, much noise was made about a so-called national party, we are told of a liberal current, constitutional aspirations, and the usual stock-in-trade of revolutionary *doctrinaires* was duly advertised by complacent dreamers. Misled and misleading, they did a deal of harm. It was wasting sympathy, and as events taught us, a move in the wrong direction; for the Egyptian people are not, and have never been for anything in rebellion, nor can they be made responsible for the crimes of Arabi and his native and foreign accomplices.[39]

A very British view of the day indeed, very much in agreement with Gladstone's Mansion House speech of 10 August 1882, in which the Prime Minister argued 'The absurdity of supposing that the movement in Egypt was a national one, and that Arabi was its soul, has been fully exposed by events.'[40] De Malortie echoed E. Dicey[41] when he said,

Arabi, the *fons et origio mali*, is simply a sanguinary incendiary, an ambitious soldier, dreaming the unsurpation of power, the true representative of military tyranny, ... who managed to make use of the fanatical disposition and credulity of the people for his own selfish ends and with the view of taking his master's place.[42]

Another writer, A.N. Montgomery, accused Orabi of being 'simply an adventurer playing, by the advice of intriguers, with the English people, for his own benefit. His only power is to excite religious fanaticism among the people.'[43] Relying on a widely held British view and some official dispatches, de Malortie opined that Orabi's accession to power would 'have revived the reign of the Mamlukes', and that he would not have dared to speak in the name of the fellah, 'without any other mandate than that of the sword'.

For it is notorious that he has only been able to carry the day by terrorizing the population, ... and by forcing the hand of the Notables, whom he wanted in order to give his acts a semblance and coating of legality.[44]

The nature of the relations between Orabi and the notables in the Egyptian Chamber of Deputies has been the subject of much controversy. Intrigues within the Chamber, as well as the utterances and behaviour of Deputies themselves after the failure of the Orabi revolt, have contributed to the confusion.[45]

In a dispatch to Lord Granville on 5 June 1882, Sir Edward Malet wrote from Cairo:

I have spoken to Sultan Pasha, President of the Chamber of Representatives on the subject, and he has told me that it is idle to deny that the Corporation acted under fear, for that the officers on this occasion went beyond their usual system of taking people separately and threatening them with death. They openly went about the streets in bands, and drove the notables before them. Their violence was such that the heads of the Corporation veritably believed, as they stated to the Khedive, that their lives, and the city itself, were in danger, unless His Highness yielded.[46]

The British view was formed, thus, of Orabi as the intimidating bully, who was reluctantly joined by many of his fellow-countrymen out of fear. De Malortie and other English writers therefore believed that Orabi was simply a mutineer, a bully who might never have been heard of if the rival European powers had not undermined the authority of the Khedive in Egypt. 'Had we not taught Egypt no longer to respect her rulers,' Malortie asserted, 'Arabi never would have been able to carry the population with him in a rebellious enterprise....'[47] He proceeded to criticize short-sighted, greedy European bondholders and Turkish intrigue. 'With such divergent interests, with intrigues in every direction, what was [Khedive] Tawfiq to do?' he asks.[48] He also attacked French inflexibility in the administration of Dual Control. At the end, however, he conceded,

Surely it needed no encouragement from outside; the flagrant wrongs inflicted on men whose bread was dependent on their profession, most of them with no other means of keeping a family, was more than enough to warrant a desperate protest.[49]

These extensive references to some of the English writing about the Orabi affair illustrate in part the feelings prevalent at that time about Orabi and his supporters, and the determination to justify the unexpected British occupation of Egypt.

In contrast to the detractors of Orabi, his supporters in the English-speaking world, chief among them W.S. Blunt, were equally upset at the arrest of the Orabi movement by the British Army. They saw in the Orabi revolt the beginning of a genuine national movement in Egypt. In short, the episode constituted a divisive issue that evoked contrasting sentiment and feeling among Englishmen and Europeans foreshadowing that which surrounded the Suez Affair nearly seventy-five years later.

What we must ask, though, is whether the Orabi episode represents the culmination of the first efforts at modernity in Egypt, or a reaction against it, and the wish to revert to Jacques Berque's native idiom.[50] What is clear is that the movement was neither sophisticated and strong nor clear enough about its political aims to command wholehearted support in order to withstand the then overwhelming force of European imperialism. Yet it is clearly part of the seemingly continuous process of the confrontation between different cultures and clash of civilizations we see occurring from time to time, whether in territorial or other forms. It is rather in the Orabists' defiance of outsiders, not in the nature or content of their movement, that Egyptians eventually came to consider them as precursors of their own nationalist movement in the twentieth century.

In the activities of a mutinous army, 1879–82, the frequent demands for a greater share in power by the representatives of the landed and other propertied classes in the Assembly and the ever bolder criticism and agitation of journalists and publicists, one sees the logical outcome of fifty years of material and social change in Egypt begun by Muhammad Ali the Great, accelerated by his grandson Khedive Ismail and further encouraged by the inexperienced

Khedive Tawfiq. But one also sees the effects of changed circumstances in the weakness of the suzerain Sultan in Istanbul, and the pressing imperial interests of the European Powers.

The defeat of Orabi marked the end of an era and the beginning of another in Egyptian modern history. Turkey's suzerainty over Egypt was diluted further to one of nominal significance so that after 1914 she was never again to be directly concerned with Egyptian affairs. The reform and reconstruction of the Egyptian administration and economy under British tutelage and control meant a further and more rapid fermentation of ideas, and it led to socio-economic change and the emergence of new political conditions. A more severe reappraisal by Egyptians of their own society followed during the period 1882–1914, characterized by a preoccupation with religious and educational reform. Yet the presence of a European great power amidst them moved Egyptians to think and organize in more secular terms. Given a measure of economic advancement and political stability and security, Egyptians now had the time to speculate on their condition and future, and the freedom to talk and write about it. This was followed by a period of intensive mass nationalist activity at the end of the First World War which ended with a measure of independence in 1922. But throughout a forty-year period (1882–1922) Egypt was largely isolated from both its Islamic and Arab neighbours, and its orientation was limited once again to the Egyptian environment.

In this first part of the book we have seen how the Napoleonic invasion opened up Egypt to the influence of Europe. Muhammad Ali soon recognized the efficacy of European methods, borrowed them as well as Europeans themselves, to build a powerful state. His most illustrious successor, Khedive Ismail, sought to transform Egypt socially and economically *via* massive – though more indiscriminate – Europeanization. This cost him money. Money, however, for Ismail was no object; but so was bankruptcy also inevitable. While he lost his throne, Egypt became collateral to a mortgage held by European creditors.

The nineteenth-century legacy of Ismail to Egypt, however, was not confined to a hundred million pounds debt. His social and cultural policy resulted in the first real fermentation of ideas among Egyptians, for foreign money and foreigners in the court of Ismail and in the various state agencies brought with them foreign and attractive ideas. These ideas taught Egyptians that they should seek three political aims: to limit and eventually remove foreign influence from Egypt; to limit the power of the ruler to their advantage; and to achieve power themselves. Gradually, resentment against strong foreign influence was transformed into resentment of the ruler, and a generation of Egyptians conscious of their claim and ability to share in power emerged. By 1880, experience in a legislative body of limited functions and representation, together with expression in crude but often forceful public media, produced a rebellious mood. Unfortunately, neither was the intellectual movement of that time mature enough, nor was leadership adequate to effect change. Possessing force, the army alone was able to produce an ineffectual, temporary explosion.

The Orabi Revolt was thus largely motivated by the personal disaffection and ambition of certain officers in the army who lacked the necessary qualities of leadership. There was no articulate or organized understanding of an Egyptian political entity seeking national emancipation. Such feelings, on the contrary, were confined to, and confused by, religious and communal sentiments. Moreover, European power was paramount. That educated Egyptians in general resented the privileged position of Turkish, Circassian and other foreign court officials and state employees cannot be doubted. That all peasants suffered under the burden of oppressive taxation, forced labour, conscription and widespread injustice is also certain. But whether their resentment was couched in the political conception of national rebellion is another matter. As one Egyptian writer suggested, they rebelled frequently against oppression, tyranny, injustice (*zulm*); not for liberty or freedom.[51]

These conditions did not lead to a political solidarity between disparate elements of the Egyptian population, for the progress and advancement of the more privileged Egyptians in the nineteenth century did not cause them in turn to lead a movement for equality, justice and the alleviation of general economic misery. The sharp division between two separate classes in Egypt continued: peasants on the one hand, and the élite of landowners dominating government on the other. What the revolution was really about was that a new Egyptian bureaucracy, landowners, professionals and army officers wished to replace in power and influence an older Turco-Egyptian aristocracy. Any sympathy the masses may have shown towards this group was not a result of the latter's identity of interests with the former but of that acquiescence which accompanies remoteness from public affairs. The very efforts of rulers to produce an Egyptian state meritocracy – to use a modern term – created conditions of conflict with a lingering non-Egyptian (that is, non-native) palace aristocracy. The revival of Arabic letters and the study of language and literature sharpened the distinction between these two groups as between Arab and non-Arab.

Encouragement of the Press, constitutional experiments, and the importation of European models in general – both in Turkey and Egypt – taught Egyptians for the first time the idea of opposition to a ruler. When the ruler was associated with foreign and religiously alien control, with economic misery and despotic government, the desire for opposition became greater. In European society, however, political enfranchisement was gradual, beginning with the upper cultivated classes and accompanied, as well as buttressed by, socio-economic change. In Egypt the process took a different course. While the influx of ideas in this period was great, the institutional direction of socio-economic change did not really begin until foreign tutelage was direct and complete. Thus, the response of the cultivated Egyptian to disaster in 1882 was reformative and speculative so long as economic and administrative responsibility rested on foreign shoulders. But because his response remained reactive and emulative, we shall see that events overtook and overwhelmed the first modern Egyptian élite of the twentieth century. Like its predecessor in the 1860s and 1870s, this élite too abdicated its social and political leadership to the more forceful and precipitate soldier and militant revolutionary.

Conservative and Liberal Response
to Europe
1882–1914

PART TWO

Conservative and Liberal Response
in Europe
1848–1914

CHAPTER 8

THE BRITISH IN EGYPT

Whoever the Orabi Revolt represented and whatever its aspirations and objectives, it brought about the British occupation of Egypt. This was the incontestable, devastating fact of power in September 1882. Its repercussions and implications, moreover, for Turkey and the European Powers were serious and far-reaching. It generated a new kind of Egyptian Question by the reform of Egypt's finances and administration and the acceleration of a national movement. It changed the nature of the relationship between Egypt and the Sudan, Egypt and Turkey, Egypt and other Arabic-speaking provinces of the Ottoman Empire. It produced a serious crisis and long-term rivalry between Britain and France in Africa, and strained the relations between Egypt and the Ottoman Porte.

Because in some respects the occupation was inadvertent, the abrupt consequence of the concatenation of events in a crisis and the outcome of the intricate convolutions of European power rivalries and diplomacy, it invited criticism and generated controversy. Observe, for instance, the confused scene in 1882: a military revolt in Egypt against the Khedive and foreign interference in the affairs of the country, an Anglo-French policy of retaining control over Egypt's finances, a scheming Sultan in Istanbul aiming to restore his authority over the province, and an on-going conference of the Powers' representatives in Istanbul attempting to arrive at a policy regarding Egypt, from which the Sultan remained studiously aloof at first. Most of the European countries sought mainly to protect their investments in Egypt and retain the capitulatory privileges of their subjects. Occupied by imperial ventures in North Africa, France was anxious to keep the Sultan out of Egyptian affairs. Britain, on the other hand, concerned as she was to safeguard her position in the Indian Ocean and Mediterranean, believed that her interests would be best served by the maintenance of the *status quo* in Egypt and, in the event of sedition, its restoration by collective European, or joint Anglo-French, action, and preferably with the

Sultan's approval; or, if need be, by unilateral action, which turned out to be the case.

It was the paralysis of the de Freycinet government in Paris and its collapse over the Suez Canal Credit Bill which kept France ultimately out of the Egyptian episode in July 1882. Orabi's 'brinkmanship', to use a contemporary expression, misled as he was by Turkish intrigue and Khedivial double-dealing and vacillation, precipitated British naval action against him in Alexandria on 11–14 July 1882. Whatever the immediate reasons for the bombardment, once committed to restore Khedivial authority and the *status quo ante* July 1882, it was inevitable that Britain follow her naval action by the landing of an expeditionary force. Rightly or wrongly, the official British view of Orabi and his movement was that of a military rebellion – a mutiny. This is clear from the copious exchange of dispatches between Sir Edward Malet, the British representative in Cairo, and Lord Granville, the Foreign Secretary, as well as from the debates in both houses of Parliament, including subsequent reports immediately preceding the trial of Orabi and his fellow-conspirators.[1]

By 14 September 1882, there were 10,000 British troops in Cairo. Between Kafr al-Dewar, Tel el-Kebir, Tanta and the Cairo Citadel an Egyptian army of nearly 40,000 men had surrendered to the invaders. The Anglo-Egyptian Question which was to last until the mid-twentieth century had been born with Orabi's trial based on a judicial 'deal' between his English lawyers and Lord Dufferin, special envoy of HM Government in Egypt (and Ambassador to Istanbul), and the controversy it engendered both in Europe and the East.

The first native opposition movement and rebellion against constituted authority had been suppressed by the force of arms of a Christian imperial power with the acquiescence, if not blessing, of the Sultan-Caliph and the Khedive. Its leaders had been tried by court-martial and exiled. The British insistence on a fair trial acceptable to them and their restraint of the native authorities from meting out their known punishment to rebels did not assuage the blow. Nor did it constitute a long-term investment in the future goodwill of Egyptians towards Britain.

In more practical terms the issue was even more complicated. Ostensibly – and soon by clear declaration – Britain occupied Egypt in order to crush the rebels and restore the legal authority of the Khedive. Implicit – and soon explicit – in these terms of reference was the temporary nature of the British mission. Its hopeless anomaly, however, was to emerge soon: that of a European power occupying a province of the Ottoman Padishah by force in order to restore his sovereignty. There was no agreement, specific or otherwise, which defined the British military and administrative presence in Egypt. Nor was the Convention of 1887, signed expressly for that purpose in Istanbul, successful in defining the situation. The Sultan never ratified it.

In the meantime, Lord Dufferin was instructed to

draw up a scheme for the restoration of the country, which would conform to a policy of withdrawing the British garrison at an early date.

In the Report which Lord Dufferin prepared and submitted to HMG, he said,

I cannot conceive anything which would be more fatal to the prosperity and good administration of the country than the hasty and inconsiderate extrusion of a larger proportion of the Europeans in the service of the Government, in deference to the somewhat unfavourable clamour which has been raised against them. For some time to come, European assistance in the various Departments of Egyptian administration will be absolutely necessary.

Observe, however, the vagaries of history, the momentum of a great power which proceeds to an act of incalculable and unforeseen consequences. On 26 December, the train carrying Orabi and his friends to exile in Ceylon left Kasr el-Nil barracks for Port Suez. Anglo-French control over Egyptian finances was discontinued over French protestations. Anglo-French collaboration in other areas of Egyptian affairs collapsed too. The French demanded a clarification of British intentions in Egypt, inaugurating a twenty-year-long hostility to British policy in Egypt, filled with intrigue and marked with pique.

Addressing himself to this situation, Lord Granville issued on 3 January 1883 a circular to the Powers, in which he defined British policy in Egypt as follows:

Although for the present a British force remains in Egypt for the preservation of public tranquillity, HM Government are desirous of withdrawing it as soon as the state of the country and the organization of proper means for the maintenance of the Khedive's authority will admit it. In the meanwhile, the position in which HM Government are placed towards His Highness imposes upon them the duty of giving advice with the object of securing that the order of things to be established shall be of a satisfactory character, and possess the elements of stability and progress.

To describe the intention of a short-lived military occupation on one hand, and the proclaimed objective of reforming and reorganizing the Egyptian government on the other as contradictory policies would be an understatement. For, as the astute Lord Dufferin realized, desired reform could not be effected unless the British occupation was prolonged indefinitely and evacuation postponed *sine die*.

On 6 February 1883, Lord Dufferin submitted his famous Report on the reorganization of the Egyptian government. Lord Cromer arrived in Cairo from India on 11 September to assume his duties as British Agent and Consul-General, three days short of a year after Lord Wolseley and a detachment of Guards triumphantly marched from Abbassia into Cairo. Queen Victoria addressed the reassembled Parliament soon thereafter that year. After reviewing briefly the expeditious suppression of the Orabi Revolt and suggesting that tranquillity had been restored, Her Majesty asserted,

and the withdrawal of the British troops is proceeding as expeditiously as a prudent consideration of the circumstances will admit.

The Queen, however, had spoken too soon, for disaster had struck in the Sudan where the Mahdi's rebel forces annihilated an Egyptian Army expeditionary force commanded by General Hicks Pasha. Two years later, Khartoum fell to the Mahdist forces and Gordon Pasha perished. The Queen was therefore forced to declare on a subsequent occasion,

While an unforeseen and calamitous necessity has thus required me to suspend the measure I had adopted, the aim of my occupation, which has been explained to you at former times, continues without change.

In short, a notorious historical contradiction had been born, namely, the myth of the temporary nature of the British occupation of Egypt which, in fact, was to be determined by two overriding considerations: progress in the reform of Egyptian administration, and the requirements of British imperial policy (at that time nearly global in magnitude) which, in turn, depended on the changing conditions of a new Anglo-Egyptian relationship. The nature and course of this relationship were largely determined by the stewardship of one man, Lord Cromer, better known to the average Egyptian as *El Lurd*. His career, which spanned twenty-four years, from September 1883 to May 1907, straddled the reigns of two British monarchs, two Khedives in Egypt, and the rise of an important historical Egyptian generation, many of whose members were his creatures, but who were to lead the opposition against the British occupation of their country under the banner of a 'bourgeois', European-style national movement. These were the Abduhs, Lutfi al-Sayyids, Zaghluls, Mustafa Kamils and their colleagues.[2]

Most of Cromer's previous experience had been in the administration of financial affairs, first in the Dual Control of Egypt and later as virtual finance minister in the government of India. Austere, though undoubting and self-assured, he approached matters of government and administration from a neat bookkeeping point of view. Such an approach tended to depoliticize politics and reduce all human affairs to questions of proper administration.[3]

While an intense and bitter controversy raged around him as to whether it would be more practical for the restoration of order and authority in Egypt that Britain proclaim a protectorate over the country her troops had just occupied, whether to carry on as before, or to evacuate and abandon the country altogether, Cromer methodically went about his task of making Egypt solvent and infusing a minimum of orderly administration in its affairs. He gave first priority to the balancing of the books. All else, in his view, was secondary. His attachment to the Indian pattern of creating a native civil service below a layer of British advisers was fastidious.[4]

Unlike India, however, Egypt was shackled by international arrangements and obligations which restricted any administration's freedom of action. It was this disability, more than any other, which Cromer set out with great determination to neutralize or overcome and preferably remove. In the long process of doing so, he transformed himself from an Agent-General appointed rather vaguely to advise and assist the Egyptians in reforming their government to their political master and virtual ruler. The British government, after all, had declared their policy to be one of speedy evacuation as soon as the necessary reforms had been carried out. But it fell to the lot of Lord Cromer to show the British government and Europe that it was impossible to discharge those responsibilities except by a slow and laborious policy of reconstruction. It was from that slowness that Cromer derived his supreme and unchallenged authority in Egypt. It was equally from that slowness that Mustafa Kamil, Saad Zaghlul and other Egyptian national leaders extracted their mandate to lead an independence movement.

To reform Egypt also meant to curb the capitulatory privileges of Europeans as regards taxation, judicial advantages and other extra-territorial prerogatives. To this extent Cromer sought inadvertently, by force of circumstances and the requirements of his policy, to free Egypt of these fetters and thus push her a step further towards independence. In his desire to keep the Turks and other European Powers out of Egypt's affairs, or from tampering with their reform, he virtually detached Egypt from Turkey and invited open French hostility until 1904. Once he had undertaken, under public pressure in Britain, to suppress the Mahdist movement in the Sudan and dilute Egyptian control over that country, he effected, by accident or design, the virtual detachment of those provinces from Egypt under the Condominium (1899), and inadvertently laid the foundations of the Sudanese nationalist independence movement in the twentieth century.

By his policies, actions and fervent belief in his reforming mission, Cromer came to formulate a British policy based on the premiss that Britain must remain in Egypt in order to keep others out and to enable her policy of reform to bear fruit. With the passage of time, the necessity of British control – at least in British eyes – became clear, and Cromer secured a free hand in ruling the country. France's hopes of dominating Egypt thus dashed, she embarked upon a hostile policy towards Britain in that country. Thus when a new national movement led by Mustafa Kamil appeared at the turn of the century, France exploited it with alacrity in the hope of regaining her lost position.

Throughout the first twenty years of the occupation, and more so later, executive authority in the country was left in the hands of Egyptians, organized in government departments and ministries. Yet political control remained exclusively in British hands. Whereas by the 1890s the country's finances had been complete rehabilitated, extensive reforms in irrigation, administration and education had been successfully introduced and the concern with Islamic regeneration dulled, the fact remained that Cromer's 'miracle' in the final analysis was possible because lurking in the background was a British garrison – the ultimate military sanction.

The combination of French hostility and intrigue until 1904, expanded education and administrative experience among Egyptians, and the imperiousness of *El Lurd* provoked native opposition to alien rule and fostered among some Egyptians the aspiration to self-government. The Aqaba, or Taba, incident and the Denshawai affair in 1906–7 promoted the first secular nationalist agitation in the country, led by Mustafa Kamil's National party and the Umma–Jarida group of the Western-educated new administrative class of Egyptians. British and French influences in education were the harbingers of a European-inspired nationalism, quite different from that of the Orabists. The accession to the Khedivial throne of the eighteen-year-old Vienna-educated Abbas Hilmi, son of Tawfiq, who was cocky, arrogant and autocratic, quick to grasp the intricacies of diabolical court intrigue, led to hysterical clashes between him and the Old Man of the Agency.[5] Political agitators, such as Sheikh Ali Yusuf with his newspaper *al-Muayyad*, Mustafa Kamil with his *al-Liwa'* and a host of other publications which mushroomed in a period of relative though characteristic British toleration, sang the tunes of independence.

Unfortunately for these rising Egyptian forces Europe by 1904 had recognized Britain as the protecting, dominant power in Egypt. Imperialism, that is, had hardened, a situation which rendered the British presence and task in Egypt 'easier' or less sinful. The combination, however, of a liberal revival in Britain and a terrible economic recession in 1906-7 spelled the end of Cromer's career in Egypt. It was time for him to go; and he did on 6 May 1907. After that, the task of his successors, Sir Eldon Gorst and Lord Kitchener, was to carry on the further administration of the country, while somehow satisfying rising Egyptian demands for a greater share in government and political control. The Great War intervened, producing a short-lived Protectorate which could not be sustained for long, until the unilateral Declaration of February 1922 proclaimed the country's independence in a special treaty relationship with Britain.

The vexing problem which confronted Gorst, Kitchener and later Allenby in Egypt arose from the fact that British policy had been based on the inevitable contradiction of preparing Egyptians for self-government while in the meantime helping them to enjoy the benefits of good British-supervised government. The latter objective was perhaps attained by the end of Cromer's term in Egypt. The former could not be withheld for too long. Cromer's successors had to deal with a new factor, even force, in Egyptian affairs which had not really developed before their arrival on the scene. Egyptian nationalism asserted itself in such a way that the policy of ruling the country in co-operation with Egyptian ministers became incompatible with that of encouraging the development of representative institutions, such as the Legislative Council and General Assembly. The complex, ailing Gorst and the imperious Kitchener in a way found themselves between the devil of Egyptian nationalism demands for greater autonomy and the deep blue sea of privileged Europeans who considered any further concessions to the Egyptians a mark of weakness.

Nevertheless, Cromer towards the end of his term seemed to encourage the newly educated professional and administrative élite of

Egyptians, the secularists, or those Jamal Ahmed has called the Girondists,[6] in their national aspirations. After all, Saad Zaghlul, the leader of the modern Egyptian nationalist movement and first elected prime minister of the new Kingdom of Egypt in 1923, was his protégé. Political parties were the result, and these represented the interests of and were dominated by the landowning and educated official élite of Egyptians who, between 1907 and 1919, promoted themselves into the governing class of independent Egypt between 1923 and 1952.[7]

What did the Egyptians think of Cromer? Clearly, there was a love–hate relationship between them and *El Lurd*.[8] English writers and administrators have capitalized on the proposition that their hegemony over Egypt helped free the fellah from the shackles and excesses of 'oriental despotism' and the burdens of proverbially traditional misery. They cite impressive achievements in irrigation and public works, Kitchener's famous Five Feddan Law, fiscal reform, provincial and local government improvements and innovations. As for the more educated clases of Egyptians, they point to their prosperity and political advancement under British tutelage. The Egyptians, on the other hand, have complained of British neglect of education and their exclusion from a fair share in the control of their country's political affairs.

Perhaps Britain's cardinal mistake and therefore predicament lay in her perpetuation of a vague justification for her presence and an ambivalent basis for her position in Egypt.[9] Before 1914, Egypt was not a protectorate of Britain. Nor was she ever a British colony or dominion. Britain in Egypt was simply, though significantly, a *presence* astride the Suez Canal and the route to India. England, it seems, came to Egypt – and eventually the rest of the Middle East – because she was in India, no more, no less. Cotton for Lancashire mills and the rest of the economic 'sorcery' was a mere though beneficient by-product of this crude reality of power.

Despite the fact that without the British presence – even experience – it is unlikely the Egyptian national movement would have developed as rapidly, and despite the British concern for the fellah for nearly forty years, when the Great War ended and came 1919, the explosion of the native uprising engulfed the whole country and was surprising perhaps to some in its bitterness. Hardship and poverty pushed the fellah to rebellion. Frustrated aspirations and bitter resentment prompted the new class of lay educated Egyptian

professionals and administrators, as well as landowners, to lead
the lower classes of townsmen and peasants in a national revolt.

Egyptians, in short – at least the aspiring and more articulate among
them, many of whom were also the beneficiaries of British tutelage
– wanted their country back. They were now alienated from their
tutors and mentors; they believed their apprenticeship was complete.

CHAPTER 9

JOURNALISM AND THE PRESS

Although certain kinds of firearms invented and developed in Christian Europe were readily accepted by Muslims to fight Holy Wars, printing was not, for with it would have followed infidel ideas that might undermine Islam. Thus, it is reported:

when Jewish refugees from Spain asked Bayezid II for permission to set up printing presses in Turkey, he consented on condition that they did not print any books in Turkish or Arabic, and confined themselves to Hebrew and European languages.[1]

By the end of the fifteenth century Jewish refugees from Spain had set up printing presses in a Muslim land. These were followed by other religious minorities – Armenians and Greeks – who set up their own. Some two hundred and fifty years later, in 1727, dispensation was received from the Shaykh al-Islam permitting the Sultan to authorize the printing of books in Turkish, and thus the setting up of the first Turkish press in Instanbul. The first book appeared in 1729.[2]

No such difficulties of religious, or other, opposition were encountered in Egypt. We noted earlier that the French conquerors not only brought with them a printing press, but that they soon inaugurated an official periodical press in order to keep the troops informed about events and the public *au courant* with policy and legislation. They also published a scholarly journal as an outlet for the findings of French scientists working in Egypt. Twenty years later Muhammad Ali founded the Government Printing Press at Bulaq.

The tradition of journalism in Egypt is one of the most long-established in the Arab world.[3] The early start given to the Press by Napoleon and subsequently by Muhammad Ali and Ismail afforded Egypt later a certain advantage in cultural, social and intellectual development among Arabic-speaking countries. The Egyptian Press has played since 1882 a leading role in publicizing and propagating the ideas of Muslim and, later Arab, emancipation movements, ranging from Pan-Islamism to demands for local independence among Arab groups everywhere. Views on the revival,

reform and unity of the Islamic community were promoted earlier
in this century through the Press, so that Muslim, Arab and peculiarly Egyptian tendencies regarding nationalism and other political
movements are reflected in the evolution of the Press in Egypt. It
was mainly through the Press that the evolution of modern Arabic
writing and literature occurred in the last hundred years. Leading
early writers were also publicists who wrote mainly for newspapers
and magazines. Their books, for a long time, were collections of their
newspaper and magazine articles.

The Press also played an important role in adapting classical
Arabic to the requirements of modern times, leading to the rise of
neo-classical literary movements. It helped transform a difficult
'dead' language into a reasonably flexible means of public communication.[4] In short, the Press performed the functions of a popular
teacher in spreading a new national language and culture that were
more attuned to the needs of an evolving society. Especially since
1900, the Press in Egypt has reflected the conflict between conservative and modernist tendencies in social thought and life. It has served
as a medium for the propagation of new ideas and movements for
social, economic and political reform, feminism, secular liberalism,
religious conservatism, trade unionism and so on. In practically no
other Arab country has the Press been as significant and crucial a
part of modern developments as it has in Egypt from the nineteenth
century until 1952 at least.

Until 1882, the embryonic Egyptian Press was crude, experimental,
didactic. Moreover, it was often official, that is, it was begun and
largely financed by the ruler and the State. Only during the British
occupation and until 1914, did the Egyptian Press come of age to
concern itself with the public debate of social, economic and political
issues. In the inter-war period (1919–39), the Press in Egypt
became more strictly partisan when political parties published their
own newspapers and magazines as essential media for the prosecution of their party political ends. After 1952, and with the demise
of parliamentary institutions, including political parties, the Press,
along with other more modern mass media, became an arm of the
state propaganda machine. All the same, it was through the Press
that generations of writers were trained in modern Egypt. Just as
significant was the emergence of a new profession – journalism –
and thus a new source of livelihood for writers.

To the extent that literature can reflect social phenomena, the rise
and development of the Egyptian Press constitutes an important

mirror of the evolution of modern Egypt. It is through these media that one can identify the beginnings of a modern Arab literature in terms of style, and the influence of European ideas as interpreted – or mis-interpreted – by leaders of Egyptian letters and opinion. A journalistic political prose opened immense possibilities for clearer and more precise expression on various social and political questions of the times through the famous *maqal*, or feature article and 'leader', in the newspapers. Style moreover was affected by modern notions of time and space: the hunger for world news so prominent among Egyptians in the 1877 Russo-Turkish war in which Egyptian troops were committed was satisfied by the use of the telegraph for rapid newsgathering. Although the telegraph came to Egypt in 1854, its use by newspapers did not begin until the 1870s, especially by such papers as *al-Ahram*. Reporters' deadlines and the composition of news stories from telegraphic dispatches introduced a new Arabic prose style that is so widely associated with newspapers today. The change in, and ferment of, ideas was thus strengthened by the parallel change in, and development of, their expression in the Press, and particularly as the latter was in turn affected by technological changes in communications and the dissemination of information.[5]

Europeans introduced printing to Egypt. But the evolution of the Press and the rise of a journalistic profession are connected with the response of a ruler like Ismail and his government to new conditions. Specific acts of policy in the 1860s and 1870s – the Assembly of Delegates in 1866; the reform of the judiciary under the leadership of Nubar Pasha and the erection of the Mixed Tribunals in 1876 both to mitigate the effects on Egypt of the privileged status of Europeans under the Capitulations and to curb the power of the Khedive; the Dual Control of England and France over Egyptian finances; the Constitution of 1881–2; all these helped the wider development of the Press and the emergence of an enlightened public opinion on matters of state policy and local and international issues of finance and politics. The cultural and intellectual renaissance of the period 1860–80, encouraged by Ismail, provided the favourable climate for the growth of these public media of communication. The efforts of its first pioneers, especially during the reign of Ismail, were largely responsible for the establishment of the Press as a permanent feature of Egyptian life and society.

Before Khedive Ismail came to the throne in 1863, the Press in Egypt was, like most other things, an official press of the State, limited to the publication of an *Official Gazette*.[6] The administrative reform of Muhammad Ali in 1813 affecting the army, agriculture and industry required weekly reports to be made to the Viceroy by the various departments of the government in Cairo and the provinces. Soon these reports were being published and circulated among state officials. This, essentially, was the beginning of the *Gazette*. A reorganization of the *Diwan*, or office responsible for the editing and publication of the *Gazette*, occurred in 1826 when Shaykh Hasan al-Attar was appointed its editor. Its circulation was extended to the ulama, state school pupils, armed forces in Egypt and those serving abroad (Crete, Syria, the Sudan), as well as to Egyptian students pursuing higher studies in Europe. It was intended to acquaint these people with government policy, give them news of government officials, and so on. Leading figures in education and literature, such as Rifaa al-Tahtawi, Adham Bey and Admad Faris al-Shidyaq, took a hand in editing the *Gazette* at some time or another. Indeed, they improved the quality of its Arabic, the selection of topics they wrote about, and news coverage. Much of this improvement was achieved under the editorship of Tahtawi.

During the reign of Muhammad Ali no one attempted to publish an independent newspaper or journal. The Press at this stage remained an exclusively state venture. Yet those directly active in the various departments of state gradually became accustomed to the usefulness of a press, despite its official character. In the period 1830–49, Muhammad Ali experimented with the publication of a military newspaper, as well as with a trade and commerce journal. Neither of these was successful and, under his successors Abbas I and Said Pasha, these early experiments in journalism were discontinued.

The revived and wider journalistic activity in Egypt during the reign of Ismail was initially inspired and financed by the Viceroy himself. In part, Ismail's encouragement of the Press was an aspect of his policy to promote his cause both at home and abroad; and in part it was an attempt to counter his detractors both domestic and foreign. Arabic papers had by then appeared in Beirut and Istanbul with Ottoman official backing and support. The most prominent and successful in terms of wide circulation throughout the Arabic-speaking countries of the Empire as far west as North Africa was *al-Jawa'ib*, edited by Ahmad Faris al-Shidyaq (1801–87). A Christian Syrian convert to Islam, Shidyaq launched his pro-Islamic paper in Istanbul in July 1862 and for twenty years after that it enjoyed the greatest circulation of any Arabic publication. It consistently defended the Ottoman Sultan and Muslim rulers generally against mounting European encroachments. Thus, Shidyaq defended Ismail when he was deposed in 1879. The paper was discontinued in 1884.[7]

In order to secure greater support among Egyptians in his diplomatic struggle for greater independence from Turkey, and in order to arouse local opinion against European financial control, Ismail experimented with a variety of institutions. In 1866, with the creation of an Assembly of Delegates, he financed the publication of the first political newspaper, *Wadi al-Nil*, to serve as a mouthpiece for his policy. He appointed its first editor, Abdullah Effendi Abu al-Su'ud, a graduate of the School of Languages which was directed by Tahtawi. Published twice a week, *Wadi al-Nil* defended the policies of the Khedive against its detractors. In the educational and cultural fields the Khedive financed and supported professional academic journals related to the activities of the first Egyptian intellectuals, teachers, scientists and officials. Such was the medical journal, *Ya'sub al-tibb* (1865), and the educational–pedagogic journal *Rawdat al-madaris* (1870) directed by Ali Pasha Mubarak, and edited by Tahtawi. Even the army published its own paper, *Al-jarida al-askariyya* and, by 1874, there was a paper of the Army General Staff, *Jaridat arkan harb al-jaysh al-misri*.

European-trained Egyptian state officials, writers and literati were being given the opportunity to express certain views publicly and gradually to influence the formation of a public opinion – limited as this obviously must have been – about matters concerning the relationship of Egypt to the Ottoman Sultan, and the position of the country in the face of increasing European financial control. Just as wider public interest in the Crimean War (1854–6) and its aftermath was a factor in the further development of the Press in Turkey, so also in Egypt interest in news of events in Europe, wars and treaties was a factor in a similar development. Soon the reaction of certain prominent Egyptians in government to the policies of the Khedive were being expressed in the 1870s in the Press for the first time.

Prominent writers like Adib Ishaq, Salim al-Naqqash, Ibrahim al-Muwailihi, Othman Galal and many others now had at their disposal not only a literary outlet but also a forum for the expression of their ideas on various subjects of the day. Despite their continued loyalty to the Islamic character of the Ottoman sultanate–caliphate, these early journalists and publicists were helping to lay the foundations of a stronger Egyptian identity which assisted the local ruling house in its demands for further separation and greater independence from Turkey. Furthermore, they were breaking the ground for the movement away from traditional learning, writing and social thought. The introduction of the 'editorial' to express, develop and argue a single idea clearly, briefly and logically was a far cry from the tortuous and encyclopedic ramblings of earlier traditional writing. More significant was the fact that these journalists were introducing Egyptians to an articulate means of criticizing established authority. Later, it was in the Press that major reform ideas were first presented: the religious reform ideas of Shaykh Muhammad Abduh, the nationalist movements of Mustafa Kamil and Saad Zaghlul, and many others. In fact, between 1900 and 1950 literate Egyptians did not as a matter of course read books; they read newspapers, magazines and periodicals. Significantly, Egyptians were introduced to the rationalism and pragmatism of European science via the Press which, after 1882, was led both by Egyptians and Syrians.[8] A direct consequence of this early journalistic activity was the appearance of private publishing companies owned and directed by Egyptian newspaper publishers and editors, so that the commercial publishing business also had its beginning in this period.

The role and contribution of Syrian émigrés in the development of Egyptian journalism did not become prominent until after the British occupation. The events of 1860 in Lebanon and the subsequent Ottoman repressive policy there drove many Syrian men of letters to Egypt. Men like Adib Ishaq and Salim al-Naqqash were followed by others like the Taqla brothers, Faris Nimr and Ya'qub Sarruf. The famous *al-Ahram*,[9] founded in Alexandria in 1875 by the Taqla brothers from Lebanon, did not achieve its leading position among the independent papers until later in the twentieth century. At its inception it was generally pro-Ottoman and upheld the policy of the Khedive. It was however the first newspaper to use the telegraph for the gathering of external news. It also introduced extensive advertising in its pages.

The appearance of the religious–political agitator Jamal al-Din al-Afghani in Egypt in 1871–9 inspired in part the earliest protest movements against the ruling dynasty, especially when European financial control was established in 1876, and gave a push to the non-governmental, non-official Press. The Syrian Salim al-Naqqash, for instance, founded in 1877 the weekly *Jaridat Misr*, edited by his fellow-Syrian Adib Ishaq, to oppose European control. This he followed with another daily, *Tijara*, which was suppressed by Riad Pasha in 1879. In 1880, Adib Ishaq published in Paris a paper, *Misr al-qahira*, in which he attacked the new Khedive Tawfiq. About the same time, the notorious Jacob (James) Sanua, mentioned in an earlier chapter in connection with the theatre, published his *Mir'at al-ahwal* in 1876, in which he heaped abuse upon Khedive Ismail. The following year (1877) his famous *Abu Naddara*, the first satirical paper written in the vernacular of Egypt, appeared in Cairo.[10] Expelled from the country by Ismail, Sanua went to Paris where he continued to publish several variations upon his *Abu Naddara* theme until his death in 1912. In 1879, Salim Anhuri founded *Mir'at al-Sharq*, edited by Ibrahim al-Laqqani, another Afghani follower. All these papers disappeared after a short life.

The Coptic minority was encouraged in the same period to publish its own newspaper, *al-Watan*, in 1877, edited by Mikhail Abd al-Sayyid. Foreign language newspapers, mainly French, were also founded, such as *Progrés*, *L'Egypte*, *Le Phare d'Alexandrie*.

The Orabi Revolt at the beginning of the next decade marked a turning point in the evolution of the Press, and so did the British occupation which followed it. Although unsuccessful, the Orabi Revolt marked the beginning of political agitation on a mass scale in modern Egypt. Right or wrong, a genuine nationalist revolt or not, the Press in Egypt reflected partisan views for the first time: pro-Orabi, anti-Orabi and pro-Khedive, and soon thereafter, pro-British and anti-British.

Parallel to the increased political activity of Assembly members against the Khedivial government and the forceful intervention of Orabi militarists in the affairs of state, was an outspoken agitation in the embryonic Press. By 1877–9, the Syrians Adib Ishaq and Salim al-Naqqash rendered their papers, named earlier, a platform for those opposed to foreign control of Egyptian affairs. In 1881, the legendary orator of the Orabi Revolt, Abdullah al-Nadim, was calling for the support of Orabi against the Khedive Tawfiq and the Europeans in his newspaper *al-Ta'if*.

Also during the Orabi rebellion certain short-lived newspapers such as *Misr al-fatat*, *al-Mahrusa* and *al-Mufid* supported the Orabists, attacked the presence of European financial controllers in the country and the Khedivial administration that harboured them. Tawfiq tried temporarily to counter the inimical Press by launching his own papers, of which *al-Burhan*, edited by the conservative Shaykh Hamza Fathallah, was an example. It should also be noted that the influx into Egypt of Syrian journalists after 1860 was not limited to revolutionaries, for the famous Taqla brothers published the *Ahram* as a moderate paper, respectful of the Sultan and sympathetic to the Khedive.

Until the financial recovery and economic expansion achieved during the first twenty-five years of the British occupation, and until the confrontation between a superior European power and Egyptians aspiring to independence was sharpened, the Press remained rather primitive. Most Egyptian historians have asserted that even at this stage of its development the Press was an instrument of nationalist agitation for an independent Egyptian state. The assertion is premature and imprecise. When one peruses the contents of many of these short-lived newspapers and magazines whether published in Egypt at the time or in exile, it is difficult to distinguish their general Islamic–Ottoman orientation from a strictly Egyptian nationalist tone. Orabi emerges first as a leader opposed to the Khedive because the latter appeared to favour European, that is, infidel, intervention in Egypt. Later, all these papers, especially some of their leading editors – Adib Ishaq, Salim al-Naqqash and Abdullah al-Nadim – deplore Orabi and his movement in no uncertain terms, and uphold the Egyptian connection with the Sultan–Caliph in Istanbul. In fact, the religious bias of the Press became most prominent in the 1890s and continued until the outbreak of the First World War.[11]

Adib Ishaq (1856–85) who, along with Salim al-Naqqash, briefly supported the Orabists, left a collection of Essays called *Selections* (*al-Muntakhabat*) in four volumes,[12] on a variety of subjects. Despite these essays, many contemporary Arab writers have hailed Ishaq as a leading Arab nationalist. In fact, by his own admission, he was a loyal Ottomanist who believed in the support of the Sultan, especially against the imperialist ambitions of the Russians.[13] In defining the nation, Ishaq argues against the linguistic bond in order to support Ottoman patriotism and loyalty. 'A nation-state (*al-umma*) is a group of people that becomes one ethnos with characteristics peculiar to it regardless of the different racial origins and linguistic differences among the people in it. It becomes known by one name to which all belong and which all defend.'[14] On the other hand, Ishaq was generally influenced by his reading about the French Revolution to write on freedom, the rights and duties of citizens and related subjects.

Al-Naqqash, who is usually credited with coining the expression 'Egypt for the Egyptians', emerges from his collected articles as anti-militarist, for he considered Orabi and his army colleagues incompetent.[15]

By 1895, a clear division in the Egyptian Press emerged. On one side stood the papers and magazines edited and published by Christian Syrian émigrés, prominent among which were the dailies *al-Muqattam* and *al-Ahram*, and the weekly *al-Muqtataf*. The Syrians Nimr and Sarruf, educated in Protestant missionary colleges in Beirut, first published their weekly *al-Muqtataf* with a view to disseminating progressive reform ideas which could serve as the basis for a secular national independence movement. Soon, however, their daily *al-Muqattam* came to be identified with British policy in Egypt, partly because Sarruf and Nimr subscribed to the idea that a stable administration, influenced and checked by an advanced European power, was the best road to reform. *Al-Ahram* of the Taqla brothers was initially critical of British policy and in favour of a continued link between an Egypt ruled by the Khedive and the Sultan in Istanbul.

Other Syrians turned their attention to literary and educational reform. Ephemeral illustrated weeklies, *al-Sharq* of Shidyaq, *Arghul* of Muhammad Najjar and *al-Mushir* of Salim Sarkis, appeared in the 1890s. Of great importance though was the founding of the monthly *al-Hilal* by Jurji Zaydan. A self-taught historian, Zaydan brought to journalism advanced techniques, and a consistently eminent presentation of contemporary educational and social problems. Besides innumerable historical romances, Zaydan produced a five-volume history of Islamic civilization, popularized the Arab–Islamic heritage, and awakened his readers to the epic nature of the Islamic success in history. In giving his magazine the title *al-Hilal* (The Crescent), Zaydan perhaps emphasized his intention to seek a rapprochement between Muslim and non-Muslim Arabs in the common cause of Arab regeneration and reform. For this he permitted writers from both religious communities to air their views on a variety of subjects and to seek greater toleration. He was assisted in this to some extent by the work of another Syrian, Farah Antoun, whose magazine *al-Jami'a* published debates between members of the Muslim and Christian communities. Despite his premature death in 1914, Zaydan was in fact most instrumental in paving the way for the reconciliation between conservative Muslim reformists (the school of Muhammad Abduh disciples) and secular modernists which prevailed in 1914.[16]

Yet, on the other side, there appeared a number of newspapers and magazines which clearly represented the conservative Muslim point of view. As such these were also anti-British and claimed to speak for the masses of Egyptians. Most prominent among these was *al Mu'ayyad*, edited by Shaykh Ali Yusuf. Until the appearance of *al-Liwa'* of Mustafa Kamil, the *Mu'ayyad* was, between 1890 and 1900, the major platform for nationalist writers. It was not merely poised against the Syrian Christian émigrés, but was also opposed to the reformed Islam preached by Muhammad Abduh in his writings and as editor of the *Official Newspaper*. Ali Yusuf received financial support from Khedive Tawfiq and later from Khedive Abbas. He preached and supported the interests of Pan-Islamism from Morocco to India. Yet his paper permitted the training of many Muslim Egyptian journalists who very soon came to dominate the field and outnumber the Syrians. It also gradually encouraged the appearance between 1890 and 1900 of more papers representing Islamic interests. Prominent among these was the weekly *al-Ustadh*, founded and edited by Abdullah al-Nadim in 1892–3. From an orator of the Orabi rebellion Nadim in his weekly turned into a reforming educational writer.[17]

Finally the Press became not only a public opinion-maker in the political sense, but a school for the evolution of a modern literary Arabic language, an upbringer of a new generation that was to wrest leadership in the twentieth century from the more traditional Egyptian. It also gave Egypt its more recent Arab orientation and its advantage over other Arabs in the development and expert use of mass media. It seemed inevitable that under the creative impetus of the Khedive Ismail era in the Egyptian renaissance, the Press would flourish. It represented an integral part of the legacy of the first Egyptian intellectuals and reformers. It soon took a leading part in the social and cultural development of the country when in the next fifty years it came to reflect many of the social and political developments which characterize modern Egypt.

The Declaration of Independence for Egypt in February 1922 was a unilateral British act. To be sure, riots, assassinations, sabotage, demonstrations and the popular uprising in the 1919 revolt played an intermittent role between 1900 and 1922, but no great number of Egyptians took up arms against the British occupying forces. The topography of Egypt of course has never permitted such overt military activities, or armed uprisings. In the circumstances, the Press, not the firearm, was the best available weapon. It was particularly effective against an adversary who permitted its use and was affected by it.

CHAPTER 10

RELIGIOUS REFORM AND ISLAMIC POLITICAL SENTIMENT

Reaction among educated Egyptians to the British occupation was not altogether one of enmity. A revulsion at the bungling ways of an army-led revolt in 1881–2 which led to foreign occupation caused many Muslim leaders to question the strength of Islamic institutions and to seek to reform them in such a way as to render them viable in the modern world. They realized that Khedivial authority had been restored in Egypt by force of British arms, and that for some time to come an Egyptian administration under the Khedive would govern under the supervision and control of the British Agent and Consul-General. While for all practical purposes autonomous until 1882, their country was not a sovereign state. Egyptians were Ottoman subjects, taxes were levied and money was coined in the name of the Sultan. Their ruler could not make political treaties with other states, or theoretically send representatives to foreign courts although in actual practice Khedive Ismail did so. Moreover, the autonomy Egypt enjoyed in administrative and financial matters was diluted when it came under European control and, after 1882, under direct British control. There was no uniform judicial system. Religious and 'national' civil courts had jurisdiction over native Egyptians, whereas Mixed Tribunals and Consular Courts dealt with foreigners protected by the Capitulations.

To this extent the religious reform movement which gathered momentum between 1882 and 1906 at least was not really concerned with the creation of an Egyptian national-state entity. Whereas much of its momentum was due to the resentment of European occupation, its original impetus came from the wider reaction of the Muslim world to an expanding European imperialism in Africa and Asia: France in North Africa, Britain in India and Africa, Russia in Central Asia, and Holland in Southeast Asia. A waning Ottoman Empire, bludgeoned by the encroachments of Christian Europe – both East and West – and partly dismembered by the successful separatism of its Christian subjects in the Balkans, further sharpened the realization among Muslims of a weak and exposed Islamic community. Reform movements in India led by Sayyed Ahmad Khan, and Young Ottoman and Young Turk ideas of constitutionalism in Turkey, also stirred Muslim leaders in Egypt.

Of obscure origins, Jamal al-Din al-Afghani (1838–97) claimed he was an Afghan. Recent research claims to have established that he was a Persian by origin and a Shiite. He was involved in political intrigue and agitation in Afghanistan, India, Turkey, Egypt and later in Europe as an agent of various rulers and states.[1] He was expelled from Istanbul in 1870, arrived in Egypt in 1871 where he was allowed to teach in the Azhar, and between 1871–9 he managed to create a following for himself among Azharites and other Egyptians. To these he imparted a distinct Islamic sentiment. His preaching about the rational–scientific reform of Islam earned Afghani the charge of agnosticism.[2] Yet, publicly at least, he insisted upon remaining faithful to the general principles of the Islamic message and teaching. Politically more significant was his call to limit the absolute powers of rulers, and his idea of the liberation of not only Egypt but all the Islamic countries from European control under the leadership of the strongest Muslim state of the time, the Ottoman Empire.[3] To this extent Afghani's activities reflected official Ottoman policy.

Until 1914, with a few significant exceptions, most Egyptian leaders firmly believed that the interests of Egypt lay in supporting the Ottoman Sultan who constituted the best guarantee against European imperialism.[4] The idea was strongly expressed in the poetry of that period, as for example by Shawqi, the Turco-Egyptian court poet,[5] and the native and popular poet Hafiz Ibrahim.[6] Ali al-Ghayati expressed his Muslim feelings in the praise he heaped upon the Caliph Abdul Hamid, especially when the latter was forced to grant the Turks a constitution in 1908.[7] In 1911, Shawqi called on Muslims to unite with the Sultan in fighting the infidel Italian invaders of Tripoli. Muharram Othman and Wali al-Din Yeken lamented the lost glories of Islam. Thus political sentiment in this period was of the kind that hardly distinguished religious belief from national consciousness.

Afghani's brand of political agitation was timely, for Islamic senti- ment was apt to increase when the European attack upon the Otto- man Empire was sustained over the years; when many members of the Egyptian ruling class were themselves of Turkish blood; when the religious leaders, ulama and others, saw in the presence of a foreign power and its influence upon the new generation a further threat to their own position in society; when even the more enlightened Egyptian leaders such as Shaykh Muhammad Abduh and Mustafa Kamil, who resented the tyranny of the Sultan and the Khedive and later came to believe in the independence of Egypt, felt that continued loyalty to the Sultan–Caliph presented a safeguard against European imperialism; when the masses were instinctively pro-Ottoman because they knew no other bond than that of religion.

This essentially Islamic reaction of the Egyptians to the events of 1882 in particular and to the world around them in general did not however develop along the militant lines preached by Afghani. A period of fiscal, administrative and judicial reform under British guidance and control had intervened which by the turn of the century had produced new and different political conditions.

The report of Lord Dufferin, at that time British Ambassador to Constantinople, prepared in May 1883 after six months' work, was to form the basis of British reform policy in Egypt.[8] The Organic Law (Decree) of 1 May 1883 provided for a partly elected and partly nominated Legislative Council to examine the Budget and all government-sponsored legislation bearing upon the administration of the country. Important as this was as a guided experiment in the debate of public business, it was not however the most significant consequence of the reform. The restructuring of the administration, the finances of the State, and the judiciary, on the other hand, was an important aspect of that reform.

Just before the occupation, Egypt was so 'internationalized' as to render sovereign action by any government practically impossible. The financial difficulties of Khedive Ismail which had led to bankruptcy and European control were compounded by the privileged position of foreigners resident in Egypt under the Capitulations, such as immunity from practically all taxation and judicial prosecution. At a time when Egypt was desperately in need of increased revenue,

The European concession-hunter and loan-monger, the Greek publican and pawnbroker, the Jewish and Syrian money-lender and land-grabber, who could always with ease obtain the protection of some European Power, had battened on the Egyptian Treasury and the poor Egyptian cultivator to an almost incredible extent.[9]

Added to these basically financial international fetters was a further legal restriction – that of Ottoman suzerainty over Egypt. At the same time, the International Commission of the Egyptian Debt placed serious limitations upon the administration of state revenue and expenditure.

Lord Dufferin in his report had recommended the appointment of British officials in advisory posts in key government departments, e.g., Finance, Interior, Public Works and Irrigation, Justice, Police and the Army. Appointments to these, especially from the Indian Service, were soon made early in Cromer's tenure of office. While they contributed to the general administrative reform of the country in the next twenty-five years, they also heightened Egyptian opposition to the Occupation.

Other major and specific measures of reform followed Lord Dufferin's recommendations. Civil and criminal codes were promulgated for the newly established Native Tribunals (*al-mahakim al-ahliyya*) in 1884. The *kurbaj* was abolished and, by 1890, the *corvée*, or conscripted labour. A form of punishment by whipping, the *kurbaj* had been used by most officials in Egypt to collect taxes and rents, to obtain evidence of crime, and to raise the *corvée* needed for the execution of public works. During the Ministry of Riad Pasha (1888–91), reforms were effectively introduced in the police and the army. There was a conversion of the Debt which lightened the financial burden on the Egyptian Treasury. In the poorer provinces, the land tax was reduced by 30 per cent. By 1891, Egypt showed a surplus in revenue.

Certain other benefits accrued to Egypt from the amendment of the 1880 Law of Liquidation in the London Convention of 1884–5. The Egyptian government was allowed to borrow nine million pounds with a European guarantee for the execution of urgent public works. In effect, the Convention removed many of the fetters placed by European states on Egyptian finances. Strict prevention of waste in administration was accompanied by the development of the country's productive capacity. A proper system of accounts, including a strict Civil List, was paralleled by a rise in cotton production through improved irrigation and better credit facilities for the farmer. Customs and Railways receipts went up. From 1884 canals in the Delta were improved as was the Delta Barrage. Whereas famine had visited Egypt in 1877, there was no danger of it ten years later.

There were marked advances in the administration of justice and public security. Apart from the reform of the new Native Courts, gendarmerie forces under provincial governors and district officers were abolished and a system of village watchmen, *ghaffirs*, introduced. Thus in 1883 the country was divided, for these purposes, into three police districts, each in the charge of a European inspector.

But by 1894, jurisdiction over crime and the police was returned to the provincial governors and district officers (*mudirs*). In great measure, this change was a reflection of several developments. One of these was the appointment of a competent British Adviser to the Ministry of Interior to provide adequate supervision of services. Another was that provincial administration had improved within the decade and was attracting officials of better calibre. The administration of prisons too was reorganized and improved. A Public Health department in the Ministry of the Interior was set up. This introduced a regular system of sanitary inspection, drainage and related services.

Yet in all these fields of administrative endeavour reform was still complicated by the international fetters restricting the conduct of Egyptian affairs. French opposition particularly was, at least until 1904, active and constituted a serious obstacle to reform. As early as 1884, this opposition manifested itself in the celebrated case of the French newspaper published in Egypt, *Le Bosphore Egyptien*.[10] Towards the end of 1883, Egyptian authority in the Sudan was on the verge of collapse as a result of the Mahdi's revolt.[11] The forces of the Egyptian expedition against the Mahdi led by General Hicks Pasha were annihilated that November. Cromer immediately pressed for the withdrawal of all Egyptian forces from the Sudan, a measure he considered necessary for his policy of rehabilitation. The British demand for the withdrawal of Egyptian troops from the Sudan precipitated a cabinet crisis in Egypt. Sharif Pasha's government was not prepared to accept such dictation by the British Consul-General. Sharif resigned and a new ministry led by the Armenian Nubar Pasha was formed in January 1884. This new government had accepted the principle enunciated in Lord Granville's famous instructions (4 January) to Lord Cromer to the effect that the Egyptian government must follow the advice of the British government in all important matters affecting the administration of Egypt and its defence, thus virtually handing over responsibility for the Sudanese question to Cromer.

Both the native Arabic Press and the local foreign Press attacked the new arrangement, charging that it meant virtual British control over the internal affairs of Egypt. Whereas the native Press had a serious interest in the retention by Egyptian Ministers of actual control over internal administration, the French Press in Egypt led by *Le Bosphore* was expressing the anxiety of resident foreigners in general over the impending reforms. Nubar, who took strict measures against the Opposition Press by applying the Press Law of 1881, also banned *Le Bosphore*. This act precipitated a diplomatic crisis between Britain and France which, at one point, also involved the Porte.

Until the resolution of the crisis in May 1885, it was clear that France had been using the *Bosphore* case to extract certain concessions from the British, via Nubar, in Egypt. To this extent the *Bosphore* incident reflected the continued rivalry between Britain and France in the Near East, and particularly French objection to the *de facto* control of Egyptian affairs by Britain.

Thus, while Britain's position in Egypt had no legal status, reform under British guidance and control was essential to Egypt's survival and well-being. Yet the interest of Europeans in Egypt, led by France, was for the first twenty years of the British occupation unfriendly – indeed, hostile – to reform. The successful introduction of the latter meant, by its nature, the erosion of the financial position and other privileges of the resident foreigner in the country who was protected by the European Powers. It equally meant the further strengthening of the British position in Egypt.

The reaction of Egyptians themselves was not solely against the British occupation authorities, but generally against all European influence. In the first few years of the occupation this reaction was viewed and expressed in religious terms. It is in this broad context of events that this reaction and response must be viewed. Other events beginning in 1894, and a new set of conditions both inside and outside Egypt after 1904, gave rise to new patterns in Egypt's response to Europe in general, and the occupying power in particular.

SHAYKH MUHAMMAD ABDUH AND ISLAMIC REFORM

Afghani's principal disciple and, for a while, collaborator, Shaykh Muhammad Abduh (1849–1905) soon abandoned his master's militancy. The son of a farmer in the Delta, his early education was entirely religious. From there he entered the Azhar in 1866 to study and train to be an *alim*. In 1872, he met Afghani and came under his influence. When in 1879 Afghani was expelled from Egypt for his political activities, Abduh was dismissed from his teaching post at Dar al-Ulum for his association with Afghani, and his political views. He was forced to return to his village and ordered to refrain from all political activity. Yet Khedive Tawfiq in 1881, probably at the recommendation of Sharif Pasha, recalled Abduh to Cairo and appointed him editor of the Official Gazette. In this capacity, Abduh resumed the pursuit of his reformist activities in education, language and religion. During the Orabi Revolt he supported the cause of the rebels and when these were tried in 1882 he also was sentenced to exile. Abduh joined his mentor Afghani in Paris in 1884, where together they published the short-lived (eighteen issues), but famous, Pan-Islamist journal *The Indissoluble Bond* (*al-urwa al-wuthqa*). When the journal stopped publication, Abduh left Paris for Beirut, where he married and settled down to the quieter life of a schoolmaster. Upon his return to Egypt in 1889, Abduh was appointed a judge in the National Courts of First Instance. He spent the rest of his life in the State's judicial service, becoming Mufti of Egypt in 1899, a post he held until his death in 1905.[12]

The brief stay in Paris and a very brief visit to London had a lasting effect upon him and he came to recognize the fact that a weak and backward society was the least equipped to bring about a successful revolution.

As an Azharite, a member of the ulama class, and by 1890 a well-known writer, teacher and judge, Abduh attained, with the aid of the Khedive and with the approval of the local British authorities, a public position in the official government Press and the educational establishment from which he could influence policy and public opinion in three crucial areas of Egyptian society. First, he sought to improve the quality of the written Arabic language both through his editorials and articles in the *Gazette* and his lectures on Arabic composition and grammar at Dar al-Ulum Teachers College. Second, he sought to reform the curriculum and administration of the Azhar educational complex. Third, he was ultimately interested in a religious reformation, i.e., a reform of religious doctrine, practice, and the legal application and interpretation of the religious law, the *Sharia*. This brought him into direct conflict with the Azhar hierarchy and other traditionalist elements in the country. His appointment to the office of Mufti of Egypt – supreme interpreter of the Sharia – was largely due to British influence.[13]

Shaykh Abduh then embarked upon a theological exercise to clear Islamic doctrine of traditional interpretations which, in his view, were inconsistent with the original ethical and religious message of Islam. His efforts in this direction were meant to encourage the individual believer to strive for a better life on earth as a measure of serving God. Abduh was not to be satisfied with less than an ethical system in which reason and the pragmatic accommodation between

Islam and modernity would supersede traditional practice and belief. He was in effect demanding that *ijtihad*, the right of the Muslim to interpret and reinterpret the rules of the Sacred Law in the light of changed conditions, be permitted.[14] If scientific and other modern knowledge were required to achieve this, then Abduh saw no conflict, or incompatibility, between science and Islam. He argued, moreover, that Muslim jurists and ulama should be educated accordingly in order to lead an evolving modern society of believers.[15]

Abduh was interested in justice as distinguished from a strict adherence to the rules of a legal code. To choose between what was reasonable, practical and just for society was for Shaykh Abduh a better – indeed more ethical – alternative than to stick blindly to traditional practices. To unleash the liberalizing force of Islamic teachings by making them more immanent to the believer was to activate the struggle of man and society for a better life.

Essentially what Abduh sought to accomplish in his *Essay on the Oneness of God*[16] was a reformation of Islamic thought. To liberalize belief and practice was to imbue Islamic faith with badly needed liveliness and make it bear directly upon the life of the individual believer and thus upon the life of society. But Kedourie has argued on the basis of his findings that another aim of all this reform activity may have been that of shackling the Muslim Institution into utter subservience to the Ruling Institution.[17]

Abduh may have been influenced by the preoccupation of his contemporary European intellectuals, from Comtean Positivists with their progressive secular conceptions of history, to Social Darwinists with their inevitable evolutionary processes of human society, to the general radical rationalist climate of the civilized world of those days.[18] However, in contrast to the secular positivists in Europe, who sought to replace theological religious doctrine with a rational scientific interpretation of universal phenomena, he insisted upon retaining the essentially Islamic character of Egyptian society while at the same time permitting it to accept the benefits of a secular ethic to guide its social and political conduct. Thus, in seeking to formulate a theological reinterpretation of Islamic doctrine by an emphasis upon its rather simplified ethical content, and by a rational commentary on the Koran, Abduh placed himself in an impossible position. He stood between the two extreme positions held by the Christian secularists Shibli Shumayyil and Farah Antoun on the one hand, who believed that the removal of religious ritual and superstition was necessary for the progress of society, and of the Azharite conservatives on the other who held that man should live according to God's law. His failure to produce a theological reformation of Islam was not, however, due to the enmity or opposition of either of these groups, but was the result of the essential contradiction in the task he undertook, namely to ascribe to Islamic doctrine possibilities that were incompatible with its very nature.[19]

To reinterpret the doctrinal and dogmatic bases of a revealed religious message entailed the danger of rejecting some of them, and changing others out of all recognition. Thus, his later religious disciples, led by Shaykh Rashid Rida (d. 1935), ended up with a movement whose basic teachings reverted to a strict orthodoxy. Until the 1930s this movement (*the Salafiyya*),[20] though not as puritanical as that of the Wahhabis of Arabia, basically preached a return to the early principles of Islam as laid down by the Prophet and as practised by his immediate successors to the spiritual–political leadership of the Islamic Community, the four Orthodox Caliphs (AD 632–61).

Like the *Salafiyya*, Shaykh Abduh wished simultaneously to defend Islam and to reconcile it with modern science. He longed to retain its original purity and simplicity of belief[21] – *tawhid*, or the oneness of God – and to effect a symbiosis between its scripture and modern rationalism, so as to produce a synthetic but viable social philosophy which would permit the conscious formation of a modern social and political reform programme. But to reform Islam, as Abduh tried, since he considered it inert, meant either to reject it as a bad social principle and replace it, or to transform it beyond all recognition. Thus the difficulty of Abduh ultimately was not simply theological, but also intellectual.[22]

Abduh's efforts were more successful in legal and educational reform, two areas of public life which were under governmental control. The office of Mufti is a state function. Thus in this capacity as Mufti Abduh applied his reformist ideas to the interpretation of the Sacred Law and specific Islamic practices: viz., the wearing of hats and European clothes, food rites and so on. In this capacity, also, Abduh was a member of the Supreme Council governing the Azhar, where he pressed for the reform of Azharite institutions and their educational curricula. Both these positions involved political power, the support or opposition of the government. So long as the latter favoured institutional reform of this kind, the social and religious ideas of Abduh had a chance of advancement. Yet this was not the kind of theological reformulation of Islam that Abduh had envisaged. Nonetheless, Abduh's reformist activities had a lasting effect upon later generations of Egyptian leaders, even though the question of the reformation of Islamic doctrine remains unresolved and perhaps is such that it can never be resolved. It was, however, largely as a result of his efforts that the government created in 1895 an Administrative Council for the Azhar on which Abduh served. The Council was responsible for both the academic and administrative supervision of the Azhar. The promulgation of a curriculum, the choice of texts, the establishment of a central library and the setting of examinations were to be supervised by this Council. So were the organization of its finances, staff appointments and contracts, and student discipline.[23]

Shaykh Abduh was equally active in the reform of religious courts and the education and training of *qadis*, or judges. As Mufti of Egypt he prepared reports on the better training of judges, the reform of legal rules to meet the needs and interests of a changing society; in short, he was anxious to ensure that the courts should seek to render justice in litigation rather than merely to apply the letter of the law. Recognizing the inadequacy of government schools to meet the increase in student population, Abduh together with others – among them Saad Zaghlul – founded the Muslim Benevolent Society in 1892. Its main purpose was to found schools for poor children which would serve as an experiment in private national education; they were meant to give pupils a modern education while emphasizing a Muslim upbringing.

Despite his failure in the theological reformation of Islam, what is interesting about Abduh is the philosophy underlying his response and reaction to the modern world, namely, that of Europe. This philosophy – whether motivated by his early passionate mysticism, or his later free-thinking rejection of all religious belief alleged by some – is significant because it continued to guide the response of at least the next two generations of Egyptian leaders after him. He rejected the political revival of the Islamic community as a first step in favour of its intellectual and religious reformation. Towards the end of our narrative we shall see that even here he was on unsure ground, and the present generation has opted so far for the reverse formula: the political revival – in fact a political revolution – of Islam to precede the transformation of the society to a modern state.

Muhammad Rashid Rida,[24] who remained the most devoted disciple of Abduh and his biographer, tried to systematize the teachings of the master into genuine theological dogma. The journal *Al-Manar*, which Rida founded in 1897 and edited until his death in

1935, served as an organ of the *Salafiyya* movement which he also headed. It began as a vehicle for the propagation of the Islamic views of Shaykh Abduh. But it was also associated with the less reformist and more fanatically Islamic daily *Al-Mu'ayyad*, published and edited by Shaykh Ali Yusuf. Although *al-Manar* disseminated the views of a progressive but orthodox Islam, it was distinctly influenced by the rationalism of the Abduh theology especially as developed in his *Essay on the Oneness of God*. It called simultaneously for the reform and improvement of the Islamic community everywhere and the political rally of Muslims around their heritage. Although it insisted upon the accommodation between reason and established religious texts, the *Salafiyya* hoped for the solidarity of an Islamic bloc of nations. It rejected the revolutionism of Afghani, perhaps because Rida suspected the political and irreligious motives of the latter, retained the idea to reform society expounded by Abduh, but strengthened the conservative requirement of facing the West and its culture with the irrational solidarity of an Islamic community.

In its reformist doctrine, the *Salafiyya*, like the Wahhabis of Arabia, argued for a return to purist origins – the Koran and the *Sunna*. They went beyond the Wahhabis in upholding the Abduh reformist principle of utilitarianism in ethics and law. Ultimately, though, the *Salafiyya* came to provide the major opposition to secularism in the 1920s and 1930s in politics, social reform and nationalist programmes. In the face of the nationalist movement led by Saad Zaghlul in 1919–23, the attack upon tradition soon thereafter, and the destruction of the Caliphate in Turkey in 1924, the *Salafiyya* were compelled to incorporate an Arab ethnic-national idea into their Islamic movement in order to accommodate the secular nationalism to which they were originally opposed.[25]

Even though the *Salafiyya* became in the first quarter of this century the spokesmen of Islamic conservatism in Egypt and the neighbouring Arab countries that were succumbing to more secular views in politics and socio-economic organization, Rida was perhaps socially more successful than his teacher Abduh. His work had a great impact upon educated Muslims in convincing them that Islam could have social significance. Societies to uphold and foster Islamic morals, organizations to propagate Islamic guidance in life, Eastern Unions, gave the impetus for the founding of more modern Islamic organizations with socio-economic reform programmes. The founding of The Young Men's Muslim Association (YMMA) in 1927 as a social, athletic and cultural counterpart of the YMCA, with its *Journal of Muslim Youth* founded in 1929 under the direction of Ahmad Yahia al-Dardiri, was not only an antidote to the religious indifference of a rising Europeanized urban generation but also a social, and intellectual – albeit unsuccessful – retort to the secular liberalism of the times. The *Salafiyya*, that is, inspired among certain groups of educated Muslims a purposeful and socially significant Islamic sentiment.

THE DEFENCE OF A MUSLIM EGYPT

Abduh's concern for religious reform underlined a conflict in the Egyptian mind which began in the 1870s: the response of Muslims to Western civilization, particularly European thought and culture. Although politically significant in the long term, it did not become a political issue until religious reform took on the character of a political conflict between conservatives on the one hand, and modernist reformers on the other. When modernists after independence in 1922 sought to replace Islamic solidarity with a secular nationalist principle, the defence of, and apology for, Islam became urgent. Yet an earlier defence of Islam appeared in Egypt simultaneously with the reformist movement of Shaykh Abduh. This was closely connected with the direct reaction of Egyptians to the British occupation. It differed from his venture in that it was directly involved in the practical political question of opposing British tutelage and influence, and in so far as it sought to rid Egypt of Britain. It preceded the more secular nationalist movement of such leaders as Mustafa Kamil and his National Party, and the other party organizations in the first decade of this century.

Tawfiq Pasha had succeeded his father Ismail as Khedive when Egypt was bankrupt. He came to govern an insolvent country, under foreign financial control, with a mutinous army, and a restless collection of notables clamouring for a greater share in power. Khedive Tawfiq soon found himself the captive and enemy of a rebellion led by the army. He just as quickly found himself back in power with the aid of a foreign conquering power – Britain – a dubious accolade at best. From 1883 until his death in 1892, his throne was propped up by British influence and force. He was naturally suspicious of any lingering revolutionaries after the Orabi débâcle. Yet he patiently worked for the implementation of certain administrative reforms proposed by the British which were largely responsible for the restoration of a sound fiscal policy in Egypt. Besides the basic reorganization of the government recommended by Lord Dufferin in 1883, the Khedive took a direct interest in the reorganization of the judiciary: the creation of the National Courts and the introduction of a Civil Code in 1883. He encouraged adult education as introduced into Egypt primarily by Syrian émigrés led by Faris Nimr and Yaqub Sarruf. He opened a Law School and a new School of Agriculture. Irrigation works were expanded in 1884, especially with the arrival of British engineers, most famous among them Scott Moncrieff. In view of the financial crisis in the country, Tawfiq Pasha permitted the creation of a revised and drastically reduced Civil List, beginning with economies directly affecting himself and his family. In Riad Pasha he found a tough administrative head for his government. But on the whole, Tawfiq had to accept a formula by which he ruled with the advice and consent of Britain – implying that he could not rule without them. British financial controllers, Ministry of Interior advisers, and technical experts in other departments of the government kept close watch over the affairs of the country. Elsewhere, a religious rebellion led by the Mahdi in the Sudan in 1884–5 threatened the Egyptian administration there. While the eventual suppression of that rebellion was directed by Britain and financed by Egypt, it led to an Anglo-Egyptian Condominium over the Sudan for which the agreement was signed in 1899. Thus the Sudan also became a bone of contention between Egyptian nationalists and British imperialists.

Despite his accomplishments in the fields of administration, in judicial and educational reform, Tawfiq Pasha came to be considered by the leaders of the movement against Britain as an English agent, a weak ruler and, for a while during the heyday of the Orabist Revolt, a traitor. Had he not been restored to power by force of British arms; had he not allowed the punishment of the Orabist leaders? Had he not permitted the appointment of foreign controllers and advisers in the government? In short, Khedive Tawfiq had accepted British hegemony in Egypt and reigned at their command and by their consent.

Young and infinitely ambitious, Abbas Hilmi (Abbas II) who succeeded Tawfiq in January 1892 soon appeared to favour co-operation with the anti-British elements of the smouldering Egyptian political movement. He was impatient with a system of government whose major feature consisted of an understanding between the Khedive and his ministers on the one hand, and the British Consul-

General on the other. He disliked a situation under which he had to govern not only with the advice of Lord Cromer but also with his approval. Abbas therefore anxiously assessed the various possibilities open to him in undermining the British position in Egypt and consequently strengthening his own. He looked both to Turkey and France as possible allies. But within Egypt he calculated on the support of anti-British groups. Prominent among these were the political Pan-Islamicists and agents of the Ottoman Sultan, who, between 1890 and 1900, depicted the struggle of Egypt to rid herself of British control as a religious one. Later, between 1900 and 1904, Abbas saw similar possibilities in the National Party led by Mustafa Kamil. His initial strategy consisted simply of leading an Egyptian independence movement with the aid of anti-British allies within Egypt, as well as in Turkey and France. The tactics were in theory just as simple, but in practice rather complicated. They involved the encouragement and financing of publicists, journalists and nationalist agitators in their campaigns against British rule, as well as playing off one against the other.

Whereas the conflict within Egypt between 1879 and 1882 was centred on the struggle for power by ambitious native Egyptians against a Turco-Egyptian official aristocracy, after the occupation it shifted to a convenient alliance between these two groups against the British. Moreover, the native Egyptians were gradually wresting leadership and the political initiative from the remnants of the Turkish aristocracy. Yet this alliance blessed by the Khedive Abbas manifested its political opposition to Britain in terms of a demand for local Egyptian independence, mixed with a lingering Islamic loyalty to the Ottoman Sultan.

Whether young Abbas was a genuine Egyptian nationalist or not is a meaningless question. His political behaviour at least until 1904 indicates, however, that he desired to get rid of British control and to free Egypt of Ottoman suzerainty. In this endeavour he found the assistance of the nationalists convenient.[26] Abbas therefore took an interest in three distinct groups early in his Khedivate. He was first interested in rallying Egyptian Army officers to his support by taking a direct hand in the reorganization of the army. This brought Abbas into direct conflict with Kitchener, Sirdar of the Egyptian Army, as early as 1894, when he supported demands by officers for higher pay.

Ever since the occupation, the administration of a smaller Egyptian Army had been in British hands. Dufferin, in his report, had fixed the army's establishment at eight battalions, four artillery batteries, and a camel corps. Its function was to support the police in maintaining internal security and to protect the frontier. About thirty to sixty British officers served in it under a British Sirdar's command. Within five years, five Sudanese battalions had been raised as a makeweight to the Egyptian peasant recruits. When Kitchener became Sirdar in 1892, this army numbered about fifteen thousand men. By then also the British administration of the Egyptian Army had come under further attack from Egyptian politicians, who were partly encouraged by the young Khedive. In January 1894, the Khedive toured units of this army in Wadi Halfa on the Egyptian–Sudanese border. In the course of his inspection he deplored the bearing and discipline of the troops in the presence of Kitchener, the Sirdar. The latter protested to Cromer and tendered his resignation. Needless to say his resignation was not accepted. Instead Cromer forced the young Khedive to dismiss his Under-Secretary of War, and to appoint in his place another recommended by Kitchener. The incident thus further tightened British control over the Egyptian Army. At the same time it was another manifestation of the bad relations between the Khedive and Cromer.

Secondly, he made financial contributions to support the activities of both Shaykh Ali Yusuf and his largest Islamic anti-British daily, *al Mu'ayyad*, as well as those of Mustafa Kamil and his nationalist associates. Thirdly, he attempted to assert his administrative authority in Egypt without the intermediary or advice of Lord Cromer. All these efforts earned Abbas the praise of the local Press, especially in the columns of *al-Mu'ayyad* and in Abdullah al-Nadim's *al-Ustadh*. Externally, he sought the assistance of the Porte. But Abdul Hamid was not of much help and, by 1904, France had reached an understanding with Britain over the Near East with the signing of the Entente Cordiale.

The period 1890–1914 is important in the history of modern Egypt partly because it reflected very well the conflict within the Egyptian community in its response to a direct confrontation with a European power. Such conflict was at that time couched in religious–communal terms; in a civilizational encounter. While the serious business of governing Egypt, restoring fiscal and administrative order after the unsettling events of 1882, was largely the responsibility of the British Consul-General, the articulation of local response to the situation was taken up by the leading publicists of the time. While Abduh groped unsuccessfully with the question of religious reform, other Muslim shaykhs and writers agitated for political action against the *status quo*, and sought to arouse public opposition to existing rule. The most prominent Egyptian in this agitation was Shaykh Ali Yusuf (1863–1913).

Born in a village in the province of Sohag, Upper Egypt, Shaykh Ali Yusuf received the traditional religious training until he entered the Azhar. In 1885, however, he cut short his studies at the Azhar to publish a newspaper, *Jaridat al-Adab*, with the financial assistance of one of his teachers. The paper was not a successful venture and stopped publication early in 1889. With a loan from the same teacher, Shaykh Ali Yusuf embarked upon the publication of another newspaper, the famous *al-Mu'ayyad*, which came to dominate the daily Islamic Press in Egypt for a quarter of a century (1889–1913).[27]

About the same time a group of Christian Syrians, namely Nimr and Sarruf, had founded a daily, *al-Muqattam*, which advocated a policy of co-operation with the British authority in Egypt, calling for gradual reform and a European outlook. The success of *al-Muqattam* further aroused the opposition of more conservative Muslims, among them Ali Yusuf. The latter identified *al-Muqattam* publishers and editors with foreign interests. The other daily, *al-Ahram*, owned and edited by the Christian Syrian Taqla brothers, founded in Alexandria in 1875, reappeared after 1882. Although it purported to be an independent paper, its policy was suspected to advance French interests in Egypt. Thus even the Press of Egypt at this time reflected the various local and international interests involved in Egypt. Both *al-Muqattam* and *al-Ahram* were associated with foreign Christian interests, whereas *al-Mu'ayyad* appeared as the sole spokesman for Muslim, and therefore, Egyptian, interests.

It is difficult to separate the activities of Shaykh Ali Yusuf in journalism and politics from the general Pan-Islamic tone set forth by Afghani and Abduh in their periodical the *al-Urwa al-wuthqa* a decade earlier. But whereas in 1883–4 *al-Urwa* was agitating for an Islamic revival against general European domination, Shaykh Ali Yusuf was by 1893–4 inaugurating a particular Egyptian–Islamic sentiment and struggle against British domination. Nor can one distinguish, at least until 1904, between the position of Ali Yusuf expressed in his paper and the position of other contemporary Egyptian political leaders. Chief among the latter was Mustafa Kamil, founder and leader of the National Party, and between 1900 and 1907 publisher and editor of *al-Liwa'* (*The Standard*), his nationalist daily which expressed his particular brand of mixed secular–Islamic nationalism. The main feature of the Mustafa Kamil programme was its demand for the evacuation of Britain from Egypt forthwith even if this required the use of force.

Until 1907 the *Liwa'* and its followers were still mainly motivated by an Islamic sentiment not dissimilar to that expounded and represented by Shaykh Ali Yusuf. This was especially so after the death of Mustafa Kamil in February 1908. At that time a fanatical Muslim, Shaykh Abdul Aziz al-Jawish, succeeded to the editorship of *al-Liwa'* and played no mean role in the extension of the Islamic national sentiment, especially during the communal conflict between Muslims and Copts in 1910–11. By this time, however, more moderate Muslim Egyptian leaders were abandoning this trend in favour of a pragmatic consideration of local Egyptian interests within the context of the social, economic and political conditions of Egypt. Furthermore, the retirement of Shaykh Ali Yusuf from journalism and politics in 1913, his death in 1914, the deposition of Abbas Hilmi in December of the same year for suspected disloyalty to the Allied war effort, all marked the end of an era in Egyptian political history. First, it marked the eclipse of the early nationalist movement which hardly distinguished between modern Egyptian national interests and demands on the one hand, and sentiments of Pan-Islamic solidarity on the other. Second, it ushered onto the Egyptian political stage a new group of leaders possessing a measure of experience in modern administration with a European educational background, and concerned primarily with the social and political emancipation of Egypt as a nation-state.

Ali Yusuf none the less was aided in his pro-Islamic and anti-British campaign not only by the Khedive Abbas but also by circumstances. The quelling of the Mahdi Revolt in the Sudan and the reoccupation of that country in 1896 under British leadership led eventually to the Anglo-Egyptian Condominium of 1899. Egypt and England were now to rule the Sudan jointly. The Condominium agreement was moreover signed on behalf of the Egyptian government by the Christian Foreign Minister Butrus Pasha Ghali. A year earlier (1898), the confrontation between British troops and a French expedition at Fashoda ended with the withdrawal of France from that part of Africa. Eventually the conclusion in 1904 of the Entente Cordiale between France and Britain which settled imperial differences between the two Powers in the East smacked to the Islamic nationalists of a conspiracy between the two European Powers to dominate the Muslim world. A crisis over the demarcation of the frontier between Egypt and the Ottoman State in the Sinai, which came to be known as the Aqaba Incident, found Egyptians, among them Shaykh Ali Yusuf, supporting the Sultan against the British even though it meant loss of territory for Egypt. They resented the fact that Britain was negotiating Egyptian territorial matters with the Porte. More explosive was the Dinshawai Incident of June 1906 from which one may date the reactivation of the Islamic versus Christian dimension of the Egyptian question, which remained serious until 1913.

The Dinshawai Incident is important not merely because of the national agitation which it aroused among Egyptians against Britain, but also because of the national mythology surrounding it, the subsequent punishments meted out to the accused, and the communal turmoil which followed it.[28] Briefly, it involved an altercation between British Army officers who, while on a march with their troops from Cairo to Alexandria, had camped in Menoufiyya *en route* to Shibin al-Kom. Five or six of them decided to take a pigeon-shooting trip in the near-by village of Dinshawai. In the course of shooting at pigeons, the wife of the local *imam* (the leader of the Friday prayer) was shot and wounded. The officers were surrounded by villagers, excitement rose among the latter and, before the local gendarmerie could sort out the trouble, two British officers were wounded. The officers in turn panicked and opened fire at the villagers. One of the wounded officers tried to march back to their camp a few miles away but died on the way as a result of head wounds received in the fracas. Another got back to the camp and the troops returned to the place where one of their officers had died and killed a bystander. Fifty-two Egyptians were arrested and brought before a special court convened in Shibin al-Kom, according to a special regulation promulgated in February 1895 relating to attacks and crimes against British Army personnel. It was, moreover, presided over by the Christian Minister of Justice Butrus Pasha Ghali, and included three British officials.

The sentences passed on the accused on 27 June 1906 were severe. Four of them were sentenced to death, many to terms of imprisonment with hard labour, and others to public flogging. The sentences were executed swiftly, publicly and perhaps brutally, the following day. While it is difficult in such incidents equitably and precisely to apportion blame upon the parties involved one thing is certain: the Dinshawai Incident helped both Shaykh Ali Yusuf and

Mustafa Kamil in their campaigns against British rule by rendering the mass of Egyptians their willing audience. The policy of *al-Mu'ayyad* which Ali Yusuf expressed in the first issue of his paper, namely to advance the interests of Egypt and the Muslims generally, was further elaborated in a series of twenty-three articles he wrote dealing with the incident. The Pan-Islamic feeling he tried to evoke in connection with the Aqaba Incident a month earlier, he now preached with greater force and vehemence against British tyranny. The Egyptians were first of all Muslims. Their treatment at the hands of European rulers as manifested by the Dinshawai Incident showed the importance of preserving their bond with the Ottoman Sultan. This, despite the fact that in 1906 popular agitation against the British had passed into the hands of Mustafa Kamil and his Nationalists. Ali Yusuf was already reconciled to a policy of supporting the Khedive who, after 1904, was gradually coming to terms with his special relationship to the British authority in Egypt. In 1906–7, the conflict between Ali Yusuf and Mustafa Kamil for the leadership of the nationalist movement in Egypt became open. Ali Yusuf came to be identified with moderate views of accommodation with Britain provided Egypt remained under Ottoman sovereignty, whereas Mustafa Kamil demanded the immediate evacuation of the British from Egypt.

INTERCOMMUNAL TENSION: THE COPTS

One significant effect of the Islamic orientation of newspapers, found in *al-Mu'ayyad* of Ali Yusuf and *al-Liwa'* of Mustafa Kamil, was the strained relationship it engendered between the Coptic minority and the Muslims in Egypt. The Copts who today number between six and eight million are, apart from this religious difference, almost indistinguishable from their Muslim compatriots. Especially in the rural areas – their largest concentration is in Upper Egypt – Coptic social life is regulated by local customs and traditions that are equally acceptable to Muslims. Their manner, language and assimilated practices are hardly distinguishable from those of Muslim Egyptians. Although Copts worship in a church instead of in a mosque, they shared for a long time with all other Egyptians a basic conservatism, including the seclusion of women, circumcision, marriage and funeral ceremonial practices, customary rules and practices regulating inheritance, and so on.

In his *Report on Egypt* Sir John Bowring said about the Copts

that they 'are the surveyors, the scribes, the arithmeticians, the meas-
urers, the clerks, in a word, the learned men of the land. They are
to the counting house and the pen what the fellah is to the field and
the plough.'[29] Having for centuries provided the clerical, fiscal and
tax-gathering services to rulers the Copts were undoubtedly opposed
to British rule at first, for the British introduced administrative
reforms which tended to dispense with the relatively primitive services of Coptic officials. Christian Syrians, moreover, were by 1890
the leaders in journalism, education and other areas of public affairs.
Yet the identification of a leading Copt such as Butrus Pasha Ghali
by Muslim nationalists with unpopular administrative policies – viz.,
the Sudan Condominium Agreement, the Dinshawai Trial – and his
assassination by Ibrahim al-Wardani in February 1910, frightened
the Copts. Ghali was also associated with the reactivation on 25
March 1909 of the 26 November 1881 Press Law by which the
Minister of the Interior was empowered to suspend newspapers without trial and to apply administrative exile sentences against their editorial staff for undesirable political activities. This he did against
Shaykh Abdul Aziz al-Jawish, editor of *al-Liwa'*, in June 1909.
Moreover, Butrus Ghali featured in the negotiations with the Suez
Canal Company to extend its concession for another forty years to
the year 2008, which the Legislative Council of the time had rejected.
The Copts therefore felt isolated and sought to defend their communal interests first against a rising Muslim tide, and second against
neglect by a foreign occupying power.

The Copts sensed, whether rightly or wrongly, that their rights
were being ignored by the authorities, that they were an oppressed
minority. These and similar feelings were expressed in their own
communal Press between 1909 and 1910, especially by their two leading papers, *Jaridat al-watan* (founded in 1877) and *Misr* (founded
in 1895). Despite the protestations of the Nationalists led by Mustafa
Kamil and their attempts to organize an Egyptian United Front (*al-
jami 'a al-misriyya*) against the British, Copts complained of discrimination, perhaps because the idea of a secular Egypt was alien
to a country in which groups still identified themselves in terms of
religious affiliation. Recalling their lower social status under previous Turkish and other Muslim rulers, Copts feared the Pan-Islamic
tendencies of the nationalist movement, especially those of the
National Party. Ever since the British occupation, they sought to
strengthen their communal life under British protection. Their Press
therefore deliberately worked for the promotion of such communal

solidarity by claiming for the Copts an 'Egyptian first' status, by entrenching the more able members of their community in key administrative jobs, and by purchasing land. Generally, they tended to isolate themselves in order to protect their interests against what they viewed as a rising Islamic national sentiment among the overwhelming majority of their compatriots.

The assassination of their lay communal leader, Butrus Ghali Pasha, by a Muslim who confessed to the murder for reasons of religious fanaticism and enmity couched in the terms of Ghali's surrender to European powers, terrified Copts further.[30] Witnessing the educational and other activities of the Nationalists – schools, newspapers – the Copts felt the need for better organization to secure their rights as a minority. The assassination of Ghali Pasha coincided with a Press war between the Coptic *al-Watan* and the Muslim Nationalist *al-Liwa'*. Shaykh al-Jawish had written a series of inflammatory editorials in the latter attacking the Copts under the title 'Islam, a stranger in its own land'. The Coptic Bishop of Upper Egypt called a General Congress which was held at Assiout on 5–8 March 1910, chaired by Bushra Hanna Bey, one of the notables of the city, and attended by leaders of the community. The delegates to the Conference demanded among other things certain specific guarantees. Sunday was to be recognized as an official holiday just as Friday was recognized as the Muslim official holiday. They demanded that there should be no discrimination in employment of Egyptians other than on the basis of merit; that provincial councils should guarantee religious instruction for Coptic pupils in elementary schools; that there should be communal representation in the councils themselves.

The Muslims responded to Coptic activity with a Congress of their own which was held in Cairo, and at which prudent delegates agreed to ask Mustafa Riad Pasha to call a General Egyptian Congress to be held in Heliopolis to which delegates from both communities should come. This Congress met on 29 April–4 May 1911. No serious decisions were taken, but delegates had the chance to discuss differences openly and to conclude a communal truce. In fact, a united front between Copts and Muslims in the national movement was not achieved – and then only temporarily – until personalities like Ali Yusuf, al-Jawish and Mustafa Kamil were long gone from the political scene, and until more moderate leaders achieved an accommodation with their Coptic compatriots.

PRELUDE TO SECULARISM

By this time, however, more discrete organizations for political action, namely, political parties, had appeared in Egypt with programmes and platforms to deal with the relationship between England and Egypt. Their very existence implied a certain amount of inter-party squabbles and competition which overshadowed for the moment at least the inter-communal conflict. Such a development was partly a consequence of, and in response to, internal policy changes following the departure of Lord Cromer and the arrival of his two successors, Eldon Gorst and Kitchener.

Although not quite successful, Gorst's liberalizing policy of relaxing direct British control over Egyptian administration coincided with a Liberal government in London. He had joined the Khedivial government service in 1890, rose to be an adviser in the Ministry of the Interior and in 1898 Financial Adviser to the government. As Consul-General (1908–11) he wanted to expand the authority of the Egyptian council of ministers and limit that of British advisers. He even tried to cut down the number of Englishmen in the Egyptian state service. Similarly, Gorst felt that local and provincial bodies should have wider powers to influence the administration of the country. For a long time the rural population was solely concerned with irrigation matters. For the rest they were at the mercy of the Ministry of the Interior and other central government departments. In short, Gorst conceived of a simultaneous political–constitutional and administrative radical reform that would give Egyptians greater responsibility in administering their country. Thus his law constituting the new Provincial Councils was promulgated in June 1909. It enlarged the powers of the councils and increased their responsibility in such local matters as the making of by-laws for public markets, the control of the Ghaffir force, local education and trade schools. Moreover their membership was made elective (two members elected from each *markaz*, or district). Only the district officer, *mudir*, remained an ex-officio member of each council. Another concession by Gorst to the Egyptians was his decision that the Legislative Council should be in permanent session every year from mid-November till the end of May, whereas before that it met every other month. The same concession encouraged members of the Legislative Council to question ministers on practically all matters of public policy.

Perhaps Gorst's liberal policy may have won over the Khedive to his side, and away from the dangers of conspiracies with the rising group of anti-occupation nationalists and the Ottoman authorities in Istanbul. Yet, despite his concessions to the Legislative Council members, his policy did not attract the nationalists in general who were interested in curtailing the power of the Khedive and his ministers. This became apparent in the Suez Canal concession crisis of 1909. The Suez Canal Company had requested an extension of forty years to its concession (from 1968 to 2008). It offered a down-payment of four million pounds to the Egyptian government and an annual share of the profits. The government needed the money and their Financial Adviser recommended that they accept the offer. When the government referred the question to the General Assembly, the nationalists opposed it, for they considered the pro-posed forty-year extension of the concession an unacceptable pro-longation of foreign influence in the country. This incident too in-dicated the division between the Khedive and a rising native group of nationalists who wished to curtail his power. It was also used by this same group to agitate further for the termination of the British occupation. What was more serious was that it became part of a series of events which heightened inter-communal strife between Copts and Muslims in Egypt.

Gorst's probably well-meaning liberal policy had unexpected con-sequences. It contributed to further political agitation that was inter-rupted only by the outbreak of the Great War, although, on the other hand, it further encouraged Egyptians eventually to abandon Islamic policies in favour of a more secular approach to the problem of Anglo-Egyptian relations and their own political development. This became clear in the rising influence of the *Jarida-Umma* group from 1909 to 1915, and the subsequent eclipse of the more extreme National party.[31]

Similarly, the evolution of Egyptian response to Europe was partly influenced by the policy of Kitchener, who succeeded Gorst in 1911. Kitchener sought to improve agriculture and the conditions of the fellahin. The storage capacity of the Aswan dam (completed in 1902) was increased, agricultural drainage in the Delta improved and some land was reclaimed in Gharbiyya province. His famous Homestead Exemption Law of 1913 protected the fellah from the consequences of being in debt.[32] Kitchener also got the Egyptian government to promulgate an anti-usury decree limiting interest on loans to peasants to 9 per cent.

One must, however, place the relatively new policies of Cromer's successors in proper perspective. Ever since the improvement of Egypt's financial condition and its administrative reform in the early 1890s, Cromer concentrated British efforts on the further development of the country's agricultural productive capacity. The improvement and extension of irrigation and other public works underpinned this policy. Hence the first Aswan dam (completed 1902) and the improvement of road and rail transport. Related to this basically agricultural economic development policy was the reform of land tax collection methods. Yet, except for the Ministry of Public Works, Cromer hardly encouraged a wide role for the government in the development of the economy. To this extent, Cromer never seriously considered minimizing Egypt's economic dependence exclusively on agriculture and particularly cotton by encouraging some diversification via industrial development. His departure in May 1907 coincided with a serious economic crisis in Egypt. A European recession at the end of a decade of unprecedented prosperity (1897–1907) affected Egypt's financial position. The year 1908 was marked by a reduction in the value of agricultural output. This was followed by a sharp fall in cotton yield in 1909. A sharp drop in land prices and the inability of many people to meet mortgage payment instalments shook the confidence of businessmen, creditors and investors.

These and other problems prompted serious consideration of a slight departure from Cromer's policies. Thus over-dependence on agriculture and particularly the cash crop of cotton was being questioned. So was the role of government in the economy. Then, some control over the largely foreign business community had to be devised. The extent of rural debt, the difficulty of many farmers in repaying debts due to a fall in the value of agricultural production led to a consideration of new schemes to control borrowing and to protect the rural debtor by legislation and even the organization of co-operatives. Thus, before Kitchener's Five Feddan Law, a concrete consequence of these considerations was the setting up by Sir Eldon Gorst of the Department of Agriculture in 1910 which became a Ministry in 1913.

Nevertheless, both Gorst and Kitchener continued basically to adhere to Cromer's vision of Egyptian economic development through extensive public works related to agriculture. A definite step towards diversification, by the encouragement of industrial development, was not taken until the Great War. The work of the Committee on Commerce and Industry appointed in 1916–17 and headed by

Ismail Sidqi was largely responsible for the creation in April 1920 of a Bureau of Commerce and Industry. This aimed largely at encouraging the development of existing trade and manufacturing enterprises. It also provided an important liaison between the government and the business community.[33]

Kitchener had something for the politicians, too. He was behind the promulgation of a new Organic Law in 1913 which provided for a larger Legislative Assembly replacing the old Legislative Council and Assembly. It also provided for a higher proportion of elected to nominated members (66 : 17) and gave new powers to the members to veto government proposals for increases in direct taxation. It further permitted members to demand of ministers justification of their legislative proposals and to call for testimony and information about them.

Whereas Gorst hoped to strengthen local government Kitchener now hoped to produce a central Legislative Assembly in which rural representatives would predominate. The attempt, however, was unsuccessful. But during the stormy, albeit short, life of this Legislative Assembly (1913–15) the leaders of the 1919 independence movement emerged.

Internal developments, however, were not the sole influence upon the evolution of the more secular response of Egyptians to Europe. In fact the period 1911–12 immediately preceding the Great War was characterized by a series of international crises in the Mediterranean, particularly North Africa. European power conflicts broke out in Morocco involving France and Germany, until France succeeded in establishing its protectorate over that Muslim imamate-sultanate. The Italians felt France had tipped the European balance of power in the Mediterranean in her favour and they proceeded to invade Tripoli.

The state of war which prevailed between Turkey and Italy in 1911 directly affected Egypt in many ways. Technically Egypt was still a part of the Ottoman Empire, and Turkey could have demanded passage for her troops to Tripoli. As Muslims, Egyptians were sympathetic to their Ottoman Sultan and Caliph, and viewed with alarm the dismemberment of his empire by Europeans. The Turkish loss of Tripoli to Italy, however, was further indication to the more secularly inclined Egyptian leaders that any help from their Ottoman suzerain and his government in their struggle against the British occupation was quite impossible.

Thus the rise of secular political groups in Egypt just before the

Great War and their leadership of the struggle for independence after 1918 was not simply or solely the result of a shift in the commitment of Egyptian leaders to certain new values and foreign ideas. The latter was accelerated greatly by the power of Europe and its ability to infiltrate and establish its influence and control over several Muslim dominions of the Ottoman Empire. The impotence of the Ottoman state successfully to forestall, or combat, this extension of European control and its inability to assist its non-Turkish Muslim subjects in their opposition to European rule (beyond conspiracy) prompted many of them to settle for the idea of territorial nationalism.

With the outbreak of World War I, the leadership of Egyptian nationalism had not only changed hands, but the new men were already concerned with ideas which departed radically from the earlier more instinctive Islamic reaction to Britain. The demagoguery and mass appeal of the youthful Mustafa Kamil who had called for a basically Islamic liberation of Egypt from alien rule, and the Ottoman–Khedivial policy of Shaykh Ali Yusuf faded away, with the emergence of men who seemed to grasp the idea that political emancipation depended upon social reform and the art of political compromise motivated by self and national interest. Their prominence between 1906 and 1914 marks the most illustrious phase of the movement for secular liberalism in modern Egyptian political history.

The essentially Islamic and conservative response of Egyptians to Europe during the first twenty-five years of the British occupation was due to several factors, apart from their traditional–sentimental inclination as Muslim men. On one hand, they came to accept tacitly, if not admitting it explicitly, British guidance and control in administrative matters. On the other, they observed that until 1904 and 1906 France and Turkey were opposed to the British occupation. In this international situation, many Egyptians felt, lay the possibility of bringing to an end British control of their affairs.

Yet during this same period it was equally apparent that Europeans generally were on the whole opposed to the quick recovery of their country. Some of them actively sought to obstruct this material recovery. An Islamic reaction to this attitude was natural and justified. When, after 1904–6, Britain had succeeded in helping Egypt to attain some measure of material development in the teeth of other European opposition, European acceptance of British control in Egypt came quickly and inevitably. With this change in international conditions affecting Egypt, e.g., the relaxation of international financial control, and the recognition of Britain's special position in Egypt, Egyptian response to Europe and particularly Britain changed too: from a conservative Islamic one to a secular liberal orientation towards political action against the occupying power.

CHAPTER 11

STIRRINGS OF SECULAR LIBERALISM

Implied in the religious reform work of Muhammad Abduh and the political writings and agitation of men like Shaykh Ali Yusuf, Mustafa Kamil and Shaykh Abd al-Aziz al-Jawish was an essentially Islamic response to Europe and, by implication, to Christendom. No matter how influenced these leaders of Egyptian opinion were by their contemporary intellectual environment in Europe, there is no doubt that the reform and political bases they envisaged for Egypt remained firmly anchored in the teachings of Islam about morality, society and order. Yet, in the case of Abduh, despite his failure to provide a new substantive basis for the attainment of socio-political modernity by Muslims, he nevertheless inspired the generation of liberal thinkers who came after him with a legacy of questioning the relationship between Islam and modern society. It is in this questioning spirit that Abduh's contribution to the development of modern Egypt lay. On the other hand, the Pan-Islamic tendencies of his contemporaries in the political field bequeathed a different tradition, one of apologia for, and defence of, Islam in the next fifty years. Thus, at the turn of the century two fairly distinct approaches to the question 'Whither Egypt?' had emerged. One approach evolved from the legacy of Muhammad Abduh which favoured a rationalist, and soon thereafter, a secular consideration and resolution of this question. Another approach stuck to a traditional Islamic treatment of the same question. Conflict between the two groups went on, until in the last twenty years a reconciliation between them by command of the revolutionary leadership of a military autocracy has been attempted, in the hope of achieving an acceptable synthesis between them.

In discussing the early attempts by Egyptian liberals during the period 1906–14 to establish a secularist tradition in education and politics, one must deal with three major groups. At one end of the spectrum was the group of extreme nationalists led by Mustafa Kamil, whose ideas were largely expressed in their newspaper *al-Liwa'* and the few emotionally loaded writings of Kamil himself.[1]

At the other was the more seriously liberal, rationalist and evolutionary group led by Ahmad Lutfi al-Sayyid, whose views were expressed in their newspaper *al-Jarida* (1906–15). Between these two extremes stood a strange group of Muslim pseudo-liberals, first represented by Shaykh Ali Yusuf until 1913, and later by Shaykh Rashid Rida. Moreover, not only was each of these groups organized for varying periods of time into political parties – the Nationalist Party of Mustafa Kamil, the Umma, or People's Party of Ahmad Lutfi, and the Constitutional Reform Party of Ali Yusuf – but each also reflected influences and predilections deriving from sources outside Egypt. Thus the leader of the Nationalists was presumably inspired by French ideas of liberty, in addition to an instinctive but often material devotion to the spiritual–religious hegemony of the Ottoman Sultan. The People's Party was more directly affected by British ideas of individual freedom, utilitarianism and gradualism in reform. Its leading members were also considered to have subscribed to the humanist element in European civilization which derived from the classical Graeco-Roman tradition. Finally, the short-lived Constitutional Reform Party, as well as all others subscribing to a nationalist interpretation of Egypt's Islamic being were, until 1918, inclined to identify their interests with those of the Ottoman Sultan-Caliph in Istanbul. At home they supported the continued exercise of autocratic rule by the Khedive.

Involvement in the first stirrings of secular liberalism in Egypt meant not just the emergence of political parties and an active reformist Press. Two very strong factors operating in the Egyptian environment at that time influenced this trend further. One was the British presence in Egypt, dominated for a quarter century by the forceful Lord Cromer. The other was the appearance of leading Syrian – mainly Christian – journalists in Egypt who boldly put forward progressive ideas of the scientific age in Europe, ranging from the Darwinian theory of evolution to astronomy. There was also the experience in the debate over public policies acquired by a rising generation of lawyers and writers in the Legislative Council and Legislative Assembly from 1883 to 1913. Although these institutions possessed limited powers they nonetheless became by 1893 forums for the expression of critical and more secular views by leaders of Egyptian opinion.

The combination of British tutelage, the waning power and influence of the leading Islamic state in Istanbul, and the continued tension between Islam and the requirements of modern political action tended to push the younger generation of Egyptian leaders in the period 1906–14 towards a more secularist view of man and society. But this secularism was not marked by an abandonment of the Islamic faith. It simply forced upon this new leadership the adoption of a practical conception of reform and politics: that of compromise and gradualism, the idea that political advancement for Egypt lay in co-operation with the dominant power – Britain. So that whereas until 1904 Mustafa Kamil, his collaborators and followers viewed the matter of Egyptian independence from Britain as constituting an international question, now most responsible Egyptian leaders considered it an issue to be resolved between Egypt and Britain.

An added impetus to this trend was the policy of the Young Turk revolutionaries in Turkey after their coup in 1908–9. In fact, before the coup, Egypt had been, at the turn of the century, one of the Young Turks' centres of propaganda and political activity. The liberal–decentralist group, particularly under Prince Sabaheddin, had been active in Egypt from 1902–6.[2] Their policy, however, after their successful coup in Turkey had certain repercussions in the Arab provinces of the Ottoman Empire. Certain Arab groups, especially in Syria, resented their relegation to 'second-class citizens' and began to think in terms of political separatism which, in turn, gave rise to local nationalist movements. A series of Turkish retreats in the face of expanding European control over Muslim dominions (the loss of Tripoli to Italy in 1911, and the course of the Balkan wars in 1912) further encouraged Arabs to seek autonomy and the decentralization of the Ottoman State. In Egypt the youthful and ambitious Khedive Abbas II entertained briefly the idea of an Arab alliance in 1909 and 1910, with himself preferably as the new Caliph. All this soon convinced the more secularist Egyptian leaders that the social and political problems of Egypt could be dealt with only within the context of an Egyptian state poised ultimately against Britain.

The status of the British occupation was itself a cumulative impetus to this trend. Even though after the occupation the European states on the whole recognized British responsibility in Egypt, the legal aspect of the Anglo-Egyptian relationship was not clear.[3] Turkey was still the nominal sovereign of the country. Soon after the occupation Britain was anxious to clarify the status of her relationship to Egypt and until the rise of German influence in Turkey early in this century, she was even anxious to end the occupation. This was the purpose of the mission of Sir Henry Drummond Wolff, who negotiated a Convention with Turkey, signed on 24 October 1885. Another Convention signed on 22 May 1887 which dealt with, among other matters, the withdrawal of British troops from Egypt and the conditions under which they would re-occupy the country, was opposed by France and Russia. Their objections and representations to the Porte succeeded to the extent that the Sultan did not ratify the Convention.[4]

Whereas the Drummond Wolff Mission did not serve to clarify the juridical relation of Egypt to Turkey and Britain, it implied that the British occupation would continue. The Mission's failure also alerted Egyptian national leaders that Britain would be the sole arbiter of the Egyptian Question, of Egypt's future; that Turkey would from that time retreat from any serious involvement in Egyptian affairs; and that consequently they would be dealing exclusively with Britain in their fight for independence, as they eventually did.

In 1906–7 there occurred in England a great shift to a radical Liberal government. By and large, this government seemed to favour the rapid development of Western political institutions in such Eastern countries as Egypt where Britain was directly involved. Besides Turkey, there had been movements for constitutional reform in other Middle Eastern countries, prominent among them the revolution in Persia in 1906. However, the greatest impetus to a secularist political movement among Egyptians in the period 1906–14 was the material prosperity and advancement of Egypt. Administrative and other reforms provided the conditions for order and stability which, in turn, led to economic prosperity. Financial restoration in Egypt was, under Cromer, complete by 1904. Projects to extend irrigation and public works had been eminently successful. Prosperity was reflected in the steady growth of the population, which by 1914 had doubled in size, from six to thirteen millions. Many more schools were opened by the government, so that by 1906 there were about 4,500 village schools under government control teaching some 170,000 pupils. In addition to these, over 500 primary and secondary schools employed over 4,000 teachers who instructed just under 100,000 pupils, 20,000 of whom were girls.

Improved irrigation and cultivation methods through British schemes of agricultural reform brought benefits to both peasant farmer and landowner. The orderly and expert administration of these projects coupled with the administrative reorganization of

218

provinces, districts and villages gave the Egyptian cultivator relative stability and security. The June 1909 Provincial Councils Organization Law represented a step towards local self-government. Kitchener did much to alleviate the chronic state of debt of the cultivator by tackling the problem of land shortage, devising means of settling farmers on uninhabited land in such provinces as Gharbiyya, and enacting the Five Feddan Homestead Exemption Law. Article Two of this law expressly prohibited the seizure for indebtedness of agricultural holdings which did not exceed five *feddans*. This exemption also applied to the farmer's dwelling house, two draught animals, and agricultural implements necessary for the cultivation of such land. However, British policy in Egypt as initiated by Cromer and continued by his successors until 1914 was primarily interested in practical administrative reform, whether in finance, agriculture or public works. Its primary aim was to raise the material standards of Egyptians, not to sharpen their political sophistication.

The combination of schools and material prosperity, particularly among the rural population, had far-reaching consequences. A growing class of literate Egyptians emerged from the countryside. Being more prosperous than before, their parents could now afford to send them to the city to study in higher institutions of learning, such as the Law School or Engineering College, as well as to the universities of Europe and England. Those who did not continue higher studies after secondary school flocked into the bureaucracy throughout the country and especially in the capital city.

A new administrative bourgeoisie with strong rural connections emerged from the many technical and leading secondary schools in Cairo, which not only represented a new intelligentsia but also a new nationalist élite.[5] As local political power began to shift due to economic and social change, away from the older Turco-Egyptian aristocracy, landowners and religious leaders to the new groups of professionals, rich cultivators and administrators, the latter group acquired great self-confidence, and with it, wider political ambitions and aspirations. Its members, moreover, had been favoured for advancement by the British authorities in the country. Their political activity was no longer confined to demands for self-government and autonomy under Ottoman suzerainty; now they demanded sovereign independence. As ministers and senior administrators in the governments guided successively by Cromer, Gorst and Kitchener, and as members of the Bar and Bench they had acquired the necessary practical education and experience for the governing of a modern state. Thus at a time when Britain was providing the conditions for greater material prosperity this new generation of Egyptian leaders – the very beneficiaries of British effort – embarked upon the strongest campaign against the British occupation until that time.

Also, by 1906, the legal and administrative link between Turkey and Egypt had for all practical purposes been completely severed. Shaykh Muhammad Abduh, who earlier in his career had helped Jamal al-Din al-Afghani to formulate the call for Pan-Islamic regeneration, was dead. The manipulative Islamic nationalism of Khedive Abbas II had been undermined by 1904, when England and France concluded the Entente Cordiale. Sir Eldon Gorst, who succeeded Lord Cromer in 1906, had embarked upon a policy of conciliating the Khedive with Britain in the hope of detaching him temporarily from nationalists such as Mustafa Kamil and Shaykh Ali Yusuf. The temporary alienation of the Khedive from the loudest nationalists of the time convinced the emerging new group of national leaders of the necessity to concentrate their efforts upon a practical identification of Egyptian political interests, independently of any Pan-Islamic or pro-Ottoman sentiments, and the urgent need to work for their realization through organized political action and, in the view of many among them, through negotiation with Britain.

Without rejecting Islam as a religion, the leaders and publicists of the new political groups abandoned the earlier Pan-Islamic ideal as a means of political advancement for a more liberal, moderate view that such advancement depended on the organization of a secular polity. This change in thinking brought them into conflict with those extremist nationalists led by Mustafa Kamil, who held that all advancement for Egyptians must begin with the expulsion of Britain from Egypt. The educated Muslim disciples of Abduh and the American and French-educated Syrian Christians, furthermore, now began with the premise that the application of science and modern European culture to the reform of their society was a prerequisite for any political advance. If this entailed a temporary accommodation with British policy which, during this period, was producing tangible material benefits for Egyptians, this new group of liberal secularists was not averse to it.

They adopted the European secular notion of the nation-state, to replace the basically religious concept of the community, or *umma*, in Islam. Party political organization, the debate of public policy issues, the development of a responsible electorate, civic responsibility, rights and obligations of a citizen in a secular state – these were now the ideas copied from Europe which would guide enlightened Egyptians to political maturity and emancipation. In short, local Egyptian patriotism, the allegiance and loyalty of individuals irrespective of religious belief or community to an 'Egyptian nation', was now the guiding principle of political action instead of the supranational and universalist formula of Islamic and Pan-Islamic nationalism of the earlier period, 1882–1906. As the intellectual basis of this secular liberal trend was European and, for this generation of leaders, specifically British and French, it was natural that the leaders of this political development in Egypt should be closer to the British than their predecessors.

Again in 1906, the loyalties of Egyptians underwent new pressures from both the turn of events and the division between their leaders reflected in further internal conflicts. That year the Aqaba Incident marked a watershed in Egyptian history and the history of Anglo-Egyptian relations. As early as January 1892, the Sultan in Istanbul wanted to separate a small area immediately west of Aqaba from the Sinai Peninsula district. At first this design of the Porte was not readily apparent. Only subsequently was the Sultan's delay in issuing the *firman* which officially recognized the succession of Abbas II to the Khedivial throne in Egypt seen as a means of exerting pressure on Lord Cromer to agree that Egypt should relinquish its administrative responsibility over that part of territory.

In 1906, Turkey had decided to extend the railway line from Ma'an south to Aqaba. For this purpose, Turkish troops occupied Taba, a point eight miles west of Aqaba. Britain, on behalf of the Egyptian government, protested this move to Istanbul, and demanded the evacuation of the Turkish garrison from Taba. The protest was based on the 1840 Treaty of London and the provisions of the 1892 *firman* to Abbas II, both of which had recognized Egyptian administrative responsibility over the Sinai Peninsula. France, in 1906, supported the British position, and her representative in Istanbul urged the Porte to meet the withdrawal demand. Finally, in May 1906, the Turkish garrison was withdrawn from Taba. A Turkish–Egyptian Commission was appointed to settle the dispute and a Frontier Agreement was reached in October 1906. It set the eastern frontier along a line running from Rafa on the Mediterranean coast in the west to a point three miles west of Aqaba. Thus, Taba was kept within Egyptian territory, whereas Aqaba remained Turkish.

Whether or not by this incident Turkey wished to reopen the Egyptian Question – the matter of her legal sovereignty over the country versus the status of the British occupation – Egyptians themselves were agitated by it. Mustafa Kamil and the public at large appeared on the side of Turkey. They considered Britain's position humiliating to themselves in so far as it emphasized total British control over the affairs of Egypt. Demonstrations, riots and an anti-British campaign in the local Arabic Press characterized public response to this incident. A religiously motivated outcry predominated.

The Aqaba Incident found the extreme Nationalists led by Mustafa Kamil and the Pan-Islamists led by Shaykh Ali Yusuf supporting Ottoman claims to the Sinai borders of Egypt against Britain. The young Khedive Abbas encouraged both, especially in the support he offered to their respective newspapers *al-Liwa'* and *al-Mu'ayyad*. Egyptian Islamic response to Europe and the British occupation was no longer reformist but appeared as a movement for independence from alien control. The struggle against Britain was if not actually viewed, at least represented, by the Khedive, Kamil and Yusuf, as a Muslim struggle against European domination.

However, the respective alliances between the young Khedive and Mustafa Kamil and Ali Yusuf may have been convenient, each motivated by highly practical considerations.[6] Affiliations and loyalties of Egyptian politicians, viz., pro-Khedive, pro-Ottoman, pro-British, or pro-French and anti-British, were reflected in domestic conflicts over such issues as the founding of a national Egyptian University in 1905–7, and the founding of a state school for religious judges. Whereas Khedive Abbas was in favour of an Egyptian University along with secular leaders because Cromer was against the project, he opposed the state school for religious judges because it was championed by Zaghlul, the Minister of Education who was a protégé of Cromer and a leading liberal administrator at that time.

A further indication of the widening split between the Khedive and his camp of conservative, Muslim-oriented leaders on one hand, and the more secular leaders emerging among the administrative cadre nurtured by Cromer on the other, was the reconciliation of Abbas with Mustafa Kamil, leader of the Nationalists in October 1906. Proof of the reconciliation was the financial contribution Abbas made for the founding of the English and French newspapers, *The Standard* and *L'Etendard* respectively, to push the line of Kamil's Arabic paper, *al-Liwa'*. It has also been alleged that at this time the

Khedive agreed to the formation of the National Party (*al-hizb al-watani*) to counter the Umma or People's Party of the *Jarida* group.[7]

Moreover, ever since 1904, a slow but steady involvement of secondary school students and those in institutions of higher learning (the Law School especially) in politics occurred. Most of them were particularly responsive to the nationalist agitation of Mustafa Kamil. They read Ali Yusuf's *al-Mu'ayyad* and Kamil's *al-Liwa'*. They congregated in cafés to discuss politics. They formed student political organizations, among them a club for graduates. Students in the Law School went on strike for the first time in 1906 to protest against certain new regulations. By 1908, student demonstrations became a factor in Egyptian politics and, by 1919, a fixed characteristic.[8]

The Islamic-orientated agitation against Britain over the Aqaba Incident at the expense of Egyptian-controlled territory, however, had awakened the liberal moderates to the realization that in the future Egyptian territory should not be negotiated by outsiders. Rather, such issues should be the concern of a sovereign Egyptian government.

Meantime, Russia, a European power, had been defeated by an emergent Asiatic power, Japan, in the war of 1905. Although this event heightened general anti-European sentiment,[9] it also suggested to the Egyptians that their political salvation lay in a national revival, reform and constitutional government.

Despite the prosperity experienced by Egyptians until that time, the general economic recession in Europe in 1906–7 caused a serious economic dislocation in Egypt which plagued the country until 1914. Whereas the extremists used this economic difficulty to sharpen their attacks upon the British in Egypt, the liberal secularists drew a further lesson from it, namely, that national economic development was an essential aspect of social and political reform; for they understood the relationship between wealth in economic resources on the one hand and political independence and power on the other. Nevertheless, extremists and moderates alike grew more critical of the extra-territorial privileges enjoyed by European residents in Egypt under the Capitulations. They saw in these an obstacle to uniform legislation and therefore a limitation to any future sovereignty, as well as an affront to their dignity and national sentiment.[10]

The moderates, however, settled for a systematic critical analysis of social and political matters as a concern of Egyptians, independently of what the enemy (Britain) did. They took the view that the elimination of Britain from the Egyptian scene would not magically eradicate problems endemic to the condition of Egyptian society. These had to be tackled anyway. Thus they came to dominate the Egyptian political scene and to lay the foundations of a national independence movement in 1918–22 which ended with the establishment of a constitutional monarchy and a parliamentary system of government in March–April 1923.[11]

THE RISE OF POLITICAL PARTIES

In 1906 three parties were formed which came to dominate Egyptian political life until 1914. All three contemplated the establishment of an independent state in Egypt; all three in one way or another entertained ideas of social reform; and all three sought to influence public opinion by widely disseminating their views in the Press. Their existence at this early date, however, also marked the political differences among the emergent groups of Egyptian national leaders in their approach to the problems of their society, the relations of their country with Britain, and their conception of the social and intellectual bases of a modern nation-state. They also reflected the major division among Egyptian leaders between the conservative, instinctively Islamic nationalists who naturally reflected, if not represented, the predominant loyalties of the masses against non-Muslim foreigners on one side, and the moderate secular liberals who wished to adopt foreign ideas and methods as the means to the attainment of an independent modern state on the other.

In the first group were the followers of Mustafa Kamil and the supporters of Ali Yusuf, since both were deeply moved by the basic ideas of Pan-Islamism expounded earlier by Afghani, namely, the position of Egypt in the Muslim world, and the importance of preserving a loyalty to the authority of the Ottoman Sultan. This intransigent position was, as suggested earlier, encouraged further by the material support they received from Khedive Abbas II, and possibly by the Porte. The Khedive on his side was interested in any Egyptian nationalist group and movement that would strengthen his position *vis-à-vis* the occupying power. He was equally opposed to secularist, British-influenced elements which thought in terms of constitutional government and, therefore, a curtailment of Khedivial power. The anti-Khedive, pro-British elements, including state officials, landowners and professionals on the other hand, saw in their co-operation with the occupying power for the attainment of gradual reform and political emancipation a safer road to power at the expense of the ruling family in Egypt. It was also the way to an end of Ottoman sovereignty over Egypt.

Thus the closest associates of Muhammad Abduh did not in 1906–7 consider the Islamic formula of political salvation feasible or useful. On the basis of events at home and abroad they showed a mistrust of the Pan-Islamic ideal. To them Egypt came first, Islam later. While they shared with the Pan-Islamists and extreme nationalists a feeling of humiliation and aspired to self-rule, they preferred the use of secular means to attain it. Self-improvement in their view had to precede the demand to exercise authority; reform had to underlie emancipation. Whereas the nationalism of the conservative and the extremist depended for its appeal upon an essentially religious identity, the moderate liberal attempted to anchor Egyptian nationalism in a clearly defined *patriotism* which provided a workable formula for the relationship between the individual and the state. This was to be perhaps the major contribution of the secularists to the political advancement of Egyptian society. Whereas the extremist desired a negative freedom from a foreign power, which he hated with religious instinct and emotion and good cause, the liberal equally desired freedom, yet one that was governed by critical reason and responsible behaviour within constitutionally defined limits and institutions.

It was under these conditions and in these circumstances that a group of moderates, including noted landowners, educators, senior civil servants, ministers and writers, founded *Hizb al-Umma* (People's Party), the first modern political party in Egypt, in March–April 1907.[12] Prominent among the founders of the party were Mahmud Sulaiman Pasha, one-time leader of the pro-Orabi Revolt Assembly, and Hasan Abd al-Raziq. Both these men, traditionally leaders in their rural provinces, were in a sense never reconciled to the domination of the Egyptian government by the Turco-Egyptian aristocracy and therefore not too keen to retain Ottoman sovereignty over their country. But the most outstanding member with whose name the Party was generally associated until 1914 was Ahmad Lutfi al-Sayyid (d. 1963), managing editor of the Party newspaper, *al-Jarida*, from its inception in March 1907 until it ceased publication early in 1915. Lutfi, moreover, soon emerged as the brain and conscience of the Party, its theoretician and publicist, so that the total output of the *Jarida* is really a record of the social and political philosophy of Lutfi.

What is significant about the Umma is that its newspaper was more important than the actual activities of the Party itself. In fact, the founding of a publishing house for the *Jarida* with a capital of twenty thousand pounds preceded the formal organization of the Umma Party. In its first issue of 9 March 1907, its managing editor, Ahmad Lutfi, wrote on the definition of its aims as follows:

Al-Jaridah is a purely *Egyptian* paper which aims to defend Egyptian interests of all kinds. It will guide the nation in its truly vital interests, by publishing whatever is conducive to the country's material and moral benefit. It will also criticise every act which affects well or adversely these interests, whether such act is private or public regardless of its source. It seeks the truth ... so that a public opinion can be formulated based on a solid foundation of wisdom and seriousness of thought.... The paper will not distinguish or discriminate between religions and races.[13]

Whereas the nationalist *al-Liwa'* was attacking other groups and newspapers, especially *al-Muqattam* until that time, *al-Jarida* now came forward with the intention of dealing rationally with Egyptian problems as a means of fostering an Egyptian national personality independent of extraneous influences. In this sense it appeared as an antidote to, and a restraining influence upon, the excesses of the Pan-Islamic nationalists. Especially when the latter were able to organize political clubs and stage strikes among secondary and law school students in the years 1904–6, the Umma, which was never a rigidly organized party but more of a spontaneous grouping of educated secularists, recognized the need for a rational approach to both reform and political action.[14] Lutfi, in particular, was convinced that unbridled extremism tended to harden the British attitude towards Egyptian national demands. And this was the case when the departing Lord Cromer disparaged the nationalists both in his farewell speech in Cairo and in his final report published some months after his departure.[15]

The editor of *al-Jarida* argued that if one of the aims of the British occupation was to prepare Egyptians for self-rule, then Egyptians could not achieve that merely by attacking the British and the Khedive. Although opposed to the autocracy of both the Khedive and British power, Lutfi argued that only through reform and movement towards the establishment of the foundations of an Egyptian nation, and by experience derived from the participation of Egyptians in public life, could both these disabilities be overcome. The ultimate aim of the Umma was independence for Egypt. They doubted, however, whether this aim could be attained either by negative attacks upon British power in Egypt, or by seeking shelter and support in Ottoman sovereignty. In their view, a healthy and reformed body politic was a prerequisite to Egyptian sovereign status.

The organization of a moderate party with an eloquent paper to express rationally critical views elicited almost immediate reaction from the extremist nationalists. Mustafa Kamil, the oratorical mesmerizer of the masses who demanded British evacuation from Egypt had, as a result of the Dinshawai Incident, attracted a great following among students, urban masses and peasants. Until this time, however, Kamil had not contemplated organized party activity. He rather preferred a heroic *zaama*, or personal leadership, to a structure that would entail co-operation with and criticism from a formal party executive. Nevertheless, the existence of the Umma Party forced him to organize his own National Party (*al-hizb al-watani*) in Alexandria on 22 October 1907. The constituent meeting of over six thousand people consisted mainly of townspeople, a large proportion of whom were students – his most ardent followers. Although Kamil harangued the crowd about the new party's demand for immediate evacuation, the actual programme he proposed for the Party was a 'me too' echo of the Umma. Kamil was forced to accept the Umma Party principle that Egyptian independence could be achieved only with genuine Egyptian effort. He did not however accept the idea of tactical co-operation and eventual negotiation with Britain on the future of Egypt implicit in the Umma programme. Moreover, Kamil soon expanded the concept of independence to include the Sudan, that is, the Nile Valley – a position to which the rather ineffectual National Party clung until 1952.[16]

Essentially, the difference between the National Party and the Umma lay in the deliberate emphasis Mustafa Kamil placed upon extremist and, if need be, violent mass political action. Until his premature death in February 1908, his whole programme was no more than the inculcation of a blind faith among his followers in one idea: the demand for British evacuation. There was little that was politically practical in his approach to the question of Anglo-Egyptian relations of the time. Yet he was partly successful in firing up an otherwise apathetic Egyptian public to realize the possibility of independence. Kamil was also successful in recruiting a large audience who followed him on faith rather than on a practical consideration of his leadership, or of the odds. Even his detractors and opponents among the Umma Party granted him this much upon his death.[17]

The death of Mustafa Kamil, however, only months after the founding of the Party, spelled its gradual political eclipse. Muhammad Farid (1868–1919), who succeeded Kamil as leader of the Party, did not possess the enthusiasm and magnetic personality of his predecessor. For a long time an exile in Geneva, Farid was never able to exert effective leadership. Instead, the Party came for a time under the control of fanatic elements, prominent among whom was Shaykh Abd al-Aziz al-Jawish, who took over the editorship of the Party organ, *al-Liwa'*, and who played a prominent part in the inter-communal strife, 1910–11;[18] so that by 1914 the National Party was no longer considered by responsible Egyptian leaders as a force in the political life of the country. This became even more apparent when in 1918–22 the struggle for independence was led by men more closely identified with the Umma moderates, as for example, Saad Zaghlul.

Exactly a month after the organization of the National Party on 22 November 1907, the Constitutional Reform Party (*hizb al-islah al-dusturi*) of Shaykh Ali Yusuf came into being. With the National Party representing extremist nationalists on one side, and the Umma Party representing a moderate but secular reform programme for national independence which did not preclude co-operation with the British authorities in Egypt on the other, the Constitutional Reform Party reflected first the views of its founder as expressed in his paper *al-Mu'ayyad* and second, sought to defend the interests of the Khedive and his court officials. At a time when Khedive Abbas had withdrawn his support from Mustafa Kamil and reconciled himself to an accommodation with the new British Consul-General; and at a time when a group of Umma secularists were seeking to curb his power and authority by demanding representative institutions, it was natural for the Khedive to wish to defend his position and safeguard his interests. Without impugning the patriotism of Shaykh Ali Yusuf, one can say that his political party aimed at an alliance between him and the Khedive which would advance his ideas while at the same time maintaining the authority of the Khedive. The Shaykh hoped in this way to rally support for the Khedive against other groups. While adopting Kamil's principle of evacuation and the Umma's demand for representative institutions, Shaykh Ali Yusuf preferred that both these aims be sought under Khedivial leadership. The 'constitutional' part of the Party's name indicated disagreement with the extremist methods proposed by Mustafa Kamil, whereas the 'reform' idea was intended to take the thunder out of the Umma programme, and satisfy the British.[19] Nevertheless, this party was no more than the creation of one man. Besides the unofficial and fitful support of the Khedive and a number of his court officials, the party had no real following in the country. It was no surprise therefore when it disintegrated as soon as Shaykh Ali Yusuf had retired from journalism and died in 1913.

THE SECULAR MODERNISTS

The party therefore with the most positively challenging programme for the creation of a strictly Egyptian national consciousness was the Umma. The writings and activities of its leading members between 1907 and 1914 laid the more solid foundations of Egyptian independence in 1922, and provided some of the leading minds and administrators who took over the responsibility of governing an independent Egypt. Above all it provided a civic forum for progressive Egyptians in the sense that they discussed publicly not only issues of policy, but the bases of reasonable political behaviour, and the education and training necessary for its achievement. What then were the major intellectual influences upon the leading members of this party; how did they respond to these influences; and in what way did they express them?

One of the principal reasons for the creation of a political party by the moderates was, besides their assessment of events affecting Egypt, their abandonment of Islam as a basis of political organization and action. Their decision to do so was not confined to practical calculations, such as approaching the British in a conciliatory spirit. Their stand was also determined by intellectual influences upon their conception of society and politics. For this, the moderate secularists drew from a European source: Graeco-Roman classical humanism chiefly as preserved and interpreted by English and French social and political thought. The beneficiaries of Abduh's call to reason and the translation efforts of an earlier generation of Egyptian *literati* were now in a position to formulate the intellectual content of their own movement by concentrating upon teaching and writing about desirable political principles for the good life, and by outlining the features of new political institutions crucial to the resolution of Egyptian problems. Law, social theory and institutions, education, the evolution of nations, any intellectual discipline which helped them to critically analyse and assess the condition of their own society commanded the interest of the secular liberals. Although the Press in this period took a definite political party coloration, *al-Jarida* was for almost eight years a major forum for the discussion of secularist views. If they were to reject the extremist and Islamic tendencies of the National Party, the Umma moderates had to formulate the idea of an 'Egyptian nation' (*watan*)[20] in terms of reason and the identification of common Egyptian interests. They had to replace vague and emotional – often aimless – rebellion with conviction governed by reason. If the British occupation was a fact, the only way to get rid of it was by acquiring the necessary power that came with education and a calm involvement in public life, not by emotional eruption. Social and economic reform was considered by this strange collection of intellectuals, landowners and state officials the surest road to national self-sufficiency. The latter in turn would render rebellion unnecessary for the attainment of independence. In contrast to the mass orientation of the extreme nationalists, the Umma considered the formation of enlightened public opinion as the function of a political élite, whose members represented real social and economic interests: an élite of intellectuals, property owners, industrialists and traders who possessed excellence in qualifications and virtue in the civic sense. They rejected violent revolution in favour of gradual reform; they opposed the panache of grandiose Pan-Islamic schemes and proposed instead an Egyptian independent state based on the principle of popular sovereignty.

Like the generation which preceded them, these liberals, whom Lord Cromer described as the 'Girondists of Egypt', began their search for a formula for progress by looking at the ways and thought of Europe. Their resort to sources outside Islam was made easier by two things. First was the backlog and cumulative effect of almost a century of reform ventured by the Muhammad Ali dynasty. Second was the dissatisfaction of Egyptian leaders with their society. Abdullah al-Nadim had tried to satirize what he called the 'loosely constructed society' in Egypt with a play on the nation, which although alluding to the evils of tyranny, was nevertheless staged in the Zizinia theatre in Egypt in the presence of the Khedive.[21] Poets depicted the havoc created by the cholera epidemic of 1902 as being partly due to the ignorance and superstition of the population. While the famous attacks upon Islam as a religion and social system by Lord Cromer, Renan and Hanoteaux in France evoked its defence by no less a Muslim reformer than Muhammad Abduh, the need to educate the public and to cure social ills was being championed by all groups alike whether extremist, conservative or progressive, as the only means to a national renaissance.[22] Although the lines of the conflict between conservatives and liberals (whose opponents referred to them as the Europeanizers, *al-mutafranjiyyin*) had now been demarcated, the whole issue of Islam and modernism was at the centre of such matters as individual freedom and representative government, the freedom of thought from undue pressure from the men of religion, the separation of state from religion, and the explosive question of the emancipation of women. Both groups were agreed on the issue of civic liberty, but the questions of freedom of thought and feminism were another matter. While some attacked the ignorance of the ulama, and others were being driven by the tyranny of Abdul Hamid closer to Europe, the general criticism of the weakness of Islam was countered by the call of conservatives for a renaissance based on purified Islam.[23]

The secularist trend, however, was gaining force and momentum because of the freshness of its ideas, the relentless influx of European ways and practices, alongside the agonizing reappraisal of Islam itself. The coming of the telephone to Egypt in 1884, the first tramline in 1897, the opening of a modern National Bank in 1897, and the sight of the first cinema in 1906 were features of modern living which made the appurtenances of European civilization even more attractive. One wonders what Egyptians thought of the institution of an annual Palace Ball in 1893. So was travel to Europe by Egyptians more frequent and common.

While this preoccupation with the ills of Islam and Muslim society was widespread, the writers who outlined the orientation of the future Umma party were seeking answers to the same questions in the humanist and scientific literature of Europe. Ahmad Fathi Zaghlul, the brother of Saad Zaghlul (who, as head of the Wafd in 1918–22, emerged leader of the independence movement), concentrated his efforts on the translation of European classics on law, politics, history, geography and philosophy. He had no intellectual or literary ambitions of his own other than to introduce Egyptians to the ideas which had guided Europe to economic and political achievement. By translating Rousseau's *Social Contract* and Bentham's *Principles of Legislation*, Fathi Zaghlul was anxious to impress upon his Egyptian readers the relationship of the individual to the State, and to various groups within it. By choosing to translate E. R. Demolins' *A qoi tient la superiorité des Anglo-Saxons* and Gustave le Bon's

Spirit of Society and Secret of the Evolution of Nations, Fathi Zaghlul was perhaps deliberately calling attention to the weakness of his own society. Thus, in the preface to his translation of Demolins, he bluntly declared: 'Compared to the nations of the West, we are weak in will and determination, in agriculture, science, culture, commerce and industry.... We are so weak that we ask the government to do everything for us; we can do nothing for ourselves.'[24]

The translations of Fathi Zaghlul constituted in themselves a clear, albeit indirect, criticism of both individuals and society in Egypt: the apathy and ignorance of the former, and the consequent backwardness of the latter. Implicit in his choice of European works was his aim of ascribing the rise of strong modern states in Europe to the conception of nationality with its corollary of individual and national rights. Individualism as a creed was considered by Fathi Zaghlul to lead to education, initiative and self-improvement. At the same time it held up the English experience as a desirable model for Egyptians to follow.[25]

An immediate effect of these translations was the Egyptian concern with Islamic decadence and a critical investigation by them of their own society. In 1902 *The Muqtataf* published a book by Muhammad Omar entitled *The Present Condition of the Egyptians and the Secret of their Backwardness.* Having divided society into the rich, those in the middle who were fairly well-off, and the poor, Omar painted a broad tableau of his epoch, and concluded that material misery was a close ally of moral and intellectual retardation. This was followed in 1903 by a little-known book on the *Evils of Spiritualist Séances (madar al zar)* by Muhammad Hilmi Zain al-Din. The following year a more serious work by Muhammad Farid Wajdi appeared. Entitled *Islam and Civilization,*[26] it denounced heresy (*bid'a*), because it gave Europeans a false idea of Islam. By discussing the psychological causes of Islamic decadence, Wajdi actually hoped to produce an apologia for Islam and prove that it could be reconciled with the laws of modern civilization. In 1906 a number of books followed the volume by Wajdi which, while showing some deference to the new scientific attitude, nevertheless argued against the adoption of Western ideas, and tried to defend Islam. Among these, one should note Ahmad Fahmi, *The Crime of Europe against Itself and The World,* and Salih Hamdi Hammad, *Civilization and Us.*

It was not, however, until the publication of *Hadith Isa Ibn Hisham* by Muhammad al-Muwailihi (1868–1930) in 1907 that Islamic literature with a social reform message deserved serious attention. Muhammad was the son of Ibrahim al-Muwailihi, a prominent journalist who had edited the paper, *The Mirror of the East* (*Mir'at al-sharq*) and the *Lantern of the East* (*Misbah al-sharq*). Having visited Italy and France, Muhammad was able in his book to combine a European-style romance with a mastery of the classical Arabic style of *al-maqama*. Before Muwailihi, only the Syrian Ahmad Faris al-Shidyaq and Nasif al-Yaziji had used this style successfully. Apart from its monumental literary appeal and success, *Hadith Isa* managed to depict the evolution of modern society and through this to reflect the serious preoccupation of Egyptians with social criticism and the formulation of values. His work also reflected the influence of European moralists like Dumas and Walter Scott.

Muwailihi, for example, depicts changes which occurred in Egypt over a generation – actually the period of the British occupation until 1908. While he describes local colour – life and society in Egypt – he also treats social problems even though in a literary medium. Thus he portrays the Turco-Egyptian aristocratic class left by Muhammad Ali Pasha and his successors. These had inherited vast tracts of land from their ancestors, some of whom were descendants of the old Mamluk princes. He mentions their displacement by the new class of Egyptian officials and their inevitable disappearance. But their economically privileged place, he suggests, had been taken by foreign adventurers. Then, Muwailihi deplores the fact that while Egypt's wealth had passed during this period into foreign hands, the new class of European-educated Egyptians had affected a superficial adoption of European social graces. He depicts the pursuit of education for the sole purpose of attaining posts in the bureaucracy, and the government as an instrument in the hands of the occupation authorities. In the bureaucratic, or official, class he distinguishes two groups, one educated in Europe which took over posts in the judiciary, education and public works (engineering, irrigation), and the free professions of medicine and law. The other group consisted of ministers recruited mainly from remnants of the old aristocracy. In doing this, Muwailihi portrays vividly the prevalence of nepotism, confusion and inefficiency in government. He then portrays women in three major roles or situations: the divorce court, the marriage ceremony (covered and hidden), and in the cabaret or dance hall and the theatre.

One of the ills of European influence Muwailihi sees in the abandonment of the *rif*, the countryside, by the landowners. Yet he praises the replacement in government positions of the old by the young. Preoccupation with public health, medicine, a wider interest in world affairs, and critical social awareness on the part of this new generation are all commended by Muwailihi. Moreover, he observes the new trends in literature, namely the tendency to portray local colour and the life of common Egyptians as well as the treatment of society's problems.[27]

The same interest in the transformation of Egyptian morality and values characterized another important contemporary work, *Layali Satih* by Hafiz Ibrahim.[28]

While this insistence upon a renaissance resting on an Islamic heritage was being publicized, another group of Egyptians was anxious to free thought from religious control and emancipate the public from tradition and superstition. An early expression of this concern exploded to the surface with the publication of *The Emancipation of Women* (*Tahrir al-Mar'a*) by the lawyer Qasim Amin (1865–1908) in 1899. Amin's ideas on the subject elicited tremendous opposition from every conservative quarter: the Azhar, the Khedive, and the extreme nationalists led by Mustafa Kamil. Briefly, Amin attacked the degraded status of women in Islam; and although he did not reject the veil for them, he deplored its use for their total segregation. Since education and freedom are the sources of every good for man, the basis of his civilization and his moral perfection, depriving women of either or both was, Amin argued, tantamount to barbarism. Women have a responsibility towards themselves, their families, and their society. It was wrong to prevent them from carrying out any and all of these responsibilities by segregating them and keeping them abysmally ignorant. The veil which, Amin conceded, did serve as a basis for morality and chastity (*iffah*), should not serve as a pretext to oppress women. Regarding polygamy in Islam, Amin attacked the degeneration of the marriage contract as interpreted by jurists to one which gave man possession of a woman's sexual services. Both the scriptures and common sense, argued Amin, considered marriage a life-long relationship between man and woman, to be governed by love and mutual respect beyond the mere sexual relationship. Here he also argued against easy divorce which in this instance meant the Muslim's repudiation of wives, because divorce in other than exceptionally difficult circumstances – without real cause – 'is not free from harm'.

In less than two years the vitriolic attacks on Qasim Amin were so numerous that he published another volume, *The New Woman*

(*Al-Mar'a al-Jadida*), as a rejoinder.[29] Here Amin indulged in a wider intellectual argument for the emancipation of women; in fact, for the advantages of westernization in general. He accused the leaders of Islam of woolly thinking, and reminded his readers of two historical facts. First, he emphasized the fact that the major accomplishment of Islam was to provide a simple but forceful faith which brought warlike desert tribes together and welded them into the nucleus of a great empire. Second, he bluntly asserted that modern science developed long after Islamic civilization had declined and the oppressive rigidity of watchdog jurists over the behaviour of Muslims had been enthroned. In short, Amin imputed blind stagnation and bigotry to his society in the face of European advance. To treat Europe as an implacable enemy of Islam was to perpetuate such ignorance since there was so much that was beneficial to learn from the West.[30]

Although Amin and his companions among the liberals, as we shall see, never rejected the truth of Islam as a religion, their attraction to the European ideas of freedom, science and civilization prompted them to reject the suggestion that the civilization of Islam was the ultimate in human advancement and progress. This, in essence, was the direction in which the legatees of Muhammad Abduh's reformist work were moving in the first two decades of this century.

The Christian Syrian émigrés who published *al-Muqqattam*, *al-Muqtataf*, *al-Jami'a* and *al-Hilal* did not confine their activities to simple journalism. At least three members of this group, namely Shibli Shumayyil, Farah Antoun and Jurji Zaydan, became prominent for their secularist views which had a great impact on the Egyptian liberal national movement. Their work caused a stir in the period under discussion not only by its novelty and boldness, but also because it appeared at a time when the movement for Egyptian reform and political emancipation was taking definite shape. Salama Musa, a leading journalist of the inter-war period, described the general social and cultural environment in Egypt at this time as follows:

In those years, about 1905 and 1906, we had no notions of culture and literature except in the form of those frozen patterns of eloquence and rhetoric that we had learnt by heart, passively and with dislike. But when I got to know Farah Antoun's magazine *al-Jamia* it conveyed to me at once a new perspective, and even a new inspiration ... a first glance at the new world of European literature ... the literature of rebellion.[31]

After stating that in those days there were three newspapers

that had good circulation, namely *al-Liwa'*, which exhorted the people to demand the evacuation of the British which was read by all the young men; *al-Mu'ayyad*, which supported the Khedive and was read by the scions of Turkish families and by the conservatives among the Egyptians; and *al-Muqattam*, which was pro-English and read by the officials,[32]

Salama Musa described the nature of cultural and social unrest amidst political disturbance. It was, he says, essentially a conflict between the scientific approach of the secularists, and the traditional view of the conservatives. The role of the *Muqtataf* periodical published by the Syrians Sarruf and Nimr, and the *al-Jamia* by Farah Antoun in that conflict was to put across to the public in popular form the new European sciences, especially Darwin's theory of evolution. A further cultural upsurge, according to Salama, was instigated by additional translations of English and French literature.[33]

The debate over cultural matters coincided with Lutfi's articulation of the idea of an Egyptian nation and nationality separate and distinct from any Islamic identity and the Ottoman State. At the same time, there was a general awareness of the need to escape the bonds of traditionalism in favour of modern scientific knowledge. The scientific ideas of Europe were being particularly publicized by Christian Syrian émigré writers and journalists. Many of these had been educated in French and American schools. They had come to the relatively free Egypt of the 1880s to escape the despotic rule of Sultan Abdul Hamid. Two young teachers of the Syrian Protestant College in Beirut, Yaqub Sarruf and Faris Nimr, moved with their literary-scientific periodical *al-Muqtataf*, which they founded in 1876, to Cairo in 1884, where it continued to be published for another fifty years. Together with a third Lebanese, Shahin Makarius, they founded the daily newspaper *al-Muqattam* five years later in 1889. Both in their periodical and newspaper they expressed their belief in the efficacy of European culture and civilization for Arab advancement, and opposed the Islamic alternative to the solution of Egyptian problems advocated by Shaykh Ali Yusuf's *al-Mu'ayyad*, which was also founded in 1889.[34]

Among those who wrote for *al-Muqtataf* were linguists interested in simplifying the Arabic language, like Amin Maaluf and Abd al-Aziz al-Bishri; translators and novelists like Farah Antoun interested in introducing Egyptians to French thought and literature; and medical scientists like Shibli al-Shumayyil, who was also a socialist, concerned with establishing the importance of science in the life of a nation.

An early graduate of the Syrian Protestant College medical school, Shumayyil (1860–1917) completed his medical training in Paris before settling in Egypt to practise. He soon took an interest in public affairs and became a frequent and most illustrious contributor to the pages of *al-Muqtataf*. Shumayyil, more than any of his contemporaries, believed that only scientific rationalism could undermine the oppressive hold of religious dogmatism. Strongly influenced by the effect of biology, especially the Darwinian theory of evolution, upon social thought, Shumayyil concluded that the basis of a polity in which liberty and justice were possible was science. The universalism and unity of being claimed by religious belief was more forcefully and truly emphasized by science. Using the concept of Social Darwinism constructed by Huxley and Spencer in England, Shumayyil attempted his own construction of a metaphysical system that would serve as the basis of a new morality for society in Egypt.

To preach the ideas of biological and social evolution as an inevitable process independent of religion was, to a society whose structure and order were still based on religious community, shocking to say the least. Shumayyil's teachings were not seen by the leaders of religion and tradition as a plea for necessary reform, but as constituting a crass materialist doctrine. This doctrine, moreover, was being advocated by a Christian to undermine Islamic religious belief. Hence it was attacked, and its advocate was branded a *dakhil*, that is, a foreign intruder.[35]

Another Christian Syrian, Farah Antoun (1874–1922), translated Rousseau's *Emile* at a time when an even greater number of Egyptian readers were being introduced to translations of English and French stories in the Press.[36] Of greater impact on the emerging liberals in Egypt was his publication of the periodical *al-Jami'a*. In his articles, Antoun was opening to Egyptians the door to the study of the European renaissance, especially as the latter was documented and represented by French literature and thought. If the scientific materialism which underlay the work of Shummayyil was shocking, the suggestion by Antoun that the basic teachings of all religions were really similar, that revelation was no more than the philosophic ability of prophets to dress truth in religious symbols for the benefit of the masses was perhaps downright insulting to devout Muslim ears. The political implications of these suggestions were more controversial than those inherent in the work of Shumayyil. Antoun was more directly concerned with the creation of a truly secular state in which all the 'sons of the nation' were equal irrespective of religious differences; a state in which temporal power was separated from spiritual authority.

Secularist notions came to Christian Arabs at this early date much more easily than to their Muslim brethren. Without minimizing their conviction in the efficacy and need of secular liberalism and scientific rationalism for the achievement of a modern culture and society, it is certain that their Christian upbringing was added motivation in that direction.[37]

Finally, Jurji Zaydan (1861–1914), another of the Syrian émigré journalists, cannot be classified among the secular liberals without some qualification. Although he studied briefly at the Syrian Protestant College, he was really self-taught. Zaydan was more attracted to history, geography, literature and ethics. The periodical *al-Hilal* which he founded in 1892 was largely devoted to these subjects. He shared with Shumayyil a concern for moral and social order based on modern education, including science. Zaydan, however, tried to apply his knowledge of Europe to the study of Arab and Islamic history and culture. Consequently, *al-Hilal* became an accessible medium of public education, widely read by literate Egyptians of all classes. It is indeed a tribute to its founder's competence and imagination that *al-Hilal* survives today after eighty-eight years of uninterrupted publication. Whereas all other periodicals begun in the nineteenth century have ceased publication, including the famous *al-Muqtataf*, *al-Hilal* has survived by retaining its interest as a medium for the popular presentation of topics with a human interest ranging from history, hygiene, education, psychology and literature to nuclear physics, the cinema and television. Thus its encyclopedic interests and range of coverage permitted *al-Hilal* to maintain its appeal to a public whose general reading interests have changed drastically since 1892.

No less significant was the evolution of Zaydan's pioneering work in this kind of journalism. *Dar al-Hilal* emerged as one of the largest publishing houses in the Arab World, which gave Egyptian and Arab readers such weeklies as *Al-Ithnayn wa'l-dunya*, the French pictorial weekly *Images* and its Arabic counterpart *al-Musawwar*. Managed by competently trained journalists, operated by a vast array of reporters, photographers and other staff, and printed with the aid of the latest techniques and most up-to-date machinery, the *Dar al-Hilal* publications are household words in the Arab world. Finally, it served as the training school of many leading Egyptian journalists and writers, including Salama Musa and Fikri Abaza.

AHMAD LUTFI AL-SAYYID

The culmination of these spirited inquiries into the ills of Islamic and Egyptian society occurred in the ideas and writings of the Jarida–Umma group, especially as expressed by its leading spokesman and theoretician, Ahmad Lutfi al-Sayyid (1872–1963).[38]

In order to appreciate fully the positive contribution of Lutfi al-Sayyid to the development of modern thought in Egypt the contemporary reader must bear in mind that he was writing at a time when Pan-Islamic – in effect, pro-Ottoman – sentiment still moved the masses against the British in Egypt, and when any suggestions of compromise or accommodation with European ways, let alone British rule, amounted to treason. To urge Egyptians to deviate from their tradition by adopting alien non-Islamic ideas and institutions was courageous. To consider European ideas essential to Egyptian reform and progress because they were superior to anything Egypt had was plainly revolutionary. Yet, Lutfi al-Sayyid was neither a rebel nor a rabble-rouser. He was perhaps the most uncompromisingly cultured man Egypt has produced in the past seventy-five years.

Affectionately referred to by at least two generations of educated Egyptians as the 'philosopher of the generation' (*failasuf al-jil*), he was not a philospher in the proper sense. He cannot be credited with any originality of thought; yet he was original in the way he tried to transmit European ideas, and in the manner in which he ventured to use these ideas as the basis for the construction of principles to guide the formation of a modern nation in Egypt. Ahmad Lutfi did not provide Egyptians with a metaphysic or an integrated intellectual system. Rather he laid down for them the basic rules for the reasoned criticism of society. Above all, he tried to impress upon his compatriots that a society without a system of values and a set of principles to guide it towards certain goals would remain hopelessly backward. And these could be acquired by modern European education.

Ahmad Lutfi was born in a village of Daqahliyya province in Lower Egypt, the son of al-Sayyid Pasha Abu Ali, a relatively prosperous village headman, or *umda*. After the usual Koranic training in the village *kuttab*, Ahmad Lutfi spent three years at the Mansura primary school, then entered the Khedivial secondary school in Cairo in 1885. With a secondary school certificate in 1889, he entered the School of Law. His formal education was thus strictly Egyptian. Among his contemporaries in law school were many leaders and future leaders in Egyptian politics: Mustafa Kamil, Qasim Amin, Saad Zaghlul, Ismail Sidqi and Abd al-Khaliq Sarwat. While in secondary school he became an avid reader. Among the works he read was Shumayyil's translations of Darwin. In law school he met Muhammad Abduh, a member of the School's Board of Examiners. While on holiday in Istanbul, his friend Saad Zaghlul introduced him to Afghani. Upon graduation from law school he entered government service in its legal department, travelling to many provinces and becoming intimately acquainted with Egyptian life and its problems. While in Geneva one summer with Muhammad Abduh, Saad Zaghlul and Qasmin Amin, he attended lectures at the university and exchanged views with his friends. He read Comte, Rousseau, Mill, Spencer and Durkheim, was morally and intellectually impressed by Aristotle and Tolstoy, and later was attracted by Locke and Bentham.

Lutfi did not stay in government service very long. Inclined more to the contemplative life of a scholar, he lacked the zest for practical politics. From 1907 until it closed down in 1915, he became managing editor of *al-Jarida*. Later that year he became the first Egyptian director of the Khedivial Library, *Dar al-kutub* – the National Library today – and turned once again to the quiet study of Greek philosophy. His brief involvement in politics as a member of Zaghlul's *wafd* (Delegation) in November 1918 proved a disappointment to himself and ended his political career. The quarrel which he witnessed between Zaghlul and Adli Yeken over the leadership of the Delegation to negotiate with Britain was a bitter blow to his optimistic liberal approach to politics. The national unity he had worked for so hard and preached about so eloquently had been shattered. From that time until his retirement in 1942 he taught philosophy at the Egyptian University and at one time served as Rector.

Ahmad Lutfi did his most important work relevant to the development of secular liberal ideas in Egypt and Egyptian nationalism while he was editor of *al-Jarida*, 1907–15. In fact, the major works he left represent collections of articles and editorials written for *al-Jarida*. Whether he discussed education, the relevance of political party activity to representative government, feminism or civic responsibility, Lutfi was arguing from the premise that an Egyptian

nation existed in territorial and historical terms. This nation, moreover, existed independently of the wider religious community of
Islam. Independence, therefore, was the aspiration of all Egyptians irrespective of class, status or education because it is the natural
inclination of all nations to seek independence. If the mass of Egyptians at the turn of the century appeared politically quiet and
quiescent, this was due, according to Lutfi, to their dismal lack of
education which, in turn, weakened their 'national character'. Such
weakness was a cumulative inheritance from generation to generation that could be remedied only by modern education.

Education, therefore, according to Lutfi, should aim first to foster
the independence of the individual as a personality trait, and second,
to imbue a desire for responsible participation by individuals in community life. These traits are essential because 'the strength of a nation
lies in its character. The cultivation of the mind and the refinement
of feeling. . . . Social, economic, and political reform depends upon
the education and upbringing of individual citizens.'[39] The reform
of society must begin with the reform of national character. The
quality of a nation is a reflection of the quality of its individual
citizens. There could be no personal or social well-being with
ignorance; only education in its widest sense (*al-tathqif*) can produce
the good life.

Closely related to Lutfi's conception of the relevance of education
to character-building was his analysis of the state of Egyptian moral
and political standards as they evolved historically. Their tragically
low state was reflected in the Egyptian worship of those in authority,
or close to it, their lack of self-respect as reflected in their utter obei-
sance to autocratic rule, their sloth and despondency. Although
many of these ills of Egyptian society were products of centuries of
despotic rule, their remedy lay in the gradual transformation of
Egyptian character through education, not political revolution. To
inculcate into Egyptians the principles of civic virtue, personal and
social responsibility was, according to Lutfi, the major task of
national regeneration. Such new habits of thought and qualities of
character were so crucial to moral and social regeneration that they
had to be developed gradually.

Lutfi insisted that one could not separate the need for education
from national independence only. Education could also lessen the
differences between individual citizens. He supported the feminist
ideas of Qasim Amin, because to emancipate woman was to educate
her and therefore bring her into the active stream of society. To

educate all citizens was to sharpen their collective consciousness and therefore strengthen the basis of national life. An educated person is better equipped rationally to assess his interests and those of his nation. And nationalism for Lutfi must rest on interest, not on vague, or fanatic, belief. This positivist and utilitarian conception of nationalism led Lutfi to argue for a more pragmatic system of education which prepared men to lead a more active life in the community. It also led him to prefer an ethical and moral training for students based on the humanistic values of modern European philosophy to the strict catechism of religious instruction – a suggestion which implied his abandonment of the consideration of how to reform Islamic society. Instead Lutfi appeared interested in discussing the modern conditions under which a civilized society – any civilized society – would flourish. Generally these conditions were inspired by his study of European culture.

From Europe Lutfi got two obsessions: an implicit confidence in the ability of reason to transform society – hence his confidence in human intelligence and the natural goodness of man, as well as his strong belief in the promise held by education for Egyptians – and the human desire for freedom. The first obsession caused Lutfi to overstate his case for rationalism in politics and rendered him an inveterate optimist regarding the creation of a polity ruled by reason. The second strengthened his plea for what he called a virtuous national life. He did not consider independence an end in itself, but a means to a virtuous national life and to responsible citizenship. The chief virtues of independent national existence were freedom, limited government, and constitutional rights. In this sense, Lutfi's political liberalism was of purely Western inspiration, so that he deplored state-controlled systems of education and urged instead that education remain the responsibility of individual citizens, that economic activity be confined in good *laissez-faire* tradition, to private enterprise.

Because he abhorred personal government and autocratic rule, Lutfi was essentially concerned with freedom, education and national character not only for their own sake, but as generators of tangible and lasting institutions. Thus, he urged Egyptians to acquire experience in public life by participating in the Legislative Assembly as reconstituted by the British in 1913. Although it possessed limited powers, it was a serious step towards self-government and was not to be disdained by Egyptians. In this context also Lutfi saw no serious objection to co-operating with the British authorities in Egypt as he also believed that a powerful state like England would relinquish its occupation of the country only if Egyptians were ready and responsible enough to rule themselves.

The elements of Egyptian nationalism developed and publicized by Lutfi in the *Jarida* constituted the core of the Umma Party ideology. Individual freedom which comes only through education and reform based on the principles and teachings of modern European civilization were the prerequisites of political liberty. The latter, in turn, could be guaranteed only by a constitutional system of government. Lutfi was thus averse to mass emotional appeals by politicians and the tactics of revolutionary action. But because of these views, neither the *Jarida* as a newspaper nor the Umma as a party were ever too popular among Egyptian nationalists. First, the task which Lutfi outlined and assigned to Egyptians for their advancement was exacting and took too long to complete. Second, it presumed an admission that European culture was not only superior, but also offered political salvation for a decadent Islamic community. Third, it proposed too rational and utilitarian a concept of nationalism to be digested by the limited powers of comprehension of the masses. Idealism and romanticism are far simpler techniques for the mobilization of mass sentimental enthusiasm.

The failure of Lutfi's views and those of his party to take root among a greater number of Egyptians is reflected in first, the very brief and isolated sway of secular liberalism in Egyptian political history (1923–52), and second, the devastatingly final way in which those leaders who experimented with it collapsed in July 1952. Yet Lutfi did not fail as a teacher and writer, for his influence on the intellectual and social climate of modern Egypt was genuine and survives today after his death. His failure seriously to influence Egyptian politics was in part due to the fact that he underestimated the political power inherent in the instinctive adherence of Egyptians to their Islamic heritage. By the same token, Lutfi's greatness, among all other advocates of social reform in modern Egypt, lies in his complete honesty and integrity. He did not equivocate on the crucial problem of his day: how to reconcile tradition and religion with modern science and European civilization. While respecting the traditional suggestion that any religion offers a basis for morality, and accepting the fact that Islam did this for the average Egyptian, Lutfi was bold and honest enough to assert that the kind of morality needed for a modern, civilized national existence must derive from non-Islamic sources – the classical philosophy of ancient Greece, the legalism of Rome, and the science of modern Europe. The tragedy of Lutfi was that, whether he knew it or not, intellectually he no longer belonged in 1914 to his native tradition.

Lutfi was advocating a European legal-political notion of citizenship contained in a territorially defined nation-state. The Aqaba Incident of 1906, for instance, had shown clearly the political inadequacy of diffuse notions of Islamic identity and unity.[40] Now, at the outbreak of the Great War, not only had the response of educated Egyptians to the European impact changed, but divisions in the ranks of Egyptian political leaders had occurred. These were the result of both differences in ideological orientation and material interests. More clearly identified political groups emerged in Egypt to lead the struggle for power in the movement for independence.

Thus, in 1914, a great distance separated the deceased Muhammad Abduh from his first disciples. The latter had abandoned his heroic illusion to bend Islam to a civilization created by non-Muslims; for they were now under the spell of European thought. They were willing to adopt not only European ideas, but the very institutions that grew in Europe. The success of the independence movement in Egypt in 1918–22 was not, however, simply the result of the social and intellectual changes which occurred in the country over a century, but also the consequence of international events. Yet, for the next thirty years, Egyptians showed a preference for the application of European ways in the conduct of their social, economic and political affairs. To a survey of the success and failure of this application and the ensuing anti-Western reaction of Egyptians after the Second World War we now turn.

PART THREE

Society, Government and Politics
1919–39

CHAPTER 12

THE STRUGGLE FOR INDEPENDENCE 1919–22

Among the great accomplishments of British guardians over Egypt in the period 1883–1914 was the creation of an efficient Egyptian administration, relatively free of major corruption and with it the initiation of a sound fiscal policy for the country. These achievements brought economic prosperity to the country. The production of cotton doubled within twenty years, while the fellah felt more secure, and the landed bourgeoisie grew more prosperous. So that at the outbreak of the war in August 1914 the country enjoyed a stable and efficient government, a solvent economy, a greatly increased production of high-quality cotton, and a Legislative Assembly. Even though this Assembly possessed limited powers, it served as a forum for the discussion of public policy matters by the new élite of educated Egyptians. It became a platform for those who wished to stir up nationalist feeling among the Egyptians. Moreover, a reasonably free Press in which both Egyptians and émigrés played a large role contributed to the wider spread of ideas of political independence.

Native financiers and entrepreneurs began to emerge from the ranks of enriched cotton-growing landowners with economic and political ambitions. Meanwhile, the extremist nationalist and Pan-Islamic leaders, Mustafa Kamil and Shaykh Ali Yusuf, had passed away from the political scene. Secular reformists, among them Ahmad Lutfi al-Sayyid and Saad Zaghlul, with reputable positions in journalism and government, came into national prominence. They believed in political emancipation through reform not revolution, a series of steps in self-government which would advance towards independence through negotiation with Britain.[1]

In addition to cultural and social developments the peculiarities of Egyptian nationalism in this period derive partly from Britain's occupation policy, from the nature of her position in Egypt, and from the unforeseen effects of the Great War. The juridical status of Egypt as an autonomous state ruled by the Muhammad Ali dynasty had been established and internationally recognized by the

247

Treaty of London (1840). Changes in the system of succession within the Muhammad Ali house, the fixing of the annual tribute payment to the Sultan were regularized from time to time by Imperial Decree from Istanbul. For all practical purposes, however, Egypt was, until 1882, an independent state. Turkey's nominal sovereignty was consistently whittled down until the British occupation in 1882 severed direct political connection between Turkey and Egypt. The occupation, on the other hand, as became clear in the events of 1906 (the Aqaba Incident), 1911 (The Italo-Turkish War in Tripoli) and 1914, did not erase all feelings of loyalty and sentiment between the Muslim population of Egypt and the Ottoman State headed by the Sultan-Caliph.

While nominal sovereignty over Egypt belonged to the Ottoman Sultan, actual power in the country was exercised by the British Agent and Consul-General through the Khedive and his council of ministers from 1883 until 1914. British control soon extended throughout the Nile Valley by the re-conquest of the Sudan after the Mahdi Revolt and was regularized by the signing in 1899 of the Anglo-Egyptian Condominium Agreement over the Sudan.

The question of the status of the British occupation, including the generally unsuccessful diplomatic attempts to raise it with Turkey in the 1880s, had remained unsettled. Britain had occupied Egypt in 1882 for two reasons: first, in order to prevent the overthrow of Khedivial rule by the Orabist rebels, and second, in order to forestall possible European intervention on behalf of subject creditors in Egypt. A combined European intervention might have endangered the security of British communications to India. It is equally certain that Britain did not at first intend a permanent occupation of Egypt. It is also certain that she wished to prevent other powers from getting a foothold astride her imperial life-line.[2] The Entente Cordiale concluded between France and Britain in 1904 did not settle the matter but it at least secured European recognition of the special position of Britain and her interests in that country. By this time, mounting Anglo-German rivalry was influencing British strategic thinking about Egypt. Moreover, the decline of British and the growth of German influence in Istanbul between 1908 and 1914 led Britain to consider the prolongation of her presence in Egypt.

If Britain then merely intended to neutralize Egypt and prevent it from falling prey to other European powers, it was essential to reform its administration in order to strengthen its finances and, in turn, satisfy European bondholders of Egyptian debts. To both these tasks the British authorities in Egypt attended with vigour, imagination and unequalled competence, though at the price of not paying equal, or even adequate, attention to other crucial matters.

British administrative reform of agriculture brought unparalleled prosperity and wealth to a small number of Egyptian landowners. The latter purchased ever larger tracts of land, so that by 1913 some thirteen thousand landlords holding over fifty *feddans* each owned between them 2·4 million *feddans* of arable land, or just under half of the total cultivated area of Egypt at that time, while one and a half million peasants, each owning five *feddans*, possessed a total of one and a half million *feddans* between them – an average of one *feddan* per fellah. Those who owned over five but under fifty *feddans* either bought more land, or were bought out by larger landowners. Given the Islamic law of inheritance, the tendency was for the small landholdings to be further parcelled out into infinitesimal holdings, whereas prosperous estates of large landowners grew bigger.[3]

This overemphasis upon the rehabilitation of Egyptian administration and finances did not derive solely from the undetermined position of Britain after the occupation, but also from the peculiar background and experience of British officials who, led by Cromer, came to administer Egypt for a quarter of a century.[4] Egypt was not a part of the British Empire: it was neither a colony nor a dominion. To this extent, Britain was not in a position either to undertake fundamental reforms in all aspects of Egyptian affairs, or to establish a clearly British civil autocracy over the country. Instead, the British found themselves supervising a basically Egyptian administration with a view to making it more efficient and less corrupt, in order to achieve certain limited ends. The charge made by Egyptians that the British neglected the social and political education of the nation should be assessed within the same context. If Lord Cromer viewed public instruction as a means of producing state civil servants, so did the vast majority of Egyptians (with the exception of the *Jarida*–Umma group) who flocked to government employment with their Secondary Baccalauréat diplomas. Yet, because of this situation, those among the students in institutions of higher learning (law, medicine, teachers' colleges), administrators and landowners who nursed political ambitions did so outside the purview of the British administrative reform programme. There was moreover, since the Orabi affair, an active publicity campaign by British liberals and anti-imperialists against the British presence in Egypt. Led by Wilfrid S. Blunt, a small group of Englishmen actively sought by writing and lecturing to vindicate the Orabists by showing the injustices of British action in Egypt. Furthermore, British liberal thought in general did have some impact upon the rising generation of the Egyptian intelligentsia of that time.

On 5 August 1914, the day following the British declaration of war on Germany, the Egyptian government of Husayn Rushdi Pasha issued a proclamation which recognized the special position of Britain at war in Egypt, and forbade all commercial and financial dealings between Egyptians and the nationals of Britain's enemies.

In 1913 cotton produce in Egypt amounted to a total value of just under thirty million pounds. In August 1914, cotton-growers, merchants and exporters were suddenly faced with the prospect of not being able freely to export their product. Britain would have to secure both its disposal and the importation of essential commodities. This uncertainty caused a minor financial and economic panic in the country which led the government to take quick steps to deal with the situation. As the shipment of gold into the country for the cotton season was unlikely in wartime, a short moratorium was imposed on all commercial loans and notes. This caused a sharp decline in cotton prices. Moreover, a decree was issued making the notes of the National Bank of Egypt legal tender. Soon the note issues of the Bank were to be backed by British Treasury Bills.[5] The crisis was not overcome, however, until December of that year, when the Egyptian government was authorized to purchase cotton on the open market on behalf of the British government, and when a decree was passed restricting cotton acreage to allow for the increase in the cultivation of cereal and other essential food crops. All the same, it is estimated that Egyptians lost over twenty million pounds in the cotton business in the first two years of the war.

The Legislative Assembly which was scheduled to reconvene on 1 November 1914 was, by a decree issued on 18 October, postponed until 1 January 1915. After other extended postponements, it was on 27 October prorogued *sine die*. Simultaneously, a law prohibiting public meetings and assemblies of five persons or more was passed. When war broke out between Russia and Turkey on 1 November, Sir John Maxwell, General Officer Commanding British Forces, Egypt, imposed martial law in the country, and declared that Britain would shoulder the whole burden of war, including the defence of Egypt. He also announced that Egyptians would not be required to participate actively in the war; they were merely required to refrain from assisting the enemy.[6] War with Turkey was formally declared on 6 November. General Maxwell immediately announced that Britain was now fighting to safeguard, among other things, the freedom and independence of Egypt. At the same time, he informed the Egyptian Prime Minister that the policy of his government was now under the supervision and control of the British military authorities.

A protectorate over Egypt was declared on 18 December 1914. Britain had now, by unilateral action, changed the legal status of Egypt, for it detached the country from Turkey permanently. As an attempt to legalize British control over the Egyptian government the Declaration may have been superfluous: such control already existed by virtue of a martial law effectively imposed by the presence of British armed forces in the country. What is significant about the Declaration for Egyptian nationalism however is the British undertaking – as distinguished from an aim already expressed in 1882 – included in its terms to consider the future status of Egypt regarding self-government. This the Egyptians took to mean that the Protectorate was a temporary arrangement to be changed after the war by bilateral agreement with Britain.

Khedive Abbas II, who had travelled to Istanbul at the beginning of the summer, was still there when war war broke out. Despite the suggestion by Rushdi Pasha that he return to Egypt immediately, Abbas hesitated and postponed his return. The British had for long suspected his intrigues at the Ottoman Porte, and did not wish for his return. He was therefore deposed on 19 December, the day after the Protectorate was declared. His uncle Husayn Kamil was appointed to succeed him with the new title of Sultan instead of Khedive.[7] He was the first Egyptian ruler of his line not to be appointed by Imperial decree of the Ottoman Sultan. Within a few days, on 21 December, the government of Rushdi Pasha moved to sever all remaining links with the Turks, by abolishing the office of Chief Qadi of Egypt – a position held by Turks appointed from Istanbul since the Ottoman conquest in 1517. The combination of martial law and protectorate status gave the British military authorities virtual legislative and executive powers in Egypt. The new Rushdi cabinet formed on the day Husayn Kamil was appointed Sultan was there simply to facilitate British rule and its prosecution of the war.

Meanwhile Lord Kitchener had left his post as British Agent and Consul-General in Egypt to become Secretary of State for War in England. He was succeeded in Cairo by Sir Henry MacMahon from the

Indian Civil Service. The task of Sir Henry was soon complicated by the increased military demands of unforeseen developments in the war against Turkey in the Sinai, the Hijaz, and the trouble with the Senusi warriors on the Egyptian–Cyrenaican border. At the end of 1914, a Turco-German offensive on the Suez Canal from Palestine inaugurating military operations in the Sinai brought the war to Egypt's doorstep. Gradually, Egypt became a huge concentration of British, Australian and other Imperial troops. In 1915 and 1916 preparations for expeditions to Gallipoli and later for the invasion of Palestine necessitated new and heavy demands by the military on the civilian population with regard to the requisition of buildings, the recruitment of labour to help lay lines of communications, transport and other facilities, the purchase and requisition of animals and fodder. As a result of these increased demands of the army upon Egyptian resources the civilian population became annoyed at the inconveniences caused by the war. Prices of consumer commodities rose, profiteering Egyptian and foreign landlords and merchants exploited the situation, and the heaviest burden fell on the peasant, salaried lower classes, and the unemployed.

Some opposition to these conditions was expressed in 1915 when students at the Law School boycotted the visit of the Sultan to their institution. Members of the National party were arrested. Extremists who viewed the acceptance of the Protectorate by the Rushdi government and the Sultan as treasonable attempted to assassinate the Sultan on two separate occasions within three months. Early in 1916 there was a demonstration in front of Abdin Palace in Cairo to protest against the recruitment of Egyptians into the Labour Corps, and the requisition of animals and fodder from the countryside. An Egyptian Labour Corps and a Camel Transport Corps had been formed early in 1916 to assist the British in the construction of a railway in the Sinai. Recruitment to the Labour Corps was voluntary at the beginning, well organized directly by the British authorities and sufficiently well paid. The following year, as the Expeditionary Force moved towards Palestine and Syria, the Labour Corps moved right along with it. Fellahin recruits got farther and farther away from their homes. More recruits for the Corps were demanded by the military. Their recruitment was delegated to the Egyptian government who, in turn, instructed provincial governors, district officers and village headmen to provide the volunteers. Many of these were, however, forcibly recruited by the local authorities. Throughout the provinces the temper of the fellah who, up to 1914, had every reason to be grateful to Britain, was now raised in anger against the British. He was being forcibly taken away from his land, home and family to serve as a labourer for troops fighting a war in defence of a foreign king and country and against the Ottoman Sultan and Caliph of Islam. By the end of the war over one and a half million Egyptians had passed into the Labour Corps.

In the towns Egyptian and foreign contractors for supplies and services to the British forces made windfall profits, and the cost of living rose sharply. When the price of cotton rose more than fourfold from the 1914 level – from four to seventeen Egyptian pounds per *kantar* – landowners sought to cultivate larger areas of their land with cotton for quick profit returns. The acreage for other crops dropped and a shortage of foodstuffs ensued. Both rural and urban masses were by the end of 1917 suffering considerable hardships as a result of the war. They resented not only the British demands made upon them and their resources, but also the harsh administration of their own governors and local masters. Many of the latter, the peasant observed, were enriching themselves quickly at his expense.

The group of intellectuals who had so actively pursued nationalist ideas in the two decades before the war were, under martial law, required to shelve their activities. The *Liwa* of the extreme nationalists was no more, and the *Jarida* of the Umma Party had ceased publication in 1915. They felt frustration and bitterness when the British encouraged less advanced Arabs in the Hijaz of the Arabian Peninsula to rebel against Turkey in return for independence. Those among the Egyptian intellectuals who were landowners viewed with apprehension the agricultural schemes of Britain to irrigate Gezirah province in the Sudan in 1917, for it implied competition for their cotton crop and the use of Nile waters to their disadvantage. Although they became unduly prosperous in war, they were gradually alienated from Britain and came to suspect her intentions regarding Egypt.

Because of the war, local native industries began to develop quickly to supply goods which were previously imported from Europe: textiles, fezes, sugar and tobacco were among them. Increased transport requirements in wartime multiplied the number of railway and dock workers. A nucleus of an industrial labour force began to grow in Cairo, Alexandria, Ismailiyya, Suez and Port Said.

Whereas before the war nationalist agitation was confined to the educated few, the war with its unforeseen consequences for the Protectorate slowly produced a general malaise and feeling of alienation from Britain among most classes of the population. The British, in public eyes, had deposed Khedive Abbas II; they had poured masses of foreign troops into Egypt; they had requisitioned buildings, crops and animals; they had conscripted over one and a half million Egyptians into the Labour Corps; in short, contrary to their promise, they had involved Egyptians in a war against the Sultan. Even though the war brought huge fortunes to a few Egyptian landowners and foreign merchants, it also brought misery to untold thousands of less fortunate Egyptians. Yet, because the declaration of the Protectorate in 1914 was also accompanied by a British undertaking to accelerate progress towards self-government, the political classes in Egypt, at least, prepared for political agitation as soon as hostilities had ended. The war on the other hand, had impressed upon Britain the paramount strategic importance of Egypt, and any political settlement with the Egyptian nationalists after the war had to be one that did not jeopardize British strategic control of the area. The impending disintegration of the Ottoman Empire made this British objective even more urgent in relation to the whole Middle Eastern area.

Sir Reginald Wingate, Sirdar of the Egyptian Army and Governor of the Sudan, replaced MacMahon at the British Residency in 1916. In ill-health for a long time, Sultan Husayn died on 9 October 1917. His only son, Prince Kamal al-din Husayn, had previously declined the succession, and Sultan Husayn's brother Ahmad Fuad (in 1923 King Fuad I) ascended the throne on 10 October.

Fuad, however, had a great political ambition. Together with Rushdi Pasha, the Prime Minister, he pressed the British for a reconsideration of the Capitulations and a look into constitutional reform as foreshadowed in the Protectorate Declaration of 1914. Fuad and Rushdi were anxious to extract political concessions from Britain in order to bolster their prestige with the nationalist leaders and the masses. Britain, on the other hand, was not in a position to refuse consideration of these demands as her refusal might have undermined a government which had collaborated with her throughout the war. The British were moreover certain that political agitation would follow immediately upon the cessation of hostilities. Much of this could be forestalled if Britain showed her willingness to live up to her intentions as formulated in the Protectorate Declaration.

The Special Commission set up in December 1917 to examine the question of the Capitulations and constitutional reform completed its work just before the end of hostilities in Europe in November 1918. It was dominated by Sir William Brunyate, Judicial Adviser to the Egyptian Government. Regarding the Capitulations, the Commission could not, and did not, accomplish anything without the consent of the European states concerned. Short of an international convention to deal with the Capitulations (as indeed took place at Montreux in 1937) bilateral negotiation between England and Egypt was unrealistic. Its formal recommendations on constitutional reform moreover were just as unrealistic and unacceptable to Egyptians.

The unjustified apprehension of Britain over the neutrality of Egypt in wartime led to the imposition of a Protectorate whose political implications made a post-war clash between Egyptian nationalist aspirants to power on the one hand, and the protecting power on the other, inevitable. Martial law and security requirements prevented the continued public dialogue between modern Egyptian reformers and national leaders, while a servile and malleable government ruled only in name by necessarily collaborating with the British military authorities. Developments elsewhere in the Middle East – the Arab Revolt headed by Sharif Husayn of Mecca – and President Wilson's Fourteen Points which emphasized the right of self-determination for all subject peoples (although certainly referring to Central and East Europeans mainly), further encouraged Egyptian nationalists to press their demands for independence two days after the armistice was signed in Europe.

The new leaders of the independence movement subscribed neither to the earlier Pan-Islamic pro-Ottoman sentimentalism of Shaykh Ali Yusuf and his collaborators at the turn of the century, nor to the romanticism of Mustafa Kamil's National Party. Rather they were closer to the secular liberal teachings of the *Jarida*–Umma group. In addition, many members of this group had by 1918 acquired an economic interest in political independence, whether as landowners, financiers, or even incipient industrial and commercial entrepreneurs. They represented the nucleus of a native Egyptian national landed and commercial bourgeoisie for whom independence promised power and status.[8]

The leader of this new movement was Saad Zaghlul, who until then was not known as a political leader, but who soon came to dominate the national political scene until his death in 1927 as the 'Father of Egyptians' and as the founder of the Wafd, the best organized mass party in the annals of modern Egyptian history. He was born in Ibiana village of the Gharbiyya province in the Delta in 1857 or 1860: the exact year of his birth is not known. His father was a prosperous landowning village headman, *umdah*, a position which gave the family prestige and local political influence. After the usual traditional schooling in the village *kuttab*, Zaghlul went to the Azhar in Cairo in 1871, the year Afghani had arrived in Egypt. In the same year a certain reorganization of the Azhar had taken place under the leadership of the then Shaykh Abbas al-Mahdi, pertaining to the system of examinations for the *'alamiyya* certificate. Zaghlul thus arrived when religious reform was in the air. He was drawn into the group of Afghani and Abduh disciples and in 1880 was appointed assistant to Abduh in editing the Official Gazette. An interest in legal reform led him to the study of law, its practice, and service in the judicial branch of the government. From the time he was appointed a judge in the Court of Appeals in 1892 Zaghlul was associated with the ideas of Abduh, Qasim Amin and Ahmad Lutfi al-Sayyid regarding the legal and administrative institutions of the country. He worked to modernize legal practice, the Sharia courts, and the administration of justice generally. He acquired a reputation for administrative ability and forthright behaviour.

Zaghlul was, it seems, an effective administrator, who aspired to a political career. While serving on the Bench he learned French and studied in the French Law School in Cairo. With an eye on political connections – always helpful in any society and especially in Egypt in those days – Zaghlul married in 1906 the daughter of the notoriously pro-British Prime Minister, Mustafa Fahmi Pasha. This union gave him an easy entrée into the inner circle of the ruling classes and the Khedivial court. It also brought him quickly to the attention of the British Consul-General. Before relinquishing his post in Cairo, Lord Cromer, impressed by Zaghlul's administrative competence, but perhaps also assured of his pro-British attitude because of his relation to the Prime Minister and his connection with the Umma Party, prevailed upon Khedive Abbas to appoint him as Minister of Education in 1906. The year was important, as we saw earlier, for the Egyptian national élite. Whether the new Liberal government in London had decided to permit the further development of Egyptian self-government, or whether Cromer was making a concession to Egyptian national sentiment after the Dinshawai Incident, is not very clear. But the appointment of Saad Zaghlul to this important cabinet post was significant for the further Egyptianization of the administration. It also gave priority to the moderate secular liberals to attain experience in government.

As Minister of Education from 1906 until 1910, Zaghlul aimed at extending literacy among Egyptians. He increased the number of schools including village *kuttabs*, and opened night schools for adults. By dint of hard work and a forceful personality, Zaghlul asserted his authority over the British advisers and ministry inspectors. He pushed for the replacement of English by Arabic as the language of instruction, and employed more Egyptians as school inspectors. His most dramatic achievement as Minister of Education and then as Minister of Justice was the founding of a school for the train-- ing of Sharia judges under the control and supervision of the Ministry. It angered, however, both the conservative Azhar shaykhs and the Khedive. In fact, Zaghlul shared with Shaykh Muhammad Abduh and Ahmad Lutfi the view that reform required the curtailment of the Khedive's power, and he was never on good terms with Abbas II. When in 1910 he was appointed Minister of Justice, a department directly relevant to Zaghlul's administrative reform interests, he soon disapproved of Gorst's policy of giving greater power to the Khedive. As he also did not get on well with Kitchener, he resigned his post in 1913 to stand for election to the new Legislative Assembly established by Kitchener.

While Minister of Justice, Zaghlul was anxious to elevate the standards of the legal profession and led the group which founded the Bar Association. But throughout his ministerial career, 1906–13, Zaghlul was also deliberately projecting his public image among Egyptians in anticipation of future political activity. He issued statements to the Press; he showed concern with 'public opinion'. As a minister in 1909 he had to defend both the reactivated Press Law and the extension of the Suez Canal Concession when these came before the Legislative Assembly. But he also insisted in upholding the right of the Assembly members to reject the proposed measures. He thus appeared as a champion of public control over government policy. When he was elected to the Assembly in 1913–14 he was not only appointed its vice-president but managed within the few months before the Assembly was prorogued *sine die* to establish himself as the leader of the opposition to the government and, by implication, to the British government which stood behind it. Moreover, in that first modern election campaign in Egypt, Saad Zaghlul ran successfully on a platform of greater Egyptianization of the administration. During the five months of the legislative session (22 January to 17

June 1914), Zaghlul was undoubtedly the leader of the secularly educated members who not only took such projects as marsh drainage,
the examination system in schools, and judicial rules for the courts
seriously, but who, in their demand for budgetary control, were
poised against the so-called notables and other aristocrats allied to
the Khedivial court. Even though the Assembly was no more than
a serious debating society, Zaghlul, and the opposition to various
government policies which he led, helped to establish the unmistak-
able existence of a definite national élite that was soon able to mobilize popular support in 1919.[9]

The success of the Allies against the Turks in 1917–18, coupled with
the attempted inquiry into the constitutional future of Egypt by the
Commission headed by Sir William Brunyate, encouraged leaders
in Egypt to consider strategy and plans for their approach to the
British authorities concerning the political future of their country.
It is reported that before his death Sultan Husayn Kamil toyed with
the idea of writing directly to King George V about this matter. The
Prime Minister, Husayn Rushdi Pasha, was also anxious to explore
the question of negotiations with Britain before the peace talks had
begun at Versailles. His position was, however, delicate and uncertain. Not only was he the head of the wartime government which
served the interests of the British Protectorate, he was also more
easily associated with the Sultan and his court than with any of the
nationalist groups, were they moderate reformist or extremist.

The intransigent National Party of Mustafa Kamil maintained its
uncompromising attitude on British evacuation from Egypt. Its
official chief, Muhammed Bey Farid, had been, along with many
of his aides and collaborators, in exile in Switzerland. Those
members of the Party who were still in Egypt lacked the quality of
leadership, despite the agitational following they claimed among
students and townspeople. The National Party was thus in no position to lead the movement for independence, let alone negotiate the
political status of Egypt with the Protecting power. A smaller group
emanating from the palace, headed by Prince Omar Tusun, a
member of the reigning dynasty, and including members of the older
ruling aristocracy such as Muhammad Said Pasha, sought to take
the initiative in negotiations with Britain. Finally, a group of
members of the defunct Legislative Assembly, headed by their
elected spokesman Saad Zaghlul, and generally associated with the
Umma Party, contemplated the formation of a 'national delegation'

to present Egyptian demands to the British authorities. While most groups felt that a delegation should approach Britain with a request to negotiate Egypt's political future, the political struggle over the constitution of this delegation began as early as September 1918.

The group led by Zaghlul was obviously against the involvement of the Sultan in these negotiations if that meant any extension of his authority, or his popularity. They were similarly opposed to the possible leadership of the Rushdi government for both economic and political reasons. The colleagues of Saad from the Legislative Council and the Umma Party represented not only the new élite of modern administrators, lawyers and other professionals, but also a new group of landowners, many of whose cotton-growing interests were linked to commercial and financial enterprises in the cities. Socially they belonged to a native and relatively recent landowning and professional class from the provinces. On the other hand, those associated with the palace and the Rushdi government, belonged to the older Turco-Egyptian and Albanian aristocracy.

There was therefore a socio-economic differentiation in the ranks of Egyptian leadership which was not only the consequence of nineteenth-century developments in education and administrative reform, but also the more immediate result of the war. In 1917, for instance, members of this new group, enriched by the war, sought to invest their capital accruing mainly from agricultural wealth in industry and commerce. Ismail Sidqi and Talaat Harb along with others founded a Committee for Commerce and Industry to encourage the development of Egyptian enterprises. Until that time the total investment in commerce and industry in Egypt was overwhelmingly controlled by foreigners and local minorities, either resident in Egypt or in Europe. In this sense, these early attempts by the new group of Egyptian liberals to encourage Egyptian economic enterprise may be viewed as proof of their realization that legal and social reform without economic strength could not lead to political advancement. It was not strange that the secular liberals were the first among Egyptian nationalist groups to recognize the relationship between politics and economics.[10] It was also no surprise that the leader of the movement for independence should emerge from a group whose luminaries began their political careers as moderate reformists, with a record of pro-British leanings as administrators in the period 1900–14 and a distaste for the unlimited power of the ruling dynasty. Such a record at least supported the notion that they, better than anyone else, could negotiate with Britain since they were closest to the British conception of government and politics: moderation, compromise and legality.

The Zaghlul group started out in this struggle for the control of the national delegation to negotiate with Britain with certain substantial advantages over other groups. Besides their training, administrative and judicial experience, the Zaghlul group had acquired some experience in electioneering for the Legislative Assembly with connections in the countryside among provincial councils, municipal authorities and local village hierarchies. Despite their economic rise and advancement in the cities, Zaghlul and his colleagues were still identified in origins and social milieux with the groups of small propertied farmers in the Egyptian countryside. Their chances for organizing countrywide support were in 1918 better than those of any other group. As administrators their knowledge of, and influence upon, the Egyptian Civil Service, especially the lower echelons, could serve them well. As the secular moderate generation of Egyptian national leaders, the Zaghlul group was more readily acceptable to the Coptic minority than any of the more extremist nationalist or Pan-Islamic groups. It seemed the group most capable of achieving communal unity in Egypt. In fact, rich Coptic landowners from Upper Egypt who had similarly benefited from the war, as well as those among them who had a share in the expanding Egyptian financial and commercial interests, joined the group at the end of the war and later became leading members of the Wafd Party and its cabinets when in power. Wissa Wasef, George Khayyat, Makram Obayd, are only a few of the Coptic leaders who became prominent in the Wafd.

The views on education expressed by Ahmad Lutfi and the administrative efforts of Zaghlul as Minister of Education were apt to attract the aspiring Egyptian student, as well as the teacher and intellectual, to this group. The feminist views of Qasim Amin and the support he received from the *Jarida*–Umma group with which the Zaghlul-led Wafd was initially identified was the only declared hope for the improvement of the status of women in Egypt, so that the participation of women in the anti-British demonstrations throughout 1919 and the later Feminist Movement organized by Huda Hanum Shaarawi were all closely allied to the Wafd.

With these advantages and potential sources of support, Saad Zaghlul set out to form an *ad hoc* delegation consisting of himself, Abd al-Aziz Fahmi and Ali Shaarawi to interview Sir Reginald Wingate and request permission for a delegation to go to London and present Egyptian national demands to the British government. They submitted their request through the Prime Minister on 11 November and were granted an interview with Sir Reginald on the 13th. In their conversation with Sir Reginald they indicated their expectation that both martial law and the Protectorate would soon be abolished; made clear their concern over the political future of Egypt; expressed their desire that Egypt should be heard in the councils of the peace talks in Paris; and referred to their expectation of independence. Wingate made it clear to them that he did not consider the interview as constituting an official conversation between Egyptians and the British government, but merely as a friendly chat. He, in fact, told the Egyptian Prime Minister that he did not consider the Zaghlul delegation which met him to have any official capacity.

Zaghlul learned from the Prime Minister that he also had requested to go to London with one of his ministers, Adli Yeken, while from the conversation with Sir Reginald he gathered that his own request to go to London would be opposed for the moment. He therefore realized that if he and his group were to lead and control any negotiations with Britain it was essential that he organize an official delegation which appeared to command popular support. Only in this way could he prevent any other delegation forthcoming from the government and palace from negotiating with the British government, and force the British government to recognize his delegation as the only representative of the Egyptian nation. On the same day of 13 November Zaghlul set out to organize a permanent delegation which could claim to speak for the nation, to be called *Al-Wafd al-Misri*, or the Egyptian Delegation.

The original members of the Wafd as organized on that day included mainly members of the old Legislative Assembly with one or two exceptions. Article Two of the Wafd's constitution described its aim as 'to seek the complete independence of Egypt by all legal and peaceful means, that is by negotiation with Britain'. Article Three stated that the delegation derived its strength (note: not authority) from the wishes of the Egyptian people as expressed directly, or through their representatives in various institutions. With an eye to political bargaining and wider support, Article Eight provided for the inclusion in the delegation of additional members (original number of fourteen) as required by the national interest.

Realizing that for the moment his, or the delegation's, private efforts to exert pressure on the British High Commissioner would be stalled or ignored, Zaghlul proceeded to strengthen his leadership by seeking to collect formal signed depositions from all representative organizations in the country to the effect that the Wafd was the official representative of the Egyptian nation solely responsible and authorized to negotiate its political future. The original text of the deposition was mild in the sense that the nation was delegating the Wafd (consisting of certain specified gentlemen) to seek by peaceful means the independence of Egypt according to the principles of justice and freedom preached by Great Britain and her Allies. At the insistence of the National Party extremists, who had to be mollified, the original text was changed to read that the delegation would seek by peaceful and legal means the *complete* independence of Egypt. But when the time came to distribute the printed deposition to the various bodies in all parts of the country, the British military authorities prevailed upon the Ministry of the Interior to stop its circulation. When Zaghlul protested to Rushdi Pasha against this interference from the Ministry of the Interior, the Prime Minister explained that he was not responsible, since under martial law such action by the authorities was quite legal. Although unsuccessful, Zaghlul had gained a tactical victory over his possible rivals in the National Party by appointing two of their members, Mustafa Nahhas and Hafiz Afifi, to the delegation. Ismail Sidqi and some Coptic notables were also added to the delegation to satisfy certain economic and communal interests in the country.

Later in November Zaghlul applied to the British military authorities for travel permits for the delegation to go to London. His application was denied but he was invited to submit proposals about the political system in Egypt within the framework of the Protectorate. Despite Zaghlul's repeated requests and protests that the proposed journey of the Wafd aimed solely at contacting the representatives of the British government, the Residency stood firm on refusal. Zaghlul and his colleagues feared that their delegation would be undermined by a decision of the Residency to deal with the Egyptian government directly, i.e., to send a delegation to London headed by Rushdi Pasha, the Prime Minister. On 6 December they tried indirect pressure tactics against the Residency by circulating the aims of the Wafd and their demands to the representatives of foreign states in Egypt in the hope of embarrassing the British government. They also appealed to President Wilson directly to assist the Wafd in appearing before the Peace Conference.

Meanwhile certain trends regarding Egyptian representation in any negotiations with Britain began to emerge. Rumours of an official delegation acceptable to Britain circulated. The names of the Prime Minister Rushdi Pasha and his closest collaborator in the cabinet, Adli Yeken Pasha, were persistently bandied about as the leaders of such a delegation. Rushdi could not afford with the tarnished record of a wartime Prime Minister to ignore the Wafd led by Zaghlul. He could not appear willing to become the favoured head of a British-picked delegation. Moreover, to appear concerned over the right of the Wafd to present their case in London and Paris was good politics, for it provided Rushdi with healthy leverage in any future struggle with Zaghlul. He therefore officially urged the British Residency to permit Zaghlul and his colleagues to go to London. He even warned them that he would refuse to go himself if the Wafd were denied the same right. He repeatedly tendered his resignation to the Sultan throughout December and it was repeatedly rejected. Initially, moreover, his own request to proceed with Adli Yeken to London was turned down by London, even though Wingate favoured the idea.

The British authorities managed somehow until the end of 1918 to keep the Wafd, as well as any other delegation, from going to London or Paris. But the year 1919 ushered in a tense atmosphere. British refusal to permit any Egyptian delegation to present their case in London or Paris weakened the Rushdi government, while it goaded the 'popular' Wafd to ever more extreme tactics. As the day approached (18 January 1919) for the opening of the Peace Conference the Wafd speeded up their public agitation to be heard. By 12 January the Wafd learned that a delegation from Syria would be permitted to go to the Peace Conference. They were indignant. At a General Congress of the Wafd held in the home of one of its members (Hamad Pasha Basil) on 13 January Zaghlul addressed the meeting on the right of Egypt to independènce. He argued that this independence was secured by Muhammad Ali the Great and recognized by Europe as early as 1840; that Turkish sovereignty had been abolished. A flurry of cables to Heads of States and the House of Commons in London followed, but without convincing any of them to lend their ears to the Wafd.

Soon the Wafd became apprehensive over British policy intentions especially when Wingate was recalled to London. Another mass rally was prepared to be held at Zaghlul's home on 31 January. General Watson, GOC British Forces, Egypt, intervened directly to prevent it. Zaghlul was summarily deprived of a public platform from which to announce further plans. On 7 February, on the occasion of a public lecture given by a European adviser to the Court of Appeals on criminal law, Zaghlul took the rostrum at the end of the lecture to attack the Protectorate and demand its end. The British authorities meantime reconsidered the matter of a government delegation proceeding to London and, in fact, invited Rushdi Pasha and Adli Yeken to do so. Rushdi, however, insisted for his acceptance upon the condition that Britain should permit any Egyptian who applied to travel to Europe to do so also. The condition naturally was unacceptable to the Residency since it meant the appearance of Zaghlul's Wafd in London and Paris. On 1 March Rushdi's resignation was accepted by Sultan Fuad. The Wafd immediately interpreted this as an indication of the palace's opposition to their cause. They therefore proceeded to lecture the Sultan in a letter they sent him the next day, urging him to lead the movement for independence. They also appealed to the representatives of foreign powers against the British obstruction of their plans to present their case before the Peace Conference.

The Wafd's activities were now considered by the British authorities as dangerous to public security in the country. While Wafdist agitation increased, the country was without a government; and a government which did not support or co-operate with the Wafd-led independence movement was difficult to form, or maintain. Wafdist pressure was creating a climate in the country from which disturbances could arise. The British authorities could not ignore the situation. On 6 March, General Watson called Zaghlul and members of the Wafd to his headquarters and warned them that their activities against the Protectorate would make them liable to the sanctions of martial law. The Wafd protested against this pressure in a cable to the British Prime Minister Lloyd George. It seems, however, that the military authorities entrusted with the maintenance of order and still possessing supreme authority under martial law were already determined to stop further Wafdist action. On 8 March, they arrested Zaghlul, Ismail Sidqi and Hamad Basil and exiled them to Malta. The remaining members of the Wafd protested this forceful measure in writing to the Sultan, and by cable to Lloyd George.

The immediate result of these strong measures was a series of demonstrations in Cairo, Alexandria and other towns, massive strikes by transport workers, judges and lawyers. Students from the secondary and professional schools joined in demonstrations alongside students from the Azhar, leading to violence, looting, casualties and arrests. Soon the provinces joined in the general protest and attempted more daring attacks upon railway and telephone communications. Attacks upon British military personnel became common occurrences, culminating in the murder of eight British officers and men on a train from Aswan to Cairo at Deirut on 18 March. A strict application of martial law, the setting up of military courts to try and punish rebels were among the strict countermeasures taken by the military authorities. They also threatened to burn and raze villages in retaliation for acts of brigandage.

By the end of March it seemed that the Wafd had succeeded in mobilizing countrywide support for their position. Implicit in this support was the temporary isolation of the Sultan from the Egyptian independence movement. In the absence of a government (Rushdi had resigned on 1 March), the Wafd emerged as the sole representative and spokesman for the Egyptians. Meanwhile, the participation of women in public demonstrations against British policy was a new development in Egyptian affairs. Although all the women involved were from the upper classes, the impression was created that the movement was genuinely national. Moreover, leaders of the Coptic community were for the moment equally involved on the side of the Wafd bid for independence. Whether the spread of the disturbances in the provinces was due to the desire based on an understanding of the average fellah for independence is unlikely. His violent participation in the events of March 1919 was probably the result of his dissatisfaction with the inconvenience he experienced during the war, whether in his recruitment to the Labour Corps or when the military authorities found it necessary to requisition his animals and fodder. He had suffered economically. Even though much of this suffering could be attributed to the dubious wartime practices of his richer compatriots and foreign residents, the fellah obviously ascribed all such vicissitudes to the British occupying forces. It was perhaps natural for the rural population to explode in the manner they did. But their action also brought them under the influence and control of the Wafd and its leader leader Zaghlul – a relationship which obtained for another thirty years.

Meantime General Allenby succeeded Wingate at the Residency, and was given special powers to deal with the deteriorating political situation in Egypt. Upon his arrival in Cairo on 25 March, Allenby declared firmly his intention to put an end to disturbances and investigate their causes. He succeeded in getting religious leaders and notables to issue appeals for calm to the public. He also met members of the Wafd to make his position known to them. But Egyptians were already disturbed at the statement by Lord Curzon, the Foreign Minister, in the House of Lords, indicating that Britain had no objection to receiving a delegation in London consisting of Rushdi Pasha and Adli Yeken. The government, however, objected to Zaghlul and the Wafd because they had no official standing. Curzon's statement also implied the unchanged attitude of Britain regarding the continuation of the Protectorate. More strikes followed, the most serious being a three-day stoppage by state employees. In the absence of an Egyptian cabinet, Allenby had to issue a new budget for the country prepared by the British authorities. This exercised Egyptian resentment further: more strikes and demonstrations followed throughout the first few days in April. Short of violent military measures it was impractical for the British authorities to put an end to the disturbances. In the meantime, however, London had become certain that the Allies at the Peace Conference would recognize the British Protectorate over Egypt. There was therefore no real danger in both releasing Zaghlul and his colleagues from forced exile and permitting Egyptians to present their case in London and Paris. On 7 April General Allenby announced the release of Zaghlul and on 9 April Rushdi Pasha formed a new Egyptian government. The Wafd finally left for Paris on 11 April.

If the release of Wafd detainees was meant to inaugurate a British policy of conciliation with the Egyptian national movement, other events frustrated it. The Wafd in Paris were shaken when the United States recognized the British Protectorate over Egypt. If Allenby hoped that his policy of conciliation would lead to negotiations for the termination of the Protectorate, policy statements in London contradicted this conception. The latter were based on the principle that if the Protectorate could not be maintained then the only concession they would negotiate with the Egyptians would be that of autonomy under a British arrangement. This attitude of the British government was strengthened by the recognition of the Protectorate in the Peace Conference in May 1919. Meanwhile in Egypt the Central Committee of the Wafd continued its activities of raising funds for the delegation and its cause in Paris, organizing local committees and generally making it difficult for any Egyptian government to govern without recognizing the Wafd as the official representative of Egyptian national demands. Further strikes by civil servants in April in support of the Wafd, for the abolition of martial law, and generally against the continued protectorate status of the country contributed to the embarrassment of the new Rushdi government which resigned on 21 April. Pressure from the Azhar and other students throughout the country contributed further to the ministerial crisis. Rushdi's resignation was interpreted by Egyptians as a recognition of Zaghlul's leadership of the national cause.

While taking forceful measures against intransigent civil servants and student organizations, General Allenby declared his willingness to hear Wafdist views provided they were not prefaced by a demand for an immediate termination of the Protectorate and the evacuation of British troops from the country. He informed the country that Britain planned to send a commission to Egypt to inquire into the possibilities of an autonomous arrangement under British protection. At the same time Lord Curzon corroborated this intention. With this, Allenby was able to have an Egyptian government formed on 21 May, headed by a pre-war Prime Minister, Muhammad Said Pasha. The latter was a known enemy of Saad, who had resigned as Minister of Justice from the Muhammad Said government in 1913 to become leader of the opposition in the Legislative Assembly. Egyptians now interpreted this development as an attempt by Britain to split Egyptian leadership over the national independence question. If Britain actually intended this, she was partly successful, for her success at the Peace Conference regarding the Egyptian question had already had its effect upon the Wafd delegation in Paris. Some members felt that the Wafd could no longer hope to accede to the Peace Conference and that consequently their mission had failed. Disagreements and splits among them followed. While Zaghlul tried frantically to seek the support of public opinion and legislators in the United States, reports of the erosion of Wafd solidarity reached Egypt. This gave the Muhammad Said government and its British supporters a chance of survival and the possibility of restoring a normal situation in the country.

The news of the appointment of a Commission of Inquiry to study the causes of disorder in Egypt and make recommendations about the political future of the country within the framework of the existing British connection led to further political agitation. Wafdist activity to organize public disturbances continued. Recourse to violence and political assassination was increasing daily. Muhammad Said Pasha sought to postpone the arrival of the Mission led by Lord Milner but failed and had to resign. His succession by the Christian Yusuf Wahba was further cause for nationalist opposition. The Wafd Committee meanwhile campaigned to ensure that Egyptians would boycott the Milner Mission. They succeeded in this to the extent that throughout the Mission's presence in Egypt between December 1919 and April 1920, even members of the Egyptian government who had conversations with the Mission pretended to do so on an informal basis.

The Mission was aware that no negotiations could be conducted with any hope of success without the involvement of the Wafd. On the other hand, Egyptian government leaders such as Rushdi and Adli Yeken were equally convinced that negotiations with Britain were inevitable and desirable. Their problem was to convince Zaghlul of this fact. Zaghlul in fact entered into negotiations with the Milner Mission in London in June 1920. A Memorandum was drafted regarding the points essential for the drafting of a treaty between an independent Egypt and the British government. Although Zaghlul rejected the Memorandum because he feared a possible negotiated treaty between Egyptian government ministers and Britain, the Milner Report made it clear that Britain had abandoned its insistence upon continued British protection over Egypt. Instead, Britain was now willing to consider a treaty arrangement with an independent Egypt provided its basic defence and other interests were accommodated. But Zaghlul had submitted his nationalist position to the Egyptian public in the hope of preventing any other Egyptian leader from entering into negotiations with Britain. He would not support the Memorandum.

The Report of the Mission was published in February 1921. The gist of its recommendations was that the Protectorate status of Egypt was no longer satisfactory. Allenby asked the Sultan to instruct the Egyptian government to send a delegation to England to negotiate a substitute relationship to the Protectorate. At this point, the nationalist struggle in Egypt turned into a political fight between the Wafd and Zaghlul on the one hand, and the Egyptian government on the other, over who would conduct these negotiations. Adli Yeken formed a new government in March 1921 approved by Zaghlul. But when Adli invited Zaghlul to participate in the negotiations with Britain, the latter insisted upon certain conditions for his participation, among them the immediate abolition of martial law and the termination of the Protectorate. These conditions were published in a Manifesto to the Egyptian people. Having done this, Zaghlul returned to Egypt on 5 April at the invitation of Adli.

But the presence of Zaghlul in Egypt created difficulties for Adli. Not only was Zaghlul the obvious popular leader, but Adli realized

that negotiations with Britain without Zaghlul would be doomed
to failure. Yet this disagreement between Zaghlul and Adli cost the
former a temporary setback, for within the Wafd itself there were
some who felt that compromise was necessary if they were not to
lose everything. They considered Adli's view of negotiation a plausible one and told Zaghlul so. Thus, the discussions over the Milner
Mission Report had the effect of drawing some members of the Wafd
away from Zaghlul and into the Adli camp. Whereas Adli needed
the participation of Zaghlul in the negotiations in order to secure
wider popular support for his government, Zaghlul's refusal to compromise had the effect of inciting further violent demonstrations
throughout the country which the British authorities and the Egyptian government tried to suppress by force. In May 1921 Adli
announced the composition of the official delegation which would
negotiate a new agreement in London. There were demonstrations
against the Adli government and unpleasant outbreaks of violence
between Egyptians and members of foreign communities in Alexandria. Even though the Adli delegation left for London on 1 July
1921, Zaghlul, who remained behind, continued his political activities in order to undermine the Adli-led delegation and consolidate
further support for himself at home. Allenby tried to strengthen the
chances of the delegation in London by deporting Zaghlul to Aden
– and later the Seychelles – in December.

Negotiations in London, however, broke down and Adli resigned.
The Deputy Premier, Abdel Khaliq Sarwat Pasha, agreed to take
office as Prime Minister on condition that Britain recognized Egypt
as an independent state. This Britain agreed to do. She felt that with
Zaghlul out of the way an agreement with Egypt, despite this concession, which would accommodate British interests, was likely. With
this done, General Allenby then recommended to the British government that a unilateral declaration should be issued proclaiming the
independence of Egypt. The government in London was, however,
reluctant to do this now that Zaghlul was safely out of the way, and
hoped for negotiations with the Egyptian government on their terms.
The effect of Zaghlul's deportation, however, was soon felt in the
renewed terrorist activities of Wafdist elements.[11] Allenby went to
London to convince the government of the inevitability of his recommendation. Returning to Egypt, he released the famous Declaration
of the British government to Egypt on 22 February 1922. The
unilateral act of the British government offered to recognize Egypt
as an independent sovereign state on condition that the vital

importance of the relations between Britain and Egypt to the British Empire be recognized. The latter were to rest on four matters absolutely reserved to the discretion of the British government until further agreement in the future. These were: the security of Imperial communications in Egypt; the defence of Egypt against all foreign aggression; the protection of foreign interests and minorities in Egypt; and the Sudan.

CHAPTER 13

EXPERIMENT IN CONSTITUTIONAL GOVERNMENT
1923–39

The British Declaration of 28 February 1922 created by its provisions an independent sovereign Egyptian state. But the political transactions from 1920 to 1922 which led the British government to act unilaterally were inauspicious. Moreover, its conditions – the Four Reserved Points – inaugurated a period of uninterrupted crisis in domestic Egyptian politics, which in part prevented parliamentary government and its institutions from taking root in the political life of the country. To say this is not to attribute all the blame to Britain. In 1922, Britain considered certain interests in Egypt as absolutely vital to the security of her empire, and insisted upon a special relationship with Egypt which, inevitably, diluted Egyptian independence and created conflict with a succession of Egyptian governments. Moreover, Lord Allenby, the British High Commissioner in Egypt, had assured the government in London that granting Egypt independence would inaugurate an era of goodwill which would permit both governments to negotiate their differences amicably. But there were also deeper reasons and more complex realities peculiar to the Egyptian socio-political environment which militated against the success of the experiment in representative government.

The failure of the Adli–Curzon negotiations in 1921 to arrive at an agreement over the new status of Egypt enabled Lord Allenby to convince the British government that only a unilateral declaration on their part could break the deadlock. Thus the 1922 Declaration ending the Protectorate was an act of the British government addressed to Sultan Ahmad Fuad. The general political situation it engendered was one of confusion. The Egyptian public aroused by the Wafdists was opposed to its provisions. Zaghlul led a vigorous attack on its shortcomings and termed it unacceptable as a formula for an independent sovereign state. The British hoped that an Egyptian government would draft a constitution after which a duly elected government, responsible to parliament, would be in a position to conduct negotiations with them for the settlement of outstanding matters.

The nationalists had assumed from 1919 until 1922 that no Egyptian government was capable, or dared, to negotiate a guarantee of British interests before the Protectorate was effectively abolished. Now they again hoped by organized opposition and mass demonstrations to intimidate any government in Egypt from proceeding with the drafting and promulgation of a constitution. For this, in itself, would constitute acceptance of the British Declaration with its Reserved Points. In short, the Declaration was issued under a cloud of mutual distrust: 'The Egyptian public distrusted the intentions of the British government, and the British distrusted the goodwill of Egypt towards them.'[1]

When, on 1 March 1922, Abdel Khaliq Sarwat Pasha formed a government whose major task was to be that of drafting a constitution for the new state, his position was a difficult one. He had accepted an unpopular responsibility at a time when he commanded neither public confidence nor the co-operation of the Wafd and other nationalist leaders. Moreover, he was in the unenviable position of having to satisfy on the one hand a new monarch anxious to retain as much power for himself as possible, and on the other a British representative vigilantly anxious about his country's interests in Egypt. Even though the British Declaration made no mention of, or recommendation as to, the form of government for independent Egypt – constitutional or other – the general expectation was that a constitutional system would be adopted. Besides the observation that such a system appeared as the accepted model for emulation by new states in the aftermath of the Great War, there were many groups among Egyptian politicians in the Wafd, the National Party, and the small band of Sarwat's colleagues who were anxious, under independence, to wrest as much power as possible from the ruling house. This latent conflict between party politicians and the palace had been endemic to Egyptian political life ever since the first attempts by notables in the legislative assemblies of the period 1876–1913 to curb the power of the Khedives.

The independence of Egypt was formally declared on 15 March 1922. Sultan Ahmad Fuad assumed the title of Fuad I, King of Egypt. Two years earlier, in April 1920, Britain, as the protecting power, had formally recognized Prince Faruq, the newly born son of Ahmad Fuad, as successor to the sultanate. This was done especially with a view to excluding a possible claim later by the exiled Khedive Abbas Hilmi. Now a series of royal decrees issued between April and July 1922 regularized the order of royal succession, recognized those considered as official members of the royal house and specifically excluded Abbas Hilmi, his family, and female members of the ruling family from any claim or accession to the throne of Egypt. Significantly also, a special decree issued on 27 July 1922 liquidated all the properties of Abbas Hilmi in Egypt, and barred him from ever returning to the country.

Meantime, serious political trouble broke out when the Sarwat government appointed on 3 April a Commission to draft a constitution. Even though the members of this Commission were recruited from various groups in Egyptian political circles, representing the old Legislative Assembly of 1913, landowners, merchants, lawyers, judges, religious leaders including those of minorities, and the intelligentsia, the government did not escape attack from the nationalist opposition groups. Both the National Party and the Wafd objected strenuously to an appointed Commission. They contended that only an elected constituent assembly representing the nation could legitimately draft the fundamental law of the land. Both of them refused to participate in the work of the Commission, consisting of thirty-two members and presided over by Husayn Rushdi Pasha, former Prime Minister under the Protectorate.

Another reason for the strong opposition to the Sarwat government was the demand for the abolition of martial law, the release of all political prisoners and detainees, as well as the demand by Wafdists especially for the return of their exiled leaders. Martial law, however, could not be lifted before Egypt and the British High Commissioner could agree on the promulgation of an Indemnities Bill to cover measures taken under military government during the war.

While the opposition charged the Sarwat government with unconstitutional acts, the Prime Minister himself gave them more ammunition. Addressing the first meeting of the Commission on 11 April 1922 he tried to justify its appointment by arguing that past Egyptian practice did not prohibit the promulgation of organic laws by the executive. As examples, he gave the consultative Assembly of Deputies of 1866; the National and Legislative Assemblies of 1883 and 1913. He further argued that an elected constituent assembly, under the circumstances, would lead to greater confusion and dissension in Egypt's political life during a delicate phase of transition. This clear indication by Sarwat of his distaste for the opposition made wider the rift between his government and a public influenced by Wafdist agitation. The King, on the other hand, expressed the opinion to various representatives of the European Press that constitutional government was not against the spirit of Islamic traditions. He was thus subtly giving notice of his direct interest in the kind of authority and powers he would be assigned under any new constitutional arrangement.

The composition of the Commission was such as to ensure proper regard for the legal propriety of measures, dexterous drafting of the articles of the Constitution, and a generally moderate balancing of political forces. Husayn Rushdi was not only an eminent jurist, but also a man of vast administrative experience. Abd al-Aziz Fahmi – one of the most active members of the Commission – was similarly steeped in the law and anxious to draft a modern liberal document which would measure up to European model constitutions. Yet no Egyptian commission, or constituent assembly, could have been completely free to draft a democratic document if it had to satisfy both an autocratically inclined Egyptian monarch and the British view of their vital interests in the country.

The Committee on General Principles of the Commission was confronted with difficult issues: the nature of the franchise, the representation of religious minorities, the important question of the separation of powers and especially the powers of ministers responsible to parliament versus those of the monarch, freedom of the Press, and education.

It soon became clear that the liberal tendencies of the Commission ran directly against King Fuad's aspirations to power. Whereas many of the members had been of the group that had sought for some time to curb the powers of the Khedives before the war and the King now, the President, Rushdi Pasha, was anxious to assign some real powers to the monarchy. This, he believed, could act as a moderating influence over extreme party factionalism.

In October 1922, a draft constitution was submitted to the government. Besides the fact that it was unacceptable to the King because of the circumscribed role it assigned to him, the government faced other complex difficulties. A provision in the draft designating the monarch 'King of Egypt and the Sudan' evoked British opposition. This was contrary to the provisions of the 28 February 1922 Declaration which had reserved the matter of the Sudan. The National Party and the Wafdists were opposed to any compromise on this point. So were the supporters of Sarwat who had meanwhile founded the Liberal Constitutionalist Party committed to support a liberal constitution and Sarwat's government.[2] The British for their part reassured Sudanese notables that there would be no change in the *status quo* of the Sudan. Principally, they maintained that the Sudan, together with the remaining Reserved Points of the February Declaration, was to be a matter for negotiation with the Egyptian government in the future.

While Sarwat and the constitutionalists wished for a speedy proclamation of the Constitution, the King sought to delay it in the hope of expanding royal powers. The British insisted upon the deletion from the constitutional text of any references to the Sudan.

Sarwat's government was moreover plagued with a spate of violence in the country fomented partly by Wafdists. Zaghlul and other Wafd leaders had been re-exiled and some of their members in Egypt arrested. Thus Sarwat earned still greater unpopularity when he had to deal harshly with the Press by reactivating the 1881 and 1909 Press laws. He closed down *al-Ahram* in August and he had prevented political meetings by opposition groups earlier in the year. Whereas throughout his tenure of office Sarwat's constitution-making was opposed – though for different reasons – by the Wafdists, the National Party, and the King alike, now in November 1922, he had come up against British opposition over the Sudan. He resigned on 29 November.[3]

Muhammad Tawfiq Nasim Pasha, a king's man, formed a new government on 30 November. During its less than three months' tenure of office, this government attempted to press the King's advantage over the constitutionalists, seek a compromise solution to the Sudan provisions in the draft constitution that would satisfy the British High Commissioner, and placate the Wafdist leadership. The King suggested that the title 'King of Egypt and the Sudan' be dropped from the text until the position of the latter territory was clarified later by agreement resulting from Anglo-Egyptian negotiations. But he insisted that the temporary inapplication of constitutional provisions in the Sudan should not affect Egypt's rights there (Article 145). The quick and strong protest of the High Commissioner led to the resignation of Nasim's government on 5 February 1923. The latter had already been faced with other difficulties when terrorist attacks on British personnel increased in December 1922 and January 1923. Finally compromise was reached over the Sudan – and not without the approval of the Wafdists.

Meantime, security was tightened with the appointment of a military governor to impose a stricter application of martial law. Zaghlul from his exile cabled his admiration of Nasim's resignation as a patriotic act against British interference. More Wafdists were arrested on Allenby's orders and their *bayt al-umma* headquarters (Zaghlul's Cairo residence) was closed down. The country remained without a government for another month, while the British liberal Press called for Zaghlul's return to Egypt as the only man capable of forming a government.

Suddenly, on 15 March 1923, a new government was formed, headed by a prominent judge and suspected royal courtier Yahia Ibrahim Pasha. It released Saad two weeks later. Other political prisoners were released by the British military authorities, and the position of Military Governor was abolished. The crisis had ended and the new Constitution was proclaimed on 19 April 1923.

But this was not exactly the same draft prepared and submitted by the Constitutional Committee. Although, like the Ottoman Constitution of 1876, it owed much to the Belgian model of 1831, it appeared to follow more closely the Ottoman model in its authoritarian provisions. Thus, it gave extensive powers to the monarchy which tended to undermine the authority of Parliament and Cabinet.[4] The monarchy reserved many powers not consonant with modern European parliamentary democracy or constitutional monarchy, which also reflected the retention of certain traditional patterns of authority. Thus the King had the right to select and appoint the Prime Minister; the right to dismiss the Cabinet and dissolve Parliament (Articles 38 and 49); he could postpone parliamentary sessions (Article 39); appoint the president of the senate and one-fifth of its members, presumably upon the recommendation of the Cabinet (Article 38, para. 2). Despite a government's majority in the Lower House, the monarch could dismiss it by decree. More dangerous was the investment of legislative power in the King and Parliament in so far as the King had to confirm all bills and could return draft bills to Parliament for reconsideration.

The constitutionalists led by Abd al-Aziz Fahmi protested these changes from the original draft and accused Nasim Pasha of introducing them. They objected further to such politically significant issues as the King's retention of privileged powers over religious institutions (such as the Azhar), *waqfs*, diplomatic appointments and military commissions. These and other factors were to undermine greatly parliamentary life in Egypt before it had begun in practice.

In May–June 1923, the way was cleared further for the first general elections. On 30 April the Electoral Law was passed providing for universal manhood suffrage and indirect elections in two stages. In

May more political prisoners were released by the British military authority, and all Wafdist detainees and exiles were released by June. Agreement on an Indemnities Bill was reached on 5 July, thus leading to the abolition of martial law in the country.

The vociferous opposition of the Wafd had by August been toned down when Zaghlul announced his intention to return from Europe in September ready to 'associate my service to the nation with service to the King'. For good measure, he also heaped praise on Nasim Pasha. Once in Egypt, his tactics to attain power consisted unashamedly of attacking all those who had held power between February 1922 and the proclamation of the Constitution as traitors, singling out among them for special abuse his long-standing enemy Sarwat. At the same time, he described the British as honourable opponents with whom one could do business.

Elections for the first Chamber were held on 12 January 1924, giving the Wafd an overwhelming majority in the first electoral stage. The party secured 90 per cent of the seats (214 members in the House), whereas the Liberal Constitutionalists and the National Party secured two seats each. Two weeks later on 28 January, Zaghlul formed the first Wafdist government. Parliament was formally opened by the King on 15 March. Yet, the first government with an overwhelming majority in Parliament governed for just over nine months, and the first elected Parliament was dissolved soon thereafter. Indeed, the beginning of parliamentary government in modern Egypt was in retrospect a microcosm of all the forces and factors that were to work against its success. These forces were not simply the role of the monarchy and the wide scope left to the British High Commissioner to influence events and interfere in domestic Egyptian politics – significant as these two major forces were – but also the political behaviour of this first Wafd majority, and the perception of government and opposition of its political leaders. Moreover, certain social and economic structural changes had occurred since the Great War which were to affect further the democratic experiment. They helped discredit the Establishment and its ruling groups; and, along with these, the whole imported parliamentary, constitutional edifice.[5]

The Zaghlulists, as Ahmad Shafiq called them, had won the elections fairly and squarely. Their following in the countryside was massive. The masses considered Zaghlul their national leader, the *za'im al-umma*, the uncompromising national hero. His opponents were equally discredited as compromisers in the eyes of the masses. Yet he also had finally come to power partly because he had compromised with the palace group and implicitly accepted the conditions governing the safeguarding of British interests in Egypt.

Once in power, Zaghlul was faced with several difficult problems, made worse by his earlier extremism and demagoguery. These ranged from curtailing the prerogatives of the King to dealing with Britain over the Sudan. While public expectations at the hands of a popular nationalist government were high, the reality of courses of action open to the government was a different and bitter one. A general amnesty, for example, that would lead to the release of scores of political prisoners, depended on further negotiations with Britain. The influx of political refugees from Tripolitania, for another example, posed an extradition problem with Italy, and the first major international law clash between an independent Egyptian government and a European state.

The Wafd in office believed in the total control and exercise of power to the exclusion of all other groups. Once elected (195 seats out of 214), Zaghlul's government viewed the nineteen non-Wafdist members of the House not as forming a weak opposition but as a group of men that had left the national pale. Similarly, administrative reorganization came to mean the dismissal of officials in the bureaucracy, of provincial and other local officers and their replacement by Wafdists or Wafd Party sympathizers.

Zaghlul's compromise in assuming power despite his Party's unquestioned electoral victory did not pass unnoticed. There was thus no reference to the 'complete independence of Egypt' in the Speech from the Throne to Parliament. During the early sessions of the House, Zaghlul clearly restrained his party colleagues from extremist pronouncements on such issues as the Indemnities Bill since it affected foreigners and foreign interests, and the British control of the Egyptian Army. He pleaded that he was tied to, and bound to respect, commitments undertaken by previous Egyptian governments – commitments he had flatly rejected before coming to power as having been made by political leaders who did not represent Egypt. Moreover, he pleaded that these matters would be subjects of any negotiations between his government and the British government.

The opposition Press which criticized Zaghlul's hesitation in power was mysteriously intimidated by the mob. Meanwhile, the struggle with the King continued over the allocation of specific powers and prerogatives, such as the appointment of senators, the control of religious institutions, etc.

In Parliament, there was no opposition to speak of and Saad ruled the House with an iron hand. He brooked no differences of opinion among Wafdist members. When a question of amending the Speech from the Throne was about to be considered by the House, Saad simply threatened to resign. Nevertheless, it soon became clear that despite his 'popular mandate' national leadership, and majority government, Saad was unable to deal satisfactorily with the basic question of complete Egyptian independence.

It was clear, for instance, that the new Labour government in London would stick by the Reserved Points of the 1922 Declaration in any negotiations with Zaghlul. Britain was even actively pursuing separate economic policies for the Sudan. As for the Egyptian Army, matters were even more complicated. An army is the foremost symbol of sovereignty. The limitations then placed upon its size, and its actual control by a British Inspector-General were humiliating to the nationalists.

Zaghlul's response to the attacks of the opposition Press was typically autocratic and disastrous for the Egyptian experiment in constitutional government. He did not hesitate to apply the sanctions of the 1881 Press Law (as revised and reactivated in 1909) against newspapers and magazines. This despite the fact that, in emphasizing the freedom of the Press, the brand-new 1923 Constitution had made a court order compulsory for the closing down of any press medium. All the same, in the case of the newspaper *al-Siyasa*, a court reversed the government's action.[6]

Zaghlul was pressed both about the Sudan and the army questions. The Egyptians had, for some time, been uneasy over British policy in the Sudan, especially over proposed irrigation schemes there. They felt that British policy aimed at creating a separate Sudanese national movement to help oust Egypt altogether, by ending the 1899 Condominium Agreement of Joint Anglo-Egyptian rule in the Sudan. As for the army, Egyptians demanded from the government the speedy removal of its British Sirdar and Inspector-General.

To both these problems Zaghlul responded by promising negotiations with Britain – much in the same way as succeeding Egyptian governments were to respond to the same, or similar, problems. Moreover, he confessed that he had no power to oppose, or change, British policy in the Sudan. Whereas since 1899 the Sudanese government budget had to be presented to the Egyptian government, now in 1924 the latter was being ignored. Moreover, there were pro-Egyptian disturbances among military school students in the Sudan in

August, and Egyptian Army units posted there were restless. As for other budgetary difficulties that year, the army featured prominently. Opposition newspapers objected to the proposed budget of the British Army of occupation in that it was not itemized so that Parliament could debate it properly. Others objected to the very idea of Egypt defraying the costs of any army of occupation, especially under a popular Wafdist government.

Other delicate matters plagued this first elected government. Prominent among them was the repeal of the Law of Associations passed by the Ali Yahia Ibrahim caretaker government in 1923 when martial law had been abolished. Wafdists at that time had opposed this law and wished it repealed. Now that they were in power they wished instead to retain it for political reasons, namely, to muzzle any opposition to their rule. The same Wafdist attitude prevailed over the freedom of the Press as evidenced in their prosecution of the opposition Liberal Constitutionalist paper *al-Siyasa*, the National Party paper *al-Akhbar*, and the weekly *al-Kashkul*.

Although the fall of the first Wafdist government did not come about until the crisis occasioned by the assassination of Sir Lee Stack Pasha, Sirdar and Governor-General of the Sudan, in November 1924, its record until that time had prejudiced its normal life-expectancy. Apart from its differences with the King over the distribution and separation of powers and prerogatives, the Wafdist concept of power, of politics and government was essentially inimical to the healthy development of parliamentary life and rule.

Zaghlul had by then become a charismatic leader, a *za'im* of the nation. It was difficult for him to countenance both opposition from other parties as well as differences of opinion among his own party members. His earlier rejection of the 1922 Declaration and his description of it as a 'national disaster', and those who negotiated it as 'national delinquents', did not make his eventual acceptance of power under its general conditions straightforward. Nor was he able once in power to resolve the issues this Declaration had raised by negotiation or otherwise. On the contrary, as in the case of the Sudan and later that of the army, Zaghlul's brief stay in power intensified the problems engendered by the relationship with Britain.

Nor did Zaghlul justify popular faith in him. He did not, for example, repeal the 1923 Law of Associations which others felt restrained free political life. He applied Party patronage to all levels of the administration reaching to the lowest level of local officers. He was unsuccessful in his talks with the Ramsay Macdonald government in September–October 1924 to reach a reconciliation between British policy, which since 1922 had been primarily interested in retaining enough control to safeguard Britain's vital interests, and Egypt's independence. He had failed to curtail the King's utilization of religious institutions for political purposes, as for example in opposing governments of the day ('We have no chief but the King,' cried the Azharites in various rallies between October and November 1924).

Sir Lee Stack Pasha was assassinated in Cairo on 19 November 1924. The British reaction was immediate and severe. In his ultimatum to the Egyptian government, the High Commissioner demanded, among other things, the withdrawal of all Egyptian Army units from the Sudan. He also informed them of the plan to extend the irrigated area in the Sudan by some 300,000 *feddans*. When Zaghlul could not accept all the demands in the ultimatum, the British Army occupied the Alexandria Customs House. Zaghlul resigned on 23 November and Ahmad Ziwar Pasha, first President of the Senate, formed a new government which acceded unconditionally to the British ultimatum. Suspected terrorists among nationalists were arrested by the British military authority, all Egyptian Army units were evacuated from the Sudan, and the British set up an independent Sudan Defence Force separate from the Egyptian Army.

Certain changes affecting parliamentary government had, however, been introduced by the first elected Wafdist government. The electoral law was amended in July 1924 to allow for direct elections, and a General Accounting Office was established (*diwan al-muhasaba*). Other acts covered the issue of banknotes, an education budget, government loans to co-operative societies, and the sale of Domain lands to small farmers.

On 25 November the King decreed the postponement of the parliamentary session by a month, at the end of which he dissolved the House. To make another Wafd electoral victory more difficult, the indirect two-stage election process was reinstated. A new party, *al-Ittihad* (Union), headed by Yahia Ibrahim was organized by courtiers and Wafd dissidents to fight the new elections on the side of wider powers for the monarch. In February 1925, redistricting for the new elections to be held on 12 March was implemented. Ismail Sidqi, the new Interior Minister, forbade civil servants to engage in political activities, and practically ordered provincial governors and district officers to help ensure the election of government-sponsored candidates. Even though the Wafd again won a majority of 116 out of a total of 214 seats, Ziwar formed a new coalition government consisting of Liberal Constitutionalists, Ittihadists and Independents. The newly elected Parliament, however, was dissolved ten days later on 23 March when, at its first meeting, Saad was elected Speaker of the House.

The Ittihad coalition government now proceeded, with the King's backing, to revise the electoral law once again, to take strong security measures against the opposition, and generally to ensure that the Wafd could not easily return to power. This policy marked the first palace coup against the Constitution and against politicians who wished to curtail the monarch's powers. Meanwhile, Allenby had resigned in May 1925 as High Commissioner and was succeeded by Lord Lloyd. The latter was a champion of the rigid safeguarding of British interests in Egypt. In July, the Egyptian government revised the Penal Code to stiffen the penalties against the Press. When the politico-religious tract by Shaykh Ali Abd al-Raziq was published in 1925,[7] a cabinet crisis arose which led to the resignation of Liberal ministers from the government and the reconstitution of the Council of Ministers as a pure Ittihadist one. A strong Law of Associations was decreed in October to which all opposition political parties objected. The dissolved Wafdist Parliament met privately in the Continental Hotel to protest all these measures and to press the government to reinstate constitutional life. Popular feeling was further aroused when the Ziwar government gave in to the Italian territorial claims over the Jaghbub oasis on the Libyan–Egyptian frontier. This was a centre of Sanusi activities and thus carried Islamic overtones.[8]

A new electoral law was published in December which introduced new financial requirements and qualifications for both electors and candidates, to which opposition political parties objected strenuously. The King was on the verge of undermining the Constitution further and Britain intervened to restore the balance. It is alleged that the High Commissioner forced the resignation of Hasan Nash'at, the Royal Chamberlain and the strong man behind the Ittihad Party government, and caused the fall of the Ziwar Ministry. Tawfiq Nasim, the second president of the Senate, formed a new government; the political parties formed a joint committee in January 1926 to co-ordinate their electoral policies. They first decided to boycott the elections held under the indirect process, and to hold a national congress instead. By February the government, under pressure, reverted to direct elections which were held in May. Again the Wafd secured a majority of the seats (165); but Zaghlul was unwilling to take on the premiership as this would have brought him immediately in direct confrontation with the difficult problem of British policy in Egypt. Instead, he agreed to a coalition government with the Liberals headed by their leader Adli Yeken. Ziwar's government resigned and Adli's government was formed in June. Parliament was convened and Saad was again elected Speaker of the House.

In its first session this Parliament abrogated all legislation passed when the House was not in session since December 1924; decided to deposit all local and provincial government funds in the new Bank Misr to boost local, native enterprise and passed a General Amnesty Bill for political crimes committed during the period December 1924–April 1926.

The second session of this Parliament reconvened in November 1926 and was occupied with the control of cotton cultivation, loans to cotton growers, and co-operative law projects. While discussing industrialization plans in 1927, Adli resigned the premiership and was succeeded by his colleague from the Liberal Party, Abd al-Khaleq Sarwat, who continued to lead a coalition government.

A new crisis involving British interests cropped up only weeks after Sarwat's government took office over the financing and control of the Egyptian Army. Deputies recommended that the British Sirdar of the army be replaced with an Egyptian, and the discontinuance of the membership of the British Inspector-General on the Army Council. The British reaction on 29 May 1927 was swift and firm, backed up by the dispatch of a British fleet detachment to Alexandria. Egypt was forced to extend the British Inspector-General's service for another five years, and agreed to enter into new negotiations with Britain. Meantime, Zaghlul died on 23 August and the Wafd elected Mustafa al-Nahhas as his successor a month later.

The Sarwat–Chamberlain negotiations of that summer produced a British proposal for a treaty of alliance. Among its draft provisions were that the Egyptian Army follow British training procedures and organization patterns; that Egypt give preference to British over other foreign nationals where needed in her service. Moreover, British troops were to remain in the country until the Egyptian Army was able to protect British imperial communications.

In the new parliamentary session which began in November 1927, Nahhas was elected Speaker of the House and Sarwat's cabinet colleagues rejected his report on his negotiations with Chamberlain. He resigned and was succeeded by the first Nahhas government on

18 March 1928. With a majority in the House, Nahhas, in office for the first time, showed his spirit of national co-operation by including Liberal Party members in his cabinet. The inconclusive and unpopular Sarwat–Chamberlain negotiations, however, were to prove a serious obstacle to the survival of this government beyond a mere three months. The previous full parliamentary session had, in the meantime, managed to complete a certain amount of legislative business. A new law for co-operatives had been passed; so was an act regulating elections to provincial councils, and one for the organization of the new State University in Cairo.

The Nahhas government, however, was pressed by Britain to reconsider the Chamberlain treaty proposal. British pressure was more effective when Parliament renewed its efforts to pass a new Law of Associations in April 1928. The High Commissioner demanded that the legislative project be abandoned on the grounds that it would endanger foreign lives and interests in Egypt. Allegedly working through the Palace, the High Commissioner engineered the resignation in June of the new leader of the Liberal Party, Muhammad Mahmud,[9] from the coalition government. A difference between the King and Prime Minister over the reinstatement and restoration of the property of Amir Sayf al-Din afforded the King the right pretext to dismiss the Nahhas government on 25 June 1928.[10] Muhammad Mahmud now formed a government in alliance with the pro-Palace Ittihad party; the King postponed the parliamentary session for a month, and on 19 July dissolved Parliament and postponed elections for three years. The country was to be governed by royal decree. Another royal coup against parliamentary life had taken place.

Meanwhile, Mahmud's government ended the privileged position of Iranian subjects resident in Egypt under an old Turkish–Iranian treaty with the signing of a Treaty of Friendship with Iran in November 1928. Relations with the Sudan were further normalized by the signing of a Nile Waters Agreement with Britain in May 1929. The effect of this agreement was to further separate the Sudan from Egypt.

The gulf between Palace and most politicians widened as the year 1930 approached. Parties were forced outside the normal channels of political activity at a time when the worst economic depression in modern times gripped the world. While the Wafd urged its followers to fight for a Constitution to which when in power they themselves had not been faithful, the Palace-appointed government of the Liberal Muhammad Mahmud introduced strict measures against the opposition. The old 1881 Censorship law was reinstated; an order was issued in March 1929 banning students from political demonstrations; a decree was issued to protect public officials from court litigation against them arising out of administrative cases, thus giving the government a free hand to deal with recalcitrant politicians. The activities of the Bar Association were curtailed by new government measures and, on 20 March, a Bill was published providing for the punishment of all those who agitated against the régime.

Yet another round of Anglo-Egyptian talks – this time between Henderson of the new Labour government and Mahmud – occurred in the summer. Britain suggested comprehensive negotiations covering all outstanding questions between the two countries with a view to arriving at a new formal treaty relationship. The Wafd opposed this scheme, insisting that no treaty could be negotiated, or concluded, before new elections were held in Egypt and constitutional life restored. The British government seemed to favour this restoration of constitutional life as a precondition for, and in the hope of, conclusive negotiations. The Mahmud government thus resigned and Adli, now no longer a Liberal Party member, but an independent, formed a new government on 20 October 1929. This was clearly a caretaker government to prepare for new elections. The Constitution duly reinstated by royal decree the following day, elections were held in December. Inevitably, the Wafd secured a majority (212 out of 235 seats. The number of deputies had in the meantime been increased on the basis of the 1927 Census).

The Wafd now, on 1 January 1930, formed their third government since independence and the second under Nahhas. They proceeded to remove provincial governors and high government officials and to replace them by Wafdists. In the fourth elected Parliament which opened on 11 January, the Wafdist House moved swiftly and confidently with a nationalist economic programme. In addition to the difficulties arising from the world economic crisis, the Egyptian Federation of Industries had been pressing for some time for protective tariffs to support their recent industrial enterprises, led by the Bank Misr group. The House also felt confident to resume talks with the British government. But the Nahhas–Henderson talks during 31 March–8 May 1930 broke down once again over the question of the Sudan. The clause proposed by Britain stipulated that future separate negotiations would determine any changes in the 1899 Condominium Agreement.

As before – and as usual – the breakdown in Anglo-Egyptian talks served as the convenient opening for anti-Wafdist politicians led by the Palace to topple the Nahhas government. The Liberals, for instance, petitioned the King at the end of May to dismiss the cabinet. At the same time, the King himself was anxious to do so for other reasons. For example, he was opposed to the proposed legislation which would have permitted courts to bring government ministers accused of undermining the constitutional system to trial. He was also quarrelling with the government over the question of Senate appointments.[11] A combination of these anti-Wafd dispositions and forces, and Britain's displeasure over Nahhas' rejection of the new Henderson proposals, converged to oust the Nahhas government from office on 17 June.

Ismail Sidqi now emerged as the 'strong man' of Egyptian politics to head a pro-Palace government which included many Ittihadists. An old supporter and erstwhile colleague of Zaghlul and a fellow-exile in the Seychelles in 1919, Sidqi later joined the Liberals and served as Minister of the Interior in the Ittihad–Liberal Coalition government of 1925. Faced with managing the affairs of the country at a time of a world economic crisis, Sidqi was determined to abrogate the 1923 Constitution. He wished to rule out the return of a Wafdist government once and for all. His assumption of the Premiership marked the third Palace coup against parliamentary government and the Constitution in less than seven years, and the longest period of rule by decree in the country. This was a crucial period in the political evolution of Egypt, for its effects were permanently damaging to the hoped-for development in parliamentary government. More important, this period laid the foundations of more violent politics in the country; alienated political leaders from the monarchy; and the public from all normal, orderly government. It made it easier for extremist, fanatic political groups to emerge and be organized, as well as to attract new elements of the population to their ranks. It permitted the Muslim Brethren, for instance, to strengthen their organization and experience a period of great development.

Sidqi proceeded immediately to adjourn Parliament. As in 1925 before, Parliament met privately 'in congress' in the Saadist Club on 26 June 1930 to protest government action. The government simultaneously instituted forceful measures against all public agitation fanned, or led, by political parties. A spate of demonstrations drew a sharp British warning to both government and Wafd about security conditions in the country, especially as their deterioration affected the lives and property of foreign residents. Royal Navy frigates were ready to back up this warning by force. All this constituted yet another pretext for the government to dissolve Parliament on 12 July. The latter, predominantly Wafdist, reverted to its old protest method and met as a 'national congress' two weeks later to register publicly its lack of confidence in the Sidqi government. With its extensive influence and following in the countryside, the Wafd moreover fomented serious trouble in the provinces and among members of provincial councils. Sidqi responded by disbanding many of the latter. Then in August there was an attempt on Sidqi's life while he was travelling on the Alexandria–Cairo train.

Sidqi also sought to deal with the deteriorating conditions of public order by the adoption of extreme administrative measures. He abolished the Constitution on 22 October 1930, and drafted another one, together with a new electoral law.[12] Both these new documents strengthened the powers of the monarch. Ministerial responsibility to Parliament was replaced by responsibility to the King. The latter moreover was to initiate legislation and have the right to veto all Parliament-enacted legislation. The electoral law raised the proportion of voters to electors from 30:1 to 50:1, thus minimizing the chances of overwhelming Wafdist electoral victories. It also introduced financial and educational qualifications for electors which tended to exclude over 80 per cent of the Egyptian population. It further excluded from parliamentary candidacy all those members of the liberal professions (doctors, lawyers, engineers, journalists and merchants) who lived outside Cairo; but qualified *umdas*, or village headmen, for it, as these could be easily controlled by the government. Finally a Royal Decree on 20 October disbanded all provincial councils, many of which were naturally Wafdist or pro-Wafdist under the last government in power. Public rallies to protest the new constitution were forcefully broken up and/or prevented by the police.

Sidqi then formed his own party, *Hizb al-shaab* (People's Party), to contest the elections.[13] This elicited the formation of a united front between the Wafd and the Liberals to combat Sidqi, formalized in the signing of a National Pact between them on 31 March 1931. The two parties called for a national congress to meet and consider their programme. The government, however, prevented the congress from meeting.

The elections of June 1931 were accompanied by violence and bloodshed. Yet the new pro-Sidqi Parliament met on 20 June. Throughout the rest of the year and the following year (1932) there was violent opposition to the government across the country. The government on its part applied strong censorship and other measures against the Press which now came under a revised Penal Code providing for severe punishment of its critics. In 1931, several laws regarding publications were decreed. These restricted the reporting of news about criminal proceedings, and the use of overcritical language when reporting government news. They also placed severe restrictions, including excessive financial requirements, on publishers and editors of newspapers and magazines. Finally, they provided for stiff sentences of up to five years' imprisonment and steep fines. Nonetheless, violent incidents continued to occur. There were attempts on the life of Sidqi, sabotage of trains, and bomb attacks on British installations and personnel.[14]

The government meanwhile faced a tremendous economic crisis. Cotton prices dipped to an all-time low from twenty-six *riyals* (approximately four shillings) per *kantar* to ten *riyals*,[15] which led to a fall in the price of all agricultural products. Economically, the country experienced four difficult years (1930–4). Debts of farmers and agriculturists were immense and interest rates high. Sidqi met this crisis in part by the establishment of an Agricultural Credit Bank in 1931. He lowered agricultural land rents to $\frac{1}{5}$ of value and later to $\frac{3}{10}$ of value; postponed the repayment of loans extended by the government to smaller farmers as well as the price of fertilizers supplied by the government to them. The government further made loans to farmers amounting to some three million Egyptian pounds against their cotton crops and used the new Agricultural Credit Bank to intervene to stop foreclosures on indebtedness and/or mortgage. But it did not lower the interest rates on loans, or the actual principal of loans. Thus interest income to the banks and the government was apparently ultimately unaffected.

Like its predecessors, the Sidqi government too had to deal with the perennial question of Anglo-Egyptian relations. By this time, there was a new coalition government in Britain and Sidqi had talks with the Foreign Secretary, Sir John Simon, in September 1932. It was then suspected that Sidqi had been anxious for talks in order to secure British support for his government and its emergency measures for the maintenance of law and order in Egypt. In any case, the British government made it clear that negotiations should follow the principles laid down in their earlier treaty proposals of 1929 and 1930. The talks therefore did not lead to any new developments or breakthrough in Anglo-Egyptian relations.

It was also alleged that the British High Commissioner had explored the possibility of a new coalition government consisting of the Wafd and Liberals in view of the deteriorating security conditions in the country which was giving rise to some anxiety among the British in Egypt. But this only led to a disagreement between Wafd and Liberals (the Wafd rejected the idea of a coalition government) and a split in the ranks of the Wafd executive itself resulting in the resignation of several members from the Party. Further incidents of violence in the country led in their turn to the resignation of Ali Maher and Abd al-Fattah Yahia from the Sidqi cabinet. Whether the resignations of these known Palace men was due to their disagreement with the Prime Minister over the need to investigate police actions against the public, or whether they were inspired by the King who may have decided that the time had come to dismiss Sidqi, was not quite clear. Sidqi resigned in January 1933 and the King invited him almost two months later in March to form a new government. This amounted to a re-shuffling of the previous cabinet minus Ali Maher and Yahia.

On 21 September the King deemed the moment appropriate to dismiss Sidqi and appoint a purely Palace Council of Ministers.[16] The new Prime Minister Abd al-Fattah Yahia included the Shaab Party members in his cabinet. This government was succeeded in November 1934 by yet another appointed one headed by Tawfiq Nasim. The King moreover ordered by Royal Decree the repeal of the Sidqi constitution and the dissolution of the Parliament elected in June 1931 without, however, restoring that of 1923. Instead he was to assume all powers for a transition period of unspecified duration.

A combination of factors came to bear in the following year (1935) upon the restoration of the 1923 Constitution. One was perhaps the desire of Britain to negotiate a new treaty with a constitutionally elected government. Another was the pressure from the Wafd and other political groups. Thus the Wafd held a General Congress in January 1935 in which they called for a return to the 1923 Constitution. A third factor was the inability of Palace-appointed governments to deal effectively either with the internal security problem or with the question of Anglo-Egyptian relations. Most important perhaps was the Italian invasion of Ethiopia in October 1935, and its annexation by Italy in 1936. Italian propaganda against Britain in Egypt and elsewhere in the Middle East was intensified. That year, too, the Spanish Civil War broke out, with prominent assistance to Franco from the Axis powers.

On the recommendation of the Nasim government the King agreed in April 1935 to a return to the 1923 Constitution. But Britain was anxious to ensure that a return to constitutional life and inevitably to another elected Wafdist government could come about only in conjunction with an undertaking by the Egyptians to seek a new treaty relationship with her. This was interpreted by many Egyptians as undue British interference in their domestic political life. More disturbances and violent incidents followed that summer and autumn. Yet British pressure had its desired effect. All political parties recognized the importance of combining the demands for return to constitutional life with an undertaking to negotiate a new treaty with Britain. The King was thus able on 12 December to decree the reinstatement of the 1923 Constitution, and the preparation for direct, single stage elections under electoral procedures obtaining in 1924.

An expression of lack of confidence in the neutrality of the Nasim government to supervise fair elections by several party leaders led to the consideration of a coalition caretaker government under Nasim. This proved difficult to achieve. Nasim therefore resigned on 22 January 1936 and the King asked Ali Maher, his Chief Royal Chamberlain, to form a caretaker government on 30 January.

In addition to the preparation for elections, a nationally representative official delegation was formed in February to conduct the treaty negotiations in London on the basis of the Nahhas–Henderson talks in 1930. Elections were set for May. Meantime, King Fuad died on 28 April and was succeeded by his young son Faruq, who acceded to the throne on 6 May. The Wafd once again secured a majority of seats in Parliament; the latter met on 8 May, and Nahhas formed his third all-Wafd government on the 10th.

Several changes in the institutions of government were introduced. A Royal Council, or Cabinet (*al-diwan al-malaki*) was instituted to serve as liaison between the monarch and the elected government. Confident as a result of their electoral victory in the prospects of a settlement with Britain, the government proceeded to push through Parliament a number of legislative acts which carried overtones of social and economic reform. Thus agricultural loans were written off up to 20 per cent of their original value. A Bill giving amnesty to all political crimes committed since the repeal of the 1923 Constitution in June 1930 and its restoration in 1935–6 was passed. It revoked the Sidqi law giving immunity from prosecution to civil servants. It passed the first Accident Compensation Act for industrial workers.

The Anglo-Egyptian Treaty was signed on 26 August 1936. To a great extent, the Treaty was a British conciliatory gesture towards Egypt, but one that Britain considered urgent and necessary in view of the mounting Axis threat in Europe, the Middle East and East Africa. Presumably the Treaty dealt with the resolution of matters concerning Anglo-Egyptian relations that had been left outstanding by the Four Reserved Points of the 1922 Declaration. In fact only one of these was cleared up, namely the protection of foreign and minority interests in Egypt. But the defence of Egypt against aggression was merely re-cast in a new formula. Instead of a British occupation, there was concluded a new Anglo-Egyptian military alliance, which stipulated the maintenance of a British garrison of ten thousand men in the Canal Zone to ensure the security of British imperial communications. As for the Sudan, the Treaty, if anything, specified that it would be left to the Sudanese themselves to choose eventually between national sovereignty and an allegiance to one or the other party to the 1899 Condominium Agreement.

Yet the Treaty produced certain new conditions. Egypt's formal independence was extended, giving her freedom in the conduct of her diplomatic affairs. The British High Commissioner was redesignated HM Ambassador to Egypt, and the Wafd government proceeded with certain Egyptianization measures in the country. Upon the retirement of the British Inspector-General of the Egyptian Army, an Egyptian officer was appointed to replace him, and the government assumed full administrative control over its armed forces. It moreover opened the doors of the Military Academy to a wider group of Egyptians. The independence status of the country was strengthened further when, as a result of the Treaty, a Convention followed at Montreux in April–May 1937 which abolished the Capitulations in Egypt and ordered the closing of the Mixed Tribunals after a transition period of twelve years had elapsed (in October 1949). The Capitulations could no longer be maintained in Egypt when they had been abolished in all the other ex-dominions of the Ottoman Empire, e.g., Syria–Lebanon, Iraq, Palestine and Transjordan since 1922; in Turkey itself by the Treaty of Lausanne in 1923; and in Iran in 1928. Egypt then also became a member of the League of Nations.

Other national gains followed quickly. In an agreement with the Suez Canal Company, the government extracted such concessions as the appointment of at least two Egyptians on the Company's Board of Directors; the raising of the annual concession payment by the Company to 300,000 Egyptian pounds; and the agreement of the Company to carry a 35 per cent Egyptian labour force in its employment. The Company moreover agreed to build roads between Suez and Port Said.

With the end of the Regency Council period and the assumption of full constitutional powers by the new King Faruq in July 1937, Nahhas formed his fourth Wafd government in August. By then, however, a further split in the Wafd's ranks had occurred which led later to the formation of the dissident Saadist Party in 1938. The government nevertheless continued confidently in its policy of further Egyptianization in founding such establishments as the Officer's Staff College, a Flight School for aviators, and other institutions.

At the same time, Nahhas was anxious to stay in power for a long time if possible – at least for the normal life of the elected Parliament. Youth organizations, especially the paramilitary Blue Shirts, were founded to mobilize party followers and the masses, as well as to intimidate and terrorize the opposition. He also did not hestitate (over-confidently perhaps) to expel Mahmud Nuqrashi, Ahmad Maher and others from the party between September and December 1937.

Egyptian politics, however, became more complicated and more devious. The question of Anglo-Egyptian relations receded to the background temporarily thanks to the 1936 Treaty. The power struggle now became sharpened and confined between King and Wafd. The new King had just reappointed Ali Maher, a trusted friend of his father, as Chief of the Royal Cabinet – a post he had held since 1935. Ali Maher, a grey eminence in Egyptian politics until 1942 – and later – was unacceptable to the Wafd. In combating the Wafd, Faruq resorted to tactics similar to those used by his father. Thus, he fought over Senate appointments, the budget, control of religious institutions, the commissioning of army officers. He sought the support of Azharites, led by Shaykh Mustafa al-Maraghi, and university students. A new extreme right (fascist) organization, *Misr al-fatat* (Young Egypt), with its Green Shirts youth organization, tended to support these forces against the Wafd. Their slogan included 'Country, Islam, and King'.[17]

Meanwhile, another grey eminence of Egyptian politics appeared on the scene in the person of Ahmad Hasanayn, whose influence upon the course of affairs was to reach its height in the war years (1940–5). He was tutor, mentor, ADC, and chief secretary and adviser to the young King. He wished to protect the interests and prerogatives of his ward, possibly via a rapprochement with the popular Wafd. But he was also ambitious enough to want to wield decisive influence and control over any Egyptian government.

A serious conflict between Nahhas and the King arose over the matter of a coronation ceremony that would entail a *baya*, the traditional Islamic oath of allegiance, to be pronounced by the Shaykh of the Azhar in the Muhammad Ali Mosque in the Citadel. The government objected on the grounds that it would be unconstitutional. The King, they argued, must take the appropriate oath to uphold the constitution, as provided for in the 1923 Constitution, as the head of a secular constitutional monarchy in which a religious *baya* had no place. The Wafd, naturally, was opposed to a public occasion that would have appealed to the traditional masses and thus secured a measure of popularity among them for the young King.[18]

A situation obtained in the autumn of 1937 – only two months after Faruq had assumed the powers of the Throne – in which government and monarch were at loggerheads. Confident after their electoral victory and their vastly improved relations with Britain, the Wafd were anxious to prevent a return to the Palace powers exerted by the late King Fuad. The King, on the other hand, noted that the Wafd had not been beyond compromise (especially in the case of the Anglo-Egyptian relationship) in order to remain in power; that its ranks were split; that its relations with minority parties were shaky, if not unfriendly. He therefore tried to array against them the full influence of the court, the old Palace guard of politicians, Ahmad Maher and his colleagues who had left the Wafd, the minority parties; and to use to his advantage the continuing internal cracks in the Wafd.

It has been alleged that the King feared a Wafdist dictatorship. He observed the activities of the Blue Shirts organization with apprehension. More important he appreciated correctly the privileged treatment of an expanded Egyptian Army officer corps at the hands of the Wafd.

In these circumstances, the Wafd government had to be cautious in power, by avoiding precipitate legislative and executive action that could conceivably have brought political victory to them over the

Palace forces. By the end of October 1937, the Palace had managed to provoke anti-government demonstrations by Azhar and university students. Ironically, the old Wafd policy of organizing student groups for its political purposes had backfired. In November, a member of the *Misr al-fatat* group attempted to assassinate Nahhas outside his home in Heliopolis. A mass rally of students outside Abdin Palace on 21 December, shouting pro-King and anti-Wafd slogans, broke the back of the Nahhas government. It was ignominiously dismissed by the King on 30 December.

A Liberal government headed by Muhammad Mahmud – his second – followed which dissolved Parliament in January 1938, and ordered new elections to be held in April. Purposeful redistricting (seats were increased to 264) enabled the government to secure a combined majority of seats. This was further made possible by the formation of the new Saadist Party in January 1938 after the expulsion of Ahmad Maher (Speaker of the House) from the Wafd. Between them the Liberals and Saadists won 193 seats (eighty Saadists), and the so-called Independents who were pro-government in any case won fifty-five. The Wafd won only twelve seats and the National Party four.

Yet the new Prime Minister found it difficult to govern, especially when he had to reconcile so many divergent interests in a coalition government. A series of reshuffled cabinets followed, until the dismissal of the Mahmud government by the King in August 1939, and the appointment of his Royal Cabinet Chief, Ali Maher, as Premier. The Saadists accepted participation in this new government, but the Liberals stayed out.

The Mahmud government passed a number of important Bills, such as a new Civil Service Act, a capital gains tax law, a new stamp duty law, and an inheritance tax law. It raised the budget of the army and approved the project for a State University in Alexandria which opened in 1942. The Ali Maher government of August 1939–June 1940 had created a Social Affairs Ministry. In view of the deteriorating international situation of the time, it decreed the organization of a Territorial Army (*al-jaysh al-murabit*) which provided for six months' military training and service for all Egyptian males.

By this time the Second World War had broken out in Europe; the danger to the Middle East and Egypt was soon to follow. Consequently, Egyptian politics took a new turn. The combination of urgent British wartime security interests and the ongoing conflict between King and Wafd – and between Wafd and all other political parties – now tended to undermine further constitutional government in Egypt. In the first eight years of constitutional life, Parliament had been dissolved four times. In the fifteen-year period 1923–38, there had been seven general elections. No parliament lasted its normal term of four years. The longest until 1938 had been Sidqi's Parliament of three years' duration (1931–4).

At the same time, social and economic changes which occurred after 1919 and particularly during the Second World War undermined certain popular traditional and religious ideas and institutions in the country. It is therefore necessary to look more closely at these developments before we return to a consideration of the final erosion and decay of the old order in the period 1940–52, and its consequences.

CHAPTER 14

THE ATTACK UPON TRADITION

In addition to the inauspicious beginning of parliamentary life under the experiment in constitutional government, Egypt faced a period of social and cultural dislocation which manifested itself in many areas. Although much of the preoccupation of successive Egyptian governments centred on the resolution of the national issue (Egypt's relationship with Britain), the relentless impact made by European ideas and other influences upon educated Egyptians soon created social crises of political significance.

It will be recalled that all political parties, especially the Wafd, looked to the constitutional arrangement as a safeguard against the excessive power of the monarch. Many of their leaders had been educated in Europe, particularly in the fields of law and the humanities. The prominent writers, journalists and publicists among them expressed views of a definite European secularist orientation. For example, Muhammad Husayn Haykal, editor of *al-Siyasa*, the official organ of the Liberal Party, Mahmud Azmi, Salama Musa and others represented views ranging from the classical liberalism of the French Enlightenment to British Socialism and Social Darwinism.

Directly involved in the debates and writings of the *literati* were such fundamental questions as individual freedom and civil liberty. In order to argue such questions these writers were led to question the utility of traditional institutions sanctioned by the consensus of the religious community and, therefore, the religion of Islam itself. Soon though, the need of a government to legislate for the maintenance of a modern state, the need to expand governmental functions and services, and a growing awareness of the need for socio-economic reform brought it in conflict not only with traditional beliefs and values, but with their representatives – the leaders of religious institutions. More complicated was the exposure of this conflict to the vagaries of struggle and competition among political groups, such as the parties and the Palace.

For some seventy-five years traditional administrative structures and legal institutions were gradually relinquished. Together with the first steps in legislative assemblies since 1866, legal codes modelled after the French codes were adopted. A new Penal Code adopted in 1863 was followed by further judicial reform under the leadership of Nubar Pasha, which culminated in the founding in 1876 of the Mixed Courts of Alexandria and Cairo to satisfy the interests of the Capitulatory Powers. Commercial and civil codes reconciling Egyptian and French Law were applied in these courts. In 1880 a new law for the Sharia, or religious, courts confined their juridical competence to questions of personal status: marriage, divorce, inheritance or succession, paternity, guardianship, and *waqfs*.

As a result of the Dufferin administrative reforms of 1883, an Organic Law was promulgated in May of that year by Khedive Tawfiq which reorganized the constitutional framework of Egypt. This served as the basis for a new Legislative Assembly and Council, whose modified version in 1913 was suspended in 1915. More significant for the further secularization of the legal structures of Egyptian society was the establishment in the same year of the National Courts. Civil and penal codes, together with codes of civil and criminal procedure to be applied by these courts, were also promulgated. By the turn of the century Egypt's judicial system for all practical purposes had been modernized along French lines.

The attack upon tradition in this instance was more direct than for instance in Turkey, where the reform and modernization of the legal and judicial system in the 1850s attempted a reconciliation between the old and the new. Thus, the *Majalla*, the civil code promulgated by the Ottoman authorities, was based upon Islamic principles. In fact, it was a codification of Hanafi law.[1] A sharp dichotomy in the Egyptian judicial system reflected a firmer supercession of the tradition. On one side stood the new Mixed and Native, or National, Courts applying codified laws and rules of procedure which were of composite origin with a predominant Western influence. Their personnel from judges to legal clerks as well as the lawyers who practised before the Bar had been trained in a basically European way. Moreover, these came to constitute a large element in the ranks of liberal progressive Egyptian leadership. On the other side stood the Sharia courts applying modified laws and rules of the orthodox Hanafi rite by judges and lawyers trained in traditional religious institutions. The non-Muslim communities, on the other hand, continued the adjudication of disputes regarding personal status of their members in their communal, ecclesiastical and consular courts.

Further attacks upon tradition occurred in other areas of

Egyptian life. The institution of a parliamentary system of government upon independence in 1922–3 and the holding of the first general elections in 1923–4 formally introduced into Egypt a system of government that was theoretically based on legal–rational foundations. Legislation became a matter of debate and compromise in the resolution of conflicting interests presumably expressed in representative institutions. It appeared one of the major areas in which the desire for the reform of all social institutions clashed with the interests of the traditionalists. Closely related to this matter was the question of the reform of religious institutions, especially the Azhar, in order to integrate this leading institution of religious learning into the modern stream of life.

These issues were all part of the wider question facing Egyptian leaders of that time, namely, if Egypt were to be a modern sovereign state, and Egyptian society were to be transformed into a dynamic modern political community, what should the role of religion be? Should the secularization of society and politics be complete? As a rule, there is a secularization problem in a polity where there is a question of separating Church and State. This, in the absence of an organized church and a clerical hierarchy has, theoretically at least, never been a problem in classical Islamic society. Rather the problem presented itself in a different way, namely, in the disparity and division between the State on the one hand, controlled by warriors, bureaucrats and notables and, on occasion, merchants, and wider society on the other, controlled by the ulama, and religious *qadis*, the interpreters of the Sacred Law. Thus in the Ottomanized Islamic society, the hierarchy of ulama under the Chief Mufti amounted to the institutional but not theological equivalent of a Church. Consequently, state reformers such as Mahmud II in Turkey and Muhammad Ali in Egypt sought to weaken the economic power of this organization by securing greater control of *waqfs* and, in this way, to bureaucratize the ulama.

Another aspect of the problem was the question of religious content in the direction of political affairs: the affairs of state as distinguished from society. A third aspect was the matter of the importance of the religious factor in any so-called national regeneration, or, plainly, the reconciliation of the Islamic notion of the universal community with the adopted modern notion of political identity territorially limited and juridically defined – the nation-state. A fourth aspect of this problem was whether religious law should continue to be the controlling standard of conduct.

Given these several dimensions of the problem, the religious debate that arose from the attack upon tradition was destined from its start to become – not unlike the Church versus State controversy in Europe – a political controversy. The conflict over this duality of ethic was compounded in Egypt throughout the modern period by the state use of religion for political purposes.

By 1924, a Constitution based on Belgian and Ottoman models was in force. It provided for a parliament which theoretically legislated like any secular law-making body. Inevitably, the question of the sources of legislation came up. Traditionally, these consisted of the Koran, *sunna*, or practice and traditions of the Prophet, and the consensus of the community – in practice, the consensus of the doctors of religious law. Traditional institutions sanctioned by the Sacred Law, such as *waqfs*, just as inevitably came under the pressure of reform. Eventually, the debate moved from the limited concern of reforming traditional–religious institutions to that of questioning their validity – their advantages over their disadvantages – for a modern polity.

Reform of the Azhar and its several educational institutions was slow in the nineteenth century. Khedive Ismail had encouraged Shaykh Muhammad al-Abbasi al-Mahdi to raise the standards of the curriculum in the training of *qadis* and ulama. The law of February 1872 regulating teaching, provided for examinations by a board of ulama appointed by the Shaykh (Rector) of the Azhar, for the *alamiyya* certificate (the highest degree conferred by the Azhar in the religious sciences), and distinguished between three grades of ulama. It also aimed at putting an end to the haphazard granting of certificates and thus at weeding out the incompetent. The law also fixed salaries for the various grades of ulama.

Led by Muhammad Abduh, reform of the Azhar went further when the law of January 1895 expanded the curriculum to include a few modern subjects. Significantly, the law established an executive board responsible for general Azhar policy and the administration of its numerous institutions; and a curriculum committee responsible for syllabi in its various faculties. It further rationalized salary scales, and provided the lines of a general policy governing student housing.

It was followed in July 1896 by a decree regulating the qualifications and duties of the Rector and those of the Council of the Azhar; conditions of student registration; courses for the elementary and *alamiyya* certificates; and employment posts for which Azhar graduates were eligible. These steps in themselves reflected the dichotomy between the advance made in secular state education and the religious institutions. But they also reflected the dissatisfaction of Azharites with the inroads made by state school graduates in all areas of state employment. After all, until the reign of Muhammad Ali the Azhar had been the major source of recruitment for teachers and government employees. It was no longer that at the turn of the century. Politically, such legislation showed the determination of the government to increase its control over religious institutions.

In 1908, more significant legislation under Saad Zaghlul, the then Minister of Education, was passed. This defined precisely the functions of the Azhar rector. It established a Supreme Council for al-Azhar and councils for religious institutions attached to it in Tanta, Alexandria and elsewhere in the country. It moreover divided teaching into three stages – elementary, secondary and higher – with four years as a minimum period of study for each stage.

Those in favour of reform felt that a leading member of the new breed of secular state administrators was attempting for the first time genuine reform of a traditional institution. Those opposed to reform viewed Zaghlul's action as a clear attempt on the part of the government and particularly the secular modernists in it to extend and strengthen their control over religious institutions. There was some truth in the contention of both sides: the issue became politically more significant in the 1920s and 1930s.

But there were difficulties in implementing this new legislation. Conservative Azhar leaders were opposed to Zaghlul's new state-controlled school of Sharia *qadis* (judges). They felt this would further reduce the job opportunities of Azhar graduates in the religious–judiciary field. They were generally unhappy about job prospects when competing with holders of state school certificates. Nevertheless in 1911 another law was passed which became the organic statute of al-Azhar until 1930. These early laws were amended in 1916 and 1920, especially in their budgetary provisions.

This pre-independence programme of Azhar reform was important in two respects, one educational, the other political. It imposed more rational curricular organization in the Azhar, and allowed the government greater control of religious institutions of learning. It further eroded the independence and authority of the Religious Establishment of the ulama.

After independence, the question of Azhar reform became a burning issue of politics. Its advocates and opponents alike were not

purely motivated by the spirit of reform *per se*, namely, the modernization of the institution in accordance with a commitment to a new
national programme on one hand, or the retention of its traditional
character in deference to the religious and cultural heritage on the
other. Rather the whole issue became in the period 1924–39
entangled in the vagaries of the struggle for power between king and
politicians. It was moreover exacerbated and complicated further
by events outside Egypt, such as the disestablishment of the *sharia*
and the abolition of the caliphate in Turkey in 1924; the relations
between Egypt and the new Saudi Arabia over the Hijaz, pilgrimage
and related matters; the domestic issue of legislative reform affecting
matters of personal status. While a national political issue, Azhar
reform also became the victim of national politics. It soon reverted
by 1924 to its instrumentalism of old: it became a pawn of partisan
politics in the traditional pattern.

One of the earliest concerns of the first elected Wafd government
was the project to found a State University. The earlier private
National University begun in 1908 was inadequate. Then in 1917
the project had been revived under Prince Fuad and a Committee
appointed to study it in detail. Its report in 1921 had recommended
that a university be established consisting of seven main faculties
and colleges: Arts, Sciences, Law, Medicine, Engineering, Agricultural and Veterinary Science, and Commerce. It also suggested the
addition of smaller departments, such as Fine Arts, Archaeology,
Education and Oriental Studies. Although schools of Law, Medicine
and Engineering had existed for a long time as separate institutions
the only institution of higher learning in Letters and the humanities
had been al-Azhar.

During the brief life of the first Zaghlul government (January
1924–November 1924), the Azharites, perhaps urged by the Palace,
agitated for reform. They were, however, primarily interested in getting consideration for posts and parity with graduates of such state
institutions as Darl al-Ulum Teachers' Training College and the
Sharia Judges School. The government appointed a committee to
study their demands. But the committee's report was not made
public. The Azharis and students of other religious institutions in
Cairo and Alexandria struck and publicly declared their support of
the King and their opposition to the government of the day in rallies
and demonstrations. The government threatened to apply the 1923
Law of Associations and the provisions of the earlier 1911 and 1920
acts governing al-Azhar if the students did not return to their studies.

With Zaghlul's government out, the new Palace-appointed Prime Minister Ahmad Ziwar proceeded to placate the Azharis whose support the King was anxious to secure. A ministerial committee on the Azhar reported in February 1925. This briefly recommended that such state institutions as Dar al-Ulum be placed under Azhar supervision – a clear reversal of Wafdist policy and a political victory over the anti-monarchy forces. It recommended further concessions to the Azharis, as for instance making the *alamiyya* certificate for purposes of employment equivalent to higher degrees conferred by any state institutions of higher learning, or by a state university. It also recommended a rise in the salaries of Azhari teachers. By this action the government clearly strengthened the King in his struggle to retain powers of appointment of religious leaders. The Azharis in return were promised posts in the central and provincial state administration.

Yet not all Azharis were loyal followers of the throne. The Wafd had its religious partisans too, who in 1925 and 1926 demanded more drastic reforms. Thus Azharis produced their own predicament *vis-à-vis* Egyptian political evolution. On one hand, they insisted simultaneously that the Azhar be reformed in such a way as not to remain inferior to the secular institutions of the state (or not be discriminated against in the area of state employment), and on the other that the government retain al-Azhar's old, traditionally pre-eminent position and role in society. Until 1961 the Azhar was to lose on both counts, and after that it ceased to have a choice.[2]

Deputies in the third elected Parliament (June 1926–June 1928) raised questions affecting the Azhar. They questioned the wisdom of retaining Sharia courts and the advantages of merging them with the National courts, thus bringing them directly under the jurisdiction and control of the Ministry of Justice. They further questioned the necessity of a Mufti* who was until then appointed by the King at a time when a secular civil law was in full force. They argued that if the post were to be retained it should become an elective one. Azhar shaykhs would elect not only the Mufti of Egypt but also the Shaykh of al-Azhar for limited periods of time. The pro-Palace forces, through the government of that time, argued in favour of retaining the post of Mufti, as Egypt was a leading Muslim state to

---

* The Mufti is a salaried appointee of the State who gives legal opinions, *fatwas*, in answer to questions pertaining to Sharia, or the Sacred Law, submitted to him by judges or private individuals.

which other Muslim communities looked for rulings on the religious law, and leadership in religious–legal matters.[3]

Yet these matters were part of a wider debate in the 1920s and 1930s over the sources of legislation for the modern, independent state of Egypt, the control, reform and/or abolition of certain traditional institutions. They came into focus in part as a result of the shock served on the Islamic community everywhere by Mustafa Kemal's attack upon Islam in Turkey in 1924–6: the abolition of the Caliphate and disestablishment of the Sharia.[4]

The question arose whether the caliphate was a necessary institution for the well-being of Muslims, and if it could be separated from political authority and office. In Egypt, ulama and others felt a caliph should be appointed. But the question was not a purely academic, religious or legal one. It was a miserably political issue, for the Egyptian ulama were also alarmed at the ambitions of King Husayn of the Hijaz, the ex-Sharif of Mecca. If there was to be a new Arab caliph in succession to the deposed Ottoman–Turkish one they felt he should be an Egyptian, namely, their own king. The consensus therefore among the caliphate advocates was that the caliph was necessary and that King Husayn of the Hijaz should not be the new *imam* of the Muslims.

The Wafd government insisted upon not interfering in this problem, realizing perhaps that to encourage the ulama in their plans would only increase the influence and power of their adversary – the King. The religious groups especially Rashid Rida, head of the *Salafiyya* movement and editor of its journal, *al-Manar*, persisted with their plans for an Islamic Congress to be held in Cairo, to discuss and resolve the issue of the caliphate.[5] Meanwhile, King Husayn of the Hijaz agitated for a similar Congress to be held in Mecca.

At the initiative and with the financial support of Hasan Nash'at Pasha, the Royal Chamberlain, several committees on the caliphate were set up in the provinces and the Caliphate Committee of al-Azhar was organized to approach the King and the government on the matter. By virtue of his constitutional control over the budget of religious institutions (Article 153), the King could quietly support this movement. Active propaganda for a Congress to meet in Egypt was carried on in the Press from 1924 to 1926. Despite the government's opposition to a Congress being held in Cairo, an Executive Council of the Congress for the Caliphate met in April and May 1926, but without much success. Meantime, King Husayn had been ousted from the Hijaz by Ibn Saud. The latter called for an Islamic

Congress to meet in Mecca to look into the matters of the Holy Places and the pilgrimage. This met in June 1926 and was attended by official delegates of the Egyptian government.

Despite this initial failure to resolve the caliphate question, it remained a central issue in Egyptian politics for a long time – at least until 1939 and then again until 1946. Thus the official Azhar journal *Nur al-Islam* carried in the early 1930s much propaganda for an Egyptian caliph. It also remained a key issue in the debate over tradition versus further modern reform. This is in part reflected in some of the literary production of the 1920s and 1930s.

Al-islam wa usul al-hukm (*Islam and the principles of political authority*), a religio-political tract by Shaykh Ali Abd al-Raqiz, was published in 1925. A judge in the Mansura Sharia Court, Ali created a stir with his tract that was to lead to his expulsion from the ranks of the ulama, produce a government crisis, and become a *cause célèbre* of Egyptian politics. More important, it further embittered the relations between King and political parties and thus undermined constitutional government further. Above all, it illustrated clearly the close connection, even under a constitutional monarchy, between religious and secular political issues which, in Egypt, could hardly be separated.

Encouraged by the actions of Mustafa Kemal in Turkey, Ali argued in his book that the caliphate was neither a basic principle nor a necessary institution in Islam. Muhammad the Prophet had not established a polity, or a state, and the Sharia was a mere spiritual–moral law having no connection with political authority, or the earthly governing of men. Islam, that is, had never provided for a particular system of government. The ulama considered this thesis a threat to their influence in state and society. Ali's friends, among the Liberals, on the other hand, hailed his tract as a point in favour of limited government versus absolute traditional authority, as represented by the King in the Egypt of the 1920s.

Bearing in mind that in 1925 all political parties, with the exception perhaps of the new pro-Palace Ittihad,[6] were in the political wilderness, any attack upon the monarch's power and his supporters was welcomed. When the Higher Council of Ulama brought Ali to trial and expelled him from their community, the *Siyasa* newspaper of the Liberals, as well as the *Akhbar* of the National Party, shrieked that this action constituted the interference of religion in the constitutional order and an attack upon the freedom of thought guaranteed by the 1923 Constitution.

As the judgement of the ulama court had to be approved by the cabinet of the day, a government crisis resulted. Abd al-Aziz Fahmi, the then Minister of Justice in the Ziwar government, was a Liberal Party member and an illustrious member of the 1922 Constitutional Committee appointed by Sarwat to draft the 1923 Constitution. He refused to pass on the judgement and was dismissed from the government. He was replaced by Ali Maher, the Minister of Education in the same cabinet.

The following year, 1926, a second *cause célèbre* broke upon the Egyptian political scene with the publication of yet another work defying basic Islamic dogma and traditional belief. In his *Fi al-shir al-jahili* (*On Pre-Islamic Poetry*) Taha Husayn, a blind ex-Azhari and professor of Arabic Literature in the State University who had also been trained in France, attempted a two-pronged attack upon tradition. First, he questioned the ulama's traditional–religious interpretation of the Koran and Prophetic Tradition on the basis of pre-Islamic poetry. Second, he argued the case for the introduction of Cartesian rational and other philosophical methods into literary criticism. Immediately, the conservative ulama, led by Rashid Rida of *al-Manar*, branded Taha an apostate and demanded his dismissal from the University. The book was withdrawn from circulation, re-edited and re-published the following year (1927) under the new title *Fi al-adab al-jahili* (*On Pre-Islamic Literature*). Later, in 1931, the new Prime Minister, Ismail Sidqi, used this incident to dismiss Taha from his university post.[7]

While this kind of liberalism reflected in the writings of initially Azhar-trained but also European-educated Egyptians was questioning traditional teachings more boldly than ever, it must be viewed within the context of the struggle for power between a monarch who wished to retain certain prerogatives of power deriving from traditional patterns of authority on one hand, and politicians who sought ever greater privileges under an imported constitutional system of government on the other. Undoubtedly some of the latter were also partly motivated by the genuine attraction of European ideas about a liberal system of government. Yet the subsequent record of their performance as a governing élite, over a period of thirty years, does not justify the facile conclusion that they had been convinced of the liberal political ethic.

Others too in the 1920s quickened the pace of the attack upon traditional Islam and its teachings with the wider discussion of such alien ideas as Darwinian and social evolution. Influenced by the earlier writings of Shibli Shumayyil (1850–1917) in the late nineteenth century,[8] several Egyptian writers now carried on the propagation of the ideas of evolution. Thus *Fasl al-maqal fi falsafat al-nushu' wa'l-irtiqa'* by Hasan Husayn appeared in 1924; Ismail Mazhar's (1891–1962) translation of *The Origin of Species (Asl al-anwa)* four years later. A general treatise on the Theory of Evolution (*nazariyyat al-tatawwur wa asl al-insan*) by Salama Musa (1887–1958) also appeared around that time.[9]

Whereas at the end of the nineteenth century the literary quarrel between the old and the new was largely over style, now the concern of the modernists was the transformation of the whole concept of literature. Before the First World War, Muhammad Abduh and his followers introduced the idea of change and development; Shumayyil, Sarruf and Farah Antoun with their journal *al-Muqtataf* now introduced a systematic cricitism of all dogmatic thought – reformist or other – and, with that, a sceptical approach to all reformism which equivocated over tradition. They were interested in discovering truth via uncompromising rationalism.[10] Their followers in the 1920s and 1930s emphasized the role of science in the modern world. Technology and industrialization became the two major characteristics of modern civilization. These in turn were possible in Western Europe because of freedom – a precondition of progress.

This brand of liberal, secular rationalism constituted a far more dangerous attack upon Islam and its tradition. Salama Musa, Ismail Mazhar and Husayn Fawzi did not equivocate over the proclamation of Man as the hero of modern civilization; over the assertion that law must be man-made if it is to be dynamic and creative. Nor did they hesitate in introducing a socio-economic interpretation of history, culture and politics. Above all, they proclaimed Western civilization as the highest stage of man's spiritual and material development; declared Islamic civilization and culture dead and useless; and advocated the adoption of Western civilization and culture without reservations as the only way for the advancement of their country.

This group of critics of tradition differed from their *literati* contemporaries like Taha Husayn, Muhammad Husayn Haykal, al-Aqqad and others in that they were influenced by the scientific theories of nineteenth- and twentieth-century Europe, as for instance Darwinism, Freudianism, etc. Moreover, their philosophical and social theories derived from Nietzsche, Henri Bergson, G.B. Shaw. H.G.

Wells, Marx and Engels, and the British Fabians.[11] Moreover, unlike the *literati*, their secular humanism and commitment to the application of science to the study of society were so strong as to lead them to an attack on Islamic reformers. Thus to them al-Afghani was an 'ignorant reactionary'. Evolution, science and a positivist philosophy constituted the formula which they advocated for the advancement of Egypt.

Efforts by Wafdist Deputies and others in politics to extend the supervision and control of the State over religious institutions through legislation continued. By 1926, there were proposals for the reform of marriage and divorce laws and the prohibition of colourful local, popular practices connected with burials and visits to cemeteries. A Wafdist Parliament in 1927 pushed through the Chamber of Deputies the repeal of the 1925 law passed by the Ahmad Ziwar government which had given several concessions to the Azharis. The men of religion appeared in full retreat before the forces of modern reform.

Thus, the measures of the Kemalist government in Turkey against Islam and its Establishment had profound repercussions in Egypt, for they came at a critical stage in Egyptian politics: when an imported system of government was being tried. Whereas in the days of Muhammad Abduh and his earliest followers the debate over tradition had been confined to the reform of Islamic doctrine and institutions, now in the 1930s Egyptians were questioning the validity of the institutions themselves, though not the Islamic faith. There was now a social aspect to the issue, namely, the disadvantages to society inherent in the retention of certain institutions. *Waqf* was one of these. It occupied Deputies, ulama, and others from 1925 onwards. Here again Turkey's action was held up as a model by the abolitionists.

Both before and after Muhammad Ali there had been a constant struggle over the control and administration of *waqf* properties. Land and other property and the income therefrom endowed for religious and charitable purposes (*waqf khayri*) never constituted as much of an intractable issue as land and other property endowed or bequeathed for private family beneficiaries (*waqf ahli*). But all property endowed as *waqf* was automatically excluded from normal commercial transactions. This placed large tracts of cultivable land outside the State's agricultural plan and economic policies, administered (often controlled) by *nazirs* (supervisor-controllers), many of whom were men of religion, and giving them great influence and power. Both these attributes were often abused by the *nazirs*. Governments therefore since Muhammad Ali (and some Mamluk Sultans before him) had always tried to increase the State's administrative control over *waqf* properties. They were inevitably opposed by the *nazirs* and, in the case of family or private *waqfs*, by the beneficiaries themselves.

Muhammad Ali managed to impose some control over family *waqfs*. Ismail established an administrative department approximating a ministry, and the Legislative Council in 1913, with the support of Kitchener, sought greater administrative control over them. But by this time members of the ruling house had acquired a great stake in the control of these endowments so that the struggle over the control of *waqfs* became one between ministers and advocates of administrative reform on one side and the king on the other.

In debating the Budget for the fiscal year 1926–7, Wafdist members of the Chamber raised the question of how *waqf* could be reformed. In fact two Deputies, Ahmad Ramzi and Yusuf al-Gindi, introduced a proposal to retain charitable *waqfs* (*khayri*) but to abolish private (*ahli*) *waqfs* altogether. The advocates of reform accepted that the *waqf* institution was peculiar to Islamic societies (even though possibly it had certain similarities with European Christian pious endowments). They also recognized one of its important functions in the past, namely, the protection of heirs to property under family *waqf* against expropiation by inimical, wilful or capricious rulers. But they also insisted that the system of *nazirs* had been most abusive of the institution. Politically, they were also objecting to the control by the royal family of vast tracts of land and other properties under the *waqf* arrangement.

By July 1928, however, Parliament had been dissolved, and the Nahhas government dismissed. Consequently, the *Waqf* Commission that had been appointed to deal with these matters had not been able to complete its work and thus resolve the issue one way or another.

In 1927, the total area of *waqf* land was estimated at 610,000 *feddans*. The same figure was estimated for 1946, when the major post-war legislation to reform *waqf* was passed. This law decreed that private *waqf* endowments should be for set terms of time, but allowed charitable (*waqf khayri*) endowments to be made in perpetuity. Then in 1952, the new Free Officers régime abolished private *waqfs* altogether.[12] If one bears in mind that private family *waqfs* represented

85 per cent of all *waqf* lands in Egypt, it meant that some 500,000 *feddans* had been inalienable and outside the pale of proper economic exploitation and commercial transactions. Their abolition constituted a serious measure of economic reform.

Traditional society inevitably came under attack in other fields too. In the heightened enthusiasm of nationalist euphoria in 1919–23 the feminist cause was revived. Whereas in the 1890s and in the Great War the emancipation of women had been almost exclusively a male interest, now, after independence, feminism became an active organizational concern of women themselves. With Qasim Amin, the question of woman's emancipation was first broached publicly. Yet, the consequences of changes in education, the influx of foreigners and the opening of foreign schools since the reign of Khedive Ismail had also contributed to bringing this problem to national attention. Malak Hifni Nasif (pseud.: Bahithat al-Badiya) in her essays, *al-Nisa'iyyat* (c. 1910, 2 vols.) first published in *al-Jarida*, argued the question of improving the conditions of women as wives and mothers both in education and marriage, but explicitly did not contemplate at all emancipation in the sense of equality between the sexes.

During the Great War Abd al-Hamid Hamdi founded the weekly journal *al-Sufur* to serve as a platform for liberal ideas, including the advocacy of female emancipation particularly from the veil, of advances and reform in education including the freer and closer association between the sexes. The small band of liberals around *al-Sufur* formed a short-lived liberal party – the Democratic Party – in 1919. It was soon absorbed in the new Wafd, and later, many of its leading members joined the Liberal Constitutionalists in 1922. It was generally conceived in the spirit of the Umma–*Jarida* group of Egyptian liberals at the turn of the century.[13]

A member of the rich upper classes, Huda Sharawi, who had been closely associated with the Wafd, founded in 1923 the first Feminist Union in Egypt. Its main concern since that time has been the reform of legal and traditional customary conditions of marriage and divorce, the further education of women and their easier entry into certain professions. The problem became once again an issue of Egyptian politics when women entered university in the early 1930s. Conservatives in Parliament and religious leaders objected to co-education and, with some instigation, male students themselves agitated for the segregation of the sexes in schools and colleges. Nevertheless since that time, educational, occupational, professional and even legal restraints on women – including the areas of marriage and divorce – have been largely removed even though the social, conventional and emotional opposition to their complete emancipation may not have completely disappeared.

Related to the feminist movement in liberal constitutional Egypt of the 1920s and 1930s were the reforms introduced after 1920 in the sphere of the Sharia and its religious courts, particularly as this applied to matters of personal status. A series of legislative acts from 1923 to 1931 ameliorated the abuses involved in child marriages and the facile repudiation of wives by husbands using the traditional formula of divorce. In 1927, for instance, draft legislation further resitricting polygamy was introduced.[14] Yet, political advance for women in terms of suffrage and the holding of elected office did not come until the 1950s. A number of feminist magazines and journals, however, began to appear from this period, wholly devoted to feminine problems. Moreover, the leading political weekly of Egypt until today, *Rose al Yusuf*, was founded in 1925 by an ex-actress, Fatma al-Yusuf.[15] Later, further strides were made by Egyptian women in Egypt in the fields of law, teaching, communications and the arts.

Generally, therefore, this liberal phase in Egyptian thought and political life in the first flush of the constitutional experiment undermined Islam not only as a basis of community and a source of legislation but also as a determinant of national feeling and identity. Though not quite successful, the introduction of a secular conception of national identity permitted the projection of a cumulative historical being of an Egyptian identity that had for very long – at least consciously – lain dormant. This was the Egyptianity which derived from a combined Pharaonic–Mediterranean cultural past.[16] Now the romantic awakening of the nation (using the parable of the Seven Sleepers of Ephesus, or the Four Inhabitants of the Cave[17]) which in turn enabled the return of the soul of an eternal Egypt became the essential premise of the new Golden Age of the Egyptian nation.[18] Islam was only one phase in the Egyptian historical experience and consciousness across several thousand years. What was even more important was the splendour of its very ancient civilization.

The tomb of Tutenkhamen had been discovered in all its dazzling splendour in 1922. Pharaonism appeared as the real legacy of the new independent state of Egypt: it was both pre-Islamic and pre-Christian, so that the spirit of the new Egypt was to be an amalgam of both the Islamic and Christian cultures, but significantly also independent of either of them. The new European-modelled Constitution with its provision for freedom of thought and the consequent questioning by Egyptians of Islamic ideas, values and institutions was further evidence of the awakening of modern Egypt.[19] This revival was simultaneously a re-awakening of the mystical past, stirring the Egyptian people to action as manifested in the eruption of the peasantry in the 1919 movement for independence.

Tawfiq al-Hakim (1899–   ) became the major exponent of this return of the spirit. In 1933, two of his major works – *Awdat al-ruh* (*The Return of the Soul*) and *Ahl al-kahf* (*The Dwellers of the Cave*) – were published. Although different, both works portrayed the reawakening of Egypt. The first, a romance in two volumes, actually written in 1926–7, was set during the 1919 uprising for independence under Wafd leadership. Its heroes are the lower-class, though literate, Egyptians. As a concession to the nationalist instrumentality of language, the author used for the first time the colloquial in the dialogue. Moreover, the classical Arabic seems to have been partly by-passed by al-Hakim because it evoked Islam whereas the colloquial emphasized an Egyptian national identity possessing a long past independent of Islam. The second, written in the form of a very long play in four acts, also emphasizes the theme of national rebirth and regeneration, after the country had slept for centuries.

The attempt to identify a peculiarly Egyptian culture was not only part of the nationalist wave, but also an integral dimension of the attack upon Islam and its values. Inevitably, the matter of the kind of education the new generation of Egyptians should receive in their liberated constitutional nation-state became an important issue, particularly in relation to the desired new culture. So did the question of social and economic reform on the basis of liberal constitutional principles.

Taha Husayn (1889–1976), who had been active in transmitting the Graeco-Roman classics to his students, published in 1938 his famous *Mustaqbal al-thaqafa fi misr*[20] (*The Future Culture in Egypt*). In it, he capped his preference for Hellenic and Roman classical culture with the thesis that Egypt had always belonged to a wider, general Mediterranean civilization. The future of Egypt's development therefore lay in retaining this old link. In effect, Taha was rejecting both the Islamic and African civilizational orbit for Egypt in favour of an older – and closer to Europe – southwest Asian and eastern Mediterranean cultural heritage.[21]

More conservative, with far less formal education, and with

limited travel experience outside Egypt, Ahmad Amin (1886–1954), a teacher of Arabic, began work in the 1920s on a more subtle attack upon tradition; yet one that was intellectually most imaginative, if not altogether successful. He produced four massive volumes (1929–52) of a literary criticism of the history of Islamic culture and civilization [e.g. the intellectual life of the Islamic community in the first century AH (AD 622–750)] – *Fajr al-islam* (*The Dawn of Islam*).[22] Also in 1929, he published a book on ethics for use in schools (*Kitab al-akhlaq*) in which he argued for a system of ethics based on reason and intuition, and against one based solely on tradition deriving from religious teachings and custom. Amin differed from his European-trained contemporaries in that he sought to deal with the problem of tradition versus modernity via a critical study of the formative aspects of Islamic culture.

After the conclusion of the Anglo-Egyptian Treaty in 1936 and the abolition of the Capitulations by the Montreux Convention in 1937, demands for domestic social and economic reform were urgently publicized. Educated Egyptians both from within the political party and ruling establishments, as well as from outside them, became concerned with the inability of successive governments to deal with long-neglected social and economic problems. They feared that political instability had been largely responsible for administrative weakness and, frequently, chaos, and they called for a rational programme of national reform and development.

In 1938, there appeared two important books in Cairo: Mirit Butros Ghali's *Siyasat al-ghad* (*The Policy of Tomorrow*) and Hafiz Afifi's *Ala hamish al-siyasa* (*On the margin of politics*). Both writers essayed an outline of a national policy for an independent Egypt emphasizing the categorical imperative of social and economic reform. What was significant about these two books was that their authors had, by the use of statistical and other data about conditions in Egypt, tried to show that unless Egyptian leaders embarked upon a rigorous national reform programme the country courted disaster. They both portrayed a general concern – for the first time among Egyptian writers since independence – over the socio-economic basis (or as Western scholars would refer to it, the 'requisites') of a representative system of government. These two books also represented the first modern attempt by Egyptians at a social–scientific, critical analysis of the country's problems. Both books presented a reasoned attack upon national weaknesses during an experiment in constitutional government.

Both authors complained about the preoccupation of party leaders with the question of independence to the exclusion of all other national domestic issues. They conceded that this narrow concern was necessary until 1936. But with the conclusion of the Anglo-Egyptian Treaty, they suggested that parties should re-orient their programmes to meet domestic reform needs.

Both authors identified the major economic problem facing Egypt on the eve of the Second World War, namely, the rapid population growth (66 per cent in forty years; from 9·7 million in 1897 to 15·9 million in 1937), and correctly forecast a population of over 20 million in 1957. Since the country until that time depended largely on its agricultural economy for a living, both writers emphasized the twin problems of landownership and land productivity. They pointed out that whereas in 1900 there were 6·8 million *feddans* under cultivation for 9·7 million people (i.e., roughly ·7 *feddan* per person), there were in 1935–7 about 8·5 million *feddans* for nearly 16 million people, or just over half a *feddan* per person. Thus, there was a real lowering in standards of living due to overpopulation and a declining land–population ratio. Related to this basic economic fact of Egyptian life were the phenomena of undernourishment and endemic disease. Other related matters of public health, education, housing and labour legislation were discussed by both writers.

In short, the purpose of the two writers was to prove the need for a national plan of reform which would not be the easy victim of political strife and instability. Yet Ghali, for example, favoured the exclusive development of the agricultural sector of the economy, and was cautious about any rapid industrialization. Moreover, he believed in a *laissez-faire* economy with a minimum of government interference other than the provision of proper conditions for the encouragement of private enterprise.

Afifi on the other hand favoured greater industrialization that would at first be directed at the expansion of a local consumer market. He also recommended a modern direct system of taxation that would help erode some of the vast disparities in income among Egyptians. He wished that both graduated income tax and an inheritance tax be instituted; and he recommended greater government expenditure on public works to provide employment in preference to the inflation of a massive Reserve Fund.

Their discussion of these matters constituted an indictment of politicians, fifteen years after independence, in their abuse of both parliamentary rule and the administrative machinery once in power for personal gain and party ends. They deplored the lack of regular institutional criteria of administration; the use of students for party political purposes; the phenomenal expansion of the bureaucracy and the consequent government spending on salaries and pensions (1937–8: 36 per cent to 41 per cent of all government expenditure). Thus, Ghali called the administration 'the property of the parties' and warned that 'personal loyalties constituted the weakness of the social system which, in turn, led to the serious economic plight of the country'. 'Social and administrative affairs in Egypt,' he argued, 'constitute the foundations of national activity. They are the operative elements in the development of the nation or its stagnation.' Unless these were reformed, he concluded, Egyptians were threatened with the destruction of a system (the new constitutional one) which they would have had no time to enjoy.[23]

Significantly, both writers were suggesting that modern secular reform was in keeping with the introduction of constitutional government irrespective of the Egyptian's Islamic faith. Despite the various historical influences upon Egypt – including that of Islam – the country remained what it was: a historical and geographical unity with its own economic and social problems which now required immediate attention by an independent national government.

The attack on tradition and the political conflict it engendered in the inter-war period had, by 1952, weakened both traditionalists and modernists without advancing constitutional government, or establishing a liberal political style and life in the country. When the soldiers eventually came to power, they proceeded to rule in a traditionally autocratic fashion, albeit using modern techniques and structures, thus putting an end to the public debate.

There were, however, other elements in the situation which had been forming throughout this period, but which did not surface until the Second World War and its aftermath. By then, the international situation had changed drastically. This change affected, among others, developments in Egypt. To a consideration of these new factors we now turn so as to round the picture that can partly explain the collapse of the old order in July 1952, or at least its successful challenge and overthrow by the soldiers.

PART FOUR

From the Old Order to the New
1930–79

CHAPTER 15

THE FAILURE OF LIBERALISM AND THE REACTION AGAINST EUROPE
1930–50

The primacy of the secular liberal view as the modern approach to the resolution of Egyptian problems in the first thirty years of this century was due in part to the influence of British power in Egypt. To this extent the steady attack upon tradition ever since the 1890s and its explosion to the surface in the 1920s and 1930s was both a consequence and a reflection of the influence of European ideas of constitutional democracy upon secular Egyptian leaders as well as of the British presence in Egypt and the Middle East.

But when there arose in Europe powers which advocated ideologies and implemented policies directed against the constitutional democracies, the effect of their confrontation echoed beyond that continent. The temporarily successful challenge Fascism and Nazism presented to the Western European democracies undermined constitutional government as a model for emulation by non-European societies. When this confrontation led to a Second World War, Europe's direct influence upon Egypt eventually came to an end.

The echo in Egypt was quite resounding. It was reflected in the rapid appearance of new social and political groups which, despite their different leadership, shared a belief in violence – the use of force for the attainment of political ends. By 1945 some of these groups accepted the use of violence for the resolution of social and political conflict as inevitable.

An extremist religio-political movement, *Al-Ikhwan al-Muslimum* (The Muslim Brethren), founded by Shaykh Hasan al-Banna in 1928, emerged as a militant force at the close of the Second World War. Advocating an orthodox Islamic view of society and politics, the Brethren did not eschew forceful modern techniques of organization for political action. They presented themselves as an alternative to the rule of the so-called secular politicians, and thus to the total imported European model of society and government. In proposing to displace the latter, they were also rejecting its values and institutions.

Other extremist organizations of the national–social variety also appeared in the 1930s, which sanctified further violent politics – and political violence. *Misr al-Fatat* (Young Egypt), which began as an association in 1933, had, by 1938–9, become a party of extreme Egyptian nationalism, mixed with religious fanaticism, and a xenophobic platform. Above all, it commanded an impressive paramilitary youth organization – the Green Shirts (*Al-qumsan al-khadra*). The party advocated the radical syndicalization and militarization of Egyptian society and politics, preached a glorious Egyptian past, and demanded an equally glorious imperial Egyptian future, justified by the manifest destiny of Egypt in the Islamic world, in the East, and in the world.

Significant about these two organizations was the varied composition of their membership, followers and sympathizers. It included professionals, students, poor urban masses, provincial town and peasant masses. Their leadership, executive and unit organization were rigid and hierarchical, based on the leader–follower principle of command–obedience.

Apart from the further dilution of direct British influence over political affairs in the country in the 1930s, there were serious domestic political, social and economic factors which contributed to, and facilitated, the emergence of new organized groups subscribing to violent ideologies. These were not only opposed to the established order, but also ready to challenge its authority by violent means.

There was first the attack on the Constitution very early in its existence. It was not only the King who, in his desire for greater power, never laid great store in the newly established parliamentary government. Party leaders too showed, in practice, their willingness to bypass and frequently subvert constitutional principles when it suited their own purposes. It is this attitude of both the Crown and politicians which explains in part the perpetuation of local traditional patterns of political life in the inter-war period. But it is also a reflection of the unreal hold which liberal European political ideas had over Egyptian leaders – a condition which inevitably caused the degeneration of political parties, if not the moral (and therefore political) bankruptcy of their leaderships.

The abrogation by Sidqi of the 1923 Constitution in October 1930 and its replacement by a new one which strengthened the monarchy came to be viewed by many Egyptians as not simply the usurpation of power by palace-supported politicians, but more significantly as a reflection of the weakness of those politicians who, until then, had been considered popular, national leaders. Yet in practical terms, this public disenchantment was not of the essence in the struggle for power and in the fortunes of constitutional government. What was more important was the fact that the Sidqi period (1930–3), during which a strong, repressive government ruled in conjunction with the monarch, kept party leaders – particularly those of the Wafd – outside the normal channels of political activity. It hardened the lines of opposition, of personal and group antipathies among the ranks of the Establishment. It also forced the eventual compromise of those original supporters of constitutional government in the Liberal and Wafd parties as a price either for sharing in, or coming to, power. Such behaviour in turn further alienated many followers of the Wafd from its leadership – and this inevitably tended to strengthen the more extremist, fanatic groups, particularly the Muslim Brethren.

The reign of King Fuad (1923–36) was marked by this continuous battle between a monarch on one side who wished to govern as well as reign and the Wafd, the popular party of national independence, on the other. In its struggle against the King, the latter both under Zaghlul and under his successor Nahhas presented itself as the champion of the Constitution, of parliamentary government and civil liberties against a monarch who wished to usurp popular power. In these circumstances, the Wafd was able to mobilize mass sympathy for its cause. But as its electoral victories, given the monarch's powers, rarely led it to power, the Wafd resorted early in its history to the organization of city and town mobs for demonstrations, to the infiltration of secondary school and university student organizations for political purposes. When the activities of Wafd-led, -organized and -financed crowds met with determined state police action and repression (including mass arrests), wanton violence increased. By 1935, just as Palace autocracy had come to an end, and the 1923 Constitution was being reinstated to make way for the return of the Wafd to power, the Wafdist leadership understandably became uneasy over the violent activities of their followers. Meanwhile, the Young Egypt association and the Muslim Brethren had been expanding their activities and strengthening their organizations. Consequently, the Wafd itself as the major nationalist party sought to impose greater discipline upon its popular following. The result was the founding of the League of Wafdist Youth (*Rabitat al-shubban al-wafdiyyin*) under the direction of the lawyer Zuhayr Sabri. It was from this Youth organization that the Wafd's paramilitary body, the Blue Shirts (*Al-qumsan al-zarqa*), was recruited.

The Wafdist leadership in the early 1930s comprised an élite of administrators, several large landowners, a few industrialists and investment financiers. Its followers included vast numbers of city petty-bourgeoisie, an intelligentsia largely influenced by European education, secondary school and university students, provincial–local administrators, village headmen, and leading local landowning families in the countryside. The Liberal Party, though with a much smaller following, did not differ greatly in its leadership composition. It too included landowners, but many more intellectuals of the generation that became prominent at the turn of the century. As for the Palace-inspired smaller parties, such as the Ittihad and Shaab of Sidqi, these were perhaps no more than deliberate structures created by Palace-appointed ministers and chief ministers to serve as political adjuncts of the administration. The Saadist and Kutla parties were both dissident splinter groups from the Wafd. Yet, the Saadist Party represented in a more direct manner the interests of the new group of Egyptian industrialists.

Only the Wafd among these parties had an extensive organization throughout the country, and a following among certain labour groups in Cairo, Alexandria and the Suez Canal area. The rural population could be depended upon at election time to follow the direction of their village headmen, local administrative officers, landlords and schoolteachers. Moreover, until 1936, the Wafd still monopolized the role of leader of the movement for complete independence and that of the spokesman of anti-British Egyptian policy.

In addition to the demoralizing effect on the Wafd which its deprivation of power for five years (1930–5) had had, there was the natural proclivity which such forced absence from power engenders in a party towards compromise for the sake of return to rule. Then, the Anglo-Egyptian Treaty had been concluded in 1936 by a Wafd government, even though this came at the end of protracted negotiations at regular intervals after 1924 by several Egyptian governments. The Treaty's provision for an Anglo-Egyptian defence arrangement and for the continued posting of British troops in the country – particularly in the Suez Canal zone – embarrassed the Wafd and led to the alienation of its more extremist followers. The Wafd could no longer claim the monopoly of a policy of national revolution (to some, this was synonymous with an anti-British policy) as it did in 1919–22, and again in 1924–5 and in 1930–5. Students, professionals and intellectuals, as well as simple city and rural masses, could now more readily be attracted by extremist national – including Islamic – groups. And, in fact, this occurred to the advantage of both the Muslim Brethren and Young Egypt organizations. Radicalism towards the extreme Right – the religious fanatic and xenophobic nationalist – in Egyptian politics had now set in partly as a reaction to the apparent failure of the liberal–constitutional forces led by the Wafd in dealing with the so-called national issue, and partly in response to Fascist and later Nazi propaganda.

The Wafd had been weakened further by internal fissions within its hierarchy. These exploded to the surface when leading members after their expulsion from the party formed their own splinter parties (e.g., the Saadists in 1938–9 led by Ahmad Maher and Mahmud al-Nuqrashi; the *al-Kutla al-wafdiyya* of Makram Obayd in 1942). The new young King, however, found himself in no time continuing the old fight of his father against the Wafd.

In part the split in the Wafd leadership reflected the inability of the party to work out a new programme. Despite its continued limitations, the 1936 Treaty marked the further independence of Egypt. The Montreux Convention of the following year was important in that it abolished foreign privileges in Egypt which had existed under the Capitulations. To this extent the purposes for which the party had initially come into existence in 1919–23 had been attained and its policies realized.

The Wafd, then, could have had no *raison d'être* after 1937 without a new programme, especially in regard to domestic political, economic and social problems. The few industrialists, for example, who acquired a new importance after the 1930 protectionist tariff legislation and the few investment financiers in the party inevitably clashed with a leadership that was largely oriented towards landowning interests, content to depend on agricultural production (especially cotton) and therefore too cautious in embarking upon new economic policy measures which favoured the further and more rapid development of industry. Personal antipathies also played a role in these internal conflicts. Common as a source of internal strife too was the matter of patronage, appointments and special considerations.

Nevertheless, the internal quarrels of the Wafd were often inspired – and instigated – by outside elements. The Palace, for instance, always viewed the Wafd as its major competitor for power in the country, and sought continuously to subvert it by exploiting its international differences. The King could easily do this as he had the power to appoint and dismiss governments. By the summer of 1937, he feared that any prolonged stay of the Wafd in power could lead to their autocratic rule at the expense of his own autocracy. The Wafd on its part had decided to avoid, if possible, participation in coalition governments which the King could easily divide and undermine at will. At the same time, it had also decided to make it difficult for any government other than a Wafdist one to govern. This they felt they could easily induce by the mobilization of their organized and extensive following to stage demonstrations and harass any administration by intimidation and violent acts if need be.

In 1937, the Wafd were convinced that they could stay in power indefinitely, given the settlement of both the question of Anglo-Egyptian relations and the Capitulations. Furthermore, they assumed that they could easily control and exploit for their purposes a young inexperienced King with meagre education. What they did not take into account was the impressive array of forces the monarch could call to his aid against them in case of need: the religious forces in the country, his courtiers, minor party politicians bitterly opposed to the Wafd and, for several years, the army.

On the eve of the Second World War the socio-economic basis of power in Egypt was straightforward. The country's economy had been overwhelmingly agricultural for thousands of years. Landownership in an overwhelmingly rural country, was the major form of wealth and basis of influence and power. A consequence of British reform was that landownership became both more profitable and more secure. The ruling houses (i.e., the king and his extended family) came to own by 1939 some 500,000 *feddans*. Under 13,000 landowners possessed two and a half million of a total six million *feddans*. Simultaneously, the number of smallholders and especially those owning under one *feddan* among the peasant farmers increased sharply. One consequence of this was a 100 per cent increase in the number of agricultural workers to approximately two million.

Native industry had been in its infancy since independence. Part of the drive for national independence after 1918 was the founding of Bank Misr in 1920 as a wholly Egyptian enterprise.[1] A purely Egyptian banking concern, it was intended to accelerate economic development through industrial investment. The Wafd, for instance, in 1922–3 called for the boycott of all foreign banks operating in Egypt in favour of the new Bank Misr. In 1924, the old Committee of Commerce and Industry became the Egyptian Federation of Industries (EFI). Yet it comprised a mixed Egyptian–foreign membership. It was nonetheless a significant development when one considers the fact that in 1914 foreign capital invested in Egypt amounted to over £250 million, most of it in land, agricultural credit, insurance and related services. Such long-established industries as sugar, cigarettes, distilleries, soap and textiles were largely controlled by foreigners too.

By 1944, deposits in Bank Misr amounted to £E.35 million; its capital and reserves had risen from £E.80,000 to £E.3 million. More important were the affiliated companies and enterprises launched by the Bank Misr group over a period of twenty years. Prominent among these were a cotton spinning company in 1921, a publishing and printing company in 1922, a river navigation company in 1925, a cinema film production company in the same year. The Mehalla Kubra spinning and weaving textile company was founded in 1927. The previous year the Bank had launched an agricultural credit establishment. Further expansion and diversification of Bank Misr enterprises occurred rapidly in the next decade. Most important of these were an aviation company in 1932, the Misr Air, a steamship navigation company, an insurance company, and a tourism company in 1934. Another large textile enterprise was founded in 1938 at Kafr el-Dawar; a pharmaceuticals company in 1939; and a silk company in 1947. Despite the diversification, however, the Bank Misr group of enterprises concentrated mainly on the expansion of the textile industry in Egypt.

Economic and industrial development was accelerated by the protectionist tariff legislation of 1930. Before this law, a free trade policy imposed an 8 per cent non-discriminatory customs duty on all imports whether these were raw materials or manufactured and finished goods. Consequently, native industry could not compete with imported foreign products. The 1930 law raised tariffs to 15–25 per cent *ad valorem*. Its most salutary effects were on the textile industry (cotton, wool, silk), on agricultural industries such as sugar, cotton-seed oil, rice refining, cereals milling, the chemical industry (soap, soda, sulphuric acid, glycerin, fertilizers, pharmaceuticals, rubber, cosmetics, ink and glass), on the manufacture of furniture, household appliances, tools, leather goods, ceramics, canned foods, and communications.

The drive for economic independence was also reflected in the agricultural exhibitions organized by the Agriculture Ministry every five years after 1924 in conjunction with the (Royal) Agricultural Society. Industrial and trade schools increased in number as did their student population from 6,000 in 1924 to 280,000 in 1939.

Two other national banking institutions were founded in this period. An Agricultural Credit Bank founded in 1931 provided short-term loans to farmers, and financed the purchase of fertilizer and farm machinery. In 1948, this became the Agricultural Credit and Co-operative Bank. Another, the Agricultural (Land) Loan Bank, began as a branch of the former in 1932, but by 1941 was operating as an independent institution.

From 1930 until 1945 there was a marked rise in industrial investment and production and a drop in investment in agricultural production. The industrial labour force rose from barely a quarter of a million in 1919 to over one million in 1939 and to almost two million in 1952. Within twenty years (1919–39), capital invested in limited industrial companies tripled from seven to twenty-four million Egyptian pounds. Capital invested in commercial enterprises increased ten times. Local textile, sugar and foodstuffs production increased while import of foreign manufactured goods dropped throughout the 1930s.

Yet foreign representation on the boards of all these new enterprises was vast. Misr Bank, moreover, was not always in a favourable competitive position *vis-à-vis* the concessionaire National Bank. Also, agricultural production never kept pace with the rapid growth of population. Together with the sharp rise in the cost of living, particularly during the Second World War, real per capita income dropped despite all these developments. The consumption of goods and foodstuffs by the vast majority of the population decreased and their health deteriorated.

Disillusionment with quarrelling politicians and a power-hungry monarchy was easily transformed into an antagonism to constitutional government in general and to its European origins in particular. A radicalism to the right of xenophobic nationalism and religious fanaticism set in, which made it possible for the Muslim Brethren, for example, to attract hundreds of thousands of followers in the late thirties, during the Second World War, and after, from both the dispossessed urban masses and the permanently miserable rural population.

There were also other factors which favoured this new radical conservatism in Egyptian society and politics. The attack of the modernists upon tradition turned out to be a short-lived affair. Such leading modernists as Taha Husayn, Muhammad Husayn Haykal and Mahmud Abbas al-Aqqad were, by the 1930s, already in hasty retreat from their earlier positions of secular liberalism and the adoption of European culture. Their reverential studies of the early fathers of the Islamic Community smacked of frantic and solicitous apologia for their earlier rationalist–secular attacks upon the religion and its cultural heritage. A romantic proclivity for the epic quality of early Islam now became a major characteristic of their writings. Taha, for example, abandoned the rationalism of his earlier literary criticism in 1926 for a romantic humanism which he saw in the Prophet's Life.[2] Muhammad Husayn Haykal, editor of the Liberal *al-Siyasa* and a leading constitutionalist in the country, published a series of books on the life of the Prophet and the first orthodox Caliphs. Effectively abandoning the liberal values of Western civilization as an ideological foundation for a modern Egypt, Haykal attempted in these volumes to prove the rational and ethical content of early Islam. He admitted the inadequacy of reason and science alone to provide happiness for man.[3] Aqqad for his part embarked upon a series of volumes on the genius of Muhammad, of the first caliphs, military commanders and leading personalities of early Islam. These volumes of *abqariyyat* were phenomenally successful in a country of limited literacy, and went into many editions. They emphasized the heroic qualities of leading men in the history of Islam, and thus the glorification of the Islamic past.[4] The effect of all these works, especially by writers who only a few years earlier had attacked Islam and its tradition in favour of a Western liberal culture, was threefold. First, it lulled the public with the comfortable belief of the supremacy of their religion. Second, it strengthened the position of the new radical conservative movements, such as the Muslim Brethren, Young Egypt and other lesser organizations who were preaching a return to Islam as the first requirement for the social, economic and political salvation of Egypt. Third, it undermined still further the failing political leadership of the ruling class that had come to power with the adoption of constitutional government – and under the implicit protection of Great Britain.

Yet it is unrealistic to overlook the encouragement which revived Islamic political activism received, especially from the monarchy and its allies. Religion, as was noted earlier, was always mixed with politics. After 1937, the struggle between king and Wafd took a new turn with the accession of Faruq to the throne. Relations between these two contenders for power deteriorated further in the forties. Both parties were always ready to involve the religious institutions and their establishment in their political quarrels. As the Wafd, however, always sought by virtue of its strong position in Parliament

325

to wrest control of religious institutions from the Crown, religious leaders tended by the dictates of self-interest to side with the Crown.

For example, when in 1927 Parliament produced legislation to bring religious schools and institutes under the control of the Ministry of Education, traditional Islamic reaction was strong. These had been controlled by the Rector of al-Azhar since 1925. The new law led to demonstrations by Azharis – not uninspired by the Crown – which were marked by the cry 'down with Parliament'. With the fall of the Wafd government in 1930, the King appointed his own man as Rector, Shaykh Muhammad al-Ahmadi al-Zawa-hiri, who produced his own reform bill for al-Azhar.[5] The same characteristics of the struggle for power between king and Wafd by making use of religious institutions was to be repeated in the 1940s when Shaykh Mustafa al-Maraghi was rector.

Religious reform, whether of the Muhammad Abduh tradition or otherwise, had reached a dead end in 1930. The attempt by Abduh's chief disciple and biographer, Shaykh Muhammad Rashid Rida (d. 1935), leader of the *Salafiyya* movement and editor of its organ, *al-Manar*, to establish on the one hand the position that Islam's revealed message was directly relevant to matters of public life and policy, and on the other that Islam was not in contradiction with values deriving from Western liberalism, had failed.

Similarly, the resort of liberal intellectuals to a romantic panegyric of early Islamic history as a source of cultural advancement to counter European values did not produce the desired effect. As the State in all its administrative functions moved relentlessly to ever more secular methods, the effect of all this was to leave the field of political agitation and popular leadership free to the activist, militant and violent Muslims.

A nationalist twist was now given to Islam which was reflected in the programme and activities of the new Muslim Brethren organization and the numerous Islamic societies which sprang up. Despite the failure of the Caliphate Congress projects in 1924–6, and the attack upon tradition by secular liberals, the role of religion in politics not only continued but did so with renewed vigour.

While Rashid Rida's *Salafiyya*[6] was by this time reflecting more the teachings of Ibn Taymiyya[7] and Muhammad Abdul Wahhab[8] than those of Muhammad Abduh and his modernist disciples, several societies and organizations were formed to emphasize the social and political relevance of Islam to modern Egypt. While Rida and the jurist Abdul Razzaq al-Sanhuri argued the question of the caliphate,[9] the new organizations recruited Egyptian youth into their clubs and inculcated in them the national–social significance of their faith and its relevance to the political future of their country.

The overtones of anti-European sentiment were, by the 1930s, already present among the rising numbers of uprooted urban masses. The political leaders of liberal constitutionalism and emulators of Western culture ceased to attract them – if in fact they ever did at any time. On the contrary, the latter felt the need to prove their respect for Islamic history and culture, and to prove its relevance to their modernist ideas and programmes.

Apart from the *Salafiyya*, the most important and active of the new organizations was the Young Men's Muslim Association (YMMA). Founded by Abdul Hamid Sa'id in 1927, it soon developed as a counterpart to the YMCA. Together with the Society for Islamic Preaching and Propaganda, the YMMA embarked upon an extensive programme of countering Christian missionary activity. This programme was almost an exact replica of the YMCA's athletics, dramatics, evening adult education classes and public lectures, educational travel, etc.[10]

Even though these organizations were no doubt involved in the political struggle between king and Wafd and between the different political parties, they were at no time themselves actual, or potential, contenders for power with an Islamic restoration in view. This objective was confined to the Muslim Brethren, the only militant political organization in Egypt in the thirties and forties to embrace the theocratic ideal of Islamic government, and to seek by violent and other means to attain it.

The Brethren began as a modest lay Muslim moral and religious association. In the first few years of its existence, it confined its activities to religious teaching among its adherents. But its founder, Shaykh Hasan al-Banna, also established himself as the Supreme Guide who, one day, would lead his followers in a purified Muslim state. His Mahdist approach appealed to a rapidly increasing membership. It believed in salvation by the purification of individual and social life under the strict leadership of the Supreme Guide. Implied in this message was the charge that the Islamic faith in its puritan, original relevance to all aspects of wordly existence was not only worth preserving and strengthening, but of being applied vigorously in the resolution of social and political problems. It also suggested that European culture and values whether as reflected in the adopted constitutional government of Egypt or in the ideas expressed by secular liberals were to be scorned, questioned and eradicated from Egyptian private and public life.

The evolution of the Brethren organization from these didactic beginnings to a violent political movement was not unnatural, given the continued inability of the liberals to deal with mounting social and economic problems. The retreat of liberalism's intellectual spokesmen in the thirties to an apologetic exegesis of Islam only encouraged the militancy of the new radical conservative groups. The inadequate performance of the governing élite facilitated further the translation of this Islamic revival into militant, violent political action. The period was, moreover, propitious for such development, when force was the rule of politics in a Nazi and Fascist Europe. The defence of Islam and its civilization through militant political action became not only an increasingly popular preoccupation but a most respectable one.[11]

A similar campaign for the purification of Egyptian social and political life was launched by a new extremist national group. Founded by a lawyer, Ahmad Husayn, as an association in 1933, Young Egypt attracted mainly young students of secondary schools in Cairo, Alexandria and other major towns. These were organized in a paramilitary youth movement, the Green Shirts, to demonstrate against the manifestations of adopted European civilization. Late in 1938, Young Egypt became a political party. It published its own newspaper, *Misr al-fatat*, which, in January 1939, carried the programme and fundamental principles of the party. It was a programme intended to appeal to the masses, for it urged the retrieval of Egypt's old glory by its youth. 'The soldiers of Egypt,' it proclaimed, were to be the new generation (*junud misr al-fatat*). They should aim to create an Egyptian empire consisting of Egypt and the Sudan, allied to the Arab states, but as the leader of Islam. It postulated that the will of the people was God's will, and demanded that Young Egypt should do away with foreign privileges in the country, nationalize foreign companies, and make Friday the official weekly holiday.

In agriculture, the party called for the increase of arable land, the doubling of production, the formation of co-operatives everywhere, the mechanization of farming, and the ready extension of state credit facilities to farmers. In industry, the party recalled the achievements of Muhammad Ali and the ancient Pharaohs. It urged the founding of an industrial bank and the further implementation of protective tariff policies. Greater encouragement of local industry was to be achieved by making all government officials and students wear clothes produced by Egyptian industry. Internal trade was to be an Egyptian monopoly. Finally, the party called for the strengthening and expansion of the industrial and commercial infrastructure such as the creation of a central bank and the development of airways and harbours.

Since Egypt was, according to the party, to lead the East and 'enlighten the world', primary education had to be free; secondary and higher education should charge nominal fees so as to permit greater numbers from the poorer classes to attend. Egyptian scholars were to be sent throughout the Arab world and the East in order to spread the 'Egyptian mentality' – Egypt's message. In this connection, the Azhar was to play an important role all over the world by opening institutes to teach Arabic and Islam. Libraries and radios were to be installed in every Egyptian village.

Socially, Young Egypt emphasized the importance of religious belief and its derivative – morality. It urged its members and followers to attack those who consumed alcohol, to combat prostitution and all forms of corruption. Military service should be compulsory so as to imbue in youth the martial spirit (*al-ruh al-askari*). Women should receive more education since they produce the future greatness of Egypt and its heroes. Youth health should be one of the primary concerns of the State. All youth should receive military training in vast athletic fields located throughout the country, with an annual mass rally in a gigantic athletic field in Cairo (the Nuremberg model?). Songs should be confined to the nationalist martial variety. Only those arts which revived past Pharaonic and Arab greatness should be encouraged. Cairo should be replanned and developed as an architectural model of a Pharaonic–Arab metropolis.

In short, Young Egypt was calling for a combination of faith and action, material sacrifice – and even death – for the sake of a powerful Egyptian empire, as the new creed of the young generation. The latter were to be the soldiers of the new Egypt who, by militant – and violent – means, would revive its past glory. Their motto was to be 'God, Fatherland and King'. Believing in Egypt above all else, the soldiers of Young Egypt would attain power and prestige for their country throughout the world.

The party, no doubt, admired the methods and achievements of Nazi Germany and had connections with Fascist Italy in the thirties. It even sent a delegation to the famous Nuremberg Rally in 1936. What is more significant is that when it changed its name in March

1940 to the Nationalist Islamic Party it produced a creed of ten principles for all its adherents and followers. These were marked by their greater religious fanaticism and anti-foreign (anti-European) tone and content. 'Do not speak except in Arabic, and do not answer anyone who addresses you in a foreign language,' was the first principle. 'Do not patronize commercial stores which do not carry Arabic signs.' Similarly, 'Do not buy anything except from an Egyptian, and do not wear clothes that are not produced in Egypt by Egyptians.'

In its letter to King Faruq proposing the new programme, the party emphasized the importance of military power, and suggested the inevitability of the use of force for the realization of national political ends. It argued that Islam was the only moral force capable of renovating Egypt (not European liberalism), and that the Sharia should be the basis of social justice. It recommended the closing down of foreign schools and Christian missions, the militarization of school organization throughout the country, and the syndicalization of all workers in the State, including government officials. It declared that Egypt was 'the heart of the Muslim world', and that the Sudan was an inseparable part of the Egyptian empire. Its new slogan in the early war years was '*Allahu akbar wa'l-majdu lil-islam*' (Allah is Great and Glory belongs to Islam).[12]

Throughout this period of the thirties the *Salafiyya*, the Muslim Brethren and Young Egypt agitated against foreign schools, the activities of Christian missions and missionaries, and attacked the work of European orientalists. Several incidents involving all three targets of conservative Muslim attack were recorded at that time.[13]

The prominence of the Palestine Question in 1936 gave added impetus to this conservative religious reaction against Europe. Both the Muslim Brethren and Young Egypt called for closer co-operation with the Arabs struggling against Zionism in Palestine, Christian missionaries, and imperialism everywhere. The *Salafiyya*, some years before, had begun to justify ethnic Arab political aspirations on the basis of the Prophet's Arabness, and to suggest that their success would be synonymous with an Islamic victory.

Many followers and members of both the Ikhwan and Young Egypt from among the secondary school students in the mid-thirties were later to be found in the radical ranks of the Egyptian Army officer corps, especially after the wider recruitment of entrants to the Military Academy in 1936–7.[14] They were influenced by many ideas propagated by Young Egypt regarding independence, agrarian reform, the purification of national life, military power, the extension of Egyptian influence into the Arab Middle East and Africa.[15]

But whereas Young Egypt emphasized the fatherland in terms of king and country with a purification campaign directed against foreign economic and political influence in Egypt, the Muslim Brethren was an Islamic movement of wider scope. It did not confine itself to Egypt. It had followers and local organizations in Syria and Jordan, for example, and maintained close contacts with parallel movements in Iran (*Fedaiyan-i-islam*) and Pakistan (*Jamaat-i-islam*). To this extent, the Ikhwan had a supra-national dimension and pretension. The attainment of power in Egypt meant for the Ikhwan the possession of a base for the further extension of its programme and activities in the Arab and Islamic world.

One of the more lasting effects of both these movements in the 1930s and 1940s was the infusion of a wider sector of the population, especially the urban lower and middle classes and students, into politics. Another was their serious contribution in sapping the strength of established authority. The terrorist activities of the Muslim Brethren, for example, in the period 1944–9 reflected the militancy generated among its members by the combination of fanatic belief and paramilitary training. They forced a succession of governments to adopt repressive police methods against both the extreme Right and even the mild Left of the political spectrum.

The existence of a huge radical political movement with a paramilitary terrorist branch to harass governments at will, outside the normal channels of the political institutions of the country, inevitably discredited both the politicians of the ruling class and the monarchy. When the régime could no longer conceal its utter failure in the Palestine War (1948–9), a general condition of sedition was generated in Egyptian politics which lasted for the next three years. It would thus be misleading to discount the impact of these activist, militant movements upon the events which led to the 1952 Free Officers movement.

The social consequences of the political and economic changes which occurred in Egypt in the inter-war period were just as complex and decisive in this reaction against liberalism and Europe. Rapid growth of population, massive immigration from the countryside to the cities, unemployment and underemployment, hardship resulting from high living costs, all were indices of the social dislocation which occurred in this period. The effect of two World Wars, the rise of industry, and the rapid growth of population constituted the social strains in Egypt which inevitably affected its political stability.

We have also noted in passing such salient facts as the drop in per capita income, and the immigration of population from the rural areas to the cities in search of employment. Cairo, during the last war, had become an inchoate heap of deprived urban proletariat who could be sharply distinguished from the few native rich and the approximately hundred thousand resident foreigners. These poor masses were huddled in native quarters, some of which, like Shubra, packed ten thousand souls to the square city block. Inflation and the rise in living costs made their conditions worse. Crime became widespread in these quarters.[16]

We have also remarked that the further impetus given to industry in the last war tended to concentrate growing numbers of industrial labour in the major cities. This in part was due to the fact that Egyptian industry was monopolistic, whether one is referring to the Bank Misr Group or the Abboud or Kotzika enterprises. The investors in these enterprises and their directors were also members of the upper classes, whether as members of the Ittihad and Shaab parties of the 1920s and 1930s, or of the Saadist Party in the period 1938–52.

Their owners, directors and even managers were also members of political parties and clubs from which were recruited the government ministers and parliamentary deputies of the constitutional period 1923–52. They monopolized such industries as sugar, cement, fertilizer, chemicals, distilleries, textiles, airlines, navigation and the cinema. Their increased industrial and commercial activities were reflected in the fact that while agricultural investment fell in this period from two-thirds to under one half of all investment in the country, industrial investment rose from a mere 9 per cent to almost a quarter of the total. Investment in banking, commerce and insurance rose from a mere 6 to 17 per cent of the total.

Although the Wafd and the Liberal parties were led by men still identified with the major landowning interests in the country, after the last war many of these too had acquired high stakes in Egyptian industry and finance.

Neither the landowning interests in the Wafd and Liberal Party hierarchies nor the industrial and financial ones in the lesser political parties appeared too concerned with facing up to the new socioeconomic problems of the country. The Wafd, for example, produced no drastic agrarian or other reforms related to agriculture and rural society in general. Industrial interests, in their turn, were slow in responding to the needs, or demands, of emerging labour groups.

These problems acquire their proper perspective and acuteness when one recalls certain general facts about Egyptian society and its economy. Farm output, for example, in this proverbially agricultural country, rose twelve times during the nineteenth century, and had doubled again by 1914. In 150 years, Egyptian agriculture was transformed from its traditional subsistence level into a profitable commercial enterprise. It managed to feed a population which in 1900 was already four times greater than in 1800 without outbreaks of famine. Most of the irrigation schemes and the extension of the cultivable area had been completed by 1914. In the next thirty-five to forty years, this area was increased by only 16 per cent and the cropped area by 30 per cent. This was obviously a much reduced rate of agricultural expansion which did not keep pace with a population that had increased by 67 per cent between 1897 and 1937, and which then almost doubled between 1937 and 1967.

Even though in 1950 one half of the cultivated land was farmed by owner-farmers, the distribution of ownership was phenomenally uneven. Six per cent of owners in July 1952 owned 65 per cent of the cultivated area, with the royal family alone in possession of approximately 600,000 *feddans*.

In 1950, industry was still making only a 10 to 15 per cent contribution to national output and employing only a tenth of the country's labour force. Nonetheless, its growth was rapid after the Great War and particularly after 1930. In the twenty-year period 1919–39 capital invested in industrial joint stock companies and commercial companies, as we noted earlier, increased rapidly. Such industries as sugar, distilleries, cotton and textiles were by then highly developed; so were public utilities.[17]

A native Egyptian bourgeoisie had slowly emerged since Muhammad Ali's reign, and more rapidly after the British occupation. Its social status and political influence derived from landed property and related wealth, both of which were strengthened during the British occupation. By 1919 they were the natural leaders of the independence movement, and the rulers of the new independent State after 1923. Following independence, this same landed bourgeoisie branched off into industry and commerce. Instead of a new mercantile, trading and industrial middle class emerging, the economic development of Egypt in the inter-war period was led by an older native propertied class turned industrialist.

The radicalization of Egyptian politics and the attack by extremists on established ruling groups was by 1945 no longer confined to conservative Islamic and national-socialist movements. While the lower classes and the dispossessed responded to the fanatical Islamic movements, the more educated lower-middle and middle groups, who for a long time followed the Wafd against the monarchy, were now becoming alienated from the old-established nationalist leadership. Within the Wafd itself a split occurred between the executive hierarchy of traditional landowning interests and the younger university and professional members. This movement was not unrelated to the emergence of acute social problems in the areas of industrial labour, agricultural workers, unemployment, inflation and high living costs. Whereas in 1919 the Wafd could subsume many of these elements and smaller interest groups into a general national movement for independence, by 1945 it had not dealt adequately with most of their problems and needs. By then, too, there were more of them. This partly explains the attraction of the Muslim Brethren and Young Egypt for many members of these groups.

The working classes, including the thousands of lowly government officials, continued to suffer economically during the last war. Labour in Egypt had not been highly organized. There had been a few strikes for better working conditions and higher wages as early as the period 1899–1910 among tobacco, railways and printing workers. In 1908 a small co-operative and trade union movement had begun: tobacco workers at the Matossian factories had formed their trade union that year; so had the tramway workers.

The indebtedness of peasant farmers prompted lawyers and a few other members of the intelligentsia to develop a co-operative movement. In 1908 Omar Lutfi (d. 1911) founded the first agricultural co-operative in the country. A proposed co-operatives law in the old Legislative Assembly in 1914 never materialized because of the Great War. Yet the number of co-operatives increased, especially in the face of higher living costs in 1914–18. A Co-operatives Law was passed in 1923, but its provisions applied to agricultural co-operatives only, placing them virtually under government control. A second law passed in 1927 was more inclusive as it covered all forms of co-operatives.

When the Ministry of Social Affairs was established in August 1939, it appointed a Special Committee to look after co-operatives' affairs, and created a special Department of Co-operatives in the Ministry.[18] In 1944, Parliament passed a new bill for Co-operatives to supersede that of 1927. The membership of the Special Committee (later an Advisory Council) was expanded to include members of Parliament and private citizens directly involved in the co-operative movement. The new law also provided for the organization of advisory councils for co-operatives in the provinces to act as liaisons between those provinces and the central Department of Co-operatives in the new Ministry of Social Affairs.

Significantly, the new bill exempted all co-operatives from the payment of stamp duty on their contractual and other transactions, as well as from commercial and industrial profits tax. It also set the conditions for financial grants from the government to co-operatives. Whereas foreigners were admitted to membership in some co-operatives, they were specifically excluded from agricultural ones. Co-operatives were also given priority over the produce of their members against loans granted by them. This was intended to encourage the further extension of credit by co-operatives to their members. Provision was made in the bill for co-operatives to accumulate profits from their transactions with non-members and to earmark these for the financing of social services. Moreover, the bill permitted co-operatives to organize syndicates in each district or province which would supervise the work of all co-operatives belonging to them. Finally, the Bill provided for the establishment of a Co-operatives Bank. This was done simply by converting the old Agricultural Credit Bank founded in 1931 into the Co-operatives Bank.

By the end of the Second World War there were over 2,500 co-operatives in Egypt with a total membership of over 800,000 and a reported total volume of business of £E.8 million.

Labour and trade unions also date back to 1908–9. The new Civil Code of 1883 gave minimum attention to labour problems. A Freedom of Individual Work Act had been decreed in 1891, but in 1899 there were already the first strikes in the tobacco, railways and printing industries. The passage of the first Child Labour Act in 1909 coincided with the organization of the first trade unions in the tobacco, tramways (1908), the handicraft industries in Bulaq (1909) and elsewhere. There were about ten such unions in 1910. This Act was not amended, however, until 1923 when special conditions and limitations were placed on the employment of minors in industry. Throughout the twenties the organization of trade unions did not advance rapidly. The various political parties sought to control industrial labour by organizing their own unions as adjuncts of their party political machines. Agricultural workers – the vast majority of Egypt's working force – were, in any case, excluded from membership in trade unions. Furthermore, the Wafd, for two decades at least, continued to control their vote via their provincial representatives and appointees and village headmen. Thus, a pro-Ittihad party union was organized in 1925 under Abdul Rahman Fahmi. In 1930, the Liberals formed their own labour union led by Daoud Ratib. In the same year, when the Ismail Sidqi government opened in November a Labour Bureau in the Ministry of the Interior (which later became the Department of Labour), the Wafd formed in December a trade union under the leadership of Prince Abbas Halim, a member of the royal family. But in 1933–4, Abbas Halim detached his union from the Wafd and formed the Egyptian Labour Party (possibly by this time inspired by the Crown). The Wafd then formed its own trade union in 1935.

A series of new laws and decrees promulgated over a two-year period (1933–5) constitutes perhaps a reflection of the national importance which problems of social reform had acquired by that time. In 1933, the Sidqi government passed a new bill to regulate the employment of women in industry and commerce. Two years later, a Palace-appointed caretaker government headed by Tawfiq Nasim followed up the elevation of the old Department of Commerce and Industry to a Ministry in December 1934 with a new bill in 1935 limiting working hours in certain industries.

This is not to imply that there was no labour movement, or any organized groups demanding social reform, outside the purview of government legislation. Until this time, however, these were confined to a few members of the intelligentsia (university students and teachers, a few lawyers and professional men). An articulated – or sophisticated – social reform and labour consciousness was not yet present among the relatively uneducated working classes, i.e., among the actual members of the rising industrial labour force. But as early as 1919, small leftist socialist groups began to appear in Cairo and Alexandria. Many of their members were foreigners (Greeks, Italians and others) resident in Egypt. In 1919, for instance, an Egyptian Democratic Party made its appearance, and in 1920 the Socialist Party of Alexandria Workers led by Mahmud Husni al-Arabi. The latter drew its support from a first Confederation of Egyptian Labour which included over twenty trade unions with some 50,000 members. Then, in 1922, the first Communist Party was founded in Egypt.[19]

All these groups demanded the usual eight-hour workday, wages comparable to those paid to industrial workers in Europe and freedom to organize trade unions and to conduct collective bargaining. Influenced by the Bolshevik Revolution in Russia, they further proposed agrarian reform, the nationalization of large estates and the distribution of land to the fellahin. They also sought to unionize agricultural workers. Moreover, they took a nationalist stand against the continued British Protectorate. Their programme constituted, at the same time, an oblique challenge to the emerging national leadership of the Wafd.

To some extent, the slow pace of governmental response to labour and social reform problems was due to the appearance of these small leftist groups so early in the struggle for the attainment of independence. The new ruling classes were unlikely to permit revolutionary ideas which demanded a profound change in the social system of the country so soon after they had attained power. Repression therefore was immediate and firm. The 1923 Law of Associations was strengthened further by the first Wafd government in order to combat such activities by these new groups. Earlier, in September 1923, parts of the Penal Code had been amended to allow the government to act effectively against those spreading 'subversive, anarchist, communist, and anti-constitutional ideas'. Disciplinary measures were introduced against any strikes by government officials, employees of public utilities, and transport services. These carried stiff fines and short prison sentences.[20]

Strikes, however, occurred in March 1924 involving clashes between workers and police on factory premises. The Wafd government arrested several persons, including alleged members of the Communist Party, most of whom were foreigners. In the following two years, the Ziwar government arrested Bolshevik propagandists and several foreign residents. The new Egyptian Nationality Law of May 1926 excluded from naturalization foreigners who held such ideas. Again, the Wafdist Nahhas government in May 1928 deported several Greeks and Italians for alleged Communist activities. These measures were intensified by the Liberal Muhammad Mahmud government in December 1928.

Industrial labour constituted at that time a minority of the country's labour force. The vast numbers of agricultural workers were nowhere near any level of political sophistication. Much of the leftist labour and Communist activity was still a monopoly of a few foreigners and still fewer members of the Egyptian intelligentsia. Indeed, many of its leaders remained foreign until 1947. But it was not long until – especially during the last war – the leftist movement acquired many adherents among Egyptians in secondary schools and universities, journalists and the free professions.

Although easy it is not quite wise to agree completely with Dr I.G. Levi, one-time Director of the Statistical Service in Cairo, that labour legislation was not the outcome of trade union pressure, but of inter-party political strife.[21] For, despite the infancy and weakness of the trade union movement in the period 1908–23, the Wafd, in its determined policy always to appear as the leader of the nation, eventually sought to satisfy (perhaps only to mollify) some labour demands. Similarly – but only when it was too late – it sought to champion social reform in all its aspects. This new orientation of political parties and governments alike became more readily apparent after 1930 with the more rapid development of Egyptian industry.

Whether politically justified or not, all parties at this time were agreed on the maintenance of the Individual Freedom of Work Act originally passed in 1891 and amended in 1923. With this, they hoped to delay, if not obstruct, the further organization of trade unions. On the surface, it seems as if the parties, led by the Wafd, considered any trade union movement which might also embrace a nationalist plank in its programme, a threat to their leadership.

It is telling however, that, whether for political and electoral reasons or not, all parties, including Palace-appointed governments with no parliamentary support to speak of, felt compelled after 1926, and particularly in the period 1930–6, to pay greater attention to social reform, including labour legislation. Thus, in the Wafdist–Liberal coalition government of Adli Yeken (June 1926–April 1927), Wafdist ministers urged further social legislation upon their colleagues. The government of Muhammad Mahmud (June 1928–October 1929) promised social reform to both the rural population (drinking water in villages, distribution of land), and the industrial workers (workers' housing, hospitals, schools). It declared that the country could easily finance these projects of reform from a £E40 million reserve fund. King Fuad thus laid the foundation stone in May 1929 of the first 150-house 'workers' town' in Cairo. Yet all these projects seemed ultimately to fizzle out.

In 1930, Sidqi's unpopular government organized the Bureau of

Labour, but as part of the Ministry of the Interior. This laid the government open to the charge that the new office was meant more for the conduct of police surveillance of labour groups and trade unions and less as a public agency to assist workers with their problems. Its budget, moreover, was very small. But it recommended to the government that a delegation from the ILO in Geneva be invited to Egypt to study labour conditions and to recommend legislation. Similarly, the King's Speech from the Throne opening Parliament in December 1931 referred to extensive plans for the implementation of compulsory elementary education throughout the country, labour legislation to protect workers against sickness and accident, and the further regulation of child labour. A Committee of Labour Legislation was set up, but under the chairmanship of the Under-Secretary of the Interior Ministry, to study reform. Among its members was the Director of Public Security. It proposed two bills, one to regulate child labour and the other the employment of women.

Meantime, the so-called Butler ILO Mission had finished its work in 1932. Its report painted a terrible picture of working conditions in the country. These consisted of a fourteen to sixteen hour workday, the employment of children under ten in appalling unhygienic conditions in factories; weekly holidays were often unknown, wages were very low and often paid (or unpaid) via the intermediacy of the *rayyis* (foreman), who was also responsible for the recruitment of labour. Moreover, management did not recognize any trade unions. The Mission recommended legislation to regulate strictly the employment of minors in industry; a definite provision for accident compensation; the recognition of trade unions; the limitation of working hours; the institution of a compulsory weekly day off; and the direct payment of wages and salaries by management, not through the foreman.

Between 1924 and 1938 a wave of strikes occurred, partly the result of the 1930 economic crisis and partly because of the slow response by the government to the need to improve working conditions. In 1933, two years after the passage of a bill regulating the employment of women in industry and commerce, a new bill was passed which fixed maximum working hours, but only in certain industries. Another bill of limited scope covering accident compensation was passed by the Wafd government in September 1936.

Meanwhile, Ali Maher's government (January–May 1936) appointed a Higher Council for Social Reform – a forerunner of the Ministry of Social Affairs founded in August 1939. A School of Social Service, to train social workers, had been opened in Cairo the same year, and one in Alexandria the following year. When the new Wafdist Parliament opened in November 1936, it featured a Speech from the Throne replete with projects for social reform. But in the summer of 1938 a serious strike at the Misr Group textile factory in Mehalla al-Kubra, involving a sit-in and occupation of the premises by workers, led to clashes with the police and scores of arrests. The outbreak of war the following year brought martial law to the country and, with it, emergency powers for any government to deal with labour – and other – unrest.

The return of the Wafd to power in February 1942 was effected by the threat of British arms. It was not, to say the least, a popular return to power for a popular national party. To this extent, the important social reform and labour legislation promulgated by this government in 1942–4 was partly motivated by a desire to retrieve lost popularity. In September 1942 trade unions were recognized as legal organizations. But the same law prohibited the formation of a federation of labour or trade unions in the country, as well as all political activity on the part of existing unions. The same bill made accident insurance compulsory. Then, in May 1944, a new individual work contract law was promulgated.[22]

From that time on it was clear that the Wafdist leadership was anxious to attract rising labour groups and an emerging leftist intelligentsia back into its ranks. It wished to repeat – if not continue – a situation in which the Wafd subsumed (as it did largely in the period 1919–39) all groups in Egyptian society under the broad banner of its national leadership. When the Wafd was out of power in the years 1945–50, it made further efforts to appear as the champion of social reform. In this way it hoped to prevent the further breaking away of its intelligentsia and student following from the party. Many of these had already been recruited by the radical Islamic and nationalist movements of the Muslim Brethren and Young Egypt who, by this time, had also adopted 'socialist' planks in their programmes. The Brethren, for instance, managed this on the Islamic basis of social justice; Young Egypt on the basis of national socialism. On the other hand, these developments were perhaps a crude indication of the acuteness of socio-economic problems facing the country in the aftermath of the Second World War.

Meanwhile, the coalition government of Nuqrashi (February 1945–February 1946: Saadists, National Party, and the Kutla of Makram Obayd) strengthened the government's security measures by creating a special section in Public Security to combat communist activities – but really against the heightened terrorist activities of the Muslim Brethren. A few months later, in July 1946, the Sidqi government carried out mass arrests of Communists in Cairo, Alexandria, Port Said and Suez. Many of these were Greeks, Italians, and Jews of various nationalities (including Egyptians).

While taking these repressive measures, all minority governments in the period 1944–9 sped to produce palliative measures of social reform. Yet in January 1946 a series of strikes in such major textile industrial centres as Mehalla al-Kubra, Shubra al-Khayma and Cairo demanded a forty-hour week, a minimum daily wage of PT 30, and paid holidays. These strikes spread to Alexandria and continued through the summer and autumn. By 1947–8, workers were resorting to the sabotage of factory premises. Both police forces and the army had to be used against them.

The strike fever spread to tramway workers who, in 1946, demanded a seven-hour day, double time for holiday work, social security and collective bargaining rights. Other public utilities followed suit, such as the strike of petrol distributors which paralysed motor transport in February 1948. Government employees went on strike next with a demand for salary revision. Worst of all, the police struck in April 1948, leaving Alexandria and Cairo virtually without public security. The male nurses at Qasr al-Aini Hospital and the Medical School complex there also went on strike to demand better working conditions and higher wages. The movement of demands for social reform now threatened to extend to the countryside with its millions of deprived fellahin.

There were parallel demands for other germinal social reform measures in and out of Parliament and the government in the period 1945–50, regarding education, inheritance laws, the limitation of landownership, village reform and progressive and graduated taxation on income. A new generation of writers calling for the total reform of Egyptian society emerged at this time. Most of them were Western-educated like their liberal predecessors and contemporaries, but what was different about them was their search for a new radicalism which accepted, among other things, Marxist ideas. Prominent among these was the literary critic Muhammad Mandur, the philosopher Abdul Rahman Badawi, the Azhari Shaykh Khaled Muhammad Khaled, the economic publicist Rashed al-Barrawi, the novelist Najib Mahfuz, the literary and cultural historian Louis Awad, the folklorist and publicist Rushdi Salih, and many others.

Many of these were leftist and radical members, or followers, of the Wafd who had increasingly become disillusioned with the party's record and leadership. In addition to their own writings, they launched a number of magazines and journals in which they expressed their radical social and economic ideas. Thus, Mandur's *al-Baath*, Rushdi Salih's *al-Fajr al-jadid*, and several others represented Egyptian *avant-garde* radicalism in the forties. Then, the publication of Shaykh Khaled's devastating attack upon the traditionalism of the religious Establishment,[23] and the more prolonged impact of Najib Mahfuz's *Trilogy*[24] gave both radicalism and a rising trend of social realism in literature a powerful impetus in Egypt at mid-century.[25]

It is against this general background of mounting social and economic problems, and the confusion of political orientation – the rise of radical conservative movements to challenge established ruling groups, as well as the emergence of a radical leftist tendency among a Western-educated intelligentsia – that one must outline the disintegration and collapse of the old Establishment and its political order. But as these developments were not the sole – or even most important – factor which undermined the Old Order, we must resume in the next chapter the political history narrative of this critical phase from the outbreak of the Second World War to the overthrow of the *ancien régime* by the military in July 1952.

CHAPTER 16

PRELUDE TO REVOLUTION
1939–52

At the outbreak of the Second World War, Egypt was governed by a coalition consisting of Independents and Saadists, headed by Ali Maher, Chief of the Royal Cabinet since 1935. Relations between the King and Wafd at that time were strained and deteriorating. Moreover, it soon became clear that Ali Maher harboured Axis sympathies which the young King Faruq also shared. British troops were soon pouring into the country. The following year, the war was very near-by in the Western Desert. Public sympathy for an Axis victory spread; Ikhwan and Young Egypt agitators organized activities which, in the view of the British military in the area, constituted serious threats to security. Many Egyptian Army officers led by their Chief of Staff, Aziz Ali al-Masri,[1] were suspected of having contacts with the enemy.

Nevertheless, bound by the 1936 Anglo-Egyptian Treaty, the Ali Maher government had proclaimed martial law in the country in September 1939 and imposed censorship. Diplomatic relations with Germany were severed, although there was no Egyptian declaration of war on that country. Certain provisions of the Penal Code were strengthened to deal with the wartime emergency. Several strict economic and monetary measures were introduced to regulate imports and exports, prices of foodstuffs, and essential and critical commodities.

Not unexpectedly the Wafd, which had been out of power since the end of 1937, submitted a Memorandum to the British Ambassador in April 1940 in which it raised the matter of Anglo-Egyptian relations in general. It was an inopportune and clumsy communication, coming as it did from the majority national party, in so far as it demanded an undertaking to the effect that after the war Britain would withdraw all her troops from Egypt and would recognize Egyptian rights in the Sudan. In short, the Wafd at a critical moment in Britain's wartime position was demanding the abrogation of the 1936 Treaty, and an advance commitment by the British government to negotiate a new arrangement over Egypt. The Memorandum also demanded that Egyptian cotton should either be permitted to be sold during the war to neutral countries or, if the British opposed such sale, for the latter to buy it at acceptable prices. Needless to say, the British government rejected all the proposals of this Memorandum. It also specifically indicated that the Wafdist communication might lead to a reconsideration of Britain's commitments under the 1936 Treaty adverse to Egypt, and, more ominously, to the interference of Britain in Egypt's domestic political affairs. It charged the Wafd with wishing to undermine Britain's economic warfare against Germany.

Perhaps, in submitting their Memorandum, the Wafd were anxious to attain several objectives. First, they wished to reassure the public, including their more radical followers, that they were still the leaders of the national independence movement and the only ones who could deal effectively with the traditional question of Anglo-Egyptian relations. Second, they were, perhaps foolishly, suggesting that while they as a party and government concluded the Treaty back in 1936, they nevertheless did not consider it as satisfactory or final. Third, the Wafd hoped to show further the inadequacy and unrepresentative character of minority governments in power since their demise in 1937 and to arouse public opinion against them. Finally, rather perversely, they were trying to convince the British that only the Wafd could govern effectively and to their satisfaction in time of war. This they assumed was inherent in their ability to generate domestic political trouble. Wartime developments soon proved that their most perverse assumption was also their most realistic consideration, for it eventually brought them to power.

Italy entered the war in June 1940. This became a most important factor affecting the British position in Egypt. Italian ambitions in the Middle East, Africa and the Red Sea had been well known for some time; they became more apparent since 1935. The Italian presence in Libya to the West, in Ethiopia and Somaliland to the south and southeast now constituted a grave danger to British security. The government of Ali Maher and the King were apparently interested in keeping Egypt out of the war. They had opted for a policy of sitting on the fence until the outcome of the hostilities became clearer. Yet Axis, especially Italian, propaganda over the years had had some effect among Egyptians and other Arabs in the Middle East.

Meanwhile the Ali Maher government had created in September 1939 a territorial army under the command of the then Minister of *waqfs*, Abd al-Rahman Azzam – a known Arab nationalist and anti-

British politician. Moreover, it is not unlikely that Ali Maher viewed this army of some twenty-five thousand men as a makeweight and future weapon against the Wafd. Nor is it inconceivable that it could have been used in guerrilla and sabotage operations against British forces and installations in Egypt had the circumstances warranted – e.g., an imminent defeat of Britain in the war. Finally, General Muhammad Salih Harb had become Minister of Defence in the Ali Maher Cabinet. A known Muslim nationalist, Harb later succeeded Abd al-Hamid Sa'id as President of the YMMA.

Anti-British propaganda campaigns by both the Axis radios and native extremist elements spread rumours of a repetition of Britain's First World War policies in Egypt, e.g., the forceful conscription of a labour corps, the requisition of food and supplies, etc. This tended to create resentment among the poorer masses of the population, panic, and a general atmosphere of open hostility.

The British made forceful representations to the Egyptian government to put an end to these developments and to bring the situation under control, which produced a government crisis. General Aziz Ali al-Masri was placed on leave and later, in August 1940, retired from active duty. Parliament meanwhile voted the break of diplomatic relations with Italy on 12 June, but noted that Egypt should not declare war on that country unless directly attacked. Ali Maher's policy of 'neutrality' in the war was upheld.

British Intelligence suspected contacts between Ali Maher and Murad Sa'id Ahmad Pasha, Egyptian Minister in Rome, who had refused to return to Egypt after Italy's entry in the war. Further British pressure on the government did not produce any results. The Maher government, for example, had issued strict orders to Egyptian Army units on the Western Desert frontier not to engage any Italian Army units. Moreover, the Chief of the Supernumerary Police, Muhammad Tahir Pasha, a Maher appointee, was suspected of being pro-Axis. Also the government wanted to declare Cairo an open city, a move unacceptable to the British military authorities.

In these difficult circumstances the King called a meeting of all party leaders, which was held on 22 June 1940 at the Palace, to discuss the crisis. A national government proposed by the Crown was rejected by Nahhas, leader of the Wafd, for obvious political reasons. But Ali Maher's government resigned and another coalition Cabinet headed by the Independent Hasan Sabri was formed comprising Saadists, Liberals, National Party members, Ittihad–Shaabists and Independents.

At this point one important change in Palace personnel occurred. Ahmad Muhammad Hasanayn was appointed in August 1940 Chief of the Royal Cabinet in succession to Ali Maher, who had vacated the post when he became Prime Minister almost a year earlier. The appointment was at the recommendation of the new Prime Minister, Hasan Sabri.[2] But in November, the Prime Minister collapsed and died in Parliament while reading the Speech from the Throne to the assembled Deputies and Senators. Hasanayn, it seems, now saw an opportunity for another try at a national government acceptable to both the King and the British. He urged the King to invite Husayn Sirri, another Independent, to form a Cabinet. This included Liberals, Independents and Ittihad–Shaabists and took office on 15 November 1940. The Saadists, who by then were the only group which openly favoured an Egyptian declaration of war on the Axis powers, refused to participate in this coalition. The Wafd, moreover, persisted in its non co-operation policy with these minority governments.

Sirry's first government lasted eight and a half months, during which time the economic situation in the country deteriorated and the Allied military position in the Western Desert became precarious. The Germans had invaded and occupied mainland Greece in April 1941 and Crete soon thereafter. At the same time the Afrika Corps had moved into North Africa to assist their Italian allies. Axis air raids on Egypt increased; the food supply situation created anxiety; hoarding followed.

In May 1941, the Axis forces were already in Sollum and Mersa Matruh on the Egyptian western frontier. At the same time a pro-Axis military coup in Iraq led to the establishment of an anti-British government in Baghdad led by Rashid Ali al-Geylani. This threatened further the British position in Mesopotamia. To the West most of the Levant (Syria and Lebanon) was still in the hands of Vichy French forces.

Repercussions in Egypt of these adverse developments in Britain's war fortunes were serious. The retired Chief of Staff of the Egyptian Army, General al-Masri, along with other Egyptian Army officers, was brought to trial in May 1941 for having attempted to reach the Axis lines in the Western Desert and thus defect to the enemy. A reshuffling in the Sirry Cabinet in July 1941 to accommodate returning Saadist ministers coincided with an improvement in the British military position in Libya. That summer and autumn the Allied forces had managed to stop the Axis advance on Egypt. Nevertheless security conditions in Egypt remained dangerous. Without Wafdist participation the reshuffled Sirry Cabinet soon found itself in serious difficulties.

Domestic conditions became critical in the winter of 1941–2. A sharp rise in living costs was aggravated by a scarcity of basic commodities such as sugar, flour, fuel and ordinary cloth for the attire used by the masses in their daily wear (*gallabiyya*). Black marketing was rampant. All this despite the efforts of the Ministry of Supply to introduce a rationing scheme. The opposition in Parliament and the country at large blamed both the government and the British for these difficult conditions. The latter were accused of providing for their troops first and consequently of consuming most of the country's cereal production, to which the government responded by limiting the land area cultivated in cotton and allocating an additional 200,000 *feddans* for cereals and basic foodstuffs production. Cost of living allowances were introduced for salaried government officials. Yet by January 1942 bread was scarce. Inhabitants of the poorer native quarters in Cairo were storming bakeries for bread.

There was also in this month a ministerial crisis. Abd al-Hamid Badawi, the Independent Minister of Finance, resigned. The crisis worsened when at British insistence the government severed diplomatic relations with Vichy France. The opposition in Parliament, led by Ismail Sidqi, raised a big fuss over this move. They recalled the services rendered by France and Frenchmen to Egypt in the past, and deplored the government's action under British pressure. Another Independent in the Cabinet, Salib Sami, the Foreign Minister, resigned. The King, moreover, who was on a tour of Upper Egypt when this action was taken, was annoyed that he was not consulted in advance, or at all. Such royal displeasure in Egypt always served as an opening for anti-government political forces to create a rift between the monarch and his ministers. The estrangement between King and Cabinet was soon rumoured. Thus despite a more pro-British – or at least a British-accommodating – policy, the Sirry government was unable to satisfy the opposition groups and the King, or to meet adequately the deteriorating economic situation in the country.

To make things worse Rommel's forces were again advancing towards Egypt. Sirry's government resigned on 2 February 1942 amidst demonstrations in Cairo shouting anti-British slogans 'Forward Rommel; Long Live Rommel.' These went on for a day or two while the country remained without a government.

The British Ambassador informed the King via the Chief of the Royal Cabinet that a government headed by Nahhas, leader of the Wafd, should be formed. The King invited Nahhas on 3 February to form a national government. Nahhas declined. In the face of this, the British Ambassador urged the King again through Hasanayn to invite Nahhas to form a Wafdist government. A hurried meeting of all party and other political leaders at the Palace on the afternoon of 4 February to seek a resolution of the crisis was superfluous, for the British Ambassador had already presented his ultimatum to Hasanayn which read as follows:

> Unless I hear by 6 pm that Nahhas Pasha has been asked to form a cabinet, His Majesty King Farouk must accept the consequences.

The assembled politicians, upon hearing the text of the ultimatum, decided to reply to the British Ambassador with a protest signed by all of them:

> The British ultimatum constitutes an attack upon the independence of Egypt, an interference in its domestic affairs, and a violation of the provisions of the Anglo–Egyptian alliance. It is therefore beyond the King's powers to accept conditions which compromise the country's independence ... etc.

This reply Note was delivered to the British Ambassador by Hasanayn. The Ambassador refused to accept it [as a response to his ultimatum] and informed Hasanayn he would be calling on King Faruq that evening. Shortly before he did, British tanks, other armour, and troops had surrounded Abdin Palace. And when the British Ambassador arrived he was accompanied by General Stone, GOC British Troops, and a detail of armed officers and men. Faced with abdication, the King had no choice but to immediately invite Nahhas to form a Wafdist government. Such was the episode which came to be known as the 4 February Incident.

Despite Nahhas's letter of 5 February 1942 to the British Ambassador stating that his assumption of the premiership did not in any way imply his or his party's acquiescence in any British interference in Egyptian affairs, the fact remained that he had come to power only because Britain had threatened the monarch with the use of armed force. Britain on her part had simply considered that at that critical moment of her wartime position a Wafdist government in Egypt was the most consonant with, and convenient to, her interests. There was no indication that the British government considered the Wafd the best hope of a government as such for Egypt.

It would be ludicrous to suggest that Nahhas was not, on 2 February, aware of the British Ambassador's intentions. The charge that Amin Othman, a leading member of the party, had acted as liaison between Nahhas and the British Embassy is not untrue, yet Nahhas remained adamant against participating in, or even leading, any national government. Hasanayn of the Palace on the other hand was hopeful that he could avert such an eventuality as the one that broke upon the King and the country on 4 February by convincing the Wafd otherwise. Finally he was forced to advise the King to accede to the British ultimatum rather than face abdication or exile, if not imprisonment.

The real effect of the 4 February Incident on domestic Egyptian politics was far-reaching. It immediately widened the rift between King and Wafd. The latter were now in power for what they hoped would be a very long time, supported by the requirements of British wartime interests. The King had been humiliated. More widely, the Wafd's standing with its more extremist followers went into serious and continuous decline, the extent of which became clear in 1950–1. Politics now became a game of revenge: the Wafd struck against all those who helped keep them out of power since 1937, and the King and Palace minions watched for the first opportunity to destroy the Wafd. Meanwhile, the public suffered in a struggle to make ends meet under adverse economic and financial wartime conditions. The extremist groups, such as the Ikhwan and Young Egypt, continued to organize and prepare their members for the day of reckoning that would surely come after the war. Significantly also the first groups of native Egyptian radical leftists began to organize and propagate their views in earnest. They too bided their time. More important, as it turned out in July 1952, the 4 February Incident did not pass unnoticed by young regular army officers. A policy of mutual destruction set in among the ruling classes that had come to power in 1923.

The new Wafd government held fresh elections in March 1942, which were boycotted by the Liberal and Saadist parties. Naturally, an overwhelming Wafd majority was returned to Parliament. In its first session this Parliament proceeded to enact several important bills, partly motivated by the desire to dilute the government's and party's pro-British record. Thus it passed a bill, first projected in 1924, to establish a General Accounting Office (*diwan al-muhasaba*), with audit and other fiscal supervisory powers over public funds. Another bill made primary education free. The party's nationalist credentials and standing were farcically rehabilitated by a bill requiring the use of Arabic in all commercial company transactions. The government also met with a measure of success when the public subscribed widely to the new issue of treasury bonds formalizing the conversion of the old Public Debt into a National Debt.[3] Another bill recognized the independence of the judiciary by making the removal of appointed judges illegal. A palliative to the rural masses consisted of a bill lowering taxation on smallholder farmers. The new Faruq University, begun several years earlier at Alexandria, was completed and in 1942 opened its doors to the first students. Other legislative measures in 1944 consisted of the famous Trade Unions Law, a Municipalities bill, a new Co-operatives Law and a project for the construction, equipping and servicing of village health units.

At the same time, however, the Wafd government made maximum use of existing emergency powers under martial law to combat its political adversaries. Whereas in 1939 Wafdist senators had opposed the introduction of martial law by the Ali Maher government, and in its Memorandum of April 1940 to the British Ambassador the Wafd Party had demanded its repeal, a Wafd government was now using these very measures to silence its opponents. It was in this way that Ali Maher was arrested and placed under forced residence; that General Salih Harb, Minister of Defence in Ali Maher's government, was exiled to the countryside.

In May 1942, Rommel's Afrika Corps began a new offensive against the British Forces in the Western Desert, aiming at the capture of Alexandria. Their advance was not checked until July, and then at a line running from Mersa Matruh, Daba and Alamein near the coast to a point west of the Qattara Depression in the south. The Axis forces were virtually at the doors of Egypt's Delta. The effect of this was immediate and Egyptian reaction hysterical – if not panicky. There was a run on grocers for hoarding of foodstuffs. More ominous was the run on banks by depositors. Foreign residents especially were prominent in this panic, many of whom began to leave Egypt for Palestine, Lebanon and Syria. Strangely enough the public was both terrified at the possible coming of an Axis occupation and at the same time pro-Axis in their sympathies. Jewish merchants sold their goods and stores to Levantine traders (Syrian and Lebanese resident in Egypt) at very low prices. 'Among the Levantines, optimism was based on the belief that the coming of the Axis powers to Egypt would eliminate Jewish middlemen and they would take over.'[4]

The position in Egypt was precarious. Axis agents and sympathizers were encouraging the public to sabotage the British war effort
in Egypt. Politicians known to be Axis sympathizers had been
arrested or placed under house arrest throughout this period. Thus
on 22 February, 1942, Abd al-Rahman Azzam, ex-Minister of *waqfs*,
was dismissed as commander of Ali Maher's vaunted, but useless,
territorial army. On 8 April, Ali Maher himself, as noted earlier,
was prohibited from all political activity and placed under house
arrest. Prince Abbas Halim, a labour union leader since the 1930s,
was arrested; so was the President of the Sporting Clubs Federation.

Prime Minister Nahhas took every opportunity to declare Egypt's
support for her ally, Britain, in the war. At the same time in the
summer of 1942 (July–October), the Wafd government was busy
covering its flanks in the event of an Axis victory. It is alleged that
the Cabinet drafted a letter to General Rommel to be delivered by
the then Governor of Alexandria, Abdel Khaliq Hassuna (later
Secretary-General of the League of Arab States). In it they assured
the general that Egypt's sympathies really lay with the Axis powers;
only circumstances were forcing Egyptians to work with the British.
Needless to say the letter never reached Rommel. First, there was
no easy way of delivering it by courier. Second, Hassuna was not
prepared to risk his life in delivering it. But the King too for his
part, who was only too anxious to remove Nahhas for being too
pro-British, was interested in appointing a Prime Minister who could
deal with the imminently victorious Axis forces.[5]

The Wafd lost no time, however, in gathering the fruits of office
despite difficult wartime conditions. Several senior administrative
personnel were dismissed or retired from government service and
replaced by Wafdists. Requests for exceptional promotions and
salary rises for Wafdist state officials were quickly introduced early
in 1942. These, however, met with the opposition of the Finance
Committee chaired by Makram Obayd, Minister of Finance. The
Committee reported that no exceptions should be made or approved,
and this led to a split between Nahhas and his Finance Minister who
was also Secretary General of the Party.

Here personal politics became complicated and devious. The
King, through the intermediary of his Royal Cabinet chief,
Hasanayn, took this early opportunity to exploit the apparent break
in the ranks of the Wafd Party hierarchy. A campaign to detach
Makram from his leader was set in motion. Its most obvious aspect
consisted of a series of invitations to Makram without the knowledge

of Nahhas to consult with the King about various trivial matters such as new banknote designs and the like. Meantime, under pressure from his wife, Zaynab al-Wakil, Nahhas supported applications from her relatives for special import licences and other government favours. This further strained relations with his Finance Minister. In May 1942 Nahhas found a way of getting rid of Makram. He submitted to the King the resignation of his government in the knowledge that the British would not countenance any other. The King immediately asked him to form a new one. Nahhas did so, but without Makram in it. Then in July 1942 Makram was expelled from the party altogether with a few of his closest supporters.

Just as Nuqrashi and Ahmad Maher, who were expelled from the party in 1937, had formed the new Saadist Party a year later, Makram now went into opposition to the Wafd by forming his own *al-Kutla al-wafdiyya al-mustaqilla* (The Independent Wafdist Bloc) party.

To a great extent, this division in the Wafd reflected the problem of leadership. Nahhas had by then been leader of the party for fifteen years. His *za'ama* (personal leadership) was so well established that disagreements over party policy were considered a challenge to his personal authority. Palace-inspired intrigue to widen the rift between the two men – Nahhas and Makram – no doubt made matters worse. The presence moreover of Fuad Serag el-Din, Minister of Agriculture since 31 March 1942, also helped. Ambitious and conservative, he eventually succeeded Makram as Secretary General of the party.[6]

1943 was another crucial year in the continued deterioration of relations between King and government. It also marked the beginning of a concerted campaign by all other political groups in the country to discredit the Wafd and bring about the downfall of the Nahhas government. Early in the year Makram published his famous *Black Book* (*al-Kitab al-aswad*), which comprised mainly a record of Wafd venality in government and politics, and which clearly constituted an indictment of its leader. Nahhas persuaded Parliament to exclude Makram from the Chamber. Makram was denied his seat. Other Deputies raised the question of the control exercised over imports and other economic policies in Egypt by the British-organized and -operated Middle East Supply Centre. The usual battle between a King and Prime Minister over appointments also arose in all its fury. Nahhas on one hand was determined to appear the champion of the Constitution against a power-hungry monarch. The King on the other hand pressed for what he considered his royal prerogatives. Demonstrations organized by the Wafd shouted slogans such as 'Long Live Nahhas; beloved of the nation; sole leader of the nation.'

An early test case in this battle came with the government's dismissal of Shaykh Mustafa al-Maraghi, Shaykh of the Azhar. He had been appointed by King Faruq in 1937 and had always been very close to the young monarch. Faruq refused to approve the dismissal while Nahhas insisted that constitutionally the Cabinet dealt with such appointments and removals. Nahhas made relations with the King even worse by his public utterances regarding the Wafd's record of protecting the Constitution against its detractors and violators.[7]

Makram's *Black Book* meantime prompted all opposition parties and groups to come together in a united campaign against the Wafd government. In February 1944 a second edition of the book was published. Its contents were even more damning than those of the first edition. Makram claimed that Nahhas had sabotaged the sovereign rights of the nation in favour of Britain. The implication was clear: the Wafd's behaviour in this respect was the price it had to pay for coming to power behind the rumble of British tanks at Abdin Palace two years earlier.

A National Front of the opposition had in November 1943 delivered a Note concerning Egypt's rights to the assembled leaders of the Allied Powers (Roosevelt, Churchill and Chiang Kai Chek) at Mena House by the Pyramids. This was an indirect attack upon the Wafd government. Now again, in February 1944, the opposition National Front circulated a manifesto to the nation regarding Egypt's rights and the injustices of British imperialism which, with the help of a Wafdist government, had reduced their country to the status of a crown colony. Again, in May, another document listed the repressive measures taken by the Wafd in the past two years against their political opponents and adversaries.

By April–June 1944, the position of the Wafd government was clearly precarious. The opposition was creating trouble among the public; the King was looking for every opportunity to dismiss Nahhas. Nahhas in turn arrested Makram as the principal anti-Wafd agitator. Undaunted, the opposition National Front debated Egypt's projected rights after the war, the revision of the state of Anglo-Egyptian relations, and the participation of Egypt in any

Peace conference or United Nations Organization. Yet, when in April Faruq approached the British Ambassador through Hasanayn to sound him out over the possible removal of Nahhas, he found him not interested in a change of government.

Sensing that his popularity was being seriously diluted, Nahhas struck back with traditional tactics. He reached out once again for the student population, especially those in the Azhar institutions. He raised, for example, the Azhar's budget, and provided equal opportunities for Azhar diploma holders in state jobs. Another palliative was produced with the publication of a five-year social reform and public works plan. With this behind him, Nahhas launched a campaign of reconciliation with the Palace. But this came too late. The whole Allied position in the war had now changed. The actual danger to Egypt from the Axis had long receded; the war was now being fought on the Western European continent with the Axis forces in retreat. In short, Britain was no longer interested in a continued Wafd government in Cairo. The King and his advisers were equally in no mood, or need, to respond to the Wafd's overtures or reconciliation. On the contrary, the King now renewed his efforts to reassert his prerogatives in administrative matters and in Azhar affairs. As soon as the British withdrew their support, Nahhas was summarily dismissed on 8 October 1944. Conveniently the British Ambassador happened not to be in Cairo on that day.[8]

Ahmad Maher, leader of the Saadist Party, formed a new government of Saadists, Liberals and Kutla members. It held new elections in January 1945 which were boycotted by the Wafd. A 125 majority of Saadist members were returned to Parliament; 74 Liberals, 29 Kutla, 7 National Party and 29 Independents. This government also released all political prisoners like Makram, Ali Maher and others. Even though it abolished Wafd patronage and extraordinary promotions for state officials, this government nonetheless retired several under-secretaries and assistant secretaries of state, directors of ministries and other high-ranking state officials who were Wafdists. It introduced new measures to meet rising living costs and relieve low salaried personnel; it improved food supply and the import of essential commodities.

When, on 24 February 1945, the government (prompted by a desire to participate in the United Nations) had secured parliamentary approval for a declaration of war against the Axis, the Prime Minister was assassinated in the parliament buildings by a fanatic. He was succeeded by his old colleague and co-founder of the Saadist

Party, Mahmud Fahmi al-Naqrashi, an engineer by training, who formed a government very similar to Maher's. It was this government which formally declared war on 26 February 1945.

So far as Egypt was concerned the war had, for all practical purposes, come to an end. In any event, it came to a formal close in Europe in May, and in the Far East in August 1945. Needless to say, both Egyptian society and political conditions in the country at the end of that war were vastly different from what they had been at the end of the Great War in 1918–19. Whereas in the period 1919–23, the Wafd, under Zaghlul, had emerged as the leader of an independence movement accepted and supported by the masses of a still politically undifferentiated Egyptian public, now in 1945–6 its successors stood discredited as the leaders of the nationalist movement. What was worse in practical terms, they emerged as the losers in their battle with the King. Thus, the Wafd now was no longer the foremost radical group in Egyptian politics; rather it was viewed by both extremist conservative–religious and emerging leftist radical groups as the embodiment of privilege partly derived from political corruption. Its preoccupation with power since 1923 and its rare attainment of it was not followed by any forceful resolution of social and economic problems. A whole generation of educated, though rarely economically prosperous, Egyptians who had placed their faith in Wafdist leadership for the fulfilment of certain hopes saw its leaders kow-tow alternately to the King and the British when their interests required them to do so.

The so-called minority parties, most of which were splinter groups from the Wafd, had never managed in this period (1923–45) to build up sizeable constituencies among the public. To a great extent their opposition to the Wafd initially reflected personal differences among erstwhile colleagues and political comrades. After 1937 this opposition had acquired some basic differences among them regarding economic policy. The Saadists, for example, represented leading industrial and financial interests in the country. Then the National Party, legatee of that nationalist firebrand, Mustafa Kamil, had remained so intransigent over the issue of the evacuation of British troops from Egypt that it could not survive the brief period of compromise politics under a constitutional experiment. The urban masses and students it had attracted in the period 1907–14 had, by 1923, transferred their allegiance to the Wafd. As for the Liberals, grouped around Adli Yeken and Abd al-Khaliq Sarwat since 1921–2, they

had assumed the mantle of the old Jarida–Umma group of intellectuals. But they, too, were a splinter group from the wider so-called
secular liberal élite that emerged in the period 1900–14. Some of
them, like Ahmad Lutfi, were members of the first Wafd, or delegation, in 1918–19. Their formal organization as the Liberal Constitutionalist Party in 1922 was in great measure the outcome of the personal break between Adli and Zaghlul over the leadership of the
1921–2 negotiations with Britain.

Another shift in the allegiance of the inchoate masses, suffering
from the deprivation and difficult economic conditions of war,
occurred in the crucial period 1945–9. This was not simply the result
of disillusionment with the old Wafd leadership and/or performance
of the various parties of the ruling establishment. It was also the
result of new factors which changed the nature and content of the
national movement. Even though the latter was still mainly taken up
in the first five years after the war with the ending of the relationship
with Britain – the evacuation of British troops from the Suez Canal
area and elsewhere in the country – it had already acquired a radical
socio-economic content. This, in turn, was influenced by the emergence of the Soviet Union as one of the two super powers after the
war, by the impact of anti-colonial independence movements in parts
of Asia, and later by the impact of the Communist revolution in
China. Simultaneously, the end of British imperial rule in India in
1947, the termination of the French mandates in Lebanon and Syria,
the Palestine Question and the emergence of the State of Israel, and
generally the recession of Anglo-French power and influence from
the Near and Middle East had an effect upon the radicalization of
the Egyptian national movement. Finally, the exhaustion of old
political ruling groups from their internecine struggle left them
divided among themselves, thus permitting the greater autocracy of
the monarch.

All this left a vacuum of leadership and power in street, factory,
school, university and the countryside at large, which vacuum was
nearly filled thunderously and violently for a time by the radicals
of the Right in the period 1945–52; by the Ikhwan and Young Egypt.
The activities of these organizations, particularly of the Ikhwan, in
seven years sapped the strength of the old establishment and made
them unable to govern. Left with no alternative, the country woke
up one morning to a military take-over of power.

The old political groups, then, had lost their hegemony after the
last war partly because they had lost their control over the organized

– and not so organized – masses of city folk, the youth in schools and universities, the increasing numbers of industrial workers, but most important, the soldiers. In turn, this was partly due to their inability to satisfy – deliberately or otherwise – some of their demands while they still claimed a radicalism in the leadership of the national movement they no longer possessed. Their leadership, that is, had been so seriously challenged – by the Ikhwan for example – that by 1952 it was no longer credible. This disability of a tarnished public image would have made no real difference in terms of the survival of these old political groups had its currency been confined to the civilian population. But it had already prompted paramilitary political groups to violent action,[9] and soon the professional soldiers to rebellion.

Ironically the old parties themselves had contributed to the political radicalism which erupted after the war. Regardless of whether they dealt adequately with any socio-economic problems or not, they had to bring them to public attention during elections. To this extent they contributed to the political – and radical political – education of the Egyptian public. The extreme and radical use of Islam for political purposes in the late 1920s and 1930s, together with the signing by Egypt on 7 October 1944 of the Alexandria Protocol for the formation of the League of Arab States and its subsequent adherence to the League's Covenant on 22 March 1945, provided the basis of a new Arab–Islamic dimension of nationalist agitation – a new political orientation for the masses. This, moreover, was more amenable to exploitation by various political groups because it was more easily understood and more readily adhered to emotionally by the masses than an already discredited, complex and essentially alien constitutional democracy.

Events moved swiftly. The Saadist-led government of Nuqrashi assumed that it could easily wrest the leadership of the national question from the Wafd. At the same time, by taking the initiative in requesting new talks with Britain, they also assumed that they would dilute the appeal of the extremist political organizations such as the Ikhwan. But their diplomatic moves in the autumn of 1945 had been preceded by their own deliberate campaign to expose the corruption of the Wafd and thus to discredit its leadership. Commissions of inquiry had been appointed to investigate the financial dealings of Wafdist Ministers during the war. The measure in itself, regardless of any findings by these commissions, suggested impropriety. A Press campaign in government and pro-government organs referred to the dictatorship of Nahhas when the Wafd was in power. This way too the Nuqrashi government was trying to take the thunder out of the Wafd's Memorandum to the British Ambassador in July of that year regarding evacuation.

On 9 June 1945 censorship was lifted from the Press; so was the ban on political associations and meetings. On 4 October martial law was abolished. Meantime, a Labour government had come to power in London in July. Very soon thereafter, in December, the Egyptian government formally requested the assumption of talks with representatives of the British government with a view to a revision of the 1936 Treaty. The British government's reply on 26 January 1946 was vaguely non-committal: it expressed their intention to look into the possibility of preliminary talks. The exchange of Notes was published in the Egyptian Press on 30 January.

What effect wartime declarations about self-determination, freedom of nations and the like (e.g. the Atlantic Charter of 1941) and the UN San Francisco Conference had in exciting Egyptian national demands is difficult to say. Yet the repercussions of this vague initial Anglo-Egyptian exchange of Notes were immediate and violent. They took the form of mass demonstrations by students in February and March 1946 of unprecedented ferocity and bloodshed.

Ever since the autumn of 1945 new radical student and workers committees had been organized for political action. Such were the Workers Committee for National Liberation, the National Committee of Students and Workers in Cairo and Alexandria, the Federation (Congress) of Egyptian Trade Unions and others. Cultural and intellectual clubs, associations and publishing houses which sprang up towards the end of the war were just as radical: the Centre of Scientific Research (*Dar al-abhath al-ilmiyya*), writers and editors grouped round the reviews *The New Dawn* (*Al-Fajr el-jadid*) and *Al-Talia* (*The Vanguard*), the Committee for the Dissemination of Modern Education and Culture, and others. What was interesting about these new groups was that they combined a programme of national liberation (i.e., the evacuation of British forces from Egypt) with the 'liberation of the exploited masses from a capitalist minority'. Marxist and Communist Party agitators had infiltrated several trade unions and student organizations, such as the Universities Alumni Association. These were also active as teachers in the New People's University founded in Cairo where they conducted night classes for workers. They were all activist and radical, and played a major role in the labour strikes and student demonstrations which followed from February 1946 until 1952.

One effect these organizations had – apart from the repressive measures they elicited from the government – was on the new tactics and programmes of the Wafd, the Ikhwan and other established political groups. All these adopted more radical social and economic reform platforms in their political propaganda. Thus, the leftist element in the Wafd took up, via the pages of the *al-Misri* newspaper, the cause of the urban proletariat. It even attacked the capitalists, discussed unemployment, and deplored the country's poor economic condition. The *al-Misri*, however, was owned and published by the brothers Abul Fath, who were not at that time devoid of political ambition. If this campaign, as well as making the Wafdist policy more radical and thus more appealing to the masses, also challenged the party's leadership, then it was in line with their own political aims.

More consistent in this respect was the monthly journal *al-Baath*, founded and edited by the Wafd leftist Muhammad Mandur in 1944–6. It provided a platform for the new generation of literary critics and other intellectuals who advocated a link between the intelligentsia and the rural and urban working masses of the country. These were alienated from 'official society' to the extent that they demanded the limitation of landownership as early as 1945 and the intervention of the State in bringing about radical economic and social change. As intellectuals, they viewed their task as one of awakening the social and political consciousness of the masses. They considered their intellectual peers and masters as 'Old Men' (*shuyukh*) who were insulated and isolated from the socio-economic problems and material needs of the vast majority of the Egyptian people. Whereas in the twenties and the thirties their peers had been interested in culture, they were now concerned with social justice, economic equality and political freedom. Their resistance to alien rule and/or influence was now coupled to their idea of a struggle for political and economic freedom from the native ruling classes – at this time identified as the leaders of the various political parties.

Similarly, the Ikhwan introduced vast social welfare schemes into their activities: insurance for workers, health care and others. Their newspaper, *al-Ikhwan al-muslimun*, came to have in 1946 a wide circulation; so did their monthlies *Al-Shihab* and *al-Talib al-misri*, the latter of which was addressed to university students. Then the Young Egypt Party conveniently became the Socialist Party of Egypt.

359

Even though both the Ikhwan and the new radical leftists appealed to the petty-bourgeoisie in the country, the former were politically more successful until 1952, having won over a great number of followers from the masses. The leftists were at a disadvantage, for not only were their leadership and spokesmen from the Western and westernized sectors of society, but their proposals for reform and change were based on a foreign ideology.

In January 1946 all parties and groups had been agitating for the abrogation of the 1936 Treaty. Inflammatory editorials in their Press organs calling the people to combat and sacrifice fanned this agitation. They publicized Britain's unwillingness to negotiate the evacuation of their bases in the country. When the exchange of Notes became public, the reaction came primarily from the younger clientèle of these groups: the student and workers organizations. Already, a serious strike of over thirty thousand textile workers in Mehalla al-Kubra and Shubra al-Khayma near Cairo had begun, which later in the summer had spread to Alexandria and elsewhere.

Student organizations sent a petition to the King urging him to accelerate the government's efforts in resolving the question of Anglo-Egyptian relations. On 9 February, several thousand Cairo University students marched in a mass demonstration from the university grounds in Giza towards Abdin Palace. They shouted such slogans as 'No negotiation without evacuation.' When they reached Abbas Bridge over which they had to cross the river to reach the city, their route was blocked by a strong police force. They clashed with this, and scores of them were injured. Moreover, the bridge was opened and several students apparently drowned in the river.

Significantly, the demonstrators were objecting to the lenient tone of the initial Note of the Egyptian government to Britain. This was typical in recent Egyptian political history: a government would intermittently revive the issue of Anglo-Egyptian relations. Having made this serious political gesture (which was rarely gauged against their capacity to see its practical implications through), the issue would move to the streets. In the process of whipping it up, the opposition groups would also conveniently aim at the government's downfall.

Typically, the incident led to a government crisis. The four Independent Wafdist Bloc Ministers resigned on 14 February and the government fell on the 15th. The King asked the reputed 'strong man' of Egyptian politics, Ismail Sidqi, to form a government on the 17th. This consisted of Independents and Liberals. At first, Sidqi adopted a permissive policy towards political demonstrations. Not unexpectedly, the various student and workers organizations assigned Thursday, 21 February 1946, as 'Evacuation Day', called for a General Strike, and announced the holding of mass demonstrations. A clash between the thousands of demonstrators and British Army personnel in Midan Ismailiyya near the Kasr al-Nil Barracks resulted in several deaths among the demonstrators. There were demonstrations that month in other cities and towns – Alexandria, Mansura, Zaqaziq and Assiut. Immediately these bloody incidents ended, the same organizations declared Monday, 4 March, as 'Martyr's Day', and a day of national mourning featuring another general strike. There were incidents on that day too in Alexandria which resulted in casualties among student demonstrators. The death toll was particularly high: twenty-eight students died in clashes with the police and in an exchange of fire with British troops in a sea-front hotel.

Soon after Lord Killearn had been replaced in February 1946 as British Ambassador in Cairo by Sir Ronald Campbell, the Sidqi government announced in March–April the composition of an official delegation to conduct talks with British government representatives. This included leaders and members of all political parties except the National and Wafd, as well as Independents. A British communiqué on the preliminary talks on 7 May 1946 indicated willingness to evacuate bases in the country if agreement on the use of the Canal Base could be reached. Official talks began on 9 May, but broke down in July. In the meantime British troops had evacuated their Cairo Citadel command post.

After a brief but unsuccessful attempt to strengthen his hand in another round of talks by the formation of a National government, Sidqi went to London for private talks with Bevin in October 1946. A draft project of a treaty was published at the end of these talks, but it was unacceptable to several members of the official Egyptian delegation set up earlier that year. The delegation was disbanded. One of the difficulties was the special Protocol on the Sudan included in the draft project to retain the 1899 Condominium arrangement. Sidqi in effect had acquiesced to the British insistence that there should be no change in the arrangements affecting the Sudan without prior consultation of the Sudanese themselves. He had thus thrown overboard the Egyptian demand of the unity of the Nile Valley included in the initial Note of the Nuqrashi government in 1945. Even though Sidqi and Bevin had initialled this draft agreement providing for a combined defence committee and a postponement of the Sudan question, the project came to nothing. The Sidqi government fell in December.

On the domestic front Sidqi had by the summer of 1946 moved forcefully against radical leftist groups. Several arrests of suspected Communists were made in July 1946. Among about two hundred and fifty arrests, there were several Alexandrian Greeks. Communist associations, and groups suspected of Communist leanings, were dissolved. Leftist publications were stopped, among them a new left Wafdist newspaper, *Sawt al-umma* (The Voice of the Nation), edited by the literary critic Muhammad Mandur. Legislation was introduced in Parliament to strengthen certain provisions of the Penal Code and thus to provide stiff sentences against subversives.

Meanwhile, the Sidqi–Bevin talks and their outcome had elicited further demonstrations by Wafd extremists and the Ikhwan. In November 1946, university students formed a National Front of Students of the Nile Valley organization. They overturned street cars and set them on fire; and they burned English books. When the police intervened to restore order, it became clear for the first time that students were armed with light weapons, hand grenades, etc. Scores of Ikhwan members were arrested. To make matters worse the British Governor-General of the Sudan declared his government's intention to prepare the Sudan for independence.

The new Nuqrashi Saadist–Liberal government took office on 9 December 1946. Talks with Britain broke down completely that month, and the Egyptian government decided to refer the question of Anglo-Egyptian relations to the United Nations Security Council. Public agitation over the Sudan question mounted rapidly: 19 January 1947, the anniversary of the signing of the 1899 Anglo-Egyptian Condominium Agreement, was a day of 'national mourning' and demonstrations. In August, the Nuqrashi government presented its case to the UN Security Council. A month later this new policy had proved unsuccessful in budging the British from their position over the Sudan. Britain adhered to the provisions of the 1936 Treaty, and insisted on bilateral talks for its revision. Moreover, it accelerated its encouragement of an independence movement in the Sudan.

It is interesting, however, that this first experience of Nuqrashi at the UN prompted him to consider the advantages of a so-called neutralist policy, i.e., one of seeking the aid of other powers as a counterweight to Britain.[10] However, Nuqrashi's performance at the UN had been undermined by the Wafd's formal Note to that international body, in which it claimed that Nuqrashi's delegation did not represent the Egyptian nation and therefore was not entitled to argue the country's case before the Security Council.

The evacuation by British forces of several air stations and other military installations in the Cairo and Alexandria areas since July 1946 could have eased the political pressure on the Nuqrashi government. The RAF, for instance, had relinquished the Helwan air station and Heliopolis airport (October 1946 and March 1947); base camps on the Alexandria–Cairo desert road were vacated in February 1947; so were other camps in the Alexandria area. Finally, the Abbasiyya and Kasr al-Nil barracks were handed over to Egypt in March 1947. Other difficulties, however, arose to plague the government, beginning in the summer of 1947.

One of these was financial and economic: during the war, Egypt had accumulated sterling balances in London of just under four hundred million pounds which had been blocked by the British government, and efforts were made by the Egyptian government to release certain amounts which were urgently required to finance imports, arms and other state expenditures. They were also required in covertible form to secure hard currencies. Interim agreements over these balances were reached in June 1947 and January 1948. But these released barely more than a fourth of the total balances available in London.

Another difficulty was the outbreak of a cholera epidemic in September. Deaths from the disease were in the thousands. Yet government measures in combating the disease were of such magnitude and efficiency that the epidemic had been arrested within three months of its outbreak. With this success, opposition groups could hardly make political capital out of this short-lived national disaster. But no sooner had this emergency passed than a new and politically more dangerous crisis arose.

On 29 November 1947, the General Assembly of the UN had passed a Partition of Palestine Resolution. As a founding member of the Arab League, the Egyptian delegation had voted against the Resolution, and the Egyptian government became committed to participate in any collective Arab action against its implementation in Palestine. Soon, however, extremist groups in Egypt used their mass public protest demonstrations against the Resolution to undermine the government further. The Ikhwan, for instance, were able to transform the Arab–Jewish conflict in Palestine and particularly the support which the Western powers gave the Partition Resolution at the UN into an Arab–Islamic Holy War against infidels.[11]

Ever since 1945, the political troubles of the country, partly reflected in a series of industrial strikes and student demonstrations against Britain, were accompanied by a campaign of violence: assassinations and attempted assassinations of public figures and government ministers. Leaders of this campaign were undoubtedly the Ikhwan. Thus, the assassination of Prime Minister Ahmad Maher in February 1945 was followed almost a year later in January 1946 with the assassination of Amin Othman (a known Anglophile) in the streets of Cairo in broad daylight. Othman's assassin had only a month earlier (December 1945) attempted to blow up Nahhas's car with a hand grenade which missed. There were similar grenade and gelignite attacks on public places perpetrated by the Ikhwan and other radical groups throughout 1946 and 1947, in both Cairo and Alexandria. One of these, a gelignite explosion in the Metro Cinema in which several people were killed, occurred on 6 May 1947, the anniversary of Faruq's accession to the throne.

More ominous was the attempt by the Ikhwan and other extremists to intimidate members of the judiciary with threats of assassination and actual bombing attacks. The Secretary of the Cairo Court of Appeals was murdered in March 1948 for his part two years earlier in the Alexandria court trial of Ikhwan 'bombers'. In April, unknown assailants tried to dynamite Nahhas's residence in Garden City.[12]

When Egyptian troops marched into Palestine on 15 May 1948 together with the troops of other Arab states, to forestall the establishment of an Israeli state, acts of violence were directed against foreign- (and Jewish-) owned commercial and trade establishments. Thus in the summer of 1948 the large department store, Cicurel, was damaged by dynamite. So was the exclusive store David Ades. Other attacks on similar establishments followed: Benzion and Gattegno's. The head offices of the largely British-owned Meadi Land Company were blown up too. An explosion in the Jewish quarter of Cairo killed a score of the inhabitants and injured many more. The offices of another large foreign-owned enterprise, Société Orientale de Publicité, were blown up in November. The year ended with a bold attack upon the Chief of Cairo Police, Salim Zaki, blown up in his car by a grenade thrown down from the roof of one of the Medical School buildings in Qasr al-Aini where striking students had barricaded themselves. In short, the violent terrorist campaign of these years was aimed at everyone: the government, the foreigners and the British in Egypt.

Fortunately for the government, the hostilities in Palestine had required the imposition of Martial Law in the country as of 15 May 1948. Under its provisions the Prime Minister also became the Military Governor of the country. Thus on 8 December Nuqrashi ordered the dissolution of the Ikhwan, a ban on all its activities, and the confiscation of its funds and property. A wide police raid on its headquarters and branch offices revealed the extent of its organization and activities. For the country, and particularly the ruling classes, the results were chilling. Its financial holdings, for instance, were vast. Its front and other activities ranged from schools and institutes, trade and labour unions, clinics, commercial enterprises such as an Arab minerals company, a publishing house, an Arab publicity company, a textiles company, insurance company and others. More dangerous were its paramilitary training centres, arms and munitions caches. Its *Jawwala* (Vigilantes) organization consisted of cells of fanatic members who were well trained in the use of small arms and explosives.

The answer of the Ikhwan to the dissolution of their organization came twenty days later. One of their members, disguised as a police officer, murdered Nuqrashi, the Prime Minister, as he was going up to his office. A new government was quickly formed by another Saadist, Ibrahim Abd al-Hadi, who had been appointed Chief of the Royal Cabinet in February 1947. The latter post had been vacant for about a year after the death of Ahmad Hasanayn in a car accident in February 1946.

Abd al-Hadi's government now comprised, in addition to Saadists, Liberals and Independents, two National Party members. It proceeded to tighten security and launched a repressive campaign against terrorist organizations. Nevertheless, violent acts of sabotage and attempted assassinations continued unabated. Then, on the evening of 12 February 1949, Hasan al-Banna, Supreme Guide of the Ikhwan, was murdered by unknown assassins.[13] On 5 May, Ikhwan members tried to retaliate with an abortive attempt on the Prime Minister's life.

Meantime, hostilities in Palestine came to an end, and Egypt had signed an Armistice Agreement with Israel in February 1949. Yet in view of the public order and security conditions in the country, Parliament approved on 15 May the government's request for the extension of martial law for another year. The performance of the

Egyptian Army in the Palestine War was, on balance, anything but creditable, let alone brilliant. The famous reception ('victory') parade laid on by the government in Cairo on 10 March 1949 to honour the returning troops that had been besieged in Faluja only papered over the cracks in the deteriorating political situation which followed what was virtually a defeat of Arab armies in Palestine. The Ikhwan, for instance, albeit proscribed, continued to lead clandestinely the agitation against the *status quo*. They distributed propaganda tracts against the government and the King. They used mosques, Azhar and state university students to disseminate their seditious literature. The government, for its part, resumed Sidqi's 1946 repressive campaign against all extremists with numerous arrests of suspected members of leftist and Communist organizations.

The cost of the Palestine War placed the government in serious financial difficulties and led to the first huge deficit in Egypt's budget in many years. Various new income tax schemes affecting capital gains and investment dividends were rejected by Parliament. Since the latter institution consisted mainly of wealthy Deputies and Senators its rejection of new tax legislation gave added impetus to anti-government agitation and propaganda. Also, the government's treatment of arrested citizens was reputedly so harsh that families of internees often suffered financial hardship.

In these difficult circumstances, the usual political remedy was sought once again by the Palace, namely, the constitution of a coalition government. This was easier to achieve now, for the Wafd, terrified by the violence of terrorism in the country, was ready to compromise. It had witnessed the flouting of state authority and power by the Ikhwan, and the near total discrediting of the Monarch's prestige. Yet the Wafd extracted its price this time too: it agreed to participate in such a national government provided Abd al-Hadi relinquished the Premiership. Thus on 26 July 1949, the Independent Husayn Sirri formed a government including members from all the major parties.[14]

The new government now sped to mollify extremists by a gesture of a return to normalcy. It released most political prisoners and promised to abolish martial law. It also appointed an all-party cabinet committee to implement an electoral redistricting scheme on the basis of the latest (1947) Population Census. But such coalitions rarely made for smooth political sailing in Egypt. The Wafd was certain of its return to power. Other parties were bound to fall out over the electoral redistricting; and they did. On 3 November 1949, the King was forced to ask Sirri to form another independent caretaker government to prepare the country for national elections.

Parliament was dissolved on 6 November and elections were held on 3 January 1950. Some re-polling for several seats was conducted on 10 January. The elections returned a Wafdist majority to Parliament, even though the Wafd polled barely 40 per cent of the votes cast.[15] Significantly, one Young Egypt Socialist and one Labour deputy were elected. Among the 38 Independents there were, this time, several who were rumoured to hold radical leftist views. There were at the time also allegations of Wafdist intimidation of and pressure on voters in polling stations in Cairo and Alexandria. In any event, Nahhas formed his seventh and last government.

Once in power the Wafd proceeded to retrench its position in the administration and the country at large. Patronage and administrative promotions were again resorted to, costing several millions of pounds. On the popular front, the government promised the palliative of an attack upon outstanding social and economic problems, such as living costs, housing, industrial and land reform. The most dazzling measure, though, was the project introduced by Taha Husayn, Minister of Education, to make all secondary and technical education gratis.[16]

The Saadist governments before them had led the way with legislation to ameliorate some of the glaring socio-economic difficulties. The Nuqrashi government, for example, had introduced a progressive taxation law; it had built more hospitals and health units in villages; it had extended drinking water to certain areas in the countryside; it had constructed a workers' city in Embaba, a densely populated industrial quarter in Cairo. An engineer himself, Nuqrashi had always been keenly interested in electrification projects. Thus he reactivated the hydro-electric scheme at Aswan. To encourage further industrialization in the country he had founded in 1947 the Industrial Bank. Relevant to this was the new law promulgated the same year to regulate Egyptian companies, requiring that all companies should be 51 per cent Egyptian owned. Furthermore, he nationalized a major public utility: the Cairo Electricity Company. He encouraged and supervised the completion of the first Egyptian Civil Code since 1883, drafted under the chairmanship of the eminent jurist Abd al-Razzaq al-Sanhuri, and published in 1948. Nuqrashi's government also produced the first serious Military Selective Service Law.

The Wafd carried on in 1950–1 with more legislation affecting socio-economic problems, but this time it dealt more directly with the welfare of the working and rural classes. There were, for instance, a Collective Work Contract Law (July 1950); a Sickness Compensation Act (August 1950); a High Cost of Living Allowance Law (February 1950); and a bill authorizing the distribution of a million *feddans* to landless peasants (May 1951).

More serious difficulties arose when the Wafd approached once again the question of Anglo-Egyptian relations, as this released organized popular groups in all their fury. In March 1950, barely two months after its coming to power, the Wafd requested the resumption of talks with the British government. These lasted on and off for nineteen months (March 1950–October 1951), and ended with the Egyptian unilateral abrogation of the 1936 Treaty and the 1899 Sudan Condominium Agreement on 8 October 1951.

Somehow, and perhaps erroneously, the Wafd felt certain it could immediately recapture its old popularity and re-impose its traditional control over the mobs. In May 1950 it had repealed martial law and by the end of that summer it had packed the Senate with its recommended appointees. It had not, however, anticipated the tenacious adherence of a British Labour government to the provisions of the 1936 Treaty and their unhesitating use of force against Egyptian guerrilla operations and sabotage to protect their installations and military personnel in the Canal zone.

To the various radical organizations and particularly to the masses of students who by that time had been infiltrated by such radical agents, the unilateral abrogation of the Treaty meant clearly that the British military presence in Egypt was illegal. More important, they now considered it open to attack by force. While Britain reinforced its garrison in the Canal, Egyptian labour (between 60,000 and 100,000 strong) at the instigation of various political groups and organizations refused to work in British camps. Egyptian railways delayed or plainly refused to transport British supplies and personnel. Egyptian customs officials delayed clearance of goods destined for British bases; so did longshoremen and stevedores. Egyptian contractors and suppliers of British troops broke their contracts; tradesmen withdrew their services and business.

Anti-British demonstrations soon flared up in Ismailiyya and Port Said, leading to clashes with patrolling British Army units. Key bridges, such as the Firdan (near Kantara) linking the Delta with the Sinai, and other vital communications points were occupied by

British forces; so was the Suez Customs House. Soon the whole Canal zone was cordoned off by British troops. All communications between Suez and other parts of the country had been cut. Moreover, they isolated the Egyptian forces posted in the Sinai, with head-quarters at al-Arish, from those west of the Canal. They virtually occupied Sharqiyya province with its vital centre of Tel el-Kebir.

Egyptian guerrilla squads were quickly formed, consisting mainly of students, peasants (especially from the Canal area), workers and a few radical members of the intelligentsia, a very few army officers and non-commissioned officers. The bulk of the guerrilla recruits came perhaps from the Ikhwan. Armed clashes between these squads and British Army units occurred for the next three months (November 1951–January 1952) and occasionally pitched battles were fought.[17]

The Wafd government were now faced with a difficult situation, partly of their own making. They had no way of really controlling these guerrilla operations by Egyptian irregulars. They were, justifiably so, perhaps, unwilling to pitch units of the Egyptian regular army against superior British forces in the Canal. Above all, they hesitated over what to do. They could have conceivably taken up the sytematic training and organization of these irregular forces pending some diplomatic resolution of their difficulties with Britain. They could, on the other hand, have attempted to prevent the guerrilla squads from operating against the British in the Canal. Disastrously, they did no more than recall the Egyptian Ambassador to the Court of St James; and while they hesitated over what to do next the British commanders had pursued mopping-up operations which ever widened the sector of their actual military control. By January 1952, it was clear that British forces were relentlessly moving towards the capital.

In these conditions, the opposition groups assumed correctly that the Wafd government was not prepared to risk armed combat with British troops. Demonstrations in Cairo and student strikes from 16 January 1952 onwards indicated clearly the opposition to both the government and the King. Furthermore, several of the demonstrating students publicly displayed their arms and used them against the police. The government realized that subversive and seditious elements had by now decided to use the Anglo-Egyptian crisis for their own political ends.

On 25 January, the British commander in the Ismailiyya area wished to clear the city of all armed Egyptian personnel including the police and gendarmerie posted there. In fact he planned a straightforward occupation of the city. He therefore handed in an ultimatum to the Egyptian police and gendarmeries (*boulouk nizam*) demanding that they surrender their arms, evacuate the governorate buildings and compound, and depart from the city. On orders from the Minister of Interior, Fuad Serag el-Din, the local Egyptian police commander rejected the ultimatum. British artillery and armour destroyed the compound and decimated its Egyptian defenders. Over fifty policemen and gendarmes were killed; many more were wounded. The next day, 26 January, the mobs burned Cairo.

Over 750 establishments were destroyed, at least thirty people lost their lives in the holocaust, and several hundred others were injured. The chaos – the breakdown of order – was complete. Martial law was quickly introduced that evening and Nahhas was appointed Military Governor-General of the country. A curfew was imposed and supervised by the military. Next day, 27 January, in the evening, the King dismissed the Nahhas government.

Another reputed 'strong man' of Egyptian politics, Ali Maher, formed an independent government with a view to restoring order. The Wafd and other political parties must have been so terrified by events that they readily gave Ali's government a vote of confidence in Parliament. Guerrilla squads and other Egyptian combatant units were withdrawn from the Canal zone; transport services and other facilities for British forces were resumed. Some reconstruction in Cairo was begun and financial compensation to owners of commercial establishments by the government was approved. The defeated Wafd tried during this time to patch up its relations with the King in the hope of returning to power soon.

But this government resigned on 1 March 1952 over the issue of the postponement of parliamentary meetings, to be succeeded by another independent government headed by Nagib Hilali. The latter hastily and desperately approved pay rises and other benefits for police and army officers – both of whose services were now obviously badly needed by any government. It dissolved Parliament on 24 March and announced fresh elections for 18 May; but later it postponed holding them indefintely.

It was now suspected that the King favoured a return to a Palace-controlled government. Hilali's Cabinet resigned on 28 June and Husayn Sirri formed a new government on 2 July. The King's interest in greater control over any government was perhaps reflected in the inclusion of his personal Press Adviser, Karim Thabit, as

Minister of State in the new Sirri Cabinet. It was during the new tenure of office of this government that a crisis arose in the army which provided the appropriate moment for the Free Officers coup on 23 July 1952.

Without suggesting that the events described in this chapter were inevitably bound to lead to a revolution against the established régime, I wish to suggest instead that the breakdown of law and order was as much the result of conditions in the country as it was the result of the Wafd's and other political parties' weak and frequently ill-considered policies. In fact, when in power, the Wafd tried to take on tasks which it could not fulfil given its resources and abilities. The moment they severed their special relationship with Britain – which had also served as a prop for their rule – they had sealed their own fate in the country. It is unlikely they had expected an army coup; it is even highly probable that this eventuality hardly crossed their minds. Perhaps after the fiasco in Palestine it should have.

When the King tried to tamper with the officer corps, the Establishment had no alternative makeweight force to the army. The police and other security forces were in a shambles. Meantime, the State's authority and the leadership of all the established political groups had been seriously challenged by paramilitary, extremist organizations, as was clearly the case with the Ikhwan. Above all, the Wafd and their opponents among the older established political parties had imprisoned themselves in the intemperate tone of their irresponsible promises which they knew very well they could not fulfil; and which only served to encourage violence in the country.

CHAPTER 17

REVOLUTION AND REPUBLIC
1952–79

Disaffection among army officers centred upon the relationship of their corps to the King. The latter had always tried to control the army through his senior military appointees, and the matter of army commissions had been a source of conflict between the monarch and the Wafd ever since independence in 1923. The Wafd at least for a while after 1936–7 had gained a measure of popularity with younger army officers when it liberalized entry into the Military Academy.

What really kept sedition out of the army was British control over it from 1882 until 1948. In 1882, the old Egyptian Army at the time of the Orabi Rebellion had been disbanded. Various military schools, founded by Muhammad Ali, expanded and improved by Khedive Ismail, were closed down. Many of the Egyptian Army units had been sent to the Sudan during the Mahdia war. Among these, some had perished in the ill-fated Hicks expedition against the Mahdi in 1883. A smaller force (about fifteen thousand) was then organized under the command of a British Sirdar. Conscription, since the introduction of the *badaliyya*[1] system, had been at a minimum. Yet both nationalists and the ambitious young Khedive Abbas Hilmi had constantly tried to expand and strengthen this army with a view to eroding British control over it. Khedive Abbas even urged some of the Egyptian Army personnel to commit acts of mutiny.

With independence in 1923, the Egyptian government wished to strengthen the army. This eventually led to the crisis of 1927 when Britain reasserted its control over the Egyptian Army by invoking the defence provisions of the 1922 Declaration. The 1936 Treaty abolished the office of Sirdar, but it provided for a British Military Mission to train the Egyptian Army. Moreover, it submitted this army to indirect British control in so far as both its training and equipment were to be exclusively provided by Britain. This state of affairs continued until 1948.

MILITARY CONSPIRACY AND COUP

Since 1936, many of the younger Egyptian Army officers had undergone Staff College and other advanced training both in Egypt and Britain. The political situation in the country, however, deteriorated at a time when British control over the army was diminishing. British troops themselves had by 1948 evacuated all centres they had occupied in the country since 1882 and retreated to their one supergarrison in the Canal area. Conspiracy and sedition in the officer corps, prompted by whatever grievances and causes, became possible. The breakdown of order in the country in 1950–1 was a most opportune time for this to happen. Above all, the new generation of officers had just lost the only war (in Palestine) the Egyptian Army had fought in sixty-five years. Rightly or wrongly, many of them believed that the politicians, the King, the *ancien régime* in its entirety were to blame for this humiliating defeat.

Ever since the February 1942 Incident, when the British Ambassador forced upon the King a Wafdist government by the threat of arms, Jamal Abd al-Nasir had frequently exchanged views with a few of his closest fellow-officers on how to rid the country of British control. Some among his colleagues who had been associated with Aziz Ali al-Masri, the old Army Chief of Staff, were involved in the latter's pro-Axis activities during the war. Others had been influenced by the extreme anti-foreign, anti-infidel views of the Muslim Brethren. A few of them were conservative Muslims by conviction and actually members of the Brethren organization. Still others had been impressed by the radical, national paramilitarism of the Young Egypt Association and, later, Party which some officers joined. Also, a very small minority among them had acquired leftist – Marxist and Communist – leanings. A strong impetus to their conspiratorial thinking generally, however, had come from their defeat in the Palestine War in 1948–9. It was their firm belief that their defeat in the field had been due mainly to the British control of Egyptian military training and arms supplies and to the involvement of the Palace and the politicians in several arms scandals.

Bonds of friendship between these officers had been cemented in the Military Academy, in various postings during the Second World War, in the Staff College, and in the attendance of other specialized military training schools. Affinity between some of them in their younger days derived partly from similar experiences in city and provincial town secondary schools in the thirties. Some of them even

shared common family backgrounds: they were sons of small landowners living in the provinces, or the sons of both lower and higher
salaried government employees. Others were sons and grandsons of
army officers. Significant perhaps was the fact that they represented
the first batch of entrants to the Military Academy who had come
from such 'middle-class' backgrounds.[2]

Apparently, nine of these officers met towards the end of 1949
and organized themselves as the constituent committee of a Free
Officers movement. These were Lieut. Col. Jamal Abd al-Nasir,
Major Abd al-Hakim Amer, Lieut. Col. Anwar al-Sadat, Major
Salah Salem, Major Kamal al-Din Husayn, Wing Comdr. Gamal
Salem, Squadron Leader Hasan Ibrahim, Major Khalid Muhieddin,
Wing Comdr. Abd al-Latif al-Boghdadi. Major Husayn al-Shafi'i
and Lieut. Col. Zakariyya Muhieddin came into this body later.[3]
In January 1950, Abd al-Nasir was elected chairman of this com-
mittee. He was re-elected to the chairmanship in January 1951 and
again in January 1952.

For the next two years, the members of this group recruited more
officers sympathetic to their cause. A campaign against the *status
quo* was launched both by word of mouth and in clandestinely
printed and distributed leaflets and pamphlets. Contacts were established with civilian elements opposed to the monarchy, particularly
among the members of the Cairo Press. What was important, however, was to attain as wide an infiltration of the officer corps as possible. The first institution in the Armed Forces establishment they
sought to control by lawful means was the Officers Club.

Elections for the presidency and board of directors of the Club
were scheduled for Thursday 27 December 1951. The Free Officers
had prepared their own slate of candidates to oppose that of the
more senior and known royalist officers. When King Faruq heard
about this he ordered the postponement of these elections. The Free
Officers nevertheless persuaded their assembled comrades (three to
four hundred officers) to proceed with the election. Moreover, in
keeping with the nationalist agitation of that period, the election was
preceded by political speeches delivered by the Free Officers to their
assembled comrades. They succeeded in getting their slate of candidates elected.

It is certain that Faruq viewed the Free Officers election triumph
in the Officers Club as a clear challenge to his control over the
army. He also suspected it as a prelude to sedition and therefore a
clear indication of the existence of a conspiracy in the officer corps.

For the next seven months he sought a way of reimposing his control.

Hilali's government of March–June 1952 had tried to placate the army and the police with pay rises and other benefits. Husayn Sirri, who succeeded to the premiership on 2 July 1952, made some effort to resolve the differences between the army and the King. He urged Faruq, for instance, to entrust the portfolio of Defence to General Muhammad Naguib. The latter, an infantry division commander who had acquitted himself comparatively well in the Palestine War (1948–9) and had been popular with the troops and some of the younger staff and line officers, had been the Free Officers' candidate for the Officers Club presidency to which he was elected in December 1951. The King rejected the proposal off-hand and Sirri's government resigned on July 20. Hilali now returned as Premier on the 22nd. But the King had virtually imposed his brother-in-law, Ismail Shirin, as Minister of War and Marine (Defence).

Shirin was not considered a professional by other army officers, even though he held the rank of colonel. To the Free Officers his appointment was clearly a royal attempt to reassert Palace control over the army. They also feared surveillance and arrest on charges of conspiracy. But they also realized that an Independent government such as Hilali's, appointed by the King, had no standing with any of the political parties. They appreciated accurately the weakened security conditions in the country which had been a consequence of the repeated governmental crises since October 1951. Above all, they appreciated the total break between Britain and the Wafd since that time and assumed, again correctly, that British armed intervention to thwart their coup was a remote possibility.

It seems the decision to carry out the coup was taken suddenly on the morning of 22 July. At midnight (22–3 July) about three thousand troops (infantry and armour) and some two hundred officers took control of the key Army Headquarters Barracks in Abbasiyya. The Army Chief of Staff, General Muhammad Farid, who had been holding an extraordinary meeting of senior officers to discuss army grievances, was arrested along with others. The GOC Armed Forces, General Muhammad Haydar, along with the rest of the government, had been in Alexandria for the summer. Troops commanded by Free Officers, their followers or sympathizers occupied the headquarters of the Frontier Force, all airports, the broadcasting station headquarters in Cairo and its relaying facilities at Abu Za'bal, the Cairo telecommunications centre, and all major roads and bridges in the city. At 7 am on 23 July, the first announcement of the take-over was made to the public over Cairo radio by Anwar al-Sadat. Strict security control was established throughout the capital, and all demonstrations – friendly or otherwise – were banned.

Hilali, the Prime Minister, also in Alexandria for the summer, abjectly informed Naguib that he was willing to accede to all of the army's demands. He was informed, however, that a new government would be formed to replace his own. Hilali resigned and the Free Officers asked Ali Maher to form a government of civil servants. The King, also in Alexandria, sought the intervention of the United States Ambassador. But by the time the latter had consulted Washington for instructions the army had occupied Alexandria too. With this accomplished, Naguib ordered Faruq on 25 July to dismiss several members of his own staff.

Terrified now, Faruq moved from Muntazah to Ras al-Tin Palace on the Alexandria seafront. But the new army rulers had ordered the captain of his seagoing yacht, *al-Mahrusa*, not to sail without their orders. The next day, Saturday 26 July, Faruq was ordered to abdicate and to leave the country permanently. His infant son, Crown Prince Ahmad Fuad, was proclaimed King and a Regency Council was appointed. At 6 pm that evening Faruq sailed on the *Mahrusa* for Italy.

Seventy years earlier, in 1882, another Egyptian colonel, Ahmad Orabi, had succeeded – but only temporarily – in challenging the ruler's control over the army. But his revolt was short-lived, for it invited a British occupation of the country. With India to the east, both Egypt and its Suez Canal were, at that time, of far greater and immediate importance to the British Empire. Now with hardly a British Empire left, it was the increased unlikelihood ever since 1945 of foreign power intervention which assured the success of the army movement in 1952.

In traditional political style all the party leaders hastened to congratulate the army for ridding the country of the 'tyrant' Faruq and to swear undying loyalty to the 'revolution'. Nahhas, the 'beloved and sole leader of the nation', raced back from his European holiday to do the same. What they did not understand was that the Free Officers were not *their clients*. They had come to power by force, and presumably in order to purify the country of all elements that had contributed to its plight since the Second World War.

CONSOLIDATION OF POWER

A series of measures which indicated the extent of the army's intention to rule followed in quick succession. A Revolution Command Council, consisting essentially of the old constituent committee of the Free Officers, was formed under the chairmanship of Nasser. It dictated interim policy to the civilian cabinet of Ali Maher, banned the practice of the government's removal to Alexandria every summer, abolished all civil titles (*pasha, bey*, etc.), and ordered all political parties to 'purify' their ranks and reconstitute their executives.

The first trouble came from the working classes. On 12 and 13 August 1952, a violent strike at the Misr Company textile factories in Kafr al-Dawar of the Delta involved over ten thousand workers. They attacked and set part of the premises on fire, destroyed machinery, and clashed with the police. When the latter could not cope with the demonstrators, the army was called in to restore order. This was achieved only after subduing the workers in a pitched battle in which several workers lost their lives and scores were injured. The reaction of the junta was quick, ruthless and brutal, for they could not countenance such violent disruption so soon after their coup. Although there has never been a clear official account of this bloody disturbance, the régime quickly set up a special military court which tried arrested textile workers. Two of the ringleaders were convicted and executed; many others were given prison sentences. What was more significant was that the régime followed this up with the arrest of nearly thirty persons on the charge that they belonged to the outlawed Communist movement. The Democratic Movement for National Liberation (MDLN), a faction of the Communist Party, reacted by denouncing the régime as a military dictatorship.

Meanwhile a government crisis arose as a result of the army's intention to introduce radical agrarian reform for the limitation of landownership and the distribution of land to peasant farmers.[4] Ali Maher's government resigned on 7 September and Muhammad Naguib headed what was still a civilian cabinet. The Agrarian Reform Law was decreed on 9 September, accompanied by a series of other measures calculated to forestall opposition from the political parties and other groups against the army régime. Thus a law for the reorganization of political parties and one abolishing all *waqfs* except those for charitable purposes (*waqf khayri*) were decreed. More indicative of the junta's intentions were the wide arrests of Palace officials and party leaders (about ninety persons altogether), even though many of these were released two months later. On the 14th, the higher civil service ranks were purged and some four hundred and fifty army officers retired. Immediate, though temporary, financial relief was secured when the new Finance Minister, Dr Abd al-Jalil al-Emari, negotiated with Britain the release of five million pounds of Egyptian sterling balances in London. To help deal with the long-range economic problems of the country a Permanent Council of National Production was organized on 2 October.

The junta also faced difficulties with the Regency Council it had appointed upon the abdication and exile of King Faruq, who were to act on behalf of the infant Crown Prince Ahmad Fuad. Consisting of three members – Prince Muhammad Abd al-Mon'em, Bahy al-Din Barakat, a liberal politician, and Colonel Rashad Mehanna, an artillery officer – the Council all but collapsed on 14 October. Suspected of Muslim Brethren connections, Colonel Mehanna was removed from the Council. At the same time, Barakat resigned from the Council, leaving only Prince Abd al-Mon'em as Regent.

Both the Muslim Brethren and the political parties sought actively throughout the period October–December 1952, to embarrass the junta: the Brethren by using the strength of their organization to demand a share in power, and the parties (particularly the Wafd) by clamouring for a new constitution and thus an early return to parliamentary government. The junta could not at first deal with both of these threats to their position simultaneously. Then the threat from the Brethren was far more serious than that from the political parties. Consequently, the new military rulers adopted a clever policy of appearing temporarily to respond to one while effectively neutralizing the other. Thus, in early November, the government decreed a general amnesty for all political criminals. This, of course, affected mainly the Muslim Brethren whose members had been the foremost terrorists in the preceding seven to eight years. At the same time, the junta decreed that all acts and measures taken by them to 'protect the revolution' could not be challenged in the courts for a period of six months. The Revolution Command Council then ordered a series of cabinet changes to bring in civilians who had not been associated with any of the old political parties.[5] It also attracted one or two leading members of the old Young Egypt association, and the National Party.[6]

Faced with the continued demand for a reinstatement of the Constitution from old party politicians led by the Wafd, the junta plunged in November–December 1952 into a countrywide campaign to drum up popular support. Several of its members, headed by General Naguib, embarked upon a whistle-stop campaign in the Delta and parts of Upper Egypt. At the same time, a Ministry of National Guidance was created on 10 November, headed by Fathi Radwan. The opposition was discomfited further when, after a re-shuffle of Naguib's Cabinet, the junta declared on 10 December the abolition of the 1923 Constitution. Two weeks later, it set up a Cor-ruption Tribunal to try public servants and members of Parliament who had allegedly abused the public trust to their own advantage. Several of those convicted were deprived of their political rights for a number of years.

The junta nevertheless felt compelled to make some gesture to-wards promulgating a new constitution and, early in January 1953, they went through the motions of preparing one. Undoubtedly, several members of the Revolution Council, perhaps all of them, may even have seriously wished a return to constitutional govern-ment. In any case, a fifty-member Commission to draft a Constitu-tion was appointed. Headed by Ali Maher, the Commission was of traditional composition: elder statesmen, lawyers, intellectuals, Azharites, lay and religious leaders of minority communities, and high-ranking army officers. The Commission, in turn, appointed its own 'Committee of Five' to report on the question, What form of government for Egypt, monarchy or republic?

The Commission, however, never had a chance to submit its report or findings, let alone a draft constitution, to the government and the people. For, in the meantime, the junta had proceeded to tighten its political control over the country. Thus, on 17 January 1953, all political parties were dissolved and banned, and their funds con-fiscated. Significantly, this measure was officially taken by the Chief of the Armed Forces who was also head of the government in his capacity as 'leader of the army movement'. With this, a three-year transition period was declared (17 January 1953–16 January 1956) during which the junta, now constituted as a Revolution Command Council, would rule. A provisional constitutional charter of general principles providing authority for the government of the RCC was proclaimed on 10 February 1953. Together with the Cabinet, the RCC became responsible for the setting of national policy.

A Liberation Rally was quickly launched to serve as an organiza-tion for the mobilization of popular support for the new régime. This was headed by Colonel Nasser. Other Free Officers such as Majors

Ahmad Tahawi and Abdullah Tu'ayma were appointed deputy secretaries-general in charge of labour affairs. Similarly, army officers were assigned to look after the Rally's youth activities and paramilitary training. Less than six months later, on 18 June 1953, the RCC decreed Egypt a republic, abolished the monarchy and put an end to the rule of the Muhammad Ali dynasty. Naguib became the first President in addition to being Prime Minister; Nasser became Deputy Premier and Minister of the Interior.

While introducing these changes, the junta brought in more of its trusted officers, and particularly members of the RCC, into ministerial positions. Similarly, expert technologists assumed the more technical ministries, e.g., Public Works. In October, Gamal Salem became Minister of Communications and Zakariyya Muhieddin Minister of the Interior. Earlier that summer Major Salah Salem had assumed the Ministry of National Guidance. Three months later in January 1954 Kamal al-Din Husayn replaced the civilian Abbas Ammar as Minister of Social Affairs.

Meanwhile, the properties and wealth of the deposed Faruq and all other members of the royal family were confiscated in September–November. Also, at this time, a permanent Revolution Tribunal was set up, consisting of three Free Officer members of the RCC – Abd al-Latif al-Boghdadi, President, Anwar al-Sadat and Hasan Ibrahim, members – to try *ancien régime* politicians.

By the end of 1953, the military régime had managed to overthrow the monarchy and, in great measure, to neutralize if not altogether destroy, *ancien régime* political leaders and groups. But its rule was by no means firmly established, widely accepted, or secure, for it still had to contend with the most powerful movement in the country – the Muslim Brethren. The latter had infiltrated deep into all sectors and strata of Egyptian society, particularly the student population, the poorer urban masses generally, and even the army. Ever since the coup in July 1952 they had hoped to exert a direct influence over the new military rulers. By June 1953, it had become clear to them that, despite their survival as a political–religious organization, they were no nearer to a direct participation in the military-controlled government. Yet they were encouraged in their prospects for they were the only remaining organized group that could conceivably challenge the new régime. Free Officer control via the Liberation Rally over various labour and other groups in the country was, in their view, too recent to be effective.

After an unsuccessful attempt by Colonel Nasser to split their Executive, the Brethren struck on 12 January 1954. Using the occasion of a memorial meeting in Cairo University to honour Egyptian dead in the Canal disturbances of 1951–2, they incited their student followers to demonstrate. Clashes followed between these and the pro-junta student members of Liberation Rally. Two days later, the government arrested the leaders and several members of the Brethren, dissolved the organization and proscribed all its activities. The Brethren went underground and soon came to control a secret apparatus in the army, which constituted an even more serious threat to the régime.

THE STRUGGLE FOR POWER BETWEEN NASSER AND NAGUIB

But the junta's rule was not solely threatened by the Brethren. It also suffered, quite naturally, from splits in the RCC, particularly differences between Colonel Nasser and General Naguib. Although not an original or active member of the Free Officer movement, the latter's eighteen months in office as Prime Minister and, since June 1953 President of the Republic, had earned him wide popularity in the country. Older than his RCC colleagues and a member of a military family (his father had been a brigadier in the Egyptian Army), he was by temperament more inclined to favour a return to constitutional government. He resented the RCC's dictation of policy, and criticized the summary sentences passed by the Revolution Tribunal on political leaders of the *ancien régime*. On 24 February 1954, Naguib resigned as President, Prime Minister, and Chairman of the RCC. Nasser was proclaimed chairman of the RCC and Prime Minister. The Presidency of the Republic remained vacant.

These changes produced an unexpected public reaction inside and outside Egypt. Himself half-Sudanese, Naguib's resignation (and suspected ouster) evoked official Sudanese representations to the Egyptian government. The nearly all-Sudanese Frontier Force was visibly displeased and threatened to mutiny. What was more serious was the dissension these events created within the officer corps. Armour officers led by Khaled Muhieddin, an original member of the Free Officers Executive and of the RCC, proceeded to challenge the Nasser faction in favour of Naguib's return to office. An extreme leftist, Khaled's interest in a return to civilian constitutional rule seemed to converge with that of the extreme rightist Muslim Brethren elements in the army. Naguib was obviously the man to lead such a move. Khaled may have also hoped to accede to the premiership under Naguib's Presidency. Anyway, Naguib was reinstated as President on 25 February but Nasser retained the Premiership – an indication that Khaled, who had risked an armed clash between his officer followers and those of the Nasser faction, had failed in his bid for power. The universities were closed down on 1 March and some hundred and twenty arrests were made, which included several Muslim Brothers, Socialist Party (the old Young Egypt) extremists, some Wafdists and Communists.

Pressure from the anti-Nasser elements within the army and the disturbances in Cairo nevertheless forced the junta to make certain concessions. These turned out to be temporary and served as time-gaining devices. Thus on 5 March the RCC voted for the election of a Constituent Assembly in July that year; for the abolition of martial law a month before elections; and the immediate lifting of censorship. Under these conditions, Naguib was reinstated on 8 March as Prime Minister and Chairman of the RCC, while Nasser reverted to his old post of Deputy Prime Minister. Then, on 25 March, the RCC decreed the restoration of political parties and the dissolution of the RCC on 24 July – the day assigned for the elections of the Constituent Assembly.

This sudden reversal of junta policy, indicating an intention to return to constitutional government, was interpreted as a clear triumph by Naguib over the RCC. It aroused opposition in the army. On 27 March, officers met to declare that their revolution was threatened by a restoration of the *ancien régime* and to insist that the RCC's March resolutions be rescinded. A similar protest came from the transport workers unions (about one million members), who went on a two-day strike. Major Tu'ayma, a Nasser supporter, who had been in charge of labour affairs in the Liberation Rally, was allegedly instrumental in organizing the strike. Predictably, the RCC in its meeting on 29 March announced the postponement of the implementation of the March 5 and 25 resolutions till the end of the 'transitional period' decreed in February 1953, i.e., till January 1956. This was followed on 5 April with a series of tough RCC measures intended to consolidate their position and 'protect the revolution'. These consisted mainly of a purge of the provincial and municipal councils, and of the Press, of so-called undesirable elements. More significant was the neutralization of civilian political leaders. On 15 April, the RCC issued a decree depriving all those members of the Wafd, Liberal and Saadist parties who had held ministerial posts in the period 6 February 1942 to 23 July 1952 of their political and civil rights for ten years. The powerful Journalists' Union Executive Council was dissolved on the same day. It was replaced by another whose members were appointed by the government.

By mid-April it was clear that the Nasser-led faction in the RCC and the army had emerged victorious from this phase of the power-struggle. But it would have been a hollow victory without the isolation of the opposition from sympathetic elements within the army. A number of officers (sixteen) were tried in April by the Revolution Tribunal for their alleged connections with civilian politicians who planned to overthrow the government. Twenty leftist officers were also tried and convicted in September 1954.

On 17 April 1954, Nasser became Prime Minister while Naguib remained President of the Republic. During the next four months more Free Officers were brought into the government and given Ministries. Thus in April, Lieut. Col. Husayn al-Shafi'i became Minister of War and Wing Comdr. Hasan Ibrahim Minister of State for the Presidency of the Republic. In August, Wing Comdr. Gamal Salem became Deputy Premier; Shafi'i replaced a civilian as Minister of Social Affairs; Artillery Major Kamal al-Din Husayn replaced another civilian as Minister of Education; General Abd al-Hakim Amer took over the War Ministry from Shafi'i; Colonel Anwar al-Sadat became Minister of State. Only two civilians were left in the government: Abd al-Mon'em al-Qaysuni for Finance and Economics, and Fathi Radwan for Communications.

The militarization of the government came at a time of heightened Muslim Brethren activities against the régime. There were disturbances and clashes with the police on 27 August which led to several arrests. Then on 26 October while Nasser was addressing a rally in Alexandria to celebrate the signing with Britain of the Evacuation Agreement, a Muslim Brother, a plumber called Mahmud Abd al-Latif, tried to assassinate him. Police and security inquiries allegedly found an extensive Muslim Brethren plot to overthrow the régime. Among the conspirators were the leaders of the Brethren Executive and several army officers. Of the latter, Lieut. Col. Abd al-Mon'em Abd al-Ra'uf was found to be the leader of a secret pro-Muslim Brethren apparatus in the army. He could not be arrested, however, as he had fled the country.

A new revolutionary tribunal was appointed on 1 November 1954 to try those accused of treason, including the arrested Muslim Brothers. It was given the name of 'The People's Court'. Wing

Comdr. Gamal Salem was appointed President of the Court, Anwar al-Sadat and Husayn al-Shafi'i members. The Court was further organized into three circuits each presided over by an army or air force officer to deal with the cases of over 700 persons accused of high treason. In all, the People's Court tried over 875 persons, and the military courts over 250 officers. Six members of the Muslim Brethren were executed, among them three lawyers, one merchant, a preacher and a plumber. Another ten were given various prison sentences. These were mainly lawyers, engineers, professors and high state officials. By 1955 there were over 3,000 political prisoners in the country.

It was alleged during the investigations and trials of the Muslim Brethren and other so-called subversive elements that President Naguib had been in close touch with them. Thus on 14 November the RCC decided to dismiss him from office and place him under house arrest.[7]

A month later, in December 1954, the High Military Court brought a number of Jewish doctors and others (fifteen persons) to trial on the charge of spying for Israel. Two of those convicted were executed in January 1955; others were given life sentences at hard labour. In the same month, the Bar Association was purged by dismissing its old Executive Council and appointing a new one.

On 16 January 1956 a new Constitution was promulgated. It consisted of 196 Articles providing for a presidential Republican system of government in which the President appoints and dismisses ministers. It also contained two new notions: first, that Egypt is an Arab nation, and second, that the State is committed to economic planning and social welfare in the interests of social co-operation among members of the nation. The real innovation introduced by this constitutional charter (it was superseded in March 1958 when Syria and Egypt entered upon a union) was that it replaced a parliamentary form of government by a presidential system. The Constitution was approved and the President elected by a plebiscite held on 23 June 1956. The Electoral Law of 3 March 1956 had provided for universal male suffrage at eighteen years of age and gave the franchise to military personnel on active duty. A law for a new unicameral National Assembly was decreed on 11 July which provided for the election of 350 members from 350 districts. The eligible age for the Assembly was thirty years and a fifty-pound (Egyptian) deposit. More important, the new legislation decreed the creation of a National Union (Article 192) to replace the Liberation Rally, which was to screen and select nominees for election to the National Assembly.

Nasser was elected President in June and proceeded to form a new government on 29 June which included more technocrats and fewer soldiers. Thus Sayyid Mar'i took over a new Ministry of Agrarian Reform, Aziz Sidki a new Ministry of Industry, and Mustafa Khalil the Ministry of Communications. Free Officers Gamal Salem, Anwar al-Sadat and Hasan Ibrahim were dropped. Wing Comdr. Abd al-Latif al-Boghdadi was entrusted with the new Ministry of State for Planning.

Whereas in 1954 Nasser used his closest associates to strengthen his position against Naguib and civilian opposition groups, now with the consolidation of his position in 1956 after the elimination of his opponents he brought more civilians into the government to head new departments concerned with economic, agrarian and social problems. Such alternation of personnel for his retention of power, or at least a pre-eminent position in the power structure of the military oligarchy, was a trade mark of Nasser's rule and political style throughout his Presidency.[8]

Further arrests and purges, especially of leftist and Communist elements, continued throughout 1955 and 1956. Internal consolidation of power by Nasser was by no means complete with his triumph over Naguib and the Muslim Brethren. Yet the two-year period 1955–7 was characterized by developments in the foreign relations of Egypt which had a direct bearing upon internal policies. It is therefore useful at this point to turn to these before outlining the economic and social policy programmes adopted by the régime in the 1950s and early 1960s.

ANGLO-EGYPTIAN AND FOREIGN RELATIONS

One of the goals set by the régime when it first came to power was the eradication of imperialism. To most Egyptians this meant the end of British military occupation of the Canal. Partly related to this issue was the status of the Sudan. It will be recalled that the Anglo-Egyptian Condominium Agreement of 1899 worked relatively well until 1924. The strained relations between Britain and Egypt after the assassination of Sir Lee Stack Pasha, Sirdar of the Egyptian Army, in November that year resulted virtually in the elimination of the Egyptian side in the Condominium. The Sudan question flared up again in the late summer of 1947 when Egypt brought the whole issue of Anglo-Egyptian relations before the UN Security Council, and again in 1950–1 when the Wafd government unilaterally abrogated the 1936 Anglo-Egyptian Treaty and declared the unity of the Nile Valley. With Naguib as nominal head of the military régime after July 1952, there was renewed hope among Egyptians that this unity could be realized. By then, however, there had arisen in the Sudan parties and groups who, with British encouragement, sought to achieve an independent sovereign Sudanese state. Talks between Britain and the new Egyptian military régime began soon after the latter had come to power, were successfully concluded and an Agreement was signed on 12 February 1953. It provided for a three-year transition period during which the Sudanese were to prepare for independence, thus ending the Anglo-Egyptian Condominium over the Sudan. This was to be determined by a Constituent Assembly, which was to choose between union with Egypt and complete independence. Egyptian and British troops were to be withdrawn from the Sudan. The country became independent in 1956.

As for the evacuation of British troops from the Canal, talks between the two countries began in April 1953, a first agreement laying down general principles was initialled on 27 July 1954, and a final one on 19 October 1954. It is significant that the Egyptian delegation to the talks was led by Colonel Nasser. The Agreement provided, among other things, for the complete evacuation of British troops from Egyptian territory within a period of twenty months from the date of signature. It declared the supercession of the Anglo-Egyptian Treaty signed on 26 August 1936, including its provisions of various special privileges and exemptions for British troops in Egypt. But it provided for the maintenance of the Canal Base in viable military condition at all times for possible use in the event of external aggression upon any member state of the Arab League that was a signatory to the Joint Defence and/or Turkey. In such an eventuality, Egypt was to offer Britain all necessary facilities for the reactivation of the Base on a war basis. Both countries recognized that the Suez Canal is an international waterway and that the right of passage as enunciated in the Istanbul Convention of 29 October 1888 would be guaranteed to all states. The Agreement was to be for a period of seven years, at the end of which the two parties were to examine changes and further arrangements.

The Agreement could not have been concluded at a more propitious time for the hard-pressed military régime. It was a boon to the Nasser forces which were then battling for supremacy against a combined civilian–military opposition led by the Muslim Brethren. Although it still tied Egypt to a British military alliance of sorts, to the general Egyptian public it meant the ultimate triumph over imperialism after nearly seventy-five years of the physical presence of British troops in the country. The last British troops left Port Said on 13 June, and on the 18th Nasser ceremoniously raised the Egyptian flag over Navy House there.

Other external events affecting Egypt and the course of the régime's yet uncharted policies were not as comforting to the junta rulers. While the final stages of the negotiations for evacuation were under way, the Israeli Army occupied al-Auja, a strategic point in the demilitarized zone (no-man's-land located in what was Mandatory Palestine) between Egypt and Israel, in September 1953. More ominous were developments throughout 1955. While Britain sought alternative security and strategic arrangements in the Middle East with the negotiation of the first stages of the Baghdad Pact (involving Iraq, Iran, Turkey and Pakistan) in January–February 1955, the Israelis mounted their successful raid on Gaza on 28 February. This was partly in retaliation for increased border raids organized by the Egyptians in the Gaza Strip. Other Israeli raids followed in May and August, on the strategic Sinai fort of Kuntilla in October, and Sabha in November of that year.

Colonel Nasser and his colleagues interpreted the Baghdad Pact as a British attempt to isolate Egypt from other Arab states and in the Middle East generally. Given the Israeli Army raids in Gaza and the Sinai, they also felt weak and exposed to the military incursions of Israel. It was essential, they thought, to seek international political support from the West and, failing that, from an emerging group of Asian states (e.g., India and Indonesia). They also considered as most urgent the purchase of arms to strengthen the Egyptian Army, which they sought first from the West, but without success.

The search for new sources of political and diplomatic support was reflected in Nasser's attendance of the Bandung Conference (18–24 April 1955) of Afro-Asian states, and the subscription of Egypt to its resolutions against imperialism and military alliances. Nasser was also instrumental in getting the Conference to adopt a resolution stating Arab rights in Palestine and support for the Yemen's position *vis-à-vis* the South Arabian protectorates. Egypt's participation in the Conference marked the acceleration of an anti-Western Egyptian policy in the Middle East and served as a forum for Nasser to condemn Israel. Moreover, it established a personal relationship between Nasser and the late Nehru of India, Tito of Yugoslavia and Chou En-Lai of China.

Faced with a military threat from Israel and a political challenge from the Euphrates, the régime, particularly after Nasser's Bandung experience, turned to the Soviet bloc for assistance. On 27 September 1955 it announced an Arms Purchase Agreement with Czechoslovakia.[9] Following so soon after Nasser's participation in the Bandung Conference, this development was considered as a clear departure in Egypt's foreign policy. The arms deal was explained by President Nasser and some of his Western apologists as the consequence of the refusal of Western Powers, specifically Britain and the United States, to supply Egypt with necessary arms. He also related his new policy to the military threat from Israel. More significantly, he declared that '... the policy of Egypt is based on complete independence, freedom of commerce with any and every state. We have resorted to this new agreement with Czechoslovakia, that is only after the United States reneged on its promise to supply us with arms and after repeated Israeli raids on Gaza. Moreover, it is a purely commercial agreement and has no bearing on policy.'

From this point onwards, Egypt's external relations and foreign policy generally veered towards the East. On 16 May 1956, she recognized Communist China and established diplomatic relations with that country. The decision was explained partly as a logical step in Egypt's liberation from a dependence on 'imperialist pacts and alliances'.

A month after the last British troops left Egypt, President Nasser attended the Brioni Conference of leaders of non-aligned states, namely, Nehru and Tito. In May 1955, soon after his return from Bandung, President Nasser had announced his adherence to the doctrine of so-called positive neutralism when, in addressing graduating cadets of the Naval Academy, he said: 'We oppose those who oppose us, and are at peace with those who make peace with us.' At the Brioni Conference, Nasser pledged his country to work against Power blocs in the world, to seek speedy disarmament, to contribute to the development of new nations, and to combat Great Power rivalries in the Middle East.

The worst breakdown of relations between Egypt and the West, however, was yet to come. Towards the end of 1955 and early in 1956, Egypt sought to negotiate massive loans from the World Bank to finance the construction of a High Dam at Aswan. The régime had staked much of its reputation and prestige – in fact, its revolutionary intentions to improve the socio-economic and generally material conditions of the population – upon a projected rapid economic development via industrialization. Closely related to its radical agrarian reform policy (see below), its national planning to raise production and per capita income, was the High Dam project. The régime, like all other governments before it since the time of Muhammad Ali, was anxious to bring ever larger areas of land under cultivation to feed the country's rapidly increasing population (over half a million yearly increase) as well as to generate enough hydro-electric power to meet the needs of their ambitious industrialization programme.[10]

Initial agreement on a $200 million World Bank loan was in sight in mid-1956. Britain and the United States indicated they would provide $70 million for the project. But on 19 July, while Nasser was in Brioni, the United States announced its withdrawal of the offer. Britain followed suit by announcing its withdrawal from the project the next day. Finally, the World Bank announced that the initial agreement no longer stood.

Reacting to such a rebuff from the West, President Nasser declared in Alexandria on 26 July the nationalization of the Suez Canal, seized the Company's assets and premises in Egypt, and appointed an Egyptian Suez Canal Authority to administer the waterway, headed by the Army Engineer Mahmud Yunis. With this act, Egypt precipitated a confrontation with Britain and France that led to the events of October–December 1956, better known in the West as the Suez War, and in the Arab Middle East as the Tripartite Aggression (Britain, France and Israel) against Egypt. For a start, Britain, France and the United States froze all Egyptian assets and funds in their countries. Despite feverish diplomatic activity in London and Cairo, Britain and France seemed determined to use force to punish Nasser's seizure of the international waterway.

The Suez War opened with the Israeli push in the Sinai on 29 October. This was followed by the Anglo-French ultimatum to Israel and Egypt to stop hostilities, and the Anglo-French landings in Port Said. Aerial bombardment of Egyptian airfields and other strategic targets began on 31 October. A cease-fire was ordered by the UN General Assembly on 2 November, which was rejected by Britain, France and Israel. Meanwhile, the United States warned Britain and France that it was categorically opposed to the use of force against Egypt. Then on 5 November the Soviet Union issued its warning

to Britain and France that it would consider the use of force if necessary to bring about an end to hostilities. On 7 November the UN
cease-fire was accepted by all the combatants. British and French
troops evacuated Egyptian territory on 22 December 1956.

Less than two weeks later, on 1 January 1957, Egypt abrogated
the 19 October 1954 Anglo-Egyptian Agreement over the Suez Canal
Base. Not only was the Canal as an international maritime waterway
now in the sole hands of Egypt and administered by her, but the
British Canal Base too. The United States, on the other hand, concerned with the deteriorating situation in the Middle East, reversed
its disengagement policy during the Suez Crisis by formulating the
Eisenhower Doctrine to combat Communist threats to the area.

Other developments which followed the conclusion of the Baghdad Pact indicated Egypt's search for alternative collective security
arrangements within the Arab Middle East. On 20 October 1955 she
signed a Joint Defence Agreement with Syria. Exactly a year later,
this Agreement provided for the posting of Egyptian troops in Syria
when the latter also veered away from the West.

All these developments in the two-year period 1955–7 marked a
turning point in the régime's external relations, characterized by the
adoption of the so-called positive neutralist policy as a reflection
of Egypt's increasing anti-Western stand. By December 1957, Cairo
was emerging as the centre of Afro-Asian solidarity conferences with
their anti-Western platforms. These coincided with Egypt's search
for rapid economic development, her option for a so-called Arab
policy in the Middle East, and the penetration of Israeli technical
assistance and trade in several countries of Africa, Southeast Asia
and the Far East. It was, for instance, in 1958 that Egypt embarked
upon an active African policy, which ended with failure in 1963.[11]

ECONOMIC AND SOCIAL POLICIES

In 1952, Egypt was a predominantly agrarian country.[12] Industry
accounted for 10 per cent of GNP. Its trading account carried a
deficit of £E. 39 million in 1951; £E. 72 million in 1952. Cotton was
the major cash export crop which earned the bulk of the country's
foreign exchange. Much of its financial and trading institutions were
still controlled by foreigners and foreign residents in the country.
The economy was generally characterized by free enterprise, with
direct state activity solely in irrigation and the railways. The distribu-

tion of income was extremely unequal, underpinned by a fiscal system which featured a low level of direct taxation, and much of government revenue derived from indirect taxes.

The Korean War boom in raw materials permitted Egypt to export all its cotton crop for 1950–1 at exceptionally high prices. Profits were handsome. But in the absence of government restrictions these led to record imports – especially of luxury items – and thus trade deficits. The following year (1952), however, world demand for cotton fell sharply and surplus Egyptian stocks could not be sold easily. Simultaneous manipulation of the Alexandria futures market had artificially inflated cotton prices, with the result that Egyptian cotton was even more difficult to dispose of.

Faced with a deteriorating economic situation, the new military régime proceeded in 1952 to impose stringent controls over budgetary expenditures, imports and trading in cotton. On 23 November it closed the Alexandria futures market (it was not reopened until September 1955), and the government offered to buy cotton at nominal support prices. The régime was also faced with the diminishing returns of a basically agricultural economy which limited the possibilities for economic development. Agricultural production had not kept pace with a rapidly rising population. Despite the improved yields of land, production per capita was falling continuously, so that alternative sources of national wealth and employment for surplus labour had to be created, particularly in industry.

For the first four years of its rule, however, all the régime could do was deflate the economy with a view to cutting down expenditures, imports and trade deficits in order to balance the budget. Pending the evolution of new economic projects for development its policy remained one of encouraging private enterprise – native and foreign – to invest and expand its activities in the country. The period 1952–4 was thus one of a liberal policy of incentives favouring foreign capital. Old laws (1947) requiring a 51 per cent Egyptian control of enterprises were reversed in favour of foreign companies. A tax exemption provision for industrial companies for seven years was intended to encourage industry and to attract investment away from land. Another law provided for the transfer of profits in foreign currency after a five-year period of investment. Minimum profits were guaranteed together with a lowering of customs dues for the import of raw materials and machinery. Dues on luxury imports were raised.

While encouraging private investment in industry, the new régime

From the old order to the new, 1930–79

also embarked upon a state policy of devising a programme for long-range economic development. For this purpose a Permanent Council for the Development of National Production was created in October 1952, consisting mainly of civilian experts and some army technicians. It was charged with drawing up plans for national development especially in the fields of irrigation and land reclamation. Similarly, the government enacted legislation to facilitate prospecting for minerals, particularly petroleum. Yet its general policy to divert investment from land into industry during this period has been adjudged a failure. The régime was in its first three to four years totally occupied with the political issues of consolidating its power and negotiating an evacuation agreement with Britain. Much of its economic policy was one of holding down expenditures and inflation. Otherwise, this policy was a continuation of the pre-1952 free enterprise system with the difference that the Free Officer régime was more committed to the state encouragement of industry.

Radical change in this period came about in the agricultural field. Committed to a redistribution of landed wealth, the régime's first reform measure was that of the Agrarian Reform Law of 9 September 1952. Previous agrarian reform bills introduced in Egypt in 1945 and 1950 had been rejected by landowner-dominated parliaments, and the September bill was introduced over the protestations of a civilian cabinet. Basically, it provided for the limitation of agricultural landholdings to two hundred *feddans* and a maximum of another one hundred *feddans* if the owner had children. The surplus land was to be taken over by the government within five years. Compensation was to be paid in bonds, and land thus requisitioned was to be distributed to farmers owning under five *feddans* in two to five *feddan* lots which could be further subdivided. Payment for the land by farmers was to be by instalments. Land belonging to the royal family, however, was expropriated without compensation. By 1960, about 500,000 *feddans* had been taken over.

Even though the Agrarian Reform Law also provided for the fixing of agricultural labour wages and the organization of co-operative societies of all sorts, its major impact at first was not an agricultural-economic one. Rather its consequences were of great political advantage to the new régime, for essentially the reform, together with its amendment in 1961 which further limited landholdings to 100 *feddans*, broke the economic and political power of the landowning groups. Its scheme of co-operatives, moreover, ultimately brought the whole agricultural sector of the economy under more direct government supervision and control.[13] This was later to fall in line with the eventual control of the total economy in all its sectors and aspects by the State.

The radicalization of the State's economic policy occurred on a large scale after the Suez War. It reflected the decision of the régime to acquire greater control of the economy simultaneously with its commitment to state planning. It also reflected the new political orientation of the régime to break away from the West in favour of a closer economic and political relationship with the Soviet bloc and certain states in Asia and Africa. The new radicalism in economic policy was not therefore simply a result of any new ideological orientation towards socialism as it was a consequence of the impact of external events upon Egypt, as well as the clear failure of the régime's earlier policy to stimulate economic development by encouraging private native and foreign enterprise.

The government, moreover, sequestrated and eventually nationalized all foreign establishments in the country. In November 1956, all British and French banks and companies were taken over, a total of 15,000 establishments. In January 1957, an Economic Organization was created to take over the functions of the old Permanent Council for the Development of National Production which was dissolved. The Organization was also entrusted with the management of the enterprises taken over by the government. At the same time, the government nationalized all banks, insurance companies, commercial houses and agencies. Planning for the economy was formally introduced; a Higher Planning Council and a Committee of National Planning were created.

Shortly before the Suez War a Ministry of Industry had been created with responsibility for such major projects as the Aswan High Dam, electrical power, a new war industry, and fertilizers and chemicals. Through the new Economic Organization the State began to participate in capital formation, especially in industry. By the 1960s the control of industry, transport, finance and trade was transferred to the State. The government budget came to account for over 65 per cent of GNP. Direct taxation rose sharply since it was first introduced in 1949, and so did revenue from a number of state enterprises.

Thus, after a commitment to comprehensive planning in 1957, the government by 1960 assumed responsibility for all capital formation when all investment had come under its scrutiny and control. A command economy, centrally controlled by the government, became the trend and after 1960 free enterprise began to disappear. Whereas in 1956–7 nationalization was directed mainly at foreign enterprises, by the beginning of 1960 the process had been extended to include Egyptian firms. Bank Misr and the National Bank were nationalized in February 1960, so was the Press in May, and Cairo transport was municipalized. In June–July 1961, the government took over by decree the entire import trade of the country and most of its export trade, including cotton, as well as local insurance and trading establishments. The steepest progressive taxation system was also introduced with the purpose of making £E.5,000 per annum the maximum income of anyone in Egypt. Soon after the break-up of the Egyptian–Syrian union in September 1961, a series of punitive economic measures followed in October and February 1962. The property of 600 of the wealthiest Egyptian families (now including Muslims as well as Copts and Jews) was sequestrated by the State; several of their members were arrested. Further nationalizations followed in August 1963. According to the National Charter of May 1962 (see below), only 'national capitalism' was to be allowed in the country. In March 1964, even contracting firms were nationalized.

Generally, much of this economic policy was dictated by political events, as in the case of the February 1962 sequestrations and the earlier seizure of Belgian property in Egypt, for example, during the Congo crisis.

Meanwhile, the first Five-Year Plan (1960–5) came into operation, aimed at doubling the national income in ten years. The mainstay of the Plan was the High Dam at Aswan. Work on the Dam began, with Soviet aid, in January 1960.[14] The first stage of its construction was completed in May 1964, when the occasion was ceremoniously marked with the visit to Egypt of Chairman Nikita Khrushchev of the USSR. The completion of the whole project in 1970 increased the crop area of the country by 25 per cent. More important, it was expected to provide 10,000 million KWH per annum of electric power. All major construction on the Dam was completed in January 1968.

Meanwhile, the High Dam at Aswan project was supplemented by the wider exploitation of natural resources, especially petroleum in southeast Egypt below the Gulf of Suez, in the Sinai (occupied by Israel in 1967), and in the Western Desert. Reclamation projects after the Suez War were planned with a view to irrigating half a million *feddans* in the New Valley, Fayyum, Beheira province, and elsewhere. Most of these development plans came to depend more heavily than ever before upon Soviet financial and technical aid, particularly after the Egyptian defeat in the June 1967 Arab–Israeli war.

Even though the number of Russian technicians working on the Dam complex was great (at one time 2,000), the Egyptian contribution was not insignificant. Much of the contracting work was carried out by the Othman Ahmad Othman firm. This, in itself, was a great opportunity for Egyptian technicians to gain greater expertise. What is equally important is the fact that cheap electric power started flowing from three of the twelve generators planned at Aswan, making it possible to close down some of the more expensive thermal power stations along the Aswan–Cairo power route. The power generated by the Dam was expected to reach 10,000 million KWH in 1972, and output of electricity tripled.

At the same time, the recent discovery of natural gas reserves in the Delta (Abu Madi fields) and the prospecting at Abu Hammad of Sharqiyya province as well as off-shore drilling near Rosetta may prove adequate for a 20–25-year supply of 5–15 million cubic metres a year. This could further ease the fuel situation in the country.

So far, the Dam has made it possible to cultivate about 200,000 *feddans* of the projected 1–1·5 million which are to be irrigated. No one, however, seriously contends that this development in itself will solve the Egyptian agricultural production/population ratio problem.

Despite all these developments, there is among responsible Egyptians now a marked reluctance to sustain the old political attitude (or myth) of the fifties and early sixties which held up the Dam project as the panacea for the ills of the Egyptian economy. Industry, in particular, has been plagued by surplus labour, low productivity and the shortcomings of bureaucratic planning. Waves of nationalization and greater state control led to complacent disregard of competition. Then, near-bankruptcy after the June 1967 war, especially the shortage of foreign exchange, reduced industrial production to a low level; several factories had in fact been idle in late 1967. The temporary loss of the Suez refinery after the Israeli artillery bombardment in October 1967 and the productive oilfields in the Sinai also created a fuel shortage, or at least, raised the price of securing it. Nevertheless the whole Aswan complex, completed in 1970, was believed to constitute a formidable base for further industrial development.

Perhaps the most significant change introduced by the new régime to the economy in the decade 1952–62 was that of rapid industrialization. Whereas in 1952 industry accounted for only 10 per cent of GNP, in 1962 it accounted for over 20 per cent. Industrialization was an economic necessity:

Agricultural productivity obviously needed to be raised, but Egypt's development strategy pointed inescapably towards industrialization. In order to meet the growing pressure of population upon a relatively fixed area of land, productive capacity and opportunities for employment had to be created outside the primary sector.[15]

Socially and politically more significant, however, was the commitment of the Egyptian government after 1956 to comprehensive planning and the rapid control the State achieved over capital formation and eventually over the whole economy in the 1960s. It has been argued that this transformation in Egyptian economic policy has been unrelated to ideological considerations, such as socialism, for instance. Rather it was the failure of private enterprise to respond to the régime's earlier liberal economic policies (1952–4) coupled with the desire of the Free Officers for rapid development which prompted the drastic change. However, the close connection between the State and the economy in Egypt's history tempered the novelty of such policies.[16]

In the area of social policy, agrarian reform initiated by the Land Reform Law of 1952 achieved with varying degrees of success two major objectives: it broke the economic and political power of the big landowners and improved the living conditions of certain groups among the rural population. The measure, however, did not quite satisfy the desired economic ends of its authors, namely, the diversion of private capital from agriculture to industry. Nor did it, at first, raise agricultural output appreciably.

Yet the Agrarian Reform Law stipulated other developments besides redistribution of large estates. It fixed minimum wages for agricultural labourers and permitted them to form trade unions; it fixed land rents and improved other tenancy regulations; and it provided for the organization of co-operatives. Regarding landownership, by July 1961, no individual was allowed to own more than one hundred *feddans* and no family more than three hundred *feddans* of agricultural land (including desert land). The 1962 National Charter indicated further limitations.[17] Land owned by foreigners was gradually expropriated in the period 1962–4.

Agricultural co-operatives had existed before the First World War. Many more were founded after independence (1923) as a result of favourable legislation. After the establishment of the Agricultural Credit Bank in 1931 with its loan facilities to individual farmers there was a slack period in the formation of new co-operatives. But the necessities of the Second World War spurred on the co-operative movement so that by 1945 there were over 500,000 members in some 2,000 co-operatives. In the 1950s, the government extended its control over co-operatives and sought to expand the scope of their activities. In 1961, co-operatives were placed under the supervision of the Ministry of Agriculture, thus further bureaucratizing their operation.

Closely related to agrarian reform has been the régime's policy of rural development. Not by any means new or original, this policy goes back to the old Fellah Department of the Social Affairs Ministry which was founded in 1939–40. Begun as an experiment to provide villagers with a comprehensive programme of social services and rural education, 150 Rural Combined Units were formed in the period 1939–52. Each of these was staffed by resident specialists (agronomists, health nurses and others), and served a population of 10,000. In 1954, the new régime reorganized the Combined Units so that each would serve a population of 15,000. By 1961, there were 250 of these Units (*wahdat mujamma'a*) serving over 1,000 villages with a population of nearly four million. The material contribution of villages to each unit consists of two *feddans* of land and £E.1,500. Personnel of the Units from agricultural experts to social workers were expected to live in the locality. But the greatest obstacle so far to the rapid expansion of the system of Rural Combined Units has been the shortage of funds and adequately trained staff. The target of the government is 865 such Units that would cover the total rural population. In 1970, there were under 400 fully operating Units.

Several other measures of social policy affecting industrial labour were introduced, including a new scheme of social services. Legislation providing for higher wages, shorter working hours and better working conditions (including popular housing for industrial workers) was enacted. In February 1962, the minimum wage was raised from PT 16 to PT 25. Earlier, in July 1961, a law was published which provided for the distribution of 25 per cent of net profits to employees and workers. Whereas in 1952 there were 400,000 workers in industry, today the figure has risen to 1·5 million.

Working hours were steadily reduced to fifty hours per week in 1957 and forty-eight hours in 1958. A new law in 1961 fixed the maximum working day in industry at seven hours (six days a week).

Labour organization, however, followed the pattern of greater government control as in other areas of national economic life. Although the earliest trade unions in Egypt were organized at the beginning of this century, the labour union movement itself was not officially recognized by the State until 1942. The law passed by a Wafdist government that year authorized the formation of trade unions by workers, but excluded state and municipal employees as well as agricultural workers from such organization. Despite the permission of trade union federations, political activities by unions were prohibited. Nevertheless, within ten years there were just under 500 registered unions with 150,000 members. In 1952–3, the new régime amended through a series of bills the 1942 law to permit all workers and employees except those in government and municipal services to form unions. It also authorized the organization of a confederation of trade union federations. In 1955 an all-Egyptian Trade Unions Congress was formed which, in 1957, was replaced by the Egyptian Federation of Labour. Although the membership of unions had, by 1958, risen to 430,000 workers in 1,350 unions, a new law in 1959 reorganized the whole trade union movement and reduced the number of unions to about sixty. This was obviously part of the régime's overall policy both to control the economy and mobilize all sections of the population in support of its new policies, and spelled greater direct state control over labour. But this was no departure from earlier Egyptian practice which had always kept labour subservient to the government.

There were, however, advances in the bargaining power of labour unions. A law in 1948 provided for compulsory arbitration in key industries. Another law in 1952 extended this rule to all industries. Yet the attainment of social benefits by industrial workers has not been mainly the result of their bargaining efforts. On the contrary, their greater control by the State made such benefits inevitably the gift of the government with the view of acquiring labour's allegiance to the régime. As early as 1936, legislation provided for the employer's liability for accidents affecting industrial and commercial workers. In 1942 – an important year for labour legislation – insurance against work accidents was made compulsory and, by 1951, further legislation provided for compensation of workers against occupational diseases. Similar social insurance, first considered unsuccessfully in 1950 to cover disability, old age, widows and orphans, was introduced in August 1955. This new law also provided for a health insurance scheme, unemployment compensation, old age pensions, death and disability compensation. It was implemented by a contributory Insurance and Investment Fund (employer: 7 per cent; worker: 5 per cent). It was further extended in December 1958 and April 1959. In 1961, workers were decreed a share in company profits and membership on the boards of enterprises.[18] Schemes were drafted in 1963–4 to extend social security and national insurance so as to provide for full health and unemployment insurance benefits. Many of these social services in the country came under the overall policy planning supervision of the Permanent Council of Public Services formed in October 1953.

POLITICAL ORGANIZATION

The National Union, formally established in May 1957, was the prelude to elections for the first legislature since the overthrow of the old régime. Elections to a National Assembly were held in July. Of 2,500 candidates who presented themselves for the 350 seats, over half were disqualified after screening by the government-appointed National Executive Committee of the Union. The elected Assembly met from July 1957 to March 1958, but only as a dutiful audience for ministerial and presidential speeches. It was dissolved in March 1958 when the union with Syria, proclaimed on 1 February and ratified by plebiscite on 21 February 1958, created the United Arab Republic (UAR).

Now a reorganized governmental structure for the UAR was created. The 1956 Egyptian Constitution was abolished and a provisional one for the enlarged Republic was promulgated by decree in March. The President announced a new government consisting of four Vice-Presidents (two Syrians and two Egyptians), a Central Cabinet for the UAR, and two Regional Councils of Ministers, one for Syria and one for Egypt. Political parties in Syria were officially dissolved and replaced by the National Union.[19]

Three and a half years later, in September 1961, Syria seceded from the union. President Nasser had to effect yet another political reorganization of his régime. A new government was formed on 18 October and a Preparatory Committee of the National Congress of Popular Forces was convened in Cairo. Its task was to prepare the ground for a National Congress which would lay down a Charter for National Action. A Congress consisting of 1,750 members elected by peasant farmers, labour, professional and occupation associations, and other community and minority groups met in May 1962 to debate the Draft National Charter presented to it by President Nasser. It approved the draft, after some lively debate, as it stood on 30 June.

Among other things, the Charter provided for the creation of a new state political structure, the Arab Socialist Union (ASU), in which the public were to participate in support of the régime's revolutionary policies. The ASU replaced the National Union, but did not differ drastically in its organization from its predecessor in so far as its pyramidal structure and organization from village and the basic units to those on the district, provincial and national level was concerned. There were, however, two innovations. One, which introduced occupational, or functional, representation, consisted of a provision that fifty of the seats in all elected ASU structures at all levels be filled by 'farmers and workers' as these two categories were defined in the National Charter. The other was a provision for elected ASU units in factories, business firms, agricultural co-operatives, ministries, professional syndicates, and state-controlled industrial enterprises. The latter provision was a logical outcome of the vast nationalization policy and industrialization programme undertaken since 1957.

The Charter represented a radical departure in Egyptian political annals. It embodied the principles of Islam, Arab nationalism and socialism. More important, it intended to create a new *Arab* society in Egypt as well as outline the basic characteristics of the desirable Muslim, nationalist, socialist Arab society everywhere.

It was also the prelude to yet another reorganization of the country's political and constitutional life. After several weeks of talks between Egypt, Syria and Iraq on Arab unity (Tripartite Talks of spring and summer 1963),[20] new decrees were announced in November 1963 providing for the election of a National Assembly in February 1964. The country was organized for electoral purposes into 175 constituencies, each to be represented by two members, one of whom had to be a worker or a farmer as defined in the Charter. All representatives had to be members of the ASU, literate and over thirty years old. Civil servants and members of local councils were disqualified from candidature. Elections were held a month later on 10 March 1964; 1,750 candidates contested the 350 seats, over 975 of whom were workers and farmers, and over twenty-five women.

As the electoral law stipulated an absolute majority for election, less than half of the members were declared elected in the first round of polls. A second round was therefore conducted on 19 March with the amended requirement of a simple majority. The final results as officially broken down indicated over half of the representatives to be workers and farmers as defined by the Charter, and eight women. The President appointed ten additional members of the Assembly, making a total of 360. Several former ministers, particularly old members of the Free Officers movement, were among those elected.

A provisional constitution embodying the principles enunciated in the Charter[21] was proclaimed by President Nasser on 23 March 1964 and the Assembly convened on the 26 March. Briefly, the new Constitution stated that the UAR is part of the Arab nation; its system of government is 'democratic socialist ... based on the alliance of the working forces of the people' (Article 1). The religion of the State is Islam (Article 5); and the economic foundation of the State is the socialist system, which prohibits any form of exploitation, and instead is based on sufficiency and justice (Article 9). It emphasized work as a right, equality, and social services. The armed forces continued to be 'entrusted with the duty of protecting the socialist gains of the nation' (Article 23).

The Constitution provided for an exceptionally strong presidential form of government. The President, who is nominated by the National Assembly (this was done on 20 January 1965 by a vote of 355 for, three abstentions, and two members not present to vote) and confirmed (i.e., chosen) by plebiscite (not by an election), is the supreme executive head of the State. He appoints vice-presidents and ministers, and dismisses them. Together with his government he lays down the general policy of the State in all fields and supervises its execution (Article 113). The President has the power to initiate and propose laws, approve them, or return them to the National Assembly for reconsideration.

The Assembly, as the legislative power in the State, is elected for five years. All ministers, though appointed by the President, are responsible to it. The Assembly may be convoked, prorogued, and dissolved by the President.

The National Assembly elected in 1964 was to act as a Constituent Assembly charged with drafting a permanent constitution for the country. Moreover, it was to be guided by the ASU which was intended to set the broad principles of national policy. By June 1967, at the outbreak of the Arab–Israeli war, the organization of the ASU and the demarcation of its exact functions had not been completed. The projected National Conference to elect a General Council for the ASU had not materialized. Thus the Assembly had completed two full sessions (November to May for each session) and yet its exact relationship to the ASU had not been made clear.[22]

Despite these constitutional strides in the political and administrative reorganization of the country there was a resumption of repressive measures by the government against the remaining richer groups in 1964, and certain political groups like the Muslim Brethren in 1965. Thus the prominent ideologue of the latter group, Sayyid Qutb, was tried for conspiracy against the régime, convicted of treason and executed in 1966. After June 1967, there was another round of purges in the armed forces following the defeat in the Sinai, trials of senior military personnel (winter 1968) for conspiring against the régime, a restructuring of the military command, and a reconstitution of President Nasser's government.

ARAB AND REGIONAL POLICY

Throughout its first fifteen years the Free Officer régime was expensively occupied in the politics of the Arab Middle East. Much of this involvement was accelerated after the Suez War in a bid for the leadership of that area. Inevitably, it entailed conflict with several leaders of other Arab states, such as Saudi Arabia, Jordan, and Iraq every now and then. An extensive – and very expensive – network of radio and other propaganda media was developed by Egypt both to project her leadership of revolutionary Arab nationalism, and to subvert rulers and régimes she considered conservative or reactionary and opposed to her interests in the area. Support of various groups, for instance that opposed to the Hashemite ruler of Jordan, was provided by the Egyptians from 1956 to 1964. The same policy was followed with respect to pro-Nasserite elements in other Arab countries too. The *Voice of the Arabs* radio station, and the more traditionally orientated *Enemies of God* programme, poured invective not only on the imperialists but more directly upon those leaders in the Arab world considered to be their agents, viz., the Saudi ruling house, the various shaykhs and rulers in the Gulf states. The call for a socialist revolution in all Arab states was made the basis of Arab unity.

Egypt's Arab leadership policy failed first in Syria for, among many other reasons, it was challenged by the Baath Party and its allies in the Syrian Army. Her sporadic attempts since 1958 at bringing about a régime in Iraq more amenable to her dictates also bore little fruit. What brought Egypt to a rapprochement with Jordan in 1964–5, the harvest year of Arab Summit meetings, namely, the military threat from Israel, was a consideration not shared as consciously and immediately by other Arab states. Nonetheless, until 1966 Egypt was considered by Arab radicals and radical groups everywhere in the Middle East as the natural leader of Arab revolution and unity. President Nasser, in turn, was looked upon as the most effective Arab leader both in the area and for projecting and representing the Arab cause to the outside world. Thus, while heads of Arab states may have opposed Egyptian policies affecting their interests, Arab nationalists within them constituted his willing audience. By the autumn of 1962, however, Egypt's radical Arab leadership had come up against an increasing resistance from other Arab states.

When, however, on 28 September 1962, officers led by Brigadier Abdullah al-Sallal in the Yemeni army carried out a successful coup which overthrew the Imam Badr and declared a republic, new possibilities for Egypt's Arab policy emerged. When, moreover, Sallal requested Egyptian military aid to sustain his new republican régime against the guerrilla forces immediately formed by the Imam Badr, who had escaped, Nasser promptly responded by sending an expeditionary force to the Yemen. The Yemen war, which for Egypt lasted from September 1962 until December 1967, and tied up over a third of her army there, proved a heavy burden on the economy, and created serious and permanent antipathies between Saudis and Egyptians, even between republican Yemenis and Egyptians. On the other hand, the Yemeni military involvement afforded Egypt a further incursion into Arab politics in the then Federation of South Arabia and Aden. It proceeded to support with money and arms various rebel nationalist groups, particularly FLOSY (Front for the Liberation of South Yemen), against the Federation structure fostered by Britain there. This policy too ended in apparent failure with the eventual emergence of the NLF (National Liberation Front), who negotiated independence from Britain in the autumn of 1967.

Relations with Syria deteriorated after the 1963 Arab Unity Talks and did not improve until the signing of a Defence Alliance in 1966. Meantime, the Cairo summits in 1964 and 1965 provided an opportunity for Egypt to patch up, but only in an unsatisfactory way, its relations with such 'enemies' as Faysal of Saudi Arabia and Husayn of Jordan. President Nasser and King Faysal tried to resolve the Yemen war, in which the Saudis were supplying the royalists with money and arms, by an unsuccessful attempt to bring the two Yemeni sides together. When this collapsed in 1965, the war in the Yemen was pursued by the Egyptian forces with greater vigour and brutality. Faysal responded by an ill-fated attempt at an Islamic bloc to counter the so-called radical policies advocated by Egypt, Syria, to some extent Iraq, and Algeria.

Committed to support liberation movements in the Middle East and Africa, the Free Officer régime extended its Arab policy to North Africa. The leaders of the Algerian independence movement against France were welcomed in Egypt, as was their revolutionary leadership and government in exile in the late fifties. They received both money and arms from Egypt. After independence in 1962, President Ben Bella of Algeria became closely allied and identified with President Nasser's radical Arab revolution and unity policies. This, despite the fact that the usual cultural–educational activities of Egypt in the other Arab states met with very little success in Algeria. Nevertheless, Egypt considered Algeria the only liberated, radical socialist Arab state in the Maghreb and generally supported Ben Bella's policy towards Morocco and Tunisia. With the overthrow of Ben Bella's régime by Colonel Boumèdienne, Chief of the Algerian Army and Deputy Prime Minister, in June 1965, Egyptian–Algerian relations became strained. They deteriorated further after the June 1967 Arab–Israeli war when, faced with a disastrous military defeat, Egypt opted during the Khartoum Arab Summit Conference in September 1967 for a less radical policy towards Israel. Boumèdienne of Algeria, in conjunction with the régime in Syria, insisted upon a policy of continued armed struggle against Israel.

Despite the bloody and indeterminate inter-Arab war in the Yemen, Egypt made a last effort to recapture the leadership of the Arab nationalist cause in 1965–6. But, again, this policy foundered upon the treacherous rocks of the Palestine Question. In the Arab Summit meeting of January 1964, even Nasser's old enemies Husayn and Faysal had temporarily welcomed the renewed attempt at peaceful co-existence between Arab states. Husayn even went so far as to recognize Nasser's leadership in dealing with inter-Arab issues. He subscribed to the Egyptian proposal to create the Palestine Liberation Organization (PLO) and the recruitment and training of a Palestine Liberation Army. This rapprochement, however, did not last very long, for the PLO came to represent primarily a potential threat to the position of the ruling dynasty in Jordan.

Then in the September 1964 Alexandria Summit Conference, Nasser and Faysal discussed the possibility of ending the Yemen war. Republican Yemenis had by then become resentful of Egyptian domination in their country and were prepared to entertain a solution. In August 1965, Nasser went to Jedda to sign an agreement with Faysal to end the Yemen war. But the conference which was provided by the agreement to take place between the two Yemeni sides and met at Harad, a village near the Saudi frontier, failed to produce agreement and came to naught. It was adjourned until February 1966, but by then both sides to the conflict had stiffened their attitudes. Meanwhile, the British publicly announced their intention to withdraw from South Arabia by 1968. This may have had a determining influence upon the decision of both Saudis and Egyptians not to abandon their clients so soon. Faysal, for example, proceeded with his Islamic peregrinations to enlist support for his project of an Islamic bloc. Egypt responded by attacking this policy as partly inspired by Western imperialists and announcing that President Nasser would not attend any more summit meetings. (Nasser: 'I shall not meet, discuss or negotiate Arab problems with reactionaries.')

Throughout the 1964–5 Arab summitry period, the Syrian Baath régime appeared resentful of its isolation from the rest of the Arab states. It accused Nasser of courting reactionary monarchs, and preached instead an exclusive alliance between Arab revolutionaries. What this meant really was that Syria was anxious to conclude an alliance with Cairo, which excluded her monarchist enemies. Then on 23 February 1966, the extreme radical cabal of Baathi officers in the Syrian Army mounted a successful coup against the Baath régime in power which was considered by them as too amenable to the idea of peaceful coexistence with reactionary Arab states. Meantime, relations between Egypt and Saudi Arabia had worsened. At this point, the new Syrian rulers pressed for an alliance with Cairo, partly by their active espousal of the PLO cause not so much against Israel as against King Husayn of Jordan. By the summer of 1966 they had forced Nasser to re-establish his relations with them even though with greater caution than at the beginning. He was perhaps forced to move towards a closer relationship when the Syrians became most active in sponsoring the PLO and other guerrilla organization (*al-Fatah*) raids into Israel. In November an alliance between the two countries was formally concluded, and in May 1967 King Husayn followed suit.

Undoubtedly, President Nasser's Arab policy in the years 1958–62 helped to radicalize the Arab nationalist movement. Its first set-back in 1962 could have led to a more permanent revulsion to Arabism on the part of Egyptians. But the Yemen five-year interlude forced Egypt to subscribe to the notion that Arab unity was not a matter of the coming together of the heads of Arab states but the battlecry of revolution. Yet, even during this later period, Egypt tried to establish a policy of coexistence with Arab states. This, however, served only to alienate the more radical Arab régimes, such as the one in Syria, and to again force Egypt to shift its ground. It was of course the military defeat in the June 1967 war which finally forced Egypt to withdraw its 'Arab revolutionary' presence in the Yemen – and thus South Arabia – and to appear once again the champion of peaceful inter-Arab coexistence. Her dependence upon massive financial aid from the reactionary monarchs and princes in January 1968 muted her Arab revolutionary cry and temporarily eclipsed her claim to the leadership of Arab Nationalism and Socialism.[23] She also became more dependent upon Soviet military aid until, by 1970, there were 15,000–20,000 Soviet military and other advisers in the country. Many of these manned anti-aircraft missile units on the Canal and elsewhere in the country; others flew air reconnaissance and defence missions, performing direct defence duties in Egypt.

FROM THE SIX DAY WAR TO NASSER'S DEATH

The effect of the defeat in the 1967 war was felt not only in the country's relations with the other Arab states and its superpower patron, the Soviet Union. Its domestic repercussions were even more significant, as they tended to discredit the Nasser régime and devalue its policies. The defeat was so massive that President Nasser felt compelled to resign from the presidency of the Republic on 9 June 1967. He announced the appointment of Zakariyya Mohieddin to succeed him. This move was seen by some as a conciliatory gesture towards the United States, with whom Egypt had severed her relations over the Six Day War, on the assumption that Zakariyya was widely believed to be acceptable to the United States. Others considered it a veiled attempt on the part of Nasser to escape responsibility. The fact remained that the magnitude of the defeat was not yet known or fully appreciated by the vast majority of Egyptians. The latter, whether spontaneously or at the instigation of Nasser's extensive and well-organized political–security apparatus, would not countenance his relinquishing office. Massive demonstrations, only surpassed in size and intensity by those at Nasser's funeral three years later, demanded that he remained at the helm.

This was, however, the outward manifestation of a nation's desperation at the moment of shattering defeat. Nasser, it seems, could not be certain of how the very same public that was clamouring for his continuation in office would react to the unfolding of the real disaster the country had just suffered in the weeks and months to come. Though numbed and dazed by the war, and its immediate aftermath, the public demanded that those responsible for the defeat be brought to justice. There followed the curious affair of the alleged conspiracy by Field Marshal Abdel Hakim Amer, Commander in Chief of the armed forces, and his military cabal – members of his political fiefdom, that is – against his close friend, the President. This occupied them throughout most of the summer until the Field Marshal was arrested and subsequently committed suicide while in custody in August 1967. The trial of several high-ranking officers, among them the commander of the air force, the Minister of War, Shams Badran, and others, followed.

In February 1968, the first riots by students ostensibly protesting the lenient sentences passed on the culprits of the Six Day War defeat took place. In fact between those and the bloodier riots later that year in November it became clear that authority was at least being insistently questioned if not challenged and the whole régime pushed towards some form of public scrutiny. Nasser was forced not only to be rid of his closest colleague, Amer, but also to dissociate himself from the vast collection of power fiefdoms that had been carved out by some of his close associates and lieutenants under his rule. In responding to the public outcry of dissatisfaction, he issued the 30 March 1968 manifesto, 'Mandate for Change', in which he proclaimed his intention to cleanse his régime of corrupt 'centres of power', liberalize its political arrangements and work assiduously for the reconstruction of a strong and healthy political order using the Arab Socialist Union, and rebuild the country's defences.

In order to deal with domestic difficulties, Nasser was forced to accommodate himself more readily with his fellow-Arab rulers since he now needed their financial support. This was apparent in the proceedings and resolutions of the Arab Summit Conference at Khartoum in September 1967. His erstwhile enemies King Faysal of Saudi Arabia and the ruler of Kuwait now offered their financial assistance to Egypt within the framework of an adopted all-Arab policy regarding Israel of 'no war, no peace, no negotiation'. It meant, however, the dilution of the Egyptian leader's radical policy in the Arab world, and his adoption of a more moderate policy towards the region. At the same time, if he were to rebuild his country's defences Nasser had to depend more heavily than ever before upon Soviet assistance, and this implied in turn a further restriction of his freedom of action both at home and abroad.

More damaging was the realization by Egyptians of the hollowness of the régime's fifteen-year-long claims to military prowess, economic and social reform, not to mention political change. The inevitable revelations during the trials of military commanders in the winter of 1967–8, Nasser's own admission regarding the existence of 'centres of power' practically constituting a state within the State, and the acrimonious differences between original members of the Free Officers Executive in the mid-sixties, all pointed to a terrible political mess of privilege and incompetence. It scandalized a long-suffering public which had lost its confidence in the probity, let alone competence, of its erstwhile youthful and enthusiastic rulers. These no longer commanded the admiration or sympathy of their vast mass constituency.

Older dormant traditional forces bestirred themselves to life and activity, especially the Muslim Brethren. Encouraged by the financial dependence of their country after June 1967 on 'upright' Islamic states such as Saudi Arabia, they were emboldened to re-engage themselves in the political life of the country.[24] There was also a wider Arab revulsion against and hostility to the régime in Egypt and Nasser's leadership. There was an outpouring of highly critical and soul-searching writing occasioned by the débâcle of June 1967.[25] Some of this was probably encouraged and subvented by the so-called conservative Arab states. Yet it reflected a real development, namely, the decline of Egypt's role in the Arab world, or at least the new constraints being placed upon it.

At the other end of the political spectrum the ASU came temporarily under the control of the leftist elements which gravitated around the person of Ali Sabry, a vice-president of the republic, secretary general of the ASU and one-time prime minister. Secret vanguard organizations within the ASU sought to establish a parallel if not alternative centre of power and attain primacy in the counsels of the President. The fall of Ali Sabry, however, in 1969, ostensibly for abusing his exalted position for personal gain, was only a reflection of the devaluation of the peculiar brand of Arab socialism adumbrated since 1962.

In the realm of practical politics, though, Nasser exhibited great reserves for survival. Though dogged by advancing illness since 1964, if not earlier, he acted on several fronts simultaneously. After an impressive rate of growth between 1956 and 1963, the Egyptian economy began to falter and decline perilously by 1968. The Six Day War ended with the Israelis in control of the Sinai Peninsula, denying Egypt half of its oil production. Revenues in hard foreign currency from the Suez Canal stopped completely when the waterway was closed during that war. Defence expenditure in the years 1967–70 swallowed up nearly a fourth of national income. Deteriorating relations with the United States during the years of the Yemen war (1962–7) deprived Egypt of much-needed American aid, especially wheat shipments. The breaking off of diplomatic relations with West Germany early in 1965 for its sale of arms to Israel denied Egypt yet another rich source of economic assistance.

A new political economy of retrenchment was clearly needed, and Nasser moved towards that in the mid-sixties. This strategy, however, was shattered by the Six Day War in 1967. Although the war pushed Egypt towards an ever greater dependence on and closer alliance with the Soviet Union, her acute economic crisis required the mending of her fences with the West. This, in turn, implied a moderation of her regional policy, especially with regard to Israel. From Khartoum in 1967 to the Casablanca Arab Summit in 1969 Nasser sought to win Arab support for a more circumspect policy of confrontation with Israel. What this meant in practice was to keep the conflict with Israel alive short of another actual armed clash. His interest in securing the support of the other Arab states, or at least the rich ones, for his policy converged with that of many of those states which were satisfied with Nasser's retreat from the regional Arab political stage. By 1969, however, Nasser was also disillusioned with his Arab allies in seeking a formula for the resolution of the conflict with Israel.

All of this set the stage for Nasser to signal his willingness for a rapprochement with the West, particularly the United States. This, however, was not a straightforward proposition. The Israelis were content with their occupation of the Sinai, West Bank and Golan in Syria. The other Arab states that had suffered from Nasser's aggressive regional policy of the previous decade were equally content with his predicament, and the 'no war, no peace' status of the Arab–Israel conflict. The reconstituted Palestine Liberation Movement had lost faith in the ability of the regular Arab armies to retrieve Palestine for them; more radical elements gained control of the Palestine Liberation Organization (PLO) and embarked upon a policy of violent action against Israel, launched at first primarily from Jordan. They were unhappy with the 'no war, no peace' situation and preferred war. Egypt, in fact, was the least happy of all parties concerned with the 'no war, no peace' formula of the Khartoum Summit. In the face of American indifference too, an initiative to break the deadlock was needed.

It was against this regional and global background that Nasser launched his war of attrition on the Suez Canal in March 1969. The gamble was very costly in lives and material, for it escalated the violence across the Canal. The Israelis, now deeply entrenched in their Bar Lev defence line along the Canal, escalated the war from mere artillery duels to intense and devastating air strikes against Egyptian positions in the Canal area and deep penetration aerial bombing of Egyptian installations and industrial sites along the Nile Valley. Though technically a failure, Nasser's strategy paid off in a sense, since the escalation of violence attracted international and, significantly, American attention. The Americans came forward with a cease-fire proposal as a prelude to a settlement on a modified version of the 1967 UN Resolution 242.[26] This came to be known as the Rogers Plan after the then US Secretary of State William Rogers.

In devising the multi-pronged strategy and policy after 1967, Nasser perhaps took advantage of the new Nixon administration (1968) announcement that it intended to follow a more 'even-handed policy' in the Middle East, and the fact that his Soviet patrons seemed quite satisfied with the post-June 1967 *status quo* and pressed him (their client) to seek a political settlement with Israel. Having severed their diplomatic relations with Israel, however, it was clear that the Soviets could contribute little towards that end. The remaining option was an American role. Nasser though wished to enter any negotiations from a position of strength. When Israeli raids became fierce towards the end of 1969, he managed, during a secret visit to Moscow in January 1970, to extract from the Soviets an effective SAM-3 missile air defence system along the Canal, with Soviet crews to operate it.

The developments of the more direct Soviet involvement in the defence of Egypt during the war of attrition created the preconditions not only of further escalation of the conflict but more ominously of a superpower confrontation. Momentarily both superpowers became interested in a negotiated settlement. At this point Nasser was able to announce Egypt's readiness to accept an American-sponsored cease-fire as a prelude to a settlement on the basis of the Rogers Plan.

Radical Arab, particularly Palestinian, reaction to this move was expectedly sharp. They realized that any settlement between Egypt and Israel would be at the expense of their own national aspirations and objectives. Consequently, they embarked upon an international campaign of terror, consisting mainly of airline hijackings. But they also forced an armed confrontation with the régime of King Hussein in Jordan, where they tended to operate openly, defying him and his army's authority. It was this showdown leading to the decimation and expulsion of the remnants of the Palestine resistance movement from Jordan which prompted the reinvolvement of Nasser – and Egypt – in the affairs of the wider Arab region. Both national interest and Nasser's own image and erstwhile role as an Arab leader impelled him to seek a settlement of the Hussein–PLO conflict at a summit meeting of Arab heads of state in Cairo in September 1970. Having managed to set inter-Arab machinery in motion in the form of a committee and having convinced the antagonists to stop the slaughter, he died of a heart attack on 28 September 1970. The Palestinians, however, had to move on from Jordan to Lebanon, creating new and explosive situations in that 'precarious republic'. But that is another story.

EGYPT UNDER SADAT

It is not possible or sensible to attempt a history of Egypt in the last ten years under President Sadat. All we can essay here is a broad outline, a sketch, of the most significant developments.

Nasser's death ended an era in contemporary Egyptian history. Within less than a year after his death, his political lieutenants were ousted from all positions of power by his successor, Anwar al-Sadat. His economic policy was in tatters; his Arab policy a controversial memory. At first imperceptibly, though relentlessly, his successor moved towards the undoing of Nasser's power élite or at least its neutralization and the construction of his own. May 1971, when in a lightning coup President Sadat established his undisputed control over the Egyptian state, was followed by July 1972 when he expelled all Soviet advisers and other personnel from the country, signalling an about-face in Egyptian foreign policy. At the same time he moved closer to an alliance with the rich, conservative Arab states, chief among them Saudi Arabia, as a prelude to the October 1973 war. At the same time an equally radical departure from the recent past was President Sadat's adoption of a different economic policy, one directed at attracting massive foreign capital into Egypt, and encouraging the revival of the private sector of the economy.

The Egyptian crossing of the Suez Canal and the political outcome of the Ramadan or Yom Kippur war provided the new basis for President Sadat's peace policy of a final accommodation with Israel. The dramatic steps which he took in the implementation of this new policy – his visit to Jerusalem in November 1977 when he addressed the Knesset, the summit meeting in America in September 1978, and the Camp David accords leading to the signing of the Egypt–Israel Peace Treaty in March 1979 – constituted perhaps the first serious act of policy taken by any Arab ruler in the thirty-year-old conflict. It is not unkind, nor does it detract from Sadat's bold and imaginative initiative, to suggest that the domestic troubles of autumn 1973 and the food riots of January 1977 underlined the urgency of resolving the burdensome external conflict if Egypt was to concentrate on the tackling of pressing economic and social problems at home.

But if Sadat's peace initiative were merely a tactical manœuvre, and even allowing for the fact that in Egypt everyone follows the ruler's cue whether he agrees with him or not, there would not have been the massive and surprisingly unsolicited support for that initiative on the part of Egyptians. One must look for more substantial reasons and deeper foundations for this initiative.

The genuine desire and real need of Egyptians for a peace settlement with Israel had been gestating at least since 1970. This was partly reflected in Nasser's own impatience and disappointment with his Arab allies in 1969–70, and in his intense feeling of insecurity over Soviet military assistance between January and April 1970, which forced him to press the Soviets into a more direct involvement in the defence of his country – at the same time as accepting the Rogers Plan for a cease-fire on the Canal. But the desire and need acquired intensity and urgency after the October 1973 war, though in an historically and nationally more characteristic way. Egyptians, for the first time in twenty-five years, reverted to a more insular perception and articulation of their national interest. Their new-formed pride in a national identity involved the memory of Muhammad Ali the Great and Ibrahim Pasha, Khedive Ismail and Orabi Pasha, and the 1919 Revolution and its leadership.

Egyptians believe historically and feel nationally that their country represents one of the oldest civilizations in the world; that their state is the oldest and most experienced in the region. To this extent they have a secular perception of – and an instinct for – survival. They view their quarrel with Israel as being mainly one over territory; they want Sinai back. They do not ignore, however, the potential rivalry between them and Israel in the region. At the same time they argue that, despite their opposition, other Arabs for the moment can do very little about Israel without Egypt's leadership and support. Nor can they deny Egypt a role in the Arab world by virtue of its sheer size, the dynamism of its experience and momentum of its human resources. On a more popular though muted level, Egyptians deplore the possibility that they 'may have missed the bus', so to speak, of the last thirty years, as a result of their involvement in a regional conflict which forced them to fight four wars against Israel and one in the Yemen. In more general, but for the moment guarded, terms one observes a quiet though perceptible determination on the part of Egyptians for a partial disengagement from the vagaries of the Middle East conflict and a thunderous readoption of the old slogans 'Egypt for the Egyptians' and 'Egypt first above all else'.

THE DOMESTIC SCENE

The poor state of the Egyptian economy in 1977 was obvious. It became clear as soon as one probed systematically into the economic, administrative, educational and other social problems of the country. Issues such as the availability of trained human resources, emigration, inflation, housing, and the relationship with the richer Arab states and foreign powers, were a few of the main preoccupations. The great burden of defence expenditure together with the pressure of population on the economy and the breakdown of services in urban areas were sources of general disquiet and insecurity.

Egypt, then, needed a peace settlement. But much of the economic mess was perceived to be the result of the *political* bankruptcy of the 1952 régime. What is interesting is that most groups of Egyptians, including the youth, recognized this and were anxious for the restoration of a plural political system. Thus secular Egyptians, civilians and soldiers, felt uncomfortable about the widespread resurgence of religio-political groups and movements among the youth, the lower ranks of army officers and the state bureaucracy. They ascribed this phenomenon in part to the connection with Saudi Arabia, and somehow hoped that in the event of a peace settlement this tie would be loosened. At the same time they suggested that one of the dangers of Israeli intransigence in the peace negotiations was the further strengthening of these extreme, fanatic groups in Egypt. 'Fanaticism', they argue, 'tends to be fought by a counter-fanaticism.' Thus, in the student-union elections of the university in the winter of 1978 the religio-political Right secured the majority of offices. On the basis of this specific instance, as well as the violent events connected with the group known as *Al-hijra wa'ltakfir*, secular Egyptians alluded to a wider nexus of trouble: the closer Egypt's involvement in the Arab political labyrinth, the more powerful the religious–traditional currents in their country's politics become.

This overall feeling explains in part the surprising enthusiasm for the new Wafd Party in January–February 1978. Young and old Egyptians alike hailed it as a much-needed mass centre political organization. They expected it to press for constitutional guarantees of civil liberties, check the excessive tendencies of one-man rule deriving essentially from the Nasser experience, help distinguish between an Egyptian state role in the Arab world on one hand, and an indiscriminate political involvement (as in Nasser's days) on the other, and promote and strengthen Egyptian national interest. Psychologically, these hopes represented Egyptians' revulsion against the twenty-five-year rule of the soldiers. At the same time, the military establishment hoped that the Wafd's return to political life would counteract the infiltration of their lower ranks by the Muslim Brethren.

After his scathing attack on the Wafd in the summer of 1977, President Sadat was obliged to allow the party's formal return to public life, partly for the same reasons but also because of external factors – the peace negotiations with Israel, and the recent policy of closer ties with the Sudan. After all, Egyptian patriotism and the so-called unity of the Nile Valley have always constituted the heart of the Wafd's political platform and programme. The as yet unknown consequences of Sadat's peace with Israel policy moreover suggested to him the advantages of the availability of an alternative government formed by a party which, surprisingly perhaps, still commands immense popularity throughout the country. It was also in keeping with Sadat's so-called liberalization programme for the restoration of democracy in Egypt. More generally, the threat of communal differences in September 1977, the acrimonious debates over the government's economic policies later that autumn and during part of winter 1978, and Sadat's dramatic visit to Jerusalem provided the kind of atmosphere for the support the new Wafd needed to press for its recognition and reinstatement. The Left was on the whole in favour of the Wafd's return because it hoped to constitute its *avant-garde* wing. On its own the Left had hardly a chance of reorganizing its ranks, outside the Khaled Mohieddin party in the People's Assembly, the National Unionist Progressive Party (NUPP).

That there was also opposition both to the Sadat régime and the return of the Wafd among remnants of the Nasserites, there is no doubt. But one must gauge the effectiveness of this opposition against the reality of domestic and international factors. On the whole, the Nasserites are a dwindling breed for the simple reason that the military believes Nasser with his policies 'destroyed the army', and the population at large believes that Nasser's economic policy at home and Arab policy abroad have been the main causes of their condition today. It is more difficult to explain the apparent enthusiasm of the young for the Wafd. They constitute a generation that never knew the Wafd. Of course many of them belong to Wafdist families. Probably their revulsion against the 1952 régime has been such that they welcomed the return of a political party associated with the Egyptian national movement – or perhaps any change was better than no change. If the alacrity with which the over 50,000 copies of the *Ahali*, the newspaper of the NUPP, were snatched from newsagents early in 1978 is any indication, Egyptians have been clearly bored with a style of government and politics which Louis Awad in 1974 described as 'government by monologue'.

At the same time the Sadat regime had already been reviewing – in many instances, undoing – the whole Nasserite economic policy, if not the Nasserite edifice itself. Legislation had been passed, and more was in the pipeline, which allowed a greater share in the economy to the private sector and which would engender serious competition for the highly bureaucratized and often corrupt public sector. Using the foreign media and his *October* magazine, President Sadat had been trying to generate an atmosphere of public concern for individual freedom and initiative, and for the further development of agriculture, while alluding to the 'errors of the July revolution' over economic policy. He was also trying to create the impression that his régime was immediately concerned with domestic matters, especially those of employment, nutrition, health and housing. There was a relative freedom for Egyptians to speak their minds openly on political issues; something that was hardly possible under Nasser. In the spring of 1978 Egypt appeared to see itself as a state with clear interests at home and abroad, not as a centre of regional revolutionary or liberation struggles.

Many wonder about who might oust Sadat from power. The simple answer is another soldier at the head of a military *coup d'état*. But coups are not as easy to organize or mount as they were twenty-five, or even ten, years ago. The army then was small. Many of its younger officers were involved in, or had connections with, radical movements going back to the 1930s and 1940s. Today the army is nearly 500,000 strong, and the officer corps is proportionately large. Many of the officers, moreover, are one- to two-year conscripts, usually with direct commissions as university graduates. Consequently conspiracies are difficult to organize and the risk of detection is high. At the same time, the periodic purging of the officer corps, a practice begun under Nasser, continues, even though it may not be as massive or frequent today. There is also a reluctance on the part of soldiers to intervene in political matters, largely motivated by the vagaries of past experience. Thus, during the terrible food riots of January 1977 Sadat's – more precisely, Mamduh Salem's – request for army intervention was turned down by the commander-in-chief of the armed forces as well as by senior commanders. The extensive changes in structure, organization and training introduced between 1964 and 1973 have greatly affected the professional and career perceptions of army officers, as well as their attitude to the role of the army in politics. These reservations cannot preclude a military coup in the future, but the circumstances will have to be truly extraordinary. Nonetheless the ever-widening gap between the few very rich and the vast majority of the poor may create conditions reminiscent, because parallel, of the period 1950–2. That many of the new rich acquired their wealth as a result of access to influence and power would only help to fuel the resentment of the rest of society. The experience in Iran in 1978–9 suggests that the massive importation of luxury commodities for the few is not economically or politically wise in the long run. But the leaders of the country appear for the moment insensitive to these sharp disparities. Another source of potential disaffection is in the officer corps. Equally affected by rampant inflation, they can see their civilian relations enriching themselves in quick-return enterprises. They also view with great suspicion the better pay and conditions and the unnecessarily sophisticated weaponry of the police, for they assume the régime might use the strengthened police force to control popular disturbances caused by economic hardship. It is noteworthy that, generally speaking, coups in the Middle East have been rare in the last decade.

THE NASSER LEGACY UNDER SADAT

The main feature of Nasser's rule was the highly personalized 'system' he devised. The brief period of collective decisions and responsibility under the Free Officer régime lasted barely two years. By November 1954 Nasser was supreme. From a *primus inter pares*, he had become a native *sultan*. The issue of his legitimacy was resolved, in a manner of speaking, by his charisma and his acceptance by an enthusiastic public. The people soon constructed their hero, and reaffirmed their loyalty and allegiance to him in a series of plebiscites from 1956 onwards. The centralization of power was also assisted by the peculiar geography of Egypt and the military élitist provenance of the régime. Political competition was eliminated – the bureaucracy was further militarized – the society mobilized and regimented. Because Nasser believed he embodied the aspirations of the Egyptians and reflected their will, he saw no need for political representation for them.

The stability Nasser provided in Egypt by his charismatic personal rule stood in sharp contrast to the instability of the institutions he experimented with. During his rule he produced five parliaments with an average life of two years. He promulgated six constitutions. His cabinets had on average a lifespan of thirteen months. Even on the ideological front, Nasser exhibited successive changes in his commitment. The stability of his sixteen-year rule derived from his charismatic autocracy, or caesarist despotism. The President became the linch-pin of the new Egyptian political order. He had the right to interfere in all areas of national, political, social, economic and cultural life of the country.

Has there been a change in this central position of the President since 1970 or 1973? Some say unequivocally that Sadat is as much of a *sultan* as Nasser in terms of power concentrated in his person.

Others argue that a great deal has changed. Neither view is warranted. What there has been is a process of reorientation, intimating a transition from an authoritarian to a plural régime of sorts, and from a denial to a recognition of civil rights. The process has been slow, gradual, at times abrasive and frustrating, with an element of stop–go in it. Above all it has been a tightly controlled process. Sadat has been able to use Nasser's legacy of autocratic rule to direct this process from a position of strength. Without it, there could have well been a Portugal-type of chaos in post-Nasser Egypt.

When did this reorientation begin? It is difficult to give an exact date, for it had already begun under Nasser in 1968–70. However, it became more perceptible when Sadat was no longer under the shadow of the founder of the Egyptian republic. In fact, Sadat's own legitimacy derived from two events: his destruction of the Nasserites who challenged his authority in May 1971 and his going to war against Israel in October 1973. Soon after this he was emphasizing the importance for Egypt of moving from arbitrary power to the rule of law. With such an orientation went the lifting of censorship, the reform of the courts, selective desequestrations of property and assets, and a less clumsy use of the security services. The next step was the introduction of a *controlled* multi-party system, under which there were limitations on party activity imposed by the law of political parties. What was being introduced under this controlled change was not so much an element of pluralism in Egyptian political life as one of *diversity*. But it was the first of its kind since 1952 and it managed also to generate an atmosphere of security while at the same time further improving Sadat's political standing in the country.

There was not, however, any fundamental change in the composition of the élite, whether in cabinet or parliament; nor in the basis of its recruitment. On the other hand, there was a firmer determination to keep the army out of politics by a greater emphasis on its professional role. In the 1976 elections the army was denied the vote and generally, it was no longer the political force it had been under Nasser. Nevertheless, there was a reluctance, born – presumably – of fear, to permit any widespread liberalization and democratization of the régime. The food riots in January 1977 led to a retreat from any further diversity, until by mid-1978 the whole process of reorientation was qualified, if not in fact arrested, and the atmosphere of security disturbed. By June 1978 it looked as if the régime was preparing the way for the army to regain its old political role.

In the face of vehement attacks by the President and the administration, the newly reconstituted Wafd Party disbanded itself. A pall of uncertainty hung over the political evolution of the country.

More marked, and perhaps lasting, have been the changes introduced by Sadat in the area of social and economic policy. 'Socialism', however defined under Nasser (say, extensive nationalization), was dropped in favour of an as yet unclear 'democratic socialism'. Egyptian rumour had it that Sadat was enamoured of the Austrian model and experience. Whatever Sadat's understanding of democratic socialism may be, he has recently (1978–9) organized his own National Democratic party. But the most important development of all the changes since 1970 and 1973 has been the Open Door Economic Policy of the Sadat régime. Before we examine this policy, however, we must look at Sadat's position and that of his régime a little more closely.

The fact must be faced that a popular revolution is not a valid option in Egypt – for several reasons, the most important being: first, the vast majority of Egypt's rather poor population lacks political organization; second, revolutionary trends can always be countered by a resort to religious symbols and the strongly held popular values associated with them; and third, Sadat is the beneficiary of an important Nasser achievement, namely, the absence of all other leadership – or at least, credible alternative leadership – in the country. To this extent, the powers of Sadat as President of Egypt have not changed since Nasser. Even though Sadat affects a different style, there is hardly anyone else in the country with enough of a power base to challenge him, not even Nasser's engaging apprentice, the journalist Muhammad Hasanein Heikal. Moreover, the difference in style between the two men is to Sadat's advantage. Whereas Nasser had no social life to speak of, Sadat, some will aver, has too much of it. Sadat leads an easier life in contrast to Nasser's austere puritanism and obsessively intense preoccupation with power. Above all, unlike Nasser, Sadat truly delegates power to his most trusted and loyal lieutenants. In a sense, Sadat is the better juggler. Although both men may be characterized as pragmatic, non-doctrinaire political types with no serious ideological commitments, their personalities could not be more different. Nasser was the typical product of urban Egypt in the 1930s, intensely brooding, secretive and reticent; whereas Sadat is essentially a *rifi*, i.e. village type, who has maintained his close links with his village and visibly retained the popular-religious inclinations of the villager.

Despite the contrasts and changes, or attempted changes since 1970, the lingering influence of Nasser did act, for a time, as a constraint on Sadat. There was, for instance, Nasser's ghost, if one may call it that, among students. There was also the memory of Nasser's charisma. More practically, there were the residual foreign policy considerations from Nasser's legacy. It can be argued that it was Sadat's desire to escape from these which led him on to the dangerous road to liberalization. In social and economic terms, Nasser's economic policy, the main feature of which was the creation of a huge public sector, gave rise to a new social stratum: an odd 'capitalist class' consisting of army officers, public-sector managers and a few remnants of the old régime, whose power was mainly due to their peculiar role as 'middle men' in the new overregulated state economy.

Sadat's decision to allow a measure of capitalism and a free market economy was linked to his political programme of liberalization. It would be a mistake, however, to suppose that capitalism and liberalism in Egypt, or elsewhere in the Arab Middle East, are synonymous. After 1973 Egypt could not seriously contemplate the restoration of the Nasserite model which, in any case, had exhausted its limits. Nor could she consider a radical socialist régime because of internal constraints and external factors, such as the growing dependence on Saudi financial help and, after the break with the Soviet Union, upon American assistance. She could, however, opt for a capitalist economy alongside an authoritarian state. All of these options, though, ran a very great risk of failure, because they could not be based on a middle-class movement. Even the comparatively small stratum in Egyptian society which approximates to a middle class would not readily commit itself to any of these options because it would place its very survival at risk. (Today even Egyptian Marxists concede the fact that there is no middle class in the country with a continuous tradition to speak of, or a working class for that matter; they even have some difficulty in identifying the petty-bourgeoisie. Only the rural lower class, if you wish the *fellah*, seems to enjoy this continuity.)

Yet real power, as in Nasser's time, rests with the military-police or complex security, not civilian, institutions. Outside the Ministry of Defence or War, and war production and supply, Sadat, unlike Nasser, has studiously avoided appointing military men to senior positions or key ministries. Nevertheless, the Vice President of the Republic is an air force officer, and perhaps for the foreseeable future the offices of President and Vice President will be filled by senior military officers. Sadat also continues to defer to the military over very important decisions, such as the one to go to Jerusalem in November 1977.

Earlier I alluded to the difference in style between the two men. Unlike Nasser, Sadat strengthened his familial ties to power – a kind of tribal ethos characterized by marriages. He married his children to the Sayyid Marei (Speaker of the Assembly) and Osman A. Osman (the most successful Egyptian contractor and now minister) families. He is not pathologically opposed to the small genteel middle class in the country, whether this is represented by its pre-1952 remnants or its post-1952 recruits. Nasser preferred and felt most comfortable with the native lower classes.

To this extent one may speak of a move to the right (although Right and Left are misleading terms in Egypt) under Sadat. Detente (whatever it means or is worth) and the reality of petro-dollars helped Sadat make this move. Even Nasser was by 1970 beginning to consider the possibility, but he always hesitated and equivocated for one important reason: he was anxious to remain a leader of the Arabs. Under Sadat there is no equivocation over the move to a free market economy, closer ties with the US, devising incentives for the small middle class, or above all, to an active policy of peaceful accommodation with Israel.

In the meantime, Sadat has allowed the selective dismantling – and discrediting – of his predecessor's legacy, including some of its institutional scaffolding and paraphernalia, as, for example, the Arab Socialist Union and its vanguard organizations which had become a veritable state within the State. I say 'selective' because the bureaucratic monster remains. So does the vast security apparatus, albeit in less clumsy form. Thus if Nasser's death marked the end of an era, Sadat's rule has yet to constitute a new one.

Egypt under Sadat could, of course, opt for a certain kind of *immobilisme*, which permits the survival of a decadent social order – incidentally, a legacy of Nasser. But since the most serious challenge to the régime comes from the staggering problems of the Egyptian economy, and from the question of whether the government under any régime can feed the teeming masses of the people, Sadat has opted for *infitah*, or the Open Door Policy. Intended, in the first instance, to attract foreign capital investment into Egypt, this policy has been possible only by the régime's abandonment of many of the provisions of a strictly state-controlled public sector economy. The

Open Door Policy thus implies a grudging recognition of the advantages of a free market – capitalist – economy for the treatment of Egypt's terrible economic and social ills. Whether capitalism as such is a viable solution for a country like Egypt, however, is a serious and complex question.

THE OPEN DOOR POLICY

There are certain basic demographic facts about Egypt that must be borne in mind. The country has a very young population: 42 per cent of its 40 million population (estimate end of 1977) are under 15 years of age. Yet the working population is about 9·5 million, or just under 25 per cent of the total population of the country. Despite the industrialization programmes of the last 25 years and the expansion of the service sector, nearly half of this working population (44·7 per cent) is still engaged on the land, 35·9 per cent in services and only 19·4 per cent in industry. In other words, the industrial labourforce in Egypt today stands at just over 1·5 million, half of them employed in the private sector, of a total population of 40 million.

The acts leading to the Open Door Policy did not really constitute the creation of a series of political institutions. Rather they established a number of political guidelines enunciated by Sadat, dating back to 1971. On 10 June 1971 he proclaimed his Plan for National Action. This was followed by a referendum and a constitution in September 1971. A further constitutional document was the 'October Declaration' of 1974, on the basis of which Investment Law No. 43/1974 was promulgated and decreed. This came to be the central feature of the Open Door Policy. Its chief purpose is to attract Arab and foreign investment capital under highly favourable – indeed, privileged – conditions. An Investment and Free Zones Authority was set up to deal with this aspect of the new law. It might be said that the elections of November 1976 and the referendum of February 1977 further formalized, if not sanctioned, the public 'acceptance' of these important measures.

It is too early to say whether the Open Door Policy has led to serious economic changes in the country, or that it has created new economic structures. What it seems to have done so far is to establish and expand a parallel market for foreign exchange, reduce exchange restrictions, reform banking laws, and to some extent decentralize the making of economic decisions. More important perhaps, it has increased the participation of the private sector in the economy and thus introduced an element of greater competition for the public sector.

Another major shift in economic policy under the Sadat régime appears to be a greater attention to agricultural development and land reclamation as a result of the recognition that massive industrialization is not feasible and cannot alone resolve Egypt's economic problems. If the monument to Nasser's rule is the Aswan Dam, with its intended dual role in the industrialization of the country and the expansion of agricultural production, further hydroelectric schemes, if they ever materialize, may well become the monument to Sadat's régime. For Sadat's nightmare remains that of feeding the 40 million Egyptians: the famous 200 million loaves of native bread he must provide every morning.

It appears then that the most basic choices in political economy the Sadat régime has made are: (a) a shift to a free market economy in the hope of attracting foreign capital investment; (b) a greater determination to strike a more reasonable and credible balance between industrial and agricultural development; (c) a decision to revitalize the existing public sector by promoting keener competition from an enlarged private sector; and (d) a conscious effort to provide for a manageable handling of the social and economic problems looming on the horizon between now and the year 2000. This, it is hoped, will be greatly facilitated by the more rapid transfer of technology to Egypt which will accelerate Egypt's economic and social development. If this is a reasonable depiction of the most recent trends, it is important to survey some of the difficulties and obstacles these plans face.

It is staggering to think that Egypt's estimated population in the year 2000 will be 60 million or over, or an increase in 20 years of 50 per cent. Although the country's total area covers 1,002,000 square kilometres, only one-quarter of this area, 38,700 square kilometres, is cultivated and inhabited. This area is only slightly larger than Belgium. Whereas along the river banks average population density is bearable at 39 per square kilometre, in the Delta it reaches suffocating proportions of 1,000 per square kilometre, one of the highest in the world. Lately much of this population has been moving to the cities, especially Cairo, at an alarming rate. Thus Cairo today creaks – has virtually collapsed – under the weight of nearly ten million inhabitants.

Although Egypt disposes of abundant and cheap labour, most of it is ill-fed, uneducated or poorly educated and trained. So the question of the manpower that is available for economic development is not straightforward. The migration propensities of the Egyptian workforce which could slightly alleviate the problem and also provide remittances back home are mainly confined to white-collar skills, and the professionally trained: teachers, doctors, lawyers, engineers, scientists. Ever since the mid-sixties scores of thousands of these have migrated to the rich oil-producing Arab countries, Canada and Australia. But this is the wrong kind of exported workforce, since it is exactly the kind of people Egypt needs to man its development programmes.

It seems clear that the collapse of municipal and other services, so crucial to the success of an Open Door Policy, has been due in part to Nasser's fatal mistake of allowing the large community of Italian and Greek craftsmen, artisans and small-scale business managers to leave the country. One is not referring to the big landowners and entrepreneurs among the resident foreign communities of pre-1952 Egypt, but to the highly skilled, wage-earning members of these communities who helped maintain public utilities, buildings and services at a cost far below that being charged by imported experts today. It can be said in mitigation that when the services of a city like Cairo were first planned and developed between the 1870s and 1930s, they were never intended to serve 9–10 million souls.

Even more serious is the deplorable condition of the state administration, with its overmanned and wasteful bureaucracy. It is not only a matter of non-existent telephones, virtually absent telecommunications, inadequate water and power services which hinder the development of a free market economy or economic development, in any area from agriculture to industry. It is also the quality of the human factor in the equation. Ever since Nasser – for political reasons – opened up higher education to all and embarked upon an ambitious educational programme for which the country had neither the financial nor human resources, the State has had each year to find jobs for thousands of university graduates, who normally expect to be absorbed into the state bureaucracy or state-owned enterprises. Security of tenure regardless of performance is not the best incentive to productive work. It is this obstructionist monster of the state machine with its red-tape, lethargy and choking legalism which has impeded a faster rate of foreign capital flow into the country. Nor should one minimize the deterrent of political uncertainty to investment. At the same time it is, literally, a tremendous chore to exist in, say, Cairo on a daily basis. No individual or corporate investor, who expects some return on his investment will put up with these haphazard and frustrating conditions.

The régime apparently hope that the Open Door Policy will alleviate the employment problem by absorbing the masses of Egyptian unemployed and underemployed secondary school and university graduates into an expanding private sector of the economy. With the greater attention to be paid to agriculture and food production, it also hopes to slow down the movement of population from the countryside to the city. The hope is to raise production by multiplying productive economic pursuits, and so lower inflation and increase the rate of savings. There are hazards in the Open Door Policy itself, if only because it brings to mind (without referring to Egypt's current indebtedness) the Khedive Ismail episode of last century. Historical parallels and analogies may be dangerous, but they remain instructive. Egypt, on the other hand, may well be trying to emulate the Brazilian experience, but there are grave dangers in such emulations.

This kind of political economy could conceivably push Egypt back to an old national interest, namely, its link with the Sudan. Apart from the traditional, historical interest of Egypt in its southern neighbour, the Sudan could become an important source of additional food for the Egyptian masses. Nasser, towards the end of his days, tried unsuccessfully to make the Sudan a recipient of Egyptian excess labour. This the Sudanese firmly resisted. But economic and political government policies have clearly led to a more immediate interest in the Red Sea.

Perhaps the greatest danger to these new policies comes from domestic factors. Educated Egyptians are aware of the fact that Egypt has been, since 1953, one of the largest recipients of foreign aid. They are equally aware of the inequitable distribution of available resources, and the glaring disparity between great wealth among the new post-1952 privileged groups and the economically deprived masses of the population. Even if these educated Egyptians number no more than two or three million, it is they who are most affected by the vagaries of the economy, especially its near 40 per cent inflation. It is from them that the greatest potential threat to the Sadat 'vision' may come, not from the masses of poor peasants and the heaps of idle and distraught city folk. It is their expectations that have been aroused by the prospect of peace, and they in turn have communicated it to the masses.

Nor should the dangers of a psychologically rooted national dis-affection of the less well-off masses be minimized. In a fragile economy the harsh economic conditions of the last thirty years were justified – perhaps argued away – by the requirements of a wartime economy, i.e. the conflict with Israel. The 1977/8 budget for example, showed a deficit of £E.1,300 million, inflation was about 40 per cent and rising, and the growing chasm between rich and poor of a magni-tude never seen before. After a peace settlement with Israel, no Egyp-tian régime can have an excuse for not attending to the country's urgent domestic problems.

The immediate need will be for austerity measures, which of course may prove highly unpopular, especially if they eliminate state subsidies for essential food commodities. Austerity measures, how-ever, without an accompanying extensive programme of economic reform, will be meaningless. Oil revenues and an anticipated rise in revenue from Suez Canal dues, once its current development pro-gramme has been completed, will help in an area that is not of imme-diate benefit to the masses, namely, that of critically needed foreign exchange. The government could, of course, point to the prospect of developing Sinai with its unexplored riches in minerals. But this can have only a long-term impact on the country's economy.

The short-term prospect, even with peace, is therefore grim. A heavy national defence burden on the budget will persist for some years, rising from the current £E.2,500 million to possibly £E.3,000 to 4,000 million in the next five years. Any quick reduction in defence expenditure will remain problematical in view of relations with neighbouring Libya and developments in the Horn of Africa affect-ing the Red Sea area. Moreover, the demobilizing of part of a huge standing army will be a very costly affair. It will require the expensive increase in pay and incentives to attract men to a regular peacetime force. And the re-deployment of 100,000 to 200,000 demobilized men may create havoc in a labour market already saturated with vast numbers of unemployed. Finally, there will be the problem of restructuring and controlling the eternal bureaucracy.

If the political economy of the country after the conclusion of a peace treaty with Israel founders upon the rocks of a stubbornly authoritarian state system, a Nasserite legacy, if you will, Egyptians may well resort to different patterns, and the Open Door Policy will have only been an interlude – an experiment that failed. Egypt is still a 'hydraulic society' which requires a master, a *rayyes*. Until the nineteenth century, plagues, famines and other natural scourges kept its population either below the optimum number, or in balance. What the Egyptians need now is a political order that can accommodate the kind of economic policy which will enable 40 million today, and 60 to 70 million people in the year 2000, to live above the subsistence level.

CONCLUSION

There are dangers lurking in the Sadat régime policy of the last five years which can affect both the domestic situation and the external relations of the country. Egypt's major problem for the foreseeable future will be that of feeding its rising population. In this respect it will continue to depend on outside assistance. Related to it is the phenomenal exodus of its skilled and trained human resources to neighbouring rich Arab countries and, since 1965–6, elsewhere overseas. A redefinition and reformulation of its political priorities both at home and abroad will depend on a resolution of some of its most pressing economic problems. In this respect, Egypt differs perhaps fundamentally from other Arab countries. Moreover, it is also more directly affected by developments in Africa.

In the meantime, the liberalization policy of the régime has opened a political Pandora's Box from which the first creature to emerge – albeit only for a few months – has been the new Wafd. Sadat has, over the last eight years, allowed the discrediting of his predecessor's régime. It is in that atmosphere that old and new forces have moved and surfaced. What may have been originally a mechanical, pro-forma liberalization policy for propaganda purposes now threatens to turn into a serious one by better organized public demand, and by the prospects – slim as they may seem to some – of peace with Israel. An immediate danger, for example, was in the early euphoria exhibited by Egyptians over Sadat's peace initiative. It was as if they were anxious, if not indeed desperate, for an escape from the labyrinth of the Middle East conflict. The reaction which set in, just before Camp David, in the face of no tangible progress towards a settlement, threatened to undermine their faith.

It seems likely, however, that Egypt will seek to strike a balance between a settlement with Israel and a role in the Arab world. Whatever the outcome, for the moment, the vast majority of Egyptians have reacted against the direction and experiments of the last twenty years and are willing to consider a less exciting, more home-oriented policy of retrenchment.

Needless to say, all of these new policy departures entailed an economic and political price at home and abroad. Although the response and reaction of the vast majority of Egyptians to President Sadat's peace initiative and policy was one of welcome relief, opposition to it continued to be spearheaded by the stirring popular religio-political movements that had lain dormant for a long time. These are led and manipulated by the resurrected Muslim Brethren who, under the liberalization programme of the Sadat régime, resumed their activities among students especially and in the press. Their *Da'wa* magazine provided a steady platform of opposition to the régime and its policy of peace with Israel.

Abroad, Sadat's peace policy provoked a sharp and concerted hostile reaction on the part of the other Arab states. Led by Iraq and Syria, these states, meeting in Baghdad in November 1978 and again in March 1979, agreed on a policy of active opposition to Egypt's efforts to implement the terms of her peace treaty with Israel. In practice, it denied Egypt Saudi and Kuwaiti economic aid and financial assistance, which Egypt tried to replace by American and West European help. In inter-Arab political terms, it caused the virtual break-up of the League of Arab States and the severing of diplomatic relations with Egypt by several Arab states. The object of this Arab policy seemed to be one of isolating Egypt on the grounds that she was seeking to conclude a separate peace treaty with Israel, to the detriment and at the expense of wider Arab and specific Palestinian interests.

By 1980, however, this anti-Egyptian Arab front appeared to be only partially effective. Domestic difficulties in Iraq and Syria affecting their move towards closer co-operation, the situation in Lebanon, the eruption of the anti-Shah revolt in Iran with its aftermath and implications for Iranian–Arab relations in Iraq and the Gulf, eroded the forcefulness of the anti-Egypt Arab policy. At the same time the inability or unwillingness of the Arab states to come up with a genuine alternative policy of either peace or war with Israel put the credibility – and effectiveness – of their opposition to Egypt in serious question. Closely involved in this opposition is, of course, the rivalry for Arab leadership. Neither Iraq, Syria nor Saudi Arabia are keen to countenance the eventual emergence of a stronger Egypt after the implementation of the treaty with Israel, including the possible attainment of autonomy for the Palestinians on the West Bank and Gaza Strip. They are also aware of the fact that the Egyptian presence in the Arab world remains massive, despite political differences between Egypt and the other Arab régimes. It is not only the training of Arab military personnel, fifty thousand Arab students in Egypt, or the export of thousands of Egyptian professionals and technical experts to the Arab countries which attests to this presence. It is also the strategic position of Egypt astride Africa and Asia Minor, or astride the Arab East and the Arab West, which concerns them. Moreover, as the oldest modern Arab state, Egypt has always been capable of formulating policies based on a balance between her national interest and her wider interest in the Arab world. Her strategic position and consequently her political posture will clearly improve with the recovery of Sinai. These are some of the considerations which render President Sadat's policy, for the time being at least, credible, and Arab opposition to it more stylish than substantive. In short, it is very difficult to deny Egypt a role in the Arab world, even if Egypt herself opts for a more national policy of 'disengagement' from the wider arena of Arab politics.

PART FIVE

The Search for a Modern Culture and Society

CHAPTER 18

EDUCATION AND CULTURE

Modern state education in Egypt is over a hundred and fifty years old; it dates back to Muhammad Ali the Great who first introduced a system of state schools to train personnel for his army and a cadre of state officials for his administration. In the reign of Khedive Ismail there were further advances and reforms.

The embryonic state school system under Muhammad Ali was military in character, organization and purpose. As in the Ottoman State of that time, modernization was attempted by an autocratic ruler in his military institution. It hardly affected the vast majority of his subjects, whose educational needs continued to be met – adequately or inadequately – by the traditional religious educational system of the Azhar, its affiliated schools and institutes in the towns and provinces, and the village and mosque *kuttab*.

By the mid-1850s and particularly during the reign of Khedive Ismail (1863–79) there was a proliferation of non-governmental private foreign missionary and community schools. English, Scots, American and Catholic French and Italian missionaries opened schools in Cairo, Alexandria, Port Said, Suez, Tanta, Mansura, Fayyum, Dimyat, Kafr al-Zayyat and Asiut. The Coptic, Greek, Italian and Jewish communities also set out about this time to organize their own school systems, financed and controlled by the members of their respective communities. Thus the Coptic Patriarchate Schools were begun in 1853–5. The Greek Community in Cairo was formed in 1856 and provided for schools and a hospital: a girls' school in Hamzawi and the famous Abet School (1860). Similarly in Alexandria they founded schools in 1855; at Mansura in 1859 under the aegis of the Ralli family who were prominent in the cotton trade; in Tanta in 1860 where Greeks had been active in the same trade since 1840. The Italians founded schools in Cairo and Alexandria in 1861–5.

Private schools for members of these communities were also opened a few years later. The Jews, for instance, established free schools in Cairo and Alexandria as well as a Talmudic school in Cairo

(1861). By 1863, the year of Ismail's accession to the Khedivate, there were over fifty such community schools. But in the country as a whole there was no modern primary system of education for Egyptians, whereas the old military schools founded by Muhammad Ali had deteriorated in quality and many of them had been closed down by his immediate successor Abbas I (1849–56). Only the Azhar and village *kuttab* carried on with their work of a traditional religious form of instruction for Egyptians.

Whereas at the end of Muhammad Ali's reign there were barely 3,000 Europeans, by the end of Ismail's there were nearly 70,000, almost half of whom were Greeks, and the other half equally divided between Italians and French. By the time of the British occupation in 1882 there were over 90,000 and at the turn of the century nearly 125,000. These were concentrated mainly in the cities and towns, engaged in commercial, banking and minor industrial enterprises. They also enjoyed the privileges of extra-territoriality under the Capitulations, which amounted virtually to a juridical and political independence from the Egyptian government. They were able therefore to lead their lives practically as self-contained self-sufficient communities, quite divorced from the mainstream of native Egyptian life.

Ismail reopened and improved the old military schools and, with his greater control over religious charitable institutions (*waqfs*), was able to introduce more rational educational aims for the few primary–elementary and private schools then existing in the country. He reactivated the Council (*Diwan*) of Schools, and appointed such competent administrators as Adham and Ali Pasha Mubarak to head it. In 1867–8, Ali Pasha Mubarak, perhaps the greatest administrative reformer in the modern history of Egypt, separated the military from the civilian schools for purposes of administration. He strengthened the Law School under a French director, also the School of Languages, and virtually created a new Polytechnic (*Muhandiskhana*). Aware of the continued importance of the *kuttab* as the only available educational facility for the vast rural population, he reorganized these and introduced examinations to fit a more rational scheme of national educational policy and school system. Then in 1867 he made provisions for three types of schools: (1) primary in Cairo and Alexandria; (2) primary in provincial capitals; and (3) village elementary schools – mainly *kuttab* – in the countryside. With the reorganization of courses, however, came greater centralized control by the State, which now extended to schools previously administered for instance by the *waqfs*. Yet in 1870–3, there were still only 70,000 school pupils in the country, most of them in village *kuttab* and foreign missionary and community schools.

The number of students in the Azhar and its affiliated institutions had risen from 5,000 in 1865 to over 15,000 in 1880; and the number of European and other community schools had risen to 130 in 1880. Yet, the main objective of school reform in this period was the training of state officials – an objective adhered to in the British occupation period 1881–1922.

By 1882, there were over twenty-five primary state schools with 4,500 pupils, over 5,000 *kuttab* with 135,000 pupils, and only one state preparatory school with less than 300 pupils. Lord Dufferin, in his report of 1883, adjudged all these schools as deficient. There were also some 200 European schools of all kinds, and a similar number of private Egyptian schools.

At the turn of the century 95 per cent of Egyptians were illiterate, and until 1920 hardly more than 1 per cent of the annual budget of Egyptian governments was ever devoted to education. Education during the British occupation had been neglected. Thus the Sub-Committee on Education of the 1920 Milner Commission had deplored the government's record in the field and declared it a failure.

A worse legacy of the nineteenth century was that created by the dichotomy in training and cultural outlook produced by the introduction of a state school system modelled on European lines and the expanded missionary and foreign community schools. These tended to produce Egyptians trained mainly in the French language, and some of the modern subjects of a European curriculum. At the same time, the vast majority of Egyptians who became literate did so in the religious *kuttab* and the traditional curricula of the Azharite institutions. The latter system was neither displaced nor thoroughly, or properly, reformed until recently. Several of the Egyptian leaders before and after independence who had been exposed to both types of education portrayed not simply this dichotomy but a peculiar cultural ambivalence manifested in their writings and political behaviour, characterized by an immobilism at dead centre (e.g., Muhammad Abduh, Saad Zahglul, Taha Husayn, Muhammad Husayn Haykal and many others). Even in the matter of foreign languages, Egyptians in the state school system were exposed primarily to French influence throughout most of the nineteenth century, but after 1882 English became, at least officially, ascendant.

With independence in 1922, educational policy became strictly a concern of the Egyptian government. As early as 1917 the administration had been considering a project for compulsory elementary education. Article Nineteen of the 1923 Constitution declared it so, and ordered all *kuttab* schooling free. The position at that time was that, in addition to centrally controlled schools, the 1909 Provincial Councils Law had permitted local authorities to set up elementary and primary schools. There were about 615 of these elementary schools, with nearly 60,000 pupils and 70 primary–preparatory schools with about 8,000 pupils.

Elementary education did not become compulsory until 1925. Total enrolment in government secondary schools then was under 10,000, and enrolment in elementary schools under 250,000. For the next thirty years (1923–52), there was a steady expansion of the state educational system. But this was uneven. Compulsory free elementary education decreed by the 1925 law to be completed in ten years fell far short of the mark, for it required an extensive building programme of schools and other facilities. In fact, it was implemented only where there were schools available. Nonetheless, expenditure on state education tripled and by 1940 came to represent 12 per cent of the annual budget. In 1945 there were nearly 4,500 elementary, primary and kindergarten schools in the country with over 750,000 pupils. In 1950 there were a million pupils in these level schools.

Yet the original aim of the 1925 law to combat illiteracy was in 1950 nowhere near fulfilment. The enrolment represented only 30 per cent of elementary school-age children in the country, and in 1960–1 only 65 to 70 per cent of them. Moreover, rapid expansion led to a highly centralized system of state control over syllabi and examinations despite the official diffusion of control represented by *waqf*-supervised schools, those technical institutes under the Ministry of Social Affairs (since 1940), certain provincial primary schools, and Azhar-affiliated institutions.

The greatest pressure on the state school system in the period 1925–50 was felt in secondary education, particularly with the formal opening of the State University in Cairo in 1925. Primary education led to prep–secondary school depending on examination results; secondary school led to employment in government departments and, after 1925, depending on examination results, to university. The pressure became so great that between one school year and another (1951/2–1952/3) the number of secondary school pupils rose from 151,000 to 182,000, representing 20 to 25 per cent of pupils going from primary to secondary education. In 1961, there were about

280,000 secondary school pupils in some 500 schools. What happened then is that there was a distinction in Egyptian educational policy between elementary and primary–preparatory schooling. The former was intended to combat illiteracy, and apply largely to the majority of the rural population. It was also meant to constitute a terminal kind of education. Many of those who managed to get into primary–preparatory schools were destined for secondary schools and eventually came to constitute a privileged group *vis-à-vis* the vast majority of elementary school children. Moreover, elementary schools never accommodated more than 35 per cent of the eligible children in that period.

In 1951, the Wafd government passed a law unifying all early schooling into a six-year elementary course leading to a certificate by examination. An earlier law in 1949 had made the first two years' tuition in the academic stream in secondary schools free, with resultant increased pressure on secondary schools. When the following year (1950) the Wafdist Minister of Education, Taha Husayn, decreed all secondary education free too, the results were nearly disastrous. Pressure on secondary schools with limited facilities in turn led to pressure on government jobs and university places. Meanwhile, the original objective of making elementary education universal in the country to eradicate illiteracy suffered. By 1951, there were 1·8 million pupils in state schools of all levels, representing an annual increase since the end of the Second World War of nearly 100,000. Secondary schools in particular manifested the drawbacks of a centralized uniform syllabus and examinations; an overemphasis on language and theoretical subjects; overcrowding because of poor and limited physical facilities; a shortage of qualified teachers; and consequent low standards of teaching.

The perception of education by most Egyptians before 1952 was one of receiving *instruction* in a packaged syllabus form, in order to pass an examination which led either to an office position in the state bureaucracy or to a place in one of the three state universities.[1] The acquisition of a school certificate was considered a ticket to a better economic future via secure state employment – tantamount to a sinecure. This situation is clearly reflected in the slow development of technical and vocational education (trade, commercial and other schools) in the period 1922–52. In 1938, for instance, there were only twenty-two such schools administered by the Ministry of Education – three in Cairo, ten in the Delta, and nine in Upper Egypt – despite the fact that such schools had been introduced by Muhammad Ali as early as 1830. Nor were these schools too successful because of the average Egyptian's conception of the purposes and ends of education – state employment.[2] At the end of the Second World War total enrolment in these schools was hardly over 20,000. Even as recently as 1962 it was barely over 80,000. This constituted a serious difficulty when the government had recently estimated that it would require initially between 60,000 and 100,000 technicians for its in-dustrialization programme, most of them in engineering and allied trades and skills.

A reorganization of technical education began in 1956 on the primary, secondary and higher levels. The last has been strengthened by the founding of Institutes of cotton, petroleum, technology and electronics.

Political trends in this period were also reflected in certain policies of the government intended to extend its control over educational institutions. The attack upon tradition discussed in Chapters 13 to 15 was reflected in the movement for reform of the Azhar after 1925. The government wished to bring that venerable centre of Islamic learning into line with modern state education and at the same time to extend its secular control over its affairs. Yet, simultaneously with the secularization of state education in Egypt, independence brought with it a conscious attempt to curtail the influence of foreign missionary, community and private schools in the country. Thus the thirties and forties saw new legislation passed to combat missionary activity in Egypt and to bring foreign schools under closer supervision and control of the Ministry of Education. In 1933 and again in 1940 such laws were passed. Among other things, the law in March 1940 required all foreign schools to teach Arabic, Islamic history and religious instruction to all their Muslim students.

The contribution of foreign and native private schools to education in Egypt since the mid-nineteenth century is noteworthy. When practically no other schools were available, it took care of over 50 per cent of the student population in the country. One student of Egyptian education estimated that in 1880 52 per cent of all students in the country attended foreign schools. In 1914 the percentage was 38; however, 54 per cent of all girl students attended foreign schools. In 1928 there were 78 American schools, 91 Italian, 74 British, 279 French, 88 Greek, and 27 others. Together these looked after nearly 70,000 pupils. In 1956, when the number of these schools was half the 1928 figure, they had a total enrolment of nearly 100,000. Even in 1961 there were over two hundred foreign schools. After their nationalization in 1958–60, these schools together with all other Egyptian private schools still enrolled over 450,000 students.[3]

Social consciousness among the educated élite produced an active interest in the educational and social improvement of the Egyptian fellah. The creation of the Social Affairs Ministry in 1939 further encouraged this concern, so that one observes the appearance of several social reform organizations and societies, as well as a series of publications devoted to the social problems of the Egyptian countryside, the fellah and his needs. A society for the renaissance of villages and the eradication of illiteracy was active by 1941; a Society of Social Affairs appeared in January 1940. Various books dealing with the fellah, with education and unemployment appeared.[4]

Projects for an Arab Encyclopedia were inaugurated with independence in 1923, and the question of the teaching of medical and other sciences in Arabic studied. The feminist movement and some of its earliest organizations attacked the problems of polygamy, marriage and divorce, female education, child care and maternity questions.[5]

Despite the flowering of the popular Press and various schools of prose and poetry in this period,[6] state educational policy consisted essentially of providing instruction in predetermined curricula to equip children with enough knowledge to permit them to secure a livelihood. There was as yet no systematic attempt to relate educational policy to national economic and social needs. Worse still, there was no conscious philosophy relating education to civic training and culture. The rural population still relegated to the traditional *kuttab* and having limited access only to elementary schooling continued to be isolated from the cities and towns. Outside the major cities there were hardly any libraries or other educational aid facilities.

In the cities, on the other hand, the alarming increase in secondary school and university graduates (representing of course a wide migration from country to town) swelled the ranks of the unemployed and underemployed. The more talented members of the intelligentsia – the intellectuals – be they newspapermen, writers or others – rankled under economic conditions not commensurate with a self-image of their own worth. Students became a 'political class' to be alternately wooed and punished by political parties and the State, their ranks a hotbed of rebellion, violence and moral destitution.

By 1952, it was clear that the economic standards of the majority of secondary school pupils rendered their average age above the normal elsewhere in the world. In their inordinately vast numbers they became an identifiable community – *al-talaba*, the student body – with a *student-anschauung* characterized by a bitter enmity against all well-to-do Egyptians and foreigners, and against the West generally; ready to be recruited into militant movements which purported neat and easy formulae of salvation (e.g., the Muslim Brethren, Young Egypt Association and the Communist Party). Cultivated by Wafdist and other politicians since independence and by politicians even before that, students acquired a sociopolitical status far more important than their actual role and capacities justified.[7]

Following the rat-race to get through a packed – and, in many respects, existentially and nationally meaningless – secondary school curriculum, the average Egyptian school-leaver went out into society armed with a weapon (*al-shahada silah*, 'a certificate is a weapon') – a high school diploma, or in the case of the university graduate a degree, expecting a job. He had memorized aspects of Islamic and Arab history, aspects of certain physical and natural sciences; learned Arabic with hypnotic parroting yet without a real appreciation or critical understanding of it, and a foreign language (English or French) rather badly. He had hardly read widely on his own, or outside the texts prescribed by his syllabus; and had been trained even less to think independently.

A £E.10 a month clerical post in a Ministry or government department was perhaps meagre reward for a BA holder. The important thing was that in the eyes of his family, relatives and friends the graduate had acquired status and perhaps £E.5 a month more than he would have received without a degree.

The Free Officer régime attempted its first comprehensive, radical reorganization of the entire educational system in 1953. As initiators of a radical nationalist régime the new governing élite were interested in the eradication of illiteracy and the further Egyptianization of education. Not only did they wish to produce a literate society, but also one alive to its national responsibilities, let alone the revolutionary tasks ahead of eventually building a socialist society and political system. Law 210 of that year rationalized all preparatory education in three stages or levels: a joint elementary–primary level compulsory for all six–twelve-year-old children; the talented among this level would move up to a four-year preparatory school (later

reduced to three years) and from there, depending on their performance, to three years of secondary school. Law 213 in 1956 decreed
free tuition for all levels of this public education, and abolished
examinations for promotion from one form (or year) to another.
But it introduced tougher requirements for advancement from
one stage to another in the school system: from elementary to
preparatory to secondary.

Aware of the instructional character of education in the country,
the new régime attempted to relate syllabi to the more acute socio-
economic problems and urgent needs of the country: to make education, that is, relevant to national goals and aspirations. Yet this
hardly went beyond the introduction of civic courses on Egyptian
society and, after the Suez War, courses on Arab nationalism and
society whose content and approach appeared more like propaganda
and less like genuine subjects of study. The integration of the educational and cultural life of the country, the régime argued, required
such measures, though they inevitably meant in effect a lowering of
academic standards.

Egyptianization was successfully accelerated and completed after
the Suez War. Before 1948 the Ministry of Education hardly exercised any control over foreign schools. That year a certain measure
of supervision was imposed over these schools as regards curricular
and administrative matters. It was, however, Law 160 in 1958, following up the sequestration of several foreign schools in the country,
which abolished all foreign schools as such. Needed as they were,
however, they were simply taken over as Egyptian private schools.
Existing Egyptian private schools, moreover, were subjected to more
direct curricular control from the Ministry of Education. The new
policy of course was based on the argument that a major source of
the educational dichotomy and cultural ambivalence in Egypt
between those Egyptians educated in foreign schools and those educated in the native state and religious schools would at least formally
be removed.

The nationalization of education, and with it presumably culture,
meant that certain jobs and services requiring a relatively high degree
of formal education and skill performed for 150 years by foreigners,
or Egyptians educated in foreign schools in Egypt – as in the commercial and technical fields – now had to be manned by properly
qualified Egyptians trained in state schools. Emphasis therefore was
placed both on the eradication of illiteracy and the promotion of
technical, trade, agricultural and commercial training of Egyptian

youth. This emphasis on technical education applied at all levels of public schooling, especially the preparatory and secondary; so was an emphasis on science advocated for all academic streams at all school levels. With these priorities went also an emphasis on foreign language training. Yet despite the reorganization of technical education in 1956 at the prep, secondary and higher levels, there were in 1962 under 150,000 students enrolled in the technical curricula of these schools out of a total school population approaching four million. This could not have been encouraging when one considers that since 1957 state-owned industrial and commercial enterprises have multiplied rapidly as a result of nationalization and sequestration measures, requiring diversified talent and qualified personnel.

Significantly, the Ministry of Education was re-designated in 1954 the Ministry of Education and Public Instruction, to emphasize the distinction between education as pedagogy and instruction; and at the same time to indicate that national needs demanded that the two be closely linked. In 1955, an estimated 50 per cent of Egyptian children were in elementary–primary schools and the régime announced it hoped to have enough schools by 1968 to accommodate every child at that level. The argument for unifying the elementary stage of public education (six–twelve years) was in order to get virtually everyone through the first four years of school at least (six–ten), and then prepare the pupils in the remaining two years for the next stage. Those academically inclined would go up to preparatory and secondary schools and those not so inclined and/or qualified would go into three years of technical and vocational preparatory training. At all stages tuition was free; where extra fees were permitted they could not, by law, exceed £E.3$\frac{1}{2}$.

The strengths and weaknesses, progress and shortcomings, and the predicament of Egyptian education, however, can all best be observed in its system of higher education. Egypt has the oldest state university of the Arab countries. The founding of a private national university in 1907–8 was opposed both by the British Agency in Egypt and the Egyptian government. But there had been several specialized higher schools and institutes of Medicine and Veterinary Science (1824), Engineering (1820), Agriculture (1829), Law (1858), Dar al-Ulum (Training College for Teachers of Arabic) (1871), another Teachers' Training College (1886), and a College of Commerce (1911). All these were incorporated in the first State University when it opened in Cairo in 1925.

In 1917, a project for a state university was introduced and a committee appointed to study and report on its feasibility. Their report first appeared in 1921. Legislation for its creation was passed in December 1924 and the university opened as Fu'ad al-Awwal (Fuad I) University in March 1925. The old Egyptian University became in effect its Faculty of Arts. Eventually, the new state university came to comprise seven basic faculties: Arts and Letters, Sciences, Medicine, Law, Agriculture, Engineering and Veterinary Science, with departments of Commerce, Education, Oriental Studies, Art and Archaeology.[8] A second state university was opened in Alexandria in 1942 (then as Faruq University), a third in Heliopolis (Ain Shams) in 1950 with an emphasis on Arabic literature and the social sciences, and a fourth in Assiut in 1957 with an emphasis on science and technology – actually, the engineering sciences.

In 1926 there was a total of just over 3,000 students enrolled in colleges and institutes of higher education in Egypt; in 1946 that enrolment had risen to over 15,000 and in 1960 to just over 80,000. It is now estimated to be over 150,000. This, in addition to some 20,000 in teacher training colleges, technical institutes, art and music schools, and some 5,000 at university level in al-Azhar and its affiliated institutions.

The emphasis the government has placed since 1952 upon the expansion of facilities for training in science, engineering and medicine has meant a wider recruitment of students to these faculties. The continuation of free secondary education and its extension to university and higher education in 1961–4 has meant at least a 50 per cent rise in secondary school graduates who enter university. Moreover, the ideological sop by the régime in 1963 which assured all secondary school graduates of a place in university further increased the numbers of those seeking places. The country was faced with a situation in which the number of university graduates had doubled in ten years without a parallel or commensurate expansion of employment opportunities. There may be in Egypt today four to five university students per 1,000 population – a ratio twice or more than that in the United Kingdom.

Despite the recognized need for science graduates and applied technicians, 70 per cent of the enrolment in higher education institutions persists in Arts, Law and Commerce subjects,[9] and only 30 per cent in Science, Medicine and Engineering. There is no problem of employment with the latter in view of the intensive state industrialization programme, especially since 1960, the rapid expansion of public and social services, construction and related areas of economic activity, and the Armed Forces. Moreover, in 1962 there were approximately 5,000 Egyptian students pursuing higher studies overseas, some on government grants but the majority at their own expense, and it has also been the policy of the régime since 1955 both to encourage the admission of foreign (especially Arab and Afro-Asian) students into the country's higher institutions (there were over 14,000 of these in 1960), and to export as many of its graduates, particularly teachers, to these countries. This naturally increases the pressure on universities. Thus, attempts to restrict entry to university only to the best qualified candidates have not produced the desired result of cutting down enrolment.

These conditions have created serious problems affecting the quality of education and standards of graduates. In Cairo University, for example, there were in 1963 some 968 staff members for nearly 35,000 students, or a ratio of 1 : 36; in Alexandria University the ratio was 1 : 32; and at Ain Shams 1 : 40. The actual average staff–student ratio in terms of teaching was 1 : 50. In Arts, however, this ratio in 1930 stood at 1 : 7, in 1950 at 1 : 6, and in 1962 at 1 : 60. State expenditure per student has not, in the past few years, exceeded £E.100 in a total budget for all four universities of £E.9 million in 1959 and £E.14 million in 1962.

Egyptian and foreign critics recognize the shortcomings of an ideologically decreed mass university educational system, when illiteracy is still about 60 per cent for the whole country (higher for women than for men), and elementary education is not yet universal; when so much can be done to strengthen middle technical and vocational education directly needed for the country's economic and social well-being. On the other hand, the same critics object to an autocratic lumping of higher with other levels of education in the name of national revolution, and to policies from the centre by decree which dictate what universities must teach.

A devastating critique of higher education in Egypt was published in 1964(?) by Dr Louis Awad, Cultural Counsellor of the daily *al-Ahram*.[10] It represents, in my view, the most detailed and best documented record of university education in the country, even though many readers might disagree with the author's interpretations and assumptions regarding the purposes of higher education. Dr Awad nonetheless argues convincingly about low standards resulting from inadequate staff both in numbers and quality, lack of time for independent study and research, lack of funds for library acquisitions and research facilities – particularly foreign exchange for the purchase of foreign publications – forced specialization determined by secondary school cumulative examination mark averages, and heavy lecture loads (seventeen to twenty-four hours per week) for teachers. Above all, he deplores the fact that students are rarely exposed to independent study. Instead, they depend heavily on lecture notes to pass examinations. He thus denigrates the student's interest in *ta'lim* – instruction – rather than *'ilm* – education that comes with independent study and research – and argues for the inseparability of these two aspects of the educational experience. He attacks Egyptian attitudes towards technical education and the low social status associated with it even though he insists upon the classic distinction between university work on one hand and advanced institutes of technology on the other. He objects to the régime's deliberate attempt at comprehensive planning for all levels and types of education. Finally, he considers it unwise for the State to pamper scientific programmes in the universities by offering them privileged facilities while ignoring the arts and the humanities. Such discrimination, Dr Awad feels, could create a gulf between the 'Two Cultures'.

With what is close to mass higher education in Egypt today (it has been estimated that 1 per cent of the population enters university), one must raise several questions relevant to the cultural aspects of education in modern Egypt. Do the Egyptians today represent a highly cultured society, modern in outlook and behaviour and thoroughly integrated into the aspects of modern education? The question is meaningless as regards the vast rural majority which even when they had completed four to six years of elementary school were until recently in danger of reverting to illiteracy because of the lack of post-school facilities, such as libraries. It is relevant to a very small proportion of educated Egyptians.

Egyptians, like other nations today which desire rapid development and modernization, have assumed that mass education is essential to the achievement of their goals. They have also assumed that the State must be the foremost agency for, and director of, this development. Consequently, as in several other countries, a complex bureaucratic state educational and cultural establishment has recently emerged, and particularly since the Free Officers came to power in 1952. Whereas until then much of the cultural and intellectual activities in the country were led both by private individuals and organizations and the State, since 1952 much of the financing, organization and direction of these activities have been taken over exclusively by the State.

In earlier chapters the debate over the questions of traditionalism versus modern reform, Western civilization and European culture versus Islamic culture as related to the wider issues of the secular state and society has been outlined. Here one must look briefly at the further expression and reflection of this debate in the actual intellectual (literary and artistic) output and cultural activities of the Egyptians themselves.

The cultural impact of Europe on Egypt in the nineteenth century was not uniform in its consequences. Two trends emerged simultaneously from the start: one traditional and therefore Arab in its linguistic emphasis and Islamic in its cultural preference; the other emulatively European. It was not until Ismail's reign that a European influence on literature and the arts was noticed. Undoubtedly, this was helped by the immigration of Syrian Christians and others to Egypt at that time, and the sharp rise in the number of resident Europeans in the country, the further expansion of education, and the British occupation after 1882.

The intellectual–cultural movement can be traced in nineteenth-century Egypt in the fields of literature (poetry and prose) and the arts (music and the theatre), the rise of academic, scientific and other societies, the rapid development of the Press, and the appearance of the first publishing concerns. It is not intended here to deal with all these activities. In poetry, for instance, one observes that until the mid-nineteenth century, Egyptian poets followed the traditional forms of rhymed verse which were largely concerned with sounds. Moreover, most of them were religious teachers. In part, poetry did not change until Egyptians began to read European literature. Yet practically all literary activity was confined to poetry, in addition to the traditional preoccupation of religious scholars with the exegesis of holy literature such as the Koran. There were no other forms of literature such as the short story, the novel and drama. Prose was concerned with rhetoric. Story-telling was strictly in the form of oral folklore.

Most Egyptians agree that Sami Pasha al-Barudi (1834–1904), a Circassian and the son of rich Mamluk parents, a cavalry officer and briefly Prime Minister during the Orabi affair, was the first modern Egyptian poet. They also agree that together with Ismail Sabri (1854–1923) and Hafiz Ibrahim (1870–1932) Barudi inaugurated a veritable renaissance of classical Arabic poetry, influenced primarily by the Abbasid poets (750–1258). Appearing at a time when Pan-Islamic notions struggled weakly against increasing European encroachments on the world of Islam, these poets emulated the Muslim classics to the extent that their poetry was long (of the *qasida* type), emotional and panegyric. It depicted the heroic qualities of Islamic society, the caliph–sultans faced as they were by the European threat. Their emulation of classical poetry, however, was essential for the revival of the language; even its reform, and the emergence of neo-classical forms.

Whereas Barudi who was identified with the so-called Turco-Circassian Egyptian aristocracy was more concerned with the Islamic community, Hafiz who was clearly not an aristocrat wrote poetry which expressed the feelings of native Egyptians though still as members of an Islamic community. Thus, while using classical poetic forms, Hafiz attempted to express the religious and social inclinations of Egyptian Muslims. He was, moreover, a more popular poet than Barudi and quite anti-European. Finally, what is interesting about these poets is that they were all government officials like practically all other intellectuals (men of letters and science) in nineteenth-century Egypt.

Perhaps the poet who is credited with carrying the renaissance begun by Barudi to its heights is Ahmad Shawqi (1869–1932). An aristocrat of mixed Kurdish–Circassian–Greek blood, Shawqi had studied law in Egypt and France before being appointed Chief of the French Section (Translation) in the Khedivial Court, and later court poet to Khedive Abbas II (Hilmi) (1892–1914). A staunch supporter of the Khedive and the Ottoman Sultan, Shawqi's popular image is that of the poet who introduced the epic into Egyptian poetry. Above all, he developed the dramatic form in poetry which Egyptians have adapted to the theatre, opera and the cinema. In fact, he may be also considered the father of the Egyptian 'operetta' and 'musical', for several of his long poems have been set to music. Among his epics one ought to mention *Ali Bey al-Kabir*, *Masra Kiliobatra* (*The Death of Cleopatra*), *Majnun Layla* (*Layla's Lover*) and *Amirat al-Andalus* (*Princess of Andalusia*), a work possibly inspired by his exile to Spain during the First World War. To this extent, Shawqi's poetry was the supreme expression of Arab–Islamic consciousness, lyrical and romantic, and its form the epitome of the neo-classical development. His influence on such nationalist poets earlier this century as Ali al-Ghayati and Aziz Abaza was great.

Generally, the poetry of the nineteenth and early twentieth century was musical and most particular about the pure classical structure of the language and its style. Nevertheless, Shawqi influenced the famous Khalil Mutran, a leader of the modernists in the thirties, who carried on with Shawqi's dramatic poetry at least, especially when the theatre in Egypt had advanced somewhat. Moreover, when these poets had a European education it was one associated with France, so that any European literature they had read was French literature.

The next generation of poets earlier this century differed from the Shawqi and Barudi school in several ways. Culturally they became exposed to a wider Europe, beyond say France and Italy, particularly Britain. They had been in varying degrees involved in the 1919–22 events. They criticized their predecessors for being blind panegyrists of court and social occasions; for their emulation of the classics; for their adherence to and interest in the linguistic gyrations of classical Arabic forms; and generally for their lachrymose romanticism and oozing lyricism. The new school combined a new Egyptian nationalist concern with a more existential poetic approach, and an interest in expressing universal meaning – if not truths. Poetry was to be a personal expression of the poet, not a panegyric of authority, or a vehicle of social preaching. Moreover, several of these new poets were also critics and prominent prose writers.

The names associated with this new school are Abbas Mahmud al-Aqqad, Ibrahim al-Mazini, Abd al-Rahman Shukri, Ahmad Zaki Abu Shadi, Ibrahim Naji and Ali Mahmud Taha. These differed from their predecessors not only in their poetry but also in their background, training and occupation. Thus al-Aqqad (1880–1965) was a schoolteacher, born in the Aswan region, who became an active Wafdist and anti-monarchist. Later, he joined the Saadist Party, wrote in its newspaper *al-Asas*, and became a senator. Under the Nasser régime he became an arch-critic of the new younger radical modernists in literature, particularly poetry. He also received the State Appreciation Prize for Literature. Al-Mazini (d. 1949) was also a schoolteacher with barely more than an elementary education. What is interesting is that Abu Shadi (d. 1892) had studied medicine in England, took an English wife, and ended up as a bacteriologist in the Egyptian Ministry of Health. He went to the United States in 1946. So was Naji (1898–1953), a native of Shubra in Cairo, a medical graduate and one of the founders in 1946 of the Union of Doctors. Only Shukri (1886–1958), originally Maghribi (North African) but born in Port Said, began the study of law until he was thrown out of Law School for his National Party activities, and ended up in Teachers' Training College and subsequently as an Inspector in the Ministry of Education. Ali Mahmud Taha (1902–49) of Mansura was perhaps the first modern poet to have studied art. He graduated from the School of Applied Arts in 1924, and later became an architect in the Ministry of Public Works. Teaching, science and the arts were a far cry from court officials, lawyers, and soldiers.

Although this group did not make a complete break with the classical Arab past, they were directly involved in Egyptian national politics and closer to a wider selection of European literature. When Abu Shadi founded the Apollo Group in 1932–3 and published its review in 1935, it attracted a variety of poets ranging from pure sensualist epicureans like Taha to existential pessimists like Naji, Abu'l Wafa and Kamil Husan al-Sayrafi. They published collected verse volumes (*diwan*) and anthologies and gave vent to a parallel renaissance in romantic and symbolic poetry in the Lebanon for instance. Nevertheless, the political situation after 1930 – the hardened autocracy of the King and the Sidqi government – forced them into greater and perhaps unbridled romanticism. Those among them, like al-Aqqad for example, who also wrote prose in the thirties and forties, portrayed perhaps an extremely romantic view of history and politics.

The deterioration of the political situation in Egypt during and immediately after the Second World War gave rise to the next school of poetry, usually recognized and referred to as that of Social Realism. Disillusionment with the romanticism of their predecessors and since the forties with the pessimism of the Apollo Group, the new Realists called for a return to topical poetry with a social message and a national goal. Faced with such explosive political issues as the relationship of Egypt to Britain, the economic plight of the mass of Egyptians, the wider involvement of their country in Arab problems, especially the Palestine Question, the Realists preferred poetry which expressed metrically and clearly political and social ideas on topical matters. They rebelled against emotional verse which excited undirected feeling. Instead, they concentrated on a vivid description of national problems, the depiction of the realities and vicissitudes of local life. The poet, so to speak, became a 'fighter for national liberation'. They were also rebelling against tradition with its classical poetic forms in favour of experimentation with metric, non-rhyming verse. Today perhaps the two leading figures who are heirs to the Realist school in this movement are Salah Abd al-Sabur and Ahmad Hijazi.

It is in the field of prose, however, that one can follow the cultural–intellectual trends in modern Egypt. It is there too that literature tries to reflect socio-economic and political problems. In Egyptian Arabic prose literature one can also follow the wider literary and cultural impact of Egypt upon the Arab world. It is, however, impossible to even survey here all aspects of prose literature in modern Egypt. One can only touch upon certain trends and their relationship to conditions in the country. Undoubtedly, as was argued in earlier chapters, the rise of journalism and the Press directly influenced the evolution of a neo-classical Arabic with which to express and interpret newly learnt European ideas. Equally, the newspapers which emerged late in the nineteenth century became the vehicles for experimentation with editorial, essay, article and short-story writing. The whole range of translation activity introduced not only the ideas of the Enlightenment, the theory of evolution, European romantic philosophy, utilitarianism and pragmatism into the country, but also the legal and scientific knowledge of modern Europe. As important was its introduction of Egyptians to the novel, short story and drama.

The literary–cultural importance of newspapers and magazines in Egypt cannot be emphasized enough. Ali Yusuf's *al-Mu'ayyad*, Mustafa Kamil's *al-Liwa'* and Ahmad Lutfi al-Sayyid's *al-Jarida* helped develop the famous *maqal*, or feature article, and an editorial style in modern Arabic. It was a new political style of writing free of the encumbrances of the old rhymed prose (*saj*), aimed at enlightening and teaching its readers. By 1938, for example, there were nearly two hundred Arabic newspapers, magazines and periodicals in Egypt, and about sixty-five in foreign languages. Publishing houses like Dar al-Hilal had become well-established institutions whose monthly *al-Hilal*, weeklies *al-Ithnein* and the pictorial *al-Musawwar* represented the library and reference works of the average literate Egyptian. This, not to speak of the monthly *al-Muqtataf*. Women's magazines proliferated after the mid-twenties which dealt with matters related to the feminist movement in Egypt and discussed personal and social problems of the Egyptian woman in general. Labiba Hashim's *Fatat al-Sharq* (Girl of the East), Rose Haddad's *Hawa' al-jadida* (New Eve), Huda Sharawi's *al-Misriyya* (The Egyptian Woman), and Doriyya Shafiq's *Bint al-Nil* (Daughter of the Nile) are some of the feminist publications which appeared in the inter-war period and after.

Even though newspapers and certain magazines became politically more partisan after independence, they nevertheless continued to serve a literary and cultural purpose too. For what newspapers allowed was the experimentation by writers with new forms of prose in publishing short stories and modern poetry. Moreover they encouraged an open debate of timely social and political issues in their pages. This was true particularly in the inter-war period in the pages of Amin al-Rafi'i's *al-Akhbar*, Mahmud 'Azmi's *a'-Istiqlal*, the Liberals' *al-Siyasa*, the Wafdist *al-Balagh* edited by Abd al-Qadir Hamza, the Independent *al-Ahram* and the pro-Wafdist *al-Misri* founded by the Abu'l-Fath brothers in 1938. Then a new type of satirical political journalism was inaugurated with the appearance of *al-Kashkul* in 1921 and the more successful weekly *Rose al-Yusuf* in 1926. The more serious periodicals, such as *al-Risala*, founded in 1933 and edited by Ahmad Hasan al-Zayyat, widened the scope of open debate over the possible rapprochement between East and West, between the classical Muslim and modern Egyptian. Ahmad Amin's *al-Thaqafa* which appeared in 1939 became an additional outlet for the more systematic discussion of Arab culture and literature.

The Press in every respect represented perhaps the sole platform for the expression of views on literary, cultural and political matters by a rising generation of young writers. It, moreover, helped form a genuinely modern style of writing. In doing so, it managed to adapt the language in such a way as to introduce and coin technical and other terms from the scientific and technological vocabulary of Europe.

In addition to the publishing activities of Dar al-Hilal, Ahmad Amin of *al-Thaqafa* and others launched in the late thirties an important publishing venture, *Lajnat al-ta'lif wa'l-tarjama wa'l-nashr* (Committee of Writing, Translations and Publishing), to encourage writing, translation and publication of serious works. Also in the last thirty years there have appeared numerous publishing enterprises such as Maktabat al-Nahda, Maktabat al-Anglo al-Misriyya, Dar al-Ma'aref, Dar al-Fikr al-Arabi and Mu'assasat al-Matbu'at al-Haditha. Cairo became the centre of Arabic publishing. Some years ago there appeared the first Arab Bibliographical Review of its kind as a quarterly publication (*Majallat al-Maktaba'l Arabiyya*) edited by Dr Mahmud al-Shiniti. For English subscribers Shiniti provided bibliographical news in his *The Arab Library, a Quarterly Journal*. Documentation centres proliferated among government departments and institutes, prominent among them being the Centre of Educational Documentation (*Markaz al-wathaiq al-tarbawiyya*). In 1961 it began publishing a Bulletin of Contemporary Trends in Education (*Al-Ittijahat al-tarbawiyya al-mu'asira*). More important, it produced a number of collected documents on education and other publications in a series on the subject.

Earlier in this century, al-Manfaluti (d. 1924), although sticking to classical Arabic, developed the modern essay with a social message to a new and clear style. He also attempted the adaptation of stories from the French which he had translated for him.[11] But the local short story and novel did not develop until later. Yet as early as 1910–14 Husayn Haykal's famous *Zaynab*, which he wrote while studying in France, became accepted as the first purely Egyptian story. It portrayed life in the countryside, used classical Arabic for narrative and description and colloquial vernacular for dialogue. A few years earlier, Muwailihi's *Hadith Isa Ibn Hisham* had stuck to more traditional forms of writing.

The Egyptian story, however, received its first real impetus with the writings of the Taymur brothers, Muhammad and Mahmud. The latter especially is considered the father of the modern Egyptian short story. Both were apparently influenced by Guy de Maupassant. As the short story advanced, there was a break with the earlier historical novel and romance of say a Zaydan, a Muwailihi or Hafiz Ibrahim which reflected symbolically social conditions, the difficulties of Islamic society influenced by European ideas, and so on. Now the writer immersed himself in contemporary life. The stories of Mahmud Taymur, for example, dealt with the life, trials and tribulations of the fellah and average Egyptian; so that a link with the already widespread folk-story telling was maintained. His brother Muhammad Taymur (1892–1921) may be said to have inaugurated this form of short story during the First World War, using the real atmosphere of local colour and dramatizing local characters in lively dialogue. He introduced a genuine element of entertainment in his stories.[12] Mahmud Taymur, however, injected an even greater element of realism to his story-telling, partly as a result of the influence Russian writers had on him and partly perhaps as a consequence of his conception of a truly national literature. Still, one feels that Taymur and, to a great extent his successors in short-story writing, dealt more with characterization and the vivid description of local colour and atmosphere than with a plot around which their characters acted.[13]

The novel, on the other hand, did not come into its own until the
1940s; even since then it has been practised successfully only by very
few writers. Yet, in Ibrahim al-Mazini (d. 1949), the concept of an
Egyptian modern novel begins to emerge, combining action in the
Egyptian countryside and milieu with the more universal 'agony'
of unrequited love and a radical pessimism about the human condition. There is a distinct introspection which tries to express the life
and soul of Egypt, so to speak. One also observes in al-Mazini the
increased influences of British writers. While critics have argued that
al-Mazini was neither original nor profound his influence can be if
only partially observed in another master of the Egyptian novel
today, namely, Najib Mahfuz.[14]

At the same time, the novel, perfected or incipient, afforded well-
known writers in other fields, such as Taha Husayn, Husayn Haykal
and Tawfiq al-Hakim in the thirties and forties, the opportunity to
depict social ills in the country, the vices of power, and the deplorable
condition of the poor in their plays, novels and stories.[15] This, not
to speak of the use of the novel for the expression of a nascent Egyptian nationalism, especially by Tawfiq al-Hakim; paralleled at that
time by the romantic–revivalist sculpture of Mukhtar.[16] Moreover,
this genre of prose permitted Egyptian writers to experiment with
a psychological approach to human character and behaviour.

A national literature in Egypt concerned with the depiction and
dramatization of native life, society and its problems developed after
1919. The favourite form of this literary expression has been, and
continues to be, the short story, despite the recent development of
the novel and drama. In part, this has been due to the ready access
writers have had to the proliferating mass media. Founded by Mahmud Taymur, it is now an accepted literary–artistic vehicle that is
strongly supported by the institutions of the State. Very few story
writers have ever been able to publish independently – or at least
to make a decent livelihood out of it. The impetus came largely from
two developments after 1952: the Nadi al-Qissa, the Short Story
Club, founded by an ex-army officer Yusuf al-Siba'i in conjunction
with the *Rose al-Yusuf* publishing complex; the *Iqra'* (Read!) Series
of Dar al-Ma'aref, and the *Kitab al-Hilal* (Book of Hilal) of Dar
al-Hilal which began in the last war. *Rose al-Yusuf*, moreover, has
been publishing monthly *al-Kitab al-Dhahabi* (The Golden Book) and
Nadi al-Qissa al-Kitab al-Fiddi (The Silver Book). Not only have

these various series published the works of older writers such as al-Mazini, al-'Aqqad and others, but also those of such masters of the modern story and novel as Yahia Haqqi who, until recently, was editor of the leading Egyptian cultural monthly *al-Majalla*, the Cultural Journal. Concerned with the cultural disequilibrium Egyptians have experienced as their traditional values have been undermined, Haqqi in much of his work has underlined the fervent hope that since the Revolution they may find a new personal and cultural equilibrium.[17] These series have also published the bitterly realistic novels of Yusuf al-Siba'i about the poorer quarters of Cairo and those of Ihsan Abd al-Quddus, for a long time editor and owner of *Rose al-Yusuf*, many of which have been the basis of film scripts.[18]

Perhaps one of the most respected novelists of the new Realist school is Abd al-Rahman al-Sharqawi, whose *al-Ard* (1954) (The Earth) has been widely acclaimed. It portrayed in great detail the perennial problems of the Egyptian peasant, including his unhappy relationship with the landlord. Later, in the early sixties, Sharqawi dabbled in a sort of pristine idea of Islamic socialism and revolution with his famous *Muhammad Rasul al-hurriyya* (Muhammad, Messenger of Freedom).

Among the contemporary writers, Fathi Ghanem, a civil servant in the Ministry of Education, who for some time edited the satirical political weekly *Sabah al-Khayr*, has devoted most of his efforts to the novel.[19] Najib Mahfuz, perhaps the leading Egyptian and Arab novelist today, has, in the tradition of Tawfiq al-Hakim in the twenties and thirties, produced the most professional novels about Cairo, its people and life. In them he portrays the changes that have occurred in the lives of the petty-bourgeois families in Cairo, highlighting the difference between one generation and another within the same families as these are influenced by new forces, ideas and developments. His famous *Trilogy*[20] was preceded by a realistic portrayal of the lives of the native Cairene who lives, loves and dies in the native quarters of the city, away from the dazzle of modern Cairo.[21] Later, he constructed shorter novels dealing primarily with the abject reduction of the poor city dwellers to lawless brigands and thieves.[22] It should be noted, if not asserted, briefly that Mahfuz is the one contemporary Egyptian novelist who has perfected the arts of careful plot construction and superb characterization. Moreover, he remains particular – and careful – about his use of classical Arabic.

Syrian émigrés had introduced the theatre and European drama to Egypt in the second half of the nineteenth century. Marun al-Naqqash, later Georges Abiad and others put on mainly French plays, translated and adapted into Arabic, in Cairo and Alexandria. Until very recently, however, there was no national theatre in Egypt for which Egyptian playwrights provided the dramatic works. There was what one might call local, folk and popular theatre practised for a long time especially in the inter-war period and until 1952 by Najib al-Rihani, Badi Khayri and Ali al-Kassar. In the main, this was a vehicle for the kind of light local comedy and farcical drama for which the vernacular was so eminently suited. Creative drama continued to be confined to the classical writings of, say, Tawfiq al-Hakim. Both he and Mahmud Taymur had perhaps a more cultured approach to drama by Western standards, but they were concerned with more universal themes.

After the mid-fifties, drama, like much other writing, became more socially topical, realistic and symbolic within the Egyptian environment. The new generation of young writers became involved in the naked description of their contemporaries in order partly to exercise their ideological preferences and predilections. At the same time they learnt how to use the elementary symbolism of a writer's, or dramatist's, art.

Although he started out as a talented, sensitive short-story writer in the early fifties, Yusuf Idris is perhaps today the leading dramatist of this generation. A medical doctor by training and a rebel by nature, his earlier short-story collections and his more recent plays in the vernacular – sometimes in a mixed classical–vernacular – elicit universal interest and response. His symbolism regarding the way man contrives systems to maintain his relations is uncanny and runs through most of his writings.[23] Along with Mahfuz, Idris has acquired an international reputation as some of his works have been translated into Russian, French and English. He is possibly the realist – some would argue, sceptic – *par excellence* among Egyptian writers today, familiar with the medical–psychological problems of his characters, as well as with their social predicament. His style also happens to be very simple, lively, and his language mischievously humorous.

A more revolutionary playwright in terms of content today is Nu'man Ashur, a young civil servant. His delightful play, *Al-Nas illi Taht* (The People Downstairs) was an instant success when first performed in 1956. It dealt with the question of an egalitarian society and was, in my view, unrealistically obsessed with the chimera of a classless society. His next play two years later, *Al-Nas illi Foq* (The People Upstairs), appeared at a time when several of the younger radicals felt that the régime, or the revolution it purported, was not radical enough. Finally, in 1963 Ashur's disillusionment with the ability and/or willingness of Egyptians to change into his vision of a new – and classless – society appeared complete in his third play, *A'ilat al-Dughri* (The Family of the Straight Man). As a bitter satirization of post-revolutionary Egyptian society, it was clothed in thick symbolism; only to be followed by Idris' *Farafir* the following year.

The development of the radio, cinema and television has provided additional outlets for the talents of several writers, directors and producers. To mention only one among many, Amin Yusuf Ghurab, a writer of peasant origin without much formal education, has proved a short-story and scenario writer of immense talent. Like many others, he too started out by contributing his stories to the weeklies like *Akhir Saa* and *Rose al-Yusuf*.[24]

Although the cinema industry in Egypt dates back to the early thirties, its rapid development since 1952 and with that the appearance of new talent among writers for it has been due in part to the establishment by the Ministry of Culture of the Cinema Development Organization in 1957. The latter in turn has established a Higher Cinema Institute to help train directors and other cinema technicians, and was instrumental in the formation of choral and theatrical groups, as well as the opening of a Ballet School and a Conservatory. Similarly television, which was inaugurated in Cairo in July 1960, transmitting then on two channels for about 150 hours a week, has similarly contributed to the training of writers for that medium, directors and producers. It has also helped the appearance of a whole new group of artists from stage designers to animators. Cairo Radio, on the other hand, with its powerful transmissions to the Arab countries, Europe, Africa and Asia has similarly employed numerous young writers in all its programmes: Home, Popular, Second, and Voice of the Arabs.

Ever since the nationalization of the Press in May 1960, the proliferation of state-financed and controlled periodical and other publications – indeed too many to be listed here – most of them under the auspices of the Ministry of Culture has accommodated, that is, employed, several leading writers of the Right, Centre and Left. Then, the founding in 1956 of the Higher Council for the patronization of Arts, Letters and Sciences has led to the organization of several cultural and literary national committees (poetry, prose, art, cultural exchange, etc.). These have launched competitions and discovered new talent, granted fellowships to young writers fully employed in other occupations which permitted them to go on sabbatical leave and pursue their creative writing and artistic work. The Council, for example, has investigated problems and difficulties in the educational, artistic and cultural fields and proposed possible programmes to meet them. Its Committee on the Theatre, headed for a long time by Tawfiq al-Hakim, dealt at one time or another with the question of theatrical facilities, the matters of a national theatre company, and the popular theatre. Its Public Relations Committee headed in the late fifties by Yahia Haqqi dealt with the problem of Egypt's cultural relations with other countries. The Music Committee headed by Husayn Fawzi made great strides in encouraging, with foreign assistance, the further advance of classical European music, as well as the greater development of Arabic–Egyptian folk music and folk-dance groups. The Committee on Poetry chaired by the late Abbas al-Aqqad created more controversy and a split between the older generation of neo-classical poets and the younger modernists. A Committee on popular dialects and popular literature under Husayn Mu'nis encouraged work on popular folk literature as an expression of the national spirit.[25]

Painting and sculpture have also received great impetus from the Council and the general atmosphere of artistic relief. Just as the younger generation of writers have appeared more intimate and personal in their expression, so too the new group of Egyptian painters since the last war portray local, individual themes in their work. And so are their colour lines and schemes a reflection of their immediate environment and their own vision. Just as in prose and poetry there has been a rebellion against the formalism and academicism of the previous generation, in painting and sculpture too one observes a similar revolt. In painting this can be seen in the works of Ramses Yunan, Inji Aflatun, Jadhbiyya Sirri, Fu'ad Kamel and others. In sculpture this new trend is quickly discernible in the works of Samuel Henry, Jamal al-Sajini and others.

The organization of learned societies, institutes and associations for the promotion of study and research in various subjects dealing with Egyptian history, geography, economics and agriculture goes back to the mid-nineteenth century. As was noted earlier, the establishment of an Egyptian Institute in the 1850s was followed by the founding of *Jamiyyat al-Maaref* in 1868 to extend education and

disseminate culture. Khedive Ismail founded the Khedivial Geographical Society, later under King Fuad the Royal Geographical
Society. Its projects of historical studies in the twenties and early
thirties on modern Egypt under the direction of Gabriel Hanotaux
are monumental and indispensable for the study of Egyptian society.
The Khedivial Library founded in 1870, later *Dar al-Kutub* and now
the National Library, became a repository of Arabic manuscripts
and books. A Society of Legislation and Political Economy has been
publishing the well-known *Egypte Contemporain* journal.

In 1932, an Arabic Language Academy was founded with both
Egyptian and foreign members, including corresponding members.
Meantime, the Coptic community had developed a Coptic Institute
related to the Coptic Museum in Cairo, as a documentation centre
of the history of Christianity in Egypt. The Cultural Register of the
Ministry of Culture for the fifties indicates the extent of translation
and publishing that has been going on in recent years. Examples of
these activities are the Thousand Books project, and the Masters
of Arabic Thought Series launched in 1955. This is not to speak of
the intellectual and cultural activities of foreign communities, long
resident in Egypt until the mid-fifties.[26]

New research centres and institutes in the social sciences and
sciences have been established by the government, particularly since
1957. Among these one should mention the National Research
Centre, the Atomic Energy Organization, the Desert Institute for
the study of water resources, soil, weather and the geophysical
characteristics of Egyptian deserts. Another important institute has
been the National Institute for Social and Criminal Research. The
Ministry of Culture, for example, has also opened Popular Culture
Institutes in several parts of the country, and Palaces of Culture.
Together with the Higher Council of Arts, Letters and Sciences, the
Ministry has sponsored state prizes in science, literature and the arts.
It has organized meetings and congresses of Arab writers, scientists
and engineers; commemorative meetings to celebrate such greats
of Arab history as Ibn Khaldun. Yet not all these government-
sponsored activities by the Ministry of Culture have had a purely
cultural motivation and intent: propaganda has often been the real
objective.

From the preceding very sketchy survey it is clear perhaps that there
has been wide cultural activity in Egypt, both related and unrelated
to the educational efforts of the State. It is, moreover, not surprising

that such activity since 1952 has been almost exclusively directed by the State or its agencies, given the context to Egypt's recent history. What is interesting is that the post-1952 régime has not encouraged one trend at the expense, or to the exclusion, of others. Rather, it seems that it has supported all of them: Egyptian, Islamic, Arab, modern radical socialist, or realist, etc. What is also clear is that despite the fantastic increase in book publishing and the phenomenal appearance of new talent, journalism remains the favourite and ready vehicle of most writing. There is, moreover, a marked adoption of the vernacular in drama and the cinema, but not in the novel and short story. This may be due, in part, to the fear that Egyptian writers with a wide following in the rest of the Arab world might not be easily understood if they adopted the Egyptian vernacular in their stories and novels.

The social role of the Press, literature and the arts generally has been emphasized in the past twenty years despite the fact that writers and creative artists have appeared more individualistic and introspective than the generation before them. There is a greater influence on them and intellectuals generally which derives from nineteenth- and twentieth-century English and Russian writers. There has also been a clear movement away from the *éclaircissement* of the turn of the century and the inter-war period to a radicalism of the Left and the Right. This in part explains the ready adoption by the intelligentsia and state leaders of cultural activities advocating radical notions of Socialism, Arab Socialism, Arab Revolution, or the more improbable Islamic Socialism. This in part explains too the attempts, say, by the novelist Abd al-Rahman al-Sharqawi and others today to carry on the secularization of religious history begun by Taha Husayn and Husayn Haykal in the thirties.

Fundamentally, many Islamic ideas and institutions remain. Despite the abolition of the Religious (Sharia) Courts in 1955–6[27] and the reorganization of the Azhar University in June 1961 into a modern state university, effectively under the President's control, the advocates of Islamic culture and tradition remain fairly active. This was particularly the case in the late fifties and early sixties if one considers the work of such writers on Islam and leaders of Muslim learning as Muhammad al-Bahi, the late Shaykh Shaltut, Ahmad al-Ahwani, and even the more moderate, the late Ahmad Hasan al-Zayyat.[28]

It is inaccurate, therefore, to assert that Islam as a political and cultural force has been relegated to the role of strictly individual belief and ethic. On the contrary, it remains a strong force in Egypt despite the greater state control over religious institutions, and the official 'abolition' of the famous religious brotherhoods (*tariqas* or *turuq*) by 1961. Life in villages and towns is still strongly influenced by it. Moreover, instinctive and historical Egyptian identification with an international, or at least an inter-Arab sentiment of Islamic solidarity, may still be a factor in their cultural and political outlook. In fact, the post-1952 régime in its revolution has not tampered with the religio-cultural Islamic foundation of society in any radical or drastic way as, for example, Atatürk did in Turkey fifty years ago. On the contrary, it has been very careful to appear the defender and upholder of this tradition. Both the activities of the Islamic Congress founded in 1954 and the involvement of the Azhar in the State's activities at home and abroad have been used to propagate Egyptian views and to advance Egypt's political leadership abroad.

A more vexing dimension of Egyptian cultural development is the Arab one. Egyptian commitment to it is deliberate and recent. If one follows intellectual and cultural trends in Egypt since independence, or at least in this century, one is struck by the fluctuating fortunes of the Arab idea among Egyptians, or in their consciousness. While Egypt was emerging as the centre of Islamic and Arab studies, as the foremost centre of Arabic publishing and Arab education, its peculiar circumstances of independence and its earlier isolation from the Arab Fertile Crescent (specifically until 1922 and more practically until 1937) permitted it to develop a local national literature. The latter tended to emulate the Enlightenment and generally Western European Liberalism. Thus in the twenties and early thirties one witnessed the Pharaonic and Mediterranean–Hellenic interpretations of culture and national identity which were put forward by Tawfiq al-Hakim in the novel, Mahmud Taymur in the short story, and Taha Husayn in social and literary history and criticism.

Yet as early as 1921 there was a pro-Arab *Rabita Sharqiyya* (Eastern Union) in Egypt organized by such members of the intelligentsia and the military as Salih Jawdat, Dasuqi Abaza, Mansur Fahmi, Aziz Ali al-Masri and others. By 1936–7, the Palestine Question was beginning to have some impact in Egypt, for by that time Egyptian politicians were in a better position to get involved in inter-Arab state politics. Egypt attended the Arab Conference at Bludan in 1937 to discuss the Palestine Question; she also participated in the London Round Table Conference on Palestine the following year.

Muhammad Ali Alluba organized a Society for Arab Unity in 1942. That and his book on Egyptian policy (*Fi al-siyasa al-misriyya*) which appeared the same year were echoes of an earlier organization on Arab unity formed by As'ad Dagher in 1938 (*Jamiyyat al-wihda al-arabiyya*). During the war there also appeared a Union of Arabism (*Rabitat al-uruba*), formed by law students at Cairo University.

At the same time, however, serious advances were being made in the study of Egyptology. This and the exploration of Egypt's deserts and its general geography coincided with the rise of a group of Egyptian intellectuals who were calling for a total adoption of Western civilization. Most outspoken among these were Salama Musa, Ismail Mazhar and Husayn Fawzi.[29] The *tarbush* (fez) controversy which led Tawfiq al-Hakim (French-oriented to the bone) to adopt his now famous beret and apparently Bohemian Left Bank existence in the middle of Cairo, was paralleled by an efflorescence of what was considered Egyptian folk music under the leadership of Mahmud Hasan Ismail and others, and the revival of Sayyid Darwish's music. Similarly the debate over the simplicity and simplification of language in terms of its Egyptianization found in the writings of Aziz Fahmi and others in the twenties and the thirties was capped by the major works which claimed a peculiar Egyptian nationalism distinct and free from Arab origins and circumstances. Thus Taha Husayn's *The Future of Culture in Egypt* (English transl. Washington 1954) (*Mustaqbal al-thaqafa fi Misr*, 1938); Abbas Mahmud al-Aqqad's, *Saad Zaghlul, sira wa tahiyya* (Saad Zaghlul, Biography and Tribute) (1936); and Subhi Wahida's, *Fi usul al-mas'ala al-misriyya* (The Origins of the Egyptian Question) (1950).

But even the leaders of this Egyptian national culture tergiversated between that and Islam and Arabism. Husayn Haykal, Muhammad Abd al-Wahhab, Ahmad Husayn, leader of the Young Egypt association, Ahmad Hasan al-Zayyat and Abd al-Rahman Azzam are some of the Egyptians who at that time began to travel around the Arab countries, go on pilgrimage to Mecca, and write books about their experiences. The formation of the Arab League in 1945, the famous though unproductive Inshass Conference in 1946, and the Palestine War in 1948–9 were all factors in the further involvement of Egypt in an Arab political–cultural direction. Literary trends, however, as represented by Naguib Mahfuz in the novel of the forties and the fifties, remained tenaciously concerned with Egyptians and Egyptian national life. Then, a revulsion against the State's involvement in Arab affairs after 1949 was reflected to some extent after the 1952 revolution in the 'Egypt first' tone of *Rose al-Yusuf* (1952–4), the propaganda output of the Liberation Rally (1953) for the mobilization of Egyptians to achieve a modern revolutionary society, the writings of Mahmud Amin al-Alem on education and the treatment of Egypt's message by Husayn Mu'nis.[30] Then the work of Rushdi Salih on Egyptian folklore and fork-art only strengthened this search for an inner local basis of Egyptian cultural strength, perhaps with a radical intention and tendency, but nevertheless indigenous. This, despite Rushdi Salih's more Arab-oriented later work, such as his *Rajul fi'l-Qahira* (A Man in Cairo) (1962).

The goals of Arab nationalism and unity and policies to attain them which were adopted by the régime in 1956–8 met with several temporary successes, but also many more setbacks and failures. Such state policy never intimated an Egyptian interest in a regional culture of, say, Arabism. Moreover, the new generation of intellectuals – writers and artists – in Egypt had been acquiring a wider Arab audience and following not because of their Arab character or message, but because of their radical, so-called socialist, and realistic orientation and predilection. So that even though Nu'man Ashur's plays and those of Yusuf Idris may have a heavily local colour, symbolism and dialogue, their radical portrayal of social and political problems, as well as psychological personal difficulties that are common to other Arab societies, appealed to a wider Arab audience. Even Salah Abd al-Sabur's verse, his *Al-nas fi biladi* (People in my Country) (1957), for example, and Kilani Sind's *Qasa'id fi al-Qanal* (Poems on the Canal) with their existential realism and anti-imperialist tone, had a wide appeal.

Holding up industrialization and mass education as requisites of something Egyptian intellectuals and the State came to call Arab Socialism may have had little to do with the question of a new Egyptian culture, but it certainly had immense appeal to the alienated, frustrated and confused Arab intelligentsia everywhere.

In the field of education generally, Egyptian authorities in the last thirty years have maintained a policy of universal elementary education in the quickest time possible; equal opportunities for all in all stages of education; the planning of educational policies on the basis of the country's needs and capabilities; the expansion of technical education; and increased support of higher education, especially in the sciences. As in the past, however, centralism in the setting of these policies remained. Following the general principle of the last twenty years of rapid Egyptianization, the development of a uniform radical national political culture, the State came to control and supervise all remaining private education.

The State, moreover, came to exercise what is virtually total control over all cultural activities in the country; and therefore over intellectual endeavour. It is largely for this reason that writers and artists were impelled to symbolism. Several among them were forced into the role of panegyrists for the solicitation of those in power and authority. Debates over such issues as 'directive' and 'directed' literature and art; 'the role of the writer in a socialist society'; government-sponsored Writers' Conferences and even Charters for Writers and Intellectuals – these were all manifestations of a closed political system seeking to bureaucratize its intelligentsia in order to use them for its own purposes. The question was not novel, but it arose in Egypt: How can a state plan intellectual and artistic creation in order to serve the so-called popular masses?

The State also pressed its intelligentsia deliberately to seek and devise a culture for a peculiar mass society it called Arab Socialist. At one time it even directed them to work towards a 'unity of ideas among them' (*nahwa wihda fikriyya lil-muthaqqafin*). As a consequence of this aggressive state cultural–educational policy there was fear of censure and opprobrium – even worse – from the Establishment; there was more bitter alienation of intelluctuals from their society; and a debilitating, dangerous ambivalence on their part towards their society. One sometimes feels that despite the relatively great attainments in education and culture, there is in Egypt (though less than in the rest of the Arab world) with all due respect a bureaucratic intelligentsia with a political consciousness, but not an intellectual élite with a civilizational potential. To a great extent, it has been state control over educational, intellectual and cultural activity which tended to reduce intellectuals to purveyors and communicators of state policies and programmes. There were thus only either of two extreme positions an Egyptian intellectual could take in recent years: total withdrawal or total involvement in what came to be known as the Egyptian Revolution. There seemed to be no position between these two extremes.

In any case, the old quarrels, such as the use of the vernacular in preference to the classical Arabic for more creative, original work persisted but in a less acute and shrill form. Yet the State continues to use the classical as the ultimate assertion of an Arab identity and Muslim cultural feeling. One also observes that under an autocratic régime since 1952, literature and the arts have flourished when with state encouragement new talent has come forward. What has not developed at all – and it had a start and a minor tradition in the inter-war period – is critical, analytical thought and research on social, economic and political problems. To explain this short-coming away by simply arguing that the State now places a premium on technology and scientific study is to insult thoughtful Egyptians.

Egyptian intellectuals, educational and cultural leaders, or the State have not resolved the question. What national culture for Egypt? Arab, Muslim, African, or plainly Egyptian, or a combination of all of these. Two new historical developments are important in this connection. Egypt, for the first time, is truly Egyptian. There are no sizeable foreign communities resident in the country any more. Here I am not thinking of such communities as come and go with foreign technical and military assistance programmes. Rather I am referring to such old communities as the Italian and Greek with their schools and hospitals, as well as their wide intellectual and cultural activities. There is, moreover, among many of the new generation of intellectual and cultural leaders a social consciousness about *class*, the relations between town and country in their society, which goes beyond the old division between ruler and ruled.

The crushing defeat of Egypt in the June 1967, or Six Day, War had inevitably serious repercussions for the Nasser régime at home and abroad, especially in the Arab Middle East. The questioning of authority, loudly and violently expressed in the February and November riots and demonstrations, followed an already manifest revulsion among Egyptian writers against a repressive political order. The suspected corruption of the new governing class gradually surfaced in some of the writings of Egyptian authors.[31] It was not, however, until after the death of President Nasser in 1970 that a pro-fusion of fiction, critical essays and polemical tracts by Egyptian writers revealed the extent of the bitter frustration and cultural atrophy.[32] The cost of the régime's Arab policies, especially in the Yemen, and its domestic programmes, ranging from industrialization to political regimentation, was gradually brought home on top of the dangerous demographic explosion with its attendant problems. Thousands of unemployed school-leavers and university graduates were only one indication of the magnitude of the country's economic difficulties and social plight. In cultural terms, moreover, it became clear that after 1970 radical nationalism and socialism were, beyond mere slogans, hardly meaningful to the vast majority of hapless Egyptians caught in the maelstrom of rapid change and the costly consequences of an activist Arab policy. The social and economic problems arising in the aftermath of the June 1967 War were made plainly visible to all Egyptians when nearly a million of their compatriots began evacuating the towns and cities in the Canal area. With the war of attrition launched by Nasser in 1969, more of these streamed into Cairo and other urban centres to inflate their populations, tax beyond endurance their limited services and creaking infrastructure, and constitute in large part a huge mass of destitute pavement, street and cemetery dwellers.

Among the basic problems which came to preoccupy leaders of opinion in culture and education by 1970 was that of the sharp decline in the new generation's proficiency in foreign languages. Another, of particular concern to the government, was the 'brain drain' resulting from the emigration of highly skilled and trained Egyptian scientists, engineers and other professionals to North America, Australia and the oil-rich Arab states. The urgent need for such scarce human resources, and that of capital investment to deal with an almost permanent – some would argue, endemic – economic crisis in the country has produced a situation somewhat parallel to that in the nineteenth century, that is, the problem of transferring technology back to Egypt.

In a broader cultural sense, the impact of the October 1973 War (also known as the Ramadan, or Yom Kippur, War) found Egyptians reverting to an earlier sense of national identity, that of Egyptianism. Egypt became their foremost consideration and top priority in contrast to the earlier one, preferred by the Nasser régime, of Egypt's role and primacy in the Arab world. This kind of national 'restoration' was led by the Old Man of Egyptian Nationalism, Tawfiq al-Hakim, who in the 1920s and 1930s was associated with the Pharaonist movement. The debate he inaugurated in 1977–8 regarding Egyptian 'neutrality' pushed to the surface yet another underlying social–cultural trend among Egyptians, the tension between old-style secular Egyptian nationalists and those still clinging to a partly Islamic-based orientation. The short-lived ferment and excitement over the official reappearance of a reconstituted, or new, Wafd Party in February 1978 reflected in part the final disillusionment with the Nasserite experiment of the preceding twenty years, with radicalism of the Left and with an expensive and debilitating involvement in Arab affairs. Alongside the wish to disengage from the wider Arab arena, supremely expressed in the new policy of peaceful accommodation with Israel, was also the desire to face, if possible, the economic problems of the country which directly affect its educational well-being and cultural development.[33]

The question, What national culture for Egypt, will not be resolved by the intellectuals alone, or in conjunction with the State. History has shown that the Egyptians are an immensely 'absorbent' people, if their evolution in Roman–Byzantine, Arab–Islamic–Ottoman and later periods is any indication. They have a kind of local social resistance, a tenacity which derives from their geographical–historical experience as a nation, both to pressure from their own State and government and to change. This resistance is not absolute, but it emerges in the sense that change occurs very slowly, almost on an *ad hoc* basis, without long-term ideological commitments. This perhaps is also the secret of the survival of Egyptians for so many thousands of years in a country which has seen so many God-Kings, Emperors, Prefects, Governors, Caliphs, Satraps, Sultans and other rulers. It is now acceptable for Egyptians, under Sadat, to claim an Egyptian political identity first and foremost. Their Arabism constitutes for them a cultural dimension of their identity, not a necessary attribute of or prop for their national political being.

NOTES

CHAPTER 1: LAND AND PEOPLE

1 See Justin A. McCarthy, 'Nineteenth-Century Egyptian Population', in *The Middle Eastern Economy*, ed. Elie Kedourie (London 1976), pp. 1–39.

2 See Tawfiq al-Hakim, *Taht shams al-fikr* (Cairo n.d.), p. 108.

3 ibid., p. 109.

4 ibid., pp. 105, 106.

5 See on this theory John A. Wilson, *The Culture of Ancient Egypt* (Chicago 1958), pp. 8–17.

6 See Gabriel Baer, 'Egyptian Attitudes towards Land Reform, 1922–55', in *The Middle East in Transition*, ed. Walter Z. Laqueur (New York 1958), pp. 80–99. See also his *A History of Landownership in Modern Egypt, 1800–1950* (London 1962), and *Studies in the Social History of Modern Egypt* (Chicago 1969). Cf. Doreen Warriner, *Land Reform in the Middle East* (London 1957).

7 See Afaf Lutfi al-Sayyid Marsot, *Egypt's Liberal Experiment, 1922–1936* (Berkeley, Los Angeles and London 1977), pp. 10–42, and Janet Abu Lughod, *Cairo* (Princeton 1971).

8 See his *Mustaqbal al-thaqafa fi Misr* (Cairo 1939).

CHAPTER 2: THE ESTABLISHMENT OF ISLAM IN EGYPT

1 A.J. Butler, *The Arab Conquest of Egypt* (Oxford 1902), pp. 433–4.

2 ibid., p. 464.

3 As recently as October 1961, the appellation Kāfūr was used by a Syrian to disparage the rule and leadership of President 'Abd al-Nāṣir of Egypt. See the poem by *Badawi al-Jabal* addressed to the Tyrant Kāfūr of Egypt, Jamal 'Abd al-Nāṣir, in *Al-Sijill al-aswad* (*The Black Record*) by Muṭṭali' (Damascus n.d.), pp. 111–13. Among other publications banned by the Baathi government of Syria after March 1963, *The Black Record* was prominently listed.

4 To emphasize power as the sole basis of legitimacy, the following certainly apocryphal story is told about the caliph al-Mu'izz. When a delegation of *sharifs*, or *ashrāf* (descendants of 'Ali) came to examine his claim to the caliphate, al-Mu'izz in response drew his sword before this august gathering and declared, 'Here is my pedigree.' Then, scattering gold among his audience, he added, 'and here is my proof.'

5 For example, Bab al-Nasr, Bab al-Futūh and Bab Zuweilā. Nasir-i Khusraw, the famous traveller, who visited Egypt in 1046–9, wrote a vivid description of

a prosperous Fatimid state. See his *Sefer name*, ed. and tr. by Charles Schefer (Paris 1881).

6 See the discussion in H. A. R. Gibb and H. Bowen, *Islamic Society and the West*, Vol. I, pts 1 and 2 (London 1950, 1957), I, pt 1, pp. 216–34; 258–75.

7 One notes that Muslim jurists and historians, such as al-Māwardī (d. 1058), al-Ghazẓali (d. 1111) and Ibn Khaldun (d. 1406), soon rationalized the usurpation of the caliphal temporal authority by these warring castes on a variety of grounds: the necessity of political power, the difference between kingdom and caliphate, etc. Cf. Al-Māwardī, *al-Ahkām al-sultāniyya* (Cairo 1880–1; new ed., 1960). French translation by E. Fagnan, *Les status gouvernementaux* (Algiers 1915); and Ibn Khaldun, *Muqaddima* (Prolegomenes), ed. E.M. Quatremere, 3 vols (Paris 1858). English translation by Franz Rosenthal, *The Muqaddimah*, 3 vols (New York and London 1958).

8 Sir William Muir, *The Mameluke or Slave Dynasty of Egypt, 1260–1517* (London 1896), p. 215.

9 See Stanford J. Shaw, *The Financial and Administrative Organization and Development of Modern Egypt, 1517–1798* (Princeton 1962), p. 22.

10 See, for instance, Aḥmad ibn 'Alī al-Maqrīzī, *Kitābal-mawā'iz wa'l-i'tibār fī dhikr al-khiṭaṭ wa'l-akhbār*, or *al-Khiṭaṭ al-Maqriziyya*, 2 vols (Bulaq 1853), 4 vols (Cairo 1906–8). French trans. by U. Bouriant (Paris 1895–1900); al-Sayyāḥ edition, 3 vols (Beirut 1959). See also his *Itt'āz al-ḥunafā' bi akhbār al-a'imma al-khulafā'*, ed. Hugo Benz (Leipzig 1909) and ed. al-Shayyal (Cairo 1948).

11 Al-Suyūṭī is known for his *Ḥusn al-muḥāḍara*, 2 vols (Cairo 1882 and 1909), and *Tārīkh al-khulafā'* (Cairo 1887 and 1964). English trans. by H.S. Jarrett, *History of the Caliphs* (Calcutta 1881); Ibn Iyas for his *History of Egypt, 1343–1522*, or *Kitāb tār-īkh miṣr*, known as *Badā'i' al-ẓuhūr fi waqā'i' al-duhūr*. There was also Abu'l-Maḥāsin Ibn al-Taghribardi who left a *History of Egypt, 1382–1469, Al-nujūm al-zāhira fi mulūk miṣr wa'l-qāhira*, 9 vols (Cairo 1929–35). Eng. trs. W. Popper, 7 vols (California 1954–63).

12 See Abd al-Rahmān al-Jabartī, *'Ajāi'b al-āthār fi'l-tarājim wa'l-akhbār*, 4 vols (Cairo 1870–1, 1882 and 1904–5), and Ali Mubarak, *Al-khitat al-tawfīqiyya al-jadida li miṣr wa'l-qāhira*, 20 pts in 4 vols (Cairo 1887–9).

CHAPTER 3: THE FIRST EUROPEAN IMPACT

1 On these uprisings and rebellions, see Louis 'Awaḍ, *Al-mu'atharāt al-ajnabiyya fi'l-adab āl-a'rabī al-hadith* (Foreign influences on modern Arabic literature), 2 vols (Cairo 1963), 'Introduction'. Dr Awad uses the evidence of Anglo-French rivalry in Egypt to argue that the Huwara 'state' set up by Humam in Upper Egypt was an attempt at a republican régime. He opines that Humam's contact with Europeans had given him some acquaintance with the revolutionary notions of republicanism current in Europe in the eighteenth century. This contention is perhaps somewhat forced. After all, the French Revolution did not break upon Europe until 1789.

2 *Letters on Egypt* (London 1786), I, p. 36.

3 ibid., I, pp. 71–3.

4 ibid., I, p. 90.

5 ibid., I, p. 99.

6 See Ali Pasha Mubarak, *Al-khitat al-tawfiqiyya*, 4 vols (Cairo 1887–1900), I. See also later editions (Cairo 1955, 1968).

7 See Jabarti, *'Ajā'ib al-āthār*, 4 vols (Cairo 1870–1, later edition, 4 vols, Cairo 1958–66), and Mubarak, *Al-khitat*, 1969 ed., I, pp. 137–55. See also Volney, *Voyages en Égypte et en Syrie*, 2 vols (The Hague 1959), and Nicolas Turc, *Chronique d'Égypte 1798–1804* (Cairo 1950). Ali Mubarak asserts the Mamluks introduced the 'politics of power' from their Tatar background, causing a division between *sharia* (the religious law) and politics. See *Khitat*, new ed. (Cairo 1969), I, p. 137.

8 *Letters on Egypt*, I, p. 158.

9 ibid., p. 136.

10 ibid., p. 381.

11 ibid., p. 99. See also II, pp. 125–9.

12 ibid., p. 124.

13 ibid., pp. 130–40.

14 ibid., p. 210.

15 ibid., II, pp. 290–350.

16 See J.A. McCarthy, *op. cit.*

17 See Jabarti, 1879 ed., II, p. 262.

18 ibid., pp. 261–65.

19 See Mubarak, 1969 ed., I, p. 244. See also Mahmud al-Sharqawi, *Misr fi'l qarn al-thamin 'ashar* (Egypt in the Eighteenth Century) 2nd ed., 3 vols (Cairo 1957).

20 See al-Sharqawi, *op. cit.*, I, pp. 97–100, and II, p. 165.

21 ibid., I, pp. 86–92.

22 *Naquib al-ashraf* was the title held by the leading member of the group of notables who claimed descent from the Prophet's family. On Omar Makram, see Jabarti, IV, p. 98.

23 Jabarti, IV, p. 299.

24 *Letters on Egypt*, I, pp. 88–9.

25 Jabarti, III, pp. 2–3; later ed., IV, p. 285.

26 ibid., III, pp. 4–5; later ed., IV, pp. 288–91. See also on this matter Bourrienne, *Memoirs of Napoleon Bonaparte*, ed. R.W. Phipps (New York 1891), 4 vols, I, pp. 166–75.

27 Jabarti, later ed., IV, p. 326.

28 ibid., pp. 326–43. Napoleon used the shaykhs to quell the native rebellion.

29 Turkey declared war on France in September 1798.

30 Jabarti, new ed., IV, pp. 345–52.

31 Text of proclamation quoted in Bernard Lewis, 'The Impact of the French Revolution in Turkey', *Journal of World History*, I, 1 (July 1953) (pp. 105–25), p. 122. See also Jabarti, new ed., IV, pp. 338–43.

32 It is interesting that the Free Officer régime built in 1953 a mosque in Ras al-Tin, Alexandria, to the memory of this 'national hero'.

33 *Jabarti, III*, p. 316 (Events of the year 1219 AH).

34 This practice was stopped by Muhammad Ali.

CHAPTER 4: MUHAMMAD ALI, THE
MODERNIZING AUTOCRAT

1 The idea of a *Nizam Jadid*, a New Order, was first conceived and implemented in Turkey by Selim III, whose reform schemes for the Empire were resumed and extended by Mahmud II of the Tanzimat period beginning in 1839.

2 Note that Muhammad Ali's rank in modern Egyptian military terminology in 1952 would have been 'bikbashi', the same rank held by President Nasser when he led the military *coup d'état* that overthrew the dynasty.

3 For a discussion of Selim III and his *Nizam-i-Cedid* reforms, see Bernard Lewis, *The Emergence of Modern Turkey* (London 1961), pp. 38–75. In connection with Egypt, see Jabarti, '*Ajā ib al-āthār*, III, pp. 241, 300, and IV, pp. 9–11, 19, 23, 34, 61, 63, 79, 222.

4 *Manners and Customs of the Modern Egyptians* (Everyman Library Edition, London 1954), p. 25.

5 *La Genèse de l'Esprit National Égyptien, 1863–82* (Paris 1924).

6 *The Founder of Modern Egypt, A Study of Muhammad Ali Pasha of Cairo* (Cambridge 1931).

7 *op. cit.* For a different socio-economic explanation of this failure, see Charles Issawi, 'Egypt since 1800; a study in lopsided development', *Journal of Economic History*, XXI 1 (March 1961), pp. 1–25.

8 See A. Paton, *A History of the Egyptian Revolution*, 2 vols, 2nd ed. (London 1870–9), II, p. 79.

9 On the notorious Citadel massacre of the Mamluk princes and chiefs, see Jabarti, '*Ajā'ib al-āthār*, IV, pp. 127–33, and Paton, II, pp. 30–5.

10 See J.H. Mordtmann and B. Lewis, 'Derebey', *Encyclopedia of Islam*, 2nd ed. (*EI²*), II, pp. 206–8; see also B. Lewis, *op. cit.*, pp. 441–2.

11 For a detailed study of Muhammad Ali's agricultural policy, see Helen Anne Rivlin, *The Agricultural Policy of Muhammad Ali in Egypt* (Cambridge, Mass. 1961). For a concise, yet more appropriate work for the general reader, see Gabriel Baer, *A History of Landownership in Egypt, 1800–1950* (London 1962).

12 Unlike the holders of *ciftlik*, or large estate farms, which by the 15th century Ottoman Sultans came to grant influential men in the provinces of Anatolia and Rumeli, the tax-farmer in Ottoman Egypt was not required by the ruler to equip and supply troops for the army. Nonetheless, the *iltizam* system in Egypt gave rise to large private landed estates. Even though Muhammed Ali abolished the system early in his reign, he very soon reverted to the practice of extensive land gifts to his officials. Coupled with *ciftliks* to members of his family, a return to large private landed estates soon occurred in the second half of the 19th century.

   See Halil Inalcik, *Ciftlik EI²*, II, pp. 32–3; see also Halil Inalcik, 'Land Problems in Turkish History', *The Muslim World*, XIV (1955), pp. 221–8.

13 For a detailed discussion of this question, see Gabriel Baer, *op. cit.* On certain aspects of social structure generally, see Nada Tomiche, 'Notes sur la hiérarchie

sociale en Égypte à l'époque de Muhammad 'Ali', in P.M. Holt, ed., *Political and Social Change in Modern Egypt* (London 1968), pp. 249–63. For an appreciation by Muhammad Ali of the need for a state agricultural policy see Rifā'a Rāfi' al-Tahtāwī, *Manāhij al-albāb al-misriyya fī mabāhij al-ādāb al-'asriyya* (Cairo 1912), pp. 207–42.

14 This Ismail Pasha, a son of Muhammad Ali the Great, should not be confused with the Khedive Ismail, the grandson of Muhammad Ali, who reigned in Egypt from 1863 to 1879.

15 For a list and description of the various military schools and colleges founded by Muhammad Ali, see 'Abd al-Rahmān al-Rāfi'ī, *'Asr Muhammad 'Alī*, 3rd ed. (Cairo 1951), pp. 386–463.

16 For biographical sketches on the members of educational missions to Europe at the time of Muhammad Ali, see Amir 'Omar Tūsūn, *Al-bi'thāt al-'ilmiyya fi 'ahd Muhammad 'Ali* (Alexandria 1934).

17 23 vols: 9 vols text; 14 vols plates (Paris 1809–28). Savary reports the manufacture of linen from flax, I, p. 67.

18 On the general question of the early influences upon Muhammad Ali regarding industrialization, see James August St John, *Egypt and Muhammad Ali*, 2 vols (London 1834). See also Shafiq Ghorbal, 'Dr Bowring and Muhammad Ali', *Bulletin de l'Institut d'Égypte*, XXV, p. 110.

19 See on this Prince Omar Toussoun, *Memoir on the Army and the Navy of Egypt* (in Arabic), Alexandria 1933. See also A. Politis, *L'Hellénisme et Égypte*, 2 vols (Paris 1930).

20 Originally, under the Capitulations, European diplomatic missions in the Ottoman Empire distributed (and sold) commercial and fiscal privileges to their subject merchants and their commercial houses. Selim III granted such privileges to local Christian and Jewish merchants who were his protected *rayahs* (subjects) so that they could compete with foreign commercial interests. Holders of these privileges, or *berats*, were known as *beratlis*, and their numbers increased appreciably in the 18th and 19th centuries. Later, this privilege was extended to some Muslim merchants. *Beratlis* had the right to trade with Europe and were entitled to certain legal and fiscal privileges and exemptions. See B. Lewis, 'Beratli', *EI²*, I, p. 1171. For texts of the earliest treaties between the Ottoman Sultan and European powers, inaugurating the Capitulations formula of extra-territoriality in the Ottoman dominions, see J.C. Hurewitz, *Diplomacy in the Near and Middle East* (New York 1956), I, pp. 1–6, 15–38. On foreign commercial agents and houses, in this period, see Clot Bey, *Aperçu général sur l'Égypte* (Paris 1840), II, pp. 328–9; and John Bowring, *Report on Egypt and Candia* (London 1840), pp. 15–17.

21 See on this subject, Charles Issawi, *op. cit.*, and Helen Rivlin, *op. cit.*

22 For parallel and often similar changes in the government and administration in Turkey during the same period, see B. Lewis, *op. cit.*, Chapter XI, 'State and Government', esp. pp. 365–72 and 378–94.

23 Rāfi'ī, *'Asr Muhammad 'Ali*, pp. 652–63.

24 See especially M. Sabry, *L'Empire Égyptien sous Mohamed Ali et la Question d'Orient* (Paris 1930); Lucien Davesies de Pontes, *Études sur l'Orient et l'Égypte* (Paris 1869); and George Antonius, *The Arab Awakening* (London 1938).

25 See Asad J. Rustum, *The Royal Archives of Egypt and the Origins of the Egyptian Expedition to Syria, 1831–41* (Beirut 1936).

26 See A. St John, *op. cit.* Burckhardt noted the common occurrence of petty independent chiefs in the empire defying their sovereign. See his *Travels in Syria and the Holy Land* (London 1822).

CHAPTER 5: ISMAIL, THE IMPATIENT EUROPEANIZER

1 Asad Jubrail Rustum quotes speeches by Ibrahim Pasha and other officers to the Egyptian Army in Syria which refer to 'Egyptian honour' and 'Egyptian courage'. It is possible that these may have been drafted by European advisers to Muhammad Ali. It is, however, difficult to assess what effect they had on troops and if they elicited the kind of feeling one normally associates with patriotism. See *The Royal Archives of Egypt and the Origins of the Egyptian Expedition to Syria 1831–41* (Beirut 1936).

2 Polygamy in this instance always produced hatred and suspicion among half-brothers in the struggle for succession and power among members of the ruling families.

3 For an interesting account of the Muhammad Ali family by one of his descendants, see Emine Fuat Tugay, *Three Centuries, Family Chronicles of Turkey and Egypt* (London 1963).

4 His death has been shrouded in mystery, and most historians suspect that he was either killed by his own guard, or at the orders of his paternal aunt in Istanbul, Nazli Hanum.

5 For Saʿīd's law, see Gabriel A. Baer, *A History of Landownership in Modern Egypt 1800–1950* (London 1962), pp. 7–10. For a parallel development in Turkey on the heels of the 1856 Hatti Humayun reform rescript, see J. Belin, 'Sur la propriété foncière en Turquie', *Journal Asiatique*, XIX (1862) 2 parts, pp. 156–212 and pp. 257–358 (including a translation of the new law of 21 April 1858).

6 See Ahmad Shafiq Pasha, *Mudhakkirātī fi nisf qarn* (My Memoirs of a Half Century), 2 vols (Cairo 1934–6), and ʿAbd al-Raḥmān al-Rāfiʿī, *ʿAṣr Ismāʿīl* (The Age of Ismail), 2 vols (Cairo, 2nd ed. 1948), esp. I, p. 30.

7 Dodwell, *The Founder of Modern Egypt* (London 1931), p. 343.

8 See J. Carlile McCoan, *Egypt under Ismail*, a romance of history (London 1889) and P. Crabitès, *Ismail the Maligned Khedive* (London 1933).

9 Edward Dicey, *The Story of the Khedivate* (London 1902), pp. 69–70.

10 See text of Mustafa Fazil's letter to the Sultan in Marcel Colombe, 'Une Lettre d'un Prince Égyptien du XIXᵉ siècle au Sultan Ottoman Abd al-Aziz', *Orient*, V (1958), pp. 23–8. See also a brief reference to this episode in B. Lewis, *op. cit.*, pp. 149–50.

11 See Chapter 7 on Constitutionalism below.

12 Shafiq, *Mudhakkirātī*, I, p. 23.

13 A leading contemporary critic has made the most straightforward and fair, though brief, assessment of Ismail to date: 'Had it not been for Ismail's inclination – despite his superficiality and arrogance (*safāha*) – to favour the arts and letters, we (the Egyptians) would not have easily emerged from the darkness.'

(The darkness, that is, in which Abbas and Sa'īd Pashas had allegedly pushed the country.) See Louis 'Awaḍ, *Al-Jāmi'a wa'l-mujtama' al-jadīd* (The University and the New Society), 'Socialist Studies' (Cairo n.d. – 1964?), p. 49.

14 One Egyptian historian of education has stated that in 1880, 52 per cent of all Egyptian students were in foreign schools at all levels. In 1914, only about 38 per cent of male students were still in these schools. But the percentage of female students in them remained high at 54 per cent. See Amīn Sāmi, *al-Ta'lim fī Miṣr* (Education in Egypt) (Cairo 1917).

15 His most celebrated Prime Minister was Nubar, an Armenian. Nubar was born in Smyrna in 1825, the son of a consular Dragoman. He studied in France for a year, then went to Egypt in 1842, where a relative of his – Boghos Bey – was Muhammad Ali's 'Minister' of Commerce. On Nubar, see J. Carlile McCoan, *op. cit.*, pp. 26–7. On his relations with the Khedive and particularly his so-called Mixed Cabinet of Egyptian and European ministers, see Shafiq, *Mudhakkirātī*, I, pp. 33–40, and Chapter 7 below. See also Ilyās Ayyūbī, *Tārīkh Miṣr fī 'Aṣr al-khidīwī Ismā'il* (The history of Egypt in the Reign of Ismail) (Cairo 1923), and Najīb Maklūf, *Nūbār Pasha* (Cairo n.d.).

16 The Khedivial Library (*al-Maktaba al-khidāwiyya*) which later became *Dar al-Kutub* (The National Library). See Cheikho, *al-Ādāb al-'arabiyya fī'lqarn al-tāsi' 'ashar* (Arab Letters and Arabic Literature in the 19th century), 2 vols (Beirut 1924–6), II, p. 72. See also Shafiq, *Mudhakkirātī*, I, *passim*, and Chapter 6, Education and the First Egyptian Intellectuals, below.

17 Edwin de Leon, *The Khedive's Egypt, The old House of Bondage under new Masters* (New York and London 1878). See also Elbert E. Farman, *Egypt and Its Betrayal* (New York 1908).

18 For example, Francis Adams, *The New Egypt* (London 1893), W. Fraser Rae, *Egypt Today* (London 1892), Moberly Bell, *Khedives and Pashas by one who knows them well* (London 1884), Elbert E. Farman, *op. cit.*, A.E.P. Brome Weigall, *Egypt, from 1798 to 1914* (London 1915), Alfred Cunningham, *Today in Egypt* (London 1912), Lady Duff Gordon, *Letters from Egypt, 1863–65* (London 1865).

19 *Egypt, Native Rulers and Foreign Interference*, 2nd ed. (London 1883), p. 67.

20 E. de Leon, *op. cit.*, pp. 327 ff.

21 Francis Adams, *op. cit.*, p. 69.

22 David Landes, *Bankers and Pashas* (London and Cambridge, Mass. 1958, and New York 1969).

23 *England in Egypt* (London 1892, 1904).

24 Blanchard Jerrold, ed., *Egypt under Ismail Pasha* (London 1879), p. 193.

25 ibid., p. 275.

CHAPTER 6: MODERN EDUCATION AND THE FIRST EGYPTIAN INTELLECTUALS

1 See the detailed and interesting depiction of social and political conditions in this period in Louis 'Awaḍ, *Al-mu'atharāt al-ajnabiyya fī'l-adab al-'arabī al-ḥadīth*, II. (Social and Political Thought from the French Expedition to the Reign of Ismail) (Cairo 1963), Introduction.

Notes

2 See Ali Mubarak, *Khiṭaṭ*, IV, p. 38.

3 Quoted in Mahmūd al-Sharqāwī, *Miṣr fi'l-qarn al-thāmin 'ashar* (3 vols in one, Cairo 1955), I, p. 55.

4 ibid., I, pp. 86–93.

5 ibid., I. pp. 57–80. See also Louis 'Awaḍ, *Al-mu'atharāt*, II; and J. Heyworth-Dunne, 'Arabic Literature in Egypt in the 18th century with some reference to poetry and poets', *BSOAS*, IX (1937–9), pp. 675–89.

6 See his *Considérations sur l'instruction publique en Égypte* (Cairo 1890), p. 69.

7 For less plausible reasons, see Jamāl al-dīn al-Shayyāl, *Tārīkh al-tarjama wa'l-ḥaraka al-thaqāfiyya fī'asr Muhammad'Ali* (Cairo 1951), p. 10. See also 'Abd al-Rahmān al-Rāfi'ī, *Tārīkh al-haraka al-qawmiyya* (3vols, 4th ed., Cairo 1955), II, pp. 312–13.

8 Law No. 103 of June 1961 for the reorganization of the Azhar University may thus produce interesting results within the next generation. See text of the Law with the Explanatory Memorandum of the Minister of State in *Majallat al-Azhar*, XXX (July 1961), pp. 237–64. A French translation of the Explanatory Memo is found in *Mélanges Institut Dominicain d'Études Orientales du Caire* (*MIDEO*), VI (1959–61), pp. 474–84.

9 Printing was already known in the Near East long before the French or Muhammad Ali introduced it to Egypt. Thus by 1728 there was a printing press in Istanbul followed soon by one in Syria. Only about 1815 did Muhammad Ali, urged by Father Rafael Zakhur and Othman Nur al-Din, seriously entertain the founding of a Government Printing Press. See Chapter 9, Journalism and the Press, below.

10 On printing and the offical press of this early period generally, see Ibrahim Abduh, *Tārīkh al-waqā'i' al-miṣriyya, 1828–1942* (Cairo 1942). For antecedents, especially the introduction of the first printing press to Egypt by Bonaparte, see also Ibrahim Abduh, *Tarikh al-ṭibā'a wa'l-ṣaḥāfa khilāl al-ḥamla al-faransiyya* (Cairo 1949). See also the lucid discussion in Louis 'Awaḍ, *Al-mu'atharāt*, II, pp. 78–91.

11 See al-Shayyāl, *Tārīkh*, pp. 205–6.

12 For a detailed description of translation assignments under Muhammad Ali, and a list of technical works translated and published – a list as impressive incidentally as the Project of One Thousand Books launched by the Free Officers Régime in Egypt since 1952 – see al-Shayyāl, *Tārīkh*, Appendix One and Two, pp. 7–40, and Appendix Three, pp. 41–53.

13 On these matters generally, see Artin Pasha, *op. cit.*; 'Izzat Abd al-Karīm, *Tārīkh al-ta'lim fī 'aṣr Muhammad 'Alī*(Cairo 1930); Ali Pasha Mubārak, *Khitat*; see also Muhammad Kāmil al-Fiqī, *Al-Azhar wa atharuhu fī'l-nahḍa al-ḥadītha*, 3 vols (Cairo 1956).

14 It should be noted that in Turkey an Imperial *irade* in 1851 formally authorized the formation of the *Encümen-i Danis* (Society of Knowledge), followed in 1860 by *Cemiyet-i Ilmiye-i Osmaniye* (Ottoman Scientific Society). Professor Bernard Lewis has suggested that the former was modelled on the *Académie Française*, and the latter on the Royal Society of England. See *op. cit.*, pp. 431–2, and his 'Andjuman' in *EI²*.

474

15 On al-Nadīm, see two recent works ʿAlī al-Ḥadīdī, *ʿAbdullah al-Nadīm, khaṭīb al-waṭaniyya* (Cairo n.d.), and Najīb Tawfīq, *Al-thāʾir al-ʿazim* (Cairo 1957), and Chapter 8 on Journalism below.

16 This Society should not be confused with the one bearing the same name and founded by Muhammad Abduh in 1892.

17 Shaykh al-Mahdī (1828–98) was appointed both Shaykh of the Azhar and Mufti of Egypt in 1871. In 1872, he introduced a scheme of an Examinations Supervisory Committee for the certificate of *ʿalamiyya* (in effect, the highest diploma the Azhar confers upon its graduates), consisting of six shaykh scholars representing three of the four schools of law, namely, Shafei, Hanafi and Maliki. See Zaydan, *Mashāhīr*, II, pp. 186–9.

18 On Othman Galal, see L. Cheikho, *Al-ādāb al-ʿarabiyya fī ʾl-qarn al-tāsiʿ ʿashar* (hereafter cited as Cheikho *Al-ādāb*) (Beirut 1924–6), II, pp. 100–2, and Jurji Zaydan, *Tārīkh ādāb al-lugha al-ʿarabiyya* (Cairo 1914), IV, p. 245.

19 Sanua was a Freemason. He had worked briefly for the Khedive in the 1860s. After his exile to Paris in 1878, he was an implacable enemy of the Khedivial rulers in Egypt. The source, or sources, of his income during exile are a mystery, though it could have been Turkey, France or others. On Sanua, generally, see Ibrahim Abduh, *Abū Naẓẓāra* (imām al-saḥāfa al-fukāhiyya al-muṣawwara wa zaʿīm al-masraḥ fi miṣr) (Cairo 1953). See also Irene L. Gendzier, 'James Sanua and Egyptian Nationalism', *Middle East Journal*, XV (Winter 1961), I, pp. 16–28; and *The Practical Visions of Yaʿqub Sanu'* (Cambridge, Mass. 1966).

20 For a biographical sketch on Ḥamūlī, see Jurji Zaydan, *Mashāhīr*, II, pp. 305–11. Generally, on singing artists of that period, see Ahmad Shafiq Pasha, *Mudhakkirati*, I, p. 60.

21 It should be noted that the first state schools opened by Muhammad Ali the Great were organized as 'military' schools. Students were subjected to rigid military discipline. Those who taught in them were also considered members of the military establishment, and held appropriate military ranks commensurate with their position in the administrative hierarchy of the school system. This was to be expected if one bears in mind that these schools were intended to serve exclusively the army in all its branches and activities. Thus the Medical School was intended to train army doctors, the Engineering School military engineers, the trade and industrial schools to supply the army, and so on. Schools at this early stage therefore were organized as military camps in permanent barracks. Even the members of educational missions to Paris under Muhammad Ali were housed together and supervised in military fashion.

22 One short biography of Ali Mubarak is by Muḥammad Aḥmad Khalafallah, *ʿAli Mubārak wa āthāruhu* (Cairo 1957).

23 For a more complete list of his works, see Zaydan, *Mashāhīr* (3rd ed. Cairo 1922), II, pp. 22–6, and *Tārikh ādāb*, IV, pp. 295–7. See also Cheikho *Al-ādāb*, II, p. 8; Sarkis, *Dictionnaire Bibliographique* (Cairo 1928), pp. 942–7; and Maurice Chemoul, 'Rifaʿa Bey', *EI¹*, III, pt 2, pp. 1155–6. See also Jamal al-din al-Shayyāl, *Rifāʿa Rāfiʿ al-Tahtāwī zaʿīm al-nahda al-fikriyya fi ʿasr Muhammad ʿAli* (Cairo n.d.); and Ahmad Badawī, *Rifāʿa al-Tahtāwī* (Cairo 1950).

24 See the references cited above in Zaydan and Cheikho *Al-ādāb*, EI, and Carra de Vaux. See also Huart, *Littérature Arabe* (Paris 1912), pp. 406–7; Vicomte

Ph. de Tarrazi, *Tārīkh al-ṣaḥāfa al-'arabiyya* (Beirut 1913), I, pp. 93–6. See also references to Ṭahṭāwī in H.A.R. Gibb, 'Studies in Contemporary Arabic Literature I; the 19th century', *BSOAS*, IV (1928), pp. 746–60; J. Heyworth-Dunne, 'Rifaa Badawi Rafi' al-Ṭahṭāwī; the Egyptian Revivalist', *BSOAS*, IX (1937–9), pp. 961–7, and X (1940–2), pp. 399–415. See also the long discussion of Ṭahṭāwī's work in Albert Hourani, *Arabic Thought in the Liberal Age, 1798–1939* (London 1962), pp. 67–83.

25 *Manāhij al-albāb*, p. 437.

26 ibid., p. 243.

27 ibid., p. 248.

28 Louis 'Awaḍ, *Al-mu'atharāt*, II, pp. 122–94, argues that Rifaa is the founder of 'bourgeois liberalism' in Egypt and the father of modern social and political thought in the country. He contends that Rifaa represented the greatest educational and cultural force in 19th-century Egypt, especially as he preached about the 'Egyptian national idea' (i.e., the idea of an Egyptian nation), the notion of a 'temporal state', and the foundations of a 'progressive bourgeois society'; the education of the citizen and his participation in politics, and the sovereignty of law. Although 'Awaḍ presents his argument brilliantly, one feels that he reads Rifaa's writing in mid-19th century rather uncritically, applying to it ideas and political concepts of the 1960s in what appears to be a slightly forced manner.

29 *Murshid al-ḥayrān ilā ma'rifat aḥwāl al-insān* (2nd ed. Bulaq 1890).

30 Ahmad Vefiq Pasha, a distinguished Turkish diplomat in the 19th century, also translated *Télémaque* and adapted certain plays by Molière. See H. Bowen, 'Ahmed Wafiq Pasha', in *EI²*, and Bernard Lewis, *op. cit.*, pp. 86–7. On Othman Galal, see Cheikho *Al-ādāb*, II, pp. 100–2.

31 On Ṣāliḥ Majdī Bey, see Cheikho *Al-ādāb*, II, pp. 18–20, and Shaykh al-Leythī, Cheikho, *Al-ādāb*, II, p. 98.

CHAPTER 7: CONSTITUTIONALISM, REBELLION AND OCCUPATION

1 See *Kitāb manāhij al-albāb*, 2nd ed. (Cairo 1912), esp. pp. 215–16.

2 For a detailed description of the first Assembly, see Jacob M. Landau, *Parliaments and Parties in Egypt* (Tel-Aviv 1953), pp. 7–27. See also the complete reference work on parliamentary life in Egypt by Muhammad Khalīl Ṣubḥī, *Tārīkh al-ḥayāt al-niyābiyya fī Miṣr min 'ahd sākin al-jinān Muḥammad 'Ali Pasha*, 7 vols (Cairo 1939). For comments on the Assembly established by Ismail, see Roderic H. Davison, *Reform in the Ottoman Empire, 1856–1876* (Princeton 1963), p. 225.

3 Ahmad Shafiq Pasha, *Mudhakkirātī fī niṣf qarn*, 2 vols (Cairo 1934–6), II, p. 29.

4 Ahmad Shafiq Pasha, *Mudhakkirātī*.

5 It is interesting to note that on 6 October 1875 the Ottoman Treasury defaulted on its payment of interest on the public debt. The Grand Vizier announced that arrangements would be negotiated with representatives of creditors for the setting up of an agency to administer the Ottoman Public Debt. This was established in 1881. See B. Lewis, 'Duyun-i-umumiyya', *EI²*, II, pp. 677–8.

Notes

6   The text of this letter is reproduced in Rāfiʿī, *ʿAṣr Ismāʿīl*, 2 vols, 2nd ed. (Cairo 1948), II, pp. 74–5. The decree was reversed by Tawfiq Pasha on 18 August 1879 when he abolished the Council.

7   On Afghani, see Muhammad Makhzumi, *Khāṭirāt Jamal al-din al-Afghani al-Ḥusayni* (Beirut 1931). For a reassessment of the role of Afghani, see Nikki R. Keddie, 'Religion and Irreligion in Iranian Nationalism', *Comparative Studies in Society and History*, IV (1962), pp. 265–95; and Elie Kedourie, *Afghani and Abduh* (London 1966).

8   See Albert Hourani, 'Djamʿiyya', *EI²*, II, pp. 428–9. For political activities of secret societies in Turkey, see B. Lewis, *op. cit.*, p. 148 and 148n, especially the Kuleli Incident in 1859; and p. 394 for the 'New Ottoman Society' of 1865.

9   Shaykh al-Bakri (1814–80) was one of the ulama who succeeded his father as Marshal of the *asyād* (those who are officially recognized as descended from the Prophet's family). As a member of the Assembly he was involved in the general movement to curtail the powers of the Khedive and against European control over the affairs of the country. For a biographical sketch, see Ali Pasha Mubarak, *Khiṭaṭ*, III, p. 124.

10 For a more detailed listing of the aims and programmes of this Society, see 'Wathāʾiq tārīkhiyya ʿan al-aḥzāb waʾl-tanẓīmāt al-siyāsiyya fī miṣr min al-ḥizb al-waṭanī ḥattā al-ittiḥād al-ishtirākī al-ʿarabī', *Al-Ṭaliʿa*, I, no. 2 (February 1965), 147–9.

11 See the revealing documentation and analysis in Elie Kedourie, *op. cit.*, pp. 22–37.

12 Another ruler, Sultan Abdul Hamid, had dealt just as disarmingly a couple of years earlier with his constitutional lot led by Midhet Pasha and the Conference of Ambassadors in Istanbul.

13 Quoted in Rāfiʿī, *ʿAṣr Ismāʿīl*, II, pp. 186–7.

14 At this time, just before the demise of Riad and Nubar, the group of Assembly Delegates who came to form the Helwan (or National) Society, led by Shaykh al-Bakri, held meetings in order to agitate the masses against Riad as the friend of Europeans, i.e., the Christians. Ismail was surely behind this agitation.

15 Is that perhaps the reason why Sharif Pasha said to Blunt in January 1882: 'It was I who created the National Party' (as agent of the Khedive?). See W.S. Blunt, *Secret History of England in Egypt* (London 1907, 1928), p. 196.

16 He referred to the Khedive derisively as *Shaykh al-ḥāra* (Leader of the Alley Boys), *al-wād* (The Boy). See Ibrahim Abduh, *Abū Naḍḍāra* (Cairo 1953).

17 On the Debt and the Law of Liquidation, see Viscount Milner, *England in Egypt* (11th ed., London 1904), p. 52.

18 See Cromer, *Modern Egypt*, I, pp. 180–1, 295, on the alleged role of Baron de Ring.

19 Quoted in Muhammad Rifaat Bey, *The Awakening of Modern Egypt* (London 1947), p. 183. See also Orabi, *Kashf al-sitār ʿan sirr al-asrār*, I (Years 1881–2) (Cairo n.d.), pp. 236–7.

20 On the impatience of France to intervene after the September 1881 army mutiny, the role of Gambetta and the inimical reaction of British officials on the spot

against the proposed delivery of the Joint Note, see Cromer, *op. cit.*, I, pp. 218–22.

21 For a list of papers publicizing the Orabist cause, see Rāfiʿī, *Al-thawra al-ʿurābiyya waʾl-iḥtilāl al-inglīzī* (2nd ed., Cairo 1949), pp. 159–60.

22 Estimates of the number of victims on both sides in the Alexandria troubles have ranged from 200 to 500. See Salim al-Naqqash, *Miṣr lil-miṣriyyīn*, V, p. 5; and Rāfiʿī, *Al-thawra*, pp. 293–4.

23 According to Turkish sources, Sultan Abdul Hamid sent his personal aide-de-camp (*yawir akram*) Darwish Pasha, carrying the Mejidi Order First Class decoration for Orabi, as well as decorations for other officers. The Sultan, it is reported, aimed at using Orabi to abolish the Khedivate and restore Ottoman control. Darwish was accompanied by Esʿad Effendi, the *ferashet vekili*. The mission however failed and Darwish returned to Istanbul 'sad and downcast'. See Kamil Pasha, *Memoirs*, p. 15. I am indebted to Professor Bernard Lewis for this reference.

24 Ahmad Shafiq Pasha, *Mudhakkirātī*, I, p. 178.

25 ibid.

26 Casualty figures among the Egyptian forces in Tel el-Kebir battle are instructive. The total Orabist force involved in this operation has been estimated between 10,000 and 15,000. Their positions were so completely overrun by the British force that over a third, between 3,000 and 5,000 troops, were killed. The rest either fled or were captured. Some have stated that the force was practically wiped out. See Rāfiʿī, *Al-thawra*, pp. 434–5, who gets these figures essentially from Blunt, *op. cit.*, p. 306.

27 Rāfiʿī, ibid., reproduces Orabi's statement on the Tel el-Kebir battle from the latter's *Memoirs*, *op. cit.*, 435–8. The statement accuses Egyptian officers of deserting their positions and described the flight of troops abandoning their posts. For a discussion of aspects of the trial of Orabists, see Mary Rowlatt, *Founders of Modern Egypt* (London 1962), W.S. Blunt, *op. cit.*, and A.M. Broadley, *How We Defended Orabi and his friends, A Study of Egypt and the Egyptians* (London 1884).

28 Jacques Berque, Egypt, *Imperialism and Revolution* (first published in French, Paris 1967; English translation, London 1972); and Mary Rowlatt, *Founders of Modern Egypt* (London and New York 1962).

29 See the interesting interpretation of the relation between Orabi and 'autochtonous landlords' in the Chamber of Deputies by A. Schölch, 'Constitutional Development in Nineteenth Century Egypt – a reconsideration', *Middle Eastern Studies*, X, January 1974, no. 1, pp. 3–14.

30 Sir Edward Malet to Lord Granville, 5 June 1882, Blue Book, *Egypt*, no. 11 (1882).

31 *The Making of Modern Egypt* (London 1906).

32 Sir Edward Malet, *Egypt 1879–1883*.

33 *Kashf al-sitar ʿan sirr al-asrar*, I (Cairo n.d.).

34 See for example, W.S. Blunt, *Secret History of the English Occupation of Egypt* (London 1907) and 'The Egyptian Revolution', *Nineteenth Century*, September 1882; A.M. Broadley, *How We Defended Orabi and his Friends* (London 1884)

and E.Dicey, 'England's Intervention in Egypt', *Nineteenth Century*, August 1882.

35 *The New Egypt*, p. 101.
36 ibid.
37 ibid., p. 103.
38 ibid., p. 112.
39 pp. 5–6.
40 Quoted in *The Standard*, 16 February 1883. Cf. W.S. Blunt, *op. cit.*, *Nineteenth Century*.
41 ibid.
42 *op. cit.*, pp. 6–7.
43 *Egypt for the Egyptians*, p. 15.
44 *op. cit.*, p. 8.
45 See Elie Kedourie, *Afghani and Abduh* (London 1966).
46 Blue Book, *Egypt*, no. 11 (1882), p. 124.
47 *op. cit.*, p. 23.
48 ibid., p. 157.
49 ibid., p. 174.
50 *op. cit.*
51 See Louis 'Awad, *Al-mu'atharāt*, II, *passim*.

CHAPTER 8: THE BRITISH IN EGYPT

1 See Sir Edward Malet, *Egypt 1879–1883*, ed. Lord Sanderson (London 1909). See also Blue Book, *Egypt*, no. 11 (1882).
2 See Chapter 11 below.
3 See Lord Cromer, *Modern Egypt*, 2 vols (London 1908). See also A. Milner, *England in Egypt*, 11th ed. (London 1904), and Robert Tignor, *Modernization and British Colonial Rule in Egypt 1882–1914* (Princeton 1966).
4 See E.R.J. Owen, 'The influence of Lord Cromer's Indian Experience on British Policy in Egypt, 1883–1907', in Albert Hourani, ed., *Middle Eastern Affairs*, No. 4 (St Anthony's Papers No. 17) (London 1965), pp. 109–39.
5 See Lord Cromer, *Abbas II* (London 1915).
6 See J.M. Ahmed, *The Intellectual Origins of Egyptian Nationalism* (London and New York 1960).
7 See Walid Kazziha, 'The Jarida-Ummah Group and Egyptian Politics', *Middle Eastern Studies*, XIII, no. 3, October 1977, pp. 373–85.
8 See Afaf Lutfi al-Sayyid, *Egypt and Cromer* (London 1968).
9 See Lord Lloyd, *Egypt since Cromer*, 2 vols (London 1933–4).

CHAPTER 9: JOURNALISM AND THE PRESS

1 Bernard Lewis, *op. cit.*, p. 41.
2 ibid., pp. 50–1.

3 See Ibrahim Abduh, *Taṭawwur al-ṣaḥāfa al-miṣriyya 1798–1851*, 3rd ed. (Cairo 1951), and Abd al-Laṭīf Ḥamza, *Adab al-maqāla al-ṣaḥafiyya fī miṣr*, 6 vols (Cairo 1950–4). See also Martin Hartmann, *The Arabic Press of Egypt* (London 1899), Vicomte Ph. de Tarrazi, *Tārikh al-ṣaḥāfa al ʿarabiyya*, 4 pts (Beirut 1913).

4 On this point see the remarks of Salāma Mūsā, *Al-ṣaḥāfa ḥirfa wa risāla* (Cairo 1958).

5 Until the 19th century journalistic writing was unknown to the Egyptians. Yet even England did not acquire the beginnings of journalistic writing until the late 18th and early 19th century, especially with the appearance of writers like Addison, Swift and Steele.

6 Under Menou, the French in Egypt published for a time an Arabic paper, *Al-Tanbīh*, containing mainly news of the administration and the Cairo Council, or *Diwan*. Its editor was Shaykh al-Khashab, Secretary of the Council. See Ibrahim Abduh, *Taṭawwur*, pp. 23–5. On printing and the Press during the French occupation generally, see his *Tārikh al-ṭibāʿa wa al-ṣaḥāfa khilāl al-ḥamla al-faransiyya* (Cairo 1949).

7 On al-Shidyaq and his career, see 'Djarida', *EI²*, II, pp. 464–77; Zaydan, *Mashāhīr*, II, pp. 74–83; and Louis ʿAwad, *Al-muʾatharāt*, I, pp. 20–48, and II, pp. 195–235. In this second volume, Awad deals extensively with Shidyaq's books in an attempt to extrapolate social and political ideas relevant to the impact of Europe on modern Arabic literature. He does not deal with his journalistic career at all.

8 Prominent among the Syrians were the group comprising Nimr, Ṣarruf and Shumayyil with their newspaper *al-Muqaṭṭam* and periodical *al-Muqtaṭaf*. Further on this, see Chapter 11 below.

9 For a history of *al-Ahram*, see Ibrahim Abduh, *Tārikh al-Abrām* (Cairo 1951).

10 On Sanua, see Ibrahim Abduh, *Tārīkh*, and I.C. Gendzier, *op. cit.*

11 See the discussion on Shaykh Ali Yusuf and his *al-Muʾayyad* in Chapter 10 below.

12 See Cheikho *Al-ādāb*, II, pp. 133–5.

13 *Muntakhabāt*, 4 parts in one volume (2nd ed., Alexandria 189?), pt. ii, pp. 54–7.

14 ibid., p. 61.

15 Only volumes IV–IX of his collected articles mainly published in his paper *al-Maḥrūsa* and entitled *Miṣr lil-miṣriyyīn* (Alexandria 1884) were available to me for examination. These fortunately cover the period of Khedive Tawfiq's early reign (IV); the Orabi-led army mutinies and revolt (V); the British occupation until 1884, and especially the mission and report of Lord Dufferin in 1883 (VI); and the record of the proceedings of the Orabists' trials (VII–IX). Orabi claimed that the expression 'Egypt for the Egyptians' was coined by Said Pasha (1856–63) in a speech in 1859. See his Memoirs, *Kashf al-sitār* (Cairo n.d.).

16 For a fuller discussion of these developments, see Chapters 10 and 11 below.

17 See *al-Ustādh*, II (first year, 7 February–13 June 1893). Among the more recent studies in Arabic of al-Nadīm are Muhammad ʿAbd al-Wahhāb Ṣaqr and Fawzī Saʿīd Shāhīn, *ʿAbdullah al-Nadim* (Cairo n.d.), and Ahmad Amin, *Zuʿamaʾ al-iṣṭaḥ fiʾlʿaṣr al-ḥadīth* (Cairo 1965), pp. 202–48.

Notes

CHAPTER 10: RELIGIOUS REFORM AND ISLAMIC POLITICAL SENTIMENT

1   See Nikki Keddie, 'Religion and Irreligion in Early Iranian Nationalism', *Comparative Studies in Society and History*, IV (1962), pp. 265–95, and *Sayyid Jamal al-Din 'al-Aghani', a political biography* (Berkeley and London 1972). See also Elie Kedourie, *Afghani and Abduh* (London 1966), pp. 7–10; Albert Hourani, *Arabic Thought in the Liberal Age* (London 1962), pp. 107–29.

2   Cromer suspected that Shaykh Muhammad Abduh was an agnostic too. See *op. cit.*, II, pp. 179–80, and Elie Kedourie, *op. cit.*, *passim*.

3   See the Arabic periodical *al-'Urwal al-wuthqā* (The Indissoluble Bond) which Afghani and Abduh edited and published in Paris in 1884 (3rd ed., Beirut 1933).

4   See Muhammad Farīd, *Tārikh al-dawla al-'aliyya al-'uthmāniyya* (History of the Ottoman State) (Cairo 1893).

5   See *Dīwān*, I and II (Cairo n.d.).

6   See *Dīwān* (Cairo 1922), 3 vols.

7   See *Waṭaniyyāt: Dīwān*, 3rd ed. (Cairo 1947).

8   For a detailed and critical discussion of the Dufferin Report, see Alfred Milner, *England in Egypt*, 11th ed. (London 1904), pp. 63–6, 140–57, 308–12. See also P.G. Elgood, *The Transit of Egypt* (London 1928), pp. 81–120.

9   Milner, *op. cit.*, p. 15.

10 For details of the incident, see Milner, *op. cit.*, pp. 97–9, and 'Abd al-'Aziz Muhammad al-Shinnāwī, *Ḥadith al-busfur ijibshyān* (Cairo 1962). There were at that time another fifteen foreign language newspapers and periodicals in Egypt, most of them French, but a few Italian, and one English – the *Egyptian Gazette*.

11 See P.M. Holt, *The Mahdist State in the Sudan 1881–98* (London 1958); and *A Modern History of the Sudan* (London 1961, 1963).

12 The major biography of Abduh is by Shaykh Muhammad Rashīd Riḍā, *Tārikh al-ustādh al-imām al-shaykh muḥammad 'abduh*, 3 vols (Cairo 1926–48). C.C. Adams, *Islam and Modernism in Egypt* (Oxford 1933) is the nearest work in English to a biography of Abduh. For various discussions of his writings and ideas in English, see Albert Hourani, *Arabic Thought in the Liberal Age* (London 1962), pp. 130–98; Nadav Safran, *Egypt in Search of Political Community* (Harvard 1962), pp. 62–75; J.M. Ahmed, *The Intellectual Origins of Egyptian Nationalism* (London 1952), pp. 35–43. Certain allusions to a *sufi* (mystical) relationship between Abduh the 'acolyte' and Afghani the 'master' are discussed in Elie Kedourie, *Afghani and Abduh, an essay on religious unbelief and political activism in modern Islam* (London 1966). See also Malcolm Kerr, *Islamic Reform* (California University and Cambridge University Presses 1966), esp. pp. 103–52.

13 On the politics of Abduh's appointment as Mufti, see Kedourie, *op. cit.*, pp. 37–9.

14 The gate of *ijtihad* was formally closed in the 10th century with the triumph of orthodoxy over the Mu'tazila. The orthodox jurist and theolgian Abu'l-Hasan al-Ash'arī (874–936) of Basra led the movement against the rationalist Mu'tazila. See 'Idjtihad', *EI*, I, pp. 694–5.

15 See Riḍā, *Tārīkh al-ustādh*. With the 'religion of humanism' emanating from Europe rampant, European-educated natives and European residents in Turkey, Egypt and other parts of the Ottoman Empire, as well as in Iran, formed secret societies and joined freemason lodges. Both Abduh and Afghani became active members of such lodges and societies. See Kedourie, *op. cit.*

16 *Risālat al-tawḥīd* (Cairo 1943) (French translation by B. Michel and Moustapha Abdel Razik, Paris 1925); English translation by Ishaq Musa'ad and Kenneth Cragg, *The Theology of Unity* (London 1966).

17 *op. cit., passim.*

18 For a view which implies such influences on Abduh, see Albert Hourani, *op. cit.*, pp. 130–60.

19 The analysis of Elie Kedourie, *op. cit.*, suggests that there was implicit in the work of both Afghani and Abduh a subtle betrayal of Islam – even an agnostic rejection of it – which resulted from their *sufi* romanticism and freemasonic rational humanism.

20 For a brief biographical sketch of Shaykh Rashīd Riḍā see Hourani, *op cit.*, pp. 222–4. For general information on the *Salafiyya*, see Malcolm H. Kerr, *Islamic Reform* (California 1966), esp. pp. 153–208.

21 Again, Kedourie's study cited earlier would suggest a more extreme conclusion, namely, that Abduh really wished to reject the prophecy of Islam for a 'religion of reason'.

22 Malcolm Kerr arrives at a similar assessment of Islamic reform in his recent work, cited above. See *op. cit.*, pp. 209–23.

23 Generally, on the Azhar and its reform, see 'Abd al-Mut'āl al-Ṣa'īdī, *Tarikh al-iṣlahfi'l-azhar* (Cairo 1943); and Muhammad Abdel Monem al-Khafājī, *al-Azhar fi alf 'ām* (Cairo 1955), 3 vols. See also Bayard Dodge, *Al-Azhar, a Millennium of Muslim Learning* (Washington D.C. 1961), and 'Al-Azhar', *EI²* I, pp. 813–21.

24 On Rashīd Riḍā and his thought, see Malcolm H. Kerr, *op. cit.* (Los Angeles, California and London 1966).

25 In this connection, the thesis by 'Abd al-Raḥmān al-Kawākibī, *Umm al-qurā* (Cairo 1931 and Aleppo 1959 – ed. by his grandson Abd al-Rahman al-Kawākibī) which argued a privileged position and central role for the Arabs in Islam is interesting. See also on al-Kawākibî, Sami Dahhan *'Abd al-Raḥmān al-Kawā-kibī* (1854–1902) (Cairo n.d.). For a critical discussion, see Sylvia G. Haim, *Arab Nationalism: An Anthology* (Los Angeles and Berkeley, California 1962), pp. 25–8.

26 Cromer has written an indictment of Abbas. See Earl of Cromer, *Abbas II* (London 1915). A set of edited memoirs of Abbas appeared in the newspaper *Al-Miṣri* in 1950. These, one suspects, are incomplete. His private papers are reportedly in a bank in Geneva, and no one outside his family has had access to them so far.

27 A detailed study in English of Ali Yusuf, his journalistic and political career is to be found in an unpublished University of London Ph.D. thesis, *Shaykh Ali Yusuf: Political Journalist and Islamic Nationalist, A Study of Egyptian Politics, 1889–1913* (1967) by Abbas Kelidar. There is no doubt that the *Mu'ayyad* succeeded *al-Jawā'ib* of Ahmad Faris al-Shidyaq as the leading Arabic

Muslim paper. *Al-Jawā'ib* ceased appearing after 1884, twenty-three years after it was first launched. It had been the leading Arabic newspaper in the Muslim world and had attained wide circulation. *Al-Mu'ayyad* was even more successful. Both papers however had the support of the wider Islamic community and propagated both an Ottoman and Islamic policy. Whereas *al-Jawā'ib* had been published from Istanbul and financed by the Ottoman Sultan, *al-Mu'ayyad* appeared in Cairo with the financial support of the Khedive Abbas II. On *al-Jawā'ib*, see Hourani, *op. cit.*, pp. 98–9, and 'Djarida', *EI²*, II, pp. 466–9 [464–76].

28 For an Egyptian version of this incident see 'Abd al-Raḥmān al-Rāfi'i, *Muṣṭafā Kāmil* (Cairo 1950), 3rd rev. ed., pp. 197–235.

29 Quoted in Cromer, *op. cit.*, II, p. 208.

30 For an interesting discussion of the assassin al-Wardani, his background, motives and political connections, see Samir Seikaly, 'Prime Minister and Assassin: Butrus Ghali and Wardani', *Middle Eastern Studies*, XIII, no. 1, January 1977, pp. 112–23.

31 Aḥmad Luṭfī al-Sayyid, leader of the *Jarida*–Umma group and spokesman for the independence of Egypt as a liberal constitutional state in 1907–9, did not consider Gorst's policy different from Cromer's. [See *Ṣafaḥāt maṭwiyya* (Cairo 1946), pp. 7–24.] He attacked Gorst's policy especially in aggravating the economic crisis of 1907, and argued that independence had to be secured by Egyptians themselves, from both the British and the personal rule of the Khedive, as the Ottomans had done in Turkey in extracting the 1876 Constitution from the Sultan and again in 1908–9. [See ibid., pp. 32–42.]

32 Further on this see Chapter 11.

33 On this subject generally and this period in particular, see the work of Dr E. R. J. Owen cited in the bibliography. See also his 'The Attitudes of British Officials to the Development of the Egyptian Economy, 1882–1922', in Michael Cook, ed., *Economic History of the Middle East* (London 1972).

CHAPTER 11: STIRRINGS OF SECULAR LIBERALISM

1 See Ali Fahmī Kāmil, *Muṣṭafā Kāmil fi arba'a wa thalāthīna rabi'an* (Cairo 1908–11), 9 parts; Muṣṭafā Kāmil, *Al-mas'ala al-sharqiyya* (Cairo 1898); Ali Fahmī Kāmil, *Rasā'il miṣriyya faransiyya* (Correspondence of Mustafa Kamil with Mme Juliette Adam) (Cairo 1909). See also Fritz Steppat, *Nationalismus und Islam bei Mustafa Kamil*, monograph from *Die Welt des Islams*, IV, no. 4 (1956), pp. 241–341. See also Aḥmad Rashād, *Muṣṭafā Kāmil, ḥayātuhu wa kifāḥuhu* (Cairo 1958).

2 See Bernard Lewis, *op. cit.*, pp. 197–203.

3 See Cromer, *Modern Egypt* (London 1908), 2 vols, and Lord Lloyd, *Egypt Since Cromer* (London 1933–4), 2 vols.

4 On the Drummond Wolff Mission, see A. Milner, *England in Egypt* (London 1904), 11th ed., pp. 117–25 (1st ed., London 1892). For a sharp criticism of this Mission, see Auckland Colvin, *The Making of Modern Egypt* (London 1906), pp. 143–58.

5 See Rāfi'ī, *Mudhakkirātī* (Memoirs) (Cairo 1952).

Notes

6 On certain specific links between Abbas II and Mustafa Kamil, and suggestions of the latter being an agent of the former in Paris, see the interesting correspondence of Kamil edited by Muhammad Anīs, *Ṣafaḥāt maṭwiyya min tārīkh al-zaʿīm Muṣṭafā Kāmil, rasāʾil jadīda li Muṣṭafā Kāmil* (New Letters of Mustafa Kamil from 8 June 1895 to 19 February 1896) (Cairo 1962).

7 On these matters generally, see Ahmad Safiq, *Mudhakkirātī fī niṣf qarn*, 2 vols (Cairo 1934–6), II, pp. 102–13.

8 See ʿAbd al-Rahman al-Rafiʿi, *Mudhakkirati*, pp. 8–36.

9 See Muṣṭafā Kāmil, *Al-Shams al-mushriqa* (The Rising Sun) (Cairo 1904). See also Ḥāfiẓ Ibrāhīm, *Dīwan* (Collected Poems) (Cairo 1922), 3 vols.

10 See a satirization of this in ʿAbdullah al-Nadīm, *Sulāfat al-nadim* (Cairo 1897–1901), 2 vols, I, p. 86.

11 See J.M. Ahmed, *The Intellectual Origins of Egyptian Nationalism* (London 1960); Albert Hourani, *op. cit.*; Nadav Safran, *Egypt in Search of Political Community* (Cambridge, Mass. 1961).

12 On the founding of *Ḥizb al-umma*, see Elie Kedourie 'Ḥizb', *EI²*, and Jacob M. Landau, *Parliaments and Parties in Egypt* (Tel Aviv 1953), pp. 137–40.

13 Quoted in Ibrahim Abduh. *Taṭawwur al-ṣaḥāfa al-miṣriyya, 1798–1951*, 3rd ed. (Cairo 1951), p. 176. See also Walid Kazziha, 'The *Jarida*–Umma Group and Egyptian Politics', *Middle Eastern Studies*, XIII, no. 3, October 1977, pp. 373–85.

14 See Rāfiʿī, *Mudhakkirātī*, p. 10.

15 *Egypt No. 1* (1907), Cd. 3394, p. 7.

16 See Rāfiʿī, *Muṣṭafā Kāmil bāʿith al-ḥaraka al-qawmiyya* (Cairo 1950), pp. 465–500. See also Ali Fahmi Kamil, *Muṣṭafā Kāmil*, 9 parts.

17 See eulogies in Rāfiʿī, *Muṣṭafā Kāmil*, pp. 267–90. See also J.M. Ahmed, *op. cit.*, p. 79.

18 His editorial attacks upon Mr Dunlop, British adviser to the Ministry of Education, often incited student demonstrations, and led the government to reactivate, on 25 March 1909, the November 1881 Press Law, whose penalties now included administrative exile sentences. Legislation was also passed to restrict student political activity of all kinds, and to cover acts of conspiracy. See Lloyd, *op. cit.*, I, pp. 89–95, 102–4.

19 On Ali Yusuf, his party, and its programme, see ʿAbd al-Laṭīf Ḥamza, *Adab al-maqāla al-ṣaḥafiyya fi miṣr* (Cairo n.d.), 5 vols, IV, pp. 148–62. See also unpublished Ph.D. thesis (London 1967) by Abbas Kelidar cited earlier.

20 Although *waṭan* was popularly understood then as the location where a man lived and/or was born in, the secularists and particularly Luṭfī among them used it as a precise connotation of the *nation-state* – a territorial, juridical unit. They wished to replace the more religious-traditional notion of the Islamic *umma* or community. See Aḥmad Lutfi al-Sayyid, *Ṣafaḥāt maṭwiyya min tārīkh al-ḥaraka al-istiqlāliyya* (Cairo 1946).

21 See *Sulāfat al-nadim*, II, pp. 33 ff. Namik Kemal, the Turkish national poet, upon return from exile to Turkey in 1871, produced a comparable patriotic play entitled *Vatan*. See Bernard Lewis, *op. cit.*, p. 154.

22 On the debate between Abduh and Hanoteaux, see Riḍā, *Tārikh*, II, pp. 401–68. See also Abduh, *Al-islām wa'l-radd 'alā muntaqidīhi* (Cairo 1928).

23 A series of articles by 'Abd al-Qādir Ḥamza entitled 'There is a Danger to us and the religion', appeared in *Al-Muqtaṭaf* magazine in March 1904, attacking the ignorance of the 'ulama. The Syrian 'Abd al-Raḥmān al-Kawākibī had published in Cairo in 1899 his *Umm al-qura* (Mother of Cities) in which he deplored the weakness of Islamic nations and called for a separation of the Caliphate from the Ottoman Sultanate since he argued that the Caliphate belonged to the Arabs as 'the best in Islam' (or 'the privileged' – those preferred by God – in Islam.). Another Syrian Christian Sulaymān al-Bustānī in his book *Dhikrā wa 'ibra* (A Commemoration and a Lesson) published in Cairo in 1908, discussed the decadence of Ottoman rule on the occasion of the Young Turk Revolution. Seven years earlier, in 1901, Kawakibi's *Ṭabā'i' al-istibdād* had appeared, which also criticized Ottoman rule as tyrannical. Shaykh Muhammad Abduh had, as early as 1880, attacked certain Muslim practices in Egypt, especially those connected with the *tariqas*, or religious brotherhood orders. See Riḍā, *Tārikh*, II, pp. 133–40. Abdullah al-Nadim in 1883 also attacked the heretical nature of some ceremonies common to religious brotherhoods, such as *dōsah* (the practice of religious brotherhood members lying flat on the ground for their venerated shaykh to ride over them while mounted on a horse, mule or donkey). See *al-Ustadh*, I, pt 2 (Cairo 1893), pp. 786–91. See also E.W. Lane, *Manners and Customs of the Modern Egyptians* (London 1895), pp. 251, 457–9; (1954 Dent ed.)., pp. 456, 474–6.

It is only fair to point out that not all the above writings were necessarily prompted by, or reflected a profound change in, the views of their authors. Thus recent research has uncovered certain practical motivations behind the published attacks of Al-Kawakibi against the Ottoman Sultan. See Sylvia G. Haim, 'Islam and the Theory of Arab Nationalism', in *Die Welt des Islams*, IV (1955), pp. 124–49.

24 See *Sirr taqaddum al-ingliz al-saksūniyyīn* (Cairo 1894), pp. 23–4. Historians of Turkey have argued a similar influence by Demolins on the Young Turk liberal Prince Sabaheddin. See Bernard Lewis, *op. cit.*, p. 199 and p. 226.

25 Another prominent Egyptian, Abdullah Pasha Fikri [1834–90], who served as Inspector of Schools in the Department of Education and as tutor to Khedive Tawfiq, represented Egypt in the Congress of Orientalists held at Stockholm in 1888. Upon his return from that trip he wrote a volume, 'A Guide to the Advantages of Europe', *Irshād al-alibbā' ilā maḥāsin ōrobbā*. He was instrumental in the establishment of a National Library in Cairo. For a short biographical sketch of Fikri, see Cheikho *Al-ādāb* (Beirut 1910), II, pp. 95–7.

26 Further editions of this book, *Al-madaniyya wa'l-islām*, appeared in 1912, 1927 and 1933. This writer has used the 1912 Amin Hindiya edition. The latter includes the Preface to a first edition dated 1898, not 1904, showing that the 1904 was a second edition.

27 Thus one of the concrete social problems mentioned by Muwailiḥi is the abuse of *waqfs* (religious trusts and bequests) for other than charitable purposes. See *Ḥadith 'isā ibn hishām* (Cairo 1907, 1923). See also a discussion of it in Ṣalāḥ al-dīn Dhuhnī, *Miṣr bayna'l-ihtilāl wa'l-thawra* (Egypt Between the Occupation and the Revolution) (Cairo 1939), pp. 8–64. On Muwailiḥi and his work, see

Saadedine Bencheneb, *Revue Africaine*, nos 380–1 (1939) and nos 382–3 (1940). See also Henri Perès, 'Les origines d'un roman célèbre de littérature arabe moderne: Hadith Isa Ibn Hisam de Muhammad al-Muwailihi', *Bulletin d'Études Orientales* (Institut Français de Damas), IX–X (1942–4), pp. 101–18. See also a series of articles by Jean Lecerf, 'Litterature dialectale', in *B.D.'E.O.* II–IV (1939–41), II, pp. 179–207, III–IV, pp. 47–172.

28 On *Layālī Ṣatīḥ* (Cairo 1906) as the model story with a social message see the brilliant concise essay in Muhammad Mandur, *Qaḍāya jadīda fī adabinā al-ḥadīth* (New Issues in our Modern Literature) (Beirut 1958), pp. 48–58.

29 Tal'at Ḥarb had written a rebuttal to the ideas of Qasim Amin in the first book *Taḥrīr al-Mar'a*. See *Faṣl al-khiṭāb fī'l-mar'a wa'l-ḥijāb* (Cairo n.d.).

30 On the further development of the feminist movement in Egypt, see Doriya Shafiq and Ibrahim Abduh, *Taṭawwur al-nahḍa al-nisā'iyya fī miṣr min 'ahd Muhammad 'alī ilā al-fārūq* (Cairo 1945).

31 *The Education of Salama Musa* (Washington D.C. 1961), English translation of *Tarbiyat Salāma Mūsā* (Cairo 1947), by L.O. Schuman, pp. 38–9.

32 ibid., p. 30.

33 ibid.

34 J.M. Ahmed refers to the *al-Muqaṭṭam* and *al-Muqtaṭaf* publicists and writers as constituting a political group. See *op. cit.*, pp. 30–1, 82–4. Among these, Nimr was popularly referred to as the 'leader of the pro-occupation group' (*shaykh al-iḥtilāliyyīn*). That they constituted one kind of political influence in Egypt at that time is certain. But that they were a real political group is doubtful. See Nadia Farag, 'The Lewis Affair and the Fortunes of the al-Muqtataf', *Middle Eastern Studies*, VIII, no. 1, January 1972, pp. 73–83.

35 On Shumayyil, see Jean Lecerf, 'Sibli Sumayyil', *B.D.'E.O.*, I (1931), p. 153. See also the works of Shumayyil, *Majmū'a* (Cairo 1909–13, 2 vols), and *Falsafat al-nushu' wa'l-irtiqa'* (Cairo 1910). For a discussion of Shumayyil, see Albert Hourani, *op. cit.*, pp. 245–53.

36 See Hourani, *op. cit.*, pp. 254–9.

37 These suggestions were made by Antoun in his study of the life and philosophy of Ibn Rushd (Averroes). See Antoun, *Ibn rushd wa falsafatuhu* (Cairo 1903). See the response by Shaykh Muhammad Abduh in his *al-Naṣrāniyya wa'l-Islām* (Cairo 1947–8). See also Rashīd Riḍā, *op. cit.*, I, pp. 805 ff. cf. the discussion of Farah Antun by Hourani, *op. cit.*, pp. 253–9.

38 See his *Ṣafaḥāt maṭwiyya* (Cairo 1946), and *Al-Muntakhabāt*, 2 vols (Cairo 1937–45).

39 *Al-Muntakhabāt*, I, pp. 8–9. Luṭfī's thought, incidentally, could have been influenced by the writings of the Turkish liberal writer Abd Allah Djewdet [1869–1932]. On Djewdet, see *EI*² Suppl., pp. 55–60.

40 For Luṭfī's view on the Aqaba Incident, see *Ṣafaḥāt*, 103–5, where he argued that Egyptian pro-Ottoman sentiment was not a necessary extension, or corollary, of Egyptian Islamic sentiment – or religious fanaticism – but a normal reaction against the lack of self-rule.

Notes

CHAPTER 12: THE STRUGGLE FOR INDEPENDENCE, 1919–22

1   See Ataf Lutfi al-Sayyid Marsot, *Egypt's Liberal Experiment 1922–1936* (Berkeley and London 1977).

2   See Edward Malet and others cited above.

3   See Gabriel Baer, *A History of Landownership in Modern Egypt, 1800–1950* (London 1962), pp. 38–9.

4   See Roger Owen, 'The Influence of Lord Cromer's Indian Experience in British Policy in Egypt, 1883–1907', in Albert Hourani, ed., *Middle Eastern Affairs* no. 4 (St Antony's Papers, no. 17) (London 1965), pp. 109–39.

5   Rāfi'ī claims that the moratorium did not affect the worst-hit farmers as they were forced to pay their debts. See *Thawrat sanat 1919* (Cairo 1946), 2 vols, I, pp. 55–7. See also Charles Issawi, *Egypt in Revolution* (London 1963), p. 31.

6   Lloyd, *op. cit.*, I, criticized this part of the Declaration for the Egyptian government later called on Egyptian sacrifices for the war effort.

7   On Sultan Husayn Kamil and the circumstances of his accession, see this writer's 'Husayn Kamil', *EI²*; P.G. Elgood, *The Transit of Egypt* (London 1928), pp. 208–29; Lloyd, *op. cit.*, I, pp. 205–20; Muhammad Sa'īd al-Kaylānī, *Al-sulṭān ḥusayn kāmil* (Cairo 1963).

8   A Committee of Commerce and Industry had been formed in 1917 by a group of Egyptian financiers and rising industrialists, led by Talat Harb (founder of Bank Misr in 1920) and Ismail Sidqy. See Anouar Abdel-Malek, *Égypte société militaire* (Paris 1962), p. 22.

9   The major biography of Zaghlul is by Abbās Maḥmūd al-'Aqqād, *Saad Zaghlul, sīra wa taḥiyya* (Cairo 1936), and his political note is discussed in Abd al-Khaliq Lajin, *Saad Zaghlul was dawruhu fi al-siyasa al-Misriyya* (Beirut 1975). See also J.M. Ahmed, *op. cit.*, pp. 52–5. See also A. Marsot, *op. cit.*, pp. 43–72.

10 See Robert L. Tignor, 'The Egyptian Revolution of 1919, New Directions in the Egyptian Economy', *The Middle Eastern Economy*, ed. Elie Kedourie (London 1976), pp. 41–68.

11 A model analysis of Zaghlul's leadership and political tactics is by Elie Kedourie, 'Sa'd Zaghlul and the British', in Albert Hourani, ed., *Middle East Papers* no. 2 (St Antony's Papers, no. 11) (London 1961), pp. 139–60.

CHAPTER 13: EXPERIMENT IN CONSTITUTIONAL GOVERNMENT, 1923–39

1   Ahmad Shafiq Pasha, *Ḥawliyyāt miṣr al-siyāsiyya: tamhīd*, 3 vols (Cairo 1926–8), III, p. 13.

2   See Maḥmūd Zāyid, 'The Origins of the Liberal Constitutionalist Party in Egypt', in *Political and Social Change in Modern Egypt*, ed. P.M. Holt (London 1968), pp. 334–46.

3   On the difficulties of the Sarwat government, see Ahmad Shafiq, *Ḥawliyyāt*, III, pp. 45–410. Shafiq did not think the Sudan question was the real cause for the fall of the Sarwat government. Rather, he emphasized the intrigues of Court politicians in the palace, led by Muhammad Sa'id Pasha, who tried to convince

King Fuad that Sarwat had liaison with the exiled ex-Khedive Abbas. See III, p. 350.

4   See *Dustur*, monograph from *El²* (Leiden 1966), pp. 11–12 and 24–32.

5   For a discussion of some of these, see Chapter 15 below.

6   See Muhammad Ḥusayn Haykal, *Mudhakkirāt fi'l-siyāsa al-miṣriyya* (Political Memoirs), 2 vols (Cairo 1952–3), I, pp. 185–200.

7   See Chapter 14 below.

8   On the affair of the Jaghbūb oasis, see Muhammad Ḥusayn Haykal, *Mudhak-kirāt*, I, pp. 229–30.

9   Muhammad Mahmud, member of a rich landowning family, had succeeded Adli Yeken to the leadership of the Liberal Party in 1928. His assumption of the leadership occurred partly as a result of the split which occurred in the party that year over the question of their participation in the coalition government. See Muhammad Ḥusayn Haykal, *Mudhakkirāt*, I, pp. 260–90.

10 Actually Nahhas was tried before the Disciplinary Committee of the Bar Association for his alleged involvement in this case, and acquitted. See Rāfiʻi, *Fi aʻqāb al-thawra al-miṣriyya* (Cairo 1949), II, pp. 75–6.

11 The question of Senate appointments provided one of the earliest disagreements between the King and the Wafd. According to the Constitution the King appointed the President and half the Senators. The other half were elected. Presumably many of the appointments to the Senate were to be made with consideration to the recommendations of the party in office as well as the other parties. They also provided the King with a means of recognizing the services of senior government officials, judges, lawyers and men of affairs.

12 See *Dustur* (Leiden 1966), p. 29.

13 On the formation of the Shaʻb party. See Haykal, *Mudhakkirāt*, I, pp. 347–8, and Muna Abul Fadl, *The Ismail Sidqi Regime*, unpublished Ph.D. thesis, University of London, 1975.

14 See Rāfiʻī, *Thawrat sanat*, II, pp. 154–7, and Haykal, *Mudhakkirāt*, I, pp. 322–60.

15 The *riyal* is a unit of account used almost entirely for transactions in cotton. It is worth 20 Egyptian piastres (a fifth of an Egyptian pound). Other vernacular common names for it have been *dollar* and *talari*. It was first used in the early 19th century (perhaps earlier) by foreign merchants who did not wish to keep their accounts or conduct their business in Egyptian currency, which was constantly fluctuating (and often depreciating) in value. The word must be derived from the Spanish *odrai* and Austrian *thaler*. Its value was fixed at 20 piastres as a result of Muhammad Ali's currency reform in 1835–6. See Crouchley, *Economic Development of Modern Egypt* (London 1938). I am grateful to Dr Roger Owen, St Antony's College, Oxford, for this information.

16 It was alleged at the time that Ṣidqi and members of his family as well as several other government officials and ministers had been involved in financial scandals over the construction of the Alexandria Corniche. The Commission appointed by the Abd al-Fattah Yahia government to inquire into this case did not come up with any serious findings to warrant any indictments. There were also allegations of, and investigations into, police brutality under the Ṣidqi government.

Notes

See Haykal, *Mudhakkirāt*, I, pp. 353–7. See also Saniya Quraa, *Nimr al-siyāsa al-misriyya* (The Tiger of Egyptian Politics) (Cairo n.d.).

17 On *Miṣr al-fatāt*, see Chapter 15 below.

18 On this episode see Muhammad al-Tabʻī, *Min asrār al-sāsa wa'l-siyāsa* pp. 57–64.

CHAPTER 14: THE ATTACK UPON TRADITION

1 On problems surrounding the codification of the *Majalla*, see 'Hasan Fehmi', *EI²*, III (1966), pp. 250–1.

2 In June 1961, the government decreed a law for the reorganization of al-Azhar intended to transform its university into a modern institution of higher learning with such faculties as Engineering, Medicine, Agriculture and Public Administration. For the text of this legislation, see *Majallat al-Azhar*, XXXIII (July 1961), pt 2, pp. 237–64. For a discussion of the political significance of this drastic reform, see my 'Islam and the Foreign Policy of Egypt', in *Islam and International Relations*, ed. J. Harris Proctor (New York and London 1965), pp. 120–57.

3 On the general question of Azhar reform, see Chapter 10 above. See also Lajnat iṣlāḥ al-Azhar, *Mashruʻ iṣlāḥ al-Azhar* (Cairo 1919); Abd al-Mutʻāl al-Ṣaʻīdī, *Tārīkh al-iṣlāḥ fī'l-Azhar*, 2 vols in 1 (Cairo 1951?); Muhammad Abd al-Munʻim Khafājī, *al-Azhar fī alf ʻām*, 3 vols in 1 (Cairo 1954–5); Muhammad Abdullah 'Inan, *Tarikh al-jami' al-Azhar*, 2nd ed. (Cairo 1958); Abdul Ḥamīd Yūnis and Tawfīq 'Othmān, *al-Azhar* (Cairo 1946); and Bayard Dodge, *Al-Azhar* (Washington, D.C. 1961). On al-Azhar and politics, see Shaykh al-Ẓawahiri, *Al-siyāsa wa'l-Azhar* (Cairo 1945). See also Ahmad Shafiq Pasha, *Hawliyyāt miṣr al-siyāsiyya*, I, p. 353, II, pp. 229–33, III, pp. 478–87, 646–50. See also 'Ali Abd al-Rāziq, *Min āthār Muṣṭafa 'Abd al-Rāziq* (Cairo 1953).

4 In March 1936, Shaykh Muhammad Sulayman, of the High Shari'a Court, delivered a lecture at the Royal Society of Economics, Statistics and Legislation, entitled *Bi ay shar' nahkum* (With which law do we govern?) in which he urged the adoption of the sacred religious law as a basis for legislation. *Égypte Contemporain*, XXVII (1936), pp. 289–365 (Arabic text), pp. 271–87 French résumé. In another lecture, delivered in April 1936, Shaykh 'Abbās al-Jamal, a lawyer in the Shari'a Courts, defended the role of al-Azhar in modern society. See ibid., pp. 385–403, and pp. 367–84.

5 On the question of the Caliphate, see Shafiq, *Hawliyyāt*, I, pp. 119–21, III, pp. 40, 147–51, 203–4, 271–82, 380–1; Elie Kedourie, 'Egypt and the Caliphate', *Journal of the Royal Asiatic Society* (1963), pts 3 and 4, pp. 208–48.

6 It should be noted that the Ittihad Party was founded in January 1925 in preparation for the elections under the Ziwar government. Further on this, see Chapter 12 above, and Shafiq, *Hawliyyāt*, II, pp. 11–29, 833–47, 1044–57.

7 It is interesting to note that Ṭaha Husayn had just been appointed, in 1925, editor of *Ittiḥād*, the official organ of the new pro-Palace *Ittiḥād* Party. See Haykal, *Mudhakkirāt*, I, pp. 227.

8 On Shumayyil's influence generally, see Amīn Rīḥānī, *al-Rīḥaniyyāt*, 3 vols (Beirut 1923–4). See also Jean Lecerf, 'Sibli Sumayyil metaphysicien et moraliste contemporain', *Bull. d'Études Orientales*, I (1931), pp. 152–86. See also Albert Hourani, *op. cit.*, pp. 245–53. Shumayyil's most influential writings were *Falsafat*

al-nushū' wa'l-irtiqā' (Theory of Evolution) (Cairo 1910) and *Majmū'a* (Collected Essays) (Cairo 1910).

9 (Cairo n.d.).

10 Faraḥ Anṭun (1874–1922) debated the question of science and religion with his major work *Ibn Rushd wa falsafatuhu* (The Philosophy of Averroes) (Cairo 1902).

11 See, for instance, Salama Musa, *Hā'ulā' 'allamūnī* (Cairo n.d.), *Muqaddimat al-sūbermān* (Cairo n.d.) and *Bernard Shaw* (Cairo 1957). See also Husayn Fawzī, *Sindbād ilā'l-gharb* (Cairo n.d.), and *Sindbād 'aṣrī* (Cairo 1938).

12 The question of public and private charitable endowments (*waqf*) in Egypt has been an important social, economic and political problem. It is, however, too intricate to deal with here in any great detail for our purposes. It is mentioned as part of the important debate in the 1920s and therefore as an aspect of the constitutional experiment. For detailed studies of the *waqf* problem in Egypt, see Achille Sekaly, *Le Problème des Waqfs en Égypte* (Paris 1929), reprinted from *Revue des Études Islamiques*, III (1929), pp. 75–126, 277–337, 395–454, 601–59. See also Gabriel A. Baer, *A History of Landownership in Modern Egypt, 1800–1950* (London 1962), esp. pp. 147–85. See also H. Cattan, 'The Law of Waqf', in *Law in the Middle East*, ed. Khadduri and Liebesny (Washington D.C. 1955), and N.J. Coulson, *History of Islamic Law* (Edinburgh 1964).

13 On *al-Sufūr*, see Rāziq, *Min āthār*, and Haykal, *Mudhakkirāt*, I, pp. 75–6. On Feminism generally, see Doria Shafiq and Ibrahim Abduh, *Taṭawwur al-nahḍa al-nisā'iyya* (Cairo 1945).

14 On the problems of marriage and divorce, see Malcolm Kerr, *Islamic Reform* (California 1966), pp. 215 ff.

15 On *Rose al Yusuf*, see Ibrahim Abduh, *Rōz al-Yūsuf* (Cairo 1961).

16 See on this Bernard Lewis, *The Middle East and the West* (London 1964), pp. 76–81.

17 For the use of this biblical theme in Egyptian romantic–national literature, see Tawfīq al-Ḥakīm, *Ahl al-kahf* (The People of the Cave), a play in four acts (Cairo 1933).

18 See Tawfīq al-Ḥakīm, *Awdat al-rūḥ*, 2 vols (Cairo 1933).

19 The first writings on patriotic ideas in Egypt were the work of Shaykh Rifā'a al-Taḥtāwī (d. 1871), as for example his *Takhlīṣ al-ibrīz ...*, or his *Riḥla* cited earlier in this book (Cairo 1905); his *Kitāb manāhij al-albāb* (Cairo 1912) also cited earlier, and his *Al-murshid al-amīn li'l-banāt wa'l-banīn* (Cairo 1873).

20 English translation by S. Glazer, *The Future of Culture in Egypt* (Washington D.C. 1954).

21 Needless to say most of these ideas have been since rejected by Egyptian leaders and the 'revolutionary intelligentsia'. Until the end of the Second World War, however, practically all the modernists with varying intensity argued in favour of Egypt's essentially European cultural link.

22 Amin continued the study of Islamic culture with the following volumes: *Ḍuḥa'l-Islām* (*The Morning of Islam*), 3 vols (Cairo 1933–6); *Ẓuhr al-Islām* (*Islam's Noon*), 2 vols (Cairo 1945–7), and *Yawm al-Islām* (*The Day of Islam*) (Cairo 1952). Interesting among his other works are his autobiography *Ḥayātī* (Cairo

Notes

1950), *Al-sharq wa'l-gharb* (East and West) (Cairo 1955), and his essays in the form of letters to his son *Ilā waladī* (Cairo 1951).

23 Ghali, pp. 8–35.

CHAPTER 15: THE FAILURE OF LIBERALISM AND THE REACTION AGAINST EUROPE, 1930–50

1 The National Bank of Egypt (*Al-bank al-ahlī*), founded in 1898, had represented in it foreign capital (largely British), and operated under concession from the Egyptian government. See Elie Kedourie, ed. *op. cit.*

2 See his *'Alā hāmish al-sīra* (On the Margin of the Prophet's Tradition), 3 vols, *Ṣaddiq Abū Bakr* (The Life of Caliph Abū Bakr) (Cairo 1942).

3 See for instance his *Ḥayāt Muḥammad* (The Life of Muhammad) (Cairo 1935), and *Al-Ṣaddīq Abū Bakr* (The Life of Caliph Abu Bakr) (Cairo 1942).

4 See his *'Abqariyyat Muḥammad* (The Genius of Muhammad) (Cairo 1942); *'Abqariyyat 'Umar* (The Genius of Caliph Omar) (Cairo 1942); *'Abqariyyat al-Ṣaddiq* (Cairo 1943); *'Ali al-safud* (Caliph Ali) (Cairo 1944); *'Amr ibn al-'Aṣ* and *Khālid ibn al-Walīd* (Cairo 1944).

For a fuller discussion of these developments, see Nadav Safran, *op. cit.*, pp. 165–80.

5 See his memoirs, *Al-siyāsa wa'l-Azhar* (Politics and al-Azhar) (min mudhakkirāt al-shaykh Muḥammad al-Ahmadī al-Ẓawāhirī (Cairo 1945), ed. Dr Fakhr al-din al-Aḥmadī al-Ẓawāhirī.

6 On the Salafiyya, see Henri Laoust, 'Le réformisme orthodoxe des *Salafiya* et les caractères généraux de son organisation actuelle', *Revue des Études Islamiques*, VI (1932), pp. 175–224. See also Malcolm H. Kerr, *op. cit.*, *passim*.

7 A theologian and jurist of the Hanbali school (1263–1328).

8 Another Hanbali puritan reformer in Arabia (1703–87) who was greatly influenced by the teachings of Ibn Taymiyya; the founder of Wahhabism in Arabia.

9 See Riḍā, *Al-khilāfa aw al-imāmā'l-'uzmā* (Cairo 1923); French transl. by Henri Laoust, *Le califat dans le doctrine de Rasid Rida* (Beirut 1938); and al-Sanhūrī, *Le Califat* (Paris 1926).

10 General Ṣāliḥ Ḥarb Pasha, a former Chief of Staff of the Egyptian Army, succeeded Abdul Ḥamīd Sa'īd as President of the YMMA. Other lay Muslim organizations at this time were: *Jam'iyyat makārim al-akhlāq al-islāmiyya* (Society of the Virtues of Islamic Morals); *Al-hidāya al-islāmiyya* (Islamic Guidance); *Jam'iyyat iḥyā'al-sunna* (Society for the Revival of the Sunna); *Jam'iyyat nashr al-faḍā'il al-islāmiyya* (Society for the Propagation of Islamic Virtues); and others.

11 The Muslim Brethren has been a most important religio-political movement in Egypt and the Arab world. It is not our intention to discuss it here at great length. There are several studies of the movement (in addition to the huge body of literature produced by its leaders and executive) in English, among them, Ishak Musa Husaini, *The Moslem Brethren* (Beirut 1956); J. Heyworth-Dunne, *Religious and Political Trends in Modern Egypt* (Washington 1950 (privately printed)); Christina Phelps Harris, *Nationalism and Revolution in Egypt* (The Hague 1964) and Richard P. Mitchell, *The Society of the Muslim Brothers* (London 1969). The

491

Brethren's first Supreme Guide, Ḥasan al-Bannā, was assassinated at the entrance of the YMMA Headquarters in Cairo in February 1949. He was succeeded by Huḍaybī, a lawyer of no great eminence. Its latest Supreme Guide, Sayyid Quṭb, and one of its most eminent ideologues, was executed by order of the Egyptian government in 1966, after he was tried and convicted of the charge of conspiracy against the régime. Professor Magdi Wahba of Cairo University has translated an intriguing and revealing autobiographical document by Hassan al-Banna, covering his early life and activities until 1943. In it Hassan reports that he began his early religious calling as a *sufi*, or mystic, and probably belonged to one of the religious brotherhoods. To my knowledge this translation has never been published.

12 On the eve of elections in October 1949, the party changed its name once more to become the Socialist Democratic Party. The most detailed recent history of the party and its programme is to be found in *al-Ṭalī'a*, I, no. 3 (March 1965), a state-owned monthly published in Cairo, and edited by Lutfī al-Khūli. See also *Oriente Moderno* (1938), pp. 491–4, and (1940), pp. 183–8. See also J. Jankowski, *Egypt's Young Rebels, 'Young Egypt'* (Stanford 1975), and P.J. Vatikiotis, *Nasser and his Generation* (London and New York 1978), especially Chapters 2 and 3.

13 See Louis Jouvelet, 'L'évolution sociale et politique des pays arabe 1930–33', *Revue des Études Islamiques*, IV (1933), pp. 429–644; and *Oriente Moderne* (1933), pp. 536–7; (1934), pp. 46–504. See also Henri Laoust, 'L'évolution politique et culturelle de l'Égypte contemporaine', in *Entretiens sur l'évolution des pays de civilisation arabe*, Centre d'Études du Politique Étrangère, no. 3 (Paris 1937), pp. 68–98.

14 See Anwar El Sadat, *Revolt on the Nile* (New York 1955), *passim*; and Gamal Abdel Nasser, *Egypt's Liberation, the Philosophy of the Revolution* (Washington, D.C. 1955), *passim*.

15 See Anouar Abdel Malek, *Égypte, société militaire* (Paris 1962), and my *The Egyptian Army in Politics* (Bloomington, Ind. 1961), esp. Chapter 3.

16 This is depicted in some of the novels by Najīb Maḥfūẓ. See his *Al-khawf* (Fear) (Cairo 1965), and *Al-liṣṣ wa'l-kilāb* (The Thief and the Dogs) (Cairo 1961).

17 On these matters generally, see Charles Issawi, *Egypt in Revolution* (London 1963) and P.K. O'Brien, *The Revolution in Egypt's Economic System* (London 1966).

18 See Umberto Rizzitano, 'Il nuovo ministero de gli Affari Sociali in Egitto', *Oriente Moderno* (1940), pp. 313–21.

19 On the Communist Party and several related groups in Egypt, see Walter Z. Laqueur, *Communism and Nationalism in the Middle East* (London 1954), pp. 36–62.

20 On the Law of Associations and its early application in this period, see Shafiq, *Hawliyyāt*, I, pp. 273–5, 857–900.

21 See his 'L'élaboration du droit social égyptien', *Égypte Contemporain* (1943), pp. 77–91, and 'Réflexions sur certains de nos problèmes économiques et sociaux', ibid., pp. 535–48.

22 On trade unionism, labour and social legislation in this period generally see M.T. Audsley, 'Labour and Social Affairs in Egypt', in *Middle Eastern Affairs* no. 1,

Notes

ed. Albert Hourani (St Antony's Papers, no. 4) (New York 1959), pp. 95–106. See also Rauf Abbas Hamid Muhammad, *al-Haraka al-ummaliyya fi Misr, 1899–1952* (Cairo 1968).

23 Particularly *Min hunā nabda'* (Cairo 1950). English translation by I.R. al-Faruqi, *From Here We Start* (Washington, D.C. 1953). The Muslim Brethren sympathizer Shaykh Muhammad al-Ghazzali countered Khaled's book with his *Min Hunā na'lam* (Cairo 1950). English translation by Ismail R. al Faruqi, *Our Beginning of Wisdom* (Washington, D.C. 1953). The Muslim Brother Sayyid Qutb also produced his famous volume, *al-'adāla al-ijtimā'yya fi'l-Islām* (Social Justice in Islam) (Cairo 1946?). English translation by John B. Hardie, *Social Justice in Islam* (Washington, D.C. 1953).

24 Although Maḥfūz's *Trilogy*, consisting of *Bayn al-qasrayn, Qaṣr al-shawq*, and *al-Sukkariyya*, was not published until 1956–7, his earlier works depicting life in the crowded native quarters of Cairo, such as *Khān al-khalili* and *Zuqāq al-mīdaq*, had appeared in 1946 and 1947 respectively. Similarly Ṭaha Husayn in three of his books all published in 1949, *Mir'āt al-ḍamīr al-ḥadīth* (The Mirror of Modern Conscience), *al-Mu'athhabūn fi'l-ard* (The Tormented on Earth), and *Jannat al-ḥayawān* (Animals' Paradise), deplored the injustices of society, depicted the misery of the mass of Egyptians, and attacked the hypocrisy of political party leaders.

25 Further on these new writers, see the discussion in Chapter 18, Education and Culture, below.

CHAPTER 16: PRELUDE TO REVOLUTION, 1939–52

1 On the political activities of Aziz Alī al-Maṣrī, see Majid Khadduri, 'Aziz Ali al-Masri and the Arab Nationalist movement', in *Middle Eastern Affairs*, no. 4, ed. Albert Hourani (St Antony's Papers, no. 17) (London 1965), pp. 140–63, and A. Sansom, *I Spied Spies* (London 1965).

2 Muhammad al-Tāb'ī suspects there was a deal between Aḥmad Ḥasanayn and Ḥasan Ṣabrī: Ḥasanayn would recommend Ṣabrī to succeed Ali Maher as Prime Minister, and Ṣabrī in return would recommend Ḥasanayn as the new Chief of the Royal Council. Tab'ī moreover argues that Ḥusayn Sirrī who succeeded the deceased Sabrī as Prime Minister in November 1940 was also an Aḥmad Ḥasanayn choice. Whatever the case was regarding these appointments, there is no doubt that the summer of 1940 marked the beginning of a political period in Egypt over which the new Royal Chamberlain, Aḥmad Ḥasanayn, had great influence and in which he played a most important role. See *Min asrār al-sāsa wa al-siyāsa al-miṣriyya (miṣr mā qabl al-thawra)* (Of the Secrets of Politics and Politicians in Egypt) (Cairo n.d.), pp. 178–200.

3 It should be noted in this connection that the *Caisse de la Dette Publique* had been abolished three years earlier on 17 July 1940. It had been founded in May 1876 to receive all revenues specified for servicing the Public Debt. These revenues comprised tax incomes from Gharbiyya, Menūfiyya, Beḥeira and Asiūṭ provinces, as well as customs and railways receipts. The *Caisse*, that is, had a claim over a sizeable portion of the State's revenues. Founded to deal with Khedive Ismail's bankruptcy, it was always administered by delegates of creditor European countries.

4 See Tāb'ī, *min asrār*, p. 301.

5 See Tāb'ī,. *min asrār*, pp. 278–80.

6 See Tāb'ī, *min asrār*, pp. 310–11 on this problem, where he also describes the constant suspicions of Nahhas regarding the King's efforts to drive a wedge between him and his colleagues in the Wafd executive. See also M.M. al-Feki, *Makram Ebeid, A Coptic leader in the Egyptian National Movement*, unpublished Ph.D. thesis, University of London, 1977.

7 See Tāb'ī, *min asrār*.

8 In describing the circumstances surrounding the dismissal of the Nahhas government, Tāb'ī,. *min asrār*, p. 324 stated: 'All these secret orders emanated directly from the Palace; for the Palace was the source of all powers.'

9 The reference here is not only to the Ikhwan organization. We shall note below the intermittent organization of student and workers' battalions for guerrilla operations against British installations in the Canal area in 1950–1; earlier volunteer formations for action in the Palestine War (1948–9). What is significant about these ephemeral attempts at popular military action is that they had been organized independently of the ruling establishment – often in clear defiance of official state disapproval. In short, the Wafd for instance, the party in power in 1950–1, did not command the loyalty or allegience of such student and worker paramilitary formations. See P. J. Vatikiotis, *Nasser and his generation*, esp. Chapter 4, and Tariq al-Bishri, *al-Haraka al-siyasiyya fi Miṣr: 1945–1952* (Cairo 1972).

10 See his public statement upon arriving in Cairo from New York on 20 September 1947, quoted in Rāfi'ī, *Fi a'qāb al-thawra al-miṣriyya* (Cairo 1951), III, p. 234.

11 Addressing a General Arab-Islamic Congress at the Azhar in December 1949, General Ṣālih Ḥarb, President of the YMMA, and ex-Minister of Defence (Ali Maher Cabinet of 1939), held a Koran in one hand and a revolver in the other and declared: 'Brothers: It is these that must speak now.'

12 These assailants, incidentally, could have been from any organization: Ikhwan, Young Egypt, or even pro-Palace elements.

13 The assassins were never caught and no new light has been thrown on the crime since. It has been popular belief ever since, however, that Special Branch security agents of the government committed the crime.

14 It is interesting to note that the Wafd, smelling an imminent return to power, publicized the party's abhorrence of violence, and its opposition to Communism, its undying loyalty to the Crown, and its firm attachment to Islam.

15 Only 2·8 million out of 4·1 million eligible voters went to the polls. The Wafd secured 288 seats out of a total of 327.

16 For further comment on this educational policy, see Chapter 18 below.

17 See references to Egyptian sources on these activities, in P.J. Vatikiotis, *op. cit.*

CHAPTER 17: REVOLUTION AND REPUBLIC, 1952–62

1 The Ottoman *bedel-i-askeri* involving the payment of a fee or levy in lieu of actual military service. The practice was introduced in the Ottoman State in 1856; the use of the term somewhat later. See H. Bowen, 'Badal', *EI²*, I, p. 855.

2 See Eliezer Be'eri, 'Social origins and family backgrounds of the Egyptian Army officer class', *Asian and African Studies*, I, no. 2 (1966), pp. 1–40. On the recruit-

ment and organization of the army after the British occupation in 1882, see Arthur Silva White, *The Expansion of Egypt* (London 1899), pp. 287–94. This chapter must be read in the light of the author's recent book, *Nasser and his Generation* (London and New York 1978).

3 Rāfi'ī, *Thawrat 23 Yulio 1952* (The Revolution of 23 July 1952) (Cairo 1959), and P.J. Vatikiotis, *op. cit.*, pp. 44–68.

4 On the Agrarian Reform Law no. 1781/1952, see al-Sayyid Mar'ī, *Agrarian Reform* (Cairo 1957), Gabriel S. Saab, *The Egyptian Agrarian Reform* (London: Chatham House Middle East Monographs 1966), and Robert Mabro, *The Egyptian Economy, 1952–1972* (London 1974).

5 For example, Abbas Ammar, a social anthropologist, who was appointed Minister of Social Affairs, and Mahmud Fawzi who was appointed Minister of Foreign Affairs.

6 For example, Fathi Radwan and Nur al-Din Tarraf.

7 For Muhammad Naguib's version of these events, see his *Kalimati Lil-tarikh* (My Record for History) (Cairo 1975). [Italian translation by Clelia Cerqua, *Memorie* (Florence 1977).]

8 For a fuller discussion of this political device, see my 'Some Political Consequences of the 1952 Revolution in Egypt', in *Political and Social Change in Modern Egypt*, ed. P.M. Holt (London 1968). See also Maxime Rodinson, 'The Political System', in *Egypt Since the Revolution*, ed. P.J. Vatikiotis (London 1968), and P.J. Vatikiotis, *Nasser and his generation*.

9 The considerations entailed in the famous arms deal with the Soviet bloc were more complicated. I have chosen, for the sake of brevity in a chapter of outline narrative, not to go into them. See, however, Keith Wheelock, *Nasser's New Egypt* (New York 1960), pp. 228–31. See also Uri Ra'anan, *The USSR Arms the Third World: Case Studies in Soviet Foreign Policy* (Cambridge, Mass. 1969).

10 On the High Dam at Aswan, see P.K. O'Brien, *The Revolution in Egypt's Economic System* (London 1966), pp. 78–9; Keith Wheelock, *op. cit.*, pp. 173–205; and Tom Little, *High Dam at Aswan* (London 1965) and Robert Mabro, *op. cit.*

11 On the foreign policy of the régime in its first eight years, see my 'Foreign Policy of Egypt', in *Foreign Policy in World Politics*, ed. Roy C. Macridis (2nd rev. ed. Englewood Cliffs, N.J. 1962), pp. 335–59; and Malcolm Kerr, 'Egypt's Foreign Policy since the Revolution', in *Egypt Since the Revolution*, ed. P.J. Vatikiotis, and *The Arab Cold War*, 3rd ed. (London 1973). See also A.I. Dawisha, *Egypt in the Arab World* (London 1976).

12 The following outline of the régime's economic policy relies heavily on two works: Charles Issawi, *Egypt in Revolution*, an Economic Analysis (London 1963), and P.K. O'Brien, *op. cit.* See also Robert Mabro, *The Egyptian Economy 1952–1972* (London 1974).

13 See O'Brien, *op. cit.*, pp. 136–47.

14 It is estimated that the Soviet Union has invested close to $400 million in the Aswan High Dam and related projects.

15 See O'Brien, *op. cit.*, pp. 302–24. In this connection, one must refer to the struggle for power in 1952–5 discussed above with its attendant purges which may have dampened the enthusiasm of private business for investment.

Notes

16 See O'Brien, *op. cit.*, pp. 200–40. See also B. Hansen and G. Marzouk, *Development and Economic Policy in the UAR* (Amsterdam 1965); B. Hansen, 'Planning and Economic Growth in the UAR (Egypt), 1960–5', in, ed. P.J. Vatikiotis. *op. cit.* See also Galal A. Amin, *The Modernization of Poverty* (The Hague 1974).

17 Law no. 104 of 1964 decreed all land expropriated under the land reforms of 1952 and 1961 state property without further payment of compensation.

18 For fuller comment on this particular point, see Galal Amin, 'Revolution and the Economic System in Egypt', in ed. P.J. Vatikiotis.

19 On the UAR and its problems, including Syria's secession from it, see Patrick Seale, *The Struggle for Syria* (London 1965), pp. 327–34; Malcolm Kerr, *The Arab Cold War* (2nd ed. London 1967), pp. 2–58; and P.J. Vatikiotis, *The Egyptian Army in Politics*, pp. 140–86.

20 For the semi-official record of the Tripartite Talks on Arab unity, see *Maḥāḍir jalsāt mubāḥathāt al-waḥda* (Cairo 1963). For an intelligent discussion of these see Malcolm Kerr, *The Arab Cold War*, pp. 58–122.

21 For the texts of the Constitution and the Charter, see Department of Information, UAR, *The Charter* (1962), and *The Constitution 1964* (1964).

22 Much of the difficulty in this relationship was inherent in the very conception and preliminary organization of the ASU. See the verbatim report of the discussions between President Nasser and the Executive Organizing Committee for the ASU in *al-Ṭali'a* (Cairo), I, 2 (Feb. 1965), pp. 9–26.

23 On Egypt and the Arab world, particularly Egypt's Arab policy under the Free Officer régime, see Malcolm Kerr, *The Arab Cold War, 1958–67*; Peter Mansfield, *Nasser's Egypt* (Penguin 1965, 1969), pp. 53–76; P.J. Vatikiotis, 'Nasser and the Arab World', *New Society* (23 December 1965), pp. 7–9; A.I. Dawīsha, *Egypt in the Arab World* (London 1976).

24 See Muhammad Jalal Kishk, *Madha yuridu al-talaba al-misriyyun* (Beirut 1968).

25 See, for example, Sadiq al-Azm, *al-Naqd al-dhati* (Beirut 1967), and Salah al-Din al-Munajjid, *A'midat al-nakba* (Beirut 1967).

26 Essentially this Resolution provided for Israel to withdraw from all occupied Arab territories in return for a recognition of its right to exist within secure boundaries.

CHAPTER 18: EDUCATION AND CULTURE

1 In 1950, the state universities were: Cairo, Alexandria and 'Ain Shams (Heliopolis). For a brief discussion of university education see below.

2 Ḥāfeẓ 'Afīfī, *op. cit.*, pp. 122–8.

3 See Amir Boktor, *The Development and Expansion of Education in the UAR* (Cairo 1963), pp. 11, 119 ff.

4 For example, 'Ibnat al-Shāṭī ('Ā'isha 'Abd al-Rahmān), *Al-rīf al-misrī* (The Egyptian Countryside) (Cairo 1936), and *Qaḍiyyat al-fallāh* (The Case of the Fellah) (Cairo n.d.). Also, 'Abd al-Ḥamīd Fahmī Maṭar, *Al-ta'līm wa'l-muta'aṭṭilīn fī miṣr* (Education and Unemployment in Egypt) (Cairo 1939). See also the bibliography to this book.

5 For instance, the activities of *Jam'iyyat al-ittiḥād al-nisā'ī almiṣrī* (Egyptian Feminist Union); the activities of the lawyer Munīra Thābit; *Dār al-ta'āwon al-*

Notes

iṣlāḥī (Centre of Co-operative Reform); and *Jam'iyyat Nahḍat al-qurā wa mukā-fahat al-ummiyya.*

6 For a brief outline discussion of these developments, see below.

7 A pattern not peculiar to Egypt, but widespread in the Arab and Middle Eastern states, as well as in certain Central and Eastern European countries. See on Egypt the interesting article by A.J.M. Craig, 'The Egyptian Students', *Middle East Journal*, VII (1953), pp. 293–9. See also Sylvia Haim, 'State and University in Egypt', in Chauncy D. Harris and Max Horkheimer, *Universität und moderne Gesellschaft* (Frankfurt 1959).

8 In 1961, Cairo University had 15 faculties, branches at Mansura, Tanta, Khar-tum and Beirut, and an enrolment of 36,000, 6,000 of whom were women. Alex-andria University had 13 faculties, 22,000 enrolment, 2,000 of whom were women. 'Ain Shams had 12 faculties with 28,000 students, 4,500 of whom were women. Asiut had 6 faculties and 4,000 students, 200 of whom were women. In addition of course were the Higher Institutes such as Modern Languages founded in 1952 (and teaching among others, Russian, Chinese, Serbo-Croat, Indonesian and other Afro-Asian languages); Physical Education; Public Ad-ministration (founded in conjunction with the UN in 1955); and several others. These enrolled in 1961–2 between 20,000 and 25,000 students. It should be noted that since July 1961 there have been two ministries of Education in Egypt, one for Public Education, and one for Higher Education.

9 Recently an average of 20,000 students have been enrolled in law faculties. There is roughly the same number of qualified lawyers in the country, not all of whom can practise. Many of them join the state bureaucracy, and the administration of state economic and industrial enterprises.

10 *Al-jāmi'a wa'l-mujtama' al-jadīd* (The University and the New Society) (Cairo n.d., 1964?). Dr Boktor has made essentially the same general criticism of edu-cational policy, especially as it relates to pre-university levels: 'While educational development is undergoing rapid quantitative expansion, there is, at the same time, a corresponding decline in quality. This is due to a lack of qualified teachers, adequate building, and budget, and to overcrowded classrooms – the usual con-sequences of mass education.' See *op. cit.*, p. 14.

11 His collected essays, *al-Naẓarāt*, were first published in Cairo in 1910–20. Another collection entitled *al-'Abarāt* first appeared in 1915 (*al-Naẓarāt*, 7th ed. Cairo 1936; *al-'Abarāt*, 10th ed. Cairo 1946). On Manfalūṭī, see H.A.R. Gibb, 'Studies in Contemporary Arabic Literature II', *BSOAS*, V:2 (1929), pp. 311–22.

12 See Maḥmūd Taymūr, ed., *Mu'allafāt Muḥammad Taymūr* (The Writings of Muhammad Taymur) (Cairo 1922).

13 See especially his collected stories: *Al-Shaykh Jum'a (Gum'a) wa qiṣas ukhrā* (Cairo 1925) (The Shaykh Jum'a and other stories); *Al-Shaykh al-Sayyid al'abīṭ* (Cairo 1926) (Shaykh Sayyid the Fool); *'Am Mitwallī* (Cairo 1927) (Uncle Mitwalli) and several other collections. For a brief discussion of the Taymurs, see Abdel-Aziz Abdel-Meguid, *The Modern Arabic Short Story* (Cairo n.d.).

14 See for example, Mazini's *Ibrāhim al-kātib* (Stories of Ibrahim, the Writer) (Cairo 1931); *Ḥaṣād al-hashīm* (The Harvesting of Stalks) (Cairo 1925); *Qabḍ al-rīḥ* (The Grabbing of the Wind) (Cairo 1928); and *Khuyūṭ al-'ankabut* (The Cobweb) (Cairo 1935), perhaps the most incisive characterization of his fellow-Egyptians.

Notes

15 Al-Hakim's *Yawmiyyāt nā'ib fi'l-aryāf* (Diaries of a Country Prosecutor) (Cairo 1937), English translation by Aubrey S. Eban, *The Maze of Justice* (London 1947); *Praska, aw mushkilat al-hukm* (Praska, or the Problem of Power) (Cairo 1939) and others. Ṭaha Ḥusayn's, *Jannat al-Shawk* (Paradise of Thorns) (Cairo 1945); *Al-Mu'adhabūn fi'l-ard* (The Tormented on Earth) (Cairo 1949), and *Jannat al-Ḥayawān* (Animal Paradise) (Cairo 1949). His autobiography *Al-Ayyām* (The Days), 2 vols (Cairo 1929–39), English translation of vol. 1 by Hilary Wayment, *The Stream of Days* (London 1948).

16 See al-Ḥakīm, *'Awdat al-rūḥ* (The Return of the Spirit, or the Resurrection), 2 vols (Cairo 1933), which depicts the life of a lower middle-class family in Cairo caught in the events of 1919 and portrays their sudden awakening to national consciousness. His play in four acts, *Ahl al-kahf* (The Cave Dwellers), published in the same year, contains a similar theme about the reawakening of Egypt.

17 See especially his famous novel *Qindīl Umm Hāshim* (Umm Hashim's Lamp) (Cairo 1944).

18 See Sibā'ī's, *Al-Saqqā māt* (The Water-Carrier is Dead) (Cairo 1952).

19 For example, his *al-Jabal* (The Mountain) (Cairo 1959), an absorbing novel about brigandage in Upper Egypt.

20 *Bayn al-Qaṣrayn* (Cairo 1956; 2nd impr. 1957; 3rd impr. 1960); *Qaṣr al-Shawq* (Cairo 2 impressions 1957; 3rd impr. 1960); *al-Sukkariyya* (Cairo 1957, 1958 & 1961). The titles represent presumably names of quarters and streets. For a discussion of this *Trilogy*, see J. Jomier, 'La vie d'une famille au Caire d'après trois romans de Naguib Maḥfūẓ', *Mélanges*, Institut Dominicain d'Études Orientales du Cairo (*MIDEO*), vol 4 (1957), pp. 27–94. See also Sasson Somekh, *The Changing Rhythm, A Study of Najib Mahfuz's Novels* (Leiden 1973).

21 Especially his *Khān al-Khalīlī*, the quarter in which is found the famous Bazaar (Cairo 1946, 1954, 1958), and *Zuqāq al-Midaqq* (Midaqq Lane or Alley) (Cairo 1947, 1955, 1957).

22 *Al-Liṣṣ wa'l-kilāb* (The Thief and the Dogs) (Cairo 1961) which has been made into a successful film; and *Al-Khawf* (Cairo 1965). For a discussion of some of Mahfūẓ's work, see J. Jomier, 'A Travers Le Monde des Romans Egyptiens: Notes et Interview', *MIDEO*, vol. 7 (1962–3), pp. 127–40. See also R.C. Ostle, ed., *Studies in Modern Arabic Literature* (London 1975), and S. Somekh, *op. cit.*

23 His first volume of collected stories, *Arkhaṣ Layālī*, was published in 1954; his other, *Ḥadithat Sharaf*, in 1958. Both his one-act plays, *Malik al-Qotn* and *Jumhūriyyat Farḥāt*, were performed by the Modern Cairo Theatre Company. His greatest success came with the performance of his controversial two-act play, *Al-Farāfir*, by the Republic Theatre in April 1964.

24 One might mention among his collections of stories *Āthār 'alā al-Shifāh* (Traces on the Lips) (Cairo 1953), *Arḍ al-Khaṭāyā* (Land of Sins) (Cairo 1958), and *Nisā' al-ākharīn* (Other Men's Wives) (Cairo 1962).

25 In 1954 appeared the major work on Egyptian folk-literature by Ahmad Rushdī Ṣāliḥ, *Al-adab al-sha'bī*. In it, Ṣāliḥ also makes a case for the vernacular in literature.

26 Such activities among the Italian and Greek communities in Egypt at least were extensive and dated back to the last century. The Greeks published at least two daily newspapers, several weeklies, and a number of periodical reviews. Gener-

ally on this, see Athanase G. Politis, *L'Hellénisme et l'Égypte Moderne*, vol. 2 (Paris 1930).

27 See Nadav Safran, 'The Abolition of the Shar'i Courts in Egypt', *The Muslim World*, vol. 48 (January and April 1958).

28 For a discussion of the reorganization of the Azhar and the work of Muslim publicists, see the author's 'Islam and the Foreign Policy of Egypt', in J. Harris Proctor, *op. cit.*

29 For a brief discussion of these, see Chapter 14 above.

30 For example, Al-'Ālem and 'Abd al-Azīm Anīs, *Fī al-thaqāfa al-miṣriyya* (Egyptian Education and Culture) (Cairo 1955), and Mu'nis, *Miṣr wa risālatuhā* (Egypt and her Message) (Cairo 1955).

31 See especially the works by Naguib Mahfuz, *Tharthara fawq al-Nil* (Cairo 1966), *al-Maraya* (Cairo 1972), *al-Hubb taht al-matar* (Cairo 1973), *Awlad Haritna* (Beirut 1967), *al-Karnak* (Beirut 1973).

32 See Louis Awad, *al-Hurriyya wa naqd al-hurriyya* (Cairo 1971), and *Aqni'at al-Nasiriyya al-sabaa* (Beirut 1975). See also, Tawfiq al-Hakim, *'Awdat al-wa'i* (Beirut 1974, 1975), and Naguib Mahfuz, *al-Karnak* (Beirut 1973).

33 The best exposition of these problems to date is John Waterbury, *Egypt* (Bloomington, Ind. 1978).

BIBLIOGRAPHY

In writing an interpretative narrative of the emergence of modern Egypt from 1800 to 1970 primarily for the general lay reader and the beginning student of Egypt, I had not intended to resort to so many explanatory and reference notes. Even though I have striven to keep them at a minimum, I now feel that the appearance of more notes than originally intended may yet serve these students of Egyptian history. In this bibliography, therefore, the intention is to provide a brief, select grouping of works mainly in English which are relevant to each part of the book, and some which provide background reading for certain parts of the book. There is such a great body of literature on Egypt that some readers will feel that I have left out too many works.

The works listed here should be considered primarily as useful for further exploration of specific historical periods and particular problems: not necessarily as highly specialized research monographs. A few of the latter are, however, mentioned in connection with certain social, economic and political problems of modern Egypt. Several of these will be found in the notes. Although this bibliography is generally one of works in English, certain books and a few articles in French are listed because of their standard importance for the study of the modern history of Egypt.

INTRODUCTION

The beginning student of Egypt will find basic information about Egypt's geography in W.B. Fisher, *The Middle East: a physical, social and regional geography* (3rd ed., London and New York 1961). In fact, for the lay reader, Hachette's *Égypte* in Les Guides Bleus series (1956) contains sound concise information about the country. General accounts of the history of Egypt before 1798–1800 are to be found in the *Précis de l'histoire d'Egypte*, vols II–III (Cairo 1932, 1933) and in Gabriel Hanotaux (ed.), *Histoire de la nation Égyptienne*, vols II–V (1926–32). S.R.K. Glanville (ed.), *The Legacy of*

Egypt (Oxford 1942–43–47–53) can serve as good background on ancient Egypt, and Sir Harold Idris Bell, *Egypt* (Oxford 1948) for Graeco-Roman and Byzantine Egypt.

While there is no single detailed study of Muslim Egypt before 1798, A.J. Butler, *The Arab Conquest of Egypt* (Oxford 1902) can be supplemented by the general work of S. Lane-Poole, *History of Egypt in the Middle Ages*, vol. V (London 1901; reprinted by Frank Cass, London 1968), which covers the period from the Arab conquest until 1517, and his *Story of Cairo* (London 1906). Entries on the Mamluks will be found in the *Encyclopedia of Islam*. References on institutions in Muslim Egypt will be found in H.A.R. Gibb and H. Bowen, *Islamic Society and the West*, vol. I, pts 1 and 2 (London 1950, 1957 and New York 1959). Further material on institutions will be found in the specialized study of Stanford Shaw, based on archival sources, *The Financial and Administrative Organization and Development of Ottoman Egypt, 1517–1798* (Princeton 1958). Relevant information can also be had from the contributions to P.M. Holt (ed.), *Political and Social Change in Modern Egypt* (London 1958), whose own book, *Egypt and the Fertile Crescent, 1516–1922* (London and Ithaca 1966), fills a great gap.

The rural population, the *fellahin*, of Egypt have been the subject of numerous sociological and anthropological studies. In fact so many, that there is at least one published bibliography in English: Lyman H. Coult, Jr, *An Annotated Research Bibliography of Studies in Arabic, English and French of the Fellah of the Egyptian Nile* (Coral Gables, Florida 1958). Only a few are listed here: W.S. Blackman, *The Fellahin of Upper Egypt* (London 1927), H.H. Ayrout, *The Fellaheen* (Cairo 1945), an English translation by H. Wayment of the French *Mœurs et coutumes des fellahs* (Paris 1938). Ayrout's book has been translated into several languages and has appeared in many editions. The classic, standard description of traditional society in Egypt before westernization had had any real impact is E.W. Lane, *The Manners and Customs of the Modern Egyptians* (London 1836, followed by many subsequent reprintings; also, Dent's Everyman's Library ed., 1954). This can be supplemented by a more modern study of folk religious practices and celebrations by J.W. McPherson, *The Moulids of Egypt* (Cairo 1941). A still more recent relevant ecological study with basic information is Gabriel Baer, *Population and Society in the Arab Eàst* (London 1964), and *Studies in the Social History of Modern Egypt* (Chicago 1969). Among studies of provincial and village life one should mention Hamed Ammar, *Growing*

Up in an Egyptian Village (London 1954), and Jacques Berque, *Histoire sociale d'une village Egyptien au XXième siècle* (Paris and The Hague 1957). Morroe Berger, *Islam in Egypt Today* (New York 1970) is a useful monograph for the study of the social and political aspects of popular religion in Egypt. Iliya Harik, *The Political Mobilization of Peasants: A Study of an Egyptian Community* (Bloomington, Ind. 1974), is an examination of the effect of the Nasser régime policies on the rural population and a discussion of the presumed changes that have taken place. Mahmud Abdel Fadil, *Development, Income Distribution and Social Change in Rural Egypt* (Cambridge 1975) is a more technical but important monograph, which again deals mainly with the post-1952 period. Janet Abu Lughod, *Cairo* (Princeton 1971) remains a standard social anthropological study of the major urban centre in Egypt. John Waterbury, *Egypt, Burdens of the Past, Options for the Future* (Bloomington, Ind. 1978) is perhaps the starkest exposition of Egypt's social and political problems as the country approaches the end of the century, based on demographic and economic considerations.

Depictions and descriptions of Egypt in the eighteenth century by travellers and others are also numerous, many of them in French. Famous among these is Savary, *Letters on Egypt*, 2 vols (London 1786). There are others such as Sonnini de Manoucourt whose *Voyages dan la haute et basse Égypte* was published in Paris in 1789. A few years ago, an English translation was published of Gustave Flaubert's travels in Egypt, *Flaubert in Egypt*, translated by Francis Steegmuller (Boston 1972). Also well known is Volney, *Voyages en Égypte et en Syrie*, 2 vols (The Hague 1959). There is a recent specialized study of guild organizations, *Egyptian Guilds in Modern Times* by Gabriel Baer (Jerusalem 1964) which is partly relevant.

Among accounts of the Napoleonic expedition and French occupation of Egypt the following based mainly on Western sources should be mentioned: F. Charles-Roux, *Bonaparte, Gouverneur d'Égypte*; English translation, *Bonaparte: Governor of Egypt* (London 1937), and *L'Angleterre et l'Expédition française en Égypte* (Cairo 1925) by the same author; P.G. Elgood, *Bonaparte's Adventure in Egypt* (London 1936); *Memoirs of Napoleon Bonaparte* by his private secretary de Bourrienne, 4 vols, especially vols 1 and 2, edited by R.W. Phipps (New York 1891); vol. V of Hanotaux's *Histoire de la Nation Égyptienne*; Gabriel Guemard's work on Napoleon's Institute of Egypt, *Histoire et bibliographie Critique de la Commission des Sciences et Arts de l'Institut d'Égypte* (Cairo 1936) and his *Les*

Reformes en Égypte (Paris 1936) covering the period 1760–1848; also the more general though readable Christopher Herold, *Bonaparte in Egypt* (New York and London 1962). Orders of the Day and other documents relating to Napoleon's sojourn in Egypt are reproduced in Alexandre Keller, *Expédition d'Égypte*, Correspondence, Bulletins et Ordres du Jour de Napoleon (Paris n.d.). Interesting is a personal memoir of the physicist Malus about the expedition, annotated and published by General Thoumas as *L'Agenda de Malus, Souvenirs de l'Expédition d'Égypte* (Paris 1892). Charles Inglis, *Operations on the Coast of Egypt 1801*, edited by J.Q. Laughton, vol. II (London 1912) describes British naval operations against the French in Egypt. There is a more general narrative, *History of the British Expedition to Egypt* by Sir Robert T. Wilson (London 1803).

There is one general study of the Beduin (a very small group in Egypt), *Sons of Ishmael* (London 1935) by G.W. Murray. There has been on the other hand a continuous stream of general portrayals of Egypt, its land and people in this century. These have been by travellers, European or British officials in the Egyptian government service, journalists and others, many of which are cited in the Notes. Here one should list Lord Edward Cecil, *The Leisure of an Egyptian Official* (London, 2nd ed. 1921); Sir Thomas Russell Pasha, *Egyptian Service 1902–46* (London 1949). Russell Pasha was Chief of Egyptian Police until 1946. Although they deal with the early 1860s, Lady Duff Gordon's *Letters from Egypt*, edited by her daughter Janet Ross (London 1902), give a vivid picture of 'land and people' in Egypt. There are also many other lesser-known published impressions of various visitors to Egypt, among them: Charles Godfrey Leland, *The Egypt Sketchbook* (New York 1874), Bayard Taylor, *A Journey to Central Africa* (New York 1854), Henry Goodman Potter, *The Gates of the East* (New York 1877), and William S. Nassau, *Conversations and journals in Egypt and Malta* (London 1882).

There are a few studies about the Copts in Egypt: William H. Worrell, *A Short Account of the Copts* (Ann Arbor, Michigan 1954); Edward Wakin, *A Lonely Minority* (New York 1963); S.H. Leeder, *Modern Sons of the Pharaohs* (London 1918). A curious work is Eliot Warburton, *The Crescent and the Cross* (New York 1845). An unpublished Ph.D. thesis on the role of the Coptic politician William Makram Obeyd in the Egyptian national movement and Egyptian inter-war politics by Mustafa el-Feki is very useful (University of London 1977).

PART ONE

For the nineteenth century up to the British occupation (1800–82), one should note especially the series of volumes and documents relating to the reigns of Muhammad Ali and Khedive Ismail, published in French under the auspices of King Fu'ad by the Royal Geographical Society of Egypt; specifically the volumes on Muhammad Ali by E. Driault and G. Douin, those by Douin on the reign of Khedive Ismail, and those by Charles-Roux on Egypt from 1801–82. Angelo Sammarco's history of this period, *Histoire de l'Égypte moderne*, 3 vols (Cairo 1933–7) is also important. Indispensable is René Maunier's *Bibliographie économique, juridique et sociale de l'Égypte moderne, 1798–1916* (Cairo 1918), and the supplement to it by G. Guémard (Cairo 1925). E. Dicey, *The Story of the Khedivate* is a useful general survey as it covers practically the whole nineteenth century. A very recent useful outline survey of modern Egypt since the French expedition is by Nada Tomiche, *L'Égypte Moderne* in the 'Que sais-je' series (Paris 1966). Other useful general introductions to the emergence of modern Egypt in the nineteenth century are G. Young, *Egypt* (London 1927) and Mohammad Rifaat, *The Awakening of Modern Egypt* (London 1947). Another by an official of the Khedivial Court is Ahmed Chafik Pacha, *L'Égypte Moderne et les Influences Étrangères* (Cairo 1931). Arthur E.P. Broome Weigall, *Egypt from 1798 to 1914* (London 1915) is a straightforward though uninteresting outline. Amusing and full of insight is Moberley Bell, *Khedives and Pashas by one who knows them well* (London 1884).

Of the more specialized studies for this period dealing with aspects of Muhammad Ali's policy, the following should be mentioned: Helen Rivlin, *The Agricultural Policy of Muhammad Ali* (Cambridge, Mass. 1961), Gabriel Baer, *A History of Landownership in Modern Egypt 1800–1950* (London and New York 1962), Moustafa Fahmy, *La Révolution de l'Industrie en Égypte et ses Conséquences sociales au 19ᵉ Siècle (1800–50)* (Leiden 1954); Shafiq Ghorbal, *The Beginnings of the Egyptian Question and the Rise of Muhammad Ali* (London 1928); M. Sabry, *L'Empire Égyptien sous Mohamed-Ali et la Question d'Orient* (Paris 1930); Richard Hill, *Egypt in the Sudan* (London and New York 1959) (this volume is also relevant to Khedive Ismail's policy in the Sudan). Finally, Henry Dodwell, *The Founder of Modern Egypt* (Cambridge 1931, reprinted 1967) is still the only single volume in English on Muhammad Ali and his policies.

A. Clot Bey, the first head of the medical school founded by Muhammad Ali in Cairo, wrote his own survey of Muhammad Ali's Egypt, *Aperçus général sur L'Égypte* (Paris 1840). Among other contemporary French writers on Egypt one may mention Felix Mengin, *Histoire sommaire de l'Égypte sous le Gouvernement de Mohammed Ali, 1823–38* (Paris 1849), and P.N. Hamont, *L'Égypte sous Méhémet Ali*, 2 vols (Paris 1843). For a description of Egypt in Muhammad Ali's time by an English traveller, there is James Augustus St John, *Egypt and Muhammad Ali, or Travels in the Valley of the Nile*, 2 vols (London 1834).

There is a plethora of works on Khedive Ismail, his financial difficulties, the Suez Canal and attendant problems. We can only list here very few. Generally, on Ismail's reign, most readable is J. McCoan, *Egypt under Ismail* (London 1889), E. de Leon, *Egypt under its Khedives* (London 1882) and P. Crabitès, *Ismail, the Maligned Khedive* (London 1933). Regarding Ismail's financial difficulties, these are illuminated by David Landes, *Bankers and Pashas* (London and Cambridge, Mass. 1958 and New York 1969). Readers might refer to the Notes for Chapter 5 where reference is made to several other works dealing with Khedive Ismail. The employment by Ismail of American army officers is dealt with by William B. Heseltine and Hazel C. Wolf, *The Blue and the Gray on the Nile* (Chicago 1961). As for the Suez Canal and its 'creator', see the readable biography by Charles Beatty, *Ferdinand de Lesseps* (London and New York 1956), Charles Hallberg, *The Suez Canal, its history and diplomatic importance* (New York 1931) and Arnold Wilson, *The Suez Canal* (2nd ed., London 1939) for a history of the Canal.

Jacob Landau, *Parliaments and Parties in Egypt* (Tel Aviv 1953) is still standard on early constitutional experiments and parties before 1882. As for the Orabi episode, in addition to the English literature on it to be found in the pages of the periodical *The Nineteenth Century*, there are several books written by supporters of Orabi: for example, W.S. Blunt, *Secret History of the English Occupation of Egypt* (London 1907), and A.M. Broadley, *How We Defended Orabi and his Friends* (London 1884). More recent sympathetic accounts of the Orabi episode and its aftermath are Mary Rowlatt, *Founders of Modern Egypt* (London and New York 1962), and Jacques Bergue, *Egypt, Imperialism and Revolution* (London 1972). See also M. Sabry, *La Genèse de l'esprit national Égyptien* (Paris 1924). Readers with a particular interest in the international administrative and judicial bodies that emerged in Egypt after 1875 will find J.Y. Brinton, *The Mixed Courts of Egypt* (New Haven, 1930) informative.

PART TWO

A general introduction to the transition from the Egypt of Muhammad Ali and Ismail to that of the British occupation is P.G. Elgood, *The Transit of Egypt* (London 1928) even though it covers the period just after independence. So are A. Colvin, *The Making of Modern Egypt* (London 1906) and S. Low, *Egypt in Transition* (London 1914). E.W.P. Newman's *Great Britain in Egypt* (London 1928) is a good general account of relations of British officials with Egyptians in the occupation period and contains an Appendix with Lord Dufferin's Scheme of Reform (1883). So is J. Alexander, *The Truth About Egypt* (London 1911). A. Milner, *England in Egypt* (11th ed. London 1904) is a detailed history of the early years of Britain's administrative record in Egypt. There is, of course, Lord Cromer's own record in his *Modern Egypt*, 2 vols (London 1908), and his *Abbas II* (London 1915). Clara Boyle, *Boyle of Cairo, a diplomatist's adventure in the Middle East* (London 1968), gives a vivid picture of British diplomatic life at the time of Cromer in Egypt. Boyle was Oriental Secretary practically throughout Cromer's office in Cairo, from 1890–1908. There is also a recent historical analysis of the British occupation, *Modernization and British Colonial Rule in Egypt 1882–1914* by Robert Tignor (Princeton 1966). An apologetic record perhaps of the events leading up to the British occupation is Sir Edward Malet, *Egypt 1879–1883*, edited by Lord Sanderson (London 1909). *Marquis of Zetland, Lord Cromer* (London 1932) is an authorized biography. There is also Afaf Lutfi al-Sayyid, *Egypt and Cromer: A Study in Anglo-Egyptian Relations* (London 1968). Interesting is Thomas S. Harrison, *The Lonely Diary of a Diplomat in the East, 1897–99* (New York n.d.). Harrison was US Diplomatic Agent and Consul-General in Egypt. Frederick C. Penfield, *Present-Day Egypt* (New York 1899), George W. Steevens, *Egypt in 1898* (New York 1898) and William B. Worsfold, *The Redemption of Egypt* (London 1899) all deal with conditions in Egypt at the height of Cromer's stewardship. Interesting too are the guides for travellers to Egypt of that period: Sir Ernest Budge, *The Nile, Notes for Travellers in Egypt* (a Thomas Cook & Son guide, London 1893), and Eustace A. Reynolds-Ball, *Cairo Today, a Practical Guide* (London 1902).

There are several studies of the religious and political ideas of the pre-1914 period. Of these one may mention, C.C. Adams, *Islam and Modernism in Egypt* (London 1933); H.A.R. Gibb, *Modern Trends in Islam* (Chicago 1947); Elie Kedourie, *Afghani and Abduh* (London and New York 1966); Malcolm H. Kerr, *Islamic Reform* (London and Berkeley 1966); J.M. Ahmed, *The Intellectual Origins of Egyptian Nationalism* (London and New York 1960); Albert Hourani, *Arabic Thought in the Liberal Age* (London and New York 1962). These in addition to the references found in the Notes.

There is one book in English on journalism and the Press in the nineteenth century: Martin Hartmann, *The Arabic Press of Egypt* (London 1899). A book, *L'Angleterre en Égypte* (Paris 1922), by Juliette Adam is interesting in connection with pre-1914 nationalism.

PART THREE

Two general surveys serve as good introduction to independent Egypt, and the period 1920 onwards: *L'Égypte Indépendante* by Le Groupe d'Études de l'Islam (Paris 1938), and Marcel Colombe, *L'Évolution de l'Égypte 1924–50* (Paris 1951).

On the struggle for independence, British policy and related matters, Lord Lloyd, *Egypt Since Cromer*, 2 vols (London 1933–4) and Viscount Wavell, *Allenby in Egypt* (London 1943) are important. There is also a recent monograph, *Egypt's Struggle for Independence* by Mahmud Zayid (Beirut 1965). John Marlowe, *Anglo-Egyptian Relations 1800–1956* (2nd ed. London 1965) is a useful survey. Basic information on these relations will be found in Royal Institute of International Affairs, *Great Britain and Egypt 1914–1951* (London 1952). The Institute's volumes, *Survey of International Affairs*, beginning with vol. I (1925) (London 1927) onwards, contain chronology of events relevant to independent Egypt and Anglo-Egyptian relations. Similarly, the recent volume edited by P.M. Holt and referred to elsewhere in this bibliography contains contributions on the Liberal Party by Professor Mahmud Zayid and on the 1923 Constitution by Professor Kedourie which are important for the understanding of constitutional developments in the inter-war period.

Some of the problems of the War and the Protectorate are outlined in P.G. Elgood, *Egypt and the Army* (London 1924) and Sir Valentine Chirol, *The Egyptian Problem* (London 1920). Another general work dealing with the Protectorate and containing interesting sketches of Egyptian nationalist leaders is Murray Harris, *Egypt under the Egyptians* (London 1925). There are also the reports of the High Commissioner on the finances, administration and conditions in Egypt and the Sudan for the period 1914–19 (London: HMSO 1920). One of the better-known accounts of independent Egypt before the Second World War is Amine Youssef, *Independent Egypt* (London 1940), and George Young, *Egypt* (London and New York 1927).

On the economic problems and development of Egypt before the Second World War, a standard work has been A.E. Crouchley, *The Economic Development of Egypt* (London 1938). A monographic study on the population problems of Egypt that is still useful is Wendell Cleland, *The Population Problem in Egypt* (Lancaster, Pa 1936). Another monograph is E.R.J. Owen, *Cotton and the Egyptian Economy* (Oxford 1969). Others find the Department of Overseas Trade publications, *Reports on Economic and Commercial Conditions in Egypt*, published by HMSO in the twenties, thirties and forties useful.

For the general phase of secular liberalism before the Second World War, in addition to the references in the notes, see Nadav Safran, *Egypt in Search of Political Community* (Cambridge, Mass. 1961); Henri Laoust, *'L'évolution politique et culturelle de l'Égypt contemporaine'*, *Entretiens sur l'évolution de pays de civilization arabe* (Paris 1937). See also Albert Hourani's work cited earlier; Pierre Cachia, *Taha Husayn* (London 1956); Walter Z. Laqueur, *Communism and Nationalism in the Middle East* (New York 1956); and Ibrahim Ibrahim, *The Egyptian Intellectuals Between Tradition and Modernity, 1922–52*, unpublished Oxford D.Phil. thesis 1967. The secular liberal movement in the inter-war period is the subject of Afaf Lutfi al-Sayyid Marsot's recent *Egypt's Liberal Experiment, 1922–1936* (Berkeley, Los Angeles and London 1977).

PARTS FOUR AND FIVE

For the period up to 1952, the book by Jacques Berque, *Egypt: Imperialism and Revolution* (London 1972) is the most comprehensive to date, though somewhat misleading. Colombe's survey volume cited earlier is more straightforward and still relevant. As for the social and political forces operating in Egypt in this period one may mention the following: J. Heyworth-Dunne, *Religious and Political Trends in Modern Egypt* (Washington, D.C. 1950); H.A.R. Gibb, 'La réaction contre la culture occidentale dans le Proche Orient',

Cahiers de L'Orient Contemporain (1951); Salama Musa, 'Intellectual Currents in Egypt', *Middle Eastern Affairs*, vol. 2 (1951); Ishak Musa al-Hussaini, *The Moslem Brethren* (Beirut 1956); C.P. Harris, *Nationalism and Revolution in Egypt* (The Hague 1964). Two more recent monographs on the radical movements of the inter-war period which came to prominence in the turbulent period before 1952 are Richard D. Mitchell, *The Society of Muslim Brothers* (London 1969) which is still the standard work in English about the Muslim Brethren, and James P. Jankowski, *Egypt's Young Rebels, 'Young Egypt': 1932–1952* (Stanford 1975). In my *Nasser and his Generation*, cited earlier, I deal extensively with Young Egypt and the Muslim Brethren, particularly their relations with the Free Officers before the latter came to power in July 1952.

On economic problems, see Charles Issawi, *Egypt in Revolution* (London 1963) cited earlier; P.K. O'Brien, *The Revolution in Egypt's Economic System* (London 1966); Gabriel S. Saab, *The Egyptian Agrarian Reform, 1952–1962* (London 1967); Robert Mabro, *The Egyptian Economy, 1952–1972* (London 1974); and Galal A. Amin, *The Modernization of Poverty, the political economy of nine Arab states 1945–1970* (Leiden 1974).

On the military *coup d'état* of July 1952 which overthrew the monarchy and the *ancien régime*, see Rashed al-Barawy, *The Military Coup in Egypt* (Cairo 1952); Anwar al-Sadat, *Revolt on the Nile* (London and New York 1957); P.J. Vatikiotis, *Nasser and his Generation* (London and New York 1978); Jean and Simone Lacouture, *Egypt in Transition* (London 1958). A most detailed account of the socio-economic aspects of the 1952 coup is the one by Anouar Abdel-Malek, *Égypte, société militaire* (Paris 1962); [English ed., *Egypt: Military Society* (New York 1968)]. See also a Marxist economic interpretation of the events after 1952 in Hasan Riad, *L'Égypte nasserienne* (Paris 1964). Also relevant is Mahmoud Hussein, *Class Conflict in Egypt, 1945–1970* (New York 1973). Eliezer Be'eri, *Army Officers in Arab Politics and Society* (New York 1970), deals with several Arab countries, including Egypt. There is also Nasser's own statement, *Egypt's Liberation: the Philosophy of the Revolution* (Washington, D.C. 1955). Miles Copeland, *The Game of Nations* (London and New York 1969) created a stir when it was first published since it argued the links between US Intelligence and the Free Officers. An attack on the post-1952 régime is Ahmad Abul Fath, *L'Affaire Nasser* (Paris 1962). A sociological analysis of the military and social change in Egypt is Morroe Berger, *The Military*

Élite and Social Change: Egypt since Napoleon (Princeton 1960). For a bibliography of English works on the post-1952 régime, see Derek Hopwood, 'Works in English on Egypt since 1952', in *Egypt since the Revolution*, ed. P.J. Vatikiotis (London and New York 1968). See also the bibliography in P.J. Vatikiotis, *The Egyptian Army in Politics* (Bloomington, Ind. 1961, Greenwich, Conn. 1975), and the notes in P.J. Vatikiotis, *Nasser and his Generation* cited earlier, where most of the books and tracts published by Egyptians after 1970 about the Free Officers and Nasser régime are cited.

There is only one modern study to date on the famous bureaucracy of Egypt, namely, Morroe Berger, *Bureaucracy and Society in Modern Egypt* (Princeton 1957).

The Arab policy of the post-1952 régime is discussed in Malcolm Kerr, *The Arab Cold War* (London 1967), and A.I. Dawisha, *Egypt in the Arab World: the elements of Arab policy* (London 1976). The Islamic dimension in the Free Officer régime's foreign policy is discussed in P.J. Vatikiotis, 'Islam and Egypt's Foreign Policy', in *Islam and International Relations*, ed. J. Harris Proctor (New York 1965), pp. 120–57. Among assessments of the régime one may mention Maxime Rodinson, 'The Political System', in P.J. Vatikiotis (ed.), cited earlier, and 'L'Égypte nasserienne au miroir Marxiste', *Temps Modernes*, vol. XVIII, no. 203 (1963), pp. 1859–87. There is also Tom Little, *Modern Egypt* (London and New York 1967), a revised, enlarged edition of his earlier book in the Benn Series (1958).

Several accounts of the Free Officer régime and Nasser's leadership of it until 1970 have appeared in the last eight to nine years. Leonard Binder, *In a Moment of Enthusiasm: Political Power and the Second Stratum in Egypt* (Chicago 1978) is an attempt to apply concepts of the ruling class and élite to the Egyptian experiment in political organization since 1952. Raymond William Baker, *Egypt's Uncertain Revolution under Nasser and Sadat* (Cambridge, Mass. 1978) is an attempt to assess the difficulties – and failure – of the Free Officer régime to transform a conspiratorial military coup into a revolution. A most ambitious essay to portray Nasser's personality and analyse his rule is Jean Lacouture, *Nasser* (1973). Anthony Nutting, *Nasser* (London 1972), and Robert Stephens, *Nasser, a political biography* (London 1971), are somewhat instant biographies with an emphasis on Nasser's foreign relations. Nissim Rejwan, *Nasserist Ideology: Its Exponents and Critics* (New York 1974) is a textual discussion of what writers and others thought Nasser and his ideology stood for. Mohamed Heikal, *The Cairo Documents: The inside story of Nasser and his relationships with World Leaders, Rebels and Statesmen* (London and New York 1973), *The Road to Ramadan* (London and New York 1975), and the *Sphinx and the Commissar* (London 1978) represent apologias for Nasser's career by the ex-Chief Editor of the *Ahram* Cairo newspaper, a close confidant of Nasser's from 1954 to 1970. Anwar al-Sadat, *In Search of Identity* (London and New York 1977, 1978), the autobiography of the Egyptian President (1970–), is interesting and revealing, especially when contrasted with his earlier writings in the 1950s and 1960s.

The most complete account in English of modern education in Egypt up to the British occupation is J. Heyworth-Dunne, *An Introduction to the History of Modern Education* (London 1939; reprinted by Frank Cass & Co., London 1968). Two Egyptian officials who dealt with education in the nineteenth century have written about it: V.E. Dor Bey, *L'Instruction publique en Égypte* (Paris 1872), and Y. Artin, *Considérations sur l'Instruction publique en Égypte* (Cairo 1894). Basic information and discussion of education in Egypt can also be found in a standard modern work, *Education in the Arab Countries of the Near East* (Washington, D.C. 1949) by Roderic D. Matthews and Matta Akrawi. A life-long student of education in Egypt, Dr Amir Boktor, has produced two major works on the subject: *School and Society in the Valley of the Nile* (Cairo 1936), and *The Development and Expansion of Education in the UAR* (Cairo 1963). The problem of centralization in education discussed by Dr Boktor in his last book is the subject of an earlier study, *The Effects of Centralization on Education in Modern Egypt* (Cairo 1936) by Russell Galt. There is also Ismail al-Kabbani, *A Hundred Years of Education in Egypt* (Cairo 1948). Statistical data on education for the first eight years of the post-1952 régime can be found in the publication of the Ministry of Education, *Education in Eight Years, 1953–60.* Information on education during the period of the British occupation can be found in several of the works mentioned earlier in this bibliography, e.g., Cromer, Lloyd, Milner and others.

For news and comment on educational and cultural activities and developments in Egypt as well as for discussions of literature, the publication of the Dominican Institute of Oriental Studies in Cairo, *Mélanges* (MIDEO) is very useful. These trends are also covered briefly in the journal *Orient* edited by Marcel Colombe in Paris, but which has unfortunately ceased publication.

Relevant to the economic aspects of education in Egypt is

Frederick Harbison and Ibrahim A. Ibrahim, *Human Resources for Egyptian Enterprise* (New York 1958) and the work of Charles Issawi. The intellectual and cultural concerns of men of letters in the pre-1952 period and immediately thereafter are well summarized in the work of Nadav Safran cited earlier. Jacques Berque, *The Arabs* (London and New York 1964), a translation of his *Les Arabes d'Hier à Demain* (Paris 1960), contains a discussion of a fair cross-section of literary and cultural matters. Two anthologies of modern Arabic prose in French translation have appeared in Paris recently: *Anthologie de la littérature arabe contemporaine: Le roman et la nouvelle* by R. and L. Makarius, and *Les Essais* by Anouar Abdel-Malek which contain selections of excerpts by several Egyptian writers. *Studies in Modern Arabic Literature*, ed. Robin Ostle (London 1976) and Mustafa Badawi, *Introduction to Modern Arabic Poetry* (London 1977) are more recent and relevant. *The Journal of Modern Arabic Literature*, edited by M. Badawi and P. Cachia, also fills an important gap in this respect.

Daniel Lerner, *The Passing of Traditional Society, Modernizing the Middle East* (New York 1958) is useful for a discussion of the distinction made today about developing states between 'cultural revolution' and a 'communications revolution'. A critical article about Egyptian intellectuals (there are several recent ones in Arabic) that may help put their predicament in perspective is 'The Egyptian Intelligentsia', by Georges Ketman in W.Z. Laqueur, *The Middle East in Transition* (New York 1958), pp. 478–86. A balanced discussion of the relationship of education to political development in contemporary Egypt is that by Malcolm Kerr in *Education and Political Development*, ed. James S. Coleman (Princeton 1965), pp. 169–94. Equally interesting and relevant to such new notions as socialism and Arab revolution is Kerr's 'Arab Radical Notions of Democracy', St Antony's Papers, no. 16: *Middle Eastern Affairs*, no. 3 (London 1963). A recent critical survey of cultural and intellectual developments in Egypt, 'Cultural and Intellectual Developments in Egypt since 1952', by Dr Louis Awad in *Egypt since the Revolution*, ed. P.J. Vatikiotis (London and New York 1968) discusses these matters in relation to developments before 1952.

The following periodicals are relevant for the study of modern Egypt:
Revue des Études Islamiques
Revue du Monde Musulman

513

Cahiers de l'Orient Contemporain
Orient (has ceased publication)
The Middle East Journal
Middle Eastern Affairs (has ceased publication)
Middle Eastern Studies
International Journal for Middle Eastern Studies
Égypte Contemporain
Oriente Moderno (for those who read Italian; important for the
    1920s and 30s)
The Information Department, Egypt, publishes various year books.
So do several of the Egyptian Ministries.

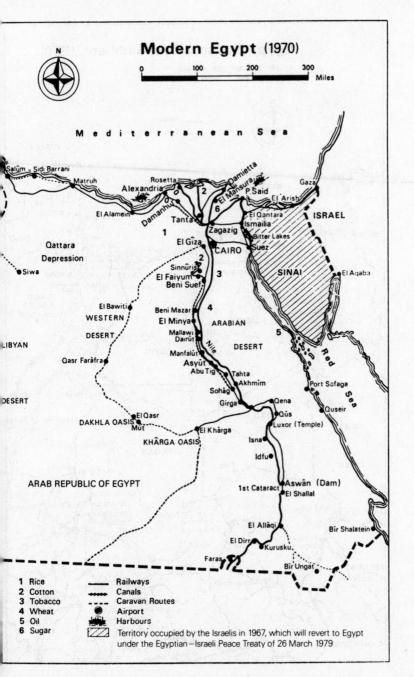

Modern Egypt (1970)

```
0        100        200        300
                                    Miles
```

N

Mediterranean Sea

Salûm · Sidi Barrani
Matruh
Rosetta
Alexandria
Gaza
El Alamein
Damanhûr
Tanta
El Arish
P Said
Damietta
El Mansura
El Qantara
Ismailia
Bitter Lakes
Suez
ISRAEL
Qattara Depression
1
Zagazig
El Gîza
CAIRO
Siwa
Sinnûris
El Faiyum
Beni Suef
2
3
SINAI
El Aqaba
El Bawiti
Beni Mazar
El Minya
Mallawi
Dairût
Manfalût
4
ARABIAN
WESTERN DESERT
Qasr Farâfra
DESERT
5
LIBYAN
Asyût
Abu Tîg
Tahta
Akhmim
Sohâg
Girga
Qena
Qûs
Luxor (Temple)
Port Safaga
Quseir
DESERT
El Qasr
DAKHLA OASIS
Mut
El Khârga
KHÂRGA OASIS
Isna
Idfu
Red Sea
ARAB REPUBLIC OF EGYPT
1st Cataract
Aswân (Dam)
El Shallal
El Allâqi
Bir Shalatein
El Dirr
Kurusku
Faras
Bir Ungat
Nile

1 Rice
2 Cotton
3 Tobacco
4 Wheat
5 Oil
6 Sugar

——— Railways
┅┅┅ Canals
- - - Caravan Routes
● Airport
⚓ Harbours
▨ Territory occupied by the Israelis in 1967, which will revert to Egypt under the Egyptian–Israeli Peace Treaty of 26 March 1979

515

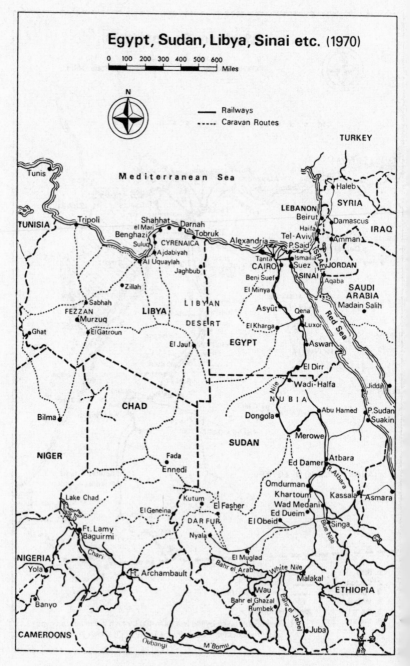

Egypt, Sudan, Libya, Sinai etc. (1970)

0   100 200 300 400 500 600
Miles

N

——— Railways
- - - - Caravan Routes

TURKEY

Mediterranean Sea

Tunis

Haleb

LEBANON
Beirut
SYRIA
Damascus

TUNISIA
Tripoli
Shahhat
el Mari   Darnah
Benghazi   Tobruk
Suluq   CYRENAICA
Ajdabiyah
Al Uquaylah
Jaghbub

Haifa
Tel-Aviv
Alexandria   P.Said
Tanta   Ismailia
CAIRO   Suez
Beni Suef
El Minya

IRAQ
Amman
JORDAN
SINAI
Aqaba
SAUDI
ARABIA

Sabhah
FEZZAN
Murzuq
Ghat   El Gatroun
Zillah

LIBYAN
DESERT

Asyût
El Kharga
El Jauf

LIBYA
EGYPT

Qena
Luxor
Aswan

Madain Salih

Red Sea

El Dirr
Wadi-Halfa

Bilma

CHAD

NUBIA
Dongola   Abu Hamed
Merowe

Jidda
P.Sudan
Suakin

NIGER

Fada
Ennedi

SUDAN

Ed Damer
Atbara

R Atbara

Lake Chad

Kutum
El Geneina   El Fasher
DARFUR
Nyala

Omdurman
Khartoum
Wad Medani
Ed Dueim
El Obeid

Kassala   Asmara

Blue Nile

Singa

NIGERIA
Yola
Ft. Lamy
Baguirmi
Chari

Banyo

Ft. Archambault

El Muglad
Bahr el Arab   White Nile
Wau
Bahr el Ghazal
Rumbek

Malakal

ETHIOPIA

CAMEROONS

Oubangi   M'Bomu

Bahr el Jebel

Juba

516

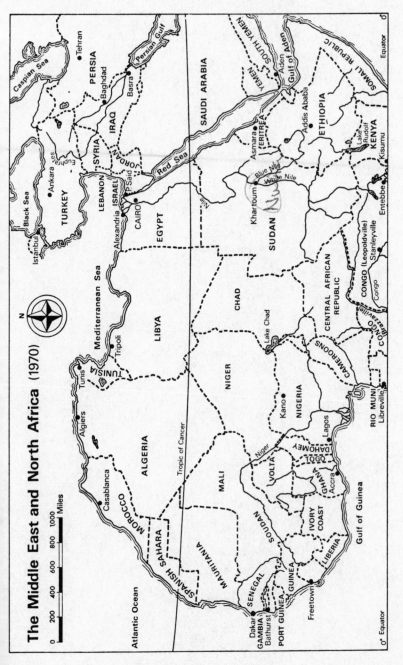

The Middle East and North Africa (1970)

517

INDEX

Abbas Pasha (Abbas I), Viceroy of Egypt, 71–2, 73, 101, 102, 181, 434

Abbas Hilmi Pasha (Abbas II), Khedive of Egypt, 174–5, 187, 200–2, 204, 217, 220, 221, 251, 253, 272, 273, 372, 447; and the National Party of Mustafa Kamil, 228; conflict with British, 202, 253; relations with Egyptian nationalists, 201–2, 222, 224, 256, 257

Abd al-Hadi, Ibrahim (Prime Minster of Egypt), 365–6

Abd al-Majid (Ottoman Sultan), 72

Abd al-Monem, Prince Muhammad, 378

Abd al-Nasir, Jamal, see Nasser

Abd al-Quddus, Ihsan, 454

Abd al-Ra'uf, Abdel Mon'em, 383

Abd al-Raziq, Shaykh Ali, 282, 304–5

Abd al-Sabur, Salah, 450, 462

Abdel Aziz (Ottoman Sultan), 74, 75

Abduh, Shaykh Mohammad, 107, 183, 186, 187, 190, 202, 215, 225, 230, 240, 244, 256, 306, 307; reformist thought and work, 193–7, 199, 220, 299, 326, 435

Abdul Hamid (Ottoman Sultan), 142, 152, 189, 202, 231, 236

Aboukir, 43

Abu Dhahab, Muhammad of Acre (Mamluk of Ali Bey the Great), 32, 33

Abul Fath Brothers, 359, 451

Abu Shadi, Ahmad Zaki, 448, 449

Aden, 66

Adham, Ibrahim Bey, 101, 103

Afghani, Jamal al-Din, 107, 134–5, 136, 183, 189–90, 198, 220, 307

Afifi, Hafiz, 262, 312–14

Agrarian Reform, 8–9, 377, 392–3, 396–7

Agricultural Credit Bank, 288, 324, 335, 397

Ahmad Fuad, Crown Prince of Egypt, 376

Ain Shams University, 443, 444

al-Ahram, 180, 183, 186, 203, 275

Alexandria University, 294, 443, 444

Ali Bey the Great, 28, 32–3, 67; and Anglo-French rivalry, 33

Allenby, General, 282; policy in Egypt of, 265–70, 271

Amer, Abd al-Hakim, 374, 383, 407

Amin, Ahmad, 312, 451

Amin, Qassim, 234–5, 240, 241, 256, 260, 309

Amr ibn al-As, 10, 12, 13

Anglo-Egyptian Treaty (1936), 291, 292, 320, 321, 322, 343; abrogation by Wafd of, 368, 372

Antoun, Farah, 186, 195, 236, 237–8, 306; his magazine al-Jamia, 186, 235, 236

Appollo Group of Poets, 449

Aqaba (Taba) Incident, 174, 205, 206, 221–2, 248

al-Aqqad, Abbas Mahmud, 324–5, 448, 454, 457, 461

Arabia (also Arabian Peninsula), 12, 20, 26, 33, 64, 253, 301; Wahhabis in, 27, 196, 198, 326

Arab-Israel War (June 1967), 402, 406, 409, 464, 465

Arab League, 357, 363, 428, 461

Arab Nationalism, 11, 406

Arab Socialism, 11, 406, 459

Arab Socialist Union, 400, 401–2, 407, 408

Arab Unity Talks, 400, 403

Ashur, Nu'man, 455–6, 462

Assembly of Delegates (also Chamber or Assembly of Deputies), 103–4, 126, 127, 131, 132, 133, 134, 140, 141, 180; and the Orabi Revolt, 142–52, 162, 273

Assiut University, 443

Aswan, 20, 57, 367; dam at, 210; High Dam, 4, 388–9, 393, 394

Atatürk, *see* Mustafa Kemal

al-Attar, Shaykh Hasan, 27, 92, 114, 181

Awad, Louis, 341; on higher education, 444–5

Ayrout, Father H. H., 9

al-Azhar, 54, 105–6, 153, 197, 234; founding of the mosque by Fatimids, 16; centre of Egyptian opposition to French occupation, 43–4; centre of intellectual activity under Mamluks, 37; role in education, 58, 91–3, 102, 434–5; Reorganization Law (1961), 106, 459; reform of, 92, 105, 194, 256, 299–302, 326, 438; in politics, 276, 292–3, 294, 304

al-Aziz, Fatimid Caliph of Egypt, 16, 17

Azmi, Mahmud, 296, 451

Azzam, Abd al-Rahman, 344, 351, 461

Badawi, Abd al-Rahman, 341

Badr, Imam of Yemen, 403

Badran, Shams, 407

Baghdad Pact, 387

Baker, Samuel Pasha, 81

al-Bakri, al-Sayyid Ali, 27, 37, 136

Bandung Conference, 387–8

Bank Misr, 283, 285, 322–3, 324, 332, 394

al-Banna, Shaykh Hasan, 317, 327

Barakat, Bahy al-Din, 378

Baring, Sir Evelyn, *see* Lord Cromer

al-Barawi, Rashed, 341

Bardisi (Mamluk Bey), 50–1

al-Barudi, Muhammad Sami Pasha, 136, 144, 146, 154, 160; Prime Minister, 149–50; poet, 446, 447

Basil, Hamad, 263, 264

Baybars, Mamluk Sultan of Egypt, 11, 26

Ben Bella, President of Algeria, 404

Bludan Conference, 460

Blunt, Wilfrid S., 156, 160, 163

al-Boghdadi, Abd al-Latif, 374, 380, 385

Boghos Bey, 62, 96

Bonaparte, *see* Napoleon

Le Bosphore Egyptien case, 192–3

Boumedienne, Colonel Houari, coup against Ben Bella regime of, 404

Brioni Conference, 388

Britain: occupation of Egypt, 106, 153–8, 333; purchase of Suez Canal shares, 129; reforms in Egypt, 171–5; protectorate over Egypt, 175, 251, 254, 258, 262, 264, 266–8, 271, 272, 273; Unilateral Declaration, 175, 187, 269–70, 271, 272, 274, 279, 291, 372; intervention in Egyptian domestic politics during Second World War, 348–9; relations with Nasser regime, 385–90; and South Arabia, 405

Brunyate, Sir William, 255, 258

Bulaq State Printing Press, 95, 99, 178

Byzantines, 12, 23, 24

Cairo, 5, 28, 32, 38, 59, 219, 253; its founding by the Fatimids, 16; Saladin's Citadel, 17; Council, *see* *Diwan*

Cairo University (*also* State University in Cairo), 222, 284, 436, 443, 444, 461

Caliphate, question in Egypt, 303–4, 326

Camp David, 412, 427

Capitulations, 86, 180, 188, 190, 223, 254–5, 312, 321, 322

Cave Mission, 78, 86, 129

Cave, Steven, *see* Cave Mission

Champollion, 83, 97

Chief Qadi, 31, 37, 251

Clot Bey, 56, 96

Colvin, Sir Aukland, 84, 155, 160

Commission for the Constitution, *1923*: 273–4; *1953*: 379

Committee of Commerce and Industry, 211, 259, 322, 378

Communist Party (*also* Communists), 336–8, 358, 366, 385, 440

Constitution: 293, 298; *1923*: Commission for, 273–4, 276, 289–90, 436; abrogation by Sidqi of, 286, 318; *1956*: 384–5, 399; provisional Constitution of 1964, 401–2

Constitutional Reform Party, 216, 228–9

Cooperative Movement, 334–5, 397

Copts (*also* Coptic Community), 10, 20, 32, 36, 37, 63, 184, 259, 262, 265, 394, 458; language and creed, 10, 12; schools, 102, 433; relations with Muslims, 204, 206–8

Corruption Tribunal, 379

corvée, 84, 87, 142, 191

Credit Lyonnais, 80

Crimean War, 72, 112, 182

Cromer, Earl of (Sir Evelyn Baring), 84, 87, 129, 130, 155, 172–5, 211, 216, 218, 219, 226, 230, 249, 256; and the Egyptians, 176, 222; and the Sudan, 192; and Khedive Abbas Hilmi, 201–2

Crusades, 17, 18, 23

Cyrus, Byzantine Prefect of Egypt, 12

Dar al-Hilal, 238–9, 450, 451, 453

Dar al-Kutub, 106, 111, 240, 458

Dar al-Ulum, 102, 106, 111, 121, 193, 194, 301–2

Delta, 3, 5, 6, 8, 14, 210, 350, 368, 395; Barrage at, 111, 191

Democratic Movement for National Liberation (MDLN/HADETU), 377

derebeys, 51, 53

Dinshawai Incident, 205, 256

Disraeli, 78, 129

Diwan (Cairo Council), 30, 32, 39–40, 41, 63, 91, 93, 126

Dual Control (Anglo-French financial control in Egypt), 88, 129, 137–8, 140, 146, 153, 156, 163, 169, 173, 180

Dufferin, The Marquis of: reforms, 170, 171, 172, 191, 200, 201–2, 297, 435

Duri, Muhammad Pasha, 119

Economic development, *1919–39*: 320–4; post *1939*: 333–4

Economic Organization, 393

Egypt–Israel Peace Treaty (1979), 412

Egyptian Army, 142, 201–2, 283, 372–4, 418

Egyptian Federation of Industries, 286, 322–3

Egyptian Federation of Labour, 358, 398

Egyptian National University, *see* Cairo University

Egyptian Trade Unions Congress, 398

Eisenhower Doctrine, 390

Elfi Bey, 50–1

England, *see* Britain

Entente Cordiale, 202, 204, 220, 248

Fahmi, Abd al-Aziz, 260, 305; and 1923 Constitution, 274, 276

Falaki, Mahmud Pasha, 119

Falaki, Ismail Pasha, 119

Farid, Muhammad Bey, 228, 258

Faruq, King of Egypt, 70, 104, 290, 292, 330, 343, 380; Crown Prince, 272; and the Wafd, 292, 293–4, 325–6, 353–4; February 1942 Incident, 348–9, 373; and officer corps, 374–6

Faruq University, *see* Alexandria University

Fatimids (*also* Fatimid Caliphate), 16, 49; conquest of Egypt, 15–17; caliphs, 28

Fawzi, Husayn, 306, 457, 461

Faysal, King of Saudi Arabia, 404, 405

fellah (fellahin), 4, 7, 25, 37, 247, 249, 252, 397, 420, 439

Feminism, 260, 309–10; feminist publications, 450–1

Fertile Crescent, 67

First World War, *see* The Great War

Foreign communities in Egypt, 102–3; schools of, 433–4, 438, 441

Free Officers, 9, 11, 396, 402, 417;
Committee of, 374, 408; July 1952
coup, 371, 373–6; and workers, 377;
and Muslim Brethren, 373, 378–9,
383; struggle for power, 377–81;
regime's relations with Britain, 385–
7; foreign policy, 387–90; Arab
policy, 402–6; educational policy,
440–5; and Islam, 459–60; and
Arabism, 461–2
Fuad al-Awwal (Fuad I) University,
see Cairo University
Fuad, King of Egypt (*also* Ahmad
Fuad), 70, 104, 272, 290, 293, 318,
338, 458; Sultan of Egypt, 254, 271;
and 1923 Constitution, 274, 282;
and Parliament and the Wafd, 281,
321–2, 327; and the University, 301;
and the Caliphate question, 303–4
Fustat, 13, 16

Galal, Muhammad Bey Othman, 106,
120, 121, 182
Geographical Society, 83, 104, 458
al-Geylani, Rashid Ali, 346
Ghali, Butrus Pasha, 204, 207, 208
Ghali, Mirit Butrus, 312–24
Ghanem, Fathi, 454
Gordon Pasha, 172
Gorst, Sir Eldon, 175, 209–12, 219,
220
Great War, The, 7, 164, 176, 210, 213,
244, 247, 250–5, 272, 277, 309, 355
Goschen–Joubert Mission in Egypt,
129
Guilds, 28, 31, 60

Hafiz Ibrahim, 189, 234, 446, 447, 452
al-Hākim bi Amrillah (Fatimid
Caliph), 16
al-Hakim, Tawfiq, 311, 454, 457, 460,
461, 465
Halim, Prince Abbas, 336, 351
Haqqi, Yahia, 454, 457
Harb, General Muhammad Salih, 345,
350
Harb, Talaat Pasha, 259
Hasan, Mamluk Sultan of Egypt,
Mosque of, 18

Hasanayn, Ahmad Muhammad, 293,
346, 348, 351, 354
Hassuna, Abdel Khaliq, 351
Haykal, Muhammad Husayn, 296,
306, 324–5, 435, 452, 459, 461
Heikal, Muhammad Hasanein, 419
Helwan Society, *see* National Society
Hicks Pasha, General, 172, 372
Higher Council for the Arts, Letters
and Sciences, 456, 458
Hijaz, 12, 62, 253, 301, 303
Hijazi, Ahmad, 450
al-Hilal, 186, 235, 238, 450
al-Hilali, Abu Zeid, 20, 26
Hilali, Nagib, 370; and the Free
Officers, 375–6
Hizb al-islah al-dusturi, *see*
Constitutional Reform Party
Hizb al-shaab, *see* Shaab Party; *see
also* Sidqi
al-Hizb al-watani, *see* National Party
Humam, Shaykh, 31
Husayn, Ahmad, 328, 461
Husayn, Kamal al-Din, 378, 380
Husayn, Kamil, Sultan of Egypt, 251,
254
Husayn, King of Hijaz (also Sharif
Husayn of Mecca), 255, 258, 303
Husayn, King of Jordan, 404, 405, 411
Husayn, Taha, 10, 305, 306, 311, 324–
5, 367, 435, 437, 459, 461

Ibn Iyas, 26
Ibn Khaldun, 26, 458
Ibn Saud, King of Arabia, 303
Ibn Tulun, 15, 17, 49
Ibrahim Bey, Mamluk ruler of Egypt,
32, 33–6, 38
Ibrahim, Hasan, 374, 380, 383, 385
Ibrahim Pasha, 62, 64, 68, 70, 96
Ibrahim, Yahya Pasha, 276, 280, 281
Idris, Yusuf, 454, 456
al-Ikhshid, Muhammad b. Tughj, 15,
17
Ikhwan, *see* Muslim Brethren
iltizam, 53–4, 55
Industrial Bank, 367
Institute of Egypt, 41–2, 83
Iraq, 346, 387, 400, 402

Ishaq, Adib, 136, 143, 182, 183, 184–5
Islamic Congress (1954), 460
Ismail, Khedive of Egypt, 56, 70, 79, 94, 105, 107, 113, 117, 121, 124, 125, 126, 136, 137, 156, 161, 164, 308, 372, 413, 425, 458; reign of, 73–84, 90, 154, 188; and the Press, 99, 128, 139, 156, 180, 181–4; educational and cultural policy, 81–3, 101–5, 107–8, 120, 299, 433, 434–5; legal codes, 119–21, 297; Assembly of Delegates, 76, 86, 136, 140, 156; financial problems, 76, 84–7, 127, 129–31, 190; deposition and exile, 141, 142; Western views of, 84–9
Ismail, Mahmud Hasan, 461
Ismail Sabri, 446
Israel, 356, 365, 384, 388, 405, 465
Italy: invasion of Ethiopia by, 289; in the Second World War, 344–5
al-Ittihad party, 281, 282, 286, 304

al-Jabarti, Abdel Rahman, 26, 27, 30, 37, 38, 40, 41, 44, 45, 91–2, 93
Jaghbub, 282
al-Jarida, 225–7, 230, 240, 243, 253, 255, 309
Jawhar, Fatimid conqueror of Egypt, 15, 16, 17
al-Jawish, Shaykh Abdul Aziz, 204, 207, 208, 215, 228
al-Jazzar, Ahmad Pasha, 42
Jomard, 42, 96
Jordan, 402, 411

Kafur, 15, 17
Kait Bey, al-Ashraf, Mamluk Sultan of Egypt, 21
Kansuh al-Ghuri, Mamluk Sultan of Egypt, 22
al-Kassar, Ali, 455
Khaled, Shaykh Khaled Muhammad, 341
Khartoum, 64; Arab Summit Conference 1967, 404, 408
Khedive Ismail, *see* Ismail, Khedive of Egypt
Kitchener, Lord: Sirdar of the Egyptian Army, 201, 202, 209, 251, 308; British Consul-General in Egypt, 175; policy, 176, 210–12, 219; and Zaghlul, 257
Kleber, General, 44
Korean War, 391
Kurayyim, Muhammad, 43
kurbaj, 84, 87, 142, 191
al-Kutla al-wafdiyya, *see* Kutla Party
Kutla Party, 320, 321, 340, 352, 354
kuttab, 91, 111, 433, 434, 436

Labour Corps, 254
Labour movement and labour unions, *see* Social reform and legislation
Land reform, *see* Agrarian reform
Lane, E. W., 52
al-Laqqani, Ibrahim, 136, 184
Law of Associations (1923), 280, 282, 284, 301, 337
League of Arab States, *see* Arab League
League of Nations, 291
Legislative Assembly (also Legislative Council), 175, 212, 216, 242, 247, 250, 257, 259, 273, 297, 308, 334
de Lesseps, Ferdinand, 72, 77
Levant, 95
Liberal Constitutionalist Party, 274, 277, 282, 283, 286, 296, 309, 320, 332, 349, 354, 355–6, 365, 382; newspaper of *al-Siyasa*, 279, 280, 296, 304, 325, 451
Liberation Rally, 379–80, 381, 382, 462
Liquidation Law (1880), 142, 191
Literature and the arts, 310–11, 446–58; poetry, 446–50; prose (short story, novel, drama), 450–6; cinema and television, 456; music, folklore and painting, 457; Egyptianism and Pharaonism, 311, 460
al-Liwa (newspaper), 175, 187, 203, 206, 207, 208, 215, 222, 226, 228, 253

MacMahon, Sir Henry, 251–2, 254
Magdi, Saleh Bey, 121
al-Mahdi, Shaykh Muhammad al-Abbasi, 105, 256, 299

Maher, Ahmad, 292, 293, 294, 321, 352, 364; his government, 354
Maher, Ali, 289, 290, 292, 294, 305, 339, 354, 370, 376, 377, 379; wartime government, 343–5, 350
Mahfuz, Najib (Naguib), 341, 342, 453, 454, 461
Mahmud, Muhammad Pasha, 284–5, 294, 337, 338
Mahruqi, Shaykh Muhammad, 37, 57
Mahmud II, Ottoman Sultan, 51, 56, 66, 298
Malet, Sir Edward, 160, 162, 170
Mamluks (also Mamluk Beys), 3, 16, 17, 18, 19–23, 25, 26, 28, 30, 31, 39, 44, 46, 50, 62, 85, 90
al-Manar, 192, 303, 305, 326
Mandur, Muhammad, 341, 342, 362
al-Manfaluti, Mustafa, 452
al-Maqrizi, 17, 26, 109
al-Maraghi, Shaykh Mustafa, 292, 362, 353
Mariette Pasha, 83, 97, 120
Mar‘i (Marei), Sayyid, 385, 421
al-Marsafi, Shaykh Hasan, 103, 121
al-Masri, General Aziz Ali, 343, 345, 346, 373, 460
Mazhar, Ismail, 306, 461
al-Mazini, Ibrahim, 448, 453, 454
Mehanna, Colonel Rashad, 378
Menou, General, 42, 45
Middle East Supply Centre, 352
Military Academy, 330, 373
Milner, Lord, 84, 87; (Commission of Inquiry), Mission to Egypt, 267–9, 435
Ministry of Industry, 393
Misr al-fatat, see Young Egypt
al-Misri (newspaper), 359, 451
Mixed Tribunals, 80, 85, 119, 120, 121, 129, 139, 180, 188, 291, 297
Mongols, 11, 14, 19; at Ain Jalut, 20; sacking of Baghdad, 20
Montreux Convention, 255, 291, 312, 321
Morea, 64
al-Mu‘yyad (newspaper), 175, 187, 198, 202, 203, 206, 222, 228, 450

Mubarak, Ali Pasha, 26, 37, 101, 109–12, 116, 118, 119, 120, 121, 182, 434–5
al-Mufattish, *see* Saddiq, Ismail Pasha
Mufti, 194, 196, 197, 302
Muhammad Ali the Great, Viceroy of Egypt, 8, 11, 26, 45, 49–69, 70, 71, 73, 77, 81, 85, 86, 89, 105, 117, 121, 124, 125, 127, 163, 263, 298, 328, 333, 372, 413; control over *waqfs*, 307–8; expedition against Wahhabis in Arabia, 51, 64; educational policy, 58, 91, 92, 93–101, 119, 433, 434, 438; printing and the Press, 95, 96, 98–100, 178, 181
Muhieddin, Khalid, 374, 381–2, 415; his National Unionist Progressive Party (NUPP), 415; his newspaper *al-Ahali*, 415
Muhieddin, Zakariyya, 374, 380
al-Mu‘izz, Fatimid Caliph of Egypt, 16
multezims, 25, 31
Mu’nis, Husayn, 457, 462
Muqabala Law, 128, 132, 133–4, 137, 142
al-Muqattam (newspaper), 186, 203, 226, 235
al-Muqtataf (periodical), 186, 232, 235, 236–7, 450
Murad Bey, Mamluk ruler of Egypt, 32, 33–6, 38
Musa, Salama, 235–6, 238, 296, 306, 461
Muslim Brethren, 286, 317, 320, 325, 327–8, 330–1, 334, 340, 343, 349, 356, 357, 359–60, 362, 363–4, 365, 366, 369, 371, 378, 380–1, 382, 383–4, 385, 387, 402, 408, 428, 440
Mustafa Fazil Pasha, 75–6
Mustafa Kamil, 137, 174, 175, 183, 190, 199, 201, 202, 203–4, 206, 207, 208, 213, 215, 217, 220, 223, 224, 227–8, 234, 240, 247, 255, 258, 355, 450; and Islamic agitation, 205; and the Aqaba Incident, 222
Mustafa Kemal, 303, 304
al-Mustansir, Fatimid Caliph, 16, 17, 20

Mutran, Khalil, 448
al-Muwailihi, Abd al-Salam, 133, 136
al-Muwailihi, Ibrahim, 103, 120, 182, 233
al-Muwailihi, Muhammad, 233; his *Hadith Isa Ibn Hisham*, 232–4, 452

al-Nadim, Abdullah, 104, 230; and the Orabi Revolt, 184, 185; his paper *al-Ustadh*, 187, 202
Naguib, Muhammad, 375, 376, 382, 384, 385; his government, 377–81
Nahhas, Mustafa, 262, 283, 284, 285–6, 290–4, 319, 337, 345, 348, 358, 364, 367, 376; his 1942–1944 government, 349–54; and the Azhar, 292–3
Naji, Ibrahim, 448, 449
Napoleon, 10, 34, 49, 93, 96, 178; expedition to Egypt, 36; invasion of Egypt, 33, 38–45, 164; impact on social life in Egypt, 45–6; policy in Egypt, 39–42, 91; Egyptian rebellion against, 43–4; Syrian campaign, 44; Institute founded by, 41, 42, 46, 83, 103
Napoleon III, Emperor of France, 75, 76
Napoleonic Code, 119, 120, 121
al-Naqqash, Salim, 106, 136, 182, 183, 184–5
Nash'at, Hasan Pasha, 282, 303
Nasif, Malak Hifni, 309
Nasim, Muhammad Tawfiq Pasha, 275, 276, 282, 289–90, 336
Nasir, Mamluk Sultan, 21
Nasser, 155, 158, 373, 374, 377, 412, 417, 419, 424, 465; and the Muslim Brethren, 373, 380–1, 383–4, 387, 402; and Naguib, 381–5; Prime Minister of Egypt, 383; President of the Republic, 384–5; foreign policy, 385–90; economic policy, 390–6; social policy, 396–9; Arab policy, 402–6; relations with Algeria, 404; and Islam, 459–60; and Israel, 387–8, 409–10; after the Six Day War, 406–11; Soviet Arms Purchase Agreement (1955), 388; and Soviet

aid, 394, 406, 409–11; and the United States, 409–10; and the Rogers Plan, 410–11
National Assembly, 384–5, 399, 400, 401
National Bank, 324, 394
National Charter, 400, 401
National Congress of Popular Forces, 399–400
National (*Ahli*) Courts, 119, 142, 191, 194, 200, 297, 302
National Party, 137, 174, 199, 201, 203, 207, 216, 223, 227–8, 230, 258, 262, 294, 340, 355, 365, 378; and independence, 252; and the 1923 Constitution, 272–5, 277; newspaper *al-Akhbar*, 304
Native Courts, *see* National Courts
National Society, 107, 134, 136–7, 140, 143, 144
National Union, 384, 399
National University, 301
Nile (also Nile Valley), 3–5, 9, 17, 24, 79, 110, 227, 248, 253, 361, 414; Nile Waters Agreement (1929), 284
Nimr, Faris, 183, 200, 203, 236
Nubar Pasha, 77, 80, 87, 119, 138, 139, 180, 297; his ministry, 130–1, 132–3, 135–6, 156, 192
Nuqrashi, Mahmud Fahmi, 292, 321, 352, 355; his first government, 340–1, 357–60; his second government, 362–5; legislation, 367

Obayd, Makram, 260, 321, 340, 351–2, 354; his *Black Book*, 352, 353
October War 1973 (*also* Ramadan *or* Yom Kippur War), 412, 418, 465
Omar Makram, *Naqib al-Ashraf*, 37, 51
Orabi, Ahmad Pasha, 107, 170, 413; Revolt, 88, 112, 141–65, 169, 372; leader of army movement, 134, 137; and the Press, 184–5
Othman, Amin, 364
Ottoman Bank, 80
Ottomans, 22, 40; in Egypt, 10, 19, 24, 25, 26; and Orabi Revolt, 147, 152

Palestine, *see* Palestine Question
Palestine Question (also Palestinians),
330, 364, 387, 404, 411, 428, 449,
460; Palestine Liberation
Organization (PLO), 404–5, 410;
Palestine Liberation Army, 405; *al-
Fatah (al-Fateh)*, 406
Palestine War (1948), 331, 364–6, 371,
373, 461
Palmerston, 66, 68
Pan-Islam (also Panislamism), 178,
201, 203–6, 207, 215, 220–2, 224–5
People's Court, 383–4
People's Party, *see* Umma Party
Permanent Council of National
Production, 378, 392, 393
Permanent Council of Public Services,
399
Pharaonism, *see* Literature and the
arts
Press Law, 193, 207, 275, 279, 284

Qadri, Muhammad Pasha, 119
Qalaun, Mamluk Sultan, 21
Qutb, Sayyid, 402

Radwan, Fathi, 379, 383
Ragheb, Ismail Pasha, 136, 152
Regency Council (1952), 376, 378
Religious Courts, *see* Sharia
Relgious orders, *see tariqas*
Revolution Command Council (RCC),
377, 379, 381, 382–3
Revolution Tribunal, 380, 381, 383
Riad Pasha, 130, 133, 138, 139, 147;
Prime Minister, 137, 142–5, 191
Rida, Shaykh Muhammad Rashid,
196, 197, 198, 216, 303, 305, 326
Rifqi, Osman Pasha, 143, 144, 149
al-Rihani, Najib, 455
Rose al-Yusuf (periodical), 310, 451,
453, 456, 462
Rosetta Stone, 83
Royal Council (*al-Diwan al-malaki*),
(also Royal Cabinet), 290, 292
Rushdi, Husayn Pasha, 250, 251, 252,
254, 258, 262, 263, 264, 266, 267,
268, 273; and the 1923 Constitution,
273

Saadist Party, 292, 294, 320, 340, 349,
354, 355, 382
Sabri, Hasan, 345, 346
Sacred Law, *see* Sharia
al-Sadat, Anwar, 374, 375, 380, 383,
384, 385; President of Egypt, 419;
peace with Israel policy, 412–13,
414; 'open door' economic policy,
419, 421, 422–7; regime of, 417–22;
and the Nasser regime, 417–22, 427;
and the United States, 420, 421; and
the Arab States, 428–9
Saddiq, Ismail Pasha (al-Mufattish),
77, 84, 128
Said, Abdul Hamid, 327
Said, Muhammad Pasha, 258, 267
Said Pasha, Viceroy of Egypt, 56, 62,
71, 72–3, 81, 83, 84, 87, 101, 102,
120, 181
Sabry, Ali, 408–9
Saladin (Salah al-Din al-Ayyubi), 11,
17–18, 19, 20, 49
Salafiyya, 196, 197–9, 303, 326, 327,
330
Salem, Gamal, 374, 380, 383, 384, 385
Salem, Salah, 374
Salih, Rushdi, 341, 342
al-Sallal, Brigadier Abdullah, 403
al-Sanhuri, Abdul Razzaq, 326–7, 367
Sanua, James (Yaqub), 106–7, 136,
140, 184
Sarruf, Ya'qub, 183, 200, 203, 236,
306
Sarwat, Abdel Khaliq Pasha, 240, 355;
his government, 272–5, 283;
negotiations with Britain, 269–70
Saudi Arabia, 405, 408, 428
Savary, Claude Etienne, 31, 34, 35–6,
37, 38
al-Sayyid, Ahmad Lutfi, 216, 225–7,
239–44, 247, 256, 356
Sayyid Darwish, 107, 461
School of Languages, 94, 95, 98, 102,
113, 114, 119, 182
Second World War, 9, 61, 244, 294–5,
317, 342, 397, 449; economic
conditions in Egypt, 313, 322, 324,
335; Axis threat to Egypt, 346–50;
Axis propaganda in Egypt, 345

Index

Selim I, Ottoman Sultan, 31, 85; conqueror of Egypt, 22, 30, 34, 74–5

Selim III, Ottoman Sultan, 51, 56; his *nizam jadid*, 49, 51

Serag el-Din, Fuad, 352, 370

Sève, Colonel (Soliman Pasha al-Faransawi), 57, 96

Seymour, Sir Beauchamp, 153

Shaab Party, 287, 289

Shaarawi, Ali, 260

Shaarawi, Huda, 260, 309–10, 450

Shafi'i, Husayn, 374, 383, 384

Shafiq, Ahmad Pasha, 227

Shafiq, Doriyya, 450

Sharia, 6, 26, 27, 29, 40, 63, 119, 196, 197, 297, 299, 300, 301, 302, 303, 304, 310, 459

Sharif, Muhammad Pasha, 119, 136, 137, 143, 157, 193; leader of Assembly of Delegates and National Society, 134; Prime Minister, 138–40, 142, 144, 146–9, 154, 192

al-Sharqawi, Abd al-Rahman, 454, 459

Shawqi, Ahmad, 189, 447, 448

shaykh al-balad, 22, 31, 35, 62

al-Shidyaq, Ahmad Faris, 181, 233; his newspaper *al-Jawa'ib*, 103, 181–2

Shirin, Ismail, 375

Shukri, Abd al-Rahman, 448–9

Shumayyil, Shibli, 195, 235, 236, 238, 306

al-Siba'i, Yusuf, 453

Sidqi, Ismail, 212, 240, 259, 262, 264, 295, 318–19, 347, 449; his governments, 286–9, 360–2; abrogation of the 1923 Constitution, 286–318; formation of Shaab Party, 287; Anglo–Egyptian relations, 288–9, 361–2; social legislation, 338–9; and Communists, 341

Sinai, 12, 221, 252, 368, 394, 409, 413, 429

Sirry, Husayn, 346, 366–7, 370, 371

Six Day War, *see* Arab–Israel War

Social Affairs Ministry, 339

Social reform and legislation, 331–42, 396–9

Socialist Party of Egypt, *see* Young Egypt

South Arabia, 387, 406; British withdrawal from, 405

Soviet Union, in Egypt, 388, 394, 406, 410, 412, 420

Stack Pasha, Sir Lee, 280, 281, 385

Stone, General Charles P., 81, 104

Sudan, 64, 85, 104, 169, 227, 253, 281, 284, 361, 385–6, 414, 425; Mahdi Revolt, 172, 174, 192, 200, 204, 248, 372; Anglo–Egyptian Condominium, 174, 200, 204, 207, 248, 291, 361, 362, 368, 385; and the Egyptian Constitution, 274–5, 279–80, 286

Sudan Defence Force, 270, 281, 381

Suez Canal (also Suez Crisis and Suez War), 71, 72, 74, 76, 77–8, 84, 85, 107, 128, 170, 176, 210, 252, 257, 292, 356, 376, 385–6, 409, 412, 426; nationalization and Suez War, 163, 389–90, 393, 402; war of attrition, 410

Suleyman, Ottoman Sultan, 31

Syria, 12, 13, 17, 18, 21, 22, 33, 252, 390, 402, 403, 409, 428; conquest by Muhammad Ali, 62, 64–5; Baath Party in, 403; army in, 403; Baath regime, 405

Syrian *emigrés*, *see* Syrians

Syrians, 98, 183, 186, 200, 203, 220; cultural and intellectual activities (in Egypt), 235–9, 446, 455

Taha, Ali Mahmud, 448, 449

al-Tahtawi, Rifaa Rafii, 92, 106, 109, 112–18, 119, 120, 126, 181

Tamerlane (Timur), 21

Taqla Brothers, 183, 203

tariqas (*turuq*: religious brotherhoods), 26, 28, 460

Tawfiq Pasha, Khedive of Egypt, 103, 119, 133, 135, 136, 137, 138, 141, 142, 156, 157, 163, 164, 193, 297; and the Orabists, 143–54; and the Press, 147, 184, 187; reign, 199–200

Taymur, Mahmud, 452–3

Taymur, Muhammad, 452

Tel el-Kebir, 154, 369

Thabit, Karim, 370

Trade Unions, *see* Social Reform and Legislation
Tu'ayma, Abdullah, 380, 382
Turkey: war with Italy over Tripoli, 212, 248; and Egypt in the Great War, 251–2
Tusun, Prince Omar, 258

ulama, 6, 26, 105, 299, 300; role in Mamluk Egypt, 35; under Napoleon, 39; under Muhammad Ali, 181, 298
Umma Party (also Umma–Jarida group), 174, 216, 222, 225–7, 229–30, 231, 243, 255, 256, 258, 259, 309, 356
United Arab Republic (UAR), 399, 401

Wadi Halfa, 3, 202
Wafd (also Wafd Party), 231, 260, 271, 272, 273, 282, 284, 287, 290, 319, 321, 332–3, 334, 355, 358, 366, 382, 414, 415, 427, 465; formation and early activities, 255, 261–5, 266, 267; and 1923 Constitution, 273–5, 277; first elections and government, 277–81; relations with Britain, 268, 285–6, 343–4, 386; and King Faruq, 293–4; Blue Shirts, 292, 299, 319; and control of religious institutions, 303, 307–8, 325–6; League of Wafdist Youth, 319; leadership, 320; and labour movement and labour legislation, 336, 350; and the Left, 337–8; and the February 1942 Incident, 348–9; and the Free Officers, 378–9; government, 340; in opposition, 359, 363; last Wafd government, 367–70; and Egyptian army, 293, 372; educational policy, 301, 437
Wahhabi movement (also Wahhabis), *see* Arabia
Wahida, Subhi, 461
al-Wakil, Zaynab, 352
waqf, 24, 31, 54, 110, 111, 118, 276, 298, 299, 307–9, 377, 434

Western Desert, 346, 350, 394
Wilson, Sir Rivers, 130, 132, 133, 137, 138–9, 155
Wingate, Sir Reginald, 254, 260–1, 265
Wolff, Sir Henry Drummond (also Mission to Turkey and Evacuation Convention), 217–18
Wolseley, Sir Garnet, 154, 172

Yahia, Abd al-Fattah, 289
Yeken, Adli, 240, 261, 263, 264, 266, 268, 269, 283, 285, 338, 355, 356
Yemen, 387, 406, 464
Yemen War, 403, 404, 405, 409
Young Egypt, 294, 317–18, 320, 325, 328–31, 340, 343, 349, 356, 359, 373, 378, 440; Green Shirts, 292, 318; view of the Sudan, 330; as the National Islamic Party, 330; as the Socialist Party, 359, 367, 382
Young Men's Muslim Association (YMMA), 198, 327
Young Ottomans, 189
Young Turks, 189, 217
al-Yusuf, Fatma, 310
Yusuf, Shaykh Ali, 175, 198, 202, 203, 208, 213, 215, 216, 220, 224, 228–9, 255, 450; Pan-Islamic publicist, 204, 206, 222, 247; and Dinshawai, 205–6; and the Aqaba Incident, 205, 222

al-Zabidi, Shaykh Murtada, 27, 93
Zaghlul, Ahmad Fathi, 231–2
Zaghlul, Saad, 135, 183, 197, 222, 228, 231, 240, 247, 255–8, 283, 286, 319, 355, 356, 435; and the 1923 Constitution, 275, 276, 277; first government, 277–81; leader of the independence movement (1919), 176, 258, 259, 260–9, 271; and reform of the Azhar, 300; new Sharia Judges School, 257, 301
al-Zawahiri, Shaykh Muhammad al-Ahmadi, 326
Zaydan, Jurji, 186, 235, 238–9, 452
al-Zayyat, Ahmad Hasan, 451, 461
Ziwar, Ahmad Pasha, 281, 282, 283, 305, 337; and the Azhar, 302

THE LIBRARY
ST. MARY'S COLLEGE OF MARYLAND
ST. MARY'S CITY, MARYLAND   20686

DT
107
.V38
1980

Vatikiotis, P.J.
   The history of Egypt.

DATE DUE			
DEC 2 1981			
APR 1 7 1982			
SE 26 '83			
NO 26 '84			
JAN 3 1989			
MAY 1 5 1989			
-OCT 0 8 1989			
OCT 2 3 1989			
DEC 11 1989			

Library of St. Mary's College of Maryland
St. Mary's City, Maryland   20686